WWW/Internet 2017 and Applied Computing 2017

Algarve, Portugal
18 – 20 October 2017

Editors:

Pedro Isaias
Hans Weghorn

ISBN: 978-1-5108-5324-9

Printed from e-media with permission by:

Curran Associates, Inc.
57 Morehouse Lane
Red Hook, NY 12571

Some format issues inherent in the e-media version may also appear in this print version.

Printed by Curran Associates, Inc. (2018)

For permission requests, please contact International Association for Development of the Information Society (IADIS) at the address below.

International Association for Development of the Information Society (IADIS)
Rua Sao Sebastiao Da Pedreira
No. 100, 30, 1050-209
Lisbon, Portugal

Phone: 351 21 3151373
Fax: 351 21 3151244

secretariat@iadis.org

Additional copies of this publication are available from:

Curran Associates, Inc.
57 Morehouse Lane
Red Hook, NY 12571 USA
Phone: 845-758-0400
Fax: 845-758-2633
Email: curran@proceedings.com
Web: www.proceedings.com

PROCEEDINGS OF THE INTERNATIONAL CONFERENCES ON

WWW/INTERNET 2017

AND

APPLIED COMPUTING 2017

VILAMOURA, ALGARVE, PORTUGAL

OCTOBER 18-20, 2017

Organised by
IADIS
International Association for Development of the Information Society

Edited by Pedro Isaías and Hans Weghorn

Associate Editor: Luís Rodrigues

TABLE OF CONTENTS

FOREWORD ix

PROGRAM COMMITTEE xiii

KEYNOTE LECTURE xvii

INVITED TALK xviii

TUTORIAL xix

FULL PAPERS

ROLE-BASED ACCESS CONTROL FOR CLOUD COMPUTING REALIZED WITHIN HAPI FHIR 3
Mohammed Baihan, Steven Demurjian, Yaira Rivera Sanchez, Adam Toris, Amy Franzis, Angela Onofrio, Geoffrey Cheng and Thomas Agresta

AN EARLY WARNING SEMANTIC-BASED MODEL FOR EMERGENCY DEPARTMENTS 15
Guilherme Wunsch, Cristiano André da Costa and Rodrigo da Rosa Righi

INTEGRATION BETWEEN ELECTRONIC HEALTH RECORDS STANDARDS USING ONTOLOGIES AND RULES 23
Matheus Henrique Wichman, Cristiano André da Costa, Alex Roehrs, Denise Bandeira and Rodrigo da Rosa Righi

DYNAMICALLY GENERATING NOSQL DATA SCHEMAS USING ARCHETYPES 31
André Magno Costa de Araújo, Valéria Cesário Times and Marcus Urbano da Silva

A STUDY TO CLASSIFY HOSPITAL ACQUIRED COMPLICATIONS BASED ON ELECTRONIC HEALTH RECORD: THE PREPROCESSING PHASE 39
Denise Bandeira da Silva, Taís Rabello, Cristiano André da Costa, Diogo Schmidt and Rodrigo da Rosa Righi

REVISITING SESAME ARCHITECTURE FOR 5G NETWORKS 47
Ioannis P. Chochliouros, Alexandros Kostopoulos, Evangelos Sfakianakis, Dimitrios Arvanitozisis, Anastasia S. Spiliopoulou, Maria Belesioti, Ioannis Giannoulakis, Anastasios Kourtis, Pouria-Sayyad Khodashenas, Jose Oscar Fajardo, Athanassios Dardamanis, Emmanouil Kafetzakis, Javier Garcia Lloreda and Jordi-Perez Romero

COMMUNICATING AND TRANSACTING WITH CHATBOTS: INSIGHTS FROM PUBLIC TRANSPORT 55
Darius Zumstein and Sophie Hundertmark

REVERSE MEDIATED INFORMATION SYSTEM: WEB-BASED RETRIEVAL OF DISTRIBUTED, ANONYMOUS INFORMATION 63
Johannes-Y. Lohrer, Daniel Kaltenthaler, Peer Kröger, Henriette Obermaier and Christiaan H. van der Meijden

AUTOMATIC IMPROVEMENT OF TERMS USED IN FOCUSED CRAWLING PROCESSES ON WEB PAGES 71
Gilson Faria Costa, Guilherme Tavares de Assis and Marcos Vinicius Oliveira Souza

AN ONTOLOGY-DRIVEN FRAMEWORK FOR DATA INTEGRATION AND DYNAMIC SERVICE COMPOSITION: CASE STUDY IN THE OIL & GAS INDUSTRY 79
Geiza M. H. da Silva, Aline M. Saettler, Kathrin R. Llanes, Paulo Ivson, Daniel L. M. Nascimento and Eduardo T. L. Corseuil

A QUESTION AND ANSWER SYSTEM FOR FACTUAL QUERIES IN PORTUGUESE ON DBPEDIA 87
Maksym Ketsmur, Mário Rodrigues and António Teixeira

A SURVEY ON ICT USAGE IN EDUCATION IN ANGOLA HIGH POLYTECHNICAL SCHOOL 95
Adelina Aleksieva-Petrova, Amoussou Dorothee and Milen Petrov

SOCIABILITY IMPACT ON LEARNER'S PERSONALITY IN CLASSROOM AND E- LEARNING ENVIRONMENTS: A COMPARATIVE ANALYSIS 103
Abdul Saboor, M. Irfanullah Arfeen and Wahbeeah Mohti

AN ANALYSIS OF INTERNET OF THINGS TECHNOLOGIES FOCUSED IN SMART HOMES 111
Renato Garcés, Jorge L. Rosero and Ángel Jaramillo-Alcázar

HOW DID THEY START USING OSS? — SURVEY OF OSS DEVELOPERS IN JAPAN 120
Jun Iio, Kenji Tsukagoshi, Masayuki Hatta and Ko Kazaana

REMOVING BARRIERS IN EGOVERNMENT: BACK OFFICE ASSESSMENT 127
Demetrios Sarantis

USABILITY ANALYSIS OF THREE MASSIVE ONLINE OPEN COURSE PLATFORMS 135
Alex de Souza Paiva, Augusto José Waszczynskyj Antunes das Neves, Beatriz Otto Ramos, Claudia Mara Scudelari de Macedo, Fernanda Domingues and Juliana Bueno

FACTORS FAVORING THE DEVELOPMENT OF EDUCATIONAL APPS. USABILITY STUDY OF MOBILE APPLICATIONS TO TEACH PROGRAMMING 142
Miguel García-Iruela and Raquel Hijón-Neira

ZERO COPY SERIALIZATION USING RMA IN THE HPX DISTRIBUTED TASK-BASED RUNTIME 151
John Biddiscombe, Anton Bikineev, Thomas Heller and Hartmut Kaiser

INTERNET VOTING USING ZCASH 159
Pavel Tarasov and Hitesh Tewari

TRAJECTORIES COMPARING BASED ON MATCHING AND DISTANCE EVALUATION WITHIN STIEFEL AND GRASSMANN MANIFOLDS 171
Amani Elaoud, Walid Barhoumi, Hassen Drira and Ezzeddine Zagrouba

GRAPH GENERATION WITH IMPOSED AND FORBIDDEN PATTERNS 179
Mohamed Amine Omrani and Wady Naanaa

A NOVEL ALGORITHM FOR SCALING DOWN LARGE SOCIAL NETWORKS 187
Delel Rhouma and Lotfi Ben Romdhane

EXPERIENCES ON OBJECT TRACKING USING A MANY-CORE EMBEDDED SYSTEM 195
Laercio Minozzo, José Rufino and José Lima

BENCHMARKING OF BARE METAL VIRTUALIZATION PLATFORMS ON COMMODITY HARDWARE 205
Duarte Pousa and José Rufino

BLIND QUALITY ALGORITHM TO ANALYZE STREAMING VIDEO CONTENTS IN 5G NETWORKS 213
Juan Pedro López, Anton Authier, David Jiménez, José Manuel Menéndez and Nuria Sánchez

METHODOLOGICAL GUIDE FOR A DATA WAREHOUSING PROCESS 221
Wilson Castillo-Rojas and Fernando Medina-Quispe

MEASURING MESSAGE PROPAGATION AND USER INFLUENCE IN TWITTER DATA 230
Vishali Narayana, Ashwin Kumar TK and K. M. George

SHORT PAPERS

USING INFORMATION TECHNOLOGY TO ACCESS MEDICAL EMERGENCY INFORMATION WORLDWIDE 241
Judith Born, Michael Storck, Jan Wohlmann, Sarah Krudwig, Alexander Vogel and Christian Juhra

APPLICATION OF DATA MINING TECHNIQUES ON OLYMPIC DATA 245
Eric Chagas Farias, Marco Aurélio Schünke, Paulo Rodrigo Pedroso da Silva and Carlos Mário Dal'Col Zeve

EXPLORING DATA USE TO IMPLEMENT E-GOVERNMENT IN HIGHER EDUCATION A CASE STUDY 251
Diego Buenaño-Fernández, Sergio Luján-Mora and W. Villegas-Ch

A COLLABORATIVE LEARNING ENVIRONMENT BASED ON THE SEMANTIC WEB PRINCIPLES 256
Adriano Ferraz da Costa, Cedric Luiz de Carvalho and Deller James Ferreira

MAILING LISTS ON THE INTERNET - A COLLABORATION TOOL THAT IS STILL ALIVE. THE CASE OF THE REDIRIS LISTS 261
Antonio Muñoz-Cañavate, Alejandro Cordero González, Pedro Hípola and Eduardo Alfredo Cardoso Miranda

DESIGNING AN EYE TRACKING EXPERIMENT TO DETERMINE COGNITIVE LOAD 267
Chris Barry, Mairéad Hogan and Ann M. Torres

AN APPROACH TO SECURE INFORMATION SHARING IN CRISIS MANAGEMENT 272
Mohamed Amoud, Siham Younoussi, Ikram Elrhaffari and Ounsa Roudies

CONCEPT AND FEASIBILITY TESTS OF SELF-SUSTAINING POWER COMPONENTS FOR AUTONOMOUS SPORT AND HEALTH SENSORS 277
Hans Weghorn

EXAMINATION OF SOCIAL MEDIA GUIDELINES AT UNIVERSITIES IN JAPAN USING AN ARTIFICIAL NEURAL NETWORK 283
Yukiko Maruyama, Ryozo Kitajima and Ryotaro Kamimura

EXTRACTION OF CLASSIFICATION RULES FROM IMBALANCED DATASETS USING GA-ILS 289
Aouatef Mahani, Sadjia Benkhider and Ahmed Riadh Baba-Ali

SAMPLING CAR-SHARING DATA TO EVALUATE URBAN TRAFFIC BEHAVIOUR 295
Andrea Trentini and Federico Losacco

REFLECTION PAPERS

INDICATORS FOR THE EVALUATION OF TECHNOLOGICAL ACTIVITY 303
Alexandre Lucas, Birger Larsen, Angel Freddy Godoy Viera and Elías Sanz Casado

THE DIGITAL MARKETING ENVIRONMENT THROUGH SEARCH ENGINE OPTIMIZATION AND WEB METRICS 307
José Ramón Saura, Pedro R. Palos-Sánchez and Juan José López

MODELING DATA CLEANING TECHNIQUES FOR BIG DATA 310
Diana Martinez-Mosquera, Sergio Luján-Mora and Fidel Parra

USER INTERACTION USING MOTION SENSITIVE DEVICES: A STUDY ABOUT BUTTON´S DIMENSION WITH KINECT AND WIIMOTE 314
André Constantino da Silva, Luis Otávio Alves Nascimento and Vinícius Simões dos Santos Silva

POSTERS

E-LEARNING AS A STRATEGY FOR IMPLEMENTATION OF PUBLIC POLICIES 321
Juliana Macedo Reis Mercês and Marcia Maria Pereira Rendeiro

SELF-TESTING IN PROGRAMMING BASICS LEARNING 325
Olga Mironova

AUTHOR INDEX

FOREWORD

These proceedings contain the papers and posters of the International Conferences: WWW/Internet 2017 and Applied Computing 2017, which were organised by the International Association for Development of the Information Society in Vilamoura, Algarve, Portugal, 18-20 October 2017.

The WWW/Internet (ICWI) 2017 Conference aims to address the main issues of concern within WWW/Internet. WWW and Internet had a huge development in recent years. Aspects of concern are no longer just technical anymore but other aspects have arisen. This conference aims to cover both technological as well as non-technological issues related to these developments.

Submissions were accepted under the following main tracks and topics:

- Web 2.0
    - Collaborative Systems
    - Social Networks
    - Folksonomies
    - Enterprise Wikis and Blogging
    - Mashups and Web Programming
    - Tagging and User Rating Systems
    - Citizen Journalism

- Semantic Web and XML
    - Semantics Web Architectures
    - Semantic Web Middleware
    - Semantic Web Services
    - Semantic Web Agents
    - Ontologies
    - Applications of Semantic Web
    - Semantic Web Data Management
    - Information Retrieval in Semantic Web

- Applications and Uses
    - e-Learning
    - e-Commerce / e-Business
    - e-Government
    - e-Health
    - e-Procurement
    - e-Society
    - Digital Libraries
    - Web Services/SaaS
    - Application Interoperability
    - Web-based multimedia technologies

- Services, Architectures and Web Development
  - Wireless Web
  - Mobile Web
  - Cloud/Grid Computing
  - Web Metrics
  - Web Standards
  - Internet Architectures
  - Network Algorithms
  - Network Architectures
  - Network Computing
  - Network Management
  - Network Performance
  - Content Delivery Technologies
  - Protocols and Standards
  - Traffic Models

- Research Issues
  - Web Science
  - Digital Rights Management
  - Bioinformatics
  - Human Computer Interaction and Usability
  - Web Security and Privacy
  - Online Trust and Reputation Systems
  - Data Mining
  - Information Retrieval
  - Search Engine Optimization

The Applied Computing (AC) 2017 conference aims to address the main issues of concern within the applied computing area and related fields. This conference covers essentially technical aspects. The applied computing field is divided into more detailed areas.

The following thirty-six areas have been object of paper and poster submissions:

Agent Systems and Applications, Algorithms, Applied Information Systems, Bioinformatics, Case Studies and Applications, Communications, Data Mining, Database Systems, E-Commerce Theory and Practice, Embedded Systems, Evaluation and Assessment, Global Tendencies, Grid Computing, Information Retrieval, Intelligent Systems, Mobile Networks and Systems, Multimedia, Networking, Object Orientation, Parallel and Distributed Systems, Payment Systems, Programming Languages, Protocols and Standards, Security, Semantic Web, Software Engineering, Storage Issues, Technologies for E-Learning, Wireless Applications, WWW Applications, WWW Technologies, Ubiquitous Computing, Usability Issues, Virtual Reality, Visualization, XML and other Extensible Languages.

These events received 167 submissions from more than 22 countries. Each submission has been anonymously reviewed by an average of four independent reviewers, to ensure the final high standard of the accepted submissions. The final result was the approval of 28 full papers, which means that the acceptance rate was 17%. A few more papers have been accepted as short and reflection papers, posters/demonstrations and a tutorial. Best papers will be selected for publishing as extended versions in the IADIS International Journal on WWW/Internet (IJWI) (ISSN 1645-7641) and in the IADIS International Journal on Computer Science and Information Systems (IJCSIS) (ISSN 1646-3692).

The conferences, besides the presentation of full, short and reflection papers, poster presentations and a tutorial, also feature one keynote presentation and one invited talk from internationally distinguished researchers. We therefore would like also to express our gratitude to Professor Paulo Ferreira, Department of Computer Science and Engineering, IST – Técnico Lisboa, Portugal and Dr. Latif Ladid, Founder & President of the IPv6 Forum, Luxembourg.

As we all know, organising these conferences requires the effort of many individuals. We would like to thank all members of the Program Committee for their hard work in reviewing and selecting the papers that appear in the proceedings.

We are especially grateful to the authors who submitted their papers to these conferences and to the presenters who provided the substance of the meetings.

This Proceedings book contains a rich experience of the academic & research institutions and the industry on diverse themes related to the Internet, Web and Applied Computing. We do hope that researchers, knowledge workers and innovators both in academia and the industry will find it a valuable reference material.

Last but not the least, we hope that everybody will have a good time in Vilamoura, Algarve and we invite all participants for the next year's edition of the International Conferences WWW/Internet and Applied Computing 2018.

Pedro Isaías, The University of Queensland, Australia
Hans Weghorn, BW Cooperative State University Stuttgart, Germany
Conference & Program Chairs

Vilamoura, Algarve, Portugal
October 2017

PROGRAM COMMITTEE

WWW/INTERNET

CONFERENCE & PROGRAM CHAIR

Pedro Isaías, The University of Queensland, Australia

COMMITTEE MEMBERS

Agostino Poggi, Università degli Studi di Parma, Italy
Alexander Troussov, Russian Academy of National Economy, Ireland
Andrea Kienle, University of Applied Sciences, Dortmund, Germany
Andreas Schrader, Insitute of Telematics, University of Luebeck, Germany
Angélica de Antonio, Universidad Politécnica de Madrid, Spain
Asadullah Shaikh, Najran University, Saudi Arabia
Bo Hu, Universität der Bundeswehr München, Germany
Christos Bouras, University of Patras, Greece
Christos Katsanos, Hellenic Open University, Greece
Cristiano Costa, Universidade do Vale do Rio dos Sinos (UNISINOS), Brazil
Demetrios Sampson, Curtin University, Australia
Diana Andone, Politehnica University of Timisoara, Romania
Dirk Bade, University of Hamburg, Germany
Dirk Thissen, Rwth Aachen, Germany
Evangelos Sakkopoulos, University of Patras, Greece
Fan Zhao, Florida Gulf Coast University, USA
Fatos Xhafa, Universitat Politècnica de Catalunya, Spain
Fernanda Lima, UNB, Brazil
Florin Pop, University Politehnica of Bucharest, Romania
Frederick Noronha, India, India
George Koutromanos, National and Kapodistrian University of Athens, Greece
George Vouros, University of Piraeus, Greece
Giuseppe Patane, CNR-IMATI, Italy
Gustavo Rossi, Universidad Nacional de la Plata, Argentina
Hector Migallon Gomis, University Miguel Hernandez, Spain
Henry Oinas-Kukkonen, University of Oulu, Finland, Finland
Holger Hinrichs, University of Applied Sciences Lübeck, Germany
Horst Hellbrück, University of Applied Sciences Lübeck Horst, Germany
James Thong, Hong Kong University of Science and Technology, Hong Kong
Jamshid Shanbehzadeh, Kharazmi University, I. R. Iran
Jan Zizka, Dept. of Informatics, FBE, Mendel University, Czech Republic
Janez Brank, Jozef Stefan Institute, Slovenia
Jessica Rubart, University of Applied Sciences Ostwestfalen-Lippe, Germany

PROGRAM COMMITTEE

APPLIED COMPUTING

CONFERENCE & PROGRAM CHAIR

Hans Weghorn, BW Cooperative State University Stuttgart, Germany

COMMITTEE MEMBERS

Alberto Ros, Universidad de Murcia, Spain
Anastasios Doulamis, National Technical University of Athens, Greece
Andrei Baranga, University of Bucharest, Romania
Andrew Adamatzky, Uwe Bristol, United Kingdom
Antonina Dattolo, University of Udine, Italy
Antonio LaTorre, Universidad Politécnica de Madrid, Spain
Aurelio Bermudez, Universidad de Castilla-la Mancha, Spain
Blanca Caminero, Universidad de Castilla-la Mancha, Spain
Bojian Xu, Eastern Washington University, USA
Carolina Yukari Veludo Watanabe, Federal University of Rondônia, Brazil
Catalin Leordeanu, University Politehnica of Bucharest, Romania
Dan Li, Eastern Washington University, USA
Dana Petcu, West University of Timisoara, Romania
Denis Gracanin, Virginia Tech, USA
Dessislava Vassileva, Sofia University St. Kliment Ohridski, Bulgaria
Elias Xidias, University of the Aegean, Greece
Enrique Árias, Universidad de Castilla-la Mancha, Spain
Francesca Lonetti, ISTI-CNR, Italy
Francesca Martelli, Istituto di Informatica e Telematica - CNR, Italy
Grigorios Beligiannis, University of Patras, Greece
Hind Castel, Institut National des Télécommunications, France
Inmaculada Medina Bulo, University of Cadiz, Spain
Ivan Jelinek, Czech Technical University, Czech Republic
Jan Krasniewicz, Birmingham City University, United Kingdom
Javier Oliver-Villarroya, Universitat Politècnica de València, Spain
Jiann-Liang Chen, National Taiwan University of Science and Technology, Taiwan
Joao Paulo Papa, São Paulo State University, Brazil
Juan J. Pardo, Universidad de Castilla-la-mancha, Spain
Kelton Costa, São Paulo State University, Brazil
Konstantinos Giotopoulos, University of Patras, Greece
Kuo-Chan Huang, National Taichung University of Education, Taiwan
Liz Bacon, University of Greenwich, United Kingdom
Luca Anselma, Università di Torino, Italy

KEYNOTE LECTURE

MAKING THE FUTURE A BETTER PLACE TO LIVE IN

By Professor Paulo Ferreira,
Department of Computer Science and Engineering,
IST – Técnico Lisboa, Portugal

Abstract

Mobile and Ubiquitous Computing is full of promises. This talk provides a critical review of the recent evolution, the directions that have been followed, and the directions we really want to follow assuming we want to make the future a better place to live in. This talk, with a systems approach will start from current observations and will provide a set of open questions and research challenges that should be addressed to make mobile and ubiquitous systems more user-friendly.

INVITED TALK

IPV6-BASED NEW INTERNET

By Dr. Latif Ladid,
Founder & President of the IPv6 Forum,
Luxembourg

Abstract

The public IPv4 address space managed by IANA (http://www.iana.org) has been completely depleted back in Feb 1st, 2011. This creates by itself a critical challenge when adding new things and enabling new services on the Internet. Without publicly routable IP addressing, the Internet of Things and anything that's part of Internet of Everything would be greatly reduced in its capabilities and limit its potential success. Most discussions about IoT have been based on the illusionary assumption that the IP address space is an unlimited resource or it's even taken for granted that IP is like oxygen produced for free by nature.

IPv6 provides enhanced features that were not tightly designed or scalable in IPv4 like autoconfiguration, IP mobility, end to end connectivity and e2e services, etc. IPv6 will be addressing the extreme scenarios where IP becomes a commodity service. This new address platform will enable lower cost network deployment of large scale sensor networks, RFID, IP in the car, to any imaginable scenario where networking adds value to commodity.

IPv6 deployment is now in full swing with some countries achieving over 50% penetration such as Belgium. The US and India have over 100 M users using IPv6 without even the users knowing it. Recently, Apple has required its apps developers to use IPv6 only for their apps starting June 1, 2016 which is a great shot in the arm of IPv6.

There are many inflections happening this decade to influence the design of the first tangible IoT, Cloud Computing, Web of Things and 5G. It will be a combination of IoT, SDN-NFV, Cloud Computing, Edge Computing, Big IoT Data, and 5G, to sift through to realising the paradigm shift from current research-based work to advanced IoT, 5G, and Smart Cities.

This talk will be devoted to analyze the transformative impact of IPv6 on the potential mix of IPv6-based IoT, SDN-NFV, Cloud Computing, Big Data, and 5G and its advanced features, highlighting the challenges and the solutions moving forward.

TUTORIAL

INTERACTION DESIGN FOR AUTOMATED GENERATION OF WEB USER INTERFACES

By Hermann Kaindl
TU Wien, Vienna,
Austria

ABSTRACT

Interaction design is considered important for achieving usable (Web) user interfaces. In this tutorial, we present our *discourse-based* approach for the specification of (classes of) dialogues. In addition, this tutorial demonstrates how graphical user interfaces (GUIs) can be *automatically generated* from such discourse-based models specifying interaction design. This generation approach is especially useful when user interfaces tailored for different (mobile) devices are needed. This tutorial also shows how *customization* can be included into the generation itself, for improved usability and user experience. Such customization involves managing transformation rules and including *custom widgets* already during the automated generation, in order to make the result persistent also in case of re-generation.

KEYWORDS

Human-computer Interaction, Usability, Mobile Web

1. BIOGRAPHY

Hermann Kaindl is a full professor, the director of the Institute of Computer Technology and a member of the senate at TU Wien. Prior to moving to academia, he has gained more than 24 years of industrial experience in software development and human-computer interaction. He has published five books and more than 220 papers in refereed journals, books and conference proceedings. He is a *Senior Member* of the IEEE and a *Distinguished Scientist* member of the ACM. He has previously held more than 60 tutorials.

2. LIST OF TOPICS

Background; Interaction design based on discourse modeling; Exercises; Automated user-interface generation; Customization of generated user interfaces.

REFERENCES

Falb, J., Kaindl, H., Horacek, H., Bogdan, C., Popp, R., and Arnautovic, E., A discourse model for interaction design based on theories of human communication. In *CHI'06 Extended Abstracts on Human Factors in Comp. Syst.*, ACM, 2006.

Popp, R., Raneburger, D., and Kaindl, H., Tool Support for Automated Multi-device GUI Generation from Discourse-based Communication Models, *Proceedings of eics'13*, ACM, 2013.

Raneburger, D., Kaindl, H., and Popp, R. Strategies for automated GUI tailoring for multiple device, in *Proceedings of HICSS-48*, IEEE, 2015.

Raneburger, D., Kaindl, H., Popp, R., Model Transformation Rules for Customization of Multi-device Graphical User Interfaces, *Proceedings of eics'15*, ACM, 2015, pp. 100-109.

Rathfux, T., Popp, R., Kaindl, H., Adding Custom Widgets to Model-driven GUI Generation, *Proceedings of eics'16*, p. 11, ACM, 2016.

Full Papers

ROLE-BASED ACCESS CONTROL FOR CLOUD COMPUTING REALIZED WITHIN HAPI FHIR

Mohammed Baihan[1], Steven Demurjian[1], Yaira Rivera Sanchez[1], Adam Toris[1], Amy Franzis[1], Angela Onofrio[1], Geoffrey Cheng[1] and Thomas Agresta[2]

[1]*Department of Computer Science & Engineering, University of Connecticut, Storrs, CT, USA*

[2]*Department of Family Medicine, University of Connecticut Health Center, Farmington, CT, USA*

ABSTRACT

Cloud computing provides services in the "cloud" to be utilized by mobile apps/users and businesses and is required in critical domains such as healthcare. Specifically, the Meaningful Use Stage 3 guidelines require cloud services to enable health-related information to be available for patients and medical providers via mobile apps that access, modify, and exchange data from multiple health information technology (HIT) systems. These HITs may: operate with cloud services, programming services, or web services; use different cloud service providers; and, employ alternate access control techniques in which mobile app developers are required to interact with many heterogeneous systems and platforms. This paper proposes role-based access control for cloud computing (RBACCC) for multiple HITs to register cloud, programming, and web services, where said services are unified into a global set of cloud services controlled via definition/enforcement. A new HIT system joining the cloud must map their services to existing global services. As a result, mobile developers can more easily interact with a unified global API to access multiple HITs. To demonstrate RBACCC, we utilize the Fast Healthcare Interoperability Resources (FHIR) standard, that models healthcare data with resources in JSON and CRUD RESTful APIs to track a patient's clinical findings, problems, allergies, etc.; this is via a proof-of-concept prototype: the Concussion Tracker mobile app for K-12 students; the ShareMyHealth mobile app for fitness data; and, the OpenEMR and MyGoogle HITs that have FHIR APIs utilizing the HAPI FIR implementation.

KEYWORDS

Cloud services, Access control, RBAC, Health information exchange, Security, HAPI FHIR

1. INTRODUCTION

Cloud computing has emerged as a de facto approach throughout society, commercial and government sectors, and research/academic communities. This is evidenced by: a review of cloud computing advances and technologies (Wang, et al., 2010); the characterization of cloud computing as a dominant technology for computing (Pallis, 2010); and, an assessment of IT funding (Shetty, 2016) and adoption (IDC, 2015). The wide usage of mobile devices means that average users understand storage and synching in the cloud. Security breaches are present (Kelion, 2016) in personal cloud storage (Wingfield, 2016) raising numerous issues in security and privacy (Takabi, et al., 2010) and, authentication, authorization, and confidentiality (Subashini & Kavitha, 2011). One emergent domain for cloud computing is healthcare, where the Meaningful Use Stage 3 (Himss, 2016) guidelines require all health information technology (HIT) systems (e.g., electronic health records (EHR), personal health records (PHR), etc.) to have cloud services to access, modify, and exchange health-related data. In particular, the Health Level 7 (HL7, 2016) organization is developing the Fast Healthcare Interoperability Resources (FHIR) (HL7, 2016) that abstracts healthcare data into 93+ Resources, which are recommended to be hosted in the cloud, to track a patient's clinical findings, problems, allergies, adverse events, history, physician orders, etc. FHIR provides health-related data sharing via RESTful Application Program Interface (APIs) so that apps can be easily built to utilize multiple HIT systems to support the explosion of mobile health (mHealth) apps for both patients and medical providers (Aitken, 2016). mHealth apps gather health data from multiple HITs that may grow and shrink over time, may operate with different paradigms (e.g., cloud, API, web services), and may employ different access control techniques. Such a setting requires mobile developers to utilize alternate paradigms (cloud, API, web services) and interact with multiple

HIT systems in a heterogeneous setting. This makes it problematic to develop easily maintained and evolved mHealth apps. This paper presents *Role-Based Access Control for Cloud Computing (RBACCC)*, realized within HAPI FHIR (University Health Network, 2016), that is capable of controlling the access to the available services of HIT systems to control which mHealth/web/desktop app can utilize which service by integrating the cloud, API, and web services of multiple HIT systems into a unified global set of services. RBAC has a strong history in healthcare HITs; where a study showed that 35 HITs used access control methods, and 27 of these utilized RBAC (Fernández-Alemán, et al., 2013). For example, an HIT system for a pharmacy would have cloud services for: a physician to submit a prescription (Rx) to the pharmacy; a pharmacist to be able to fill Rx; notification via text/phone to the patient that Rx is available; the insurance company to access information on Rx for approval and payment; the physician to have the Rx inserted into his/her EHR; the patient to access medications in the PHR; and, so on. RBACCC can ensure that the mHealth/web/desktop app and its authorized users are restricted to particular services. The problem is that there is currently no solution that allows cloud services to be controlled on this basis, complicated by the fact that cloud services may be from different cloud suppliers that may not be compatible with one another, making it difficult to develop and evolve mHealth/web/desktop apps. The work presented herein on RBACCC extends our previous work on the overall framework for secure and interoperable cloud computing (Baihan & Demurjian, 2017).

To address the aforementioned issues, this paper proposes *role-based access control for cloud computing (RBACCC)* so that multiple HITs can register services and security requirements for use by mobile, web, and desktop apps. Such services are unified into a set of global cloud RESTful services within an integration layer to facilitate the bi-directional mapping of services to/from HITs and exchange of information. The global services allow app developers to work with a single paradigm and unified interface. RBACCC provides one-stop shopping to the app side with global cloud services that transparently connects to the services from multiple sources. In healthcare, an mHealth app would utilize a set of global cloud services via an integration layer (e.g., HAPI FHIR) that provides a common way to interact with multiple HITs and their specific cloud, API, or web services. To demonstrate our work, we utilize the Connecticut Concussion Tracker (CT^2) and ShareMyHealth mHealth apps and the OpenEMR and MyGoogle HITs. CT^2 is a joint effort of computer science, neurobiology, medicine, and nursing departments of the University of Connecticut to support a new law to track concussions for kindergarten to high school (CT Legislature, 2014). ShareMyHealth provides patients with means to manage and share health, medical, and fitness data across multiple HITs. The OpenEMR (OpenEMR, 2016) is an open source EHR fronted with a FHIR server that maps FHIR API calls to web-services of OpenEMR. The MyGoogle API has also been fronted with a FHIR server that maps Google fitness data to/from FHIR Resources. In summary, the work in this paper highlights our development efforts for stakeholders to utilize FHIR as a bridge from CT^2 and ShareMyHealth to OpenEMR and MyGoogle, where using RBACCC allows one to define a global resource that can be easily utilized by both apps. The remainder of this paper has six sections. Section 2 provides background on RBAC, APIs, and HL7/FHIR. Section 3 provides a healthcare scenario for use in examples in the paper and explains CT^2, ShareMyHealth, GoogleFit, and OpenEMR. Section 4 defines a model for RBAC for cloud computing (RBACC) with examples via the healthcare scenario of Section 3. Section 5 illustrates the realization of RBACCC for a cloud computing setting with the HAPI FHIR implementation, introducing interceptors that intercept API calls and then perform RBAC checks against defined permissions. Section 6 reviews related work and compares and contrasts to our RBACCC. Section 7 has concluding remarks.

2. BACKGROUND

To support the material in the paper, this section reviews: RBAC, application programmer interfaces (API), and, the Health Level Seven (HL7) and FHIR standards. RBAC (Ferraiolo & Kuhn, 1992) is a well-known access control model in the field of IT system security in which a user may access a system's object via a role. RBAC consists of: objects that represent functionality for a system; operations that are defined on objects; permissions that are the allowed operations on the different objects; roles that represent a set of responsibilities for a user of the system to capture the defined permissions; and, users assigned a role during a session of a system. RBAC elements can be organized into relations: a role-user relation to assign users to roles; a role-permission relation to assign permissions to roles; a role-session relation to assign sessions to roles; a user-session relation to assign users to sessions; and, an operation-object relation to assign objects to operations. Moreover, RBAC supports a number of constraints that can be defined to restrict a user playing a specific role with further constraints.

Developers of a system may create API to provide system functionalities without exposing the actual underlying implementation. An API can be programmatic, web-based, or cloud based and could interact via a HTTP request to generate a response in a format such as Extensible Markup Language (XML), JavaScript Object Notation (JSON) based on the inputs. Cloud services are the APIs that define how cloud consumers can utilize cloud resources such as software. The API diagram in Figure 1 illustrates the API call. First, an API consumer initiates an HTTP request to the API. The API then uses the consumer's inputs to create and send a request that the Back-end system understands. After that, the API request is processed by the Back-end system which creates a response (in the Back-end system format) to be sent to the API. Finally, the API receives such a response and converts it to a common format (e.g., JSON or XML) and sends the new response to the API consumer. APIs mostly designed using Representational State Transfer (REST) (Fielding, 2000) or Simple Object Access Protocol (SOAP). A RESTful API, the dominant choice in the cloud, utilizes HTTP requests to interact with API consumers and Back-end system (Rouse, 2014). RESTful requests are frequently referred to as CRUD for create, read, update, and delete or from an HTTP perspective POST, GET, PUT, and DELETE.

In support of the interoperability and exchange of health care data, the international Health Level 7 (HL7) (HL7, 2016) organization has provided health information exchange standards including: HL7 Version 2, (HL7, 2016) that lacked the tools to satisfy evolving interoperability requirements of state-of-the-art healthcare systems; and, HL7 Version 3 (HL7, 2016) to address V2 deficiencies and introduced concepts that increased its adoption complexity. More recently, in 2011, the HL7 Fast Healthcare Interoperability Resources (FHIR) was introduced to enable interoperability and integration with state-of-the-art technologies with a particular focus on making healthcare data easily available to mHealth apps via API. FHIR has adopted REST (Fielding, 2000) style to represent all of the entities and procedures in healthcare setting as Resources (Bender & Sartipi, 2013) that logically partition and abstract the HL7 standard into 93+ resources such as Patient (see Figure 2), Medication, and Observation. FHIR resources (HL7, 2016) can hold any type of information that FHIR deals with to be exchanged from one system to another. For example, an app may use the Patient resource to store and exchange information about patients back and forth with different HIT systems. Each FHIR resource has five main properties: a unique URL for identification purposes; common metadata; a human readable section; predefined data elements; and an extension element that enables adding new data elements. FHIR provides three formats: UML for a diagrammatic representation of the resource, XML that is an HL7 schema, and JSON to facilitate a programmatic exchange via a RESTful API. FHIR supports REST services to retrieve and modify data in the Resources, via: *Create*, *Read, Update*, *Delete*, and, *Search*. FHIR involves the concept of *FHIR server* to provide a set of RESTful CRUD services to access a particular HIT system and to make calls to the API of the HIT that retrieves data that can be packaged as FHIR resources.

3. A HEALTHCARE SCENARIO

To assist in explaining the RBACCC and its implementation, this section presents a healthcare scenario that has two mHealth client apps (CT^2 and ShareMyHealth) and two HIT systems (OpenEMR and MyGoogle). To begin, CT^2 is a mHealth app (Figure 3) for Android and iOS devices. The CT^2 app allows the user (e.g., parent/guardian, coach, athletic trainer, school nurse) to report and manage the concussion incidents of students from kindergarten through high school. The CT^2 contains seven tabs ('Login', 'List', 'Student', 'Cause', 'Symptoms', 'Follow-up', and 'Return') where: the 'Login' tab allows the user to enter a concussion, to retrieve an open case, or to find a student by name; the 'List' tab which contains the list of students the user has permission to view and, for each student gives him/her the option to add a concussion or edit an existing one; the 'Student' tab allows the user to input the student's general information (e.g., name, birthdate, school, and the date of concussion); the 'Cause' tab allows the user to specify how and where the concussion occurred; the 'Symptoms' tab allows users to record the symptoms the student had within 48 hours and other pertinent data; the 'Follow-up' tab allows users to record the status of the student over time; and the 'Return' tab allows users to specify when the student can return to school activities. Both versions (Android and iOS) of CT^2 utilize an API (services) to manage CT^2 data as given in Table 1. Services CT_1 and CT_2 are used to: add/modify a student concussion status, and, retrieve such status information, respectively. CT^2 utilizes CT_3 and CT_4 services to: retrieve all information about a student, and create/update new student information, respectively. Services CT_5

and CT_6 provide ways for the CT^2 to: create/update a student follow-up summary, and retrieve follow-up information, respectively. Finally, by calling services CT_7 and CT_8, CT^2 can: retrieve all information about a student concussion, and add/modify new student concussion information, respectively. CT^2 defines four roles (see Table 2): Coach, Nurse, Trainer, and Parent. All of the four roles can access: all GET services CT_2, CT_3, CT_6, and CT_7; and two PUT services CT_4, except Coach, and CT_8. Moreover, Trainer has an additional PUT service (CT_5) while Nurse has access to all PUT services.

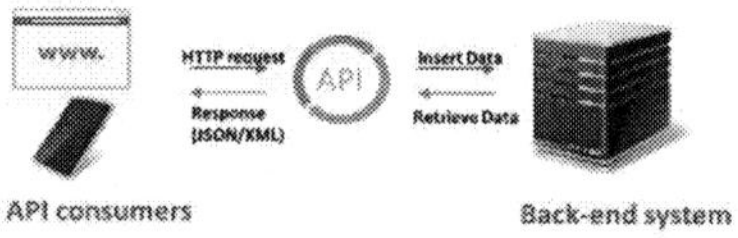

Figure 1. Simple API Diagram

{ "resourceType": "Patient",
"id" : "1",
"meta" : { "versionId" : "1", }
"text": { "status": "generated", },
"identifier": [{"system": "http://www.hitsys.org","value": "10" }],
"name": [{"family": "Levin","given": "John" }],
"gender": {"text": "Male" },
"birthDate": "1985-02-12" }

Figure 2. FHIR Patient Resource Example (JSON)

Figure 3. CT^2 Mobile Application

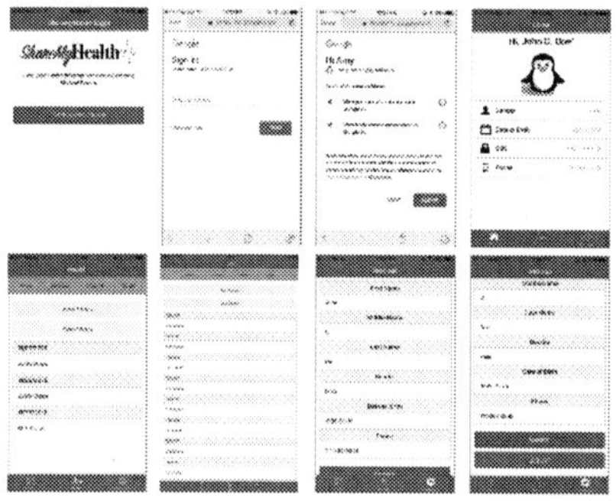

Figure 4. ShareMyHealth Mobile Application

ShareMyHealth is an mHealth app (Figure 4) developed over the last year, by a team of undergraduate students at the University of Connecticut, for Android and iOS devices. ShareMyHealth provides patients with a means to manage and share their fitness data across multiple systems. Patients can gather data from multiple sources (e.g., MyGoogle, OpenEMR, etc.) that can then be made available to medical providers. The first row of Figure 4 contains screens: *Welcome* for the initial opening of the app; *Sign In with Google* to authenticate the user credentials to access his/her fitness data, such as Google Fit API (via MyGoogle system); *Initial Access* for the user to define fitness data; and *Home* where the user sees their basic information and can access their "*Health*" and "*Settings*" pages. The second row of Figure 4 contains screens: *Health View* for viewing information on steps, calories, weight, and height; and a *Settings* page to view setting such as name, gender, date of birth, etc.; and, a second setting page that to modify information. Pressing the "View Steps" button utilizes the user's Google API Token to pull their data from the Google Fit cloud (via MyGoogle system). When a user presses the "Sync Steps" button, the app packages the data into Google Fit via MyGoogle system which in turns sends the information into OpenEMR via OpenEMR API. Settings such as name, gender, etc., are updated by direct calls from ShareMyHealth to OpenEMR.

Table 1. CT^2 Services

Sid	Service Name
CT_1	PUT /CT2/concussion/status statusINFO
CT_2	GET /CT2/concussion/status statusID
CT_3	GET /CT2/student studentID
CT_4	PUT /CT2/students/add studentINFO
CT_5	PUT /CT2/followup/add followupINFO
CT_6	GET /CT2/followups followupID
CT_7	GET /CT2/concussion/student studentID
CT_8	PUT /CT2/concussions/add concussionINFO

Table 2. CT^2 Roles

Rid	Role	CT^2 services
CT_{R1}	Coach	CT_2, CT_3, $CT_6 - CT_8$
CT_{R2}	Nurse	$CT_1 - CT_8$
CT_{R3}	Parent	$CT_2 - CT_4$, $CT_6 - CT_8$
CT_{R4}	Trainer	$CT_2 - CT_8$

Table 3. ShareMyHealth Services

Sid	Service Name
SMH_1	PUT /SMH/newMeasure/mID mINFO
SMH_2	GET /SMH/Measures/mID
SMH_3	PUT /SMH/newPatient/pID pINFO
SMH_4	GET /SMH/Patients/pID
SMH_5	PUT /SMH/Users/uID Token

Table 4. ShareMyHealth Roles

Rid	Role	ShareMyHealth services
SMH_{R1}	Patient	$SMH_1 - SMH_5$
SMH_{R2}	Physician	SMH_2, SMH_4, SMH_5

ShareMyHealth has access to a RESTful API (SMH_1 to SMH_5 services, see Table 3). Moreover, the ShareMyHealth API makes calls (via MyGoogle system) to: Google OAuth API that prompts the current user (patient) to allow ShareMyHealth access to the user's Google Fit data; Google REST Fit API to access measurement data (step, height, weight, and calorie); and OpenEMR API to read and update patient data. Specifically, ShareMyHealth utilizes services SMH_1 and SMH_2 to add/update and read a patient's measurements data, respectively. ShareMyHealth calls services SMH_3 and SMH_4 to add/update and read a patient's demographic information. In addition, service SMH_5 is used to grant ShareMyHealth app (using its Token) an access to the user (patient) fitness data. ShareMyHealth has two roles (see Table 4): Patient, that has access to all five services, and Physician, that has access to all services but SMH_1 and SMH_3.

OpenEMR (OpenEMR, 2016) is an open source Electronic Health Record (EHR) system and a medical practice management app that can be utilized by any health/medical organization around the world. OpenEMR is a Meaningful Use Stage 2 certified (Himss, 2016) and is expected to be a Meaningful Use Stage 3 EHR certified soon (Himss, 2016). In addition to a web-based interface, OpenEMR has a RESTful API from which we have selected a subset of eight services as shown in Table 5. Services $OEMR_1$ and $OEMR_2$ enable an app (or a user via an app) to add/update a note about a patient, and, retrieve information about such a note, respectively. An app may utilize services $OEMR_3$ and $OEMR_4$ to: retrieve patient information, and, create/update new patient information, respectively. Services $OEMR_5$ and $OEMR_6$ provide ways for an app to: create/update a patient follow-up summary, and, retrieve information about such a follow-up, respectively. Finally, by calling services $OEMR_7$ and $OEMR_8$ an app can: retrieve patient condition information, and, add/modify new patient condition information, respectively. Moreover, the OpenEMR system defines eight roles (see Table 6): Patient, Physician, Coach, Nurse, Trainer, Parent, CT^2, and MyGoogle in which the last two roles are designed for CT^2, and MyGoogle, respectively. The roles Nurse, Trainer, and Parent can access: all GET services $OEMR_2$, $OEMR_3$, $OEMR_6$, and $OEMR_7$; and two PUT services $OEMR_4$ and $OEMR_8$. Moreover, Trainer has an additional PUT service ($OEMR_5$) while Nurse and Physician roles have access to all PUT services. In addition, the Physician can only access $OEMR_2$ and $OEMR_4$ services, while the Patient role can access the services $OEMR_1$, $OEMR_2$, $OEMR_3$ and $OEMR_4$. The Coach role can access all services except $OEMR_1$, $OEMR_4$, and $OEMR_5$. Moreover, the MyGoogle role is restricted to access $OEMR_1$ and $OEMR_2$ services, while the CT^2 role can access all services.

Table 5. OpenEMR Services

Sid	Service Name
$OEMR_1$	PUT /OpenEMR/updatepatientnotes noteINFO
$OEMR_2$	GET /OpenEMR/getnotes noteID
$OEMR_3$	GET /OpenEMR/getallpatients patientID
$OEMR_4$	PUT /OpenEMR/addpatient patientINFO
$OEMR_5$	PUT /OpenEMR/addvisit visitID
$OEMR_6$	GET /OpenEMR/getvisits visitINFO
$OEMR_7$	GET /OpenEMR/getlist conditionID
$OEMR_8$	PUT /OpenEMR/addlist conditionINFO

Table 6. OpenEMR Roles

Rid	Role	OpenEMR services
$OEMR_{R1}$	Physician	$OEMR_2$, $OEMR_4$
$OEMR_{R2}$	Patient	$OEMR_1$ – $OEMR_4$
$OEMR_{R3}$	Coach	$OEMR_2$, $OEMR_3$, $OEMR_6$ – $OEMR_8$
$OEMR_{R4}$	Nurse	$OEMR_1$ – $OEMR_8$
$OEMR_{R5}$	Parent	$OEMR_2$ – $OEMR_4$, $OEMR_6$ – $OEMR_8$
$OEMR_{R6}$	Trainer	$OEMR_2$ – $OEMR_8$
$OEMR_{R7}$	CT^2	$OEMR_1$ – $OEMR_8$
$OEMR_{R8}$	MyGoogle	$OEMR_1$, $OEMR_2$

Table 7. MyGoogle Services

Sid	Service Name
MG_1	PUT /MyGoogle/fitness/dataSources/dsID dsINFO
MG_2	GET /MyGoogle/fitness/dataSourcess/dsID
MG_3	PUT /MyGoogle/newPatient/pID pINFO
MG_4	GET /MyGoogle/Patients/pID
MG_5	PUT /MyGoogle/Users/uID Token

Table 8. MyGoogle Roles

Rid	Role	MyGoogle services
MG_{R1}	SMH	MG_1 – MG_5

Finally, MyGoogle is a HIT that we developed to act as a middle layer between the ShareMyHealth app and two HIT systems: OpenEMR; and Google Fit (Google. 2017) which is an open HIT system for sharing and managing patient fitness data (e.g., step, height, weight, and calorie) that is maintained in the Google Fitness Store (in the cloud) that enables multiple apps to access such data via Google Fit APIs. Google Fit consists of two APIs: Fit REST API to add/update patient fitness data; and Google OAuth API to authenticate apps to access users' fitness data. MyGoogle HIT has an API (Table 7) to access OpenEMR API and Google Fit APIs and acts on behalf of apps. MyGoogle API consists of five services. MG_1 and MG_2 enable an app to add/modify and read users' fitness data from/into Google Fitness Store via Fit REST API, respectively. MG_3 and MG_4 add/update and read a patient's demographic information from/into OpenEMR via OpenEMR API, respectively. MG_5 utilizes Google OAuth API to authenticate an app (using its Token) to access a user' fitness data. In addition, MyGoogle defines one role, i.e., SMH, (see Table 8) which is designed to be assigned to ShareMyHealth app. The SMH role can access all MyGoogle API services.

4. AN RBAC MODEL FOR CLOUD COMPUTING

This section presents the RBACCC model for cloud computing that provides a single view of global services to mobile/web/desktop apps and allows those global services to be authorized according to an RBAC policy. The first set of definitions (Defns. 1 to 14) is associated with a large-scale enterprise application comprised of clients and systems with users and roles.

Defn. 1: An *Enterprise Application,* $EA=<EA_{ID}, EA_{NAME}, EA_{CS}, EA_{SS}, EA_{OT}>$, has a unique identifier (EA_{ID}), name (EA_{NAME}), sets of client apps (EA_{CS}) and systems (EA_{SS}), and a set of object types (EA_{OT}) that are the different abstractions of data. EA allows multiple clients (mobile, web, desktop) to interact with multiple systems via APIs (cloud, web, programmatic) that operate on instances of EA_{OT}.

Defn. 2: An *object type* (OT), is defined as a two-tuple $OT=<OT_{ID}, OT_{NAME}>$ and is a data abstraction that represents the structure of a particular kind of information in an EA.

Defn. 3: Each object type, OT_j, has a set of objects j_n instances, $OI_j=<oi_1, oi_2, oi_{jn}>$.

Defn. 4: Let $o=\{read, insert, update, delete\}$, be the set of operations that can be performed against an object type OT in the EA. For permissions, each will be assigned to individual roles.

Example: An enterprise application for health information exchange (EA_{HIE}) would allow apps for patients, family members, medical providers, insurance companies, etc. (e.g. CT^2 and ShareMyHealth), to interact with OpenEMR and MyGoogle (from Section 3) via cloud, web, or programmatic APIs. FHIR resources (e.g., XML schemas) are the OTs for EA_{HIE} whose instance will be accessed via CRUD services.

Defn. 5: A *client* in an EA is a mobile, web, or desktop app that includes, as part of its functionality, cloud-based services, web services, or a programming API of services.

Defn. 6: A *system* in an EA provides functionality for use by clients via cloud-based services, web services, or a programming API.

Defn. 7: A *role, r,* is defined as a two-tuple $r=<r_{ID}, r_{NAME}>$ where r_{ID} is a unique id and r_{NAME} is a name.

Defn. 8: $R_{C/S}=\{r_1, r_2, .., r_j\}$ is as set of j roles for a client/system where $r_j \in R_{C/S}$ and $r_j=<r_{IDj}, r_{NAMEj}>$.

Defn. 9: A permission, p, is defined as a three-tuple $p=<p_{ID}, p_{OT}, p_O>$ where p_{ID} is a unique identifier, p_{OT} is the involved OT (Defn. 2), and p_O is the operation (Defn. 4). Note instances are authorized at runtime.

Defn. 10: A role permission, *rp*, is defined as a three-tuple $rp=<rp_{ID}, p_{ID}, r_{ID}>$ where p_{ID}, r_{ID} are the IDs of the involved permission (Defn. 9) and role (Defn. 7), respectively.

Defn. 11: Each role r has a *role-permission set (RPS)* $RPS_r=\{rp_1, rp_2, .., rp_k\}$ of role permissions (Defn. 10).

Defn. 12: A *user, u,* is defined as $u=<u_{ID}, u_{NAME}>$, where u_{ID} is a unique identifier and u_{NAME} is a user name.

Defn. 13: Let $U_{C/S}=\{u_1, u_2, .., u_j\}$ be the set of j users for a client/system, where $u_j \in U_{C/S}$ and $u_j=<u_{IDj}\ u_{NAMEj}>$.

Defn. 14: Each *user* $u_j \in U_{C/S}$ can be assigned a role $r_j \in R_{C/S}$ for a *user role assignment (ura),* $ura_k=<u_j\, r_j>$, that signifies that a user is limited to playing that role and the authorized permissions. Note that a user can be assigned multiple roles but only plays one role in any session with a client/system.

Defn. 15: The *user-role-assignment set* ($URAS_{C/S}$) for a client/system, $URAS_{C/S}=\{ura_1, ura_2, \dots, ura_k\}$ is the set of all k user role assignments (Defn. 14), that contains an entry for relevant user/role combinations that are applicable for RBAC in support of any client/system.

The next set of definitions is systems/clients for RBAC.

Defn. 16: A cloud, web, or programming service of a client or system, denoted σ, is defined as $\sigma=<\sigma_{ID}, \sigma_{NAME}, \sigma_{SIG}>$ with unique ID, name, and signature for each service. A signature σ_{SIG} is further defined in two different ways based on the type of API:

i. Web/cloud: $\sigma_{SIG}=<\sigma_{METHOD\_TYPE}, \sigma_{URI}, \sigma_{INPUT\_VARIABLE}>$ where $\sigma_{METHOD\_TYPE} \in \{create, read, update, delete\}$ is the type of CRUD method, σ_{URI} a unified resource identifier URI, and $\sigma_{INPUT\_VARIABLE}$.

ii. Program: $\sigma_{SIG}=<\sigma_{METHOD\_NAME}, \sigma_{RETURN\_TYPE}, \sigma_{PARAMETER}>$ where σ_{METHOD_NAME} in the call name, σ_{RETURN_TYPE} is the return type, and $\sigma_{PARAMETER}$ are the parameter names/types.

Defn. 17: A *system* $S^i=<S^i_{ID}, S^i_{NAME}, S^i_{API}, S^i_{Rs}, S^i_{RPSs}, S^i_{Us}, S^i_{URASs}>$, $S^i \in EA_{SS}$ is identified by a unique identifier, name, and API, respectively, where a given S^i_{API} is comprised of a set of i_j API services $S^i_{API}=\{\sigma^i_1, \sigma^i_2, .., \sigma^i_j\}$ with each σ_j as given in Defn. 16 along with sets of roles S^i_{Rs}, role permission sets S^i_{RPSs}, users S^i_{Us}, and user-role assignment set S^i_{URASs} (Defns. 8, 11, 13, and 15 respectively).

Example: MyGoogle, and OpenEMR are in EA_{SS} where there are RESTful cloud services for MyGoogle, and RESTful web services for OpenEMR. Below we define each of these systems with the signature σ_{SIG} as a placeholder for readability in the top of Figure 5.

Defn. 18: A *client app,* $C^i \in EA_{CS}$ is defined as $C^i = <C^i_{ID}, C^i_{NAME}, C^i_{API}, C^i_{Rc}, C^i_{RPSc}, C^i_{Uc}, C^i_{URASc}>$ with unique identifier, name, C^i_{API} the set of i_j API services $C^i_{API} = \{\sigma^i_1, \sigma^i_2, .., \sigma^i_j\}$ with each σ_j as given in Defn. 16, and, sets of roles C^i_{Rc}, role permission sets, C^i_{RPSc} users C^i_{Uc}, and user-role assignment set C^i_{URASc} (Defns. 8, 11, 13, and 15 respectively).

Example: ShareMyHealth with RESTful cloud services and CT^2 with RESTful web services are in EA_{CS}. In the middle of Figure 5, each of these clients has the signature σ_{SIG} as a placeholder for readability.

- S^1=<s_1, **MyGoogle**, S^1_{API}, $S^1_{R_S}$, $S^1_{RPS_S}$, $S^1_{U_S}$, $S^1_{URAS_S}$>, where $S^1_{API}=\{\sigma_1^{S^1}, \sigma_2^{S^1}, \sigma_3^{S^1}, \sigma_4^{S^1}, \sigma_5^{S^1}\}$ in which $\sigma_1^{S^1}$=<MG_1, NewDataSource, σ_{SIG}^{MG1}>, $\sigma_2^{S^1}$=<MG_2, ReadDataSource, σ_{SIG}^{MG2}>, $\sigma_3^{S^1}$=<MG_3, NewPatient, σ_{SIG}^{MG3}>, $\sigma_4^{S^1}$=<MG_4, ReadPatient, σ_{SIG}^{MG4}>, $\sigma_5^{S^1}$=<MG_5, AppAuth, σ_{SIG}^{MG5}>, σ_{SIG}^{MG1} = <PUT, /MyGoogle/fitness/dataSources/dsID, dsINFO>, $S^1_{R_S}=\{r_1^{S^1}\}$ in which $r_1^{S^1}$=<MG_{R1},SMH>, $S^1_{RPS_S}$={<p_1, $r_1^{S^1}$, $\sigma_1^{S^1}$>, <p_2, $r_1^{S^1}$, $\sigma_2^{S^1}$>, <p_3, $r_1^{S^1}$, $\sigma_3^{S^1}$>, <p_4, $r_1^{S^1}$, $\sigma_4^{S^1}$>, <p_5, $r_1^{S^1}$, $\sigma_5^{S^1}$>}, $S^1_{U_S}=\{u_1^{S^1}\}$ with $u_1^{S^1}$=<1,ShareMyHealth>, $S^1_{URAS_S}=\{ura_1^{S^1}\}$ with $ura_1^{S^1}$=<$u_1^{S^1}$, $r_1^{S^1}$>.
- S^2=<s_2, **OpenEMR**, S^2_{API}, $S^2_{R_S}$, $S^2_{RPS_S}$, $S^2_{U_S}$, $S^2_{URAS_S}$>, where $S^2_{API}=\{\sigma_1^{S^2}, \sigma_2^{S^2}, \sigma_3^{S^2}, \sigma_4^{S^2}, \sigma_5^{S^2}, \sigma_6^{S^2}, \sigma_7^{S^2}, \sigma_8^{S^2}\}$ in which $\sigma_1^{S^2}$=<$OEMR_1$, updatepatientnotes, σ_{SIG}^{OEMR1}>, $\sigma_2^{S^2}$=<$OEMR_2$, getnotes, σ_{SIG}^{OEMR2}>, $\sigma_3^{S^2}$=<$OEMR_3$, getallpatients, σ_{SIG}^{OEMR3}>, $\sigma_4^{S^2}$=<$OEMR_4$, addpatient, σ_{SIG}^{OEMR4}>, $\sigma_5^{S^2}$=<$OEMR_5$, addvisit, σ_{SIG}^{OEMR5}>, $\sigma_6^{S^2}$=<$OEMR_6$, getvisits, σ_{SIG}^{OEMR6}>, $\sigma_7^{S^2}$=<$OEMR_7$, getlist, σ_{SIG}^{OEMR7}>, $\sigma_8^{S^2}$=<$OEMR_8$, addlist, σ_{SIG}^{OEMR8}>, σ_{SIG}^{OEMR1} = <PUT, /OpenEMR/updatepatientnotes, noteINFO>, $S^2_{R_S}=\{r_1^{S^2}, r_2^{S^2}, r_3^{S^2}, r_4^{S^2}, r_5^{S^2}, r_6^{S^2}, r_7^{S^2}, r_8^{S^2}\}$ in which $r_1^{S^2}$=<$OEMR_{R1}$,Physicion>, $r_2^{S^2}$=<$OEMR_{R2}$,Patient>, $r_3^{S^2}$=<$OEMR_{R3}$,Coach>, $r_4^{S^2}$=<$OEMR_{R4}$,Nurse>, $r_5^{S^2}$=<$OEMR_{R5}$,Parent>, $r_6^{S^2}$=<$OEMR_{R6}$,Trainer>, $r_7^{S^2}$=<$OEMR_{R7}$,CT^2>, $r_8^{S^2}$=<$OEMR_{R8}$,MyGoogle>, $S^2_{RPS_S}$={<p_1, $r_1^{S^2}$, $\sigma_1^{S^2}$>, <p_2, $r_1^{S^2}$, $\sigma_4^{S^2}$>, <p_3, $r_2^{S^2}$, $\sigma_1^{S^2}$>, <p_4, $r_2^{S^2}$, $\sigma_2^{S^2}$>, <p_5, $r_2^{S^2}$, $\sigma_3^{S^2}$>, <p_6, $r_2^{S^2}$, $\sigma_4^{S^2}$>}, $S^2_{U_S}=\{u_1^{S^2}, u_2^{S^2}\}$ with $u_1^{S^2}$=<1,John>, $u_2^{S^2}$=<2,Sara>, $S^1_{URAS_S}=\{ura_1^{S^2}, ura_2^{S^2}\}$ with $ura_1^{S^2}$=<$u_1^{S^2}$, $r_1^{S^2}$>, $ura_2^{S^2}$=<$u_2^{S^2}$, $r_2^{S^2}$>.
- C^1=<c_1, **ShareMyHealth**, C^1_{API}, $C^1_{R_C}$, $C^1_{RPS_C}$, $C^1_{U_C}$, $C^1_{URAS_C}$>, where $C^1_{API}=\{\sigma_1^{C^1}, \sigma_2^{C^1}, \sigma_3^{C^1}, \sigma_4^{C^1}, \sigma_5^{C^1}\}$ with $\sigma_1^{C^1}$=<SMH_1, NewMeasure, σ_{SIG}^{SMH1}>, $\sigma_2^{C^1}$=<SMH_2, ReadMeasure, σ_{SIG}^{SMH2}>, $\sigma_3^{C^1}$=<SMH_3, NewPatient, σ_{SIG}^{SMH3}>, $\sigma_4^{C^1}$=<SMH_4, ReadPatient, σ_{SIG}^{SMH4}>, $\sigma_5^{C^1}$=<SMH_5, AppAuth, σ_{SIG}^{SMH5}>, for example σ_{SIG}^{SMH1}=<PUT, /SMH/newMeasure/mID, mINFO>. $C^1_{R_C}=\{r_1^{C^1}, r_2^{C^1}\}$ with $r_1^{C^1}$=<SMH_{R1},Patient>, $r_2^{C^1}$=<SMH_{R2},Physician>, $C^1_{RPS_C}$={<p_1, $r_1^{C^1}$, $\sigma_1^{C^1}$>, <p_2, $r_1^{C^1}$, $\sigma_2^{C^1}$>, <p_3, $r_1^{C^1}$, $\sigma_3^{C^1}$>, <p_4, $r_1^{C^1}$, $\sigma_4^{C^1}$>, <p_5, $r_1^{C^1}$, $\sigma_5^{C^1}$>, <p_6, $r_2^{C^1}$, $\sigma_2^{C^1}$>, <p_7, $r_2^{C^1}$, $\sigma_4^{C^1}$>, <p_8, $r_2^{C^1}$, $\sigma_5^{C^1}$>}, $C^1_{U_C}=\{u_1^{C^1}, u_2^{C^1}\}$ in which $u_1^{C^1}$=<1,Sarah>, $u_2^{C^1}$=<2,Nasser>, $C^1_{URAS_C}$={<$u_1^{C^1}$, $r_1^{C^1}$>,<$u_2^{C^1}$, $r_2^{C^1}$>}.
- C^2=<c_2, **CT^2**, C^2_{API}, $C^2_{R_C}$, $C^2_{RPS_C}$, $C^2_{U_C}$, $C^2_{URAS_C}$>, where $C^2_{API}=\{\sigma_1^{C^2}, \sigma_2^{C^2}, \sigma_3^{C^2}, \sigma_4^{C^2}, \sigma_5^{C^2}, \sigma_6^{C^2}, \sigma_7^{C^2}, \sigma_8^{C^2}\}$ with $\sigma_1^{C^2}$=<CT_1, NewStatus, σ_{SIG}^{CT1}>, $\sigma_2^{C^2}$=<CT_2, ReadStatus, σ_{SIG}^{CT2}>, $\sigma_3^{C^2}$=<CT_3, ReadStudent, σ_{SIG}^{CT3}>, $\sigma_4^{C^2}$=<CT_4, NewStudent, σ_{SIG}^{CT4}>, $\sigma_5^{C^2}$=<CT_5, NewFollowup, σ_{SIG}^{CT5}>, $\sigma_6^{C^2}$=<CT_6, ReadFollowup, σ_{SIG}^{CT6}>, $\sigma_7^{C^2}$=<CT_7, ReadConcussion, σ_{SIG}^{CT7}>, $\sigma_8^{C^2}$=<CT_8, NewConcussion, σ_{SIG}^{CT8}>, for example σ_{SIG}^{CT1}=<PUT, /CT2/concussion/status, statusINFO>. $C^2_{R_C}=\{r_1^{C^2}, r_2^{C^2}, r_3^{C^2}, r_4^{C^2}\}$ with $r_1^{C^2}$=<CT_{R1},Coach>, $r_2^{C^2}$=<CT_{R2},Parent>, $r_3^{C^2}$=<CT_{R3},Nurse>, $r_4^{C^2}$=<CT_{R4},Trainer>, $C^2_{RPS_C}$={<p_1, $r_1^{C^2}$, $\sigma_2^{C^2}$>, <p_2, $r_1^{C^2}$, $\sigma_3^{C^2}$>, <p_3, $r_1^{C^2}$, $\sigma_6^{C^2}$>, <p_4, $r_1^{C^2}$, $\sigma_7^{C^2}$>, <p_5, $r_1^{C^2}$, $\sigma_8^{C^2}$>, <p_6, $r_3^{C^2}$, $\sigma_2^{C^2}$>, <p_7, $r_3^{C^2}$, $\sigma_1^{C^2}$>, <p_8, $r_3^{C^2}$, $\sigma_4^{C^2}$>, <p_9, $r_3^{C^2}$, $\sigma_6^{C^2}$>, <p_{10}, $r_3^{C^2}$, $\sigma_7^{C^2}$>, <p_{11}, $r_3^{C^2}$, $\sigma_8^{C^2}$>}, $C^2_{U_C}=\{u_1^{C^2}, u_2^{C^2}\}$ in which $u_1^{C^2}$=<1,Sarah>, $u_2^{C^2}$=<2,Alie>, $C^2_{URAS_C}$={<$u_1^{C^2}$, $r_1^{C^2}$>,<$u_2^{C^2}$, $r_3^{C^2}$>}.
- G^1=<g_1, **EA$_{HIT}$GCCC**, G^1_{API}, $G^1_{R_G}$, $G^1_{U_G}$, $G^1_{URAS_G}$, $G^1_{RRPS_G}$>, where $G^1_{API}=\{\sigma_1^{G^1}, \sigma_2^{G^1}, \sigma_3^{G^1}, \sigma_4^{G^1}, \sigma_5^{G^1}, \sigma_6^{G^1}, \sigma_7^{G^1}, \sigma_8^{G^1}, \sigma_9^{G^1}\}$ in which $\sigma_1^{G^1}$=<gs_1, NewObservation, σ_{SIG}^{gs1}>, $\sigma_2^{G^1}$=<gs_2, ReadObservation, σ_{SIG}^{gs2}>, $\sigma_3^{G^1}$=<gs_3, NewPatient, σ_{SIG}^{gs3}>, $\sigma_4^{G^1}$=<gs_4, ReadPatient, σ_{SIG}^{gs4}>, $\sigma_5^{G^1}$=<gs_5, NewUser, σ_{SIG}^{gs5}>, $\sigma_6^{G^1}$=<gs_6, NewEncounter, σ_{SIG}^{gs6}>, $\sigma_7^{G^1}$=<gs_7, ReadEncounter, σ_{SIG}^{gs7}>, $\sigma_8^{G^1}$=<gs_8, NewCondition, σ_{SIG}^{gs8}>, $\sigma_9^{G^1}$=<gs_9, ReadCondition, σ_{SIG}^{gs9}>, for example σ_{SIG}^{gs1}=<PUT, /GCCC/Observation/id, obINFO>. $G^1_{R_G}=\{r_1^{G^1}, r_2^{G^1}, r_3^{G^1}, r_4^{G^1}, r_5^{G^1}, r_6^{G^1}, r_7^{G^1}, r_8^{G^1}, r_9^{G^1}\}$ with $r_1^{G^1}$=<G_{R1},GPhysician>, $r_2^{G^1}$=<G_{R2},GPatient>, $r_3^{G^1}$=<G_{R3},GCoach>, $r_4^{G^1}$=<G_{R4},GNurse>, $r_5^{G^1}$=<G_{R5},GParent>, $r_6^{G^1}$=<G_{R6},GTrainer>, $r_7^{G^1}$=<G_{R7},GCT^2>, $r_8^{G^1}$=<G_{R8},GMyGoogle>, $r_9^{G^1}$=<G_{R9},GSMH>, $G^1_{U_G}=\{u_1^{G^1}, u_2^{G^1}\}$ with $u_1^{G^1}$=<1,John>, $u_2^{G^1}$=<2,Ali>, $G^1_{URAS_G}=\{ura_1^{G^1}, ura_2^{G^1}\}$ with $ura_1^{G^1}$=<$u_1^{G^1}$, $r_1^{G^1}$>, $ura_2^{G^1}$=<$u_2^{G^1}$, $r_2^{G^1}$>, $G^1_{RRPS_G}$={{$\sigma_{gp_1}^{G^1}$, $\sigma_{gp_2}^{G^1}$, $\sigma_{gp_3}^{G^1}$},{$\sigma_{gp_4}^{G^1}$, $\sigma_{gp_5}^{G^1}$, $\sigma_{gp_6}^{G^1}$, $\sigma_{gp_7}^{G^1}$, $\sigma_{gp_8}^{G^1}$}} with $\sigma_{gp_1}^{G^1}$=<$r_1^{G^1}$, $\sigma_3^{G^1}$>, $\sigma_{gp_2}^{G^1}$=<$r_1^{G^1}$, $\sigma_4^{G^1}$>, $\sigma_{gp_3}^{G^1}$=<$r_1^{G^1}$, $\sigma_5^{G^1}$>, $\sigma_{gp_4}^{G^1}$=<$r_2^{G^1}$, $\sigma_3^{G^1}$>, $\sigma_{gp_5}^{G^1}$=<$r_3^{G^1}$, $\sigma_3^{G^1}$>, $\sigma_{gp_6}^{G^1}$=<$r_2^{G^1}$, $\sigma_5^{G^1}$>, $\sigma_{gp_7}^{G^1}$=<$r_3^{G^1}$, $\sigma_4^{G^1}$>, $\sigma_{gp_8}^{G^1}$=<$r_2^{G^1}$, $\sigma_5^{G^1}$>.

Figure 5. MyGoogle and OpenEMR Systems, ShareMyHealth and CT^2 Clients, and the EA.HITGGGC Global Resource

The RBACCC model for cloud computing also provides the means to represent a unified set of global services encapsulated into one Global Resource for a given EA and its systems so that the clients are able to utilize a set of shared global services rather than specific services for each system that may be in different formats (e.g., cloud services, web services, programmatic API services in different languages, etc.). Although, grouping multiple systems services attracts app developers, in a domain such as healthcare, to create useful and rich apps (i.e. apps with many features) in an easy and efficient way (i.e. avoid effort duplication), it also creates one great target to the attackers to illegally access a large set of crucial and sensitive data, through services, such as electronic health records of large number of patients. Thus, an access control mechanism should be developed and utilized to restrict services access only to the authorized users and their apps. Moreover, since there is a demonstrated need to protect such global services there must be a shift in focus on the concept of RBAC permissions from objects and operations (in the traditional RBAC model) to permissions that define individual global services that are authorized by role to make invocations (calls) on objects. In this paper, we propose such an access control mechanism, i.e. the RBACCC model. Figure 6 shows the proposed RBACCC model that consists of four elements: Roles; Users; Sessions; and Permissions (i.e. the defined service calls on objects), and four relations: User-Role (i.e. which user assigned to which role); Role-Permission (i.e. which role authorized to which service in which each service calls a specific object); User-Session (i.e. which user is active in the current session); and Role-Session (i.e. which role of the current user is active in the current session).

Given Figure 6, we revise the Defns. 8, 13, 14, and 15 to version 2 (v2) that includes G (for global) as an option for a role set, user set, user role assignment, and user-role assignment set.

Defn. 8: (v2) Let $R_{C/S/G} = \{r_1, r_2, .., r_j\}$ be defined as the set of j roles for a given client/system/Global Resource where $r_j \in R_{C/S/G}$ and $r_j = <r_{IDj}, r_{NAMEj}>$.

Defn. 13: (v2) Let $U_{C/S/G} = \{u_1, u_2, .., u_j\}$ be defined as the set of j users for a given client/system/Global Resource, where $u_j \in U_{C/S/G}$ and $u_j = <u_{IDj}\ u_{NAMEj}>$.

Defn. 14: (v2) Each *user* $u_j \in U_{C/S/G}$ can be assigned a role $r_j \in R_{C/S/G}$ for a *user role assignment (ura),* $ura_k = <u_j\ r_j>$, where a user is limited to playing that role and authorized permissions. Note that a user can be assigned multiple roles but only plays one role in any session with a client/system/Global Resource.

Defn. 15: (v2) The *user-role-assignment set* ($URAS_{C/S/G}$) for a client/system/Global Resource, $URAS_{C/S/G}=\{ura_1, ura_2, \ldots, ura_k\}$ is the set of all k user role assignments (Defn. 14v2), the relevant user/role combinations that are applicable for RBAC in support of any client/system/Global Resource.

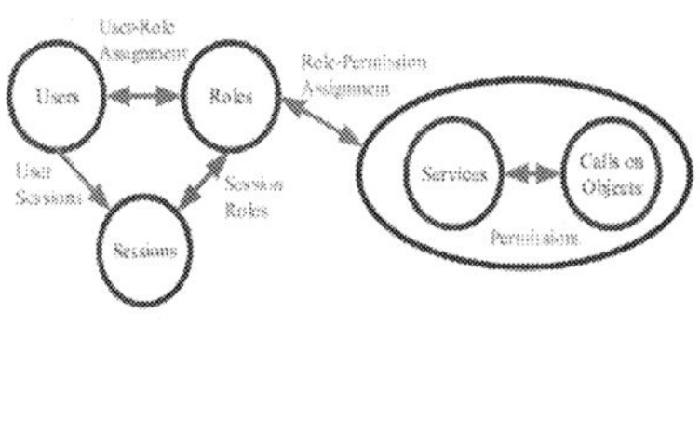

Figure 6. The RBACCC Model

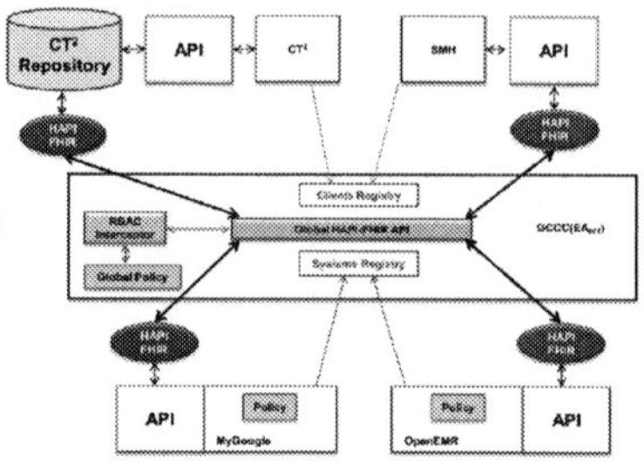

Figure 7. Integration Architecture of GCCC(EA_{HIT})

Defn. 19: A *global resource,* G^i represents a set of global services to which Clients/Systems services map.

Defn. 20: For a global resource, G^i, a *global service permission,* $\sigma^i_{gp}=<r^i_{IDk}, \sigma^i_{IDj}>$, binds a jth service $\sigma^i_j=<\sigma^i_{IDj}, \sigma^i_{NAMEj}, \sigma^i_{SIGj}>$ of G^i_{API} by identifier, σ^i_{IDj}, to a role $r^i_k \in G^i_{RG}$ by identifier, r^i_{IDj}.

Defn. 21: For a global resource, G^i, and a role $r^i_k \in G^i_{RG}$, a *role permissions set,* $RPS_{r^i_k}=\{\sigma^i_{gp1}, \sigma^i_{gp2}, .., \sigma^i_{gpn}\}$ contains all of the n global service permissions σ^i_{gpj} associated with a role.

Defn. 22: For a global resource, G^i, the *resource role permissions set,* $G^i_{RRPSG}=\{RPS_{r^i_1}, RPS_{r^i_2}, \ldots, RPS_{r^i_m}\}$ contains all of the role permission sets for the m roles in G^i_{RG}.

Defn. 23: A *global resource,* $G^i=<G^i_{ID}, G^i_{NAME}, G^i_{API}, G^i_{R_G}, G^i_{U_G}, G^i_{URAS_G}, G^i_{RRPS_G}>$, is identified by a unique identifier, name, and cloud API, respectively, where a given G^i_{API} is comprised of a set of i_j API services $G^i_{API}=\{\sigma_{i_1}, \sigma_{i_2}, .., \sigma_{i_j}\}$ with each σ_j (Defn. 16) along with sets of roles $G^i_{R_G}$, users $G^i_{U_G}$, user-role assignment sets $G^i_{URAS_G}$ (Defns. 8v2, 13v2, and 15v2 respectively), and a resource role permission set, $G^i_{RRPS_G}$ (Defn. 22).

Example: The global services in Table 9 are organized into one Global Resource EA_{HIT}.GCCC with global roles (Table 10) as given at the bottom of Figure 5.

Table 9. GCCC Global Services

Gid	Service Name
gs_1	PUT /GCCC/Observation/id obINFO
gs_2	GET /GCCC/Observation/id
gs_3	PUT /GCCC/Patient/id ptINFO
gs_4	GET /GCCC/Patient/id
gs_5	PUT /GCCC/User/id usINFO, Token
gs_6	PUT /GCCC/Encounter/id enINFO
gs_7	GET /GCCC/Encounter/id
gs_8	PUT /GCCC/Condition/id cnINFO
gs_9	GET /GCCC/Condition/id

Table 10. GCCC Global Roles

RiD	Role	GCCC services
G_{R1}	GPhysician	gs_2, gs_4, gs_5
G_{R2}	GPatient	$gs_1 - gs_5$
G_{R3}	GCoach	$gs_2, gs_3, gs_7 - gs_9$
G_{R4}	GNurse	$gs_1 - gs_4, gs_6 - gs_9$
G_{R5}	GParent	$gs_2 - gs_4, gs_7 - gs_9$
G_{R6}	GTrainer	$gs_2 - gs_4, gs_6 - gs_9$
G_{R7}	GCT²	$gs_1 - gs_4, gs_6 - gs_9$
G_{R8}	GMyGoogle	gs_1, gs_2
G_{R9}	GSMH	$gs_1 - gs_5$

Defn. 24: The Global Cloud Computing Configuration $GCCC=<G, R, U, URAS, RRPS>$ where $G=\{G^i \mid \textit{all i resources}\}$ is a set of all global resources in which each G^i as in Defn. 23, $R=\{G^i_{R_G}|_{all\,i}\}$ of all role sets from all i global resources, $U=\{G^i_{U_G}|_{all\,i}\}$ of all user sets from all i global resources, $URAS=\{G^i_{URAS_G}|_{all\,i}\}$ of all user role assignment sets from all i global resources, and $RRPS=\{G^i_{RRPS_G}|_{all\,i}\}$ of all resource role permission sets from all i global resources.

Given GCCC, the next part of the model involves the definitions of mappings of roles, users, and services from clients/systems to the global resource, specifically:

Defn. 25: Client/System Roles to Global Roles Mapping $CSRGRM_{GCCC_i}=<C^{ID}_{R_C}/S^{ID}_{R_S}, G^{ID}_{R_G}>, C^i_{R_C}/S^i_{R_S}$ mapped to $G^i_{R_G}$

Defn. 26: Client/System Users to Global Users Mapping $CSUGUM_{GCCC_i}=<C^{ID}_{U_C}/S^{ID}_{U_S}, G^{ID}_{U_G}>, C^i_{U_C}/S^i_{U_S}$ mapped to $G^i_{U_G}$

Defn. 27: Client/System API to Global API Mapping $CSAGAM_{GCCC_i}=<C^{ID}_{API}/S^{ID}_{API}, G^{ID}_{API}>, C^i_{API}/S^i_{API}$ mapped to G^i_{API}

Example: Table 11 contains the mappings of roles and services of MyGoogle, OpenEMR, CT², and ShareMyHealth. Table 11a is for the role mapping where the client role and system role could map to the same global role, as shown for the first six rows, e.g., SMH_{R1} and $OEMR_{R2}$ rows are the Patient role for Client/System, respectively, that maps to the global Patient role G_{R2}. Tables 11b to 11e map CT², ShareMyHealth, MyGoogle, and OpenEMR services, respectively, to global services. Note that for the purposes of this paper, we omit discussion of security policy and mapping processes by the security officer.

The final set of definitions involve the introduction of the interceptor concept which is utilized to enforce RBAC by intercepting each call from a client or system to a global service in order to have the global service test RBACCC permissions on objects and on services thereby performing appropriate security enforcement checks. To begin, we define an interceptor as follows:

An interceptor, *I*, is defined as a programmatic mechanism that is able to intercept a service call from a client app to an API in order to perform appropriate security enforcement checks.

Defn. 28: User-Role Enforcement Check: For a global resource, G^i, a user $u^{ID} \in G^i_{U_G}$ can utilize a role $r^{ID} \in G^i_{R_G}$ iff the entry $<u^{ID}, r^{ID}>$ exists in the User-Role set $G^i_{URAS_G}$.

Defn. 29: Role-Service Enforcement Check: For a global resource, G^i, a user with a role $r^{ID} \in G^i_{R_G}$ can access a global service $\sigma^i_{ID} \in G^i_{API}$ iff the entry $<r^{ID}, \sigma^i_{ID}>$ exists in the role permissions set $RPS_{rid} \in G^i_{RRPS_G}$.

Defn. 30: The RBAC Interceptor is a programmatic security enforcement check utilizing Defns. 29 and 30 that is able to determine at runtime if the requested API call on a global service can be executed for a user u^{ID} (Defn. 12) with a role r^{ID} (Defn. 7).

Table 11. Mapping Tables to Global Services

a. Mapping of Client/System to Global Roles

Client Rid	System Rid	Global Rid
CT_{R1}	$OEMR_{R3}$	G_{R3}
CT_{R2}	$OEMR_{R4}$	G_{R4}
CT_{R3}	$OEMR_{R5}$	G_{R5}
CT_{R4}	$OEMR_{R6}$	G_{R6}
SMH_{R1}	$OEMR_{R2}$	G_{R2}
SMH_{R2}	$OEMR_{R1}$	G_{R1}
	$OEMR_{R7}$	G_{R7}
	$OEMR_{R8}$	G_{R8}
	MG_{R1}	G_{R9}

b. Mapping of CT[2] Services to Global Services

Sid	Gid	FHIR CRUD/Resource
CT_1	gs_1	PUT Observation
CT_2	gs_2	GET Observation
CT_3	gs_4	GET Patient
CT_4	gs_3	PUT Patient
CT_5	gs_7	PUT Encounter
CT_6	gs_8	GET Encounter
CT_7	gs_{10}	GET Condition
CT_8	gs_9	PUT Condition

c. Mapping of SMH Services to Global Services

Sid	Gid	FHIR CRUD/Resource
SMH_1	gs_1	PUT Observation
SMH_2	gs_2	GET Observation
SMH_4	gs_4	GET Patient
SMH_3	gs_3	PUT Patient
SMH_5	gs_5	PUT User

d. Mapping of MyGoogle Services to Global Services

Sid	Gid	FHIR CRUD/Resource
MG_1	gs_1	PUT Observation
MG_2	gs_2	GET Observation
MG_4	gs_4	GET Patient
MG_3	gs_3	PUT Patient
MG_5	gs_5	PUT User

e. Mapping of OpenEMR Services to Global Services

Sid	Gid	FHIR CRUD/Resource
$OEMR_1$	gs_1	PUT Observation
$OEMR_2$	gs_2	GET Observation
$OEMR_3$	gs_4	GET Patient
$OEMR_4$	gs_3	PUT Patient
$OEMR_5$	gs_7	PUT Encounter
$OEMR_6$	gs_8	GET Encounter
$OEMR_7$	gs_{10}	GET Condition
$OEMR_8$	gs_9	PUT Condition

5. RBACCC REALIZED WITHIN HAPI FHIR

In this section, we discuss the realization of RBACCC in HAPI FHIR in three parts. The first part, the mapping process, is intended to enable clients (CT^2 and ShareMyHealth - see Defn. 18) to utilize systems' (MyGoogle and OpenEMR - see Defn. 17) services securely via the RBACCC and GCCC. This is accomplished by leveraging our prior work that identified and explained a set of blueprints for the design and development of FHIR servers in which an mHealth app can interacts with multiple HIT systems via FHIR through the design, implementation, and usage of FHIR servers (Baihan, et al., 2017). Specifically, FHIR requires that information in CT^2 and ShareMyHealth are mapped to/from FHIR resources and information provided by OpenEMR and MyGoogle via a mapping to/from FHIR resources and, exchanged through shared resources via the CRUD FHIR APIs defined for each resource. In support of this activity, we utilize our prior work to yield an integration architecture in Figure 7. Briefly, we explain Figure 7. First, each HIT system (i.e., MyGoogle and OpenEMR) creates a FHIR API (which consists of a subset of the 93+ FHIR resources) in front of their API (see Defn. 16), and modifies its RBAC policy to be defined against its FHIR API. Second, each HIT system registers (see Defn. 17): the system's name and a brief description, the FHIR API, and the RBAC policy into EA_{HIT} (see Defn. 24) using the Systems Registry component (in the middle of Figure 7). Third, the security officer of the EA_{HIT}:

creates a global resource (see Defn. 23) that includes: global FHIR API, based on MyGoole and OpenEMR FHIR APIs; and global roles (see Defn. 8v2), in which each global role is annotated with the name of the origin system, against the global FHIR API (see Figure 7), based on systems' RBAC policies (see Defn. 17). Fourth, each client (CT^2 and ShareMyHealth): creates a FHIR API (at the top of Figure 7) in front of their API (see Defn. 18). Next, each client registers (see Defn. 18) the client's name and a brief description in EA_{HIT}, using the Clients Registry component, and reconfigures its FHIR API to call the global FHIR API (see Figure 7). Finally, the EA_{HIT} security officer performs actions that (see Defns. 25-27): associates each registered client with a registered system based on the descriptions of the client and system; and defines a global user, for each client, to which the appropriate global role is assigned that should be annotated with the same system's name that the client is associated with. Note that the FHIR API of each system/client converts data between the system/client data format and FHIR data format, while the global FHIR API simply sends the FHIR instances back and forth between the associated clients and the systems. Also note that if two systems register the same FHIR service or role name, EA_{HIT} can differentiate between them based on the system's name that they come from.

The second part involves the implementation of FHIR APIs and the customization of the HAPI server interceptor so that it is adapted to support RBACCC checks (Defns. 29 and 30) that determine if a service is authorized by user/role. The FHIR APIs of CT^2, ShameMyHealth (top of Figure 7), MyGoogle, OpenEMR (bottom of Figure 7) and the global FHIR EA_{HIT} API (middle of Figure 7) in EA_{HIT} were implemented utilizing the HAPI-FHIR reference library (University Health Network, 2016). To implement each of these HAPI-FHIR APIs (Figure 7), the HAPI *RestfulServer* and HAPI *IResourceProvider* classes were used. Moreover, the Clients Registry, Systems Registry, and Global Policy components (Figure 7) are simple RESTful APIs, which were implemented using the JAX-RS Java library (Hadley & Sandoz, 2009). The Clients Registry and Systems Registry components support: adding systems/clients HAPI-FHIR APIs and discovering corresponding FHIR APIs, while the Global Policy component enables the security officer to add/modify the global policy (Defns. 23). Moreover, the RBAC interceptor (Defn. 31 - middle of Figure 7) was implemented by extending the HAPI *InterceptorAdapter* class to retrieve the global policy from the Global Policy component and enforce it on each access request at runtime. Figure 8 presents a sample of the global policy (Table 10) in JSON format.

The third part involves two access scenarios of usage that can be initiated by the ShareMyHealth and CT^2 apps. In the first scenario (Figure 9), EA_{HIT} would reject a request from the ShareMyHealth app to access the global service (PUT Condition) or gs_8 (see Table 9). In the second scenario (Figure 10), the request from the CT^2 app to access the same global service gs_8, would be allowed by EA_{HIT}. These two decisions were made based on the defined global policy (Defns. 23 - Figure 8). Note that the two requests were made with the Postman tool (Postman, 2013) instead of directly made them from the ShareMyHealth and CT^2 apps in order to present a clear view of the response the requests can have in different scenarios. To complete the discussion, we explain the pseudo-code of an interceptor (Defn. 31) that is utilized at runtime to check security permissions (See Defns. 29 and 30) of all calls to global services. Figure 11 has the RBAC enforcement code realized within the *incomingRequestPostProcessed* method of the HAPI *InterceptorAdapter* class. First, this method starts by retrieving a secure Token (line 3), from a HTTP header (Authorization) of the request parameter, that is passed to the *extractUser* function that can obtain the user credentials (i.e. user Id, see Defn. 13v2, and role Id, see Defn. 8v2) from the Token (line 5). After that the RBAC policy (Defns. 23), which is in the JSON format (see Figure 8), is retrieved by calling the RBAC policy URL (line 7). Then, the details of the requested resource (resource name, see Defn. 2, and HTTP method, see Defn. 4) are obtained from the requestDetails and request parameters, respectively, in which such details along with the RBAC policy are passed to the *getResourceId* function that returns the Id of the requested resource (lines 8 to 10). In line 13, the user credentials and the RBAC policy are passed to the *checkCredentials* function (see Defn. 29) to determine whether the user has the claimed role (see Defn. 8v2). If the check fails, the value of the accessDecision variable becomes false (lines 26-29). However, if the user passed this check, the associated role Id, the resource Id, and the RBAC policy are passed to the *checkPerm* function (see Defn. 30 - line 18) that returns true if the user with such role can access the requested resource or false otherwise. Based on the result of the *checkPerm* function, the variable accessDecision is assigned and returned as the result of the *incomingRequestPostProcessed* method (lines 19-24 and 30).

6. RELATED WORK

In this section, we review related work. The first group involves data-based RBAC. One effort (Tang, et al., 2012) proposed an RBAC model with an owner role to enable the data owner to grant a user access to their data and to update the owner data in cloud, with a user role. Another effort (Wang, 2011) proposed a cloud-based RBAC that authorizes permissions to data in cloud with roles that assigned to cloud users. A final effort (Takabi, et al., 2010) proposed a framework for cloud computing environments that has an access control module that protects a provider's data in cloud using classic RBAC. Our proposed RBACCC approach contrasts with the three aforementioned efforts by focusing on role permissions against cloud services as opposed to data. The second group involves RBAC in a cloud setting at API level. One effort (Sirisha & Kumari, 2010) proposed an API-based RBAC model for cloud services that defines permissions against cloud services where permissions are authorized to roles assigned to users. Their approach is similar to our RBACCC since both models defines permissions against API, however, our model is more fine-grained since permissions are assigned to different CRUD methods of cloud services, and their model allows/denies access to all CRUD methods. Another effort (Wonohoesodo & Tari, 2004) proposed a Web Service (SOAP)-based RBAC model in which a role assigned to service consumer is authorized to: a SOAP service, and a parameter of a SOAP service with an access mode (e.g., read, write, execute, modify, and delete). A final effort (Feng, et al., 2004) also proposed a Service (SOAP)-Oriented RBAC model that authorizes SOAP services to roles that are assigned to users, where when a user activates a role, an Actor is created that enables the user to access SOAP services authorized to the role. These last two efforts are similar to RBACCC since they are API- based; our approach with a cloud-based RESTful API is more versatile and in sync with increasing emphasis of cloud-based computing in the marketplace.

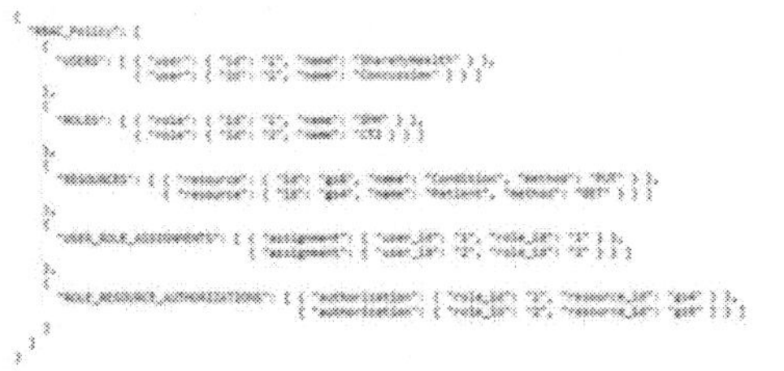

Figure 8. A Global Policy Sample in JSON

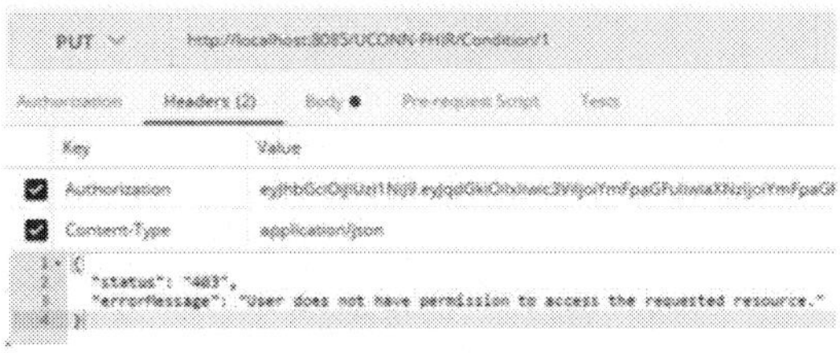

Figure 9. GCCC Rejected ShareMyHealth Request

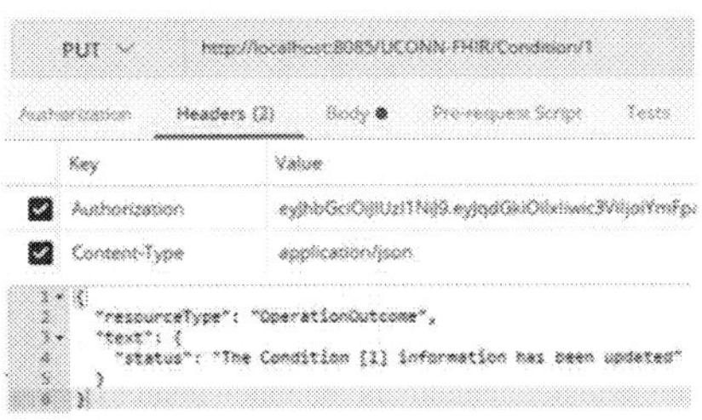

Figure 10. GCCC Allowed CT² Request

```
//Serves as Access Control Interceptor function
public boolean incomingRequestPostProcessed(requestDetails, request, response){
      secToken = request.getHeader("Authorization");
      // Retrieves the user id and role id of the current user
      [userId,roleId] = extractUser(secToken);
      // Retrieves the RBAC policy from the RBAC URL
      RBAC_Policy= HttpGet(RBAC_Policy_URL);
      resourceName = requestDetails.getResourceName();
      httpMethod = request.getMethod();
      resourceId = getResourceId(httpMethod, resourceName, RBAC_Policy);
      // check if the user has the claimed role
      verifiedUser=false;
      verifiedUser=checkCredintals(userId, roleId, RBAC_Policy); // true or false
      // check if the user (role) can access the requested resource and method
      verifiedPerm=false;
      accessDecision=false;
      if(verifiedUser==true){
        verifiedPerm=checkPerm(roleId, resourceId, RBAC_Policy); // true or false
        if(verifiedPerm==true){
                  accessDecision=true; // allow user request
        }
        else {
                  accessDecision=false; // deny user request
        }
      }
      else{
        // Error Message: User could not be verified
         accessDecision=false; // deny user request
      }
   Return accessDecision;
   }
```

Figure 11. Interceptor Pseudo Code

7. CONCLUSION

This paper has presented RBACCC that enables systems to: register cloud, programming, and web services that are mapped to a set of global cloud services; and define security policies that are mapped to a global policy. Section 2 supported this paper with background on RBAC, APIs, and HL7/FHIR, to support a healthcare scenario of two clients and two systems in Section 3. Based on this, Section 4, presented a model for RBACCC with examples in healthcare. Section 5 illustrated the usage of RBACCC in cloud setting within HAPI FHIR, extending its interceptor to intercept API calls and perform RBAC checks. Section 6 compared and contrasted our work with various RBAC approaches. RBACCC is an important first step to transition RBAC to a cloud setting at a service level to control who calls which service. Our future work involves extending GCCC to include MAC and DAC and to unify with related efforts (Rivera Sanchez, et al., 2017a; 2017b) from the mobile app perspective in terms of RBAC and service-based control.

REFERENCES

Aitken, M., 2016. Patient apps for improved healthcare: from novelty to mainstream. http://www.imshealth.com/en/thought-leadership/ims-institute/reports/patient-apps-for-improved-healthcare.

Baihan, M., Rivera Sánchez, Y., Shao, X., Gilman, C., Demurjian, S., & Agresta, T., (in press). A Blueprint for Designing and Developing an mHealth Application for Diverse Stakeholders Utilizing FHIR. Contemporary Applications of Mobile Computing in Healthcare Settings. www.igi-global.com/publish/call-for-papers/call-details/2287

Baihan, M., and Demurjian, S., (in press). A Framework for Secure and Interoperable Cloud Computing. Accepted in Springer Research Advances in Cloud Computing. http://www.cloudbus.org/racc/

Bender, D. and Sartipi, K., 2013, June. HL7 FHIR: An Agile and RESTful approach to healthcare information exchange. In Computer-Based Medical Systems (CBMS), 2013 IEEE 26th International Symposium on (pp. 326-331).

CT Legisltature, 2014, An Act Concerning Youth Athletics And Concussions. Hartford, Connecticut, USA.

Feng, X., Guoyan, L., Hao, H. and Li, X., 2004, September. Role-based access control system for web services. In Computer and Information Technology, 2004. CIT'04. The 4th International Conference on (pp. 357-362).

Fernández-Alemán, J.L., Señor, I.C., Lozoya, P.Á.O. and Toval, A., 2013. Security and privacy in electronic health records: A systematic literature review. Journal of biomedical informatics, 46(3), pp.541-562.

Ferraiolo, D. & Kuhn, R., 1992. Role-Based Access Control. Proc. of the NIST Comp. Sec. Conf., 1992, pp. 554-563.

Fielding, R. T. 2000. Architectural styles and the design of network-based software architectures. Doc. Diss. Irvine: CU.

Google. 2017. https://developers.google.com/fit/overview

Hadley, M. & Sandoz, P., 2009. JAX-RS: Java™ API for RESTful Web Services. Java Specification Request (JSR),311.

Himss. 2016. Meaningful use stage 2 Overview. https://www.cms.gov/regulations-and-guidance/legislation/ehrincentiveprograms/downloads/stage2overview_tipsheet.pdf

Himss. 2016. Meaningful use stage 3 final rule. http://www.himss.org/ResourceLibrary/genResourceDetailPDF.aspx?ItemNumber=44987

HL7. 2016. FHIR Overview. http://hl7.org/fhir/overview.html

HL7. 2016. Health Level Seven INTERNATIONAL. http://www.hl7.org/index.cfm?ref=nav

IDC. 2015. Public cloud computing to reach nearly $70 billion in 2015 worldwide. https://www.idc.com/getdoc.jsp?containerId=prUS25797415

Kelion, L., 2016. Apple icloud security celebrity breach. http://www.bbc.com/news/technology-29237469

OpenEMR. 2016. What Is OpenEMR. http://www.open-emr.org/

Pallis, G., 2010. Cloud computing: the new frontier of internet computing. IEEE internet computing, 14(5), pp.70-73.

Postman. 2013. About Postman. http://www.getpostman.com/

Rivera Sánchez, Y., Demurjian, S., Conover, J., Agresta, T., Shao, X., & Diamond, M., 2016. RBAC for Mobile Applications. Ch. 6 in Mobile Application Development, Usability, and Security, S. Mukherja (ed.), IGI Global.

Rivera Sánchez, Y., Demurjian, S., & Gnirke, L., 2017a. An Intercepting API-based Access Control Approach for Mobile Applications. In *The 13th International Conference on Web Information Systems and Technologies*.

Rivera Sánchez, Y., Demurjian, S., & Baihan, M., 2017b. Achieving RBAC & MAC on RESTful APIs for Mobile Apps using FHIR. In *The 5th IEEE International Conf. on Mobile Cloud Computing, Services, and Engineering*.

Rouse, M., 2014. REST. http://searchmicroservices.techtarget.com/definition/REST-representational-state-transfer.

Shetty, S., 2016. Gartner says cloud computing will become the bulk of new IT spend by 2016. http://www.gartner.com/newsroom/id/2613015

Sirisha, A. and Kumari, G.G., 2010, December. API access control in cloud using the role based access control model. In Trendz in Information Sciences & Computing (TISC), 2010 (pp. 135-137). IEEE.

Subashini, S. and Kavitha, V., 2011. A survey on security issues in service delivery models of cloud computing. Journal of network and computer applications, 34(1), pp.1-11.

Takabi, H., Joshi, J. & Ahn, G., 2010. Securecloud: Towards a comprehensive security framework for cloud computing environments. In Computer Software and Applications Conf., IEEE 34th Annual (pp. 393-398). IEEE.

Takabi, H., Joshi, J. & Ahn, G., 2010. Security and privacy challenges in the cloud. IEEE S&P, 8(6), pp.24-31.

Tang, Z., Wei, J., Sallam, A., Li, K. & Li, R., 2012, May. A new RBAC based access control model for cloud computing. In International Conference on Grid and Pervasive Computing (pp. 279-288). Springer Berlin Heidelberg.

University Health Network. 2016. About HAPI FHIR. http://hapifhir.io/index.html

Wang, L., Von Laszewski, G., Younge, A., He, X., Kunze, M., Tao, J. and Fu, C., 2010. Cloud computing: a perspective study. New Generation Computing, 28(2), pp.137-146.

Wang, Z., 2011, October. Security and privacy issues within the Cloud Computing. In Computational and Information Sciences (ICCIS), 2011 International Conference on (pp. 175-178). IEEE.

Wingfield, E., 2016. Personal cloud will be a $90 billion a year business by 2020. http://www.cloudwedge.com/personal-cloud-will-be-a-90-billion-a-year-business-by-2020/

Wonohoesodo, R. and Tari, Z., 2004, September. A role based access control for web services. In Services Computing, 2004.(SCC 2004). Proceedings. 2004 IEEE International Conference on (pp. 49-56). IEEE.

AN EARLY WARNING SEMANTIC-BASED MODEL FOR EMERGENCY DEPARTMENTS

Guilherme Wunsch, Cristiano André da Costa and Rodrigo da Rosa Righi
Programa de Pós-Graduação em Computação Aplicada (PIPCA), Brazil
Universidade do Vale do Rio dos Sinos (UNISINOS), Brazil

ABSTRACT

This article presents the elaboration of a computational model that uses the protocols of vital signs deterioration to integrate an early warning system (EWS) in the process of patient triage that is already widely used in the emergency department. It was conducted the elaboration of a model that was evaluated with the implementation of a prototype. This evaluation was performed on a scenario created to analyze the model's behavior. We identified that this model reached the expectations, showing that the EWS behaved correctly. Thus, it was possible to verify that the model could detect significant changes in the vital signs of the patient, notifying the nurse when necessary and potentiating the patient's life chances.

KEYWORDS

Triage, Early Warning System, Emergency Department, Internet-Of-Things, Ubiquitous Healthcare, Situation Awareness

1. INTRODUCTION

Triage is a process performed in hospitals to sort patients according to their care needs. With the increasing demand for emergency services, there was an increase in the flow of patients at the doors of the emergency department, making it necessary to reorganize this workflow so that the care was provided according to the necessity of care and no longer in the order of arrival (Brasil, 2004). Nowadays, complete triage protocols have been widely used in hospitals. In addition to these protocols for triage, protocols for clinical deterioration of patients and early warning system (EWS) have also been widely used in hospital emergencies. Its main function is to detect changes in the physiological status of patients in relation to their vital signs (Day & Oldroyd, 2010).

According to the National Institute for Health and Clinical Excellence (NICE) the vital signs register is insufficient and incomplete. The main likely causes are: pressure at work, lack of awareness of the relationship between deterioration of vital signs and acute deterioration of the patient's condition, and over-confidence of the professionals (Christensen, et al., 2011). In this sense, we can verify that an EWS isn't just an available indicator but it's an important to assist the healthcare provider in decision making.

This study aims to elaborate a computational model using the protocols of triage and vital signs deterioration protocols. That's, to develop a system of triage, patient monitoring and alerts that aims to support nurses in the emergency department. This model sought to integrate into a single solution the concepts of ubiquitous healthcare and Internet-of-things, also making use of web semantic and situation awareness.

This article is structured in the following. The next section presents the theoretical background. The third describes the related works. On the other hand, the fourth section presents the proposed. Subsequently, the fifth section presents the evaluation methodology. Finally, the conclusion is presented in the sixth section.

2. BACKGROUND

Triage is a process of identifying patients who need treatment according to their risk potential. Its main objectives are: To evaluate the patient as soon as he/she arrives at the emergency department, humanizing care; Decongest the emergency department; Reduce the time for medical care, causing the patient to be care early according to its severity; Determine the primary care area, and forward the patient directly to the referred specialties according to protocol; Inform waiting times; Promote information about the service to the patients; and return information to family (Brasil, 2004).

Currently, complex triage protocols such as the Australasian Triage Scale (ATS), the Canadian Triage and Acuity Scale (CTAS), the Manchester Triage System (MTS) and the Emergency Severity Index (ESI) have been widely used in worldwide hospitals. In addition, patient clinical deterioration protocols and EWS have already begun to be used in hospital emergency departments.

The primary function of an EWS is to detect changes in the physiological status of patients in relation to their vital signs. Any significant changes should generate alerts for the rapid response team (Day & Oldroyd, 2010). An EWS consists of a series of checklists and standardized clinical parameters, constituting a simple tool to identify patients at imminent risk of death, thus benefiting from admission to the ICU, as shown by several studies (Tavares, et al., 2010).

The most commonly used physiological parameters are the heart rate, respiration rate, temperature, level of consciousness and urine output (Day & Oldroyd, 2010). In an emergency department, the EWS can be used throughout a traditional triage system to identify the risk of deterioration in patients who needs rapid intervention (Day & Oldroyd, 2010). The most used are MEWS, SEWS, GMEWS, Worthing, ViEWS and NEWS.

We know that the physiological parameters used by these protocols can be easily obtained through wearable sensors (Patel, et al., 2012), which are widely used in the Internet-of-Things. This concept of the Internet-of-Things promises to create a world where all the surrounding objects are connected to the Internet and communicate with each other without the human intervention. According to Blake (Blake, 2015), the Internet-of-Things for healthcare has recently emerged as an approach to personalized healthcare.

The advent of new communication technologies, mobile technologies and the integration of several sensors into smart devices enabled doctors and healthcare professionals to access patients' records from anywhere at any time. This evolution can be defined as ubiquitous health (Yu, et al., 2008). The goal of this emerging concept is to bring medical services closer to both sides. From this definition derives another concept: a ubiquitous healthcare system implies in an environment that patients can receive medical treatment at any time, as well as being able to transmit information pertinent to their health remotely. This purpose of maintaining healthcare ubiquitously is called by some authors as ubiquitous healthcare (Gelogo & Kim, 2013).

3. RELATED WORK

We conducted a systematic literature review with the objective of defining the related works. This research was focused on three pillars: emergency triage, Internet-of-Things, and model (ie, which models were designed to be used during the emergency department triage process that incorporate some element of the Internet-of-Things). For this, we used the following search string *(triage AND ("emergency department" OR A&E OR "emergency room")) AND (wearable OR IoT OR "internet of things") AND (method OR approach OR system OR framework OR model OR middleware)* in these sources of research libraries: ACM Digital Library, CiteSeerX Library, Elsevier B. V. ScienceDirect, Google Scholar, IEEE Xplore Digital Library, IET Digital Library, JMIR Publications Library, PubMed, Scientific Electronic Library Online and Springer Science.

With this research method, it was possible to discover in the literature models that are proposed to monitor the vital signs of patients in the emergency department (Fernández-López, et al., 2010) (Ko, et al., 2010) (Fleming, et al., 2008) (Niswar, et al., 2013) (Ayyagari, et al., 2009), with the same purpose of the model that we developed in this study. These models use the Internet-of-Things to monitor patients through sensors that measure vital signs directly in patients. It was also possible to find other models that use these same vital signs sensors to patients triage (Kumaran & Nsenga, 2016) (Skolnik, et al., 2016).

On the other hand, some models go beyond, providing a decision support system, in other words, when the system provides some information that supports the healthcare professional to choose which conduct should be taken to a particular circumstance, for example, or models that help throughout the emergency department flow in general; controlling the patient queue, the medication that may be prescribed according to some allergy presented and the available resources in the hospital at the care moment (Claudio, et al., 2014) (Agarwal, et al., 2015) (Wunsch, et al., 2017) (Wunsch, et al., 2016).

Table 1. Comparative Between Related Works

Reference	IoT	Triage	Monitoring	Decision Support	Health management	Early warning
(Claudio, et al., 2014)	Yes	Yes	Yes	No	No	No
(Wunsch, et al., 2017)	No	Yes	No	Yes	Yes	No
(Kumaran & Nsenga, 2016)	Yes	Yes	No	No	Yes	No
(Fernández-López, et al., 2010)	Yes	No	Yes	No	No	No
(Schmidt, et al., 2016)	Yes	No	No	Yes	No	No
(Agarwal, et al., 2015)	Yes	No	Yes	No	No	No
(Sravani & Kumar, 2015)	Yes	Yes	Yes	No	No	No
(Cox, et al., 2008)	Yes	No	Yes	No	No	No
(Ko, et al., 2010)	Yes	Yes	Yes	No	No	No
(Salman, et al., 2014)	Yes	Yes	No	Yes	No	No
(Fleming, et al., 2008)	Yes	No	Yes	No	No	No
(Niswar, et al., 2013)	Yes	No	Yes	No	No	No
(Ayyagari, et al., 2009)	Yes	No	Yes	No	Yes	No
(Skolnik, et al., 2016)	Yes	Yes	No	Yes	No	No
(Chen & Pompili, 2011)	Yes	No	Yes	No	No	No
(Wunsch, et al., 2016)	Yes	Yes	Yes	Yes	Yes	No

The Table 1 brings, ordered by the title of the article, a comparative between the related works to facilitate the understanding of the characteristics of each one. The characteristics are: IoT (if the model uses some element of IoT), triage (if the model implements some method for patients triage), monitoring (if any technique for monitoring patients is used), decision support (decision-making support for health professionals), health management (providing support in health management), early warning (if any early warning protocol is implemented). An important point to note is that, even when worrying about monitoring patients in an emergency, none of the proposed models supports an EWS.

Thus, these models don't worry in employing clinical deterioration protocols to support an EWS during the triage in the emergency department. Based on this observed gap, the present work sought to add an EWS to the model initiated by Wunsch in (Wunsch, et al., 2016) and improved in (Wunsch, et al., 2017). Therefore, its objective was to elaborate a model to patient triage and monitoring with an EWS that can be used in the hospital's emergency department.

4. PROPOSED MODEL

The general architecture of the proposed model sought to integrate the previously described gap to a previously developed model, called UbiTriagem (Wunsch, et al., 2016) (Wunsch, et al., 2017). This model maintained its original architecture of distributed systems, called service-oriented architecture (SOA). Thus, as observed in Figure 1, the business rules and data stored by the model are in this service, which is described later. On the other hand, clients are distributed applications on mobile devices that can be used by both nurses and patients (while waiting for a service).

4.1 Client Layer

In the hardware domain, as previously described, mobile devices are used by nurses or patients to interact with the service. Vital signs sensors such as temperature, heart rate, pulse oximetry, are placed on patients, where through their mobile device (which is used in that case as a bridge between the sensors and the application service) collect the vital signs so that can be processed and analyzed.

On the other hand, in the software domain, we can observe the client layer. This layer is an application installed directly on the mobile devices of nurses and patients. It's divided into three modules based on their actors. The nurse module aims to provide them an easy and usual way of interacting with the model. Into this module, the nurse can perform the triage or retriage of a patient, in addition to follow the progress of the emergency department queue and receive notifications of the pertinent situation.

Also on the client layer there is the patient module, whose objective is to receive, concentrate and modularize the vital signs received from wearable sensors placed on the patients. This module does not perform any analysis on vital signs. It's only used as a bridge to retransmit this information that can be interpreted to the model service. In addition to this function, the patient module is also responsible for humanizing care, informing patients about their position in the queue and about the triage protocol.

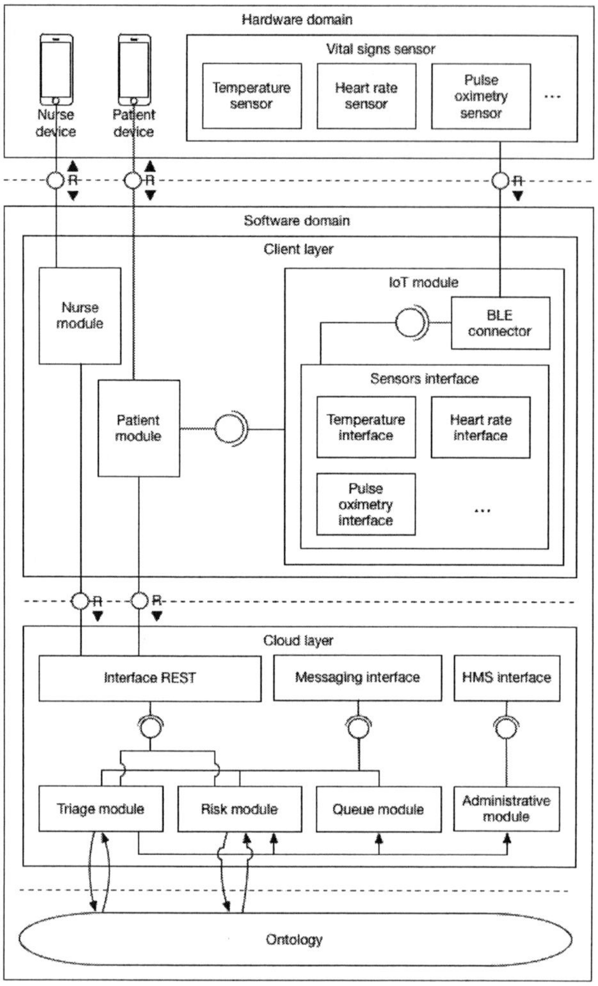

Figure 1. General Architecture of the Proposed Model

Finally, vital signs are measured from sensors that can be accessed via the IoT module. This information is collected through a Bluetooth Low-Energy (BLE) connector and specific interfaces to access each sensor. Each interface could access each sensor and modularize its data which will be later interpreted by the service. This modularization is a very important step because it ensures that the service can interpret the data extracted from the wearable sensors.

4.2 Cloud Layer

Located in the service of the proposed model, the cloud layer, on the other hand, has a REST interface, capable of connecting all of solution clients. As such, it is the default interface so that all mobile applications can access the model service in a simple and effective way. Through it should traffic all the information regarding the triage process and EWS of the emergency department.

The messaging interface is responsible for sending notifications alerts to the clients of the solution. It manages this through an indirect communication service known as publish-subscribe. In this case nurses and patient subscribe notification lists and whenever a notification is published on your list, they will receive it immediately. These notifications are: patient arrivals, needs for triage or retriage, vital signs deterioration alerts (for nurses) and estimation time for care (for patients).

The last interface module with the model service is the Hospital Management System (HMS) interface. It aims to integrate the proposed solution with legacy hospital management systems. Thus, information from nurses, such as name, ID and login; and of patients, such as name, gender, age, ID and medical records are synchronized between the proposed model and the HMS used by the health institution.

The administrative module aims to managing all the administrative information of the model, persists them temporarily and synchronizes them whenever necessary with the HMS through the HMS interface. It can be said that this is one of the most important modules of the model, since it manages all entities of this model.

However, the queue module organizes the entire attendance queue. Its organization is made by priority, according to the triage protocol used in the emergency department. Therefore, it allows the nurse to be alert in the remaining time that each care is performed, notifying him if the service deadline is close.

The risk module is the main module regarding the EWS. It has the mission of analyzing and detecting significant changes in patients' vital signs, received at real time, and sending notifications to the nurse's device, if necessary. These alerts are sent to the nurse based on the result of the reasoning performed in the specific ontology, that is a formal and explicit specification of a knowledge, of the clinical deterioration protocol used by the hospital. In this case, the nurse should then trigger a rapid response team to perform the care of the patient at risk.

In Figure 2 it is possible to note the developed ontology model that should provide the basis for the implementation of the clinical deterioration protocol ontology. The classes of this ontology are represented by oval figures. Solid arrows represent the hierarchy between classes and subclasses, while dotted arrows are used to represent the properties between the instances of those classes. The individuals of this ontology are, for example, the protocol scores, vital signs, attendance and patient.

Each Vital Sign is associated with a Score through an affirmation property. Rules should be used to associate individuals of the Risk class (WithoutRisk and AlertRisk) with the class Attendance based on the score (Score0, 1, 2, ..., N) obtained through the vital signs. Table 2 shows how the alert rules are derived from the combination of possible scores. This example was based on the NEWS protocol, but may be converted to any other clinical deterioration protocol. The NEWS defines that it is recommended to trigger a rapid response team when any vital signal has a score of 3 (on a scale of 0 to 3) or when the sum of all vital signs scores is equal or greater than 5 (Williams, et al., 2012). The combination of the scoring classes associated with the patient's vital signs will generate a result, which refers to the patient's risk of deterioration, for example, generating an Alert risk (when a nurse should be notified) or Without risk. That is, if the combination of the score classes associated with each vital signal has at least one Score3 class, the patient is at Alert risk (Rule #1). Rule #2 defines alert condition to the patient that has three associated Score2 classes and so on. These rules are all possible combinations in which according to the NEWS protocol the patient would be at risk of alertness. The Rule #6 is the exception which is the negation of the other rules.

Finally, the triage module is responsible for receiving and providing information about the triage process to all solution customers. Thus, this module receives and processes the patients' vital signs through the wearable devices. In order to process vital signs there is a subsystem directly connected to the ontology of the triage protocol used by the emergency department and, through a reasoning technique in this ontology, can infer the patient's triage. This module is also responsible for interpreting all vital signs collected in real time, analyzing them and, again, by reasoning on the same ontology, evaluating if there was any change in the patient's triage and then triggering a notification to the nurse if is necessary.

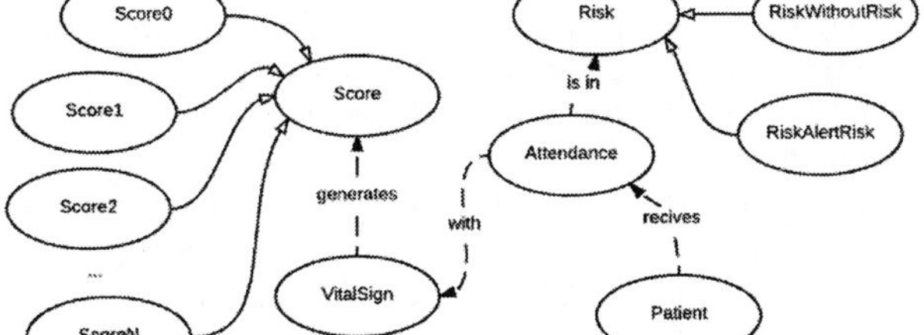

Figure 2. Ontology Model for the EWS

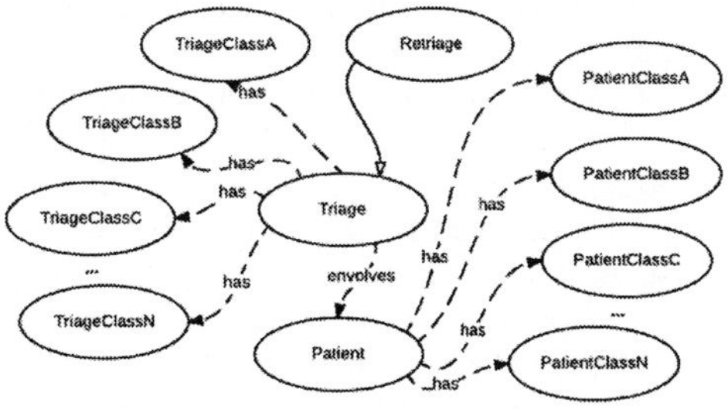

Figure 3. Ontology Model for the Triage

This ontology should be implemented according to the triage protocol used by the hospital. A base model of this ontology can be seen in Figure 3. Note that in the diagram developed in Figure 3, the individuals of this ontology are, for example, presentations, discriminators and symptoms of patients who are inserted into (TriageClassA, B, C, ..., and N). The individuals are also, for example, age groups, gender and other patient information related through their respective classes (PatientClass A, B, C, ..., and N). These individuals are related through rules and properties of transitivity with their respective categories of triage so a reasoner can infer the triage based on the information obtained from the patient.

Table 2. Derived Rules for the Possible Combinations that Generate a Risk Result

Rule	Combination	Result
#1	Score3	Alert risk
#2	Score2 **and** Score2 **and** Score2	Alert risk
#3	Score2 **and** Score2 **and** Score1	Alert risk
#4	Score2 **and** Score1 **and** Score1 **and** Score1	Alert risk
#5	Score1 **and** Score1 **and** Score1 **and** Score1 **and** Score1	Alert risk
#6	Any other possible combination	Without risk

5. EVALUATION

The use of scenarios for the evaluation of ubiquitous applications has been accepted by the scientific community (Wunsch, et al., 2016). Moreover, with the use of this methodology in the health area it is possible to make a more conscious decision, since the human factor is eliminated and focused only on the real problems involved (Westergren, et al., 2014); it can provide cost and time savings and ethical issues are not involved, for example, applying two different protocols (the reference and the test protocol) in the same patient. Thus, in order to evaluate the proposed model, a hypothetical scenario was created that describes a situation of a patient who arrived at the emergency department and was properly triaged by the nurse. After some time in the waiting room, she presented significant changes in his vital signs and the EWS notified the nurse who promptly took the proper conduct with the patient. The following scenario describes it:

"A 55-year-old woman enters the emergency department complaining of shortness of breath. She reports that she has felt nausea and she has vomited too. She has no chest pain and her pulse is 86 beats per minute, regular, and her blood pressure is 140/90. She is very calm and reports that she looks for the emergency because it's causing some discomfort to her. She was usually triaged by the nurse. The patient was equipped with wearable vital signs sensors and was sent to the waiting room. When she is waiting for her care, she began to feel severe chest pains. Her pulse rate was increased to 140 beats per minute and her blood pressure to 220/140. The nurse was notified at the same time. The nurse soon realized that the patient was having a heart attack and immediately contacted the hospital's rapid response team."

To evaluate this scenario, we used the prototype developed by Wunsch (Wunsch, et al., 2017). In the developed prototype, we used an ontology from Manchester protocol, which is one of the most used in the world and it's very common in emergencies of Brazilian hospitals. In addition, an ontology was developed for the EWS based on NEWS (Williams, et al., 2012). This ontology was created and evaluated through the Protégé, which has available the HermiT reasoner, so we can perform inferences on this ontology.

During the triage of the patient, the vital signs were measured and no alert status was generated by the EWS, as can be seen in Figure 4. According to NEWS, the sum of vital signs scores for this case would be zero, so no alert should be issued. Soon after, the service begins to listen for vital signs changes that was sent through the patient interface. When a change in vital signs was simulated with 140 beats per minute and 220/140 of blood pressure, based on the reasoning performed in the ontology, a state of alert was generated, according to Figure 5. Also, according to the NEWS protocol, the sum of the scores of the patient's vital signs changed to 6. In this case, a state of alert was issued.

In this scenario elaborated for the evaluation of the model, the patient was initially triaged and no alert state was generated, since their vital signs were normal. However, during the waiting, the patient's pulse and blood pressure measurements changed because she was having a heart attack. At that same moment, the nurse received a notification and when evidencing the patient's condition, it took as a conduit to contact the rapid response team so that the patient was attended quickly.

With this, it was possible to evaluate that the model behaved as expected, showing that the EWS acted properly. That is, when, through situation awareness, it was detected that the vital signs, measured through wearable sensors, experienced significant changes. In this case, the prototype confirmed that the model could detect, in a ubiquitous way, these changes, notifying the nurse and potentiating the patient's life chances.

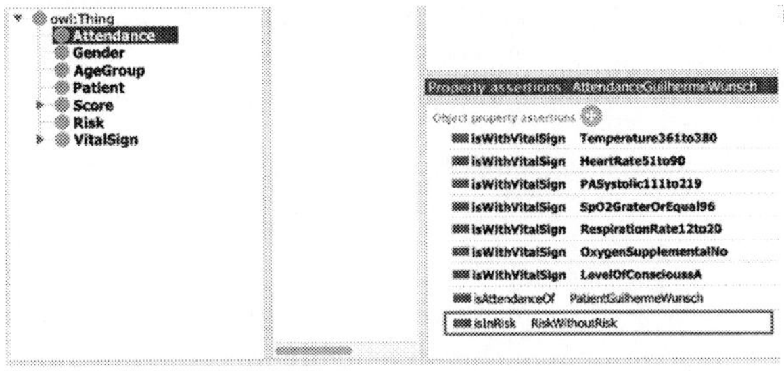

Figure 4. Result of the Evaluation with Regular Vital Signs: without Risk

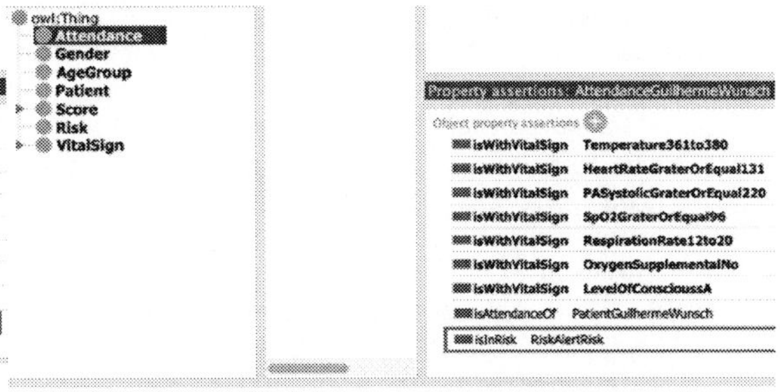

Figure 5. Result of the Evaluation with Significant Changes in the Vital Signs: Alert Risk

6. CONCLUSION

This study aimed to develop a computational model to be used by nurses during the process of patient triage in the emergency department in hospitals using the concepts of ubiquitous healthcare and the Internet-of-Things. Records of insufficient and incomplete vital signs caused by work pressure, lack of knowledge of the relationship between deterioration of vital signs and acute deterioration of the patient's state, and the overconfidence of the professionals was the main motivation of the present study.

Different from the related works, the present proposal focused on a gap found that was the implementation of an EWS during the process of patient triage. This was the main scientific contribution of the proposed model. This was possible to be done from health data collected directly from the patients with the use of wearable sensors of the Internet-of-things and making use of situation awareness through a technique of reasoning performed on an ontology.

During the evaluation, a prototype was developed whose purpose was applying it into a fictitious scenario developed specifically to evaluate the use of the proposed model. With this, it was possible to evaluate that the model reach the expectations, showing that the EWS behaved correctly. Thus, it was possible to detect that the vital signs experienced significant changes and, in this case, we confirmed that the model could detect these alterations, notifying the nurse and potentiating the patient's life chances.

As a future opportunity for related work, a case study can be conducted with patients in a controlled environment to analyze how the model would behave in a simulated evaluation, in order to evaluate attributes such as usability and perception value of this model. Afterwards, the model could be submitted for evaluation in a real emergency department in order to compare the reliability of the model with the systems traditionally used in hospitals.

ACKNOWLEDGEMENT

The authors would like to thank CAPES, CNPQ and FAPERGS for the support given to this research.

REFERENCES

Agarwal, S., Rani, A., Singh, V. & Mittal, A., 2015. FPGA based wireless emergency medical system for developing countries. *Information and Computer Technology (GOCICT), 2015 Annual Global Online Conference on*, pp. 80-84.

Ayyagari, D., Fu, Y., Xu, J. & Colquitt, N., 2009. Smart personal health manager: A sensor ban application: A demonstration. *Consumer Communications and Networking Conference, 2009. CCNC 2009. 6th IEEE*, pp. 1-2.

Blake, M. B., 2015. An Internet of Things for Healthcare. *IEEE Internet Computing,* Issue 4, pp. 4-6.

Brasil, M. d. S. S.-E. N. T. d. P. N. d. H., 2004. *HumanizaSUS - Acolhimento com avaliação e classificação de risco. Um paradigma ético-estético no fazer da saúde.* 1 ed. Brasília: Editora MS.

Chen, B. & Pompili, D., 2011. Transmission of patient vital signs using wireless body area networks. *Mobile Networks and Applications,* 16(6), pp. 663-682.

Christensen, D. et al., 2011. Nurse-administered early warning score system can be used for emergency department triage. *Dan Med Bull,* 58(6), p. A4221.

Claudio, D., Kremer, G. E. O., Bravo-Llerena, W. & Freivalds, A., 2014. A dynamic multi-attribute utility theory-based decision support system for patient prioritization in the emergency department. *IIE Transactions on Healthcare Systems Engineering,* 4(1), pp. 1-15.

Cox, P. et al., 2008. Investigation of photoplethysmogram morphology for the detection of hypovolemic states. *Engineering in Medicine and Biology Society, 2008. EMBS 2008. 30th Annual International Conference of the IEEE*, pp. 5486-5489.

Day, A. & Oldroyd, C., 2010. The use of early warning scores in the emergency department. *Journal of Emergency Nursing,* 36(2), pp. 154-155.

Fernández-López, H., Correia, J. H., Simões, R. & Afonso, J. A., 2010. Experimental evaluation of IEEE 802.15. 4/ZigBee for multi-patient ECG monitoring. *International Conference on Electronic Healthcare*, pp. 184-191.

Fleming, S., Tarassenko, L., Thompson, M. & Mant, D., 2008. Non-invasive measurement of respiratory rate in children using the photoplethysmogram. *Engineering in Medicine and Biology Society, 2008. EMBS 2008. 30th Annual International Conference of the IEEE*, pp. 1886-1889.

Gelogo, Y. E. & Kim, H.-K., 2013. Unified Ubiquitous Healthcare System Architecture with Collaborative Model. *International Journal of Multimedia and Ubiquitous Engineering,* 8(3).

Ko, J. et al., 2010. MEDiSN: Medical emergency detection in sensor networks. *ACM Transactions on Embedded Computing Systems (TECS),* 10(1), p. 11.

Kumaran, S. & Nsenga, J., 2016. Design of a Multi-Priority Triage Chair for Crowded Remote Healthcare Centers in Sub-Saharan Africa. *The International Symposium on Intelligent Systems Technologies and Applications*, pp. 903-911.

Niswar, M. et al., 2013. Performance evaluation of ZigBee-based wireless sensor network for monitoring patients' pulse status.

Patel, S. et al., 2012. A review of wearable sensors and systems with application in rehabilitation. *Journal of neuroengineering and rehabilitation,* 9(1), p. 21.

Salman, O. H., Rasid, M. F. A., Saripan, M. I. & Subramaniam, S. K., 2014. Multi-sources data fusion framework for remote triage prioritization in telehealth. *Journal of medical systems,* 38(9), p. 103.

Schmidt, T. et al., 2016. Factors related to monitoring during admission of acute patients. *Journal of clinical monitoring and computing,* pp. 1-9.

Skolnik, A. B. et al., 2016. Teletoxicology: Patient Assessment Using Wearable Audiovisual Streaming Technology. *Journal of Medical Toxicology,* 12(4), pp. 358-364.

Sravani, K. & Kumar, P. S., 2015. Human Health Behavior Detection using Bio Sensors and Classification by Wearable Tags in Smart Spaces.

Tavares, R. C. F. et al., 2010. Validação de um escore de alerta precoce pré-admissão na unidade de terapia intensiva. *Revista Brasileira de Terapia Intensiva,* 20(2), pp. 124-127.

Westergren, H., Ferm, M. & Häggström, P., 2014. First evaluation of the paediatric version of the Swedish rapid emergency triage and treatment system shows good reliability. *Acta Paediatrica,* 103(3), pp. 305-308.

Williams, B. et al., 2012. National early warning score (NEWS): Standardising the assessment of acute-illness severity in the NHS. *London: The Royal College of Physicians.*

Wunsch, G., da Costa, C. A. & da Rosa Righi, R., 2016. Um modelo ubíquo para retriagem de pacientes baseado na Internet das coisas. *Anais do XXXVI Congresso da Sociedade Brasileira de Computação*, pp. 1176-1185.

Wunsch, G., da Costa, C. A. & Righi, R. R., 2017. A Semantic-Based Model for Triage Patients in Emergency Departments. *Journal of medical systems,* 41(4), p. 65.

Yu, W. D., Gummadikayala, R. & Mudumbi, S., 2008. A web-based wireless mobile system design of security and privacy framework for u-Healthcare. *10th International Conference on e-health Networking, Applications and Services, 2008. HealthCom 2008*, pp. 96-101.

INTEGRATION BETWEEN ELECTRONIC HEALTH RECORDS STANDARDS USING ONTOLOGIES AND RULES

Matheus Henrique Wichman, Cristiano André da Costa, Alex Roehrs,
Denise Bandeira and Rodrigo da Rosa Righi
Programa de Pós-Graduação em Computação Aplicada (PPGCA)
Universidade do Vale do Rio dos Sinos (UNISINOS)

ABSTRACT

The Information Technology (IT) applied to healthcare has the potential to bring several benefits to patients as well as physicians. A kind of system which attempts to improve the healthcare process is the Electronic Health Record (EHR). However, with the emergence of different standards, a way to establish communication between them is needed. Although some works have addressed the interoperability issue, most of them are based on the use of custom tools to exchange data between EHRs. This paper proposes the development of an ontology, called HIGO (Health Information Gathering Ontology), which captures the common information between each EHR. After, we use the Semantic Web Rule Language (SWRL) to create rules that feed this ontology. The method evaluation was done with vital signs data, represented using *open*EHR and FHIR (Fast Interoperable Health Resources) standards. As result, using the HIGO ontology and SWRL rules, we were able to query both standards without being necessary to develop specific queries for each one.

KEYWORDS

Interoperability, openEHR, FHIR, Ontology, Electronic Health Record, Semantic Web

1. INTRODUCTION

The Information Technology (IT) applied to healthcare has the potential to bring several benefits to patients as well as physicians. The benefits include: better support in decision making from the medical staff; cost reduction; better engagement of the patient during the treatment, decrease in the rate of human errors during procedures, in addition to others (Buntin et al, 2011). A kind of Health Information System (SIS) which attempts to improve the healthcare process is the Electronic Health Record (EHR). According to ISO / TR 20514 (ANSI, 2005), an EHR is a shareable digital repository of information about a patient. Although the EHR has the role of allowing continued, efficient and qualified care, its adoption has not yet reached all the health establishments. A group of factors contribute to hamper the implementation of these solutions. We could cite the high cost to develop an EHR, no investment in infrastructure and the lack of interoperability with legacy systems (Khalifa, 2013).

To solve the interoperability issue, some solutions have been developed. In addition to paper records, the use of defined sets of electronic messages (Kalra, 2006), transmitted through the EDIFACT (EALS, 1988) or HL7 protocols (HL7, 2017) was adopted. Most health facilities have adopted these messages to transfer financial data, between health insurance companies and hospitals, and for organization and administration of the services provided. Although this method of communication provides certain interoperability, few messages have been developed to share the clinical data among other stakeholders.

Considering the problems of previous solutions, the *open*EHR standard (2017) was developed to be a flexible and modular EHR. This standard minimizes the problem of EDIFACT / HL7 messages by using a two-layer architecture. In this way, it can be used to store any kind of information about a procedure performed. The *open*EHR architecture separates generic properties of an EHR into a layer known as the Reference Model, while the instances containing the data are stored in another layer, called Archetype Object Model.

Another initiative, to achieve the interoperability, is the FHIR (Fast Interoperable Health Resources) (HL7, 2017), developed with focus on the communication needs that modern systems require and to possibly be a substitute for HL7. Unlike HL7, the FHIR has strong support on Web standards such as JSON, XML and HTTP, making it easier to integrate with systems hosted on remote machines, as well as having good flexibility to adapt to advances in healthcare processes. However, despite the collaboration from the *open*EHR team during the creation of the FHIR, the two standards work completely apart.

In this context, this paper proposes the use of OWL (Ontology Web Language) (Welty et al, 2002) for creating ontologies that can fill the space between *open*EHR and FHIR. One of the reasons for using an ontology is that it allows the sharing of information among different software agents, making them suitable for the task of interconnecting different systems (Noy and McGuinness, 2001). Although there are works that also address the interoperability, the treatment of both standards through ontologies is incipient. The developed method starts from the mapping of each specification to a separate ontology. Next, a third ontology is used to generically capture the concepts represented in each standard. Finally, the SWRL (Semantic Web Rule Language) language is used to create rules which converts instances from each standard to members of this last ontology. In order to evaluate the proposed method, data from vital signs was used, since through this information it is possible to identify in advance deteriorations in the clinical state of the patient (Elliott and Coventry, 2012). Vital signs were used also because this kind of data uses extensively the base types from each EHR, unlike observations with multimedia resources (e.g. a MRI image), where the electronic record is used only as a proxy, since the data is stored in another place.

The rest of this article is organized as follows. Section 2 discusses similar approaches. In Section 3 some of the concepts used in this article are reviewed. Section 4 describes the mapping process to create an ontology for each standard. The ontology proposed in this article is detailed in Section 5. In Section 6 the results of the evaluation are reported. Finally, conclusions of this work are reported in Section 7.

2. RELATED WORK

Some efforts have already been made by the scientific community to address the interoperability between heterogeneous health systems. The work done so far is based on the mapping of health records to ontologies. Afterwards, custom tools are developed to create relations between them.

Bicer et al. (2005) works to create a mapping between messages from versions 2 and 3 of the HL7 standard. EHR version 2 of HL7 uses plain text messages and version 3 is based on the Reference Information Model (RIM) specification, the mapping to an ontology helps to create a consistent representation of both standards. In this work, a tool was developed, called OWLmt (OWL Mapping Tool), to aid in the mapping.

Martínez-Costa el al. (2010) emphasizes the interoperability between *open*EHR archetypes and the ISO 13606 standard (Kalra and Lloyd, 2008). Because the two specifications follow the two-layer architecture, the proposed solution is based on the transformation of openEHR archetypes into ISO 13606 models and vice versa.

Oliveira (2016) proposes a method for converting HL7 messages into openEHR. The proposed method consists of analyzing the messages and developing compatible archetypes. The conversion of the data is done through a tool, called CDOT (Clinical Document Online Translator), which receives a JSON representation of the HL7 message and performs the conversion to *open*EHR, based on the archetypes developed for each type of message. The mentioned method does not use ontologies.

Although there are works that seek to develop interoperability among medical records, no alternatives were found that addressed the data exchange exclusively through ontologies. In addition, there were no studies that emphasized the use of FHIR in conjunction with *open*EHR.

3. BACKGROUND

This section briefly discusses the concepts and technologies used to achieve the results of this work. Section 3.1 describes the foundation of the Electronic Health Record. Afterwards, section 3.2 presents the definition of interoperability. Finally, section 3.3 introduces the concept of ontology, strongly used in this paper, as well as the OWL language and SWRL rules.

3.1 Electronic Health Record – EHR

Defined by ISO / TR 20514 (ANSI, 2005), the Electronic Health Record (EHR) can be understood as a repository, in digital format, where health data regarding a patient is stored. The content of an EHR may include vital signs data, weight and height history, medications, allergies, as well as test results and procedures performed (Roehrs et al, 2017). This information has the function of assisting the decision-making process of the medical team, making the healthcare dynamic, efficient and at a lower cost (Menachemi and Collum, 2011).

3.2 Interoperability

Despite the potential benefits of EHR, the use of distinct standards has brought the problem of interoperability between systems. Interoperability can be defined as the ability of different applications to communicate with each other, allowing the exchange of information in a precise, efficient and consistent manner (Iroju et al, 2013). In order to establish a communication channel between both sides, the agents should use the same message format. To standardize these messages, some EHR specifications have emerged, firstly the *open*EHR and later, the FHIR.

3.3 Ontologies, OWL and SWRL Rules

According to Guarino et al. (1998), an ontology can be understood as the set of axioms designed to capture a certain conceptualization. To represent an ontology, it is necessary to use a formal language, known by machines, such as the Ontology Web Language (OWL). OWL is an ontology description language that has gained strong support from the academic community, consequently, several tools have been developed to use this language, such as the Protégé editor (2017).

The healthcare processes can best be described when using rule-based systems (Lezcano et al, 2011). Although OWL facilitates interoperability between systems, the language still lacks a rule structure, which could increase the expressiveness of an ontology. As a solution, the Semantic Web Rule Language (SWRL) have emerged, which aims to fill the gap left by OWL. The SWRL allows the extraction of implicit information in an ontology. Generally, a SWRL rule is composed of two blocks, one called antecedent and another consequent, both connected by a logical implication. Whenever the conditions in the antecedent are true, the consequent block will necessarily be true.

4. MAPPING HEALTH RECORDS

In order to store health records in a knowledge base, it is necessary to convert each standard specification into an own ontology. After this step, instances containing clinical data can be created within each ontology.

One way to obtain these ontologies is to perform the conversion from the XML Schema Definition (XSD) files of each standard, since both standards use the Extensible Markup Language (XML) for data representation. These files are sets of metadata that make explicit the formalisms involved in an XML document (Bray et al, 1997). By doing transformations on these XSD files, we could define a mapping which converts the XSD to OWL ontologies.

The method adopted to translate the XSD to OWL follows the approach proposed by Bohring and Auer (2005). In this method, the XSD structure is reproduced in the OWL language manually by creating a mapping table between both languages. The mappings created cover the most part of XSD specification. In Table 1, the mappings between XSD and OWL structures can be seen.

In general, every time an xsd:complexType element is found in the XSD, its conversion to OWL is done through a new class, along with its properties. When the property contains other elements, not just a literal value, it is converted through an owl:ObjectProperty. For attributes and properties whose values are literals, the translation was made to an owl:DatatypeProperty property. Cardinality constraints are represented with the help of the owl:allValuesFrom construct. We adopted the use of the prefix "dtp_" for data type properties and "obp_" for object properties, to avoid name conflicts.

In Figure 1, the ontologies generated for the *open*EHR and FHIR standards, respectively, can be visualized. In the case of FHIR, the main types of data (e.g. observation, request for examination, list of medications, etc.) are called **resources**, to translate these ones an ontology for each was created. Therefore, a basic ontology was generated containing the types and structures common to all resources as well as an ontology for each resource, which is later imported into the main ontology.

Table 1. XSD-OWL Mapping

XSD	OWL
xsd:complexType	owl:Class
xsd:attribute	owl:DatatypeProperty
xsd:element	owl:DatatypeProperty, owl:ObjectProperty
xsd:minOccurs, xsd:maxOccurs	owl:allValuesFrom

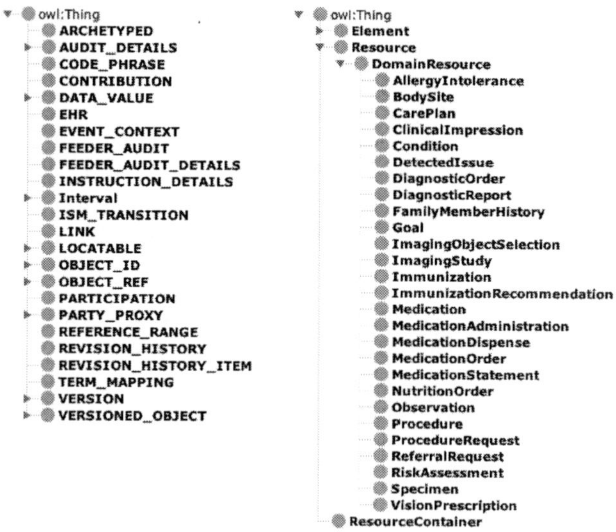

Figure 1. *open*EHR (on left) and FHIR (on right) Ontology

Another step to translate an HER is the insertion of the data in the previously ontology. To accomplish this task, a converter was developed that automatically creates the instances. However, prior to conversion, it is necessary to group all the ontologies that are part of the same standard into a new one that has the same namespace. The converter receives as input the XML and the consolidated ontology corresponding to the standard used, after it creates the instances appropriately within the ontology.

5. PROPOSED ONTOLOGY

To create a layer grouping information from *open*EHR and FHIR, we use a third ontology, called HIGO (Health Information Gathering Ontology). This last ontology captures the generalities of both standards, exposing a consistent interface for data extraction. The developed ontology does not store data, however, its classes are used to map equivalent structures between standards, allowing to gather information of both standards. Because EHR specifications have differences in expressiveness and structure, there will be objects which cannot be mapped directly with rules. To address this issue, other ontologies can be employed to translate these objets before using them in HIGO ontology.

The development of the HIGO ontology was based on an analysis of *open*EHR archetypes, since this standard is more expressive. The vital signs chosen for representation were those cited by Elliott and Coventry

(2012). To obtain the archetypes, we searched on the *open*EHR Clinical Knowledge Manager (CKM) archetype repository (2017) for observation archetypes that were appropriate for representing these signals. Table 2 lists the archetypes found and the medical concept represented by each one.

Table 2. Selected Archetypes

Concept	Archetype
Blood pressure	openEHR-EHR-OBSERVATION.blood_pressure.v1
Hear beat	openEHR-EHR-OBSERVATION.pulse.v1
Body temperature	openEHR-EHR-OBSERVATION.body_temperature.v1
Respiration rhythm	openEHR-EHR-OBSERVATION.respiration.v1

The archetype selected for blood pressure stores the two pressure measurements on distinct properties: systolic (systolic) and diastolic (diastolic). These properties store instances of type DV_QUANTITY, which is used to store quantities, allowing you to specify the unit, magnitude, and precision. Before creating any archetype-specific class we created a higo:Observation class, child of owl:Thing, which will serve as the parent class for this and for the other archetypes. After, for blood pressure, we created the higo:BloodPressure class, child of higo:Observation. For the two components of blood pressure, two object properties were created: higo:systolic and higo:diastolic. In the higo:BloodPressure class was used the owl:subClassOf property to restrict the values of these properties, allowing only instances of type higo:Quantity. Finally, the class higo:Quantity was created, which is used for quantitative values, similar to type DV_QUANTITY. This class has the properties higo:magnitude and higo:units, designed to express, respectively, the magnitude and unit of a quantity. Other information present in the archetype had to be ignored because was not possible to find matches in the FHIR that would allow an accurate mapping.

The representation of the other archetypes followed the same routine, since the only information relative to vital signs which are present in both standards is the value of the observation. The metadata present in these archetypes will not be represented because there is no consistent mapping between all of them. The process of representing heart rate, body temperature and respiratory rate is described below:

- **Heart Beat:** Initially, the class higo:HeartBeat was created, child of higo:Observation. Next, the higo:rate property was added to the ontology. In the class we created earlier a restriction was added so that the property higo:rate accepts only values of type higo:Quantity;
- **Respiration Rhythm:** Similar to the previous archetype, here the higo:Respiration was created. An restriction also was added on the property higo:rate to only allow quantities;
- **Body Temperature:** For this archetype, the higo:BodyTemperature class was added. After, the higo:temperature property was created and added to the previously created class. Just like the others, the constraint added also requires a quantity as value for the higo:temperature property, but the value also has to have an appropriate unit of measure to express temperatures.

The HIGO ontology can be visualized in Figure 2. In addition to the classes cited above, a higo:Patient class was added to identify which patient each observation refers to. This class contains basic information (name, email, and gender) and a list of identifiers used by *open*EHR and FHIR to represent the patient.

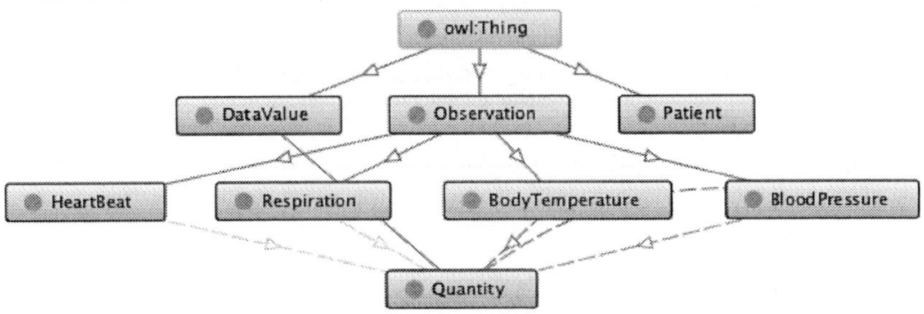

Figure 2. HIGO Ontology

6. EVALUATION

The method presented in this paper attempts to address the problem of interoperability between different EHR standards by the use of the OWL language. To evaluate it, we started from the scenario where physicians, on several occasions, need to investigate in detail the health record of a patient, in the search for anomalies. Although, due to many factors, that record can be fragmented between several stakeholders and in different formats, making necessary to develop specific query routines for each HIS. Given this scenario, we evaluated whether the use of the HIGO ontology, in conjunction with SWRL rules, allows to merge data from heterogeneous systems. The evaluation was performed by mapping the data to instances within the ontologies of each standard. Subsequently, SWRL rules were used to classify these instances into members of the HIGO ontology.

The data for evaluation is composed of blood pressure readings from three patients, extracted from the MIMIC-III database (Johnson et al, 2016). Table 3 shows the selected blood pressure readings. In the MIMIC-III readings, dates were changed to make impossible to identify the patients. Systolic and diastolic blood pressure values are both in millimeters of mercury (mmHg). We chose to represent the first 5 rows of each table in *open*EHR, while the others are represented in the FHIR.

Table 3. Blood Pressure Readings

Patient	Date	Diastolic	Systolic
188	2161-07-02 17:45	60	117
188	2161-07-03 02:00	68	130
188	2161-07-03 13:00	61	127
711	2185-03-22 14:10	94	152
711	2185-03-22 21:52	73	130
711	2185-03-23 07:00	73	121
1709	2118-01-04 12:02	102	168
1709	2118-01-04 14:15	88	120
1709	2118-01-04 17:00	81	136

After data preparation, instances for each record were created using the tool described in Section 5. These instances were added to a separate ontology. In this ontology, the ontologies of *open*EHR and FHIR previously developed, besides the ontology HIGO, were imported.

To classify the data, eight SWRL rules were required, each half being dedicated to a standard. The rule of Figure 3 looks for observations in the FHIR, whose code matches the blood pressure in the LOINC terminology. The instances found are classified as higo:BloodPressure instances. The rule of Figure 4 looks for the systolic component and then classifies this as a higo:Quantity, for the diastolic the process is similar, changing only the LOINC code and the property for higo:diastolic, rather than higo:systolic. After finding the instances of the components, the rule in Figure 5 extracts the magnitude and unit values for the appropriate properties in the HIGO ontology.

```
fhir:Observation(?obs) ∧ fhir:obp_code(?obs, ?code) ∧ fhir:obp_coding(?code, ?coding) ∧ fhir:obp_code(?coding,
?coding_code) ∧ fhir:obp_system(?coding, ?coding_system) ∧ fhir:dtp_value(?coding_code, "55284-4"^^xsd:token) ∧
fhir:dtp_value(?coding_system, "http://loinc.org"^^xsd:anyURI) ⇒ higo:BloodPressure(?obs)
```

Figure 3. Rule to Classify Observations from FHIR

```
higo:BloodPressure(?bp) ∧ fhir:obp_component(?bp, ?comp) ∧
fhir:obp_valueQuantity(?comp, ?qty) ∧ fhir:obp_code(?comp, ?code) ∧
fhir:obp_coding(?code, ?cod) ∧ fhir:obp_code(?cod, ?cod_code) ∧
fhir:obp_system(?cod, ?cod_sys) ∧ fhir:dtp_value(?cod_sys, "http://loinc.org"^^xsd:anyURI) ∧ fhir:dtp_value(?cod_code,
"8480-6"^^xsd:token)
⇒ higo:systolic(?bp, ?qty) ∧ higo:Quantity(?qty)
```

Figure 4. Rule to Classify the Systolic Component in FHIR

```
higo:Quantity(?qty) ∧ fhir:obp_unit(?qty, ?unit) ∧ fhir:dtp_value(?unit, ?unit_value) ∧ fhir:obp_value(?qty, ?value) ∧
fhir:dtp_value(?value, ?value_value) ⇒
higo:magnitude(?qty, ?value_value) ∧ higo:unit(?qty, ?unit_value)
```

Figure 5. Rule to Classify Quantities in FHIR

```
openehr:OBSERVATION(?obs) ∧
openehr:dtp_archetype_node_id(?obs, "openEHR-EHR-OBSERVATION.blood_pressure.v1") ∧ openehr:data(?obs,
?data) ∧ openehr:events(?data, ?event) ⇒ higo:BloodPressure(?event)
```

Figure 6. Rule to Classify Observation in *open*EHR

```
higo:systolic(?obs, ?systolic) ∧ higo:diastolic(?obs, ?diastolic) ∧ higo:magnitude(?systolic, ?systolic_value) ∧
higo:magnitude(?diastolic, ?diastolic_value)
⇒ sqwrl:select(?obs, ?systolic_value, ?diastolic_value)
```

Figure 7. SQWRL Query

In the case of *open*EHR, rules similar to those of FHIR are used, however, modifications are required. These changes are caused by the fact that one observation allows the storage of several readings simultaneously. The rule in Figure 6 gives the initial classification of the observations.

After executing the rules mentioned above, we can now access the data of both standards through the HIGO vocabulary. The Semantic Query-Enhanced Web Rule Language (SQWRL) was used to query the data (O'Connor and Das, 2009). An example of a query that looks for the observations of blood pressure is presented in Figure 7. The results of this query can be visualized in Figure 8. For the processing of the SWRL rules and execution of the cited query, the Pellet reasoner (Sirin et al, 2007) was used. As can be observed, the results of the query included data from both standards while the query involved only terms from the HIGO ontology. Therefore, the use of the HIGO ontology, together with SWRL rules, proved to be satisfactory for extracting data from heterogeneous patterns.

SQWRL Queries | OWL 2 RL | S9

obs	systolic_value	diastolic_value
:3506997_POINT_EVENT_1	"152.0"^^xsd:double	"94.0"^^xsd:double
:3506997_POINT_EVENT_2	"130.0"^^xsd:double	"73.0"^^xsd:double
:3443883_POINT_EVENT_3	"127.0"^^xsd:double	"61.0"^^xsd:double
:3443883_POINT_EVENT_2	"130.0"^^xsd:double	"68.0"^^xsd:double
:3443883_POINT_EVENT_1	"117.0"^^xsd:double	"60.0"^^xsd:double
:6767101_Observation_1	121	73
:5748781_Observation_1	168	102
:7018790_Observation_1	120	88
:5517797_Observation_1	136	81

Figure 8. Results from the SQWRL Query

7. CONCLUSION

The Information Technology has the potential to bring several benefits to healthcare processes. These advances include the optimization in the resource management, support in the decision-making, and, most importantly, the collaboration to improve the quality of the treatment offered. In order to achieve these goals, the exchange of information between health systems becomes essential so that physicians have at their disposal all the data that may be needed.

This paper proposed a method to achieve interoperability between heterogeneous systems through the use of ontologies and semantic rules. The present study dealt with the extraction of vital signs observations from two different systems. In order to search for this data, only one query was necessary, since an intermediate ontology was used that aggregated the data of both standards into a single one. The method presented was divided in two steps: (1) the translation of the structure of each HIS into an own ontology and (2) the creation of rules to connect structures from the standards with the HIGO ontology. Although this work focuses on health systems, the proposed method is not only limited to this area, but can be used in other applications that require interoperability

After the evaluation, the method showed that it is possible to use ontologies to extract information from different sources. As future work, it is intended to develop new rules covering other vital signs, as well as to investigate the possibility of extending the HIGO ontology to other types of information, besides the observations.

ACKNOWLEDGEMENT

The authors would like to thank Santander Universidades, CAPES, CNPq and FAPERGS for supporting this research.

REFERENCES

ANSI, I., 2005. TR 20514 Health informatics–Electronic health record—Definition, scope and context.

Bicer, V. et al, 2005. Artemis message exchange framework: semantic interoperability of exchanged messages in the healthcare domain. *In ACM Sigmod Record*, Vol. 34, No. 3, pp 71-76.

Bohring, H., Auer, S., 2005. Mapping XML to OWL Ontologies. *In Leipziger Informatik-Tage*, Vol. 72, pp 147-156.

Bray, T. et al. 1997. Extensible markup language (XML). *In World Wide Web Journal*, Vol. *2*, No. 4, pp 27-66.

Buntin, M. B. et al, 2011. The benefits of health information technology: a review of the recent literature shows predominantly positive results. *In Health affairs*, Vol. 30, No. 3, pp 464-471.

EALS Rules, 1988. ISO-9735. *ISO, Geneva, Switzerland.*

Elliott, M., Coventry, A., 2012. Critical care: the eight vital signs of patient monitoring. In *Br J Nurs*, Vol. 21, No. 10, pp 621-625.

Guarino, N., 1998. Formal ontology and information systems. *In Proceedings of FOIS*, Vol. 98, No. 1998, pp. 81-97.

Health Level 7 (HL7). *HL7 Website.* Available on http://www.hl7.org/. Accessed in Aug. 2017.

Health Level 7 (HL7). *FHIR Website.* Available on https://www.hl7.org/fhir/. Accessed in Aug. 2017.

Iroju, O. et al, 2013. Interoperability in healthcare: benefits, challenges and resolutions. *In International Journal of Innovation and Applied Studies*, Vol. 3, No. 1, pp 262-270.

Johnson, A. E. et al, 2016. MIMIC-III, a freely accessible critical care database. *Scientific data*, Vol. 3.

Kalra, D., 2006. Electronic health record standards. *In IMIA Yearbook of Medical Informatics 2006.*

Kalra, D., Lloyd, D., 2008. *ISO 13606 electronic health record communication part 1: reference model.*

Khalifa, M., 2013. Barriers to health information systems and electronic medical records implementation. A field study of Saudi Arabian hospitals. *In Procedia Computer Science*, Vol. 21, pp 335-342.

Lezcano, L. et al, 2011. Integrating reasoning and clinical archetypes using OWL ontologies and SWRL rules. *In Journal of biomedical informatics*, Vol. 44, No. 2, pp 343-353.

Martínez-Costa, C. et al, 2010. An approach for the semantic interoperability of ISO EN 13606 and OpenEHR archetypes. *In Journal of biomedical informatics*, Vol. 43, No. 5, pp 736-746.

Menachemi, N., Collum, T. H., 2011. Benefits and drawbacks of electronic health record systems. *In Risk management and healthcare policy*, Vol. *4*, No. 47.

Noy, N. F., McGuinness, D. L., 2001. *Ontology development 101: A guide to creating your first ontology.* Available on http://liris.cnrs.fr/amille/enseignements/Ecole_Centrale/What%20is%20an%20ontology%20and%20why%20we%20need%20it.htm. Accessed in Aug. 2017.

O'Connor, M., Das, A., 2009. SQWRL: a query language for OWL. *In Proceedings of the 6th International Conference on OWL: Experiences and Directions-Volume Vol. 529*, pp. 208-215.

Oliveira, R. C., 2016. *Transformation of clinical data from HL7 messages to openEHR compositions.*

openEHR. *openEHR Website*. Available on http://www.openehr.org/. Accessed in Aug. 2017.

Protégé. *Protégé Website.* Available on http://protege.stanford.edu/. Accessed in Aug. 2017.

Roehrs, A. et al, 2017. Personal health records: a systematic literature review. *In Journal of medical Internet research*, Vol. 19, No. 1.

Sirin, E. et al, 2007. Pellet: A practical owl-dl reasoner. *Web Semantics: science, services and agents on the World Wide Web*, Vol. 5, No. 2, pp 51-53.

Welty, C., et al, 2004. *Owl web ontology language guide.,* W3C. Available on http://www. w3. org/TR/2004/REC-owl-guide-20040210. Accessed in Aug. 2017.

DYNAMICALLY GENERATING NOSQL DATA SCHEMAS USING ARCHETYPES

André Magno Costa de Araújo, Valéria Cesário Times and Marcus Urbano da Silva
Center for Informatics, Federal University of Pernambuco, Recife, Brazil
Av. Jornalista Aníbal Fernandes, s/n - Cidade Universitária

ABSTRACT

The creation of databases for Electronic Health Records (EHR) has traditionally been done through relational database management systems (RDBMS). Using relational databases guarantees a referential integrity of the data, however, it hinders the extension and evolution of the data schemas due to the constant changes in the clinical concepts of the healthcare sector. This article presents a cloud service that dynamically creates NoSQL data schemas from a health informatics standard (i.e., openEHR archetype) that homogenizes data attributes, terminologies and EHR constraints. In order to achieve this, we designed a cloud architecture and specified a set of algorithms that demonstrate how NoSQL data schemas are generated in document and column family paradigms from reading archetypes. To validate the proposed service, we generate NoSQL data schemas from openEHR repository archetypes, and process a set of write-and-read data transactions on the generated data schemas.

KEYWORDS

Applications in Healthcare, frameworks for Big Data, Archetypes, e-Health, Internet Architectures

1. INTRODUCTION

Recent research in the area of Healthcare informatics show that the software industry and Academia have been debating how to improve the flexibility and evolution of Health Information Systems (HIS) (Lee et al. 2013). In this context, the creation of a data schema for the storage of Electronic Health Records (EHR) is considered an important activity in the life cycle of a HIS and has been the object of several research studies (Thomas et al. 2005 and Dinu & Nadkarni 2007).

According to Garde et al. (2007), the data schema of a healthcare application should store the different types of data that model EHR, such as structured, unstructured data and images (Jumaa et al. 2010). As mentioned by Jeffrey et al. 2012, the data requirements of EHR are dynamic, heterogeneous, and change constantly due to the natural evolution of their life cycle. Continuous change of data requirements leads to a dependency on a software development team that is able to make changes to the data schema and consequently to the business rules and graphical interface of the application. In addition, another problem that affects health data storage is the lack of uniformity in modeling and allowing the exchange of EHR information among HIS (Jeffrey et al. 2012).

Currently, Health Level Seven (HL7) and openEHR standards are important initiatives to improve the development and data exchange between health applications (Buck et al. 2009). The HL7 standard provides a set of specifications aimed at standardizing information exchange between HIS (Huang et al. 2003), while the openEHR architecture standardizes data attributes, terminologies and constraints using archetypes (Freire et al. 2016).

The dual architecture of openEHR aims to create a single EHR, preserving the patient's history and clinical data, and being able to share and reuse information across healthcare domains (Bernstein et al. 2005). The main characteristic of the dual architecture is the separation of the information in which the EHR consists from the terminologies and vocabulary associated with the clinical data. The specification of dual architecture is generated through archetypes and templates. An archetype is represented by a computational expression (i.e., Archetype Definition Language) which models and standardizes the data attributes, and the EHR terminologies and constraints, while the templates represent the graphical interfaces for user interaction, generated at runtime from archetypes (Buck et al. 2009).

Several works have used the openEHR architecture to represent clinical concepts of health applications (Chen et. al 2009), to build graphical user interfaces for recording the clinical data of patients (Georg et al. 2013) and to map archetypes in relational databases (Araujo et al. 2016).

Nevertheless, we noticed that little attention has been given to investigating how to dynamically build flexible data schema for HIS using archetypes. In that sense, this work specifies a cloud service capable of building NoSQL data schemas from data attributes, terminologies and constraints which are present in the archetypes. The main idea of the service hereby proposed is to build data schemas from a healthcare informatics standard (i.e., archetypes), which standardizes EHRs and allows health applications to store and manage the EHR using a web-based solution. In order to achieve this, we have designed a cloud architecture and specified a set of algorithms which exemplify how elements of archetypes are extracted (i.e., data attributes, terminologies and constraints), and how the NoSQL data schemas are generated in the document and column family paradigms. In this work, the document and column family models were chosen because of their ability to store and maintain the same representation of the hierarchical data types (i.e., ITEM_TREE) as specified in the archetypes. Moreover, we focus on the use of archetypes, since Späth & Grimson (2010) reported the use of this approach as essential to achieve standardization of EHR.

To assess the service proposed in this paper, we employed a set of archetypes from the openEHR repository to generate the NoSQL data schemas, and processed a set of write-and-read data transactions on the generated data schemas.

The remaining sections of this article are organized as follows: Section 2 describes the basic concepts used for the development of this work and brings an analysis of the main related work. Section 3 presents and discusses the proposed service, while Section 4 demonstrates the construction of NoSQL data schemas using archetypes. Finally, Section 4 introduces the final considerations of this article along with indications of future works.

2. BACKGROUND AND RELATED WORKS

This section contextualizes the basic concepts of archetypes (Section 2.1) and HL7 (Section 2.2) and brings an analysis of the main related works (Section 2.3).

2.1 OpenEHR Archetypes

The specification of archetype-based EHR consists in organizing its components through a two-level modeling approach (Bernstein et al. 2005). The first, called information, represents the stable level of the model from which systems and software components can be built (e.g., XML schema, UML or OWL). At this level, data have no semantic characteristics and only the data types that are chosen to represent them are known. The second level called knowledge consists of domain-driven definitions represented as archetypes and templates.

An archetype consists of a computational expression based on a reference model and represented by domain constraints and terminologies (Buck et al. 2009) (e.g. data attributes of a blood test). A template is a structure used to group archetypes and allow their use in a particular context of application. It is often associated with a graphical user interface (e.g., a GUI used by a professional for defining the elements of a leukogram list, such as leukocytes and neutrophils).

In an archetype, the specification of attributes is achieved through data entry builders named generic data structures. Such structures allow the representation of EHR data heterogeneity through the following types: ITEM_SINGLE, ITEM_LIST, ITEM_TREE and ITEM_TABLE.

ITEM_SINGLE models a single data attribute such as a patient's weight, height and age. ITEM_LIST groups a set of attributes in a list. A patient's address containing number, street and zip code for example. ITEM_TREE specifies a hierarchical data structure that is logically represented as a tree. It can be used, for instance, to model a patient's physical or neurological evaluations. Finally, ITEM_TABLE models data elements by using columns for field definition and rows for field value respectively. Each attribute of a data structure is characterized by a type of data and can have a related set of associated domain constraints and terminologies. The terminologies give semantic meaning to clinical data and can be represented as a set of Health terms defined by a professional.

2.2 Health Level-7

Health Level-7 (HL7) refers to a set of international standards to transfer clinical and administrative data between software applications used by various healthcare providers. The standard follows the conceptual definition of the application interface model, represented by the seventh layer of the OSI model, providing support to plug-and-play functionalities when used to integrate two or more health systems (Huang et al. 2003).

The HL7 standard provides specifications aiming to standardize the exchange and transportation of information between health systems, with the objective of making such systems interoperable (Huang et al. 2003). HL7 is highly recommended to organizations seeking interoperability between internal and external systems of public health. The standard provides quality, efficiency and effectiveness in the delivery and sharing of medical information.

The standard document used for integrating different health computing applications is called Clinical Document Architecture (CDA), is coded in XML format and, defines the structure and semantics of documents related to clinical care by promoting the standardization of terms in health. A CDA document is composed of levels used for recording free text information, data given by a domain specialist and, code generated by a computing platform (Marco et al. 2005).

2.3 Related Works

In the section, we conduct an analysis of the main related work in the domain of archetype mapping in databases.

One of the pioneering works in the field of archetype mapping was developed by Späth & Grimson (2010). They mapped a set of archetypes for a legacy database and exposed the lack of tools and methodologies that would have helped in modeling archetypes in a database. Using an automatic approach, Georg et al. (2013) specified a set of rules to map archetype data attributes in a relational database, generating templates in a specific problem domain. However, the proposed solution could not map archetypes with hierarchical data structures (i.e. ITEM_TREE).

The openEHR foundation offers a free solution in which the data attributes of an XML archetype are serialized in a Database Management System (DBMS). Node+Path uses Entity- attribute-value (EAV) (Dinu & Nadkarni 2007) approach to store the path (i.e., address) of an attribute in the first column, while the value of such attribute is stored in the second column. Yet, this solution requires the creation of complex logical sentences for data manipulation that may compromise the performance of the application. The persistence solution proposed by Wang et al. (2014), specifies a set of mapping rules, extracts the archetypes attributes and stores them in tables of a relational data schema. However, the terminologies and constraints specified in those archetypes are not considered.

Freire et al. (2016) evaluated the performance of the NoSQL database in the storage and retrieval of clinical data generated from the openEHR specifications. Two main aspects were evaluated. First, the size of the space allocated for storing the data. Second, the processing time of a set of queries. For the study, four legacy relational databases were used to generate clinical data documents in JSON and XML format. The results show that the JSON storage space is smaller than XML. In addition, it was verified the low performance of XML in relation to JSON when processing a set of queries for data recovery. Although the works presented in this section represent a major advance in the state of the art, it is clear that none of them proposes the dynamic generation of NoSQL data schemas using archetypes. The use of NoSQL database is justified by two points. First, NoSQL databases have greater flexibility to create run-time data schemas. Second, they have data structures that facilitate the representation of the heterogeneity of the health sector data. In addition, the results presented by Freire et al. (2016) indicate good NoSQL database performance. The main motivation for the proposed solution is to develop a tool capable of dynamically creating NoSQL data schemas to support the development of health applications based on openEHR archetypes.

3. GENERATING NOSQL DATA SCHEMAS

This section introduces the NoSQL data schemas generation service and is organized as follows: Section 3.1 describes the architecture and main components developed, while 3.2 discusses the algorithms implemented to extract the elements of the archetypes and generate the NoSQL data schemes.

3.1 Architecture and Overview

The cloud service proposed in this paper consists in a web-based solution that, by reading archetypes, extracts data attributes which define the EHR, the terminologies which provide semantic meaning to clinical data, and the specified constraints related to data attributes. Figure 1 depicts the architecture and components developed to generate the NoSQL data schemas. The extractor component reads and collects the elements of each archetype, while the generator component receives as input the elements extracted from the archetypes and dynamically generates data schemas.

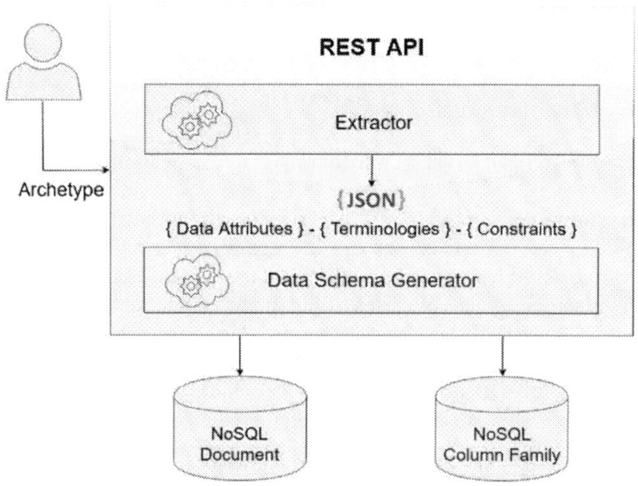

Figure 1. Architecture of the NoSQL Data Schema Generation Service

Figure 2 shows the graphical interface developed to support the generation of data schemas from the information contained in the archetypes read. Through the graphical interface, the user can select the desired archetypes and configure the generation of data schemas in one of the two paradigms selected in this work. When the data schema generation feature is triggered, the application employs both components shown in the architecture of Figure 1. The explanation of how the data schemas are generated is carried out by three algorithms described in section 3.2.

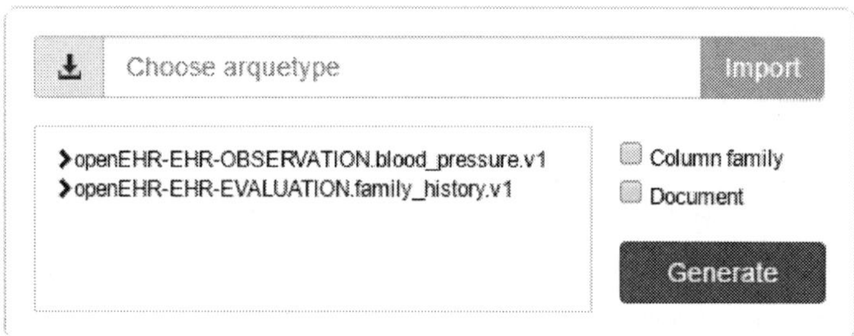

Figure 2. Graphical User Interface of the Data Schema Generator

3.2 Algorithms for Generating Data Schemas

To exemplify how data schemas are generated, we have specified an algorithm that demonstrates how data attributes, terminologies, and constraints are extracted from archetypes, and two other algorithms that describe how data schemas are generated according to the document and column family paradigms. The definition of each algorithm is given in the following paragraphs.

The *Extractor* algorithm shown in Figure 3 is initialized by receiving as input an XML archetype and subsequently creating an instance of the archetype stored in the memory to validate and extract the necessary information. The metadata of the XML archetype describes how the elements are organized and which relationships exist among them; for that reason, they are the first pieces of information to be extracted. In line 5, the *Metadata* variable stores the metadata of the XML archetype that was extracted via the *GetMetaData()* function.

```
1  public void Extractor(string XmlFile)
2  {
3      XmlDocument XmlDocument = new XmlDocument();
4      XmlDocument.LoadXml(XmlFile);
5      MetaData MetaData = GetMetaData(XmlDocument);
6      List<Element> Elements = GetElements(XmlDocument);
7      List<Terminology> Terminologies = new List<Terminology>();
8      List<DataAttribute> Attributes = new List<DataAttribute>();
9      foreach (Element Element in Elements)
10     {
11         if (!string.IsNullOrEmpty(Element.DATATYPE))
12         {
13             DataAttribute Attribute = new DataAttribute
14             {
15                 INDEX = Element.INDEX,
16                 CODE = Element.LABEL,
17                 DATATYPE = Element.DATATYPE,
18                 CONSTRAINT = Element.CONSTRAINT
19             };
20             Attributes.Add(Attribute);
21             if (    Element.DATATYPE == Const.DV_ORDINAL
22                 || Element.DATATYPE == Const.DV_CODEDTEXT)
23                 foreach (var item in Element.Terminologies)
24                 {
25                     Terminology Terminology = new Terminology
26                     {
27                         PARENT = item.PARENT,
28                         CHILD = item.CHILD,
29                         VALUE = item.VALUE
30                     };
31                     Terminologies.Add(Terminology);
32                 }
33         }
34     }
35     ColumnFamilyGenerator(MetaData, Attributes, Terminologies);
36     DocumentGenerator(Attributes, Terminologies);
37 }
```

Figure 3. Extractor Algorithm for Archetype Elements

Having the XML archetype instance store in the memory, the next step is to identify, validate and extract the data attributes, data types, terminologies and constraints. To achieve this, we divided the process into two phases. Firstly, one extracts all elements from the archetypes through the function *GetElements*(), to subsequently store the items that were found in the variable *Elements* in line 6. Afterwards, all these items in the *Elements* variable are scanned and the data attributes, types, terminologies and constraints are identified.

The loop spanning line 9 to 20 captures only the elements that carry data types. These items are characterized as elements that allow for data entry in an archetype (i.e., data structure). In that case, these elements are added to the data schema. For each element that carries a defined data type, its position (i.e., index), description, type and constraints are stored. The *Attribute* variable located in line 13 of the *Extractor* algorithm stores this new set of elements, comprehending data attributes, types and constraints.

In an XML archetype, a data attribute may contain one or more terminologies. The organization of such terminologies is managed using a multi-level hierarchical structure. To know which terminology belongs to each data attribute, it is necessary to identify the parent element and its respective children. The loop initiated in line 23 identifies and classifies the terminologies of a hierarchy of parent-child types of element. At the end of the loop, the terminology list is stores in the variable *Terminology,* as shown in line 31 of the *Extractor* algorithm.

In lines 35 and 36 of the *Extractor* algorithm, the algorithms responsible for generating the document and column family data schema are called. The definition of each algorithm is given next.

As it can be seen in Figure 4, the algorithms responsible for generating the document and column family data schemas receives as input the elements extracted by the *Extractor* algorithm.

```
1  public void DocumentGenerator(
2      List<DataAttribute> ListDataAttributes,
3      List<Terminology> ListTerminologies)
4  {
5      DataBase dataBase =
6        new DataBase("AttributesDocuments");
7      TerminologyCollection terminologyCollection =
8        dataBase.Create_TerminologyCollection("TerminologyCollection");
9      ConstraintsCollection constraintsCollection =
10       dataBase.Create_ConstraintsCollection("ConstraintsCollection");
11     AttributesCollection attributesCollection =
12       dataBase.Create_AttributesCollection("AttributesCollection");
13     foreach (DataAttribute DataAttribute in ListDataAttributes)
14     {
15         attributesCollection.AddColumn(DataAttribute.CODE,
16                                        DataAttribute.DATATYPE);
17         constraintsCollection.AddColumn(DataAttribute.CODE,
18                                        DataAttribute.CONSTRAINT);
19         if (ListTerminologies.Any(q => q.PARENT == DataAttribute.CODE))
20         {
21             List<Terminology> Terminologies =
22                 ListTerminologies.Where(q =>
23                 q.PARENT == DataAttribute.CODE).ToList();
24             terminologyCollection.AddColumn(DataAttribute.CODE,
25                                             Terminologies);
26         }
27     }
28 }
```

a) Document Generator

```
1  public void ColumnFamilyGenerator(
2      MetaData MetaData,
3      List<DataAttribute> ListDataAttributes,
4      List<Terminology> ListTerminologies)
5  {
6      DataBase keySpace =
7        new DataBase("AttributesFamily");
8      TerminologyFamily terminologyfamily =
9        keySpace.Create_TerminologiesFamily("TerminologyFamily");
10     ConstraintsFamily constraintsFamily =
11       keySpace.Create_ConstraintsFamily("ConstraintsFamily");
12     AttributesFamily attributesFamily =
13       keySpace.Create_AttributesFamily("AttributesFamily");
14     foreach (DataAttribute DataAttribute in ListDataAttributes)
15     {
16       attributesFamily.AddAttributes(DataAttribute.CODE,
17                                      DataAttribute.DATATYPE);
18       constraintsFamily.AddAttributes(DataAttribute.CODE,
19                                      DataAttribute.CONSTRAINT);
20       if(ListTerminologies.Any(q=>q.PARENT == DataAttribute.CODE))
21       {
22           List<Terminology> Terminologies =
23               ListTerminologies.Where(q =>
24               q.PARENT == DataAttribute.CODE).ToList();
25           terminologyfamily.AddAttributes(DataAttribute.CODE,
26                                           Terminologies);
27       }
28     }
29 }
```

b) Column Family Generator

Figure 4. Algorithms for Generating Data Schemas

Having these elements, the algorithm named document generator creates a database (line 5) and a set of collections to separately store the data attributes, terminologies and constraints of the archetypes, as shown in the code spanning from line 7 to 12 in Figure 4a. Afterwards, it moves on to inserting elements of the archetypes in its respective collections. The loop initialized in line 13 and concluded in line 28 scans the list of archetype elements and adds in the attribute collection (line 15) the code, description, and type of data. Regarding the collection of constraints (line 17), the attribute reference and constraint description code is stored. Finally, in case the data attribute has one or more terminologies, line 24 shows the attribute reference code is stored in its collection along with the list of discovered terminologies.

The algorithm shown in Figure 4b is responsible for generating column family data schemas. It receives as input the elements extracted from archetypes and creates a database (i.e., keyspace) when it begins running. This is done to group the data schema column families. The code snippet ranging from line 8 to 13 shows the creation of the column families used in the data schema. After creating the column families, the algorithm inserts code, description and data type in the attribute family collection (line 16), whilst the constraints family (line 18) stores the data attribute reference code alongside the constraint description. Finally, the terminology family (line 25) stores the data attribute reference code with its respective terminologies.

4. RESULTS

In this section, we demonstrate the creation of NoSQL data schemas using archetypes. In order to do that, we installed Microsoft's cloud computing platform (i.e., Azure) and chose ArangoDB DBMS to generate document data schemas, while family column data schemas are generates in DMBS Cassandra. In this example, we used family history and blood pressure archetypes, both are available in openEHR's repository.

Ensuing the configuration of the application on the cloud platform, we imported archetypes, and the generated data schemas can be seen in Figures 5.

Having generated the data schemas, we evaluated whether the data attributes, terminologies and constraints were present in the generated data schemas. Concerning the *Family History* archetype, we identified 17 data attributes, four terminologies and a single constraint, while the *Blood Pressure* archetype contains 15 data attributes, seven terminologies and three restrictions. In the *Family history* archetype, we verified that three out of 17 attributes were overlooked by the Extractor algorithm. It is worth noting that the attributes which were not imported are all *Slot* types, which is an openEHR standard data type. *Slot* types indicate the content from another archetype is to be reused. For example, if a specialist needs to insert a patient's address into an archetype, an alternative is to insert the Slot type and link an archetype which already contains that information to it, such as the *openEHR-DEMOGRAPHIC-ADDRESS.address archetype*.

Document Data Schema　　　　Column Family Data Schema

Figure 5. Generated Data Schemas from Archetypes

As the Slot type does not represent a data entry attribute in an archetype (i.e., text, ordinal, boolean, count, quantity, date and time), the extractor algorithm did not consider the attributes that contain this type of data.

The specified terminologies and constraints in the Family history archetypes had all its items imported. Besides, the Family history archetype contains multi-level hierarchical structures to represent its data attributes. The proposed algorithm has proved effective in extracting data attributes from archetypes regardless of the quantity of hierarchical levels present. Finally, the *Blood pressure* archetype had all its data attributes, terminologies and constraints imported by the algorithm.

Having finished this activity, we assessed the processes of writing transactions and reading data from the generated data schemas. Our goal in this assessment is not to measure database performance, but to evaluate whether insert, update, delete, and select operations are performed correctly. Initially we composed a routine to include 10,000 records in the databases previously created. The routine receives as an input parameter data extracted from a legacy application, establishes a connection to the DBMS, and inserts the records into the generated data schemas.

Following the record insertion, we processed a set of data transactions, i.e. update, select, and delete. Overall, 10,000 records were included in the databases and five query, update and delete instructions were executed. The results obtained in the DBMS have shown that all transactions were processed correctly.

5. CONCLUSION

In this article, we presented a cloud service that dynamically creates NoSQL data schemas from a Healthcare standard that homogenizes the EHR. We have specified a set of algorithms that demonstrate how data attributes, terminologies, and constraints are extracted from archetypes, and how data schemas are generated in document and column family paradigms. Furthermore, we introduced the web application developed and demonstrated the creation of NoSQL data schemas from the archetypes available in the openEHR repository. Finally, we processed a set of transactions for data reading and writing on the data schemas created, and the results obtained showed that the transactions were correctly processed.

As future works, we will evaluate the performance of database document and column family created from archetypes. In addition, we will generate HL7 messages using the proposed data schemas.

ACKNOWLEDGEMENT

This work was partially supported by Fundação de Amparo à Ciência e Tecnologia do Estado de Pernambuco (FACEPE), under the grants APQ-0173-1.03/15 and IBPG-0809-1.03/13.

REFERENCES

Araujo, A.M.C. et al. 2016. PolyEHR: A Framework for Polyglot Persistence of the Electronic Health Record. *Proceedings of Int'l Conf. Internet Computing and Internet of Things*, pp. 71-77, 2016.

Bernstein, K. et al. 2005. Modelling and implementing electronic health records in Denmark. *In International Journal of Medical Informatic*, V.74(2-4), pp. 213-220.

Buck, J. et al. 2009. Towards a comprehensive electronic patient record to support an innovative individual care concept for premature infants using the openEHR approach. *In International Journal of Medical Informatics*, V.78(8), pp.521-531.

Chen, R. et al. 2009. Archetype-based conversion of EHR content models: pilot experience with a regional EHR system. *In BMC Med Inform Decis Mak*, V.(9):33, pp. 1-12.

Dinu,V. and Nadkarni, P. 2007. Guidelines for the Effective Use of Entity-Attribute-Value Modeling for Biomedical Databases. *In International Journal of Medical Informatics*. V.76(11-12) , pp. 769-779.

Freire, S.M, et al. 2016. Comparing the Performance of NoSQL Approaches for Managing Archetype-Based Electronic Health Record Data, in *PLOS ONE* 11(3):e0150069, 2016

Garde, S. et al. 2007. Expressing clinical data sets with openEHR archetypes: A solid basis for ubiquitous computing. *In International Journal of Medical Informatics*, V.3:S334-41 , pp. 334–341.

Georg, D. et al. 2013. Towards plug-and-play integration of archetypes into legacy electronic health record systems: the ArchiMed experience. *In BMC Medical Informatics and Decision Making*, V.(13):11, pp. 1-12.

Huang, E.W et al. 2013. Design and implementation of a web-based HL7 message generation and validation system, *In International Journal of Medical Informatics*, V.70(1), pp. 49-58.

Jeffrey, A. L, et al. 2012. Method of Electronic Health Record Documentation and quality of primary care"; J Am Med Inform Assoc, V.19(6), pp.1019-1024.

Jumaa, H. et al. 2012. An XML-based framework for automating data exchange in healthcare. *Proceedings of IEEE International Conference on e-Health Networking Applications and Services (Healthcom)*, pp.264 – 269.

Lee K. k., et al. 2013. Alternatives to relational database: Comparison of NoSQL and XML approaches for clinical data storage. *In Computer Methods and Programs in Biomedicine*, V.110(1), pp. 99-109.

Marco E, et al. 2005. A Survey and Analysis of Electronic Healthcare Record Standards. *In ACM Computing Surveys*, pp. V.37(4) , pp. 277–315.

Späth M. B. and Grimson J. 2010. Applying the archetype approach to the database of a biobank information management system. *In International Journal of Medical Informatics*, V.80(3) , pp. 205-226.

Wang, L. et al. 2014. Archetype Relational Mapping Based on openEHR, *In Chin J Biomed Eng*, V. 2014(4) pp. 1-18, 2014.

A STUDY TO CLASSIFY HOSPITAL ACQUIRED COMPLICATIONS BASED ON ELECTRONIC HEALTH RECORD: THE PREPROCESSING PHASE

Denise Bandeira da Silva, Taís Rabello, Cristiano André da Costa,
Diogo Schmidt and Rodrigo da Rosa Righi
Applied Computing Graduate Program, Universidade do Vale do Rio dos Sinos (Unisinos), São Leopoldo, RS, Brazil

ABSTRACT

The conception of measures to prevent illnesses acquired by patients when they are hospitalized, called Hospital Acquired Complications (HACs), are a challenge these days. Prevention can be achieved through the creation of standard policies and procedures to be followed by hospital agents, as well as by algorithmic analyzes of available hospitalization data, to anticipate cases of HACs. This work extends the preprocessing phase of an application of the machine-learning model for predicting the occurrence of HACs using temporal clinical data. The original work achieved good results in the analysis phase, but they argue that it would be necessary to increase the volume of data with which the results were made so that those results could be generalized. They used the MIMIC II database (Multiparameter Intelligent Monitoring in Intensive Care) and this work aims to convert the application developed to make use of the MIMIC III (Medical Information Mart for Intensive Care) database, which has a much larger data volume. However, this article focuses only on the preprocessing phase. The conversion was successful and the application now retrieves data from the MIMC III according to the needs of the prediction model. The next step of this work is to use the retrieved data and re-test the original model and verify the possibility of generalization of the results.

KEYWORDS

EHR, HAC, MIMIC, Health Informatics, Machine Learning

1. INTRODUCTION

HACs (Hospital Acquired Complications) are complications that can affect hospitalized patients after admission to hospital. Most commonly, these problems are caused by infections associated with health care and other issues that arise as side effects from other treatments, such as surgeries. (Warner at al., 2016). In the United States, it is estimated that approximately 1 in 25 inpatients in hospitals have at least one health-care-associated infection, analyzing data over a single day. (Magill et al., 2014). There are not enough studies in Latin America, but some surveys indicate that the incidence of deaths from infection-related problems is like that reported in studies done in North America (Ruiz and Castell, 2016).

Much effort has been made to prevent the occurrence of HACs. In fact, nowadays, the actions in this regard constitute a national priority in the United States. (Anderson, J. et al., 2014). Among the documented efforts are the public health care guidelines that result from collaborative work on the creation of practices for the implementation of infection prevention routines in hospitals. Despite this, the prevention of HAIs (healthcare-associated infections) and HACs are still a challenge. (Magill et al., 2014; Anderson, J. et al., 2014).

Another approach to the problem are the studies performed using algorithms. However, the algorithmic solutions for the prediction of HACs, using machine learning techniques, for example, have variable results. In some cases, the results are accurate, but in others, variations in the data conditions or the analyzed situation generate non-appropriate results for generalizations. It is therefore important to improve the methods, as well as teste them as much as possible (Van Mourik et al., 2015; van der Ploeg et al., 2014).

This article extends the work by Warner et al. (2016) with the purpose of preparing the data to allow the proposed model to be tested in a database with greater volume of data. The article (Warner at al., 2016) presents a Machine Learning model to predict the occurrence of HACs in advance, using temporal clinical data. Their results are promising but, according to the authors, such results could not be generalized and the model needs to be retrained to achieve more general results. Originally, the work applied the MIMIC II database (Multiparameter Intelligent Monitoring in Intensive Care) (Saeed et al., 2011) in the development and testing of the predictive model. The work proposed here aims to the conversion of the data preprocessing phase so that the predictive model developed by them can be trained with the current version of the clinical database MIMIC III (Medical Information Mart for Intensive Care) (Johnson et al., 2016), which is an evolution of MIMIC II.

Therefore, this work is related to the data preprocessing phase, where the objective is to prepare the MIMIC III data, which is significantly larger than the MIMIC II, to re-test the predictive model defined by Warner at al. (2016) and generate results more accurate and possible to be generalized. It should be noted that this work deals with the preprocessing phase only, where several adjustments were necessary to cope with the changes in MIMIC schema (version III vs version II).

The remainder of this article is organized as follows: section 2 presents the MIMIC database, identifying the differences of MIMIC II with respect to MIMIC III; section 3 presents the preprocessing phase of the data, focusing on the changes made in the extraction code to obtain the data from MIMIC III instead of MIMIC II, which shows the main contribution of this work; section 4 shows the results obtained with the conversion and makes an evaluation of these results; and finally, in section 5, the final considerations of this work are presented, as well as the future work are proposed.

2. MIMIC

The MIMIC (Multiparameter Intelligent Monitoring in Intensive Care) data set (Goldberger et al., 2000) is intended for intensive care research, containing unidentified, patient-related data hospitalized at Intensive Care Units of the Beth Israel Deaconess Medical Center in Boston, Massachusetts, USA. The first version of the MIMIC had data on 90 patients, which were collected between 1992 and 1990. (Moody and Mark, 1996). Since 2001, the data were grouped in MIMIC II, which contained 32,536 patients (40,426 inpatients) admitted to ICUs. (Saeed et al., 2011).

The MIMIC III (Medical Information Mart for Intensive Care) (Johnson et al., 2016) is an evolution of MIMIC II and contains data from more than 40,000 patients (approximately 58,000 patients), the data were collected from 2001 to 2012. The meaning of the initial MIMIC acronym has been changed to give the database more visibility as a data source for research in the medical area. Several publications have been produced over MIMIC database, more intensively since MIMIC II version was launched. (Celi et al., 2016).

Research in the medical field requires new data models to be accessible for analysis. The constant evolution of these models is a necessity, mainly in the sense of allowing the reproducibility of the researches carried out. (Collins and Tabak, 2014). The present work constitutes an extension of a research already done, but with the aim of making possible the generalization of the results already obtained.

2.1 MIMIC III

MIMIC III has data from more than 38,000 patients who were hospitalized at Beth Israel Deaconess Medical Center in Boston, Massachusetts, between 2001 and 2012. It includes information on demographics, vital signs, laboratory tests, procedures, medication administration, discharge records, imaging studies, and mortality information provided by external governmental sources. Figure 1 gives a general and complete overview of the data source of MIMIC III. (Johnson et al., 2016). The data from the different sources are gathered in a repository and, before being included in the MIMIC database, are deidentified and converted to the necessary formats for the MIMIC III schema.

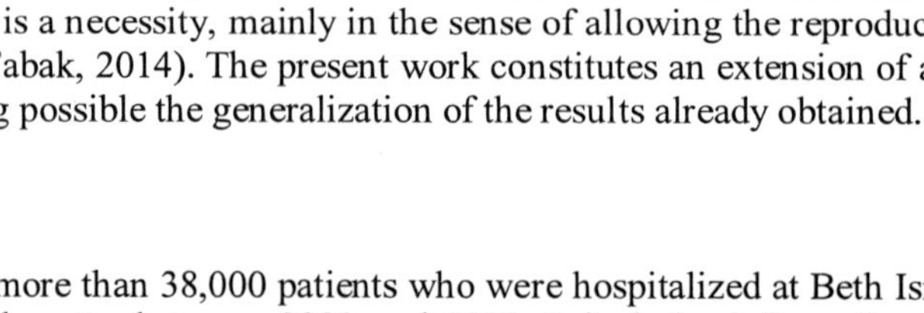

Figure 1. MIMIC General View. Adapted from (Johnson et al., 2016)

Access to MIMIC data (any version) should be formally requested through a documented process on the Physionet (https://mimic.physionet.org/gettingstarted/access/). The retrieval of the database is approved after performing some required steps.

Available through 26 CSM (Comma-Separate Value) files, the database contains detailed information on approximately 58,000 hospital admissions, encompassing around 40,000 distinct patients, aged sixteen years and over, admitted to one of the five adult intensive care units (ICUs) of the Beth Israel Deaconess Medical Center (CCU - Coronary Care Unit, CSRU - Cardiac Surgery Recovery Unit, MICU Medical ICU, SICU Surgical ICU and TSICU - Trauma Surgical Intensive Care Unit), such data are summarized in the Table 1. Of the total number of patients, approximately fifty-six percent are male and the mortality rate in units is eight-and-one-half percent. (Johnson et al., 2016).

Table 1. Summary of available data in MIMIC-III

Distinct patients	38,597
Hospital admissions	49,785
Average age of patients:	65.8
Male patients	27,983 (55.9%)
ICU length of stay, median days	2.1
Hospital length of stay, median days	6.9

The MIMIC data are organized around 4 main elements: Patients, Hospital admissions, ICU stays and Patient events. Figure 2 shows a view of the MIMIC III database schema, presenting the tables, their attributes and the relationships between them. The complete MIMIC data schema is relatively large and has therefore been presented partially in this article. The Figure presents a view of how events are assigned to patients. The schema attributes subject_id and hadm_id have a central role in identifying the records and relationships between tables. As can be seen, the MIMIC schema has many tables and this can sometimes be a problem at the time of retrieving data, because queries with joins between some large tables can become too time consuming. This aspect was impressive in the accomplishment of this work and will be pointed out later.

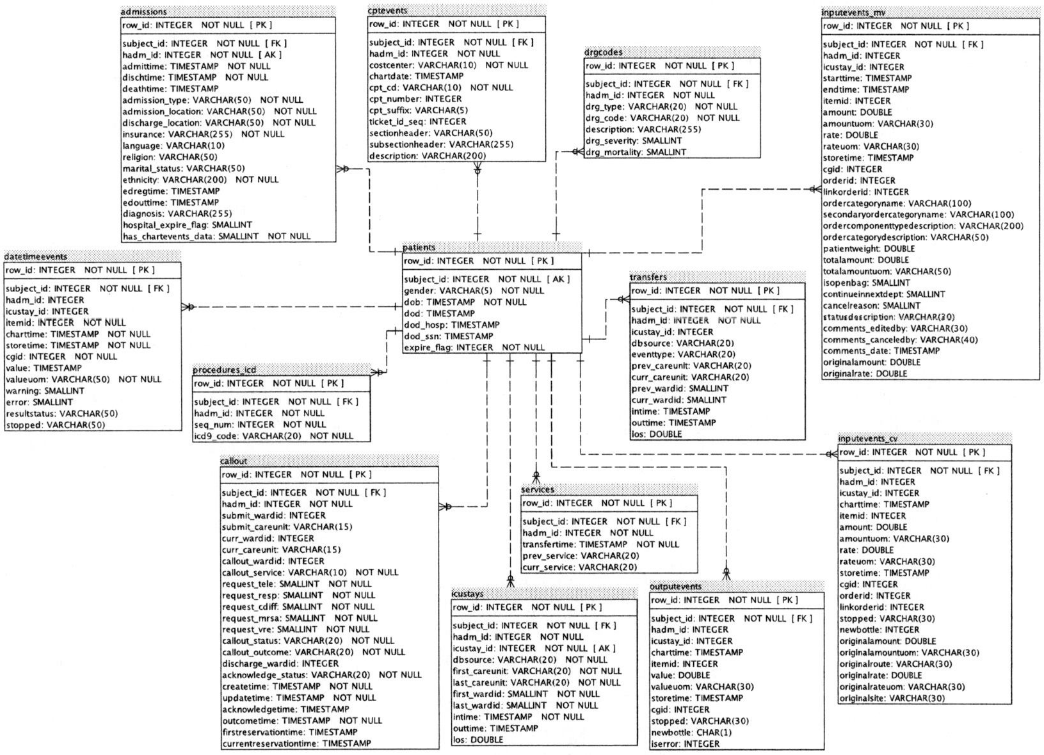

Figure 2. Relational schema MIMIC III – Patient events

2.2 MIMIC II vs MIMIC III

MIMIC III incorporates the MIMIC II data, which were collected between 2001 and 2008, plus data collected between 2008 and 2012. Furthermore, in MIMIC III, the content of the database, the data collected from the original systems, were reviewed to improve the quality of data.

The main changes made to the MIMIC III database, in relation to MIMIC II, are the modifications in the database schema, to turn it clearer and more precise. Some changes were also made in the data sources, some data were from local databases, from ICUs databases, for example, and these sources were changed to the administrative databases from hospital.

Table 2 presents the changes in more detail. Such a view is important because of the interest of many researchers, including the authors of this article, to run developed applications for MIMIC II in MIMIC III.

In the context of this work, the analysis of these changes took a preponderant role, since the original preprocessing code was developed for MIMIC II. And, as the objective of the research presented here is to investigate to what extent the methodology developed by them can be generalized from tests on a database with greater data volume, the code conversion to make use of MIMIC III was necessary. The code conversion will be presented in the next section of this article.

Table 2. MIMIC II schema vs MIMIC III schema (https://mimic.physionet.org/mimicdata/whatsnew)

Concept	MIMIC II (table)	MIMIC III (table)
Measure type (ITEMID)	D_CHARTITEMS, D_IOITEMS, D_MEDITEMS	D_ITEMS
Patient admissions		New information included: admission and outcome time; outcome location; diagnosis at admission; time of entry and exit in the emergency
Sequence of patient admissions in hospital	CENSUSEVENTS	TRANSFERS
Patient demographics	DEMOGRAPHIC_DETAIL	ADMISSIONS
Groups of Patients with Diagnostics Related (DRG)	DRGEVENTS	DRGCODES (more details added)
International Classification of Diseases (ICD)	ICD9	DIAGNOSES_ICD
Administration of medicines	IOEVENTS, MEDEVENTS	OUTPUTEVENTS INPUTEVENTS_CV INPUTEVENTS_MV
Prescriptions	POE_MED, POE_ORDER	PRESCRIPTIONS
Patient identifier (SUBJECT_ID)	MIMIC II version 2.6	Same values
Hospital admission identifier (HADM_ID)		New values generated
ICU admission identifier (ICUSTAY_ID)		New values generated
New Tables		CALLOUT, PROCEDURES_ICD, INPUTEVENTS_CV, INPUTEVENTS_MV, OUTPUTEVENTS
Tables Removed	COMORBIDITY_SCORES, DEMOGRAPHICEVENTS, D_DEMOGRAPHICITEMS, D_CAREUNITS, D_CODEDITEMS D_PARAMMAP_ITEMS, ICUSTAY_DETAILS, PARAMETER_MAPPING, WAVEFORM_*, D_WAVEFORM_SIGNALS	

3. PREPROCESSING MODEL

In the work that underlies this research, there is a data preprocessing phase, which aims to collect the information of interest from the MIMIC on which the prediction method created will is applied. This preprocessing phase is divided into two parts. The first one consists of the creation of a data structure with the data of interest for the application of the prediction model; queries are carried out on the MIMIC database and its results are manipulated through programs written in the R programming language (https://www.r-project.org) to achieve this. The second part of the preprocessing phase is where the analysis and control cases are collected for the application of the prediction model itself.

3.1 MIMIC data for the Prediction Model

In the first part of the preprocessing, the steps applied for data extraction are as follows:

- All adult admissions with admit and discharge dates;
- All adult admissions with admission and discharge dates and at least one registered prescription;
- All adult admissions with admission and discharge dates and at least one medication event;
- All adult admissions with at least one lab order within -48 hours of admission
- Determine the first event recorded after each admission;
- Determine the last event recorded before each discharge;
- Calculate the difference, in hours, between discharge and admit times;
- Add, for each admission, information on demographic, gender, ethnicity, age at time of admission, and date of death;
- Add the information on the disease code (ICD-9-CM) to each admission.

An example of the final data structure generated from the realization of this first part of the preprocessing is shown in Figure 3.

hadm_id	subject_id	admit_dt	disch_dt	first_lab	first_poe	last_poe	first_event	last_event	diff	gender	age	ethnicity	dod	elix.index	icd9string
12	8652	11/09/25	22/09/25	11/9/25 19:15	11/9/25 18:00	22/9/25 18:00	11/9/25 16:15	22/9/25 15:00	262.75	M	84.23038	WHITE	8/15/28	2	{410.41,605,440.21,496,427.31,428.0,4
98	8799	10/09/24	12/09/24	10/9/24 6:38	10/9/24 17:00	12/9/24 20:00	10/9/24 3:38	12/9/24 17:00	61.36666667	F	27.54625	WHITE	NA	3	{250.11,536.3,337.1,250.51,362.01,785
141	8777	06/06/39	11/06/39	6/6/39 4:10	NA	NA	6/6/39 1:10	11/6/39 6:00	124.8333333	F	88.15777	WHITE	NA	2	{996.01,746.86,E885.9,285.9,458.9,250
324	8654	06/09/69	14/09/69	6/9/69 9:56	NA	NA	6/9/69 6:56	13/9/69 21:00	182.0666667	M	56.75439	WHITE	NA	3	{428.0,440.22,250.00,V10.46,V45.81,27
333	8284	29/06/70	02/07/70	29/6/70 16:43	29/6/70 19:00	2/7/70 22:00	29/6/70 13:43	2/7/70 19:00	77.28333333	M	76.82994	WHITE	NA	2	{428.0,427.31,784.3,438.83,745.5,434.1
339	8174	30/04/85	01/05/85	30/4/85 13:31	30/4/85 18:00	1/5/85 21:00	30/4/85 10:31	1/5/85 16:53	30.36666667	M	56.57151	BLACK/AFRICAN AMERICAN	NA	3	{244.0,285.1,578.9,275.41,998.11,E878
372	8317	01/07/90	04/07/90	30/6/90 21:50	NA	NA	30/6/90 18:50	4/7/90 6:50	84	F	67.00559	WHITE	NA	4	{V45.82,401.9,250.00,591,599.0,276.5,2
446	8192	17/08/66	25/08/66	17/8/66 14:30	NA	NA	17/8/66 11:30	25/8/66 6:50	187.3333333	F	79.97225	WHITE	10/6/66	2	{V43.3,577.1,733.00,518.89,428.0,427.3
455	8151	05/09/99	10/09/99	5/9/99 12:30	NA	NA	5/9/99 9:30	9/9/99 21:00	107.5	F	87.45827	UNKNOWN/NOT SPECIFIED	9/10/99	1	{401.9,562.12,276.2,507.0,294.8,427.31

Figure 3. Sample with MIMIC II data

3.2 Analysis and Control Cases

Over the data structure presented in Figure 3, the analysis and control cases are then selected. The cases of analysis are constituted by adult patients, who have records of diseases ICD-9-CM (International Classification of Diseases, Ninth Revision, Clinical Modification (ICD-9-CM) indicative of HACs; these codes were identified previously and manually by the group of researchers responsible for the work. Finally, the same number of patients were randomly selected to constitute the control cases.

3.3 Converting the Preprocessing Phase from MIMIC II to MIMIC III

In the first stage of the preprocessing phase, the original code developed by Warner at al. (2016) considered a set of MIMIC II tables. However, since the MIMIC III schema is different from MIMIC II, other tables needed to be used to create the correct data set from MIMIC III.

Based on the changes made to the MIMIC III database schema in relation to the MIMIC II schema, presented in the Table 2, it was possible to identify the changes that should be made in the original code to make the same code to access the MIMIC III tables. Briefly, the following classes changes were made in the original code:

- Identify the new data sources in the MIMIC III tables;
- Alter attribute names and tables, which have changed in MIMIC III;
- Create new temporary tables to match for the MIMIC III structure;
- Standardize some data types;
- Optimizes some SQL queries for access to MIMIC III data.

During the conversion process, some difficulties were found and they were not related to the changes in the MIMIC schema. Among them, one can cite a specific difficulty in relation to the type of data for storing dates and the way in which data of this type is retrieved from the database and manipulated in R.

Another one was the difficulty faced with the size of some tables in MIMIC III, which make the execution of some queries slow down. For example, one query between the tables LABEVENTS and ADMISSIONS, which, in MIMIC II, have around 509 thousand and 1,038 registers, respectively; and, in MIMIC III, 27 million and 58,976 records, respectively. Although the MIMIC data is only accessed once, when performing the preprocessing and data collection procedures to generate the analysis and controls cases, this delay in the execution was considered as a difficulty for this work development. One improvement to be considered would be the creation of intermediate and index tables, which would make it possible to perform such queries in a faster and optimized way. This can be effectively addressed as a future work, as the MIMIC project is expected to continue to evolve to incorporate more data in the future.

4. EVALUATION

Conversion of the preprocessing phase code has been carried out and the changes promoted have made it possible to consistently retrieve MIMIC III data with the same information that was programmed to be retrieved by the original MIMIC II code. Figures 4 and 5 demonstrate this coherence. They present two views of data retrieved from the two databases, by means of the original code and the modified one, respectively, on patient admissions under numbers 8001, 8002, 8005, 8008, 8009, and 8010. Patients 8003, 8004, 8006, and 8007 do not appear in these visions because they were not retrieved by the extraction code according to the criteria defined and presented in section 3.1.

hadm_id	subject_id	admittime	dischtime	dischtime - admittime	first_lab	first_poe	last_poe	first.event	last.event	diff	gender	age	ethnicity	dod	elix.index	icd9string
5880	8001	15/01/89	17/01/89	2	14/1/89 22:30	15/1/89 2:00	17/1/89 6:00	14/1/89 20:30	17/1/89 2:21	53.85	F	84	WHITE	17/01/89	3	{E934.2,431,427.31,714.0,
20142	8002	03/08/12	22/08/12	19	3/8/12 16:40	NA	NA	3/8/12 13:40	22/8/12 5:40	448.00	M	84	UNKNOWN/NOT SPECIF	29/08/12	2	{584.5,428.0,038.42,574.9
710	8005	28/03/17	23/04/17	26	28/3/17 19:45	28/3/17 20:00	23/4/17 21:00	28/3/17 16:45	23/4/17 18:00	625.25	M	76	WHITE	28/08/17	2	{493.20,070.54,486,518.5,
17417	8008	14/01/77	17/01/77	3	15/1/77 1:12	NA	NA	13/1/77 22:00	16/1/77 22:00	72.00	F	42	WHITE	NA	4	{747.81,311,780.39,401.9,
21445	8009	20/10/14	04/11/14	15	20/10/14 23:20	NA	NA	20/10/14 21:20	4/11/14 7:48	346.47	F	82	WHITE	05/03/19	3	{790.92,426.89,518.5,E93
2887	8010	24/03/24	14/04/24	21	24/3/24 10:00	24/3/24 14:00	14/4/24 20:00	24/3/24 7:00	14/4/24 17:00	514.00	F	79	WHITE	24/05/24	7	{357.6,E947.8,693.0,401.9

Figure 4. Sample with MIMIC II data

hadm_id	subject_id	admittime	dischtime	dischtime - admittime	first_lab	first_poe	last_poe	first.event	last.event	diff	gender	age	ethnicity	dod	elix.index	icd9string
165786	8001	2/12/92 0:39	3/12/92 12:00	1.47	1/12/92 22:30	2/12/92 0:00	4/12/92 0:00	1/12/92 22:30	3/12/92 22:00	47.50	F	84	WHITE	03/12/92	3	{E934.2,431,427.31,714.0,2
148543	8002	26/8/41 14:45	14/9/41 14:31	18.99	26/8/41 15:40	NA	NA	26/8/41 15:40	14/9/41 14:31	454.85	M	84	UNKNOWN/NOT SPECIF	21/09/41	2	{584.5,428.0,038.42,574.91
187976	8005	5/3/60 18:22	31/3/60 16:45	25.93	5/3/60 18:45	5/3/60 0:00	31/3/60 0:00	5/3/60 18:45	30/3/60 21:00	602.25	M	76	WHITE	05/08/60	2	{493.20,070.54,486,518.5,4
156472	8008	19/12/32 19:33	22/12/32 10:52	2.64	20/12/32 1:12	NA	NA	20/12/32 1:12	22/12/32 10:52	57.67	F	42	WHITE	12/11/42	4	{747.81,311,780.39,401.9,3
131424	8009	27/8/64 15:31	11/9/64 19:03	15.15	27/8/64 22:20	NA	NA	27/8/64 22:20	11/9/64 19:03	356.72	F	82	WHITE	10/01/69	3	{790.92,426.89,518.5,E935
145447	8010	3/4/72 14:34	24/4/72 15:53	21.05	3/4/72 10:00	3/4/72 0:00	24/4/72 0:00	3/4/72 10:00	23/4/72 21:00	491.00	F	79	WHITE	03/06/72	7	{357.6,E947.8,693.0,401.9,

Figurc 5. Samplc with MIMIC III data

It can be observed that the two visions, although representing the same patients' **admission**s, have differences in some attributes. These differences appear because of changes made to the MIMIC III data and are only related to attributes that have dates and calculations related to those dates. The other attributes, patient identification (subject_id), gender, age, ethnicity, and disease codes (elix.index and icd9string) have the same values in both views.

In relation to the **admission** identification (hadm_id), the difference between the two visions is explained by a change made in MIMIC III, where all values of this attribute were generated again in the database, within a new range of values, ranging from 100,000 to 199,999.

Another difference can be seen in relation to the dates recorded for the same patients in the two visions. In MIMIC III, these dates were generated again for each patient, besides the admtime and dischtime dates were completed with the time (hour) in which the action did happen. Since, in MIMIC, the data are deidentified through an automated process, such a process, when re-performed, changes the dates, but remains in line with the reality of the moment when each activity related to the patient occurred. To verify this, we include a column in each of the views, which computes the difference between the admission (admittime) and discharge (dischtime) dates. As can be noticed in the two views, the same difference remains for each patient, with only a small variation caused by the addition of the time information, which was not present in MIMIC II, and was included in the MIMIC III registry.

In relation to the amount of data retrieved from the two databases, the difference was quite significant. A summary of the volume of data retrieved in the main stages of preprocessing is presented in table 3. The two factors that influenced the difference between the amount of data retrieved from MIMIC III in relation to the II where the fact that MIMIC III has more data than MIMIC II and the storage of more precise information in MIMIC III, such as the record of the patients' admission time, for example.

Table 3. Volume of data retrieved with MIMIC II versus MIMIC III

Data	**MIMIC II**	**MIMIC III**
Total distinct adult admissions	**781**	**48,250**
Total distinct adult admissions with at least one medication prescription	**641**	**44,059**
Total distinct adult admissions with at least one medication event	**599**	**45,841**
Internals with at least one exam requisition within the first 48 hours	**780**	**48,144**
Analysis cases sealed in the preprocessing phase	**243**	**13,110**
Control cases sealed in the preprocessing phase	**188**	**2,622**

The current state of development of the preprocessing code allows the data for the analysis and control cases to be retrieved from MIMIC III, thus allowing the prediction model by Warner et al. (2016) to be applied to obtain the prediction results with a suitable volume of data. The code adapted in this work was made available to the authors of the original article, whom are analyzing it to issue its considerations. The new results to be generated with the prediction model executed on the MIMIC III data will be the object of another publication, perhaps jointly between the group of researchers of the original project and the authors of this work.

5. CONCLUSION

The design of measures to prevent illnesses acquired by hospitalized patients is a challenge. Prevention can be achieved through the creation of policies and standard procedures to be followed by hospital agents, as well as algorithmic analyzes of data available on hospitalizations. In Warner et al. (2016), a method is proposed to predict the occurrence of HACs in advance, using temporal data from the MIMIC II database. However, the results of the analyzes produced could not be generalized because of the volume of data processed in the model's execution.

The objective of the work presented here was to extend the preprocessing phase presented in Warner et al. (2016), aiming to convert the extraction code developed by the authors to make use of the MIMIC III database, an evolution of the MIMIC II, with higher data volume. With this, it is expected to be possible to re-test the proposed prediction model (Warner et al., 2016) and evaluate the generalization capabilities of the model.

The extraction code was converted and it was possible to retrieve the same information from the MIMIC III database, which were retrieved from MIMIC II. The original code worked with an initial base of 781 admissions stored in the MIMIC II database and generated 243 cases of analysis and 188 cases of control. The converted code worked over an initial base of 48,250 admissions contained in MIMIC III and, after applying the preprocessing phase and generated 13,110 cases of analysis and 2,622 control cases, a data volume significantly higher than those identified in the MIMIC II database. It can be said that the volume of data retrieved from MIMIC III is between 15 and 50 times greater than the volume of data retrieved from MIMIC II.

The results obtained demonstrate that it is possible to convert applications developed for MIMIC II database to make use of MIMIC III. Some difficulties were encountered during the process of converting the code, but they could be overcome with some effort. Improvements to the volume, richness and clarity of the data contained in MIMIC III, in relation to MIMIC II, stimulate the development of new research or the continuation of previous ones, which can be evidenced in this work. Therefore, it is considered that a fundamental contribution of this work lies in the fact that health databases, well-structured and documented, can be used despite of their schema or volume evolution, thus allowing research in the medical area also continue to evolve and the effort to convert already developed applications is minimal or at least possible to be realized.

The next stage of this work consists in carrying out the same analyzes of the original work (Warner et al., 2016), applying the prediction model developed by them, but on the new MIMIC III extracted dataset. It is expected that the significantly larger volume of data contained in the new extractions could allow the generation of more accurate results from the prediction model.

ACKNOWLEDGEMENT

The authors would like to thank CAPES, CNPq and FAPERGS for supporting this research.

REFERENCES

Anderson, J. et al, 2014. Strategies to prevent surgical site infections in acute care hospitals: 2014 update. *Infection Control & Hospital Epidemiology*, 35(S2), pp.S66-S88.

Anderson, J. et al. (2014)

Celi, L.A. et al, 2016. Datathons and Software to Promote Reproducible Research. *Journal of medical Internet research*, 18(8).

Collins, F.S. and Tabak, L.A., 2014. NIH plans to enhance reproducibility. *Nature*, 505(7485), p.612.

Goldberger, A.L. et al, 2000. Physiobank, physiotoolkit, and physionet. *Circulation*, 101(23), pp.e215-e220.

Johnson, A.E. et al, 2016. MIMIC-III, a freely accessible critical care database. *Scientific data*, 3.

Magill et al. (2014)

Magill, S. et al, 2014. Multistate point-prevalence survey of health care–associated infections. *New England Journal of Medicine*, 370(13), pp.1198-1208.

Moody, G.B. and Mark, R.G., 1996, September. A database to support development and evaluation of intelligent intensive care monitoring. *In Computers in Cardiology*, 1996 (pp. 657-660). IEEE.

Ruiz, G.O. and Castell, C.D., 2016. Epidemiology of severe infections in Latin American intensive care units. *Revista Brasileira de terapia intensiva*, 28(3), pp.261-263.

Saeed, M. et al, 2011. Multiparameter Intelligent Monitoring in Intensive Care II (MIMIC-II): a public-access intensive care unit database. *Critical care medicine*, 39(5), p.952.

van der Ploeg, T. et al, 2014. Modern modelling techniques are data hungry: a simulation study for predicting dichotomous endpoints. *BMC medical research methodology*, 14(1), p.137.

Van Mourik, M. et al, 2015. Accuracy of administrative data for surveillance of healthcare-associated infections: a systematic review. *BMJ open*, 5(8), p.e008424.

Warner, J. at al, 2016. Classification of hospital acquired complications using temporal clinical information from a large electronic health record. *Journal of biomedical informatics*, 59, pp.209-217.

REVISITING SESAME ARCHITECTURE FOR 5G NETWORKS

Ioannis P. Chochliouros[1], Alexandros Kostopoulos[1], Evangelos Sfakianakis[1], Dimitrios Arvanitozisis[1], Anastasia S. Spiliopoulou[1], Maria Belesioti[1], Ioannis Giannoulakis[2], Anastasios Kourtis[2], Pouria-Sayyad Khodashenas[3], Jose Oscar Fajardo[4], Athanassios Dardamanis[4], Emmanouil Kafetzakis[5], Javier Garcia Lloreda[6] and Jordi-Perez Romero[7]

[1]Hellenic Telecommunications Organization S.A. (OTE), [2]NCRS "Demokritos", i2CAT[3], UPV/EHU[4], SmartNet S.A.[4], ATOS[5], ORION Innovation Private Company[6], UPC[7]

ABSTRACT

SESAME proposes the Cloud-Enabled Small Cell (CESC) concept, a new multi-operator enabled Small Cell that integrates a virtualized execution platform for deploying Virtual Network Functions (NVFs), supporting powerful self-x management and executing novel applications and services inside the access network infrastructure. A dedicated architecture has been proposed for that purpose. In this paper, we take into account recent research challenges in order to discuss the latest innovations, as well as the updates of the corresponding architecture. Such updates include the SC-Common VNF as fun-in/fun-out module, the progress in SESAME Small Cell functional splits, and the placement of "Self-x" features and wireless backhauling. Furthermore, to promote future improvements, we analyze the functional description of the related architectural components.

KEYWORDS

5G; Cloud-enabled Small Cell (CESC), Network Functions Virtualization (NFV), Multitenacy, "Self-x" properties

1. INTRODUCTION

The transition towards the realization of the much promising "5G era" implicates for a multiplicity of challenges and opportunities for the electronic communications market sector. In this context, the actual EU-*funded* SESAME project promotes the concept of the Small Cells (SCs) virtualization and their utilisation and partitioning into logically isolated "slices", offered to multiple operators-tenants. The main aspect of this innovative feature which is referred to as "*multi-tenancy*" is about the capability to "accommodate" multiple operators under the same infrastructure, by satisfying the profile and requirements of each operator separately, thus creating opportunities for further market growth (Chochliouros, 2016). Moreover, NFV (Network Functions Virtualization) permits virtualization of software-based network functions, which implicates for a multiplicity of network-related benefits: in fact, instead of installing and managing dedicated hardware devices for networking and servicing functions, these are realized as "software components" and deployed on commodity or special hardware infrastructures. Network elements are thus expected to become "*computing equivalent*" equipment that gathers programmable resources, interfaces and functions, based on virtualization technologies. Thus, NFV improves elasticity in provisioning network services while, *simultaneously*, enhancing scalability and reducing time to market (ETSI, 2012). To further enhance the virtualization capabilities of the Small Cell deployment, so that to include not only network capacity resources but also edge processing capabilities, a micro-scale virtualized execution infrastructure is proposed by SESAME, in the form of a "Light Data Centre" (Light DC). The Light DC concept will be considered to build a clustered infrastructure with high manageability and will be optimized to reduce power consumption, cabling, space and cost (Blanco, 2016).

1.1 The SESAME-based Approach

The architecture provided so far by the SESAME project (see Fig.1), acts as a "*solid reference point*" for 5G multi-tenant small cell infrastructures with mobile edge computing (MEC) capabilities.

It combines the current 3GPP ("The Third Generation Partnership Project") framework for network management in RAN (Radio Access Networks) sharing scenarios and the ETSI NFV framework (ETSI, 2012) for managing virtualised network functions. The Cloud-Enabled Small Cell (CESC) offers virtualised computing, storage and radio resources and the CESC cluster is considered as a cloud from the upper layers. This cloud can also be "sliced" to enable multi-tenancy. The execution platform is used to support VNFs (Virtual Network Functions) that implement the different features of the Small Cells, as well as to support the mobile edge applications of the end-users.The SESAME project develops the concept of Small Cell as-a-Service (SCaaS), which leverages on the separation between traditional market roles, with the aim of maximising the opportunities offered by opening SCs to multi-tenancy. This latter concept in opposition to typical mobile operators who deploy their own network infrastructure in competition with others, encourages both traditional and new market entrants to "share the infrastructure". In this case, operators can differentiate based on their service offers rather than on network connectivity. This flexible and dynamic system allows operators to reduce CAPEX and OPEX as required in the next generation of mobile networks (Costa, 2016).

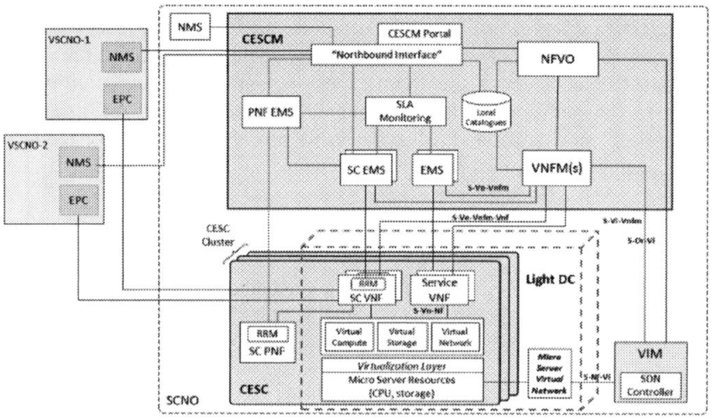

Figure 1. SESAME essential architecture and component's interactions

2. RECENT INNOVATIONS AND UPDATES IN THE SESAME ARCHITECTURE

2.1 Conceptual Approach

The most important innovations proposed in the SESAME architecture focus upon the novel concepts of virtualising Small Cell networks by leveraging the paradigms of a multi-operator (multi-tenancy) (Khan, 2011) enabling framework coupled with an edge-*based*, virtualised execution environment (Fajardo, 2016). SESAME falls in the scope of these two principles and promotes the adoption of Small Cell multi-tenancy (Oueis, 2015); that is, multiple network operators will be able to use the SESAME platform, each one using his own network "slice". Moreover, the main idea is to endorse the deployment of SCs with some virtualized functions, with each SC containing also a micro-server through appropriate fronthaul technology (Peng, 2015). A micro-server is based on a non-x.86 architecture using 64-bit ARMv8 technology. Together with the SC, they "form" the Cloud-Enabled Small Cell and a number of CESCs form the "CESC cluster" capable to provide access to a geographical area with one or more operators (Goratti, 2016).

The overall SESAME system architecture is as shown in Fig.1 and foresees the split of the SC physical and virtual network functions (Hoffmann, 2011), respectively Physical Network Function (PNF) and VNF (Virtual Network Function), based on the Multi-Operator Core Network (MOCN) requirements and associated Radio Resource Manager (RRM) and Operations and Management (OAM) features, which need to be supported. Also within the related architecture's scope is to identify, model and analyse security issues (Vassilakis, 2016) from the early stages of system design and software development, as well as to model and analyse threats and vulnerabilities in existing software and protocols (Mouratidis, 2013) that will be used in the SESAME system. Moreover, the SESAME project proposes a micro-scale virtualized execution infrastructure in the form of a Light DC (Tso, 2016) to enhance the virtualization capabilities of the Small Cell deployment, providing high processing power at the network edge. The Light DC concept (Bari, 2013) which encompasses the micro-servers of the different CESCs in a cluster, provides a high manageable architecture optimized to reduce power consumption, cabling, space and cost. To achieve these requirements, it relies on an infrastructure that aggregates and enables sharing of computing, networking and storage resources available in each micro-server belonging to the CESC cluster. The Light DC infrastructure also provides the backhaul and fronthaul resources for guaranteeing the requirements for connectivity in case of multi-tenancy scenarios. The hypervisor computing virtualization extensions enable access of virtual machines to the hardware accelerators for providing an execution platform that can support the deployment of VNFs. Different types of VNFs can be deployed through the Virtual Infrastructure Manager (VIM), for carrying out the virtualization of the Small Cell, for running the cognitive/"Self-x" management operations (Blanco, 2016) and for supporting computing needs for the mobile edge applications of the end-users. The combination of the proposed architecture allows achieving an adequate level of flexibility and scalability in the edge cloud infrastructure (Son, 2014). Finally, the CESC Manager (CESCM) is a component with an overall knowledge of the virtual and physical resources, responsible for the deployment, monitoring, configuration and orchestration of the Light DC cloud environment and radio access functionalities, over a single/multiple CESC cluster(s) with a minimum cluster size of one CESC. The main challenge to address is to design a uniform platform where the radio access management task (e.g. transmission power control, packet scheduling, handover and cell reselection thresholds, etc.) and NFV management responsibilities (e.g. VNF/service instantiation, lifecycle management, policy management, etc.) can be handled in an orchestrated way (Riggio, 2015).

2.2 Evolutionary Steps of the Main Architecture

From the perspective of the high level architecture, the main SESAME evolutions are related to the detailed functionality of the CESCs and described as follows, *per case*.

Evolution 1 – SC-Common VNF as fun-in/fun-out module: SESAME has previously specified (SESAME, 2016) the functional split of the SC in physical functions (SC PNF) and virtualised functions (SC VNF). Further design decisions have led to the introduction of a new functional entity, named SC-Common VNF (SC-C-VNF). The SC-C-VNF can be seen as "*one of the virtualised SC VNF functions*", but for clarity reasons it has been decided to define it as "*a new element in the SESAME architecture that resides between the SC PNF and the different SC VNFs*". With this design decision, there is a unique SC-C-VNF per CESC, which performs control-plane multiplexing and coordination functions from the SC-PNF to the virtualised world. Each SC-VNF supports a single VSC Network Operator (VSCNO) and maintains its own control and user plane connections to the VSCNO's core network. This design enables a flexible functional split for the SC. Depending on different parameters (e.g., fronthaul capacity, processing power, business decisions, etc.), one SC could implement a higher level functional split while others could go for a lower level functional split. The essential SESAME CESC design provides a good basis for prototype-*oriented* and research-*oriented* activities in the framework of the entire project effort.

Evolution 2 – Progress in SESAME Small Cell functional splits: SESAME has progressed in the definition of the SC functional split (Harutyunyan, 2016). Although this has not a direct impact on the high level architecture components, it has an impact on the definition of the interfaces between the SC PNF, the SC-C-VNF and the SC VNF components. Two alternative functional splits are addressed as follows: (i) S1-level functional split, *and*; (ii) RLC (Radio Link Control) – MAC (Medium Access Control) functional split. Each one implicates a series of capabilities and requirements (related to the underlying resources needed). The former functional split is considered for the SESAME intended proof-of-concept (PoC) and the latter for research and prototyping activities.

Evolution 3 – Placement of "Self-x" features: The analysis of different "Self-x" functionalities has leaded to the specific identification of the most convenient components to support these functionalities (Aliu, 2015). The design decisions do not implicate a modification of the high-level architecture, since the different alternatives are supported at different functional elements. Centralised "Self-x" features are supported at CESCM level though the SC VNF EMS (Element Management System) and SC PNF EMS modules. Distributed "Self-x" features are supported at CESC level though the SC VNF and SC PNF modules.

Evolution 4 – Wireless backhauling: In the original approach of the SESAME Architecture (SESAME, 2016), the CESC Cluster has been established by means of wired connections between the different CESCs. As an evolution to support a wider range of deployments and enhanced resiliency models, it has been introduced the possibility of connecting the different CESCs through wireless links. In this way, the different CESCs in the cluster can be connected in an *ad-hoc* way, and enabling one or several of them to serve as providers for the backhaul connection to the vEPCs (virtualised Evolved Packet Cores). In order to cope with the SESAME requirements, the wireless fronthauling/backhauling system is designed to support multi-tenancy and is driven by SDN (Software-Defined Radio) operations (Astuto, 2014), allowing the implementation of SDN rules (Sun, 2015) based on different metrics such as wireless link quality, processing capacity, etc. From a high level architecture standpoint, the wireless fronthauling/backhauling system resides at the same level than the wired system, while the SDN Controller resides at the VIM level since the VIM is the component in charge of managing the consolidated set of resources in a CESC Cluster.

3. FUNCTIONAL DESCRIPTION OF UPDATED SESAME ARCHITECTURAL COMPONENTS

In the following paragraphs we discuss, one-by-one of the previously identified evolutionary steps of the main SESAME-*based* architecture and we focus upon the functional description of their corresponding architectural components.

The SC-C-VNF as fun-in/fun-out module: The SC-Common VNF top-level functionality consists of the following: 1) S1 Multiplexer: (i) Accepts a single S1 connection request from the PNF; (ii) creates up to six S1 connections to each SC-VNF; (iii) routes S1 messages from the PNF to the appropriate SC-VNF (and vice-versa*), and;* (iv) performs a small amount of identity translation, and; 2) Cell-wide Admission Control in the Virtualised domain. The SC-Common VNF likewise performs cell-wide admission control with regard to the number of User Equipments (UEs) permitted.

An architectural update is that the SC-Common VNF no longer performs management of the front-haul bandwidth across each of the connected SC-VNFs. This function has been moved into each individual SC-VNF, which is now self-policing. This change has simplified the implementation by removing the need for a separate interface between the SC-Common VNF and each SC-VNF.

The SC-VNF top-level functionality consists of the following features and/or "components": (i) Traffic shaping; (ii) Tenant-specific AC (Admission Control) based on limits applied to the specific tenant; (iii) GTP (GPRS Tunnelling Protocol) TEID (Tunnel Endpoint Identifier) Management within the CESC; (iv) Congestion control via blind handover (not supported by the PoC demo); (v) DSCP (Differentiated Services Code Point) marking per QCI (QoS Class Identifier) – (not supported by the PoC demo), *and*; (vi) S1AP (Application Protocol) routing to and from the Core Network (CN). As described above, the SC-VNF now polices its own fronthaul bandwidth utilisation. This is based upon two configurable parameters: *Max Uplink Bandwidth* and *Max Downlink Bandwidth*. Fronthaul bandwidth utilisation is controlled in two ways: (i) A new Guaranteed Bit Rate (GBR) bearer is not admitted if, by so doing, *Max Uplink Bandwidth* or *Max Downlink bandwidth* would be exceeded, *and*; (ii) The SC-VNF continuously monitors the current bandwidth in use by the virtual cell across all bearers and, *if necessary*, discards packets for non-GBR bearers in order to bring the total throughput within the configured limit. In addition, the SC-VNF is configured with a per-tenant limit, *Max UEs*, which defines the maximum number of concurrently active UEs that it supports. Thus, for UE admission, control is exerted at two levels: (i) If the total configured capacity of the cell as a whole has been reached, the SC-Common VNF rejects a new user admission regardless of whether or not the VSCNO's individual limit has been reached, and; (ii) If admitted by the SC-Common VNF the SC-VNF will reject a new user if the maximum capacity allocated to the associated VSCNO has been reached. Similar behaviour applies to bearer admission where the SC-Common VNF monitors the cell as a whole and the SC-VNF polices a VSCNO's individual share.

Functional Split: The work included in (SESAME, 2016) have already surveyed the possible type of functional splits which have been advocated in different fora, with specific attention to the Small Cell Forum (SCF) activities. In this regard, also 3GPP has recently realised studies and promoted proposals regarding functional split options and so, requirements have been submitted (such as, *inter-alia*, those in (3GPP, 2016). For the next generation of virtualized small cells, the studies made by 3GPP have begun in *Release 1* (which comprises of around 170 high-level features and studies) and fall within the activities towards completion of *Release 1*, and are part of the wider work on virtualisation of the Radio Access Network (RAN). For the sake of completeness, the possible functional splits are: above the Packet Data Convergence Protocol (PDCP), between the PDCP and the RLC and between the RLC and the MAC. This latter split is further differentiated between the separation between high-MAC and low-MAC. The last functional split is focused on the Physical (PHY) layer, distinguishing also in this case between high-PHY and low-PHY. It is known that each of the functional splits carries *pros and cons*, with more or less stringent requirements in terms of aggregate data rate and latency. It is worth reminding that due to the functional split, the protocol stack is divided in central and remote small cell functions. The central function is the part of the protocol stack subject to virtualization, which is hence implemented as VNF (or a chain of VNFs), whereas the remote function is referred to as PNF. One central VNF can be connected to multiple remote PNFs provided that the required timing and throughput constraints are fulfilled for a given functional split. The link between a SC VNF and the SC PNF is called the *fronthaul*, whereas the link between the central VNF and the vEPC is called the *backhaul*.

The overall SESAME architecture can "suit well" different type of functional splits, bearing in mind that a functional split at the MAC layer (high or low), as well as at the PHY layer (high or low) are the most demanding in terms of latency and aggregated throughput requirements between VNF and PNF. Indeed, scheduling of Resource Blocks (RBs) occurs every Transmission Time Interval (TTI) or, in other words, every 1 ms therefore carrying computational intensive tasks depending also upon the number of connected UEs. On the other hand, baseband processing usually involves complex operations that can drain a significant amount of computing power. In the context of SESAME, the "atomic" network component, (that is, "the CESC"), is the junction of a small cell and a micro-server computing node through the logical S1 interface (VNF-PNF connection). The collection of several CESCs constitutes the edge cloud environment developed by SESAME, referred to as "the CESC cluster" with the cloud of interconnected micro-servers that identify the local exemplification of the Light DC. Since one of the most important objectives of SESAME is to deliver a cost-effective solution, the MAC/PHY functional split might add a high load to the micro-server environment. Indeed, a micro-server connected to a small cell is a one-to-one relation between them. In this regard, small cell VNFs should be executed over a single micro-server with the addition of service VNFs that can better exploit the edge-cloud environment.

Referring to (SESAMEb, 2016), service VNFs include virtualised video transcoding unit (vTU), virtualised Deep Packet Inspection (vDPI), virtualised context aware routing (vCAR) and virtualised caching (vCaching). On the other hand, small cell VNFs depend on the particular type of functional split adopted. It is anyway important to mention that small cell VNFs are most likely to be deployed within the same micro-server for each CESC. Independently of the specific functional split, the virtualised small cell has to be able to manage the multi-tenant environment and the S1 incoming/outgoing traffic on a per tenant basis (i.e., VSCNO). Besides the micro-server constraints, the medium used to implement the S1 interface is the first real bottleneck. In this regard, the work in (SESAMEb, 2016) has addressed already the core requirements for each VNF and the achievable performance depending on the implementation solution for the S1 interface (e.g. optical fibre or copper). From an implementation standpoint, two functional splits are under research in SESAME considering that a hybrid Light DC environment will be composed of the interconnection of different micro-server technologies: ARM-*based* and x.86-*based*.

"Self-x" Functionalities: The "Self-x" or Self-Organizing Network (SON) functionalities in the context of SESAME were categorized and explained in (SESAME, 2016). However, the initial SESAME architecture did not "depict" them explicitly. In this respect, Fig.2 presents an update of the SESAME architecture that includes these functionalities. As shown in Fig.3, the PNF EMS and SC EMS include the centralised "Self-x" functions (cSON) and the centralised components of the hybrid SON functions. In turn, the dSON functions - or the decentralised components of the hybrid functions - reside at the CESCs. Concerning the dSON functions, they can be implemented as a PNF or, if proper open control interfaces with the element (e.g. the RRM function) controlled by the "Self-x" function are established, they can also be implemented as a VNFs running at the Light DC.

In addition, a mapping of the specific Radio Resource Management (RRM) functions and "Self-x" functions of (SESAME, 2016), in the different components of the architecture of Fig.3 has taken place. This kind of mapping depends in general on the selected functional split between the physical and virtualized functions. In this scope, RRM functionalities such as the packet scheduling or the power control, which involve the lower layers of the protocol stack, can only be included in the SC VNF when functional split at MAC or PHY levels is considered. Regarding self-planning functions, which involve decisions for deploying new cells or for changing the spectrum assigned to each cell, they are likely to follow a centralized implementation at the EMS given that they operate in the long term and they need to consider the vision of the whole network. The same applies to self-healing, and to SON coordination functions. Regarding the self-optimisation functions, different cases can be identified; for example, some functions like Coverage and Capacity Optimization (CCO) functions or energy saving, will likely be executed at the EMS level following a centralized SON approach, because they require a view encompassing multiple cells. Instead, other functions like the Automated Neighbour Relationship (ANR) will follow a decentralized approach, possibly supported by a centralized component in case of hybrid SON. In the case of ANR, the decentralized component, which acts over the neighbour lists used at RRC level, will be placed at the SC PNF or the SC VNF depending on the position of this layer in the functional split, as shown in the table. In turn, other functions like Mobility Robustness Optimisation (MRO), Mobility Load Balancing (MLB) or Optimisation of Admission control, which act over the handover and admission RRM functions running at the SC VNF, will likely be executed at the SC VNF as well, possibly supported by a centralized component at the SC EMS in case of a hybrid SON approach.

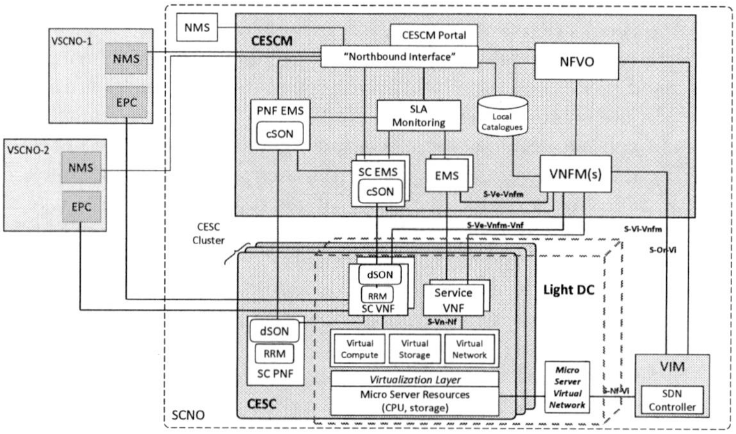

Figure 2. Update of the SESAME architecture in relation to "Self-X" functionalities

Wireless Backhaul: The wireless backhaul (Chia, 2009) is a flexible and cost efficient alternative to wired backhauls to interconnect the SCs of a SESAME deployment with each other and with the core network. Providing every SC with a wired, high bandwidth connection (e.g., fibre) to the core networks is very costly and very limited when choosing locations where SC has access to the required backhauling infrastructure. Further, the deployment requires a careful planning or even new infrastructure, making solutions very rigid. The wireless, SDN-based backhauling architecture designed in SESAME avoids these technical issues. In this part we detail the main design choices made for the SESAME wireless backhauling architecture. The main task of the backhaul is to provide connectivity for the S1 tunnels that are established between the SC-VNF of each tenant and its corresponding S-GW. Additionally, in SESAME the wireless backhauling infrastructure needs to be virtualized, so that a per tenant-*based* slicing of the physical radio resources can be applied. The SDN controller, that monitors the state of the network, offers interfaces to other SESAME modules, takes routing decisions and is based on OpenDayLight (ODL). This was chosen because of it is open source, the good support from the community, and the availability of software bundles that served as a basis for the OpenFlow (OF)-*based* communications between the agent nodes of the network and the SDN controller. OpenVSwitch (OVS) is used in the agent nodes to virtualize the wireless radio interfaces. The different components of the SDN architecture (ODL, OF, OVS) have been designed to work with wireless interfaces (originally OVS is intended for wired interfaces). On each backhaul node (corresponding to a CESC), virtual interfaces are created on top of the physical interfaces for every tenant that is operating on the CESC. Virtual switches belonging to a tenant then are interconnected to form a wireless mesh. As a result, every tenant "owns" a virtualized backhaul network that is composed of its virtual switches plus the virtual links between the switches. The slicing of the virtualized physical radio links across the backhaul network is handled by a scheduling software module developed for Linux. This module can be dynamically loaded during runtime and it will be configurable via an API that tells the module which part of the link share each of the virtual interfaces gets. (i.e., on a *per-tenant* basis). The software module requires minimal interaction with the underlying MAC (for Wi-Fi this is IEEE 802.11) for high precision bandwidth calculations. Further, the ODL controller will provide an API from/to other SESAME components that is used to: (i) Configure the shares each tenant has of the wireless backhaul; (ii) Set up new end-to-end data flows between SCs and a gateway node that connects the wireless backhaul to a tenant's vEPC, *and*; (iii) Notify SCs when a tenant may be reaching the limits of the available backhaul capacity.

4. CONCLUSIONS AND OVERVIEW

The SESAME platform targets to take advantage from the existing NFV infrastructure – that provides a virtualization platform to network functions enhancing it with new computing/storage resources and creating a virtualization environment for a wide range of applications running at the mobile network edge. In this paper, based upon the initial SESAME architecture we have discussed, *in detail*, recent innovations and evolutionary steps covering: (i) SC-Common VNF as fun-in/fun-out module; (ii) progress in SESAME Small Cell functional splits; (iii) placement of "Self-x" features, *and*; (iv) wireless backhauling. We have further realised a functional description of the corresponding updated architectural components, as identified above, with the aim of providing a "more reliable and concrete" architecture able, to ensure the proper realization of the original SESAME's aims and specific targets.

ACKNOWLEDGEMENT

The paper has received funding from the European Union in the context of the 5G-PPP / H2020 RIA Action under Grant Agreement (GA) No.671596 (the "SESAME" project).

REFERENCES

3GPP TS 32.130 v13.0.0: "Telecommunication management; Network sharing; Concepts and requirements (*Release 13*)", January, 2016.

G. Aliu, A. Imran, M.A. Imran, and B. Evans, "A Survey of Self Organisation in Future Cellular Networks", *IEEE Communications Surveys & Tutorials*, vol.15(1), pp.336-361, 2015.

B. Blanco, J.O. Fajardo, and F. Liberal, "Design of Cognitive Cycles in 5G Networks". *In Proceedings of AIAI-2016 Int. Conf.*, IFIP AICT vol.475, L. Iliadis and I. Maglogiannis, Eds. Springer International Publishing Switzerland, pp.697-708, 2016.

S. Chia, M. Gasparroni, and P. Brick, "The next challenge for cellular networks: Backhaul", *IEEE Microwave Magazine*, vol.10(5), pp.54-66, 2009.

I.P. Chochliouros, et al., "Challenges for Defining Opportunities for Growth in the 5G Era: The SESAME Conceptual Model". *In Proceedings of the EuCNC-2016*, Athens, Greece, June, 2016.

C.E. Costa, and L. Goratti, "SESAME Essential Architecture Features". *In Proceedings of the EuCNC-2016 Conference*, Athens, Greece, June, 2016.

European Telecommunications Standards Institute (ETSI), *"Network Functions Virtualisation - Introductory White Paper"*, 2012.

J.O. Fajardo, F. Liberal, et al., "Introducing Mobile Edge Computing Capabilities through Distributed 5G Cloud Enabled Small Cells". *Mobile Networks and Applications*, vol.21(4), pp.564-574, 2016.

I. Giannoulakis, et al., "Enabling Technologies and Benefits of Multi-Tenant Multi-Service 5G Small Cells". *In Proceedings of the EuCNC-2016 Conference*, Athens, Greece, June, 2016.

L. Goratti, et al. "Network Architecture and Essential Features for 5G: The SESAME Project Approach". *In Proceedings of AIAI-2016 Int. Conf.*, IFIP AICT vol.475, L. Iliadis and I. Maglogiannis, Eds. Springer International Publishing Switzerland, pp.676-685, 2016.

D. Harutyunyan, and R. Riggio, "Functional Decomposition in 5G". *In Proceedings of AIMS 2016*, LNCS 9701, R. Badonnel *et al.*, Eds. Springer-Verlag New York, pp.62-67, 2016.

M. Hoffmann, and M. Staufer, "Network virtualization for future mobile networks: General architecture and applications". *In Proceedings of the 2011 IEEE International Conference on Communications Workshops (ICC-2011)*, Kyoto, Japan, June, pp. 1-5, 2011.

A. Khan, et al., "Network sharing in the next mobile network: TCO reduction, management flexibility, and operational independence". *IEEE Communications Magazine*, vol.49(10), pp.134-142, 2011.

D. Mavrakis, "Why Fronthaul Matters – A Key Foundation for Centralized and cloud RANs", *White Paper. Ovum*, 2015.

H. Mouratidis, S. Islam, C. Kalloniatis, and S. Gritzalis, "A framework to support selection of cloud providers based on security and privacy requirements". *J. Syst. Softw.*, vol.86(9), pp.2276-2293, 2013.

A. Oueis, E. Calvanese Strinati, et al., "Small Cell Clustering for Efficient Distributed Fog Computing: A Multi-User Case". *In Proceedings of the IEEE 82nd Vehicular Technology Conference (VTC Fall)*, Boston, US, September, pp. 1-5, 2015.

M. Peng, C. Wang, V. Lau, and H.V. Poor (2015, April): "Fronthaul-Constrained Cloud Radio Access Networks: Insights and Challenges". *IEEE Wireless Communications*, vol.22(2), pp.152-160, April, 2015.

R. Riggio, A. Bradai, et al., "Virtual Network Functions Orchestration in Wireless Networks". *In Proceedings of the 11th International Conference on Network and Service Management (CNSM)*, Barcelona, Barcelona, Spain, November 09-13, IFIP/IEEE, 2015.

SESAME 5G-PPP Project, D2.2 "Overall System and Architecture", 2016.

SESAME 5G-PPP Project, D4.1 "Light DC Architecture Design", 2016.

I. Son, D. Lee, J.-N. Lee, and Y.B. Chang, "Market Perception on Cloud Computing Initiatives in Organizations: An Extended Resource-based View", *Information & Management*, vol. 51(6), pp.653-669, 2014.

S. Sun, L. Gong, B. Rong, and K. Lu, "An intelligent SDN framework for 5G heterogeneous networks," *IEEE Communications Magazine*, vol.53(11), pp.142–147, 2015.

F.P. Tso, S. Jouet, and D.P. Pezaros, "Network and server resource management strategies for data centre infrastructures: A survey". *Computer Networks*, vol.106, pp.209-225, 2016.

V. Vassilakis, I.P. Chochliouros, A.S. Spiliopoulou, *et al*, "Security Analysis of Mobile Edge Computing in Virtualized Small Cell Networks". *In Proceedings of AIAI-2016 Int. Conf.*, IFIP AICT vol.475, L. Iliadis and I. Maglogiannis, Eds. Springer International Publishing Switzerland, pp.653-665, 2016.

COMMUNICATING AND TRANSACTING WITH CHATBOTS: INSIGHTS FROM PUBLIC TRANSPORT

Darius Zumstein and Sophie Hundertmark
Institute of Communication and Marketing, Lucerne University of Applied Sciences
Zentralstrasse 9, 6002 Lucerne, Switzerland

ABSTRACT

Chatbots as a new information, communication and transaction channel enable businesses to reach their target audience through messenger apps like Facebook, WhatsApp or WeChat. Compared to traditional chats, bots are not handled by human persons, but software is leading through conversations. Latest chatbots developments in customer services and sales are remarkable. However, in the field of public transport, little research has been published on chatbots so far. With chatbots, train customers find out timetables, buy tickets and have a personal, digital travel advisor providing real-time and context-relevant information about trips. Chatbots collect and provide different data about users and their journey in public transportation systems. They include travel, product, service and content preferences, usage patterns, demographic and location-based data. Chatbots have different advantages and high potential for both companies and mobile users. They enable new user touch points, reduce service, sales and support costs, one-to-one marketing, new data collections and deep learning. Using chatbots, smartphone users can reach a company anytime and anywhere. The questioned users of a chatbot prototype are remarkably open to new mobile services and they quickly adapt to this innovative technology.

KEYWORDS

Chatbots, chat, bots, messenger services, digital communication, digital customer services, conversational commerce

1. INTRODUCTION

1.1 The Rise of Chatbots

The number and variety of chatbots strongly increased in the last couple of years. Today, more than 34’000 chatbots are available in the Facebook messenger (Statista 2017), and the potential global annual revenue generated by chatbot transactions is estimated up to 32 billion US Dollars (Business Insider 2017a).

However, chatbots as a new, personal, interactive and disruptive information, communication and transaction channel not only generate high revenues, they also reduce costs: The potential annual salary savings created by chatbots is about 12 billion US Dollars in insurance sale, 15 billion for financial services and sales representatives and even 23 billion for common customer service personnel in the US market (Business Insider 2017b).

1.2 Outline and Research Method

To better understand the use, importance and the challenges of chatbots in the context of public transport, the research project and this paper is divided into four sections: After a motivating introduction, the term chatbot is defined and its technical functioning explained in **section 2**. **Section 3** outlines the benefits and challenges of chatbots. In the main **section 4**, the research results of chatbots in the public transport sector are presented. The empirical study was separated in two online surveys: The first focused on 134 customers in the public transport sector and asked about their general preferences and habits queries the timetable and to buy tickets. Moreover, questions about the potential of a digital travel advisor including personalized information and offers were asked. In the second survey, 84 test users of an innovative prototype were asked about their experiences with the new chatbot. Furthermore, the potential for a travel advisor or other personalized offers of a public train company was evaluated. Finally, **section 5** of this paper gives a conclusion and an outlook.

2. THE USE OF CHATBOTS

2.1 Definition

The word "chatbot" consists of the terms "chat" and "robot". Originally, the term "chatbot" was used for a computer program, which *simulates human language with the aid of a text-based dialogue system*. Chatbots contain a text input and output mask, which allows mobile users to communicate with the software behind them, giving them the feeling of chatting with a real person (Wang & Petrina 2013).

Since the introduction of smartphones and mobile applications (apps), the term "chatbot" is increasingly used for *messenger apps* rather than for pure computer programs (Atwell & Bayan 2015).

2.2 Operating Mode of Chatbots

Generally, chatbots have quite similar technologies and architectures. Figure 2 shows the technical process of a chatbot, when a mobile user makes a request until the appropriate answer is sent by the chatbot.

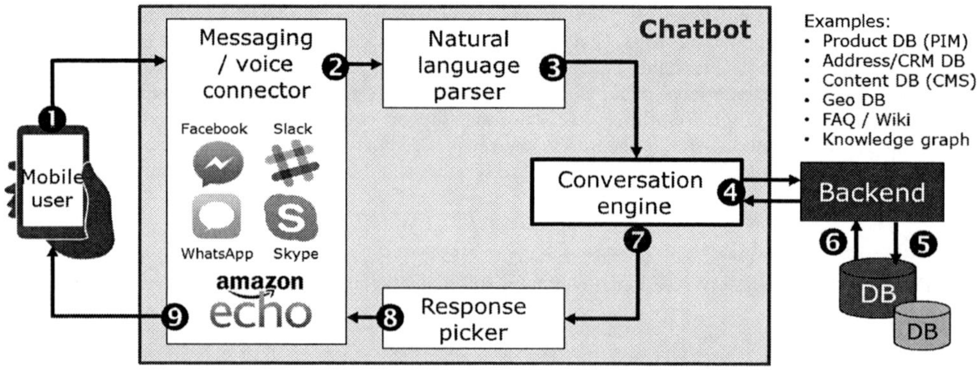

Figure 1. Operating mode of chatbots (Source: Following Weidnauer 2016)

The process starts with a *user's request* (see step 1 in Figure 1) using a messenger app like Facebook, Slack, WhatsApp or Skype, or an app using text or speech input (e.g. Amazon Echo in step 2). The user request is recorded by a so-called *Natural Language Parser* (NLP; 3) and is translated into the programming language of the conversation engine. Following, the *conservation engine* analyses the question and redirects it to the backend (4). The *backend* is linked to one or several databases (DB), which give a result to the corresponding query. Once the appropriate result has been found in the backend (5 and 6), the conversion engine forwards it to the *response picker* (7). Now the answer, which is still in the programming language of the chatbot, is translated into the natural language of the user and sent to him to user interface (see 8 and Weidnauer 2016).

Chatbots and language parsers use semantic patterns and keywords to analyze the requests of users and to edit them as accurately as possible. By matching databases stored in the backend, chatbots recognize patterns or regularities and combine them. This process is also called *machine learning*. In addition, many chatbots use the technique of deep learning, a subcategory of machine learning.

The chatbot starts with the analysis of the main core themes and then goes into the depth of the topic. If the user starts the conversation with a question, the chatbot first tries to analyze the main topic and then uses the funnel principle to narrow down the topic more closely (Dempt 2016). Software tries to understand the text of the user by regular and data-driven semantic procedures. *Rule-based methods* attempt to automatically recognize data expressions. *Data-oriented methods* work similarly to content analysis of qualitative social research. Deductive categories are built in advance and then the texts of the users are coded using these categories to assign them quickly to the related topics (Trendone 2016).

As soon as the chatbot has solved the user's request, it has to provide the right answers as quickly as possible. For this purpose, various database entries are stored in the backend (see figure 1 on the right): These can be Customer Relationship Management (CRM) systems, Enterprise Resource Planning (ERP) systems, Content Management Systems (CMS), Product databases or Information Systems (PIM) or another internal or/and external database. The chatbot matches the given question with the databases in the backend and provides the user with the requested information or suggestions (Dempt 2016).

2.3 Application Fields of Chatbots

The fields of applications of chatbots are manifold: Very popular are *calendar assistants and chatbots for reserving or purchasing event tickets* (for 68% and 64% of the responses in figure 2). *Searching and buying products online* using chatbots are very popular too (e.g. H&M, chatShopper & eBay). Moreover, 58% of the asked users are using chatbots for *booking hotels, trips and flights* (e.g. KLM & Austrian Airline chatbot).

This paper focuses on chatbots used for **searching and booking train trips**. Other fields are chatbots for news (for instance the CNN chatbot), weather (e.g. Hi Puncho), traffic (e.g. Traffic News & Traffic Jam) and financial chatbots (e.g. Trading Bot). Finally, many chatbots are used for *customer and delivery services*.

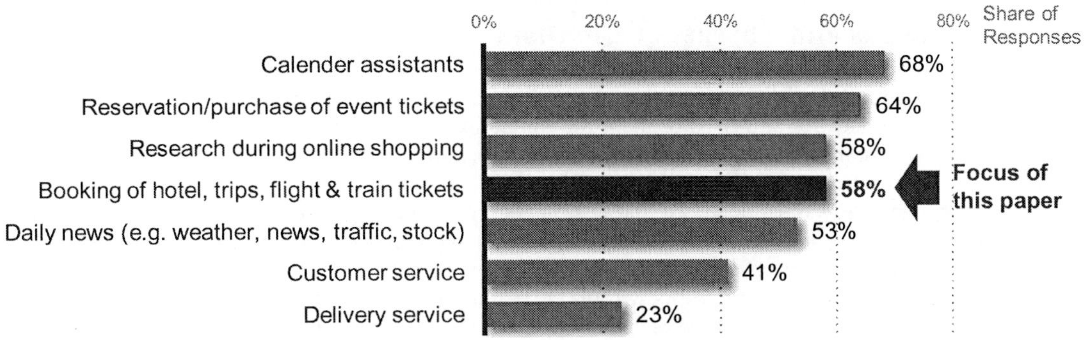

Figure 2. Fields of applications of chatbots (Source: Statista 2017b)

3. BENEFITS AND CHALLENGES OF CHATBOTS

3.1 Strengths and Benefits of Chatbots

Chatbots have two different type of consequences for companies: On the one hand, chatbots change the way of informing, communicating and transacting between the company and its customers or other stakeholders. On the other hand, they influence the organization, communication and collaboration within the company.

Thanks to messenger apps and chatbots, most businesses have new ways to interact with their customers through *one-to-one communication*. Users usually use the messenger apps for private purposes among friends and colleagues. Companies have now the chance to enter this private communication channel for businesses. Using chatbots, consumers and businesses can communicate *24 hours day, 7 days the week*, independent of working or opening hours. Companies can save on personnel costs in customer services and do not take the risk that they cannot be reached outside their business hours, and they do not miss customers' requests.

Looking at the collection of user and usage data, the use of chatbots leads to new potentials for providers. Companies get to know their customers in a new way. In many cases, users link their social media profiles with their messenger profiles, so that companies can get direct *insights into user interests, responses and profiles*. If this is not the case, the chatbot can send the necessary information or questions during the dialog with users. In addition, the chatbot stores individual user preferences based on the users' purchase history, inquiries and other activities. These new data collections give companies the opportunity to address their customers in a targeted manner, and the customized offers can be targeted directly and personally to users.

Apart from the advantages of communication and transaction, chatbots also offer new potentials within the company. For example, chatbots are used for *supporting and training purposes for employees*. Another example is the digital onboarding of new staff members. Instead of a long onboarding of colleagues, chatbots take over the introduction of new team members, internal communication, standard processes and tasks.

Chatbots allow customers to get in contact with companies whenever they want so, without having to pay attention to time zones and to *opening times and waiting loops of call/service centers*. Chatbots are promising for international and digital companies like online retailers or web shops. Customers sometimes buy products in different countries and they do not want to be dependent to local time zone or foreign languages. A further advantage is personal one-to-one communication. So far, users often *must search and browse a website for a long time* to find the right information like product, price, service or contact information. In the case of complaints or other customer service inquiries, chatbots are helpful, straight-forward and efficient.

In a best-case scenario, the chatbot knows its users like a good friend and offers them appropriate offers, solutions and services at the right time. Depending on the permissions the user gives to the chatbot, he will be informed automatically and proactively on specific inquiries and demands. In public transport, the *chatbot as a travel companion* is a promising service compared to other ones. In future, customers can automatically be informed by push notifications about delays and other relevant information directly on users' mobile phone.

3.2 Weaknesses and Threats of Chatbots

In contrast to the many benefits of chatbots, researchers, developers and providers of chatbots should also be aware of the disadvantages and risks of the new applications. Today, customers are very *familiar to receive or request information from companies using phones, newsletters, e-mails, apps or websites*. Messengers are mainly used for private communication among friends and colleagues.

However, companies must be aware that customers are used to other communication channels and that it will therefore *take some time to adapt* before getting used to the new communication and buying methods. In a transition phase, classical (offline and online) channels still must be provided and the customers should be motivated and incentivized to use the new tools. It is important that companies can be found in messenger apps like Facebook or, in the case of standalone apps, in the Apple and Google app store.

Another important topic for both providers and users is data protection. If companies offer a stand-alone chatbot app, they are responsible for protecting and handling customer data adequately. This is just like with traditional apps and websites. However, if companies offer their chatbot on a third-party platform, data are also sent to operators and platforms like Facebook, WhatsApp, Slack or WeChat. Chatbot developers and operators should ensure both *data privacy and data protection*. When it comes to payment processes, where bank or credit card data are insert, data protection is crucial. Communicating with customers, companies try to collect as many user data as possible, to store them and to use them for further transactions or marketing offers. Users need to be aware that providers of chatbots and messenger platforms will *collect personal data*.

Furthermore, some consumers may fear that they will miss other offers because of personalized offers are selected by a bot only. To reduce this risk, users should ask chatbots for *other offers outside of their preferences*. Table 1 summarizes some important strengths/opportunities and risks of chatbots.

Table 1. Advantages and risks of chatbots for providers and users

	Strengths & Opportunities	Weaknesses & Risks
For providers/ companies	- 24/7 customer service (anytime/anywhere) - New & direct customer contact points - New methods & types of data collection - High amount of personal user/usage data - Personalization & automation of communication - Reduction of service & support costs	- Malfunctioning chatbots & unanswered questions - Investments in IT infrastructure & chatbot tools - Extension of IT & analytics architectures - Lack of awareness & acceptance by users - Information security & data protection - Image & reputation risks
For users/ customers	- 24/7 customer services & support - One-to-one communication on personal device - High convenience & ease of use - Time- & cost-savings - Reduction on relevant information & services - Relevant offers based on user preferences	- Privacy - Data protection of personal & sensitive data - Lack of experience & understanding - Biased personalized information - Artificial/non-human conversation - Social isolation & ethical concerns

4. RESEARCH RESULTS ON CHATBOTS IN PUBLIC TRANSPORT

4.1 The New Chatbot of the Swiss Railway Company BLS

Since the beginning of April 2017, the chatbot of the Swiss Railway Company BLS is publicly available in the Apple app store (an Android version in Google play is following soon). Previously, it was treated as a prototype and was available for internal developing and testing only.

The first chatbot version of BLS allows its users to *buy individual tickets*, day tickets in Switzerland and additional tickets in the BLS tariff area. Furthermore, it offers the possibility to simple *query the timetable of all trains*. The user can request both core functions by chatting with the bot within the native app.

Unfortunately, the conversation with the chatbot is quite static now. The customers cannot enter free texts, but choose from various response options only. Furthermore, the chatbot is not yet functioning as a permanent travel companion. In future, the chatbot will be able to process free, imitated conversations by the user and provide regular information on travel histories or other travel-related offers like a travel companion.

4.2 Methods of Ticket Purchases and Experience with Chatbots

In the first survey, following question asked was asked to 134 participants: "Which method do you currently use most frequently to buy your tickets?" (multiple answered where possible). The responses showed that almost every second customer still is using the ticket machine to purchase tickets and *43% use an app to buy tickets* (compare Figure 3a). However, every fifth passenger still uses the ticket counter at the train station, where they have personal contact with a sales and service staff member.

To purchase train tickets, the *website is used by 12%* of customers only. Obviously, passengers are used to use apps before, during or after their journey. In the last years, websites as point of sales lost in importance in public transports. Finally, travel centers are also very seldom visited to purchase tickets (2%).

The results show that ticket machines, which are available at every train stations, and apps are the both most widely used methods to buy tickets. Digital channels as the (mobile) website, which are mostly used at home or at the office, are less and less used for buying tickets.

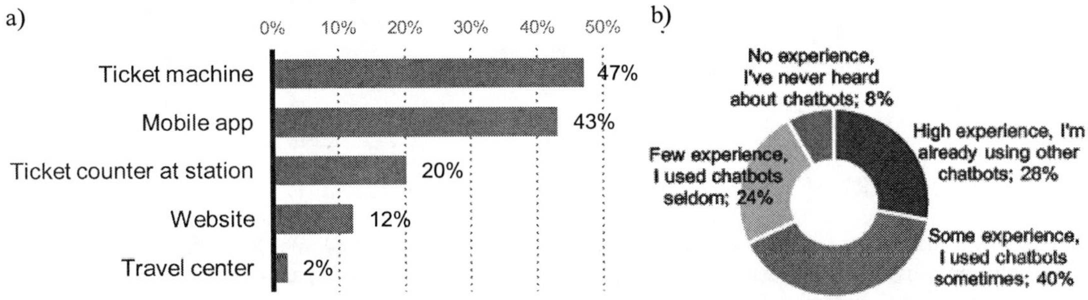

Figure 3. a) Methods of ticket purchase in public transport and b) experience with chatbots (n=134)

Secondly, in the participants of survey were asked, if they are familiar with chatbots or if these applications are (completely) new to them. Figure 3b shows that most *participants already know chatbots:* 28% of the "high experienced respondents" are using chatbots in other application fields. 40% have at least some experience and used chatbots sometimes. 24% have few experience with chatbots and did not used them often. 8% of the users had never heard about the term "chatbot". These responses show that chatbots are not completely new to customers, but this type of applications is already popular.

The answers reflect and confirm the results of the literature: Chatbots are not new to most of people, but just a minority is using them regularly and intensively. Furthermore, literature research shows that chatbots *generally get great acceptance from most users*. Regarding the survey, it is certainly helpful for many mobile users that they are familiar with chatbots.

However, many mobile users and customers still must learn this new information and communication system. Public transport customer – mobile user in general – must adapt their habits, their searching and buying behavior to chatbots, which takes some time, learning, practice and communication efforts.

4.3 Digital Services and Real-Time Information in Public Transport

Considering the registration and onboarding process of the BLS chatbot, the test users were happy: 80% were (very) satisfied (in figure 4a). The timetable and ticket access provided by the bot also have seen as positive and there was no problem with the payment process. However, the payment process and especially the ticket offering should and will be improved in a future version of the chatbot.

In future, a chatbot in public transport will serve as a travel companion, as a personal digital consultant. To find out whether the users would like travel support, the participants were asked whether they want *real-time information* during the trip, such as delays or transfers. Figure 4b shows that customers answered very united to this question: *84% of mobile users always want real-time information and updates* about their trips. 12% of the respondents would like to receive information only if they explicitly ask for it, and insignificant 4% have indicated that they do not want to receive real-time information at all. One reason for the high level of consensus is the fact that other companies are already providing order or delivery status information, e.g. e-mail or SMS notifications about a customers' mail, parcel or product. After completing a payment or buying process, customers are asked whether they wish to be informed by e-mail, SMS or by a push notification in mobile apps, for instance in the case of *train delays, next connections or changes of the rail track*. The chatbot will provide real-time and highly relevant information to its user in the form of *chat messages*. This means that the customer does not have to enter his e-mail address or phone number, but gets the information directly from the chatbot as a *push notification* referring directly to text in the messenger app.

The comparison with other providers and the detailed analysis of the prototype showed that the chatbot should not provide timetables and tickets only, but also serves as a personal travel companion, as a *robot adviser providing context- and location-based information during a customer journey in public transport*.

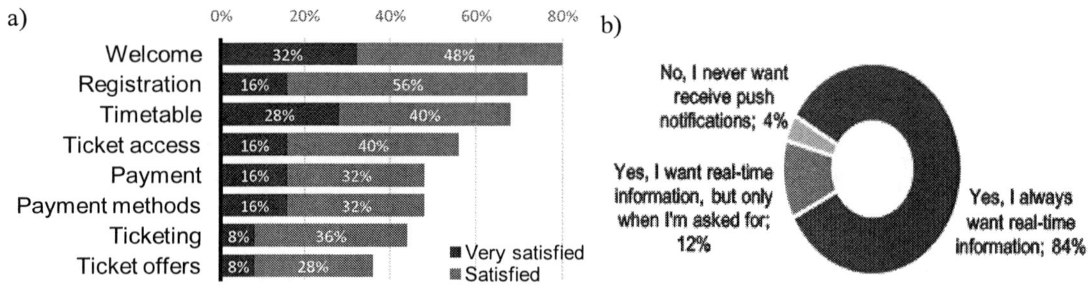

Figure 4. a) User satisfaction with the BLS chatbot and b) demand for real-time travel information (n=84)

4.4 Future Usage of Chatbots in Transportation

Users will continue to use a (chatbot) prototype only, if she/he is satisfied after an initial test phase and if the new solution provides high customer (added) value. Therefore, the participants were asked at the end of the online survey, whether they will continue to use the chatbot for buying tickets or for timetable information.

The answers in Figure 5a show that the chatbot prototype has convinced many, but not all users: *40% of respondents would continue to use it*. In contrast, 48% are not quite sure and probably prefer other methods. 12% will switch back to the previous method of searching trains and buying tickets (using common apps or the ticket machines at the station). Considerin g the answers of the previous questions, this result is plausible.

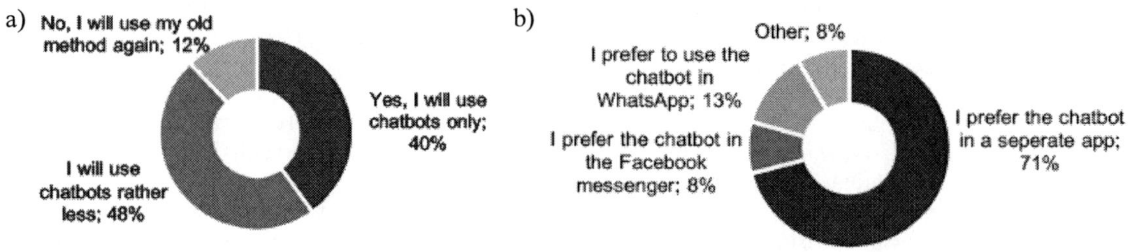

Figure 5. a) Future usage of chatbots in transportation and b) chatbots in apps or in messengers (n=84)

On the one hand, the users miss the entry of different ticket preferences and on the other hand, the chatbot do not offer all kind of tickets available. Since chatbots like the BLS prototype still have functional or technical deficits and still are in their infancy, many users will not (yet) use the chatbot regularly. At the same time, the chatbot hast to be improved and extended so that customers can use it for all inquiries and receive value.

A chatbot can be provided as a standalone app or as an integration into a messenger app like the Facebook messenger, WhatsApp or Slack. Therefore, respondents were asked if they prefer to use the chatbot as a separate app or as a chatbot in a common messenger. Figure 5b shows that users have a clear opinion to the this question: *71% prefer the chatbot as a stand-alone app.* 13% of the participants wish to integrate it into WhatsApp and 8% prefer an integration in the Facebook messenger only, probably for privacy reasons.

This results differ from literature research. This states that the trend goes to messenger apps like Facebook messenger or WhatsApp, and away from apps. In most European (national or local) public and private transport systems, customers are used to use a *mobile app to looking for time tables and to buying the next flight, train, metro or bus ticket*, often displayed in the wallet of the iPhone or Android mobile phone.

5. CONCLUSIONS AND OUTLOOK

Today, thousands of organizations – like the Swiss Railways companies BLS and SBB – are developing and providing chatbots for mobile smartphones. In future, chatbots can complement or even replace traditional information, communication and sales channels like newsletters, websites, sales desks or hotlines.

With chatbots, both companies and users can initially, directly and personally contact at anytime and anywhere, what is not possible in this manner with traditional channels like websites, newsletter or hotlines.

In addition, chatbots can communicate context- and location-based to prospects and existing customers and allow personalization as well as one-to-one marketing (see table 2).

Table 2. Chatbots versus traditionnel communication channels

	Chatbot	Website	Social Media	App	Hotline	Newsletter
Contacting by companies	++	– –	++	+	+	++
Contacting by users or customers	++	+	+	+	++	– –
Customer service outside the service hours	++	++	–	–	– –	– –
Communication to new customers (acquisition)	–	++	+	–	+	– –
Communication to customers (retention)	++	+	++	+	+	++
Communication among users	+	–	++	+	– –	– –
Machine/deep learning (Artificial Intelligence)	++	–	+	+	– –	– –
Personalization / 1-to-1 marketing	++	+	+	+	++	+
Context-/location-based services	++	–	+	++	– –	– –

Legend: ++ strength + possible – difficult – – weakness (not possible)

However, it must be ensured in digital marketing and digital business that chatbots can understand and edit most of user requests without human help. If this is not possible, a customer consultant should be available in the background and service the customer. Native apps and (mobile) websites will continue to persist despite the rise of chatbots and still be used by mobile users. Some of the app features and functionalities probably will be replaced by chatbots and other intelligent assistants like Siri or Amazon Echo.

However, a complete replacement of apps, websites and web shops cannot be observed so far. Most users are still used and bound to conventional communication and transactional channels like mobile apps and websites. This setting will probably continue for a couple of years. Since current chatbots still are not able to adequately cover all features, chatbot technologies and their applications should be developed and improved by researchers, by the software industry and by digital businesses. The same applies to social media channels: They offer many functions that chatbots currently do not cover yet and it is questionable whether they will provide them in near future. Thus, corporate social media and chatbots will co-exist and used by digital users.

Nevertheless, chatbots and their markets are rising, new fields of applications and usage are growing very fast. Companies and researchers must invest, investigate, test and develop chatbots further. Chatbots are one of the next generation intelligent information and communication systems which make our lives easier and more convenient.

REFERENCES

Atwell, E., Bayan, A.-S. (2015). ALICE Chatbot: Trials & Outputs. In: *Computación y Sistemas, vol. 19.*

Business Insider (2017a). *Here's how chatbot metrics differ from traditional apps*, BI Intelligence, Available: www.businessinsider.com/heres-how-chatbot-metrics-differ-from-traditional-apps-2016-10, accessed 24th of June 2017.

Business Insider (2017b). Facebook has opened up analytics and developer tools for Messenger bots, BI Intelligence Available: http://www.businessinsider.com/facebook-opens-analytics-developer-tools-for-messenger-bots-2016-11, accessed 24th of June 2017.

Christensson, P. (2009), Avatar, Available: http://techterms.com/definition/avatar, accessed 24th of June 2017

Coniam, D. (2008). Evaluating the language resources of chatbots for their potential in English as a second language. In: *ReCall* (20), pp. 98-116.

De Pietro, G., Gallo, L., Howlett, R., & Jain, L. (2016). Smart Innovation, Systems and Technologies. Switzerland: Springer International Publishing Switzerland.

Dempt, F. (2016). *Futuregram.* Available: http://futuregram.trendone.com/index.html#einstieg, accessed 24th of June 2017

Gill, A., & Oberlander, J. (2002). *Taking Care of the Linguistic Features of Extraversion,* Availble: http://hfac.gmu.edu/-cogscilfinaLind_files/gilLOberlander.pdf, accessed 24th of June 2017

Hill, J., Ford, W., & Farreras, I. (2015). Real conversations with artificial intelligence: A comparison between human–human online conversations and human–chatbot conversations. In: *Computers in Human Behavior* (49), pp. 245-250.

Jia, J. (2009). CSIEC: A computer assisted English learning chatbot based on textual knowledge and reasoning. In: *Knowledge-Based Systems*, pp. 249-255.

Laurel, B. (1997). Interface Agents: Metaphors with Character. *Software Agents*, pp. 67-77.

McNeal, M., & Newyear, D. (2013). Chatbot Creation Options. *Library Technology Reports* (49).

Mena, J. (2012). *Machine-to-Machine Marketing (M3) via Anonymous Advertising Apps Anywhere Anytime (A5),* Auerbach Publications, New York.

Reeves, B., & Nass, C. (1996). *The media equation: how people treat computers, television and new media like real people and places.* Cambridge University Press, New York.

Statista (2017a). Statista, VentureBeat, 11/2016. *The number of chatbots for the Facebook Messanger*. Available under: https://de.statista.com/statistik/daten/studie/662144/umfrage/anzahl-der-verfuegbaren-chatbots-fuer-den-facebook-messenger/, accessed 24th of June 2017.

Statista (2017b). Statista, Bitkom, 11/2016. *For which fields would you use chatbots?* Available under: https://de.statista.com/statistik/daten/studie/660267/umfrage/umfrage-zu-einsatzmoeglichkeiten-von-chatbots-in-deutschland, accessed 24th of June 2017.

Trendone (2016). *Futuregram.* Available: http://futuregram.trendone.com, accessed 24th of June 2017.

Van Lun, E. (2016). *Chatbots.* Available: https://www.chatbots.org/chatbot/, accessed 24th of June 2017.

Wang, Y., & Petrina, S. (2013). Using Learning Analytics to Understand the Design of an Intelligent Language Tutor. In: *International Journal of Advanced Computer Science & Applications* (11), pp. 124-131.

Weizenbaum, J. (1966). ELIZA - A Computer Program For the Study of Natural Language Communication Between Man And Machine. In: *Communications of the ACM* (9).

Woods, J., & Abdul-Kader, S. (2015). Survey on Chatbot Design Techniques in Speech Conversation Systems. In: *International Journal of Advanced Computer Science and Applications* (7).

Zumstein, D., & Hundertmark, S. (2017). Chatbots are Coming – Opportunities and Risks for Online Marketing (in German), In: *Online Marketing Conference,* 17th of August 2017, Bern.

REVERSE MEDIATED INFORMATION SYSTEM: WEB-BASED RETRIEVAL OF DISTRIBUTED, ANONYMOUS INFORMATION

Johannes-Y. Lohrer[1], Daniel Kaltenthaler[1], Peer Kröger[1], Henriette Obermaier[2], and Christiaan H. van der Meijden[3]

[1]*Institut für Informatik, Lehrstuhl für Datenbanksysteme und Data Mining, Ludwig-Maximilians-Universität München, Germany*

[2]*Bavarian State Collection for Anthropology and Palaeoanatomy, Munich, Germany*

[3]*Institut für Medizinische Informationsverarbeitung, Biometrie und Epidemiologie, Ludwig-Maximilians-Universität München, Germany*

ABSTRACT

In this paper, we describe the Reverse Mediated Information System, a new communication architecture that is particularly designed for the needs of archaeo-related disciplines, to bring geo-spatial and temporal data together again. Archaeological data of excavations is spread in data sources of offices, collections, and institutes. This data is important for archaeological questions, but cannot be accessed directly by all participants. In addition, the location of available data sources is often unclear. Our architecture lets individual databases connect to a central application that acts as a communication interface between the users and the data sources, without the need of a central administrator to manage the connections manually. It enables the users to retrieve data from anonymous data sources, independent of their file scheme and the underlying system. Therefore, we enable querying databases that were previously inaccessible.

KEYWORDS

Information System, Distributed Databases, Anonymous Databases, Architecture, Communication, Archaeology

1. INTRODUCTION

Conventional scientific research on prehistoric, historic, and sub-recent human legacies is done in the context of archaeological excavations. The unearthing is documented by archaeologists in detail. Specialists from different areas of expertise like archaeologists, zooarchaeologists, anthropologists, archaeobotanists, geographers, etc. describe, categorize, and analyze the findings and produce a huge amount of data with spatial and temporal information. Analyzing all this data shall reconstruct the cultural heritage, i.e., the environment as well as the human way of life in ancient years.

Mostly, archaeological excavations in our dense populated region are so-called rescue excavations initiated by building activities. Typically, authorities for the protection of ancient monuments control these activities. In case of signs of human made changes of the surface of the bulldozed earth they initialize archaeological excavations. These authorities may be institutions of the federal state, the town, or homeland societies (hereinafter referred to as "offices"). Another possibility that leads to an actual archaeological excavation may be the continuance of an excavation started in former times or the knowledge of a (pre)historic landmark that shall be investigated in that way.

Depending on staff, financial possibilities, and level of digital development, data from these excavations is collected and stored in databases by these institutions. The data usually consists of all kinds of general archaeological information like geo-spatial information, often temporal dating on the basis of specific findings, and a rough description of the found objects (in terms of text, photos, and even 3D scans).

Afterwards, the movable findings are transferred to specialized collections or specialists like anthropologists for human remains, zooarchaeologists for animal bones, archaeobotanists for rests of plants, and archaeologists for artifacts. The findings are packed separately in units according to the archaeologically defined context, which can be the place inside the grid of the archaeological area.

The specialists do corresponding investigations specific to each research field. Typically, this information is collected decentrally in subject-specific databases. Archaeological data and data collected by the specialists build the basis for detailed analyses. The flow of archaeological data is sketched in Figure 1.

The problem we are dealing with is that the specialized collections and specialists do not have all data that is available about a specific finding. This is a severe limitation for their research since a comprehensive analysis can only be done when considering the entire context of a finding. Sometimes, even temporal and spatial data is not available because this information is only saved completely in the databases of the offices and archives by default. Though this data can be retrieved by the archaeologists by manual requests, the retrieved data is not saved in the data scheme of the corresponding database system. Most often this data is sent in Excel sheets or CSV files, as well as scans and images. An automatic query system for the data exchange does not exist, so each request is aggravating, time consuming, and needs the work of a reviser that manages the requests.

Archaeological data is diverse and complex, most often spatial information is enriched with temporal information and further data on the findings, like isotopic fingerprints, morphological measures, etc. Analyzing this data provides challenges and interesting topics for data scientists in different fields. Archaeologists would greatly benefit from query processing interfaces and analysis methods working with such kind of complex data. Probably the highest hurdle towards this digital revolution of archaeological research is simply the technical gap described above.

In this paper we close this gap by proposing a Reverse Mediated Information System that is based on the concept of common Mediator based systems. It enables the provision of new data components without the need of a central administrator to manage the connections manually. It enables the users to search for more information about specific excavation contexts or findings that is spread through databases of offices, collections, and institutes.

In summary, the main contributions are as follows: First we discuss the challenges of the current situation of archaeo-related sciences (cf. Chapter 2). We list a set of requirements that should be addressed by an architecture for distributed data management of anonymous data sources (cf. Chapter 3) and discuss existing solutions and approaches for these systems (cf. Chapter 4). Then we describe the concept of our architecture, including the process of the initialization, registration, and the user search (cf. Chapter 5). Finally, we describe a case study with real archaeological data to be retrieved by the architecture (cf. Chapter 6).

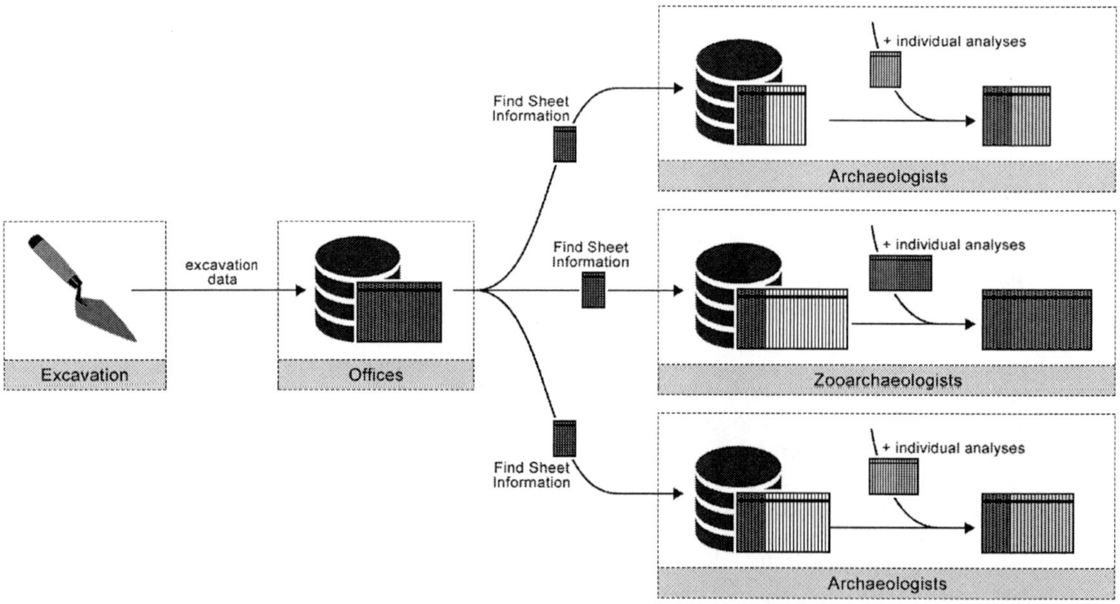

Figure 1. The basic flow of archaeological data: The data from the excavation is partly passed from the offices to the specialized collections and specialists, who perform individual analyses on the findings and save the results in their databases. The results of these analyses are not accessible from the offices. In sum, neither the offices nor the specialized collections have all available information about their findings

2. PROBLEM FORMULATION

For archaeological analysis it is not only interesting to analyze data from a single archaeological sub-domain. Considering the data from other sub-domains and the basic context information data from the offices would enable more complex and more comprehensive analysis than currently possible. In principle, enriched geo data is available, but in practice it is not easily accessible for every scientist because of the following reasons:

- **No direct access:** There is no direct external access available to data of most of the specialized databases. Data has to be gathered from the offices manually. The owner of the database has to be contacted with the parameters to search for, which is time consuming. This hinders a more detailed data selection.
- **Anonymous databases:** Data is spread over databases that – in some circumstances – are not known to all scientists. Archaeological data is not always gathered by state offices, there are also numerous city offices, local institutes, and freelancers that are gathering data as well, but do not exchange their data with the state offices. Still it would be interesting to be able to include this data in analyses as well, even if the archaeologist does not know that there exists any data in these data sources.
- **Individual database schemes:** The databases of the offices, the specialized collections, and self-employed workers have their own architectures and individual database schemes. Although they usually have identical basic information, these are saved in different ways. These cannot be standardized to a commonly used database scheme for all archaeological databases.
- **No consistent way to exchange data:** As it is common practice, data is exchanged by using Excel or CSV files that have to be formatted before being able to be used for analyses. This method can be aggravating, time consuming, and error-prone, but it is still common practice.
- **Regional and individual approaches:** There are regional and individual approaches for the filing of findings. They not only vary in the way they are excavated, but also how and which data is recorded in the databases. Furthermore, there are numerous individual solutions even on a local level.

Especially considering geo data would enable users to ask much more complex questions than it is currently possible. Therefore, we describe a solution to bring spread data together again. We achieve this without the need of a single central database, but by keeping the necessary system of distributed databases.

3. REQUIREMENTS

In this Chapter, we discuss the requirements of an infrastructure that is necessary for bringing together spread data in more detail. The infrastructure should address the following issues:

- **User Access:** Users must be able to retrieve information from distributed data sources from any local machine. This may be a web interface or an embedded solution within an existing application.
- **Independent Search:** The data sources must not have a predefined data scheme. Each data source must be searchable independently from their content even if the table and column descriptions are different for the same meaning, e.g. different labeling or languages.
- **Standard Information:** Dependent on the subject, the definition of few standard information is meaningful. Especially for information that must be part of each data set in a specific topic, such as unique IDs or spatio-temporal information.
- **Anonymous Data Sources:** The data that can be fetched by the users might be queried from multiple anonymous data sources. The users should not worry about which specific data source they should query. The system should fetch all matching data that is available in the connected data sources.
- **Easy Provision of Data:** Allowing an easy provision of – not only, but also – scientific data, administrators of data sources must be able to register their data to the distributed database system to be able to be queried. At the same time, these administrators must also be able to remove their data source from the distributed database system.
- **Rights Management:** The administrators of each data source must be able to define specific access rights for their data. Firstly, they should be able to set parts of the data source not to be searchable, e.g. if single columns in a database should be set private. Secondly, it must be possible to define the access rights, e.g. if the users should be allowed to search, but not to read the actual data.

- **Independent Database Formats:** The distributed database system should not be limited to a specific kind of database format. Each data source should be accessible independent of the underlying management system. All SQL-based database systems should be accessible.

Let us add that the data of the distributed databases is not intended to be edited by the users. This architecture is solely aimed for retrieving data.

4. RELATED WORK

In the traditional database search, information is stored in one single database. Data is retrieved by using a specific query language that is supported by the Database Management System (DBMS). In general, the basic idea of merging data from numerous databases, physical or virtual, is not a new one. In the following we recapitulate existing approaches for such infrastructures in the context of the requirements.

Over the years, it got necessary to store more and bigger amounts of data, or to separate logical information into own databases. So data was stored in different databases while each database may hold different sets of information. To make these heterogeneous databases searchable, the information was merged in central repositories. The management system has the task to retrieve and update the integrated data from the disparate sources. The users only query the central repository. These **Data Warehouses** (DW) made it possible not to have to update or extend existing databases to store new types of information. But they produce a large stream of data to query and update the central database if data is updated frequently in one of the heterogeneous databases. (Immon, 2005)

Another approach for this procedure was achieved by using **Federated Information Systems** (FIS) or **Federated Database Management Systems** (FDBMS). They map multiple database systems into a single federated database. There is no actual data integration in the constituent disparate databases as a result of data federation. The virtual data of the FIS/FDBMS is queried directly by the user. It decomposes the query into subqueries for each of the federated databases. Finally, it composites the result sets of the subqueries (Heimbigner and McLeod, 1985; Sheth and Larsen 1990). Most of the Federated Information Systems use the **Mediator concept**, "a software module that exploits encoded knowledge about some sets or subsets of data to create information for a higher layer of applications" (Wiederhold, 1992). Mediators allow the addition of new databases unknown to the user by adding a Mediator layer which is responsible to translate the queries to the designated database. While the user can still query data without knowing the amount and structure of the queried databases, the Mediator needs to know all connected databases. The Mediator is extended if a new database is added. (Wiederhold, 1994; Wiederhold, 2013)

While all of these methods are sufficient for many areas of application, none of them covers all of the requirements stated above. Especially, none of the available solutions provides the ability to add a new data source to the system without the need of a central system administrator.

Therefore, we consider the concept of the "**Internet of Databases"** that keeps the individual scientific databases, which "are for the scientists more interesting. [...] They have their database developed in their own way. They are modular, so that every user can connect and use tools in the way they want" (van der Meijden, 2012) and they are used to. These databases are connected with a simple application where meta information is managed. For our architecture, we extend the concept of the Internet of Databases and adjust it to meet our requirements described in Chapter 3. Therefore, we propose an infrastructure based on this concept to achieve a dynamic solution for retrieving data from anonymous databases.

5. REVERSE MEDIATED INFORMATION SYSTEM

Traditional web services that specialize on the retrieval of distributed data generally are configured individually to specific, directly connected data sources or use APIs for the sources. They each have different methods to access the data but the type of data that is returned mostly overlaps. E.g. the data for flight price comparison websites is standardized for the user output while each airline stores data in their own way.

In our approach we want to allow diverse data to be searchable. The results are returned unstandardized to the users, independent of the actual data scheme of the source and without the user know the potential data sources. We describe the components of the architecture below.

5.1 Architecture

The Reverse Mediated Information System (ReMIS) consists of three layers. The **Application Layer** consists of a web service that provides an input mask for the users to request data by specifying search parameters. An embedded solution is also possible to enable data retrieval directly in other applications. The **Server Layer** holds a stand-alone Mediator-like Server Application that allows data sources to register themselves to the service. It accepts requests from users and forwards them to the registered data sources, and also sends the results back to the users. Finally, the **Data Layer** stands for the servers with the data sources. Each data source runs a stand-alone Connector Application that is configured for the corresponding database. It accepts user requests from the Server Layer and translates it to a query to fetch the data from the data source. At the end, the fetched data is send back via the Server Layer to the users using a unified data structure, like JSON or XML. This allows the data to be used in other applications directly as well.

While we aim to allow diverse data, we still want to be able to search for specific parameters which are guaranteed to be stored in each connected data source. These parameters are called **Minimal Search Parameters** (MSP) and are defined in the Server Application. They are dependent on the research field that is covered by the ReMIS. However, a Server Application may define more than one set of parameters which can be selected by the users. They must be mapped for each connected data source individually to the corresponding fields.

5.2 Configuration

To setup a data source for the ReMIS an initialization process is necessary to connect a specific data source to the system. The Connector Application must be configured, therefore several steps are required. These are described below and sketched as a sequence diagram in Figure 2.

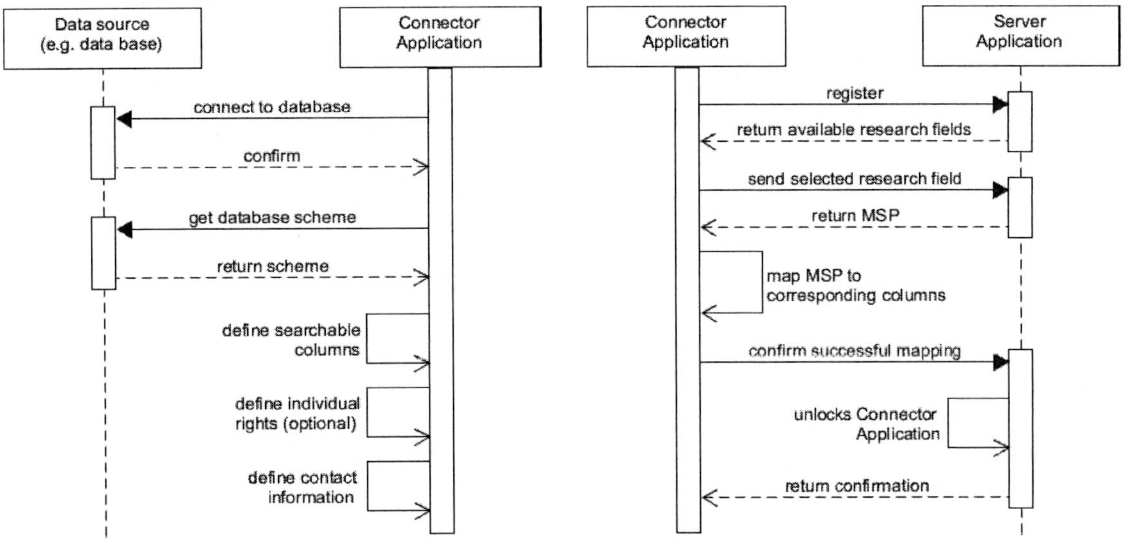

Figure 2. Sequence diagram of the Initialization Process (left) and the Registration Process (right)

In the first step, the connection of the Connector Application to the underlying data source must be established. The Connector Application then retrieves the database scheme to allow the users to select the tables and columns that in general can be returned by a search. All columns that were excluded are completely private, they cannot be considered by the Server Application, and therefore are not able to be retrieved by the users at all. If the data is not stored in one single table in the database, the different tables can be merged to one data set by mapping corresponding columns considering e.g. foreign keys. In the next step, special and optional rights can be defined which limit the visibility for specific datasets. The available rights are *Full-Public* (no restrictions, all columns are returned), *Partially-Public* (columns can be searched, but not all of them be returned as a result), *Numeric-Public* (returns only the number of found entries, no details of the entries are communicated), *Hidden* (users only get the information that there are or are not entries matching the query), and *Private* (entries will be ignored in the search). These rights can limit a dataset from being returned at all or to block specific columns for certain (maybe temporal) cases, e.g. for sensible or unpublished data. Finally, contact information can be defined which users can use to get in touch with a person in charge. All information that was set in the initialization process is saved locally in the application of the Data Layer.

After the Connector Application was initialized and the data source is connected to the system, the Connector Application is registered with the Server Application. Once a registration request is sent, the Server Application returns the options for the available research fields (e.g. "Archaeology") from which one is selected in the application of the Data Layer. Then, the Server Application sends the corresponding Minimal Search Parameters to the Connector Application, which must assign each of the parameters to a column in the local data source. These parameters must not each be mapped to a single table if the tables were connected during the initialization process before. If all parameters are mapped a confirmation is sent to the Server Application that activates the Connector Application and the corresponding data source. Then the registration process is completed and the Connector Application can receive search requests via the Server Application. If further research fields should also be considered, they can optionally be added the same way.

5.3 Search

To search for data the users start the web service by browsing the URL of the Server Application. The Server Application offers a web interface to the users in which they first select the research field for which they want to retrieve information. Afterwards a search mask is loaded with all parameters of the corresponding Minimal Search Parameters. The users fill out the parameters and the search request is sent from the Server Application to all connected Connector Applications. Then each Connector Application translates the user request to the individual, local data source, dependent on the mapping defined during the configuration. Then, the query is executed and the result is gathered while respecting the selected tables and columns as well as the specified rights set in the configuration file. Finally, the result is sent back to the Server Application which aggregates the results and forwards them back to the users to be displayed in the web interface. The full search process is sketched as a sequence diagram in Figure 3.

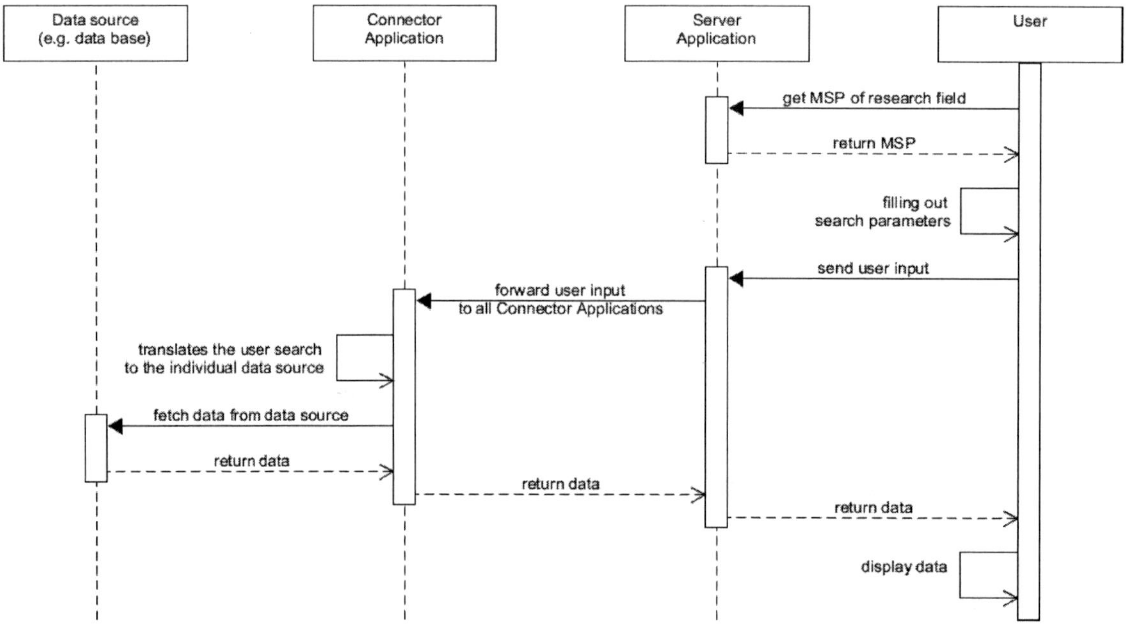

Figure 3. Sequence Diagram of the Process to Fetch Data from the Single Data Sources

6. CASE STUDY: RETRIEVING ARCHAEOLOGICAL DATA

For a case study, we use real archaeological data of three database applications in archaeo-related sciences: *OssoBook* (a scientific database for zooarchaeological findings), *ExcaBook* (a database for homogeneous capturing and administration of archaeological excavations, used by the Bavarian State Office for Monument and Sites[1]), and *ArchaeoBook* (an inventory database for archaeological objects, used by the Bavarian State Archaeological Collection[2]).

For each of these applications a Connector Application was configured to connect the data sources to the ReMIS architecture. For our case we required the research field "Archaeology" to be supported. The Server Application was initialized to require the Minimal Find Sheet information as the values for the Minimal Search Parameters. These are values that are always known in an excavation, which include the Feature Number of the excavation (which is centrally assigned by the Bavarian State Office for Monuments and Sites), the Find Sheet Number, and location information (excavation place and x-/y-coordinates).

The interested user can use the ReMIS web interface to request data from the connected data sources which they do not need to know that they exists. The search mask – that can be viewed in Figure 4 (left) – offers the opportunity to select the research field "Archaeology". Then the corresponding Minimal Search Parameters are loaded and can be entered, which actually consist of the values of the Minimal Find Sheet.

We want to retrieve information about the excavation "Marienplatz-Haltepunkt" in Munich, Germany, of which we know the excavation number "M-2011-13-1". We enter this number into the corresponding input field of the web interface and click the "Retrieve Data" button. In the background, the ReMIS architecture will now query information from all connected databases – that means the Server Application will send the user request to the Connector Application of each of the registered databases. In our case the Connector Application of *OssoBook*, *ExcaBook*, and *ArchaeoBook* will each receive the user requests and will then translate it to the local database scheme considering the mapping of the configuration. Then the query with the translated mapping is executed, and the retrieved information is sent back to the Server Application.

The result is then passed to the web interface which displays the information in table form to the users. Due to the different data schemes of each data source, the information from each data source is displayed in an own, collapsible block. In our search, we received information from the databases *OssoBook* and *ExcaBook* which is displayed to the users in the browser. However, there was no information stored in *ArchaeoBook* for the selected excavation number and therefore no data was returned from its Connector Application – so it is not included in the result view.

A screenshot of the result view is shown in Figure 4 (right). The users can now view and sort the results directly in the browser, but can also export the data to XLS, XLSX, or CSV files for further analysis in spreadsheet application or other tools.

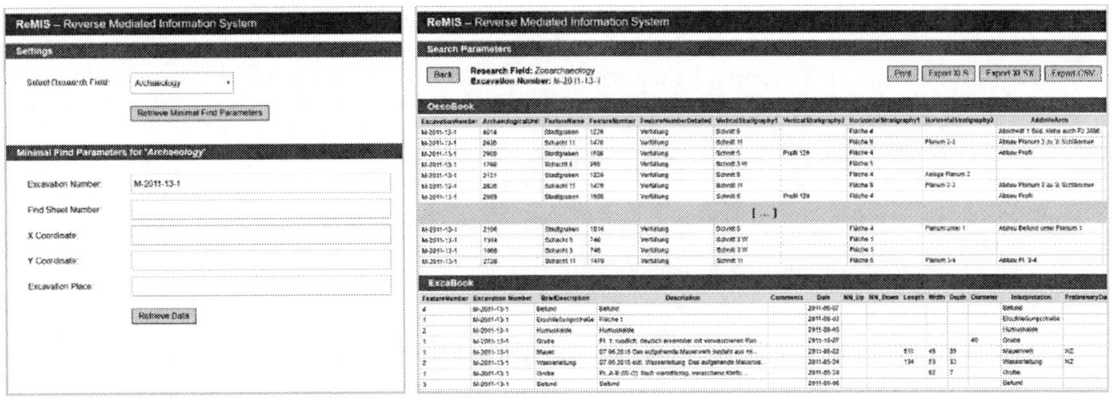

Figure 4. Screenshots of the Search Mask (left) and the Shortened Retrieved Result (right) of the Web Service of ReMIS

[1] http://www.blfd.bayern.de/
[2] http://www.archaeologie-bayern.de/

7. CONCLUSION & FUTURE WORK

In this paper, we introduced the concept of a new architecture, the Reverse Mediated Information System (ReMIS), motivated by the need to search distributed data of archaeological findings together with further contexts from multiple heterogeneous sources. We described the concept of the architecture where users can retrieve data without the need of a single central managing instance knowing about the existence of specific databases where the data is actually saved. It should be mentioned though, that this concept is not limited to the archaeo-related context. Other sciences can also benefit from this architecture.

While this architecture has many benefits for the users to gather data from distributed archaeological databases, there are also some improvements and extensions that can be addressed in the future.

In the first approach of the concept, the search possibilities for data are limited to the information of the Minimal Search Parameters. In future developments, different and more complex search options are possible. The Server Application could request all connected databases for their individual database schemes. The columns of this schemes could be displayed in the user interface as own input fields. Therefore, the user has more options and the possibility of a more detailed and individual search through the connected databases.

Data can be saved in different formats, e.g. geo data can be stored by defining coordinates or the name of the place, or different time or date formats. Currently we imply that data is entered in the same format, but this might not be the case in other working environments. Therefore it is necessary to provide a possibility to translate these different formats so that a uniform comparison is possible.

At present, the system is designed to be used for the clear excerpt of structure for archaeological data where most of the data sources are trustworthy. In future, the system should also be adaptable by extern archaeologists and institutes, maybe also a full-public approach. Therefore a verification should be considered to avoid wrong configured Connector Applications and spam.

The current system is developed having a small user base in mind. For applications in which a large amount of requests is executed every second, additional load balancers should be added.

Finally, the result of our architecture is returned in JSON or XML format. This allows the data to be reused in extern or embedded analysis tools (like Lohrer et al., 2016) as well. These applications profit by not only providing the available local data for their analysis, but also by considering fetched results from ReMIS.

REFERENCES

Heimbigner, D. and McLeod, D., 1985. *A federated architecture for information management.* ACM Transactions on Information Systems 3:3. ACM New York, USA, pp. 253–278.

Inmon, W. H., 2005. *Building the Data Warehouse*, 4th. John Wiley & Sons, New York, USA.

Kaltenthaler, D., Lohrer, J.-Y., Kröger, P., van der Meijden, C., Harrington, C., Marzinzik, S., Claßen, E., Schwarzberg, H. and Gebhard, R., 2017. *ArchaeoBook v5.6.0.* [Software] http://xbook.vetmed.uni-muenchen.de/

Kaltenthaler, D., Lohrer, J.-Y., Kröger, P., van der Meijden, C., Granado, E., Lamprecht, J., Nücke, F., Obermaier, H., Stopp, B., Baly, I., Callou, C., Gourichon, L., Pöllath, N., Peters, J. and Schibler, J., 2017. *OssoBook v5.6.0.* [Software] http://xbook.vetmed.uni-muenchen.de/

Kaltenthaler, D., Lohrer, J.-Y., Kröger, P., van der Meijden, C., Wanke, T., Sassen, I., Jantos, S., Rahm, A., Wanninger, R., Haberstroh, J. and Sommer, S., 2017. *ExcaBook v5.6.0.* [Software] http://xbook.vetmed.uni-muenchen.de/

Lohrer, J-Y., Kaltenthaler, D., and Kröger, P. (2016). *Leveraging Data Analysis for Domain Experts: An Embeddable Framework for Basic Data Science Tasks.* In: Proceedings of the 7th International Conference on Internet Technologies & Society 2016. Melbourne, VIC, Australia, pp. 51–58.

Sheth, A. P. and Larson, J. A., 1990. *Federated Database Systems for Managing Distributed, Heterogeneous, and Autonomous Databases.* ACM Computing Surveys 22:3.

Wiederhold, G., 1992. *Mediators in the Architecture of Future Information Systems.* IEEE Computer 25:3, pp. 38–49

Wiederhold, G., 1994. *Interoperation, Mediation, and Ontologies.* In: Proc. Int. Symposium on 5th Generation Computer Systems (FGCS94), Workshop on Heterogeneous Cooperative Knowledge-Bases. Tokyo, Japan, pp. 33–48.

Wiederhold, G., 2013. *Mediators, Concepts and Practice.* In: Özyer, T. et al. Information Reuse and Integration in Academia and Industry Springer, Vienna, Austria, pp. 1–27.

van der Meijden, C., 2012. *The Internet of Databases – Generalizing the Archaeo Informatics Approach.* [Online Video] 8 October 2012. Available from: https://www.microsoft.com/en-us/research/video/the-internet-of-databases-generalizing-the-archaeo-informatics-approach/

AUTOMATIC IMPROVEMENT OF TERMS USED IN FOCUSED CRAWLING PROCESSES ON WEB PAGES

Gilson Faria Costa, Guilherme Tavares de Assis and Marcos Vinicius Oliveira Souza
Department of Computing – Universidade Federal de Ouro Preto – Ouro Preto, MG, Brazil

ABSTRACT

The great popularity and, specially, the fast Web growth have led to the proposal and analysis of new techniques for helping users to locate effectively the needed information in a satisfactory time, without much difficulty. Traditional crawlers are not capable to identify relevant sub-spaces on Web related to a specific theme; however, focused crawlers are capable to solve, effectively and efficiently, the mentioned problem. Usually, a focused crawler process requires, as an input parameter, a well-defined set of terms that express the desired topic of interest; depending on such set of terms, the effectiveness of a crawling process may not be satisfactory. In order to automatically improve the set of terms necessary to perform focused crawling processes related to a genre-aware approach, we propose two strategies in this work. Our experiments generated results that improved precision and F1 measures by up to 88.9% and 32.1%, respectively, in crawling processes that considered not well-defined sets of terms as input parameter.

KEYWORDS

Automatic Improvement of Terms, Web Crawling, Focused Crawling

1. INTRODUCTION

Web's intense growth due its great popularity have led to new techniques proposal and analysis in order to help users locating the needed information effectively in a satisfactory time, without greater difficulties. Information access on Web is basically made through search engines that exploit the Web's graph structure in order to locate relevant pages to a specific search (Menczer et al. 2004). To allow this, a typical search engine uses a specific program, named crawler, which crawls the largest possible number of Web pages, generating an indexed pages collection. In this case, a traditional crawler crawls Web pages starting by seed-pages set and following the links on it, visiting other pages. Such a process continues with new pages, whose new links are followed until get a sufficient number of pages or reach some specific goal. Another program, named indexer, reads the collected pages and create an index based on the words on the pages. Each search engine uses its own algorithm to create its index aiming to return relevant results for user's searches.

The challenge of identifying specific and relevant Web sub-spaces, according to a theme, is typically referred to intelligent construction in a crawling strategy (Pant and Srinivasan, 2005). This intelligence is usually achieved by the use of heuristics, which guide the crawling process and aim at determining whether a page is relevant or not to a specific topic of interest. In this case, the crawlers are named focused or topical crawlers. Many focused crawler strategies (Almpanidis et al. 2007; Chakrabarti et al. 1999; Johnson et al. 2003; Pant and Srinivasan, 2005) make use of text classifiers to determine such relevance with additional cost of having to train the classifiers. Furthermore, due to generality of the situations where these strategies are applied, the crawlers reach low recall and precision levels: generally between 40% and 70%.

On focused crawler context, the work presented in Assis et al. (2009) (see Subsection 2.1) aimed to propose a framework that allows the construction of effective, efficient and scalable focused crawlers, requiring no training or any kind of preprocessing. Specifically, the proposed approach to focused crawling is useful in situations where the topic of interest can be expressed by two distinct set of terms: the first set describing genre aspects of the desired page's genre[1] and the second related to the subject or content of these pages. Therefore, following this approach, a specialist must specify sets of content and genre terms to

[1] By genre, according to Assis et al. (2007), it is meant to be the kind, the specie or the style of the specific documents.

represent the topic of interest. In the experiments carried out to validate the genre-aware approach, the authors noticed that, depending on the sets of terms specified, the effectiveness of a crawling process may not be satisfactory. In addition, the presence of similar terms in the sets, involving the same prefix or different only in the plurality, was observed. Thus, the automatic improvement of the original sets of terms can lead to new sets of more precise and non-redundant terms, improving the effectiveness of crawling processes, that is, the correct determination of a greater number of pages relevant to the desired topic of interest.

The solution for the mentioned problem is not trivial; so, in order to solve it, we propose two different strategies: the first one based on query expansion techniques (Carpineto and Romano, 2012) and the second based on natural language processing techniques (Gonzalez and Lima, 2003; Indurkhya and Damerau, 2010).

The rest of this paper is organized as follows. Section 2 addresses related work. Section 3 presents the proposed strategies for automatic improvement of terms to be used in focused crawling processes. Section 4 describes the experimental evaluation on the defined strategies and the results obtained. Finally, Section 5 concludes the paper and gives some directions for future work.

2. RELATED WORK

Our proposed strategies, in this work, aims to automatically improve the sets of content and genre terms to be used on focused crawling processes following a genre-aware approach. Therefore, works related to this paper are divided in two subsections: the genre-aware approach to focused crawling and the automatic improvement of terms applied to information retrieval systems.

2.1 Genre-aware Approach to Focused Crawling

The genre-aware approach to focused crawling presented in (Assis et al. 2009; Assis et al. 2007 considers a set of heuristics to guide a crawler, in such way that it allows the separate analysis of the genre and the content of a Web page. The set of heuristics has been designed with two main objectives: improving the level of F1 of the crawling process (effectiveness) and speeding up the crawling of relevant pages (efficiency).

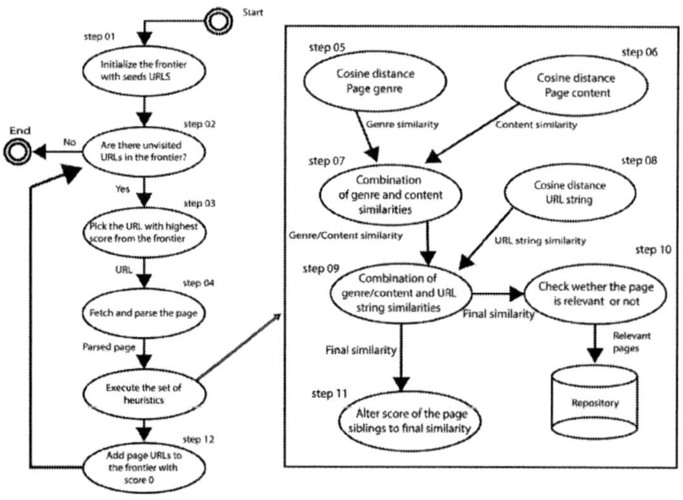

Figure 1. Functioning model of the genre-aware approach to focused crawling (Assis et al. 2009)

The Figure 1 illustrates the functioning model of the genre-aware approach to focused crawling. As we can see, firstly (step 01), a priority queue called Frontier is initialized with the URLs of the seed pages (a set of pages from which to start the crawling), setting the URL scores to 1. For each URL in Frontier (step 02), the corresponding page is visited (step 04) and its content analyzed (steps 05 to 09). It has used the cosine measure (Baeza-Yates and Ribeiro-Neto, 1999) to determine the similarity between the current page and the set of terms that represent the pages of interest. This measure is calculated separately to each set of terms (steps 05, 06 and 08), generating a specific similarity score between the current page and the sets of terms that represent, respectively, the genre, the content and the URL string of the desired pages. Each URL string term is related to the page genre or to the desired content. Then, these scores are combined into a final single one (steps 07 and 09) and compared with a given threshold defined by an expert. If this final score is greater or equal to this threshold (step 10), the visited page is included in the set of relevant pages. Next, if the current page is considered relevant, the scores of URLs in Frontier that correspond to pages siblings of the current page are changed to final score (step 11). Finally, the links previously extracted from the current page are inserted into Frontier (step 12) having their scores set to 0.

Three important improvements were proposed for the genre-aware approach. The first one (Mangaravite et al. 2012) proposes the use of link-context of the Web pages that will be visited by the crawler, in order to define their priorities (initial scores) in the Frontier, allowing the crawler to visit the relevant pages as soon as possible; such improvement generated 100% of efficiency increase. The second one (Mangaravite et al. 2014) proposes several heuristics to semi-automatically generate seed-pages for a specific topic based on its genre and content terms; results showed that the efficiency of the genre-aware approach improves to 53%. Finally, the third one (Siqueira et al. 2016) proposes three different strategies to automatically determine similarity threshold values used to classify the crawled Web pages as relevant or not relevant according to a specific topic of interest; the best strategy showed, as the best result, 100% of precision and 98% of F1.

2.2 Automatic Improvement of Terms Applied to Information Retrieval Systems

Information retrieval systems retrieve relevant documents in a collection through queries usually formulated by users. These queries are a set of terms used to describe a particular information need. According to Carpineto and Romano (2012), user queries often use an insufficient number of terms and may use a terminology different from that used to index the collection's documents. Thus, several techniques are explored to improve query terms, with the aim of making information retrieval systems able to retrieve a set of documents that better satisfy the user's information needs.

A widely used solution is the application of query expansion techniques, which, according to Aly (2008), seek to reformulate the user query by adding a set of new terms related to those that were originally established. In this context, Chartree et al. (2013) developed a work that explores an automatic method of query expansion based on association matrix. The proposed method, based on the vector model, was tested in a search engine and obtained an efficiency increase of 14.3% when compared to the same search engine without the application of the proposed method.

Another work, developed by Araujo and Pérez-Agüera (2008), proposes a method for automatic query expansion based on natural language processing, genetic algorithm and thesaurus consulting. This method works as follows: given an initial set of terms, a new set is formed including new related terms, derived from a thesaurus, in addition to the original ones; then, the stemming technique is applied to this new set; as the new set formed can be very large, an evolutionary genetic algorithm is applied to make the selection of terms that will effectively be part of the new query. The method proposed by Araujo and Pérez-Agüera (2008) obtained a precision gain of 15.2% compared to the baseline used by them. In our work, these techniques were studied and analyzed, making possible the development of the strategies described in Section 3.

3. STRATEGIES FOR AUTOMATIC IMPROVEMENT OF TERMS USED IN GENRE-AWARE FOCUSED CRAWLING PROCESSES

As already mentioned, the main goal of this work is to propose strategies for the automatic improvement of the sets of terms used on focused crawling processes based on genre-aware approach (Assis et al. 2009). The following subsections present two proposed strategies to achieve this end.

3.1 Strategy Based on Association Matrix

This strategy (see Figure 3) aims to automatically improve the sets of terms by using a query expansion technique based on association matrices. In the context of this work, association matrices were used to measure the association between the terms of the Web pages present in the set of seed-pages.

Thus, two-dimensional matrices were used in such a way that, in the columns and rows, were arranged all the terms of the considered pages; so, each matrix entry, inherent in a specific row and column, corresponds to the association between the terms arranged in that row and column. One of the possible ways to calculate the association between terms is to consider the statistical term co-occurrence (Carpineto and Romano, 2012). The Jaccard coefficient was used to calculate this association and this is given as the ratio of the number of documents, in the considered collection, containing the terms t_i (row of the association matrix) AND t_j (column of the association matrix) by the number of documents containing the terms t_i OR t_j.

$$s_{i,j} = \frac{n}{(\sum_{p=1}^{n} d_{i,j}) + 1} \quad \begin{cases} d_{i,j} = Distance(t_i, t_j) & if \quad Distance(t_i, t_j) \leq k \\ d_{i,j} = k + 1 & if \quad Distance(t_i, t_j) > k \end{cases}$$

Equation 1. MinorDistance for Association between Terms

Additionally, we propose a new metric for calculating the association between terms, which considers a distance boundary between two terms that are in the same document. This new metric was called MinorDistance and consists of calculating the association between two terms from the Equation 1, where: s_{ij} is the similarity between the terms t_i and t_j considering all pages p that contains both terms; n is the number of pages that have the terms t_i and t_j; k is the pre-established maximum distance between the terms t_i and t_j; $Distance(t_i, t_j)$ is a function that returns the distance, in number of terms, between t_i and t_j present on the same page p; $d_{i,j}$ is the smallest distance between the terms t_i and t_j present on a page p, being at most k+1.

Considering the proposed strategy, according to Figure 3, initially (step1), the original sets of content and genre terms are used to generate the set of seed-pages, using the best heuristic proposed by Mangaravite et al. (2014). Then (step 2), the association matrix is generated using the content of the Web pages present in the seed-pages set. Following (step 3), the improved sets of terms are generated by selecting, in the association matrix, the most similar terms to the original content and genre terms. Next (step 4), a new set of seed-pages is generated, using, as input parameter, the improved sets of terms. Finally (step 5), the sets of terms generated in step 3 and the seed-pages set generated in step 4 are used to start the genre-aware focused crawling process.

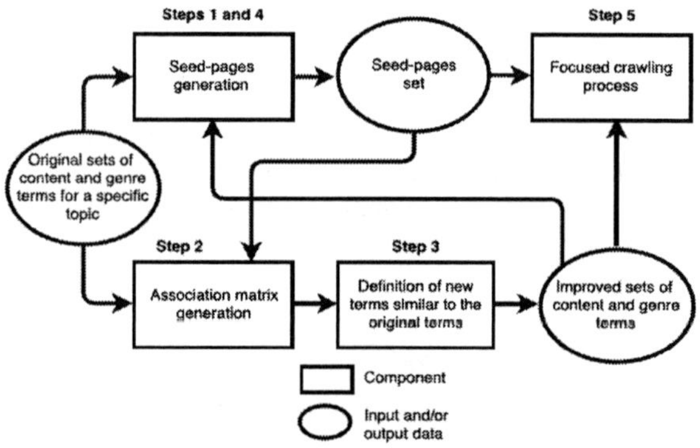

Figure 3. Strategy Based on Association Matrix

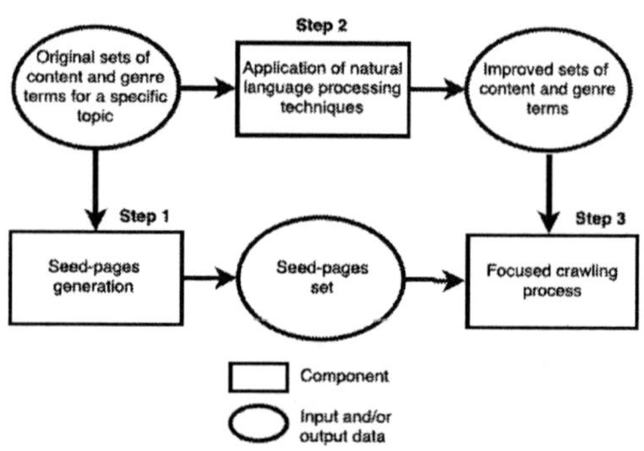

Figure 4. Strategy Based on Natural Language Processing

3.2 Strategy Based on Natural Language Processing

This strategy (see Figure 4) aims to improve the sets of content and genre terms by applying natural language processing techniques in the sets of terms for a specific topic of interest. For such strategy, among the possible techniques of natural language processing, were tested stopwords removal and stemming. In this context, the removal of stopwords (Manning et al. 2008) consists in eliminating, from the original sets of terms, the words that have little relevance to describe the topic of interest. Regarding the application of stemming (Orengo and Huyck, 2001), the improvement happens through the representation of the original terms of content and genre by their respective stems. Additionally, a "pluralization" technique was applied, which consist in performing number inflection in the original sets of terms, so that all terms are represented in plural form. Figure 4 illustrates the working architecture of this strategy.

According to Figure 4, initially (step 1), the original sets of content and genre terms are used to generate the set of seed-pages, using the best heuristic proposed by Mangaravite et al. (2014). Afterwards (step 2), the improved sets of terms are generated by applying the mentioned natural language processing techniques to the original sets of terms. Finally (step 3), the seed-pages set (generated in step 1) and the improved sets of content and genre terms (generated in step 2) are used to start the genre-aware focused-crawling process following the genre-aware approach.

4. EXPERIMENTAL EVALUATION

In order to validate the strategies proposed on subsections 3.1 and 3.2, we performed an experimental evaluation described on Subsection 4.1; the obtained results are described and analyzed on Subsection 4.2.

4.1 Experimental Setup

In our experiments, genre-aware focused crawling processes were conducted in order to crawl pages related to two distinct topics: "syllabi of database courses" and "trip to Paris". The experiments used the same sets of content and genre terms presented in Siqueira et al. (2016) and Mangaravite et al. (2014). These sets of terms (presented in Table 1 as "original sets") define the topics in a detailed and complete way. Additionally, to verify the results by applying the proposed strategies on smaller and less detailed sets, new and small sets (presented in Table 1 as "reduced sets") were defined by selecting a few terms from the original sets.

Table 1. Genre and Content Terms Specified for Each Topic

Topic	Genre terms	Content terms
Database syllabi (original sets)	syllabus, course, credits, professor, requirements, tentative schedule, program content, objectives, description, planning, class, scores, exams, works, required text, textbooks	database, databases, dbms, database systems, database management, data modeling, data model, entity-relationship, conceptual model, relational model, logical model, relational algebra, relational calculus, sql, data definition, triggers, silberschatz, navathe
Database syllabi (reduced sets)	syllabus, tentative schedule, planning	database, dbms, sql
Trip to Paris (original sets)	trip, accommodation, stay, passages, tourist packages, travel guides	Paris, Arc de Triomphe, Eiffel Tower, Louvre, Notre-Dame Cathedral, Seine River, Musée d'Orsay, Disneyland Resort Paris, Basilica of Sacré Cœur, Panthéon
Trip to Paris (reduced sets)	trip, accommodation, passages	Paris, Eiffel Tower, Louvre

Table 2. Baselines Used for Each Topic and Sets of Terms

Topic	Precision[2]	Recall	F1
Database syllabi (original sets)	0.667	0.511	0.579
Database syllabi (reduced sets)	0.353	0.657	0.459
Trip to Paris (original sets)	0.761	0.638	0.694
Trip to Paris (reduced sets)	0.707	0.363	0.479

[2] According to Manning and Schütze (1999), precision is a measure of the number of items selected correctly by a system, recall is the proportion of target items selected by a system and, finally, F1 is the harmonic mean between precision and recall.

For each topic, firstly, a crawling process was effectively performed considering its original set of terms. After such crawling processes, a log was stored for each topic containing: the set of seed-pages generated by the best heuristic proposed by Mangaravite et al. (2014) (9 seed-pages for database syllabi and 14 seed-pages for trip to Paris); the URL and HTML code of all valid pages visited by the crawler (4026 Web pages for database syllabi and 3825 for trip to Paris); the similarity value calculated between each visited page and the sets of content and genre terms; and an answer set, specified by an expert, containing the relevant pages among all of those visited by the crawler. Once the crawling processes were completed and the logs obtained, we estimated, for each topic, the best empirical similarity threshold in order to achieve the highest F1 value. After that, new crawling processes were performed involving the pages contained in the logs and the reduced sets of terms in order to evaluate the efficiency of the use of these reduced sets of terms. The results obtained on those processes are presented on Table 2 and used as baselines for this work.

After the baselines were obtained, finally, we performed a set of distinct crawling processes, where the strategies presented on Section 3 were applied using the sets of genre and content terms (Table 1) and considering the seed-pages and the visited Web pages sets contained in the logs.

For the strategy based on association matrix (Subsection 3.1), considering the Jaccard coefficient to calculate the similarity between terms during the construction of the association matrix, a total of 460 simulated crawling processes were performed by varying the following parameters: sets of terms (Table 1); number of seed-pages considered to construct the association matrix (ranging from 1 to 9 seed-pages for database syllabi, and 1 to 14 seed-pages for trip to Paris); and number of terms selected to compose the improved sets of terms (ranging from 1 to 10 improved terms for each original term in both topics). Regarding the same strategy, considering the MinorDistance metric that was proposed, 352 crawling processes were simulated by varying the following parameters: sets of terms (Table 1); number of seed-pages considered to construct the association matrix (1, 2, 3, 5 and 9 seed-pages for database syllabi, and 1, 2, 3, 5, 9 and 14 seed-pages for trip to Paris); number of terms selected to compose the improved sets of terms (1, 2, 5, and 10 improved terms for each original term in both topics); and the maximum distance between terms (k from Equation 1 considered as 1, 2, 5 and 10 terms). Related to the strategy based on natural language processing (Subsection 3.2), 28 crawling processes were performed, considering the variation of the following parameters: sets of terms (Table 1); and 3 natural language processing techniques applied to the terms (combinations between stemming, stopwords removal and pluralization).

4.2 Experimental Results

Table 3. Best results obtained by the application of the strategy based on association matrix in the original terms sets

Topic	Association between terms	Number of seed-pages	Number of selected terms	Precision (proximity to baseline)	Recall	F1 (proximity to baseline %)
Database syllabi (original sets)	Jaccard	1	8	0.800 (120.0%)	0.467	0.590 (102.0%)
		2	2	0.831 (124.6%)	0.431	0.567 (98.1%)
		8	6	0.913 (137.0%)	0.307	0.459 (79.3%)
Trip to Paris (original sets)	Jaccard	5	7	0.933 (122.6%)	0.175	0.295 (42.5%)
		5	8	0.783 (102.8%)	0.225	0.350 (50.4%)
		8	5	0.781 (102.6%)	0.313	0.446 (64.3%)
Database syllabi (original sets)	MinorDistance (k=1)	2	1	0.845 (126.8%)	0.438	0.577 (99.7%)
	MinorDistance (k=1)	2	5	0.939 (140.8%)	0.336	0.495 (85.5%)
	MinorDistance (k=2)	5	2	0.806 (120.8%)	0.423	0.555 (95.9%)
Trip to Paris (original sets)	MinorDistance (k=2)	2	10	0.676 (88.8%)	0.313	0.427 (88.8%)
	MinorDistance (k=2)	14	5	0.688 (90.3%)	0.413	0.516 (74.3%)
	MinorDistance (k=5)	14	5	0.682 (89.6%)	0.375	0.484 (69.7%)

The proposed strategies to automatically improve the sets of content and genre terms were applied in the focused crawling processes described on Subsection 4.1. Tables 3 and 4 present the best results regarding the application of the strategy based on association matrix (Subsection 3.1) on the sets of terms presented in

Table 1, and, similarly, Table 5 presents the best results regarding the application of the strategy based in natural language processing (Subsection 3.2) on the same sets of terms.

By analyzing the experiments that were performed and considering the best results presented in the Tables 3, 4 and 5, it is possible to observe, in general, that: (1) considering the complete sets of terms for both topics and the strategy based on association matrix (Table 3), few results (F1 measure) were good; (2) considering the reduced sets of terms and the same strategy (Table 4), a greater number of good results (F1 measure) was obtained, which is justified by the lack of important terms in such sets that were located by applying of the proposed strategy; (3) considering the metric MinorDistance used in the strategy based on association matrix (Tables 3 and 4), the best results appear when the maximum distance between terms was set to 1 or 2 terms; (4) for the strategy based on natural language processing (Table 5), the stopwords removal technique generated the best results; (5) considering the evaluation measures, in many cases of both topics, although the improvement in F1 was not satisfactory, there was a significant improvement in the precision value (improvement of up to 88.9%) that, in practical situations, corresponds to the most important measure.

Table 4. Best results obtained by the application of the strategy based on association matrix in the reduced terms sets

Topic	Association between terms	Number of seed-pages	Number of selected terms	Precision (proximity to baseline)	Recall	F1 (proximity to baseline %)
Database syllabi (reduced sets)	Jaccard coefficient	8	5	0.596 (169.0%)	0.474	0.528 (115.1%)
		8	6	0.523 (148.3%)	0.489	0.506 (110.1%)
		8	8	0.547 (155.0%)	0.467	0.504 (109.7%)
Trip to Paris (reduced sets)	Jaccard coefficient	1	1	0.775 (109.6%)	0.388	0.517 (107.8%)
		8	1	0.630 (89.0%)	0.638	0.634 (132.1%)
		8	3	0.741 (104.7%)	0.500	0.597 (124.6%)
Database syllabi (reduced sets)	MinorDistance (k=2)	1	2	0.563 (159.7%)	0.518	0.540 (117.6%)
	MinorDistance (k=1)	1	5	0.439 (124.4%)	0.526	0.478 (104.2%)
	MinorDistance (k=5)	2	5	0.667 (188.9%)	0.394	0.495 107.9%)
Trip to Paris (reduced sets)	MinorDistance (k=2)	3	1	0.417 (59.0%)	0.663	0.512 (106.8%)
	MinorDistance (k=2)	3	10	0.700 (99.0%)	0.263	0.382 (79.7%)
	MinorDistance (k=5)	3	10	0.574 (81.1%)	0.488	0.527 (109.9%)

Table 5. Best results obtained by the application of the strategy based on natural language processing

Topic	Natural language processing techniques applied	Precision (proximity to baseline)	Recall	F1 (proximity to baseline %)
Database syllabi (original sets)	Stopwords removal	0.645 (96.8%)	0.438	0.522 (90.2%)
	Stopwords removal AND pluralization	0.493 (73.9%)	0.511	0.502 (86.7%)
Database syllabi (reduced sets)	Stopwords removal	0.396 (112.2%)	0.569	0.467 (101.7%)
	Stemming	0.242 (68.5%)	0.526	0.331 (72.1%)
Trip to Paris (original sets)	Stopwords removal	0.781 (102.6%)	0.625	0.694 (100.1%)
	Stopwords removal AND pluralization	0.750 (98.5%)	0.450	0.563 (81.1%)
Trip to Paris (reduced sets)	Stopwords removal	0.469 (66.3%)	0.663	0.549 (114.6%)
	Stopwords removal AND pluralization	0.628 (88.8%)	0.338	0.439 (91.6%)

Additionally, analyzing the sets of improved terms generated by the experiments, it was noted that, in many cases, the content and genre terms get mixed. This can directly influence the efficiency of a crawling process, since the genre-aware focused crawling approach is useful in situations where the topic of interest can be expressed through two distinct sets of terms: one describing genre aspects of the desired pages and the other describing the content of these pages.

5. CONCLUSION

As presented in Section 4, the experiments performed, in order to validate the strategies proposed for the automatic improvement of the sets of terms used in genre-aware focused crawling process, showed that the proposed strategy based on association matrix was the one that presented good results. This strategy achieved an improvement of up to 88.9% in terms of precision and 32.1% in terms of F1 when applied over sets of content and genre terms that do not describe a topic of interest in a complete and detailed manner.

As future work, we intent to: (1) perform new validation experiments, involving new topics, to define the best parameters for the strategy based on association matrix; (2) develop a method to prevent the terms of content and genre from blending throughout the proposed strategies; (3) evaluate proposed strategies on different focused crawling approaches.

ACKNOWLEDGEMENT

This research was partially funded by research grants from PIBITI/CNPQ. Furthermore, it was carried out on the GAID/UFOP Laboratory.

REFERENCES

Almpanidis, G. et al., 2007. "Combining text and link analysis for focused crawling – an application for vertical search engines." *Information Systems,* 32(6):886-908.

Aly, A. A. (2008). Using a query expansion technique to improve document retrieval. *In International Journal "Information Technologies and Knowledge.*

Araujo, L. and Pérez-Agüera, J. R., (2008). Improving query expansion with stemming terms: a new genetic algorithm approach. *In European Conference on Evolutionary Computation in Combinatorial Optimization*. pp. 182–193.

Assis, G.T. de et al., 2009. A Genre-Aware Approach to Focused Crawling. *World Wide Web*, 12(3), pp.285–319.

Assis, G.T. de et al., 2007. Exploiting genre in focused crawling. *In Proceedings of the 14th International String Processing and Information Retrieval.* Santiago, Chile, pp. 62–73.

Baeza-Yates, R. and Ribeiro-Neto, B., 1999. *Modern information retrieval.* Vol. 463. New York: ACM press.

Carpineto, C. and Romano, G., 2012. A survey of automatic query expansion in information retrieval. *ACM Comput. Surv.*, 44(1):1:1-150.

Chakrabarti, S. et al., 1999. "Focused crawling: a new approach to topic-specific Web resource discovery."Computer Networks 31.11 (1999): 1623-1640.

Chartree, J. et al., 2013. Query expansion using association matrix for improved information retrieval performance. *In Proceedings of the International Conference on Information and Knowledge Engineering (IKE)*, p. 1.

Gonzalez, M. and Lima, V. L. S. (2003). Recuperação de informação e processamento da linguagem natural. *In XXIII Congresso da Sociedade Brasileira de Computaçao*, Vol. 3, pp.347–395.

Indurkhya, N. and Damerau, F. J., 2010. *Handbook of natural language processing, volume 2.* CRC Press.

Johnson, Judy, Kostas Tsioutsiouliklis, and C. Lee Giles. "Evolving strategies for focused web crawling." ICML. 2003.

Mangaravite, V. et al., 2012. Improving the Efficiency of a Genre-aware Approach to Focused Crawling Based on Link Context. *In 8th Latin American Web Congress*. pp. 17–23.

Mangaravite, V. et al., 2014. Semi-automatic generation of seed pages in genre-aware focused crawling. *In Proceedings of the 13th International Conference WWW/Internet (ICWI)*. pp. 51-58.

Manning, C. D. et al.,2008. *Introduction to Information Retrieval.* Cambridge University Press, New York, NY, USA.

Manning, C. and Schütze, H.,1999. *Foundations of statistical natural language processing (Vol. 999).* Cambridge.

Orengo, V. M. and Huyck, C., 2001. A stemming algorithmm for the portuguese language.*In spire*, Vol.8, pp.186–193.

Menczer, F., Pant, G. and Srinivasan, P., 2004. Topical Web Crawlers: Evaluating Adaptive Algorithms. *ACM Transactions on Internet Technology*, 4(4), pp.378–419.

Pant, G. and Srinivasan, P., 2005. Learning to Crawl: Comparing Classification Schemes. *ACM Transactions on Information Systems*, 23(4), pp.430–462.

Siqueira, G. O. d. et al., 2016. Automatic determination of similarity threshold for focused crawling processes on web pages. *In Proceedings of the 15th International Conference WWW/Internet (ICWI). WWW.*

AN ONTOLOGY-DRIVEN FRAMEWORK FOR DATA INTEGRATION AND DYNAMIC SERVICE COMPOSITION: CASE STUDY IN THE OIL & GAS INDUSTRY

Geiza M. H. da Silva[1], Aline M. Saettler[2], Kathrin R. Llanes[2], Paulo Ivson[2], Daniel L. M. Nascimento[2] and Eduardo T. L. Corseuil[2]

[1]*Departamento de Informática Aplicada- Universidade Federal do Estado do Rio de Janeiro, Av. Pasteur, 296, Urca – Rio de Janeiro-RJ – CEP: 22290-240 – Brazil*

[2]*Instituto Tecgraf/Pontifícia Universidade Católica do Rio e Janeiro, Rua Marquês de São Vicente, 225, Rio de Janeiro/RJ – CEP 22451-900 - Brazil*

ABSTRACT

Integrating heterogeneous data sources is a difficult task, particularly with regard to numerous systems that need to share information and cooperate towards a common goal. This is the kind of software environment within Oil & Gas companies. As a result, there is an increasing need for more complex services capable of integrating multiple functionalities and distributed systems. This scenario brings forth the challenge of building new composite services at runtime, which allows a set of services to interact with each other but act as a single entity. We propose an ontology-driven semantic framework to tackle both these issues: interoperability between different data sources and dynamic service composition. The solution is based on a Service Oriented Architecture that combines web services with an ontology. It describes the data domain and business processes. We analyze the proposed solution with two scenarios related to Oil & Gas process plant construction. The decentralized and generalist nature of the software architecture enables its widespread application to other domains, each with its own ontology of business terms and processes.

KEYWORDS

Data integration; Semantic Web; Dynamic Service Composition; Service Oriented Architecture

1. INTRODUCTION

Oil & Gas industrial projects involve several areas of knowledge during Process Plant Construction. In this context, incomplete specifications lead to a large number of changes that can cause waste, rework and lack of materials during execution (Sacks, Radosavlejevic and Barak, 2010). The disciplines of the executive project are physically and financially measured by issuing documents, which hinders the flow of information, creates inconsistencies between projects and consequently rework during the completion phase (Bew,Underwood and Storer,2008).

These engineering projects have many changes during its lifecycle, which comprise different technologies, processes, materials and people. The enterprise information system requires a long time for change and, when altered, increases exposure to failures and raises the levels of risk. To perform the fewest possible modifications in the software, when the business processes change, a layered software architecture must be able to control, in an independent way, the main activities/events of those business processes.

Also worth mentioning is the diversity of technological platforms, data sources and other automated components that must be integrated to implement effective engineering information systems. One of the obstacles to perform this integration is the heterogeneity of data and data sources used by them. These heterogeneities can be classified as (Bishr,1998):

- Syntactic heterogeneity: the same attributes can appear in several databases under different names;
- Semantic heterogeneity: the same attribute name can represent different concepts in different databases; and
- Schematic: different data models and types in different data sources.

In the engineering process, many organizations have domain experts who are the keepers of best practices associated with their work processes. As organizational knowledge is part of the Company Asset, its representation, storage, transfer, implementation and adaptation is extremely important.

In this paper, we focus on the interoperation between different data sources and the dynamic composition of the computational services to support the business processes of an organization. In doing so, we propose an ontology-driven semantic framework, based on a Service Oriented Architecture (SOA), that combines web services and an ontology containing the terms of the domain and the description of its business processes.

To analyze the proposed solution, we conducted a case study involving two scenarios: the integration of multidisciplinary data sources in a collaborative and distributed environment; and the dynamic composition of services that support business process related to the construction area of Oil & Gas industry. The proposed framework enables the interoperation between the data sources intervening in Process Plant Construction by hiding their semantic, schematic and syntactic heterogeneities. Besides that, it provides the dynamic composition of services, which guarantees low coupling and high cohesion of the solution.

Both characteristics ensure the framework can be easily tailored to changes occurring in enterprise environments, which facilitates management and improves production processes. The decentralized and generic implementation of the solution allows it to be embedded in external systems from a variety of different domains, whenever an ontology containing the specific terms and processes for each domain can be used.

The paper is organized as follows: Section 2 covers the related works. Section 3 describes the proposed framework and its components. Section 4 presents the case study that is composed of two scenarios of the Oil and Gas industry. Finally, Section 5 contains the conclusions and the future works.

2. RELATED WORK

Several previous works have addressed the problem of integrating heterogeneous database systems (Spanos, Stavrou, and Mitrou,2012) or data sources, using mapping functions or ontologies. In (Köhler, Philippi and Lange,2003), the authors propose pairwise translation between synonyms of a molecular biology domain, which was specified with an ontology. Other works use a mapping from a central vocabulary to specific attributes, which is more efficient. In (Petrovic, Burcea and Jacobsen, 2003) mapping functions were proposed to translate attributes to a "root" concept in order to achieve semantic matching in a publish/subscribe system.

An ontology-based system was also developed to automatically transform general queries into specific ones in order to search in multiple data sources (Arens, Hsu and Knoblock, 1996). In this case, the data sources were defined according to a general domain (which was specified as a hierarchical terminological knowledge base) and there were links between the concepts in each data source and the concepts in the general domain. The query modifications were based in direct mappings (between a concept in the domain and a concept in the data source) and in mappings from a concept to a more general or to a more specific class in the data sources.

A similar approach is the Ontology-Based Data Access (OBDA), which is a database integration architecture, where ontology is linked to a source database, thus acting as an intermediate layer between the user and the stored data. It hides the structure of data sources, and enriches incomplete data with background knowledge (Spanos et al, 2012). The ontology is connected to data sources through a declarative specification given in terms of mappings the ontology's classes and properties views over the data (SQL). One example of these systems is the *Ontop system,* which exposes relational databases as virtual RDF graphs by mapping the terms in the ontology to the data sources. These virtual RDF graphs can then be queried using SPARQL, by translating the SPARQL queries into SQL queries over the relational databases. The translation process is transparent to the user (Calvanese et al., 2017).

Another related work connected multiple ontologies to enable information searches in several and independently developed repositories (Mena, Illarramend, Kashyap and Sheth, 2000). These ontologies were connected by synonym, hyponym, hypernym, overlap, disjoint and covering relationships.

An additional application of semantics is in automatic service composition. One research defined a relationship between pairs $\{P, S\}$ of services, where P is a predecessor of S, and performed a breath-first-search in order to create the service composition (Gu, Xu, Yan and Luo, 2009). A similar approach dynamically created a Directed Acyclic Graph (DAG) that represented a service composition, based on input and output parameters of the search query and of the composite services (Srividya, Bansal, Blake and Gupta, 2008). Situation calculus (a logical language for representing dynamic systems) and description logic were also used to represent causal links between services (Lécué, Léger and Delteil, 2008).

3. ONTOLOGY-DRIVEN SEMANTIC FRAMEWORK

This section presents the proposed framework to address the challenges related to the integration of heterogeneous data sources and the dynamic composition of web services, providing a detailed computational description of its components and functionalities.

A. Architecture

To implement the ontology-driven semantic framework, we propose a SOA-based architecture that contains three layers: Enterprise Service Bus (ESB) layer, Semantic & Logic layer, and the Data layer. Each is composed by a set of services that can have multiples operations (see Figure 1).

Enterprise Service Bus Layer - it includes all services that can be accessed by external applications. These services are independent from one another. A service does not know of the existence of others unless they are integrated through a composition process. A service can invoke external web service from the ESB.

Semantic & Logic Layer -it consists of Semantic, Logic and Integration functionalities.

- The Semantic functionalities contain three main operations that call other operations belonging to the data service that access the ontology in the Data Layer. The first one retrieves all services described in the ontology. The second, given a term, returns its mapping with the data sources where the term appears and the specific attribute name that represents it. The third extracts metadata that encodes the dependencies between the web services that are present in the logical formula and creates a nested structure of these services.
- Logic functionalities, given a logical formula that describes a service, it is interpreted and a XML file containing the orchestration scenario is generated. This represents the composition of the services involved in a particular business process. It is implemented by functions that call operations at the Semantic funcionalities.

The Integration functionalities performs the integration of multiple data sources incorporated in the framework using the data services from Data Layer and the information about mapping terms provided by the Semantic functionalities. In addition, it allows executing transactions spanning those different data sources.

Data Layer- it comprises the set of services that provide access to each particular data source connected to the framework. Whenever a new data source is incorporated, a new data service should be created to access it. Each service contains a set of configuration parameters to stablish the communication with the data source, e. g., the location where the data source is hosted and the type of data source. Thus, it is possible to provide access to multiple sources, like Excel or CSV and multiple databases. One of the data sources connected to the framework and accessed through the Data Layer is the proposed RDF ontology. It contains a set of terms of the domain (Process Plant Construction) in a standardized way and their mapping according to the data source where they appear, and also contains the metadata about the dependencies between the web services involved in business processes of this domain.

The layers of the proposed architecture were implemented using the components of WSO2 middleware platform[1] which provides support for implementing SOA acting as service containers. The ESB and Semantic & Logic Layer were implemented using the WSO2 Enterprise Service Bus, that supports multiple transport and message formats. The Data Layer was implemented using the WSO2 Data Services Server, a component that allows creating services to access multiples data sources.

B. RDF Ontology

The ontology, which was written using the editor Protegé[2], is the heart of the semantic framework and is composed by three ontologies: one depicting the domain, other describing the data sources and the latter encoding dependencies between the web services involved in the business processes (Semantic Web Service Ontology).

The Domain Ontology has concepts and properties to represent the business domain in a neutral language. The Data Sources Ontology stores the identification of the data sources elements connected to the framework and a mapping from their concepts to the Domain Ontology terms. Some concepts can be formed by the concatenation of two or more attributes, in this case, the mapping is from a list of attributes to the domain concept. The usage of the ontology in the framework allows the integration of several data sources and an efficient search/update of the terms, besides preventing inconsistencies.

The Semantic Web Service ontology has the services/operations that can be called and its metadata, e.g., Servers, Endpoints, etc (See Figure 2). It also includes classes related to business processes. The services can have as pre-requisite, or can be composed by, one or more services and/or operations. It allows the

[1] http://wso2.com/ Acessed: 6th June 2017

[2] http://protege.stanford.edu/

implementation of dynamic service composition. To express composition and precedence relations, the ontology uses the object properties: *isComposedBy* and *hasPreRequisite*, respectively (Section 3. C and Section 4. B). In this context, the queries represent an analogy with business process activities, where each one is implemented by a service.

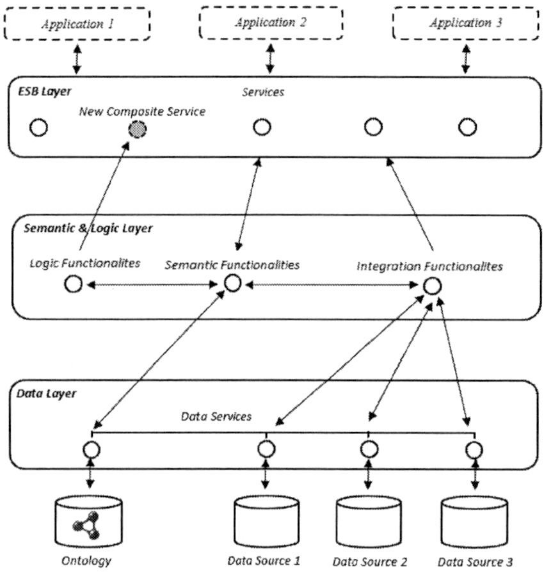

Figure 1. Ontology-driven semantic framework architecture

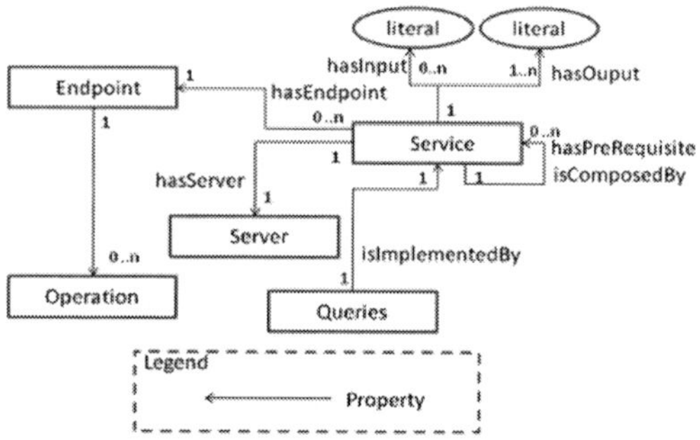

Figure 2. The concepts of Semantic Web Services ontology. Subconcepts have been omitted for clarity

Taking into account the fact that the Ontology is located at the Data Layer (Figure 1), we used a feature called punning, where some classes were modeled as instances.

The ontology can be adapted in several ways, for example, it can be extended to attend other parts of the business process or other areas. It simplifies the addition of new data sources: instead of adding a mapping from the new data source to each existing one, it needs to add a single mapping, from the ontology to the new data source concepts.

C. Semantic Data Integration

In the industrial production environment, most of the processes are automated, i.e., based on computer systems. Usually these systems consume data from different and several data sources. For this reason, the integration of those heterogeneous data sources is a mandatory and difficult task.

Aiming to solve the problems related to semantic, syntactic and schematic heterogeneities, in our solution we propose a semantic data integration approach based on SOA. The system uses the Semantic functionalities and Integration functionalities from *Semantic & Logic Layer*, the data service to access the ontology; and other data services to access the specific data sources containing the data required for the integration.

Any service deployed in the ESB Layer that needs to integrate data from multiple sources communicates with *Semantic functionalities* passing, as parameter, the terms over which it wants extract information and the specific type of information required. The *Semantic functionalities* call the service that accesses the ontology, which then retrieves the data sources where the terms appear and the specific attribute names that represent them on each data sources. Then the data services associated with the data sources involved in the mapping are accessed, in order to capture, update or delete the punctual information about the attribute names specified in the mapping. The *Integration functionalities* filters these data and returns them to the specific service from ESB that starts the integration request. See Figure 1.

D. Dynamic Composition of Services

The creation of composite services from other distinct and distributed services at runtime can be achieved using several different techniques (Mennie and Pagurek, 2000). In our solution, the dynamic service composition is based on a semantic approach that includes three main services: a specific service from *Semantic Functionalities* and *Logic Functionalities* from *Semantic&Logic* Layer and the *data service* to access the ontology from *Data Layer*.

Once the user requests a composition of activities, a new particular composition scenario is generated, it will be a new service and it must be included, together with the formula that describes its semantics, at the Semantic Web Service Ontology. These logical formulas were written using Description Logic, involving web services and conjunction connectives ($\sqcap$). Afterwards, the *Semantic functionalities* are called, passing the logical formula as parameter, then the service that accesses the ontology is called, to find inside it the pre-requisites of all services presented in the logical formula.

In the ontology semantic model, each service has as pre-requisites other services and/or operations, which must be executed before it. To run any service, all of its pre-requisites must be previously run, which, in turn, are composed by other services or have their own pre-requisites. Thus, each logical formula representing a more complex service composed by two or more services, triggers a recursive process. It is worth to mention that when the conjunction connective is used between two services that are prerequisite of another, it is interpreted as the union ($\cup$) of the prerequisites outputs; but when it connects the services to express that one service is a composition of other two services, it is interpreted as intersection ($\cap$) of the outputs.

Example I: *ServiceZ* is ComposedBy *ServiceC* and isComposedBy *ServiceM* and isComposedBy *Service R*. The *ServiceC* hasPreRequisite *ServiceA* and hasPreRequisite *ServiceB*. The *ServiceM* hasPreRequisite *ServiceI* and hasPreRequisite *Service J* and hasPreRequisite *Service K*. The *ServiceR* hasPreRequisite *ServiceV* and hasPreRequisite *ServiceW* and hasPreRequisite *ServiceX* and hasPreRequisite *ServiceY*. See Figure 3.

ServiceZ $\sqsubseteq$ **isComposedBy(*Service C*)** $\sqcap$ **isComposedBy(*Service M*)** $\sqcap$ **isComposedBy(*Service R*)**

ServiceC $\sqsubseteq$ **hasPrerequisite(*ServiceA*)** $\sqcap$ **hasPrerequisite(*ServiceB*)**

ServiceM $\sqsubseteq$ **hasPrerequisite(*ServiceI*)** $\sqcap$ **hasPrerequisite(*ServiceJ*)** $\sqcap$ **hasPrerequisite(*ServiceK*)**

ServiceR $\sqsubseteq$ **hasPrerequisite(*ServiceV*)** $\sqcap$ **hasPrerequisite(*ServiceW*)** $\sqcap$ **hasPrerequisite(*ServiceX*)** $\sqcap$ **hasPrerequisite(*ServiceY*)**

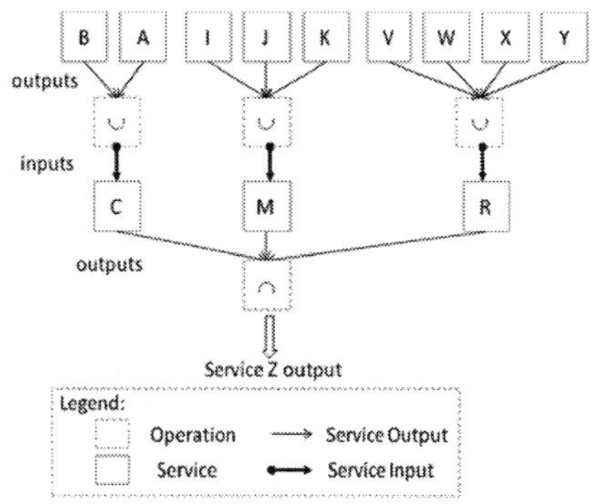

Figure 3. Example logical formula and the triggered orchestration scenario

The *Semantic and Logic Functionalities* interpret the logical formula that is in the *Semantic Web Service Ontology*, verify its pre-requisites or compositions, and generates a XML file containing the service orchestration scenario. This XML is deployed into the ESB Layer as a new service ready to be consumed by other applications. This new service must be a valid, capable of carrying out the set of operations from each service that it includes.

This architecture enables the dynamic composition of services that support the business processes. It allows multiple services to communicate and interact one with another and to provide an enhanced service.

4. CASE STUDY

To evaluate the framework, a case study with two scenarios related to the Process Plant Construction in the oil and gas industry was employed. The first scenario covers the integration of multidisciplinary data sources and the second, the dynamic composition of services that support the business processes of the domain.

A. Scenario 1: Integration of Multiples Data Sources

The goal of this scenario is to integrate different data sources of an enterprise, and verify if they are consistent. The data sources were generated by the PDMS[3], SPPID[4] and ControlTub[5] tools. PDMS is a 3D design software for accurate and clash-free plant design. SPPID is a graphical tool to develop and manage the

[3] Plant Design Management System - http://www.aveva.com/ Acessed: 6th June 2017

[4] Smart Plant Piping and Instrumentation Diagram - http://ppm.intergraph.com/products/engineering-and-schematics-product-family/smartplant-p-and-id Acessed: 6th June 2017

[5] http://www.isiengenharia.com.br/ Acessed: 6th June 2017

smart plant piping and instrumentation diagrams with focus on the plant asset. It is critical that the SPPID is kept up-to-date, accurately reflecting the as-built plant because other disciplines base their design decisions on its data. ControlTub is a tool used to control the fabrication and assembly of industrial pipelines.

In this context, inconsistencies are easy to appear, since the information system is composed by many applications. The stored information can be redundant and appear under different attribute names in the data sources. For example, if some information of an object is modified, this action must be spread to all databases where it appears, regardless of the way it is represented in each database. Thus, the goal is to verify the consistency among PDMS, SPPID and ControlTub data sources (Excel, Oracle and PostgreSQL respectively). Given a concept will be verified if the data sources store the same instances of it.

The consistency is verified by applying the proposed framework using the algorithm presented below:

1) The user enters a concept as in input to a Java application (it consumes a service from the ESB Layer).

2) The ESB service invokes the Semantic functionalities, that call the data service to access the domain ontology to extract all the databases that store the concept.

3) For each database, these functionalities informs which of its attributes correspond to that concept.

4) Given the correct attributes, the Integration functionalites invokes services in the Data Layer in order to retrieve the instances corresponding to these attributes in the databases.

5) The Integration functionalites then verify if the set of instances retrieved by the data services for each database are the same.

This scenario shows that more than verifying data consistency, it is possible to perform the semantic integration of data from multiple data sources, even in different formats, to extract more complex information using the proposed framework.

B. Scenario 2: Dynamic composition of services that support the business processes

A critical factor in Process Plant Construction is the sequencing of pipe spool fabrication, which is usually overlooked (Hu and Mohamed, 2012). A spool is a small pipe segment (containing tubes, bends, etc.) preassembled to be welded to other spools to complete a line (isometric), used during the construction of Process Plant. It can be fabricated in several alternative sequences that are often decided by shop foremen based on experience. It is rare that these alternative sequences are compared and evaluated. For this reason, for the purpose of this scenario, we select, within the whole mechanism of Process Plant Construction, the processes of fabrication and transportation of spools. Figure 4 summarizes these processes.

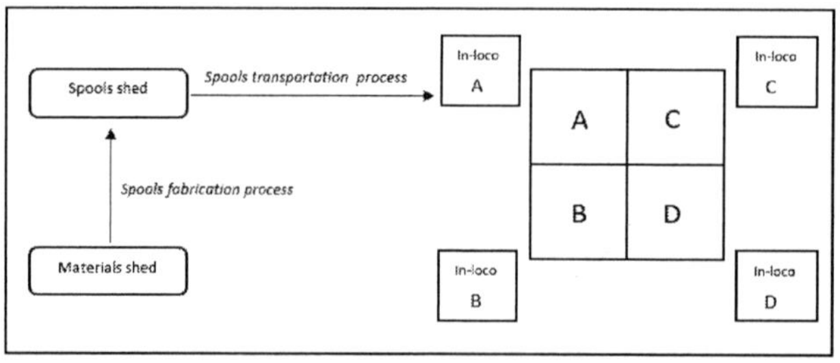

Figure 4. Spools fabrication and transportation process

First, the spools are fabricated, then are stored in the spool shed, and subsequently transported to the site where the industrial assembly will be performed. To coordinate and execute these processes, some restrictions must be taken into account. For instance, to start the manufacturing of spools, it is necessary to know the available volume of space in the spool shed for storage and the priority of each spool pending to be manufactured. The priority of a spool is associated with the priority of the constructability area where it will be assembled.

The constructability areas are divided geographically and classified into A, B, C and D, where A is the highest priority area and D is the lowest priority area. Depending on the available capacity in the shed and the priority of spools, the spools to be produced are selected and the fabrication order is generated.

The constructability areas A, B, C and D have their respective *in-loco* areas to store their spools before starting the assembly process. To transport the spools from the shed to the *in-loco* areas, the following restrictions must be considered: the volume of the spools stored in the shed, the volume of the trucks that will be used to transport the spools, and the size of the *in-loco* area of each constructability area. Then, satisfying these restrictions, the spools to be transported are computed and the transportation order is generated.

In this scenario, the part of the ontology regarding the dependencies between the services is used, which allows the dynamic service composition. Also, three independent services were deployed in the ESB Layer of our framework, which support activities related to the spools fabrication and transportation processes:

1. The *PipesToProduce* service returns pipes that are ready to be produced, based on some values of its attributes. This flow is divided in two parts. The first one is responsible for making several calls to the data service: a pipe, in order to be produced, has to satisfy several independent conditions, each one related to one of its attributes and represented by a query made to the Data Services Server. Since all conditions must be simultaneously satisfied, the second part of the service is responsible for aggregating all answers and computing its intersection. The final list contains the pipes that can be produced.

2. The *SpoolsFabricationOrder* service receives a list of pipes and returns which spools can be fabricated and their fabrication order. A spool can be fabricated if it fits inside the spools shed. This service makes two calls to the services in the Data Layer: the first one to a query that takes a list of pipes as input and returns the diameter, length, weight and priority area of its spools. The second one have no input parameters and simply returns the available volume in the spools shed. Finally, the responses to these queries are aggregated and processed in order to calculate which spools can be fabricated based on their volume and priority areas.

3. The *SpoolsTransportationOrder* service receives a list of spools (with their attributes: weight, diameter, etc.) and returns which ones can be transported to *in-loco* areas. For this computation, the volume and weight restrictions supported by the available trucks and containers, and the capacity of their respective *in-loco* areas are taken into account. This service makes two calls to the Data Layer: the first selects the available trucks and containers, and their supported volumes and weights. The second call selects the available volume in each *in-loco* area. The results are used to determine which spools can be transported.

Note that spools from pipelines that are not ready to be produced cannot be fabricated. Similarly, spools that were not fabricated cannot be transported to *in-loco* areas. Thus, to run the *SpoolsFabricationOrder* service we need to run the *PipesToProduce* service first, and to run the *SpoolsTransportationOrder* service it is necessary to run the *SpoolsFabricationOrder* service previously. These restrictions can be discovered accessing the ontology, which makes explicit that *SpoolsTransportationOrder* has *SpoolsFabricationOrder* as pre-requisite and *SpoolsFabricationOrder* has *PipesToProduce* as pre-requisite.

Once the services representing the business processes are developed and registered in the ontology, it is possible to perform dynamic service orchestration. The steps for this particular scenario are:

1) The user wants to compose a service that is: "the spools that can be fabricated" and "the spools that can be transported to assembly areas". This selection is represented by the following logical formula: ***SpoolsFabricationOrder*** $\sqcap$ ***SpoolsTransportationOrder***

2) When the composition is requested, the system searches into the ontology the services' pre-requisites in a recursive way and then interprets the logical formula and executes the services sequentially. For example, ***SpoolsTransportationOrder*** *has* ***SpoolsFabricationOrder*** *as pre-requisite (****SpoolsTransportationOrder hasPreRequisite SpoolsFabricationOrder****), and* ***SpoolsFabricationOrder*** *has* ***PipesToProduce*** *as pre-requisite. In that sense, including only* ***SpoolsTransportationOrder*** *in the logical formula is sufficient, because internally* ***SpoolsFabricationOrder*** *and* ***PipesToProduce*** *services will be executed. Even if the user doesn't know the precedence order of the services, our system is able to identify it and create the right scenario for each case.*

3) The system generates a XML file containing the service orchestration scenario that includes ***PipesToProduce, SpoolsFabricationOrder*** *and* ***SpoolsTransportationOrder*** *services. This XML is deployed into the ESB layer as a new service, which is ready to be consumed by other applications.*

This scenario demonstrates how the proposed framework enables dynamic service composition to represent complex business processes. It shows that is possible to plan automatically the spool fabrication sequence, considering several engineering and logistics aspects of Process Plant Construction.

5. CONCLUSIONS AND FUTURE WORK

This work proposes an ontology-driven semantic framework to address the challenges related to the integration of heterogeneous data sources and the dynamic composition of web services. This solution is based on SOA and semantic web technology. It includes an RDF ontology, describing the terms stored in the data sources connected to the framework and web services involved in the business processes in a standardized way. This structure is simpler than the one presented in (Mena et al., 2000). The description of the business processes can be considered as an organizational knowledge asset. This work also includes a logic-semantic interpreter component for dynamic orchestration of web services.

In this approach, the ontology also simplifies the addition of new data sources: instead of adding a mapping from the new data source to each existing one, it is only necessary to add a single mapping: from the domain ontology to the new data source concepts. This mapping does not affect the behavior of services and queries that were previously inserted, that access relational databases (Spanos et al., 2012) and (Calvanese et al., 2017) or other data source. The dynamic service composition based on a semantic approach allows the automatic generation of a new service, to be included at the ESB, from the formula that describes its semantics, stored in the Semantic Web Service Ontology. This translation happens just once and allows multiple services to communicate and interact with each other to provide an enhanced service.

The case study involved two scenarios related to Process Plant Construction in the Oil & Gas industry, which corroborate the usefulness of the proposed framework. The decentralized and generic implementation of our solution can be embedded in external systems from a variety of domains, whenever an ontology containing the specific terms and events of domain business processes is used. Moreover, it allows its structure to be expanded in order to satisfy requirements that are more complex. These flexibility contrasts with the work in (Köhler, Philippi and Lange, 2003).

Future works include: (1) extending the logical language of the logic-semantic interpreter by adding the disjunction connective; (2) programming visual interfaces to facilitate service orchestration and to update the proposed ontology with new terms; (3) developing new case studies in other areas of Oil & Gas industry and (4) studying the possibility to apply program synthesis, where services will be extracted from logical proofs to enable semi-automatic service discovery.

REFERENCES

Arens, Y., Hsu, C. & Knoblock, C.A.(1996).Query processing in the sims information mediator. *Advanced Planning Technology* , 32,78-93.

Bew, M.J.,Underwood, J.W. & Storer, G. (2008). Going BIM in a commercial world. *eWork and eBusiness in Architecture, Engineering and Construction*, 17, 542-555.

Bishr, Y.(1998). Overcoming the Semantic and Other Barriers to GIS Interoperability. *International Journal of Geographical Information Science,* 12(4), 299-314.

Calvanese, D., Cogrel, B., Komla-Ebri, S., Knotchakoc, R., Lanti, D., Rezk,M., Rodriguez-Muro, M. & Xiao, G. (2017).Ontop: Answering SPARQL queries over Relational databases, *Journal Semantic Web,*.8(3), 471–487.

Gu, Z., Xu, B., Yan, Y., Luo, S.(2009). A Qos-driven approach for semantic service composition.*.IEEE Conference on Commerce and Enterprise Computing*, 00, 523-526, doi:10.1109/CEC.2009.44

Hu, D. & Mohamed, Y.(2012). "Pipe spool fabrication sequencing by automated planning. *American Society of Civil Engineers.* Construction Research Congress.

Köhler, J., Philippi, S. & Lange, M.(2003). SEMEDA:Ontology based semantic integration of biological databases. *Bioinformatics,* 19(18), 2420-2427.

Lécué, F., Léger, A. & Delteil,A.(2008). DL reasoning and AI planning for Web service composition. *Web Intelligence and Intelligent Agent Technology*,IEEE/WIC/ACM International Conference,1, doi: 10.1109/WIIAT.2008.344

Mena, E., Illarramend A.,Kashyap, V. & Sheth A.P. (2000). OBSERVER: An approach for query processing in global information systems based on interoperation across pre-existing ontologies. *Distributed and parallel Databases,* 8(2), 223-271.

Mennie, D. & Pagurek, B. (2000). An architecture to support dynamic composition of service components. *Systems and Computer Engineering*. Carleton University, Canada.

Petrovic, M., Burcea,I. & Jacobsen, H.,(2003).S-ToPSS: semantic Toronto publish/subscribe system. *Proceedings of the 29th international conference on Very large data bases*, 29. VLDB Endowment.

Sacks, R., Radosavlejevic, M. & Barak, R. (2010). Requirements for building information modeling based lean production management systems for construction. *Automation in Construction*,19(5), 641–655.

Spanos, D.E., Stavrou, P. & Mitrou, N.(2012). Bringing relational databases into the semantic web: a survey. *Journal Semantic Web,* 3(2). 169–209.

Srividya, K., Bansal, A., Blake, M.B. & Gupta, G.(2008).Generalized semantics-based service composition. Web Services. ICWS'08. *IEEE International Conference on. IEEE,* doi: 10.1109/ICWS.2008.118

A QUESTION AND ANSWER SYSTEM FOR FACTUAL QUERIES IN PORTUGUESE ON DBPEDIA

Maksym Ketsmur[1], Mário Rodrigues[2] and António Teixeira[3]
[1]*DETI – University of Aveiro*
[2]*ESTGA / IEETA – University of Aveiro*
[3]*DETI / IEETA – University of Aveiro*
Campus Universitário de Santiago, 3810-193, Portugal

ABSTRACT

The creation of generic natural language query and answering (QA) systems is an active goal of the Semantic Web since it would allow people to conduct any query using their native language. Current solutions already handle factual questions mostly in English. The aim of this work was to develop a QA system to query knowledge bases (KB) such as DBpedia using factual questions in Portuguese. This involves representing Portuguese queries in terms of the KB ontology using SPARQL. The process of constructing a SPARQL query representing the natural language input involves determining: (1) the type of answer that is being sought - a person, a place, etc. - which is done by looking at the Portuguese equivalent of the Wh- words; (2) the main topic of the question - which person, place, etc. - obtained by morphosyntactic analysis to discover the potential subjects of the question; and (3) the properties that can be mapped to the KB ontology for creating a SPARQL query as precise as possible.

The system was tested by with 22 questions without guarantee that the answer was in the KB. The correctness of the answers was verified, and was verified if the answer existed in the KB when the system did not produced results. A correct answer was produced in 67% of times that the answer existed in the KB, and for the remaining the system failed to produce an answer. Results show that this approach is promising and further investigation should be done to improve the system. The robustness observed fosters future work to expand the system to answer questions of other types.

KEYWORDS

Question Answering, Portuguese, Knowledge Base

1. INTRODUCTION

The predominant form of search on the internet is the use of keywords. However, the use of this form of information search is often inadvertent to express the true intention of the user (Song, D. et al., 2015). The traditional keyword searching returns an extensive list of possible results, where the user must to spend some time to find the desired information. On one hand, a greater amount of information allows users to compare results and convey some conclusion, yet, makes the search more difficult, due to the quantity and growth of online information nowadays. So, a need for systems that allow anyone to perform structured search becomes increasingly needed (Hirschman, L. et al., 2001; Navigli, R. et al., 2012).

Using a well-structured search allows to better understand users' intent, returning the desired answer and not a list as in traditional approaches. With this, a need to develop new semantic search systems arise, allowing the user to carry out a structured search using the natural language that allows to identify users' intention and the semantics that allows combining distinct sources of information to obtain an answer. Increasingly, the information is provided in the form of Linked Data, which consists of using the Web to interconnect different sources of information. These can be as diverse as the databases of two different organizations in different geographic locations. Technically, Linked Data refers to data published on the Internet in a way that can be understood by both humans and computers (Damljanovic, D. et al., 2011; Unger, C. et al., 2012).

Semantic web data is published in RDF (Resource Description Framework) form, which is a standard for expressing data graphs and sharing them with other people and, perhaps more importantly, with machines. A large collection of tools and services emerged around the RDF (Bizer, C. et al., 2009; Segaran, T. et al., 2009). RDF is a language to express data models using triples, which are constituted by subject, predicate, and object. In addition, it adds several important concepts that make these models more accurate and robust, removing the ambiguity when transmitting semantic data between machines (Segaran, T. et al., 2009).

The main goal of this study is to develop a QA system that allows users to get the desired information using natural language as a query. The characteristic points of this system are the use of Portuguese language as the base language, and being designed to operate directly over already existing knowledge bases (KB), being for the moment instantiated in the popular DBpedia.

The paper continues in section two with the background and the relevant related work. The third section explains how the QA system works and the fourth section shows representative results and discusses them. The paper ends with the conclusions in section 5.

2. BACKGROUND AND RELATED WORK

The first step in the development of QA systems is to understand how users search information and what kind of answer they expect (Hirschman, L. et al., 2001). Different types of questions can be asked and can be identified per the type of answer: factual, opinion, and abstract (Hirschman, L. et al., 2001). The different types of questions can be done in different ways, such as indirect requests or even commands. "I would like to list all presidents of Portugal" is considered as an indirect request and "Name all presidents of Portugal" is considered as a command (Hirschman, L. et al., 2001). However, this can bring some difficulties to systems that heavily depend on identifying terms such as Who, Where, When and What in users' queries. For example, by identifying the word Who in the query, the system will determinate that the user wants to know about some human or organization, or the word Where that will indicate that the answer will be about some location. These types of systems cannot respond to the questions asked in indirect request form or even commands. Also, the user is not expected to perform search in a structured way, which in this case makes the autosuggest a good feature during the construction of the query, as seen in the TR Discover system.

Not all types of questions are similar, there is evidence that some types are more difficult than others, such as Why and How tend to be more difficult to analyze because they require understanding of text and relations between entities (Hirschman, L. et al., 2001). The identification of the correct expected answer type reduces the number of possible answers, making the system more efficient and precise (Breck, E. et al., 2000). Different systems use distinct approaches to form the answer that is shown to the user. Answers can be formed in two ways, extraction or generation. In the first, the fragment that contains the answer is extracted from the original document and presented to user, while in the second the answer is extracted from multiple sentences or from several documents (Hirschman, L. et al., 2001).

The ability of identifying users' intention implies a natural language analysis where the main challenge is to understand the user intent that may be ambiguous. In addition, natural language processing aims to achieve a natural language analysis like humans, using different techniques that allow to identify entities, actions, relation between entities, etc. in a natural language sentence (Hirschman, L. et al., 2001; E. Liddy. et al., 2001). Many evaluations of semantic search systems referred that users prefer to use free natural language during the search rather than controlled inputs or view-based searches. Although the flexibility offered by this approach is a significant advantage, it can also become very complex (Kumar, A. et al., 2016). Allowing users full freedom in choosing terms increases the difficulty of these tools to disambiguate the search and understand the users' intent (Elbedweihy, K. et al., 2013).

Word sense disambiguation aims to understand what the terms mean. While for humans it is easy to understand the meaning of a word, for a machine it is a difficult task (Guha, R., et al., 2003; Lopes, L.S. et al. 2005; Elbedweihy, K. et al., 2013). Therefore, the use of semantic search tools is essential to match the document content with users' intention (Hoffart, J. et al., 2011). Semantic search systems adopt different search approaches, ranging from natural language (free or guided) to visualization-based interfaces (forms or graphs). Each of these strategies provides different levels of user flexibility, query language expression and support during the query formulation (Elbedweihy, K. et al., 2013).

However, as mentioned earlier, flexibility makes it difficult to map terms with concepts, properties and ontological entities. One of these difficulties is polysemy (a word with more than one meaning) and synonymy (multiple words with the same meaning). While the first affects accuracy by providing false correspondences, the second affects recall by causing the lack of true semantic correspondences. In this way, both use the word disambiguation techniques (Elbedweihy, K. et al., 2013). For example, to answer the question "How tall is ...?", the query term tall needs to be mapped to the height property in the ontology. However, the term tall is polysemous and has different meanings including (from WordNet): "Great in vertical dimension", "High in stature", "Tall people", "Tall buildings", etc. (Elbedweihy, K. et al., 2013). In this way, the term must be disambiguated, and the correct meaning identified before gathering the related terms, among which there may be named entities, which must also be disambiguated in case multiple matches are found.

Furthermore, as in the example of the term tall, named entities can refer to several real-world entities, requiring disambiguation, which is usually done using the query context and the structure of the ontology in which the term occurs. That is, to identify the meaning of the term, is necessary to consider the phrase in which it occurs and the structure of the ontology. For example, in the question What river does the Brooklyn Bridge cross? The terms Brooklyn Bridge and Brooklyn would be mapped to the resources of DBpedia, res: Brooklyn Bridge describing the bridge and res: Brooklyn describing the city in New York, respectively. The first resource can be correctly selected based on an ontological structure that shows that crossings of properties connect a river to a bridge and not to a city (Elbedweihy, K. et al., 2013). In fact, identifying the correct meaning of a polysemic word is necessary for the process of query expansion, which is often used by search systems to find matches between search terms and ontology (Elbedweihy, K. et al., 2013).

Some approaches consider all meanings of a polysemic word and use their related terms for query expansion. However, this increase the noise and irrelevant matches, affecting accuracy. On the other hand, in the disambiguation approach described by (Lopez, V. et al., 2006), a specific synset of WordNet (list of synonyms) is considered relevant only if one of its meanings exists in the synonyms, hyperonyms, hyponyms, holonyms or meronyms of an antecedent or a descendant of synset (Elbedweihy, K. et al., 2013). Typically, in these systems, only lemmatization is performed, which consists of a morphological transformation that modifies the word for its base form or dictionary form, the lemma (Liu, H. et al., 2012), and part-of-speech (POS) tagging, whether it is a noun, an adverb, an adjective, etc. (Elbedweihy, K. et al., 2013; Berant, J. et al., 2013). After, each term is stored with its lemma and POS tagging, except previously recognized named entities that are not lemmatized. In addition, the position of each term is stored in relation to the rest of the query (Elbedweihy, K. et al., 2013).

Semantic search systems use semantic databases that can be queried using SPARQL language, since it is the recommended language by W3C for RDF (Resource Description Framework) querying. The terms generated in the disambiguation stage of the query go through the process of matching properties and ontology concepts. After gathering all correspondences of candidate ontologies that are syntactically similar to a query term, they are sorted using two string comparison algorithms described by (Winkler, W., 1990; Philips, L., 2000). The first depends on comparing the number and order of common characters by assigning a high score to the terms that are parts of each. This is useful since concepts and ontology properties are usually named in this way. For example, the term population and the total Population property receive a high similarity score using this algorithm (Yao, X. et al., 2014). At this stage, the query can be interpreted in terms of a set of ontology concepts, properties, and instances that need to be interconnected. The semantic data are presented in the form of triples, constituted by subject, predicate and object. In this way, given the object (the query) are the predicates and subjects, where the predicates present the relation between object and subject.

Given that our system is intended for Portuguese, we have analyzed some systems working for Portuguese. The question classification done by Branco et al. (2008) is per semantic category of the right answer. The major factor that differentiates the (Branco et al., 2008) system from other systems, is the way the answer is extracted. This system acts as a client of search engines, submitting the list of keywords obtained in previous phase and retrieving relevant documents. The most similar system to ours is the one of Quaresma, P. et al. (2004) since the semantic representation of the query is obtained using the ontology of concepts and a KB with some general world knowledge. Finally, the system IdSay (Carvalho et al., 2008), is an open domain QA system for Portuguese. Its current version can be considered a baseline version, using techniques from the Information Retrieval (IR) area.

All these systems are intended to answer the factual or definition questions made in Portuguese natural language. Although they use some identical methods such as natural language processing and question type classification, they differ from the developed system in terms of the form of answer extraction, using the extraction from the text or collection of texts, whereas our system uses the semantic database as DBpedia.

3. DEVELOPED SYSTEM

This section aims to present and describe the developed system, different phases of analysis and processing of information will be addressed to answer the user's question. The architecture of the developed system consists of 6 distinct processing steps. Figure 1 contains a representation of all processing steps for the example question “Onde nasceu o Albert Einstein?” (Where was Albert Einstein born?) to help better understand the processing steps description of this section.

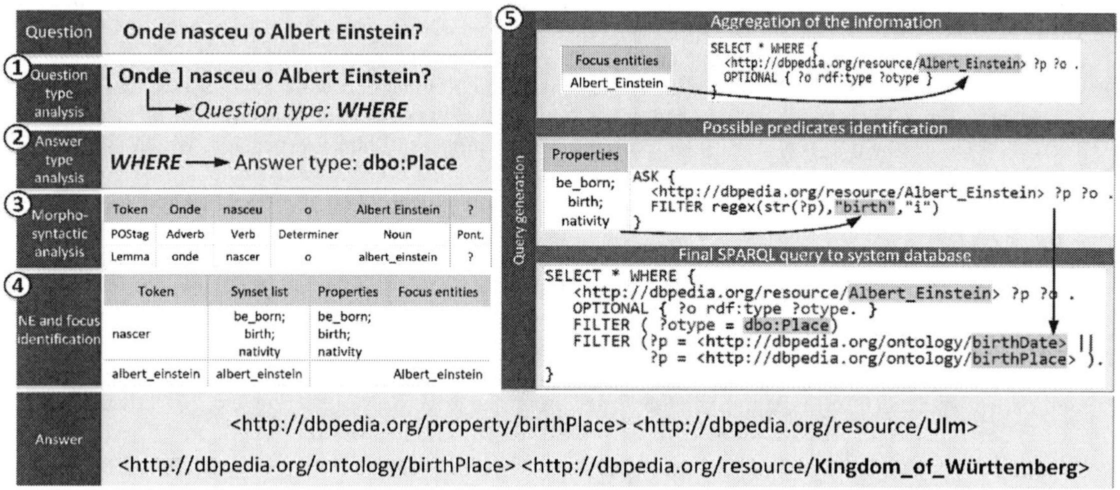

Figure 1. The question answering process exemplified with the question “Onde nasceu o Albert Einstein?” (Where was Albert Einstein born?)

The first step is to identify the question type. Many different types of questions exist, among which are being considered three types: causal, list, and definition. The identification is based on word patterns made by combinations of Who, Who is/are/where, When, Where and How much.

The next step is for determining which kind of KB object classes are expected as an answer: for instance, if the question type is “where” then the answer expected if of class Place or equivalent. The answer classes are obtained using an answer type taxonomy and a set of rules mapping question types to answer classes, the same way Pasca, M. and Harabagiu, S. (2001) did. The answer class can be any class of the ontology or xml datatype. Possible top level classes and datatypes of DBpedia were identified and the answer type class set is: *Person*, *Agent*, *Place*, *Game*, *Dog_breeds*, *Eukaryote,* and *Abstract* class. The mapping rules can define that some answer types have more than one answer class or datatype, for example a question that contains word *Which*, that can be asked about anything, the mapping rule point to the list of answer classes and/or datatypes. The answer class is directly used in the SPARQL query generated at the end of this process to filter the possible answers to improve the answer accuracy.

The third step of processing is a morphosyntatic analysis of the input query phase including tokenization, lemmatization, POS tagging, number and named entity identification, and syntactic dependency parsing. One of the key features of this module is the dependency tree construction that allows to understand the relations between different words of the phrase which in turn will allow to identify the focus entities of the sentence, taking another step in identifying what is being queried.

After having the syntactic dependency tree and all input tokens characterized, the fourth processing step aims to identify all possible named entities or concepts in the input query. To perform this, BabelNet is used to obtain the possible *synsets* of the concepts that exist in the input phrase. This practice is common in QA systems since using other words representing the same concepts, that might exist in the KB but not necessarily in the input query, broadens the coverage of the system. The concept of *synsets* comes from WordNet and consists of unordered sets of cognitively synonymous words and phrases. BabelNet allows to obtain English synsets of Portuguese words, then use them to query DBpedia. Querying DBpedia is only possible using English terms because its ontology is expressed in English. It was found that the best BabelNet source to extract synsets of nouns is Wikipedia. The focus entity is a synset that represents an entity of one of two types: (1) named like people, organizations, and cities; and (2) concepts such as light, water, star, etc. In case of multiple candidates then is selected the one closer to the dependency tree root.

The fifth step is about information aggregation and consists of constructing a first SPARQL to know the list of properties of the focus entity in DBpedia. The properties that can represent the remaining synsets identified in the input phrase will become filters in the second and final SPARQL. This final SPARQL also contains a filter to restrict the answers to the answer type classes identified in the second step. This query aims to retrieve the possible answers from the system's triple store and the answer is presented to user.

3.1 Software Tools

In our system, the most important part of processing is identifying of the user intent. For this two different Natural Language Processing tools was used, Freeling and Maltparser. FreeLing is a C++ library providing language analysis functionalities (morphological analysis, named entity detection, PoS-tagging, parsing, Word Sense Disambiguation, Semantic Role Labelling, etc.) for a variety of languages among which Portuguese is available but not for syntactic dependency parsing. FreeLing also provides a command-line front-end that can be used to analyze texts and obtain the output in the desired format (XML, JSON, CoNLL). In our case the CoNLL output format is important to perform the correct output for the Maltparser.

MaltParser is a system for data-driven dependency parsing, which can be used to induce a parsing model from treebank data and to parse new data using an induced model. The Maltparser was trained using CG-converted UD Portuguese treebank and Freeling output. The CG-converted UD Portuguese treebank is originally based on an improved and enriched version of the 7.4 dependency version of the revised Bosque part of the Floresta Sintá(c)tica treebank (cf. Linguateca.pt). 7.4 was in 2006-2008 aligned with a new live run with the PALAVRAS parser to propagate morphological features from unambiguous to ambiguous words, and to add what the Floresta team called "searchables", i.e. tags for features distributed across several tokens, such as NP definiteness and complex tenses. The public treebank only used this for the constituent version, which was the one actively revised by the Floresta team until 2008 (Linguateca.pt version 8.0).

To store all extracted information, the Jena Triple Store was used. Apache Jena (or Jena in short) is a free and open source Java framework for building Semantic Web and Linked Data applications. The framework is composed of different APIs interacting together to process RDF data. Also, the web page to manage the database and executing of SPARQL query is available.

3.2 Knowledge Bases

BabelNet is both a multilingual encyclopedic dictionary, with lexicographic and encyclopedic coverage of terms, and a semantic network which connects concepts and named entities in a very large network of semantic relations, made up of about 14 million entries, called Babel synsets. Each Babel synset represents a given meaning and contains all the synonyms which express that meaning in a range of different languages.

The major advantage of this KB is aggregation of different semantic sources in one, that allow perform synsets identification that is common among different databases. As the information extaction abous focus entity is made by querying the DBpedia, the right synset is must to be identified. In this case, was determined that DBpedia encodes concept and named entities in the same way as Wikipedia which is a part of possible BabelNet sources. In this way, extracted synsets from Wikipedia can be directly used to query DBpedia.

Additionally, the synset identification is made using Multilanguage WordNet, because of Portuguese input. Using BabelNet allow us querying different semantic databases from the same location. DBpedia is a crowd-sourced community effort to extract structured information from Wikipedia and make this information available on the Web. DBpedia allows you to ask sophisticated queries against Wikipedia, and to link the different data sets on the Web to Wikipedia data.

4. RESULTS AND DISCUSSION

Our system was evaluated using a set of factoid questions as for now it was not possible to find a golden collection for Portuguese Q&A systems based on an existing knowledge base. An effort was made to cover different domains to allow understanding which question is the easiest to answer.

Qual é a altura do Michael Phelps? (How tall is Michael Phelps?) The answer is unique and according to DBpedia is 1.83. This type of question is simple to analyze and information about the focus entity Michael Phelps is available. For the property *altura* there were two synsets, pitch and height. The process of identifying of possible predicate determinates the ontology property *height* which corresponds to the answer.

Quantos golos marcou o Cristiano Ronaldo?(How many goals did Ronaldo score?) The answer to the question consists of a set of properties which in general have no meaning. The answer is: Goals – 84; Nationalgoals – 7; Nationalgoals – 1; Nationalgoals – 5; Goals – 248.

In this case is only possible to conclude that the sum of all goals of Cristiano Ronaldo is 248. Probably the property *nationalgoals* indicates the total goals when playing for Portugal, but in this case, we have 3 different objects to the same property, which makes difficult to understand what is the meaning of each.

Qual a profundidade do Mar Mediterrâneo?(How deep is the Mediterranean Sea?) The answer to this question is like the answer about Cristiano Ronaldo, where a list was returned. But in this case the properties have a compressive meaning for user which not only correctly answers the question returning the maximum depth of 5267 meters as also return additional information of average depth.

Qual a profundidade do Oceano Atlântico?(How deep is the Atlantic Ocean?) After changing the entity of previous question, still no able to get the answer. The correct entity and its properties were successful identified, but the property that contains *depth* does not exist in the list of predicates for this property. To find the correct answer, the DBpedia page of *Atlantic_Ocean* was analyzed. Every subject on DBpedia contains the property *sameAs* that corresponds to this entity in our sources. In the list of *sameAs* result, the page of *Atlantic_Ocean* on Wikidata was found. There the property *deepest point* was identified and possibly is the correct answer. The problem there is the use of expansion methods to find out the answer, using the *sameAs* property. But even using this expansion method, the *deepest point* property would not be identified using the *depth* property. Thus, in the answer to this question there was a main problem, no existence of the same properties for different entities, that is, whereas in the previous question *depth* property was identified, for Atlantic Ocean no, being that the system correctly identified all the necessary information to get the answer.

Qual é a velocidade da luz?(What is the speed of light?) In the case of this question, there are two nouns *velocidade (velocity)* and luz (*light)*. What is important here is to identify the true focus entity, which is only possible by analyzing the dependency tree. The focus entity *light* was correctly identified, while the synsets for the *velocity,* being a noun were extracted from Wikipedia. This extraction of synsets from Wikipedia only returned a *velocity* synset, which is considered a concept. This extraction is considered good since Wikipedia extraction is only carried out on Named Entities or Concepts. In this case, *velocity* could also be extracted from WordNet, which in addition to Velocity extracted another synset *Speed.* The greater problem in answering this question is the absence of such information in the data source, present in most cases.

Quem foi a mulher de Napoleão Bonaparte?(Who was the wife of Napoleon Bonaparte?) The problem identified in this question was the inconsistency of the semantic representation of the entity Napoleon Bonaparte. Seen to be a noun, the synsets were extracted from Wikipedia by getting synset Napoleão_Bonaparte being a Portuguese representation. As mentioned before, DBpedia uses the same representation of Named Entities and Concepts as Wikipedia, which is considered a true statement. Thus, the problem consisted of misidentification of the synset. The synset for *Napoleão Bonaparte* corresponds to the Portuguese representation Napoleão_Bonaparde, while the English representation in DBpedia is Napoleon.

As seen previously there are some flaws that may cause the lack of response to the question. The failures that have been presented are in general the lack of information implies a lack of response. Given that the data source chosen for extracting information DBpedia, contains a lot of information but it is not persistent in all entities as seen in the example of the Mediterranean Sea and Atlantic Ocean, where one entity had depth and other not. Another type of failure corresponds to the meaning of properties that the DBpedia uses, as seen in the example of Cristiano Ronaldo, having 3 properties *national goals* that did not explain exactly its meaning. The identification of synsets also presented some flaws, where sometimes the amount of synsets is too few to get the answer. With all this, analyzing 22 questions, among which the system could correctly answer 10 questions (45%), answers to 7 questions do not exist in the DBpedia and Named Entity were not identified by Freeling in 4 questions. In general, the system produced a correct answer in 67% (10/15) of times that the answer existed in the KB, and thus it performs a good analysis of users' question.

5. CONCLUSION AND FUTURE WORK

In this study was presented a system that aims to answer the questions made in Portuguese natural language. A study was carried out identifying possible modules and forms of information processing. Most systems of this type are intended for English natural language, and the tools used in these systems are not always the best for Portuguese. Considering this, the part of natural language analysis with the purpose of identifying the users' intention was made by Freeling. The use of BabelNet was also not a common choice for synsets identification, but it was a good choice since this dictionary aggregates information from different data sources. Thus, it was not necessary to carry out the communication independently with WordNet, Wikipedia and others. The step about determining the focus entity using the DBpedia data source is one of the common sources among systems of this type, also having a SPARQL endpoint making this process simple and fast. One of the greatest difficulties was the identification of the true intention of the user as well as the expansion of the meaning of the word, that is, the identification of synsets. There were cases where synsets could not always be obtained in English for a word in Portuguese, being an easier task in systems of the English genre.

One advantage of this system is that it can be adapted to other languages without many changes, since the natural language processing tool is multilingual, the BabelNet synsets identification tool is also multilingual and DBpedia provides information in 125 different languages. However, at this moment the system has some limitations regarding the difficulty of identifying some named entities, as well as the lack of information in DBpedia, which in some cases can be a problem or not, depending on the question focus entity.

The system presented good results in answering the questions which had answer in data source, returning concrete results or a list of results if it existed in the data source. Since this list is much smaller than the list of results returned using the common keyword search.

Given the limitations that the system presents, it is necessary to improve the identification of Named Entities or Concepts. After the question was asked, the system could interact with the user, verifying that the named entity was correctly identified or not, thus performing module training. Likewise, a feedback could be collected at the end of the user getting the response, indicating if it was correct answer or not. Some seen systems store the answers to the questions when they were right. So, when the question is asked, the search is done first in the answers already given and only later in the database of the system. This solution could be useful for the developed system, thus reducing waiting time for complete processing of the question, and on the other hand the data size will grow significantly.

Some problems exist in the identification of the correct synsets for Portuguese words, which in some cases could only be obtain in Portuguese. One of the solutions could be to translate beforehand Portuguese to English and then perform synset identification. In domain-dependent systems like TR Discover use an auto-suggest mechanism during the query construction, thus guiding the user. It would be rather complicated to implement these mechanisms in our system due to its open domain nature.

The system has several aspects that can be improved, both in the natural language processing part and in the information query part. Also, the system can implement user feedback at each processing stage, for example, there are cases where the entity is mistakenly identified or even unidentified, in which case additional control and improved processing could be implemented. In addition to the brief answers to questions, the system could provide some additional information or a more extensive response, which involves the use of information extraction techniques that was not used in this study. The already answered questions could be stored and, then, when a question is made, the answer would be searched firstly in the database of the already given answers. This approach can both bring advantages, such as reduce the response time, as well as disadvantages, namely extra processing in the response search. In addition, some user's feedback was needed to make sure that the answer was correct or not. Given that the system is based on ontology, the use of new data sources is simpler to implement and can be used to obtain the missing information in DBpedia. Also, for better user experience the system could provide a web interface presenting short answers and its references.

REFERENCES

Berant, J., Chou, A., Frostig, R., & Liang, P., 2013. Semantic Parsing on Freebase from Question-Answer Pairs. In EMNLP (Vol. 2, No. 5, p. 6).

Bizer, C., Lehmann, J., Kobilarov, G., Auer, S., Becker, C., Cyganiak, R., & Hellmann, S., 2009. DBpedia-A crystallization point for the Web of Data. *Web Semantics: science, services and agents on the world wide web*, 7(3), 154-165.

Branco, A., Rodrigues, L., Silva, J., & Silveira, S., 2008. Xisquê: An online qa service for portuguese. *In PROPOR* (Vol. 8, pp. 232-235).

Breck, E., Burger, J. D., Ferro, L., Hirschman, L., House, D., Light, M., & Mani, I., 2000. How to evaluate your question answering system every day and still get real work done. *arXiv preprint cs/0004008.*

Carvalho, G., De Matos, D. M., & Rocio, V. (2008). Idsay: Question answering for portuguese. In *Workshop of the Cross-Language Evaluation Forum for European Languages* (pp. 345-352). Springer, Berlin, Heidelberg.

Damljanovic, D., Agatonovic, M., & Cunningham, H., 2011. FREyA: An Interactive Way of Querying Linked Data Using Natural Language. *In ESWC Workshops* (Vol. 7117, pp. 125-138).

Elbedweihy, K., Wrigley, S. N., Ciravegna, F., & Zhang, Z., 2013. Using BabelNet in bridging the gap between natural language queries and linked data concepts. *Proc. 2013 Intern. Conf. on NLP & DBpedia*. CEUR-WS. org.

Guha, R., McCool, R., & Miller, E., 2003. Semantic search. *In Proceedings of the 12th international conference on World Wide Web* (pp. 700-709). ACM.

Hirschman, L. and Gaizauskas, R., 2001. Natural language question answering: the view from here. *Natural Language Engineering*, 7(4), 275-300.

Hoffart, J., Yosef, M. A., Bordino, I., Fürstenau, H., Pinkal, M., Spaniol, M., Taneva, B., Thater, S., & Weikum, G., 2011. Robust disambiguation of named entities in text. *Proc. of Conf. Empirical Methods in NLP*. ACL.

Kumar, A., Irsoy, O., Ondruska, P., Iyyer, M., Bradbury, J., Gulrajani, I., Zhong, V., Paulus, R., & Socher, R., 2016. Ask me anything: Dynamic memory networks for natural language processing. *Proc International Conference on Machine Learning* (pp. 1378-1387).

Liddy, E.D., 2001. Natural Language Processing *in Encyclopedia of Library and Information* Science, *2nd Ed,* New York: Marcel Decker Inc.

Liu, H., Christiansen, T., Baumgartner, W. A., & Verspoor, K., 2012. BioLemmatizer: a lemmatization tool for morphological processing of biomedical text. Journal of biomedical semantics, 3(1), 3.

Lopes, L.S., Teixeira, A.J., Quinderé, M., and Rodrigues M., 2015, From Robust Spoken Language Understanding to Knowledge Acquisition and Management. *Proc. of 9th European Conf. on Speech Communication and Technology.*

Lopez, V. et al., 2006. Poweraqua: Fishing the semantic web. *The Semantic Web: research and applications*, 393-410.

Navigli, R., and Ponzetto, S., 2012. Multilingual WSD with just a few lines of code: the BabelNet API. *In Proceedings of the ACL 2012 System Demonstrations* (pp. 67-72). Association for Computational Linguistics.

Pasca, M., & Harabagiu, S., 2001. High performance question/answering. In *Proceedings of the 24th annual international ACM SIGIR conference on Research and development in information retrieval* (pp. 366-374). ACM.

Philips, L., 2000. The double metaphone search algorithm. C/C++ users journal, 18(6), 38-43.

Quaresma, P., Quintano, L., Rodrigues, I., Saias, J., & Salgueiro, P. (2004). University of Évora in QA@ CLEF-2004. In *Workshop of the Cross-Lang Eval Forum for European Languages* (pp. 534-543). Springer, Berlin, Heidelberg.

Segaran, T., Evans, C., & Taylor, J., 2009. Programming the Semantic Web: *Build Flexible Applications with Graph Data.* " O'Reilly Media, Inc.".

Song, D., Schilder, F., Smiley, C., Brew, C., Zielund, T., Bretz, H., Martin, R., Dale, C., Duprey, J., Miller, T., & Harrison, J., 2015. TR Discover: A natural language interface for querying and analyzing interlinked datasets. *In International Semantic Web Conference* (pp. 21-37). Springer, Cham.

Unger, C., Bühmann, L., Lehmann, J., Ngonga Ngomo, A. C., Gerber, D., & Cimiano, P., 2012. Template-based question answering over RDF data. *In Proc. of the 21st international conference on World Wide Web* (pp. 639-648). ACM.

Winkler, W., 1990. String Comparator Metrics and Enhanced Decision Rules in the Fellegi-Sunter Model of Record Linkage.

Yao, X. and Van Durme., 2014. Information Extraction over Structured Data: Question Answering with Freebase. In ACL (1) (pp. 956-966).

A SURVEY ON ICT USAGE IN EDUCATION IN ANGOLA HIGH POLYTECHNICAL SCHOOL

Adelina Aleksieva-Petrova[1], Amoussou Dorothee[2] and Milen Petrov[3]
[1]*Technical University of Sofia, Faculty of Computer Systems and Technologies, Sofia, Bulgaria*
[2]*ESPU - High Polytechnical School of Uige, Uige, Angola*
[3]*Sofia University "St. Kl. Ohridski", Faculty of Mathematics and Informatics, Sofia, Bulgaria*

ABSTRACT

The main objective of the paper is to conduct a survey and analyze the results for usage and understanding utilization of Information and Communication Technologies (ICT), clustered in different target groups of users in High Polytechnical School of Uige, Angola. To achieve that goal there are selected the most widely known ICT tools and distributed into seven main categories: learning management systems, blogging, social networks, e-book tools, file sharing tools, wiki tools and video tutorial tools. The results of the survey based on 441 answers from teachers, administrative stuff and university/undergraduate and graduate students. The main hardware tools used to access the Internet are divided to mobile devices and desktop computers. As result the most used ICT tools are web-based, grouped in two separated categories: social networks and file sharing tools.

KEYWORDS

Education, ICT, ICT Tools, Learning Systems

1. INTRODUCTION

Information and communication technology (ICT) is the main factor for the most of the new developments and is driving force of new industry. It is also a prerequisite for its high productivity and competitiveness. Without ICT, there is no innovation and when the activity is more innovative and oriented towards the right use of ICT, the more likely it is to be competitive (Slavinski & Benkova, 2013).

The changes in society as a consequence of the emergence of ICT have also changed the way we learn and the way we teach. Teachers and students are aware of that most of the conventional learning methods have been obsolete due to the fact it failed to adapt to the new conditions imposed by ICT. This is the reason that learning and teaching are still challenging today. The education is one of the most important areas in our society and is obliged to respond positively to that challenge.

In the last decade, great efforts have been made to integrate ICT in the educational process. That is the main reason for many problems to rise in the implementation of ICT technologies in education such as: insufficient training of the teachers and lack of the desire and motivation to follow and introduce the latest technologies and methodologies in learning.

In order to address those problems current paper aims to discover and define the level of the adoption and understanding of different ICT tools by different target groups with users in the particular school - High Polytechnical School of Uige, Angola - in order to contribute to their effective implementation in the learning process. The paper is structured as follows. The next section contains an overview of the main trends in the field of eLearning. Section 3 defines, explains and conducts of the study, and last but not least, section 4 analyzes the results from the collected data. In the last section conclusion and future work are defined.

2. RELATED WORK

With the flourishing of ICT more educational institutions are integrating it into their learning systems to support and enhance the learning process (Proserpio & Gioia, 2007). Realization of the potential of ICT and its implementation into teaching is associated not only with the physical equipment of the educational institutions and universities, but also with precise formulation of objectives and as a matter of a corresponding philosophically and psychologically based, and pedagogically and didactically elaboration of teaching material (Semradova & Hubackova, 2013). Some research studied the effect of integration of ICT in classroom and define four effective functions for integration: dynamic content presentation, information access, creation and sharing, interaction and reflection (Pheeraphan , 2013).

Other researchers has analyzed prospective teachers' perceptions about their professional development regarding the use of ICT for in offering an educational response to students with specific support needs and how the use of these tools in an inclusive school context fosters reflexive teaching practice, generating new communication channels and teamwork, methodological updating and improvements in digital competence (Palomino, 2017).

On the other side other research tries to define and find out how the perceptions of students, motivations and their success rate those study with ICT based technology supported environments. The conclusion is that it has improved the motivation and success of students (Sari, 2014). The student activities are very important in order to indicate the motivation and success of students. The study focuses on a method for improving interaction in the classroom by monitoring students' activities and there is proposed system where all the activities are stored and interaction of the students in the class through which the level of interaction of the student can be made (Choudhury, et al., 2016).

In recent years Internet innovations are more closely related to Web 2.0 which represents free or very low-cost interactive Web services, designed to facilitate real-time collaboration and information sharing. Web 2.0 changes the environment in which modern learning takes place and creates prerequisites for a new model for its implementation. The teachers challenge is to implement and experiment strategies for integrating Web 2.0 technologies and tools into the learning process.

The usage of ICT in learning process stimulate teachers' creative abilities both in creating content and combining different channels and sources of knowledge. The students have the opportunity to have personal learning spaces, to participate in the creation of learning content and to train themselves and others by using the Internet as repository of educational resources and as accessible communication environment. The tools like eRubrics, concept maps, project-based learning, ePortfolios, and virtual learning environments are used as ICT-based tools to promote students' active learning and awareness in their learning processes. The combination of all of these strategies foster the student's active participation in the way that students become involved in their learning through a reflexive process to acquire a high level of competencies (Gámiz-Sánchez, 2017).

Ongoing research on construction of client-server and service-oriented software for generation of audio-lectures can use as outcome current survey and analysis (Petrov, et al., 2017).

3. IMPLEMENTATION OF THE STUDY

The study here is done by designing a questionnaire survey which evaluates the degree of the usage of the ICT by the various participants in the learning processes at the High Polytechnic School Uige - ESPU, Angola. To achieve that goal, we have used a method with questions, where answering and collecting the answers allows us to apply the necessary analysis and conclusions.

The construction of the text inquiry has been based upon the standard "6 - models" belonging to Testing Service System (TSS), proposed by the company TestCraft (Ellafi, et al., 2004). This survey method was chosen because it is aimed at a wide range of users – teachers, administrative stuff and students. Following the basic principles for creating inquiry at the TSS, such a study is made up of the experience of target groups according the described and applied strategy.

The first two stages are collecting questions and construction of the questions and their answers. The collection and design of the questions for the questionnaire is an important process where the aim is to select appropriate targets for questions, so that the answers to which will allow us to accurate analyses of results for usage and understanding of ICT. The next stage is compilation of inquiry for which is chosen a multiple choice questions as appropriate for obtaining the answers and for processing and calculation of data. Next step is management of inquiry and to choose a suitable environment in which to allow an opportunity for feedback. The last two stages are analysis of the results of the inquiry and measuring and assessing the depth of the inquiry. Transfer of results to Excel provides an excellent opportunity for automatic visualization and graphical data processing. We apply appropriate statistical methods, based on the distribution of points according to obtained answers, percentages, arithmetic data, charts and graphs.

The survey includes three main groups of stakeholders: teachers, administrative stuff and students. The first part of the questionnaire relates to the personal information and consists of the following variables: name (optional), age, gender and education (secondary, bachelor, master or doctor). The academic staff (trainee assistant, assistant, senior assistant, associate professor or professor) is assigned to the group of teachers. Students are from 5 year graduate education and from following specialties: Computer Engineering, Accounting and Management, Nursing, and Agronomy at last. The second part of the questionnaire aims to define which hardware devices are used to connect to the Internet, the main purpose being to determine the types of devices that are most commonly used. The third part is related to the use and knowledge of ICT tools in the learning process. The first question is to list the names of the ICT tools it uses in the learning process. The second question provides a list of ICT tools that are categorized and the participants are asked to point out the well-known ones. The last question to the participants is whether they believe in the educational potential of ICT tools.

ICT tools are divided into seven main categories: learning management systems, blogging, social networks, e-book creation tools, file sharing tools, wiki tools and video tutorial tools. In each categories are selected the most widely used tools such as choice is based from the ranking of systems (Hart, 2017).

Learning management systems (LMS) include various technologies to provide communication, delivery of learning contents and management of the learning process. The list of learning tools is: Moodle, dotLRN, Caroline, Dokeos, Atutor, Telduc, WebCT, and DeskEaD. Blogs are web2.0 tools that can be used in a learning process. Platforms like Blogger and Wordpress have become popular with their versatility of use. All selected blogs are free of cost, some of which are open source. Only Live Journal has an extra charge. Social networks are structures made up of people or organizations linked to one or more kinds of relationships that share common values and goals. One of the main features of the definition of networks is their openness, allowing for horizontal and non-hierarchical relations between the participants. The most popular social networks are selected: Facebook, Google+, Instagram, Linkedln, WhatsApp, Myspace. E-books means a book in digital format. It may be an electronic version of a book that has been printed or made only in digital format. Video tutorial tools provide the ability to record and process video. File Sharing is the activity of providing files that are accessible to other users by downloading over the Internet as well as into smaller networks. This category also includes open source and freeware tools (Dropbox, Google Drive, Slide Share, YouTube, 4Shared, Zoho, Flickr). Wiki is a collection of web pages that are created and edited by users with authorized access to them. The individual pages are linked by hyperlinks, and thus all can be considered as a single project. They are suitable for collaborative work between lecturers and students. Wikis can be used to create learning content by several lecturers and teamwork of students on a common task. This is a tool for increasing the activity of the trainees. Students can work on a joint project and publish their materials and results through Wikis tools.

4. ANALYSIS OF THE RESULTS

In the survey participated 441 participants - 22 were teachers, 26 were administrative stuff, and 393 were students. Students showed the highest interest in the study and represented 89% of the target group.

In search for the Internet access devices used in a teacher category, the most used devices for the access to the internet was – in first place that was laptop, and then the mobile phones come on second place. The third place is for desktop, the fourth is for tablet, and finally iPads device. In the group of the 26 administrative stuff surveyed, the most commonly used device for accessing the Internet is the mobile phone, followed by the laptop, iPad, desktops, and finally tablets. The fact that desktop computers are not among the top three most commonly used Internet access devices shows the widespread penetration of the mobile devices within that category. There are two possible reasons behind that result. The first one is the institution does not have an Internet access in suitable areas of the school. The second reason is that the study maybe is done at a time when there was an interruption in the delivery of an Internet and teachers and administrators are unable to use other devices than personal mobile Internet access.

Among the most commonly used devices for Internet access in the category of students were mobile phones, then laptops, tablets, iPads and finally we have desktops (Figure 1).

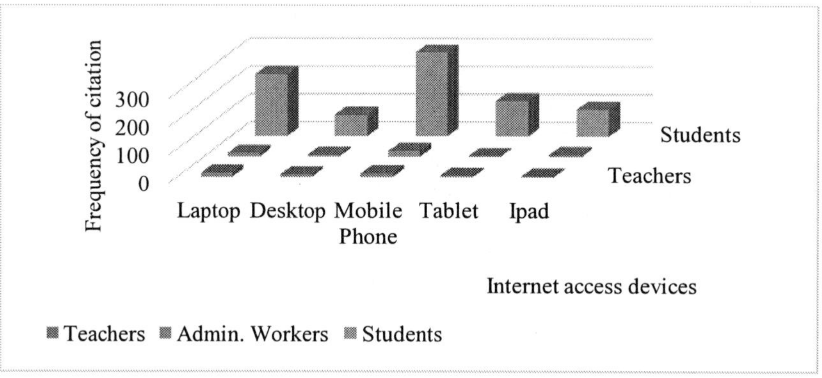

Figure 1. The Frequency of Devices used for Access to the Internet

In conclusion, in ESPU, the three most commonly used devices for Internet access are mobile phones, laptops and tablets. Last, but not least, there are iPad computers as Internet access devices of the same institution. Finally, there are desktop computers as devices to access the Internet in the same institution.

The second question, "*What are the ICT tools that the interviewee has already used?*" Aims to determine the effective use of ICT tools by respondents in the learning process. The percentage of respondents to this question for different groups of participants is different: 82% for teachers, 57.7% for administrative staff and 64% for students.

Social networks (Facebook, Instagram and WhatsApp) and file sharing tools are the most widely used tools among teachers, followed by wiki tools and blogs. There is no mention of the use of training management systems and video lesson tools.

For administrative workers, the percentage of social network users is higher than teachers, followed by file sharing tools, blogging, and learning management systems. Among tools for creating books, video tutorials, and wiki tools, there are no answers (Figure 2).

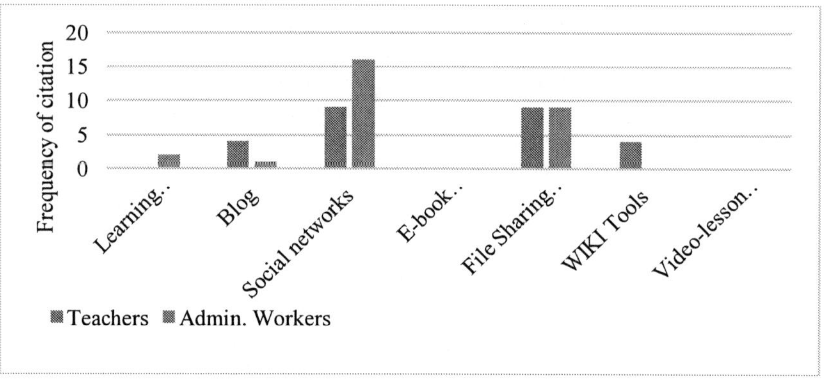

Figure 2. ICT Tools used in the Learning Process by Teachers and Administrative Workers

Among the students most widely used are social networks, followed by file-sharing tools, wiki tools, learning management systems, and blogging (Figure 3).

When providing a list of tools, all 26 surveyed administrative workers and all 393 students surveyed were able to identify at least one tool. In the side of the teachers, 96% had at least one tool.

Teachers and administrators have listed Moodle and Caroline as tools they know, with the Moodle (60%) percentage highest than the other tools. The teachers also mentioned the Telduc and DeskEaD tools with about 14% recognizable, which do not appear in the replies of the administrative workers. They in turn have named Atutor, dotLRN, Dokeos and WebCT as familiar learning management systems.

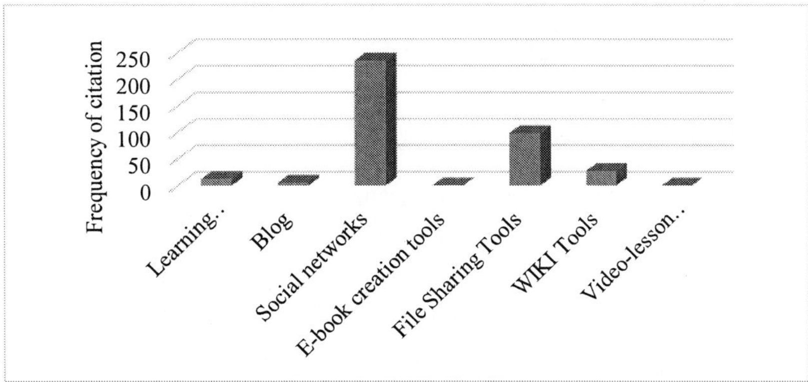

Figure 3. ICT Tools used in the Learning Process Students, Separated by Categories

Students on the other side have identified all content management platforms as familiar but the highest is Moodle's percentage (63%), which is significantly higher than the Atutor second-ranked system (9%). Other systems have significantly lower percentages of 2% to 5% of recognition. The summary graph of results in this category is shown in Figure 4.

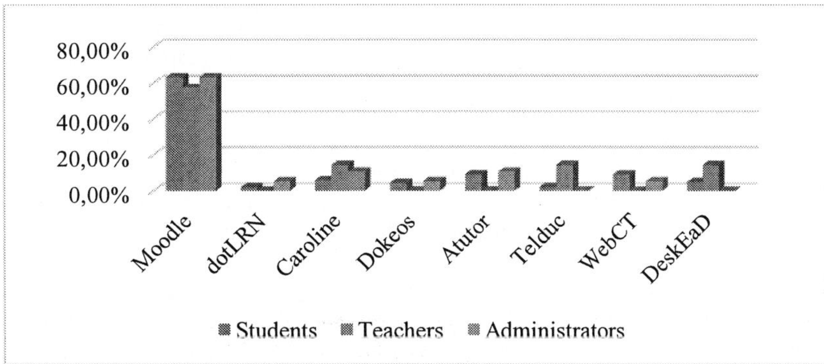

Figure 4. Percentages of LMS Awareness among the Various Participants in the Study

From blogging tools, teachers and administrative workers have first mentioned WordPress (38%), followed by Live Journal (19%) in Teachers and Blogger (23%) in administrative workers, followed by Blog, BlogSpot, and Tumblr. In the group of students, the highest recognition rate is the Blog tool (29.70%), followed by WordPress (21.12%), Blogger (15.51%) and BlogSpot (15.18%).

The widespread overlap of social networks in our daily lives can be seen in the reporting of social networking results. In the social networking category, there is no system that is not known to be familiar, both by the teachers and the administrative staff, and by the students (Figure 5a, b, c). The most popular social network remains Facebook, followed by Google+, Instagram and WhatsApp. Among the teachers, the reference to the professional social network Linkedln is significantly higher.

From the wiki category tools, teachers have indicated Wikipedia in the first place with the highest percentage - 80%. The percentage of the wikispaces (13.33%) and Wetpaint (6.67%) is significantly lower. Similarly, students share similarly distributed wiki tools: Wikipedia (82.55%), wikispaces (12.76%), and Wetpaint (3.65%).

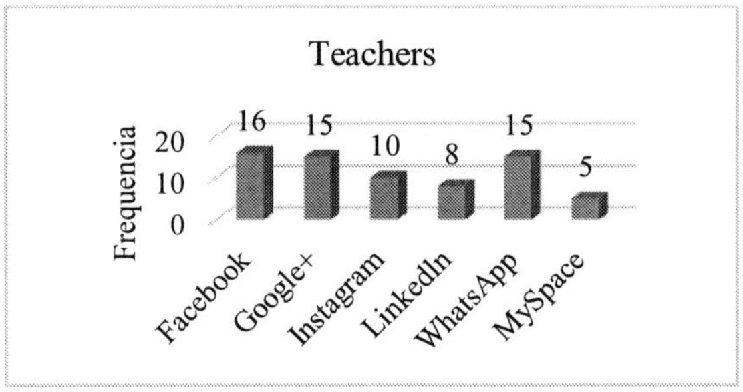

Figure 5a. Social Networks Familiar to Teachers

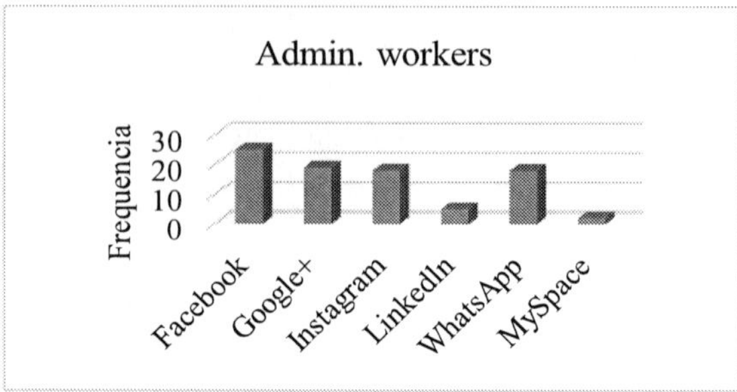

Figure 5b. Social Networks Familiar to Admin. Stuff

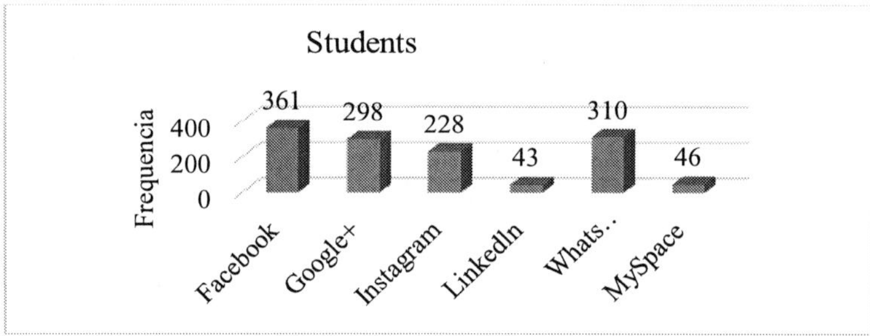

Figure 5c. Social Networks Familiar to Students

In the eBooks category, teachers have listed My E-book Builder, Papyrus, 3D Pack, Youblisher, and Book Builder, and CamTasia, Camtudio, Koyote, Scream Flow. Administrative workers have considerably less recognition of e-book creation tools, which can be explained by the fact that this is not an inherent feature of their professional activity, as opposed to teachers. Of the six listed tools, they listed only three of them: My Ebook Maker, 3Dpack, and Book Builder. Only a small number of students have identified the following e-book creation tools: My Ebook Maker, 3D Pack, Youblisher, and Book Builder. In the category of video tutorial tools, these are: Camtasia (35%), Camtasia Studio (30%), Camstudio (20). The other tools are also mentioned, but they are within 3 to 5 percent cognition.

About File sharing tools, teachers and administrators are often referred to as Youtube, Google Doc / Drive, Dropbox, and Slide Share as familiar platforms. Half of the administrative workers have indicated Youtube, while they are about 28% for teachers. However, teachers have significantly higher recognition rates for Google Doc / Drive (25%) and Dropbox (21%). The 4-Shared (10%) and Flicky (3%) tools are the other listed systems that are known but with a significantly lower recognition rate. More than half of the students said they knew Youtube (54.41%), compared with Google Doc / Drive and Slide Share by 13%. Dropbox is indicated by 12% and 4-Shared by only 5.73%. In order to determine the effective use of ICT tools during educational activities, we summarize the data obtained in the software tools group (Figure 6).

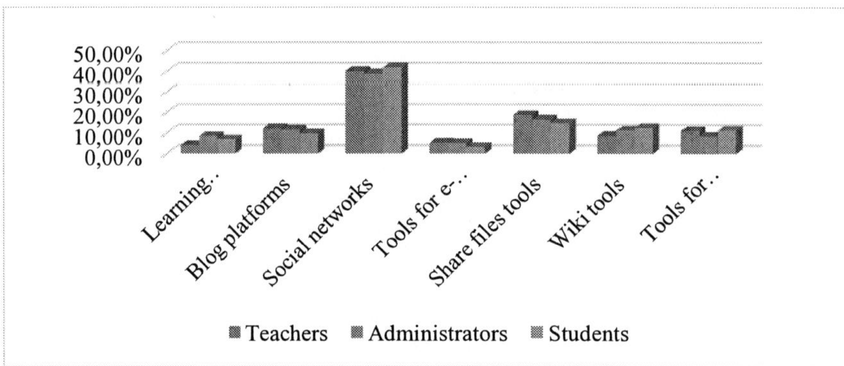

Figure 6. Percentage of Recognition of ICT Tools by Category for All Participants

The last responded question is "Do you believe in the educational potential of ICT tools?". For teachers, 82% believe strongly and 18% have abstained from expressing their opinion on the issue. Of the surveyed 26 administrative workers, 25 believe in their educational potential (96%) and one abstained (4%). For 393 students surveyed, 14% refrained from giving their clear opinion, 3% said they did not believe, and 83% believed. By comparing the three groups of participants for this issue, the greatest trust in the educational potential of ICT tools showed the administrative workers, which they may have explained with the fact that they are indirect participants in the training processes. Teachers and students who are directly involved in these processes show approximately the same belief (82%) in the educational potential of ICT tools. The latter is also the highest percentage of abstentions to answer this question.

5. CONCLUSION AND FUTURE WORK

The latest ICT trends in education are closely related to the existing variety of web and internet tools. There is huge challenge for teachers and students to overcome technical gap and integrate them into the learning process to improve the quality of learning by using benefits of the tools. The paper examines a study conducted by 441 participants among teachers, administrative stuff and students at the ESPU - High Polytechnical School of Uige, Angola. The main objective is to determine the level of use and knowledge of different ICT tools by different actors in the learning process.

Unlike the low participation of teachers and administrative workers in this study with their low levels of participation, students demonstrated greater interest and placement with 89% participation. Despite this fact, the processing and analysis of the data from this study allowed us to reach the following conclusions regarding the use to make some basic conclusions about ICT in teaching and learning at ESPU.

The main hardware tools used to access the Internet are mobile devices that are also personal devices. Among the software tools, the most widely used and recognized devices are web-based in social networking and file sharing categories. This requires consideration of the integration of this type of tools into the learning process in order to increase the efficiency of learning and motivating students. Wiki tools and blogs are the other two categories that can help in learning.

Software desktop tools are mainly used in the video lessons category. This is understandable due to the fact that video processing requires a lot of resources and is not as good for the web.

The topic of extracting text from a variety of sources such as documents and images is also up-to-date to allow editing and setting up a presentation using learning. As future work we will investigate usage of ICT tools enabling the ability to generate audio speech and audio playlists as learning materials. Our team is currently working on development of a platform which facilitates usage of ICT technologies in many domains (also in higher schools). The platform is based on autonomous web-service compositions.

ACKNOWLEDGEMENT

Research, presented in this paper was partially supported by the DFNI I02-2/2014 (ДФНИ И02- 2/2014) project, funded by the National Science Fund, Ministry of Education and Science in Bulgaria and FNI-SU-128-2017 project of Sofia University “St. Kliment Ohridski” (Bulgaria) “Secure and re-usable software architectures for Technology-enhanced learning”.

REFERENCES

Choudhury, N., Venkatesh, T., Bhattacharya, S. & Sarma, S., 2016. Avabodhaka: A System to Analyse and Facilitate Interactive Learning in an ICT Based System for Large Classroom. *Procedia Computer Science*, Volume 84, pp. 160 - 168.

Ellafi, A., Bo Ch., Iswara R., 2004. *TESTCRFT – Assessment Software*, University of Twente.

Gámiz-Sánchez, V.-M., 2017. ICT-based Active Methodologies. Procedia - Social and Behavioral Sciences, 21 February, Volume 237, pp. 606-612.

Hart, J., 2017. Top tools for learning 2016. [Online] Available at: http://c4lpt.co.uk/top100tools/ [Accessed 1 June 2017].

Palomino, M. d. C. P., 2017. Teacher Training in the Use of ICT for Inclusion: Differences between Early Childhood and Primary Education. *Procedia-Social and Behavioral Sciences*, Volume 237, pp. 144 - 149.

Petrov, M., Asenov, A. & Aleksieva-Petrova, A., 2017. Software Server for Automatic Generation of Audio Lectures (uListenSrv). International Journal of Advanced Corporate Learning, 10(1), pp. 55 - 74.

Pheeraphan , N., 2013. Enhancement of the 21st century skills for Thai higher education by integration of ICT in classroom. *Procedia-Social and Behavioral Sciences*, 103(365 - 373).

Proserpio, L. & Gioia, D. A., 2007. Teaching the virtual generation. *Academy of Management Learning & Education*, 6(1), pp. 69 - 80.

Sari, A., 2014. Influence of ICT Applications on Learning Process in Higher Education. *Procedia - Social and Behavioral Sciences*, Volume 116, pp. 4939 - 4945.

Semradova, I. & Hubackova, S., 2013. Incentives to Develop the Use of ICT in the Process of Education. *Procedia - Social and Behavioral Sciences*, Volume 89, pp. 517 - 522.

Slavinski, A. & Benkova, B., 2013. Godishnik Telecommunications in NBU. [Online] Available at: http://eboTelex.nbu.bg/dtk08-09/Inn%20ICT.pdf [Accessed 01 06 2017].

SOCIABILITY IMPACT ON LEARNER'S PERSONALITY IN CLASSROOM AND E- LEARNING ENVIRONMENTS: A COMPARATIVE ANALYSIS

Abdul Saboor[1], Dr. M. Irfanullah Arfeen[2] and Wahbeeah Mohti[3]

[1]PhD scholar, Superior University, Lahore, Pakistan

[2]Postdoctoral Fellow, United Nations University UNU-EGOV, Guimaraes, Portugal, and Assistant Professor, QASMS, Quaid-i-Azam University, 45320 Islamabad, Pakistan

[3]PhD scholar at Department of Management, Universidad de Evora, Portugal

ABSTRACT

The purpose of this study is to compare the sociability and its impact on learner's personality traits, in classroom and E-Learning settings to provide an insight for HRM decisions. We proposed that student's sociability level differ between classroom and e-learning environments. We also identify that sociability is a good predictor for extroversion and openness to experience. For this cross sectional explanatory research about 534 respondents' are identified with purposive sampling method. Results point out that there is significant difference in learner's sociability, extroversion and openness to experience, in classroom and E-Learning environments. The study also established that sociability has statistically significant and positive relationship with openness to experience and extroversion. As there is not even a single study so far that have compared educational environment by using aforementioned variables in reference with development of personality, so the study is unique and a valuable contribution both in educational psychology and for decision making in HRM as well. The study will assist managers to find suitable personal for job. It will also help for training and development plan formation.

KEYWORDS

Learner's personality, HRM decision, Sociability, E-Learning, Classroom, Education

1. INTRODUCTION

1.1 Background of the Study

Technological innovations have very speedily redefined the human interaction as well as how they will teach their new generations. Information technology (IT) has created new opportunities for education. Everything is available for just a click and physical attendance at library is no more necessary, assignments can be moved to and from professors, students can choose and study courses of their choice online and social networking has shortened distances very much. More than 1000 institutes provides e-learning (EL) options around the globe (Sharma & Kitchens, 2004) access by the stakeholders (Surjono, 2009). Advantages of EL for learners include an increased accessibility to information, personalized instruction, content standardization, better content delivery, self-pacing, interactivity and flexibility (Bhuasiri, Xaymoungkhoun, Zo, Rho, & Ciganek, 2012). It reduces costs and improves tracking, among other benefits for faculty (Yang, Chung, Hwang, Li, & Yao, 2017). Oztekin, Delen, Turkyilmaz, and Zaim (2013) concluded that e-learning has huge potential and can reduce costs in comparison to a traditional classroom environment after initial course development. Despite these benefits, EL is still in its infancy in developing countries which experience challenges unique from developed countries. Many developing countries have expressed an interest to implement EL but face obstacles in infrastructure, resources, information access (Tarhini, Hone, Liu, & Tarhini, 2017). It was also observed that despite of regular attendance of both the system, trainee's involvement was actively boosted by classroom based (CB) education system while EL education system usually restrained it (Caspi, Chajut, Saporta, & Beyth-Marom, 2006). It was found that the EL could not entertain all the expectations of learning groups, development of their social knowledge, social interactions and good hands on competencies that were primarily required (Kreijns, Kirschner, and Jochems (2002). Differences in student's personality association with learning environments have also come to surface (Carro & Sanchez-Horreo, 2017). Better results in EL were given by introvert students while on the other hand better performance in CB was shown by extrovert students (Hung & Chou, 2015). A number of personality traits are linked with educational commitment which mainly includes conscientiousness, openness to experience (OE) and extroversion (Komarraju & Karau, 2005). Komarraju and Karau (2005) indicated that OE elucidate huge variances of people committed to study than other personality traits. Researchers yet find student's personality development as an area of interest. In student's personality development, sociability is rated as a major factor and regrettably it is a challenge for education system to teach these personal qualities (Garrison, 2011).

Benefits of EL in comparison with that of traditional CB are suspicious and advanced investigation is required in relation with student's personality development. The purpose behind teaching must not be limited to passing the examination instead its aim should be to produce professionals of good quality having effective communication, good administrative skill, high sociability, when they are put in professional life. Tough EL is better than conventional CB in many ways yet it has a disadvantage of non-contribution in personality building and gloomy aspect of online study has not been probed so far by even a single study on it. That's why this study is very important because it will highlight neglected side of education system which is implicit in nature but of a huge weightage in professional career.

1.2 Study Objective

To what extent student's sociability effect student's personality traits (Extroversion, Openness to experience). And, to compare this impact between classroom based and E –learning environments.

This study planned to explore following hypotheses:

H1: Level of Sociability is high in classroom base students than e-learners.

H2: Classroom base students are high on personality trait extroversion than E-Learners.

H3: Classroom base students are high on personality trait openness to experience than e-learners.

H4: Sociability has a higher positive relationship with openness to experience in class room based students than e-learners.

H5: Sociability has a higher positive relationship with extroversion in class room based students than e-learners.

1.3 Significance of the Study

Presently, there is no strong proof available over the student's characteristics under study. Though connotation of these attributes with instruction environment has been shown by some of the students. That's why; this study is unique and paramount in its nature. Consequently, it is a worthy input in educational psychology as well helpful in decision making process related with human resource development and human resource management (HRM).

2. LITERATURE REVIEW

Traditional non-computer based approaches to the personalization of learning materials (based on learning styles) have involved domain experts in the production of multiple resources to enable a best fit to individual learners (Delgado-García et al., 2016). The use of technology can assist in the profiling of the learner and the retrieval of resources which best fit their individual learning styles (Buttussi & Chittaro, 2017). According to Alsultanny (2006) EL is an effective way of providing a just-in-time learning method by proposing a vigorously changing technical setting that target to substitute antiquated time-place content learning. Normally, "e" in e-learning stands for electronic, however it would better stand for "evolving, everywhere, every time and everybody" (Gregory et al., 2013). Teaching institutes are not only supposed to transfer skills and knowledge in the light of already defined curriculum but they also impart personality building and skills development of the students which is a hidden but counterpart of the curricula (Corno & Anderman, 2015). An asynchronous roadmap is used by almost all the online programs in which main tool for a student is listening or watching of a lecture by her/himself (Purcell, Heaps, Buchanan, & Friedrich, 2013). Students behavior has been linked in each design by a number of studies along with determining competency of asynchronous design with that of synchronous. It was held by Chou (2012) that in synchronous set, a greater ratio of social communications took place while students of asynchronous group were noted be more auguring in assignments that were task-oriented. Masoumi and Lindström (2012) held students who get registration under online courses are more autonomous in handling their issues than that of classroom based system merely because of having no relation with fellows makes them to be more decisive. Mroczek and Little (2014) stained that individuality is a composition of natural psychology discipline and with reference to particular human being, development can be successfully made in the areas like remembrance, learning theory, insight, remembrance (Mai & Mai, 2002). Individual evaluation must be made to take benefit of classes based on internet (Kim & Schniederjans, 2004).

2.1 Sociability

Eysenck (1981) put forward a theory and proposed that stimulation is considered as a fundamental element of extroversion by which extroverts get inspired to engage and stimulate social activities on account of having intrinsic desire for sociality. Holland (1997) elucidated the type of socials person as who are sympathetic, caring, liberal, accountable and responsive. Social persons like to select actions dealing with others like updating them, coaching, curing, explaining and building (Krupnov, Novikova, & Kozhukhova, 2013). These preferences incline to human relationships competencies and let them make their choice in choosing their professions like as psychotherapy and or coaching (Basak & Ghosh, 2014). Social persons have tendency and like to support others in situations like institutional service, mutual dealings or medicinal support (Mehmood, Khan, Walsh, & Borleffs, 2013). Yang, Tsai, Kim, Cho, and Laffey (2006) made comparison of effects of mixed style of learning and online education methods on learner's level of involvement and accomplishing of tasks. They showed a constructive relation between sociability in online learning and motivation. Pachucki, Lena, and Tepper (2010) revealed student's perceptions regarding their creative contribution which they expressed during their college life. In observing effects on creativity, it was proved that daily routine experience and social interactions play a major part.

2.2 Extroversion

First time, Jung (1923) introduced the term extrovert persons were put in the category of more sociable and having good relations with other people. In EL setting, learner's expectations and requirements differ relatively, from the face to face teaching method (Kim, Song, & Lee, 2017). Introverted persons have much motivation and attraction towards online education when compared with extroverts (Rekabdar, Behrouzi, & Hakhverdian, 2015). Biner, Bink, Huffman, and Dean (1995) reported that there is no link between students personality and E-learning environments .Conversely, Kim and Schniederjans (2004) documented remarkable links among students achievement and big five modal of personality. Asendorpf and Wilpers (1998) observed that social relationships are affected by personality but its inverse relation could not be proved (Baltes & Schaie, 2013). In the past, Lucas and Diener (2001) proposed extra sensitivity of extraverts in social situations than introverts and it's a good advantage to the extroverts.

2.3 Openness to Experience (OE)

There are six factors affect the OE: Aesthetics, vision, feelings, thoughts, ethics and actions. Zuckerman (1994) stated that five of these feature position for inner types of skill seeking, while Actions are symbolized as an outer type, despite of the fact that an interest in varied experience is carved by all of them (McCrae & Costa Jr, 1989). Moreover, unique ideas are triggered by openness directly to more willingness (Walczuch & Lundgren, 2004). Openness was noted to be an appropriate predictor for proficiency of training (Barrick, Mount, & Strauss, 1993). A positive connotation between OE and sociability was noted by researchers (Furnham, Jensen, and Crump, 2008). People having high trait of OE produce more new ideas and are highly absorbing to new training and skills (Barrick & Mount, 1991). Organizational changes are adopted by them easily (LePine, 2003) that's why marketing jobs are more suited to extrovert people who adjust as per situation promptly (Wanberg & Kammeyer-Mueller, 2000). It is realized on the basis of literature review that in organizations extroversion and openness has much overtone with HRM than other traits of personality. Therefoere, in our proposed model only these traits have been included (see Figure 1).

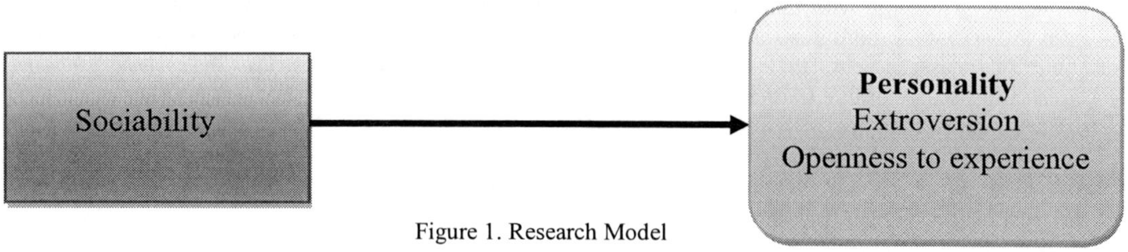

Figure 1. Research Model

3. METHODOLOGY

3.1 Sample Selection

Population comprised of students of management sciences of COMSATS Lahore & Vehari Campuses, University of Management & Technology Lahore and CFE Campus Lahore for CB while Virtual University Campuses of Lahore, Multan & Vehari for EL. In this study purposive sampling method was used keeping in view its helpfulness in taking a uniform sample, whose units share the same characteristics. In this study, sample has been made over those students of Master's program, who had completed at least 2 semesters and was jobless.

3.2 Sample Size

With the help of WHO Manual calculated a sample size of 534 students (267 students in each group), having 80% power of test and 95% confidence level with expected satisfactory performance in classroom to be 92.3% and in EL environment 84.6% by using formula as given below (Malhotra, 2008).

"n = (Zα/2+Zβ)2 * (p1(1-p1) + p2(1-p2)) / (p1-p2)2". The critical value of the Normal distribution at $\alpha/2$ is $Z\alpha/2$ is (e.g. with confidence level 95%, critical value is 1.96 and α is 0.05), while at β, $Z\beta$ is the critical value of normal distribution. Moreover, p1 and p2 are the proportions of both groups.

3.3 Instrument Development

Paper form survey was made by using questionnaire. Instruments for sociability are adopted from the work of Cheek & Buss (1981). For personality traits measurement, it is adopted from John & Srivastava (1999). In order to reduce biasness and liking/disliking of the researcher, a self- administered and structured questionnaire was used. To make it more reliable and in response items with a view of an ease to administer data, Seven Point Likert scale was adopted that contains options varying from strongly disagree to the range of strongly agree having neutral item in the middle (Jaeschke, Singer, & Guyatt, 1990).

4. RESULTS AND DISCUSSION

4.1 Results

In this cross sectional, explanatory research, 534 forms were distributed among the students. 471 questionnaires were received back which comes to 88% of the total. After scrutiny, incomplete /improperly filled 45 questionnaire forms were ruled out, so at final 426 forms were used in making final analysis which comes to the tune of 79.7% of the sample size. It contained response from 216 CB students and 214 EL.

Age of majority of the students was in the range of 20-25 years (n=360, cumulative percentage of 84.50) while only 9.39% had ages between 26-30 year bracket. There were 18 respondents from age bracket 31-35 years. Only 8 students had age 36-40 years (1.88%).

In order to evaluate the reliability of the study and to identify scale consistency, Cronebach's Alpha test was used. The value for sociability on Cronebach's Alpha value came.805, while it value was .758 for eight items Alpha scale for extroversion. Ten items scale Alpha value for openness to experience was noted to be .810. Peterson and Kim (2013) stated that, a scale is reliable if it's value of reliability coefficient is >0.7. It is evident from below given table 5, all the values of Cronebach's Alpha are within acceptable range.

For testing out the relationship of sociability with personality traits OE and extraversion, Pearson's coefficient of correlation (r) was used. An abstemiously high relationship was held between extroversion and sociability at the 0.01 level (2-tailed). Moreover, a modest positive relationship for extraversion and sociability was given by correlation value (r=.507). Same as, the coefficient of correlation value (r= .458) indicate a positive correlation between OE and sociability. Summary of the findings is given in table 1.

Table 1. Correlation/ Cronebach's Alpha

Variable	**1**	**2**	**3**
1. Sociability	**(.805)**		
2. Extroversion	.507**	**(.758)**	
3. Openness to Experience	.458**	.412**	**(.810)**

**. Correlation is significant at the 0.01 level (2-tailed). () Contains Cronebach's Alpha Values

For testing the level of sociability between two groups, the t test was undertaken. For sociability, the mean score (5.21±1.12 vs. 4.35±1.43) was high in CB in comparison with EL. Hence our first hypothesis is proved. That we acknowledged as H 1: "Level of Sociability is high in classroom base students than e-learners". Results have been combined in below table 2.

Table 2. Comparison of sociability between the Groups

	Mode of Study	N	Mean	Std. Deviation	Std. Error of Mean	*P* value
Sociability	CBES	212	5.2057	1.17798	.08090	.000
	ELES	214	4.3505	1.43215	.09790	

Alike opinion was made in terms of outcome variables. The mean score for Extroversion (4.79±1.06 vs. 4.34±1.24) and OE (5.05±1.01 vs. 4.63±1.16) was also expressively high in CB students in comparison with EL. Thus, our 2nd hypothesis H2: "Classroom base students are high on personality trait extroversion, than e-learners" proves true. It has been proved by the results that CB students are high on personality traits and OE as well. Therefore our third hypothesis H3: "Classroom base students are high on personality trait openness to experience, than e-learners" is proved as well. Results have been amassed in below table 3.

Table 3. Comparison of Extroversion and Openness to Experience between the Groups

	Mode of Study	N	Mean	Std. Deviation	Std. Error of Mean	*P* value
						.000
Extroversion	CB	212	4.7948	1.06389	.07307	
	EL	214	4.3440	1.23951	.08473	
Openness	CB	212	5.0547	1.01277	.06956	.000
	EL	214	4.6341	1.15840	.07919	

An ominously high positive impact (R square) with OE was given by regression analysis (.325 vs. .101; p=.000), in CB students in comparison with EL. Resultantly, our 4th hypothesis is proved that was stated as H4: "Sociability has a higher positive relationship with openness to experience in classroom based students than e-learners". It was also shown by regression analysis that Sociability had knowingly high positive impact (R square) with extroversion (.322 vs. .169; p=.000) in CB students while comparing with EL. Hence our 5th hypothesis is also proved that was stated as H5: "Sociability has a higher positive relationship with extroversion in class room based students than e-learners". Results have been summarized table 4 below.

Table 4. Results of Linear Regression

	Mode of Study	Dependent Variable	R Square	Standardized Coefficients Beta	*P* value
Sociability	CB	Extroversion	.322	.571	.000
	EL		.169	.416	
Sociability	CB	Openness	.325	.573	.000
	EL		.101	.324	

Hypotheses were tested with the help of t-test and regression analysis. Hypothesis were supported for $p<0.05$.

4.2 Discussion

The very purpose of the study was to compare the CB with EL with respect to learner's sociability and its impact thereof, on personality traits (extroversion, openness to experience) of students. It is evident from results that sociability level is high in students of class room based traditional education system in comparison with learners on web (Sánchez, Salinas, Contreras, & Meyer, 2011). Moreover, it is also proved that there is a positive association between sociability and openness to experience (Furnham et al., 2008). Statistically significant association of sociability with extroversion is also very clear (Bradham, Dalme, & Thompson, 2016). Thus the instant research strengthens the prior research in this sphere. However, this study is unique as it makes comparison of sociability effect between face to face learners in traditional class room system and that of web learners. Moreover, exploration about sociability effect on both the types of learner's personality has also been made in this research. Results showed that students that have high score in sociability have propensity to score high in extroversion and that of openness to experience on personalities big five model (Ibrahim, Aulls, & Shore, 2017). It is also proved that sociability has higher positive influence on personality traits of class room based students that that of e-learners. Thus, it is necessary that the teachers should adopt and use teaching methodologies having more interaction with the students and among the students.

5. CONCLUSION AND RECOMMENDATION

5.1 Conclusion

As a conclusion, it is held that sociability is a virtuous forecaster for student's personality traits and in comparison with e-learning; Class-room based education is superior in expressions of student's sociability and its effects on their personality. Though traits of personality are almost established when observed across the time, yet it is a challenging point for the decision makers to make their employees a low cost and valuable asset for the organization. For example, sociability is of key value when it is intended to hire a person for marketing job and similarly openness to experience and extroversion should be given due weightage while bringing some innovation and change or establishment of new business plan. If at this time, new hiring is not required, even then Manager must make this sorting within existing work force for not only their development rather their proper and beneficial placement as well. Now E-Learning is also established in Pakistan up to a greater extent as most of the universities are using Learning Management System (LMS). In this nexus, it is pertinent to mention Virtual University of Pakistan that is totally using LMS should make some alteration in teaching methodology by introducing a good blend learning so as to help out the students personality development and enabling them to compete the students of traditional class room based learning system.

5.2 Limitations of the Study

In the recent past, in web based education system virtual class-rooms have been introduced so as to create a sense of traditional class rooms to give students an prospect of sharing their ideas and getting rid of loneliness & shyness (Subramaniam & Kandasamy, 2011). However, such students have not been included in this study and are a limitation to this study. Therefore, recurrence of this study is needed among those students so as to effectively evaluate the effectiveness of such virtual class rooms and their role in personality development. Researchers might also include other remaining side of personality from Big Five Model, in future, so as to bring a clearer picture. Moderator variables should like social and financial position of the student's should be used. Non accounting of socioeconomic variable of is a major limitation in this study, so it must be used as moderator in future studies. A limitation point is this, the data collection was made from that of Central and Southern Punjab, in future researches, collection of sample should be made from a large area so as to bring good results and understanding from this phenomena.

ACKNOWLEDGEMENT

This paper is a result of the project "SmartEGOV: Harnessing EGOV for Smart Governance (Foundations, methods, Tools) / NORTE-01-0145-FEDER-000037", supported by Norte Portugal Regional Operational Programme (NORTE 2020), under the PORTUGAL 2020 Partnership Agreement, through the European Regional Development Fund (EFDR). It was also supported in part by funding from Tallinn University of Technology, Project B42; OGI - Open Government Intelligence project in the EU Horizon 2020 framework program, grant agreement 693849.

REFERENCES

Asendorpf, J. B., & Wilpers, S. (1998). Personality effects on social relationships. Journal of personality and social psychology, 74(6), 1531.

Baltes, P. B., & Schaie, K. W. (2013). Life-span developmental psychology: Personality and socialization: Elsevier.

Barrick, M. R., Mount, M. K., & Strauss, J. P. (1993). Conscientiousness and performance of sales representatives: Test of the mediating effects of goal setting. Journal of Applied Psychology, 78(5), 715.

Basak, R., & Ghosh, A. (2014). Personality Traits and Different Career Stages–A Study on Indian School Teachers. Procedia-Social and Behavioral Sciences, 140, 506-510.

Bhuasiri, W., Xaymoungkhoun, O., Zo, H., Rho, J. J., & Ciganek, A. P. (2012). Critical success factors for e-learning in developing countries: A comparative analysis between ICT experts and faculty. Computers & Education, 58(2), 843-855.

Biner, P. M., Bink, M. L., Huffman, M. L., & Dean, R. S. (1995). Personality characteristics differentiating and predicting the achievement of televised-course students and traditional-course students 1. American Journal of Distance Education, 9(2), 46-60.

Bradham, C. U., Dalme, F. C., & Thompson, P. J. (2016). Personality traits valued by practicing nurses and measured in nursing students. Journal of Nursing Education, 29(5), 225-232.

Buttussi, F., & Chittaro, L. (2017). Effects of different types of virtual reality display on presence and learning in a safety training scenario. IEEE transactions on visualization and computer graphics.

Carro, R. M., & Sanchez-Horreo, V. (2017). The effect of personality and learning styles on individual and collaborative learning: Obtaining criteria for adaptation. Paper presented at the Global Engineering Education Conference (EDUCON), 2017 IEEE.

Caspi, A., Chajut, E., Saporta, K., & Beyth-Marom, R. (2006). The influence of personality on social participation in learning environments. Learning and Individual Differences, 16(2), 129-144.

Delgado-García, J. M., Sánchez-Campusano, R., Fernández-Lamo, I., & Gruart, A. (2016). Dynamic Patterns of Cortical Activation During Different Types of Learning Tasks and Unpredictable Situations Advances in Cognitive Neurodynamics (V) (pp. 119-125): Springer.

Eysenck, H. J. (1981). A model for personality: Cambridge Univ Press.

Garrison, D. R. (2011). E-learning in the 21st century: A framework for research and practice: Taylor & Francis.

Gregory, S., Gregory, B., Reiners, T., Fardinpour, A., Hillier, M., Lee, M., . . . Grant, S. (2013). Virtual worlds in Australian and New Zealand higher education: Remembering the past, understanding the present and imagining the future.

Holland, J. L. (1997). Making vocational choices: A theory of vocational personalities and work environments: Psychological Assessment Resources.

Hung, M.-L., & Chou, C. (2015). Students' perceptions of instructors' roles in blended and online learning environments: A comparative study. Computers & Education, 81, 315-325.

Ibrahim, A., Aulls, M. W., & Shore, B. M. (2017). Teachers' roles, students' personalities, inquiry learning outcomes, and practices of science and engineering: The development and validation of the McGill Attainment Value for Inquiry Engagement Survey in STEM disciplines. International Journal of Science and Mathematics Education, 15(7), 1195-1215.

Jaeschke, R., Singer, J., & Guyatt, G. H. (1990). A comparison of seven-point and visual analogue scales: data from a randomized trial. Controlled clinical trials, 11(1), 43-51.

Jung, C. G. (1923). Psychological types: or the psychology of individuation.

Kim, E. B., & Schniederjans, M. J. (2004). The role of personality in web-based distance education courses. Communications of the ACM, 47(3), 95-98.

Kim, J., Song, H., & Lee, S. (2017). Extrovert and Lonely Individuals' Social TV Viewing Experiences: A Mediating and Moderating Role of Social Presence. Mass Communication and Society, 1-21.

Kreijns, K., Kirschner, P. A., & Jochems, W. (2002). The sociability of computer-supported collaborative learning environments. Educational Technology & Society, 5(1), 8-22.

Krupnov, A. I., Novikova, I. A., & Kozhukhova, Y. V. (2013). System-Functional Model of Personality Traits. Academic Journal of Interdisciplinary Studies, 2(9), 407.

LePine, J. A. (2003). Team adaptation and postchange performance: effects of team composition in terms of members' cognitive ability and personality. Journal of applied psychology, 88(1), 27.

Mai, L.-W., & Mai, L.-C. (2002). The personality attributes and leisure activities of taiwanese internet users. International Journal of Applied Marketing, 1(1), 69-82.

Malhotra, N. K. (2008). Marketing Research: An Applied Orientation, 5/E: Pearson Education India.

Masoumi, D., & Lindström, B. (2012). Quality in e-learning: a framework for promoting and assuring quality in virtual institutions. Journal of Computer Assisted Learning, 28(1), 27-41.

Mehmood, S. I., Khan, M. A., Walsh, K. M., & Borleffs, J. C. (2013). Personality types and specialist choices in medical students. Medical teacher, 35(1), 63-68.

Mroczek, D. K., & Little, T. D. (2014). Handbook of personality development: Psychology Press.

Oztekin, A., Delen, D., Turkyilmaz, A., & Zaim, S. (2013). A machine learning-based usability evaluation method for eLearning systems. Decision Support Systems, 56, 63-73.

Pachucki, M. A., Lena, J. C., & Tepper, S. J. (2010). Creativity narratives among college students: sociability and everyday creativity. The Sociological Quarterly, 51(1), 122-149.

Peterson, R. A., & Kim, Y. (2013). On the relationship between coefficient alpha and composite reliability: American Psychological Association.

Purcell, K., Heaps, A., Buchanan, J., & Friedrich, L. (2013). How teachers are using technology at home and in their classrooms. Washington, DC: Pew Research Center's Internet & American Life Project.

Rekabdar, S., Behrouzi, P., & Hakhverdian, A. (2015). The Effect of Using Metacognitive Strategies on Reading Achievement of Iranian Intermediate Extroverted vs. Introverted Learners.

Sánchez, J., Salinas, A., Contreras, D., & Meyer, E. (2011). Does the new digital generation of learners exist? A qualitative study. British Journal of Educational Technology, 42(4), 543-556.

Sánchez, M. M., Rejano, E. I., & Rodríguez, Y. T. (2001). Personality and academic productivity in the university student. Social Behavior and Personality: an international journal, 29(3), 299-305.

Sarwar, A., Hameed, S., & Aftab, H. (2013). Study to Explore the Impact of Personality Traits on Employee Turnover in Public and Private Sector. Middle-East Journal of Scientific Research, 16(9), 1249-1254.

Sharma, S. K., & Kitchens, F. L. (2004). Web services architecture for m-learning. Electronic Journal of e-Learning, 2(1), 203-216.

Subramaniam, N. K., & Kandasamy, M. (2011). The virtual classroom: A catalyst for institutional transformation. Australasian journal of educational technology, 27(8), 1388-1412.

Surjono, H. D. (2009). The Development of an adaptive eLearning System based on learning style Diversity of Visual-Auditory-Kinesthetic. Paper presented at the International Seminar on ICT for Education, Yogyakarta State University, Indonesia.

Tarhini, A., Hone, K., Liu, X., & Tarhini, T. (2017). Examining the moderating effect of individual-level cultural values on users' acceptance of E-learning in developing countries: a structural equation modeling of an extended technology acceptance model. Interactive Learning Environments, 25(3), 306-328.

Walczuch, R., & Lundgren, H. (2004). Psychological antecedents of institution-based consumer trust in e-retailing. Information & Management, 42(1), 159-177.

Wanberg, C. R., & Kammeyer-Mueller, J. D. (2000). Predictors and outcomes of proactivity in the socialization process. Journal of applied psychology, 85(3), 373.

Zuckerman, M. (1994). Behavioral expressions and biosocial bases of sensation seeking: Cambridge university press.

AN ANALYSIS OF INTERNET OF THINGS TECHNOLOGIES FOCUSED IN SMART HOMES

Renato Garcés, Jorge L. Rosero and Ángel Jaramillo-Alcázar
Facultad de Ingeniería y Ciencias Agropecuarias, Universidad de Las Américas, Pichincha, Quito EC170125, Ecuador

ABSTRACT

The Internet of Things (IoT) is quickly becoming a reality, connecting everything around us to the Internet, transforming ordinary objects or devices in smart devices, which act according to conditions or parameters. Through this revolution of Internet, the home is becoming smart. This article introduced the technologies required for Smart Home (SH) IoT deployment, summarizing some applications and domains and proposing a new graphical IoT classification, in order to identify where the technologies could be implemented. Also, defines some analysis parameters for a SH deployment based on some studies and summarizes the technologies with these parameters in a table. It concludes explaining the main characteristics of technologies for SH and the growing technology.

KEYWORDS

IoT, IoT Technologies, IoT Applications, Analysis Parameters

1. INTRODUCTION

Nowadays, we live in a revolutionary world motivated by a new concept, IoT. This is a new technological model that refers to everyday objects connection to Internet, so they can be identified and managed by other devices. This concept was proposed by Kevin Ashton at MIT's Auto-ID Center in 1999, where RFID field and sensor technologies investigations were made (Cisco, 2017). Through this growing wave of IoT, we could transform objects or devices, which had a preprogrammed automatic behavior, in intelligent ones that send and receive information to and from Internet respectively. Those allow them to act according to certain conditions or interests (Roselli et-al, 2015). These data are relevant because their impact will generate endless opportunities in different areas in which they are implemented, such as business sector, health, homes, smart cities, etc. (Ma, 2014; Kafle, 2016).

By 2020 is expected that 200,000 million devices will be connected, which means that there would be 26 devices by each person (Cisco, 2017). The IoT purpose is simple and oriented to connect objects around us between them and directly to the Internet (Roselli et-al, 2015; Mayordomo et-al, 2011). So, it is necessary to care about the internal objects inside the home, such as appliances, services, like the bulbs that are already connected to the Internet. Also there are external objects like sensors, being the most visible and almost all the time connected to the intelligent cities. These devices are constantly measuring external parameters such as temperature, energy, light, humidity, etc.

Over the last years, the IoT researches have been growing thanks to the penetration of the technology. Here is an overview with the most relevant works referent to the topic of this paper. In 2011, (Mayordomo et-al, 2011) described the main challenges and some technologies that can contribute to make the IoT happen. Also, (Shen and Liu, 2011) analyzed the technologies, applications and issues of IoT. In 2012, Yuxi Liu and Guohui Zhou introduce the concept of this technology, the basic properties, characteristics and discussed the key technologies. (Liu and Zhou, 2011). In 2014, (Suresh et-al, 2014) analyzed the history, the way of deployment, performance and applications. The technology evolution, the difference respect to Internet and also summarizes the challenges of IoT (Ma, 2014).

Furthermore, in 2015 (Kraijak and Tuwanut, 2015) presented an overview of IoT, generic architecture and protocols, applications, security and privacy concerns, implementation and its future trends. Also, (Roselli et-al, 2015) summarized the most important technologies (RFID, Green Electronics, Wireless Power Transfer and Energy Harvesting), concurrently participating to build the technological platform needed for an implementation of IoT. An overview of the IoT with emphasis on enabling technologies, protocols and application issues was made (Al-Fuqaha et-al, 2015). In 2016, Sujin Issac Samuel made a review of connectivity challenges in IoT SH, describing the standard protocols used in SH network, discussing the connectivity challenges and the protocols and finally giving the typical infrastructure for the smart home network (Samuel, 2016). Then (Shah and Yaqoob, 2016) published a paper that give a basic understanding of IoT to the reader, its technologies and applications and the open issues that is facing which needed to resolve for near future.

In this paper we are going to analyze IoT technologies, the ways of deployment, performance analysis and applications. We propose some analysis parameters for IoT deployment in SH. The paper is organized as follows: Sections 2 describes the actually IoT technologies with some technical parameters and applications. Section 3 shows IoT applications and some classifications. Some analysis parameters for IoT deployment are described in Section 4. Finally, Section V concludes this study and proposing some future work.

2. IOT TECHNOLOGIES

2.1 Radio Frequency Identification – RFID

It is a wireless technology, which uses electromagnetic or electrostatic coupling in a specific portion of the electromagnetic spectrum, to identify a person, animal or object (Fernandez et-al, 2006). An RFID system is generally composed by an antenna, an integrated circuit and a battery (Fernandez et-al, 2006). It uses two transmission classes: inductive coupling and passive backscatter. The first one is used at low frequencies (LF) between 125-134 KHz and high frequencies (HF) at 13.56 MHz, respectively. While at higher frequencies, such as UHF frequencies in the ranges of 433 MHz, 865-956 MHz and 2.45 GHz the passive backscatter is used. The main applications of RFID are transport and logistics, manufacturing, retailing, agriculture, health care, medicine, payment transactions and inventory control (Fernandez et-al, 2006; Jia et-al, 2012).

The main advantages of RFID are that the line of sight is not necessary thanks to the location of the label is less restricted. Furthermore, there is a greater reading range, compared to other similar technologies. In addition, labels may have read-write memory. Also the RFID tag can store large amounts of data. Moreover, this technology facilitates the unique identification of objects and labels are less sensitive to adverse conditions. However, this technology faces several challenges such as collision problems that may exist between tags and readers, due to electromagnetic interference. Another challenge is the security and privacy of unprotected tags that may be vulnerable to listening, traffic analysis, forgery, or denial of service. That is why many researchers and scientists are currently working on implementing low-cost security and privacy protocols, because a lot of lightweight solutions have been proposed, but they remain expensive and vulnerable and do not solve security problems (Jia et-al, 2012).

2.2 Near Field Communication – NFC

This short-range wireless connectivity technology facilitates transactions, digital content exchange and one-touch device connection. It uses magnetic field induction for these purposes, operates at 13.56 MHz and has two modes of operation: active and passive. The first one, generates its own radio frequency field. It allows to read and send information. The second one uses the radio frequency field, generated by an active device and contains information that other authorized devices can read (Kumar, 2010). Moreover, NFC has two roles that define how active and passive devices respond during communication. The first one is, the Reader/Writer and card and the second one is the Initiator and target role. The first role happens between an active device that sends a request and receives information and a passive device that answers that request sending information. The Reader/Writer is the active and the NFC card is the passive device. In the second role, NFC can create peer-to-peer sharing between devices. The device that sends the invitation is the initiator and the one that receives the instructions and responds, is the target (NFC org, 2017).

The current applications include the use of wireless data transfer such as wireless keys, electronic money, electronic tickets, data documents and mobile commerce. On top of the current applications, it also applies to the use of touching to confirm and act upon the users request such as touch and-go, touch-and-confirm, touch and-connect, and touch-and explore (NFC org, 2017; Fayloga et-al, 2007). In this context, security is one of the great challenges of technology because data transferred through radio waves can be interrupted, analyzed and modified. In the other hand, to avoid collisions NFC use the principle listen before talk, when the initiator needs to communicate, first make sure that there is no other communication in progress to avoid an interruption. However, if two targets respond at the same time, the collision will be detected by the initiator (Kumar, 2010).

2.3 Bluetooth

It is a standard wireless technology for the exchange of information at close range. The IEEE standardizes Bluetooth like 802.15.1. This allows to create a personal area network (PAN) of devices and operates in 2.4 GHz free band. When two or more devices want to communicate, they should first be paired. Bluetooh devices communications take place in a piconet network which operates in a short-range. One device takes the role of master when a connection is established, while other devices are slaves. Those kind of networks are dynamic and automatically established while devices go inside or outside of a coverage area (Bluetooth, 2017).

The way people and devices are connected is being transformed by Bluetooth in many markets such as: automotive, consumer electronics, home automation, medical health, smart phones, PC peripherals and wearables. (Silicon Labs, 2017; Bluetooth, 2017).

2.4 Weightless

Understood like a wireless technology that offers connectivity for low-power wide area networks (LPWAN) designed specifically for IoT. It operates in the free band of 1 GHz and also in licensed spectrum (Weightless, 2016). The technology could be applied in many fields like smart grid, automotive, transport, healthcare, asset tracking and smart cities. (Webb, 2012).

2.5 Zig Bee

As a requirement for low-power for machine to machine (M2M) networks, an open global standard technology called Zig Bee was developed. It operates with IEEE 802.15.4 physical radio specification and unlicensed bands, including 2.4 GHz, 900 MHz and 868 MHz (Zigbee, 2004). This system has three type of devices: the coordinator, the router and the final device. The first one, forms the root of the network tree and can connect to other networks; there is only one per network. The second one, runs application functions and can act as an intermediate router by transporting data from other devices. The last one, only has functionality to communicate with the parent node. It does not relay data from other devices. They are less expensive to manufacture than a coordinator or router because they require minimal amount of memory (Zigbee Alliance, 2017).

Zigbee is being deployed in smart homes with devices that allow home automation, security and energy management applications to home. Also is used in residential and commercial lighting applications. Finally is used in industries to monitor, control, inform and automate the delivery and use of energy and water in the industries (Zigbee Alliance, 2017).

2.6 Wi-Fi

This network technology uses radio waves to allow data transfer at high speed over short distances. The term Wi-Fi suggests wireless fidelity (Wireless Fidelity). It operates in the 900 MHz, 2.4 GHz and 5.8 GHz radio spectrum bands. Wi-Fi networks do not have wired physical connections between the transmitter and the receiver, the transmission is done using radiofrequency (RF) technology, in which an antenna transform an RF supplied current into an electromagnetic field is that is capable of propagating through the air. The fundamental element of any wireless network is the access point (AP), whose main objective is to emit a signal that devices can detect and tune. For this, the devices must have wireless network adapters (Wi-Fi Alliance, 2017). Thanks to its massive penetration, Wi-Fi is been deployed in remote wireless monitoring and management of lights, climate control, appliances, door and garage locks, manufacturing control, maintenance, medical devices and hundreds of more applications (STMicroelectronics, 2015).

2.7 Z-Wave

It is an RF-based interoperable wireless technology specially designed for control, monitoring in residential and light commercial environments. Z-wave is based on a mesh topology and operates in the sub band of 1GHz, defined specifically for each country. The physical and media access control (MAC) layers are defined by ITU-T recommendation G.9959. Each device in the network could act like a signal repeater. The devices can communicate point-to-point up to 36 meters, and can achieve 100 meters with signal jump. A Z-wave network can support up to 232 devices (Z-Wave, 2017). All networks should be identified by an ID and each device must have a node ID. The network ID, has a length of 4 bytes and is the common identification of all nodes belonging to the logical network. The node ID has a length of 1 byte and is the address of the device. Some of the applications fields of Z-wave are house management, home security, media and smart devices. A central controller is required to configure and control a network. (Smarthome, 2017).

2.8 X10

This communications protocol operates through domestic power lines and is low bandwidth. The technology supports 256 devices on a single power line, house codes are written from letter A to P and each unit has a decimal number between 1 and 16 (Buyya and Dastjerdi, 2016). X10 devices send around one command per second, and the commands require less than are as 1/100 of the bandwidth of a dial-up connection. These commands are as simple as "Device A1: turn on". An X10 system is made up of 3 types of devices: the controllers, the wireless controllers and the modules. The first type devices send addresses and commands through the network to control the modules. The second ones transmit a signal to a central receiver, which transforms it into X10 signal for the network. The last devices, control modules of lights and equipment. There are four different types of them and they are: plug-in modules, integrated switches, micro modules and modules for DIN rail mounting. Modules receive the commands from the controllers through the network (Smarthome, 2017).

2.9 Long Term Evolution LTE

Long Term Evolution has been consolidated as one of the fastest technologies available (Verizon, 2017). LTE or E-UTRAN is the access part of the Evolved Packet System (EPS). High spectral efficiency, high peak data rates, short response time and also flexibility in frequency and bandwidth are the main requirements for the new access network. The EPS is based on IP. Real-time services as well as data services will be carried over the IP protocol. The IP address is assigned when the mobile is switched on and is released when the mobile is switched off (3GPP, 2017). LTE offers new business opportunities to non-traditional technology manufacturers based on Internet-connected devices that have never been connected before. These elements can create great efficiency in homes, businesses, transportation, energy, agriculture, health care, security and more. The LTE IP architecture is ideal for IoT applications thanks to the built-in security along with robust and scalable traffic management capabilities. However the main differentiator for LTE in IoT is the economic factor because it is significantly more efficient than 2G and 3G and therefore the transport of data in LTE can be realized a lower cost per bit (Tassin, 2017). LTE technology enable a wide range of IoT services, many providers are developing their own solutions in many fields like wearables, smart cities, smart homes, media devices and other solutions (Qualcomm, 2017). Nokia for example, offers IoT solutions like vehicle telematics, agriculture, tracking, smart grid, smart metering, smart city, smart home and medical devices (Nokia, 2017).

2.10 EnOcean

It is a wireless technology that uses a combination of power collection and very low power wireless communications. It allows the creation of innovative sensor solutions without the need for maintenance. It was developed in 2012 and standardized in the ISO / IEC 14543.3.1.x standard. Through which it defines the frequency of operation of the devices according to geographical location as follows: 868 MHz for Europe and China, 902 MHz for North America and 928 MHz for Japan. The modules use the principle of energy collection, in which they derive energy from the environment, to feed the different sensors. The technology includes power converters that translate variations of movement, light or temperature into electrical energy. EnOcean offers solutions for sustainable building and home automation and so to make buildings more energy-efficient, more flexible and lower in cost (EnOcean Alliance, 2017).

3. IOT APPLICATIONS

The IoT has been transforming the way we live, there are several fields in which IoT can be implemented. However, for a better understanding, some authors have decided to categorize it into many segments. Gubbi, Buyya, Marusic and Palaniswami categorize the IoT in Personal and Home, Utility and Mobile. In the first category, they said that the collected information is used by the owner of the network and should be considered health care devices, control of household items such as air conditioners, refrigerators, washing machines, etc. The Utility category, where the collected information is used in the optimization of services. It is generally used in companies to monitor the factory resources such as energy, water use, etc. Finally, Mobile is focus on smart transportation and smart logistics (Gubbi et-al, 2013).

The IoT should be divided in consumer, commercial and industrial. Consumer refers to smart phones, smart cars, smart clocks, and also smart thermostats, smart appliances, smoke detectors, etc. In addition, commercial focuses on inventory control, interconnected medical devices, manufacturing line trackers and other components that help businesses run better. The last class includes aspects such as electrical meters, pipe monitors, manufacturing robots and other devices and systems that help the production process and give manufacturers the ability to act quickly and preventively (Buijserd, 2017).

Furthermore, (Shree, 2017) focuses more in a smart home and talks about wearable, media, home automation and smart appliances. Wearable refers to smart phones, personal Bluetooth devices and other devices that together can form a PAN. Media is considered a set of devices that allow the operation of music and movies. Next class allow us to monitor and manage our home remotely. Additionally, smart appliances will be presented in every home in the near future and every moment there is a requirement to fill, simply press buttons or click to send a request to the local vendor or any online store.

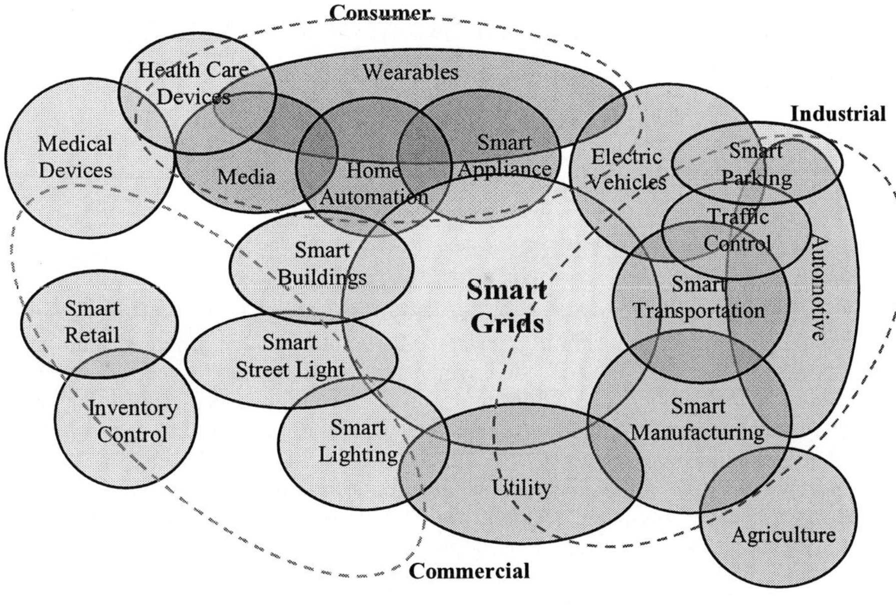

Figure 1. IoT Applications involved in Smart Cities

Finally, (Sundmaeker et-al, 2010) stablished three specific domains: industry, environment and society. Industry refers to transactions (financial/commercial) between companies and organizations. The second class refers to protection, monitoring and development of natural resources. The last class refers about development and inclusion of people, cities and society. Applications such as building & home automation, smart cities, smart manufacturing, automotive, wearables and health care could be deployed with IoT (Texas Instruments, 2017). For (Intel, 2017), the main IoT applications are automotive, retail, industrial, smart video, energy, smart buildings, health care and smart cities.

Additionally, these authors classified IoT in different domains depending of the network characteristics, the applications or simply based in the IoT solutions that they provide. Therefore, for our opinion the principal domains of IoT are consumer, commercial and industrial where all the applications in these IoT domains are directly related, as shown in Figure 1. While some applications could be part of one, two or three domains: in consumer & commercial, we considered media which is related with smart home, smart buildings and sometimes with health care devices. On the other hand, a wearable could be a health care device but a health care device is not necessarily a wearable. In addition, in commercial & industrial the inventory control helps to businesses and is necessary in industries. Finally, smart grids could be implemented in smart homes, smart buildings and also in companies to provide an efficient energy resources. All of these applications we could find in a Smart City. Consequently, Table 1 is an overview about the technologies studied in Section 2 and the IoT applications where they could be implemented.

Table 1. IoT Classification and Technologies

IoT Applications	**IoT Technologies**									
	RFID	NFC	Bluetooth	Weightless	Zigbee	Wi-Fi	Z-Wave	X10	LTE	EnOcean
Media			X			X	X			
Wearable		X	X			X				
Home Automation	X	X	X		X	X	X	X	X	X
Smart Appliances	X		X	X		X			X	
Inventory Control	X	X								
Health Care Devices	X	X	X	X	X	X			X	
Automotive	X	X	X	X		X			X	
Agriculture	X			X					X	
Smart Cities	X	X	X	X	X	X	X	X	X	X
Smart Grids			X	X	X		X		X	
Smart Manufacturing				X	X	X			X	
Smart Transportation				X		X			X	

4. ANALYSIS PARAMETERS

Choosing connectivity for an IoT project requires careful consideration of their characteristics, advantages and disadvantages that a specific technology offers. Many authors have proposed analysis parameters that should be considered before an IoT deployment. According to (Samuel, 2016) interoperability, self-management, maintainability, bandwidth and power consumption are critical for an implementation. Al-Fuqaha et al, mentioned the following parameters: availability, reliability, performance, management, scalability, interoperability and security (Al-Fuqaha et-al, 2015). Additionally, they have proposed parameters for industrial IoT such as: technical challenges, standardization, information security and privacy protection, energy, latency, throughput, scalability and topology (XU et-al, 2014). Consequently, we decided to choose some measurable parameters, which do not depend of the IoT application, from the studies above which we considered important for a home IoT deployment. These are described below:

A. Coverage

It refers to the ability to cover a certain distance. This factor must be chosen based on the application of IoT that is going to be implemented. For example, in a home environment the coverage required is less than in an industrial environment.

B. Frequency Band.

It is a specific range of frequencies in the radio frequency (RF) spectrum. The band usage is regulate by the International Telecommunication Union (ITU).

C. Standard

It is a set of rules that products must have, procedures or research that generate an environment of stability and quality for the end user benefit. It is very important for a technology to have standards in order to not be linked only to certain equipment or manufacturers. And also allow interoperability.

D. Capacity

It is one of the great challenges of IoT. Due to increasing numbers of people and devices, the amount of data has increased considerably resulting in the need for bandwidth in modern homes.

E. Topology

It refers to how nodes are connected in the network and how they communicate. The network topology impacts directly in the performance and cost of the network. Also, knowing the topology helps to solve connectivity problems easily.

Table 2. IoT Technologies with Analysis Parameters

IoT Technology	Coverage [m]	Frequency Band [Hz]	Standard	Capacity [bps]	Topology
RFID	0.1 to 200	125K - 134 K (LF), 13.56 M (HF), 433 M, 865M - 956 M, 2,45 G	ISO 18000	400 K	P2P
NFC	less than 0.2	13.56 M	ISO/IEC 14443 or ISO/IEC 18000-3	400 K	P2P
Bluetooth	1 to 10	2.4 G	802.15.1	4 M	Star
Weightless	2 K	1 G		200 to 100 K	Cellular Network
Zigbee	10 to 20	2.4 G, 868 M and 900 M	802.15.4	250 K	Star, Mesh, Tree
Wi-Fi	32 in, 95 out	2.4 G	802.11	150 M to 600 M	Star
Z-Wave	36 to 100	908.4 M and 916 M	UIT-t G.9959	100 K	Mesh
X10	15	120 K		120	Mesh
LTE	variable	700 M to 2.7 G		300 M	Cellular Network
EnOcean	30 in, 300 out	868 M, 902 M and 928 M	ISO/IEC 14543.3.1.x	125 K	Mesh

Table 2 is a brief summary of the technologies with our analysis parameters. On the other hand, there are also non-easily quantifiable parameters that need to be considered and depend directly of the IoT application such as: energy consumption, security, scalability and cost. Nowadays, Bluetooth and Wi-Fi are the more suitable technologies for IoT consumer applications. The main advantage of Wi-Fi is the existing infrastructure in homes for connection, however a major limitation is its high power consumption. On the other hand, the main advantage for Bluetooth is its low power consumption but it does not have an internet gateway. Therefore, there are already advances in this field. In the near future, LTE will be the dominant technology in almost all IoT applications fields as a result of the constant cellular networks growing. Nowadays, it is not the dominant technology because the high cost per bit that an IoT deployment should represent for the end user.

5. CONCLUSIONS

The need to interconnect devices to the Internet is increasing every day. Therefore, IoT will give us the ability to automate, monitor and control everything around us. In this analysis, we review the current technologies that enables the deployment of IoT. In addition, some quantifiable analysis parameters were exposed that must be evaluated before a specific deployment. The infrastructure installed in the homes by Internet Service Providers would provide a great advantage for Wi-Fi technology consequently end nodes and access points should be implemented to allow a greater growth of the network if it is required. Most of the reviewed technologies above are wireless, therefore they give greater mobility and availability to end users. These technologies also operate in free frequency bands, which do not require special permission to be implemented and subsequently used. Consequently, the implementation of devices and systems with these technologies are ideal for homes, because we can have equipment transmitting on these frequencies without having to ask for permission and the payment associated with its use. In addition, the technologies mentioned above have the ability to complement each other in order to build an IoT complete system and soon Internet of Everything. Finally, it should be emphasized that no technology is better than another one, just one of them may be suitable or not for certain deployments. This paper provides the basic guidelines and a macro view of the technologies that allow the interconnection of household devices to the Internet, for the future development of devices by appliances manufacturers. In a future work, we would analyze technologies with non-easily quantifiable parameters presented above in a specific IoT application. Before a deployment, it is necessary to make a deep review of the technology, advantages and limitations depending of the final device use.

REFERENCES

Al-Fuqaha, A., Guizani, M., Mohammadi, M., Aledhari, M. and Ayyash, M. (2015). Internet of Things: A Survey on Enabling Technologies, Protocols, and Applications. *IEEE Communications Surveys & Tutorials*, 17(4), pp. 2347-2376.

Bluetooh (2017). *Bluetooth | Bluetooth Technology Website.* [online] Bluetooth.com. Available at: goo.gl/2c5dDF [Accessed 22 Aug. 2017].

Buijserd, R. (2017). *Dividing the world in 3 IoT Categories - Data Management Experts.* [online] Data Management Experts. Available at: https://goo.gl/xKnCGi [Accessed 22 Aug. 2017].

Buyya, R. and Vahid Dastjerdi, A. (2016). *Internet of things.*

Cisco (2017). [online] Available at: https://goo.gl/mrdGUx [Accessed 22 Aug. 2017].

EnOcean Alliance (2017). [online] Available at https://goo.gl/dctLvz [Accessed 22 Aug. 2017].

Fayloga, R., Logan, V. and Ramirez, D. (2007). *Near Field Communication.* [online] Available at: https://goo.gl/7Ez8gJ [Accessed 23 Aug. 2017].

Fernández., Rodriguez, C. and Muñoz (2006).

Gubbi, J., Buyya, R., Marusic, S. and Palaniswami, M. (2013). Internet of Things (IoT): A vision, architectural elements, and future directions. *Future Generation Computer Systems*, 29(7), pp.1645-1660.

Intel (2017). The Internet of Things (IoT) Starts with Intel Inside®. [online] Intel. Available at: https://goo.gl/MtwpH9 [Accessed 23 Aug. 2017].

Jia, X., Feng, Q., Fan, T. and Lei, Q. (2012). RFID technology and its applications in Internet of Things (IoT). *2012 2nd International Conference on Consumer Electronics, Communications and Networks (CECNet).*

Kafle, V., Fukushima, Y. and Harai, H. (2016). Internet of things standardization in ITU and prospective networking technologies. *IEEE Communications Magazine*, 54(9), pp.43-49.

Kraijak, S. and Tuwanut, P. (2015). A survey on internet of things architecture, protocols, possible applications, security, privacy, real-world implementation and future trends. *2015 IEEE 16th International Conference on Communication Technology (ICCT).*

Kumar, A. (2011). Near field communication

Jianguo Ma (2014). Internet-of-Things: Technology evolution and challenges. *2014 IEEE MTT-S International Microwave Symposium (IMS2014).*

Mayordomo, I., Spies, P., Meier, F., Otto, S., Lempert, S., Bernhard, J. and Pflaum, A. (2011). Emerging technologies and challenges for the Internet of Things. *2011 IEEE 54th International Midwest Symposium on Circuits and Systems (MWSCAS).*

MX Alliance (2004). *ZIGBEE – AN INTRODUCTION.* [online] Available at: https://goo.gl/nUqJTH [Accessed 22 Aug. 2017].

NFC Org (2017). *About Near Field Communication.* [online] Available at: https://goo.gl/RvAs9c [Accessed 22 Aug. 2017].

Nokia (2017). *LTE Evolution for IoT Connectivity.* [online] Resources.ext.nokia.com. Available at: https://goo.gl/ZF17vq [Accessed 23 Aug. 2017].

Qualcomm (2017). IoT | Internet of Things Devices & Security | Qualcomm. [online] Qualcomm. Available at: https://goo.gl/NiympF [Accessed 23 Aug. 2017].

Roselli, L., Mariotti, C., Mezzanotte, P., Alimenti, F., Orecchini, G., Virili, M. and Carvalho, N. (2015). Review of the present technologies concurrently contributing to the implementation of the Internet of Things (IoT) paradigm: RFID, Green Electronics, WPT and Energy Harvesting. 2015 IEEE Topical Conference on Wireless Sensors and Sensor Networks (WiSNet).

Samuel, S. (2016). A review of connectivity challenges in IoT-smart home. 2016 3rd MEC International Conference on Big Data and Smart City (ICBDSC).

Shen, G. and Liu, B. (2011). The visions, technologies, applications and security issues of Internet of Things. 2011 International Conference on E-Business and E-Government (ICEE).

Shree, P. (2017). Categorizing Internet of Things and Understanding them better. [online] Startup Success Stories. Available at: https://goo.gl/2iPZPt [Accessed 23 Aug. 2017].

Silicon Labs (2017). [online] The many flavors of bluetooth IoT connectivity. Available at: https://goo.gl/ezZHTg [Accessed 23 Aug. 2017].

Smarthome (2017). What is ZWave? | Z-Wave Home Automation Products | Z-Wave Home Control. [online] Smarthome.com. Available at: https://goo.gl/yuZj2B [Accessed 23 Aug. 2017].

STMicroelectronics (2015). Wireless connectivity for IoT application. [online] Available at: https://goo.gl/xYAH3j [Accessed 23 Aug. 2017].

Suresh, P., Daniel, J., Parthasarathy, V. and Aswathy, R. (2014). A state of the art review on the Internet of Things (IoT) history, technology and fields of deployment. 2014 International Conference on Science Engineering and Management Research (ICSEMR).

Sundmaeker, H., Guillemin, P., Friess, P., & Woelfflé, S. (2010). Vision and challenges for realising the Internet of Things. Cluster of European Research Projects on the Internet of Things, European Commision, 3(3), 34-36.

Tassin, K. (2017). LTE and the Internet of Things. [online] 3gpp.org. Available at: https://goo.gl/Tje2AK [Accessed 23 Aug. 2017].

Texas Instruments (2017). Application areas for the internet of things. [online] Available at: https://goo.gl/JD49ZL [Accessed 23 Aug. 2017].

Verizon (2017). 4g lte: Here and abroad. [online] Available at: https://goo.gl/jYgDFi [Accessed 23 Aug. 2017].

Webb, W. (2012). Understanding Weightless: Technology, Equipment, and Network Deployment for M2M Communications in White Space. Cambridge University Press.

Weightless, S. I. G. LPWAN Technology Decisions: 17 Critical Features. 2016-12-07]. https://goo.gl/E2bmtE

Wi-fi.Alliance (2017). History | Wi-Fi Alliance. [online] Wi-fi.org. Available at: https://goo.gl/VUwFBE [Accessed 23 Aug. 2017].

Xu, L., He, W. and Li, S. (2014). Internet of Things in Industries: A Survey. IEEE Transactions on Industrial Informatics, 10(4), pp.2233-2243.

Zigbee Alliance (2017). The Alliance | Zigbee Alliance. [online] Zigbee.org. Available at: https://goo.gl/v12hdW [Accessed 23 Aug. 2017].

Z-Wave (2017). About z-wave technology - z-wave alliance. [online] Available at: https://goo.gl/zs5PtW [Accessed 23 Aug. 2017].

3GPP (2017). LTE. [online] 3gpp.org. Available at: https://goo.gl/uQcYyq [Accessed 23 Aug. 2017].

HOW DID THEY START USING OSS? — SURVEY OF OSS DEVELOPERS IN JAPAN —

Jun Iio[1], Kenji Tsukagoshi[2], Masayuki Hatta[3] and Ko Kazaana[4]
[1]*Chuo University, 742-1 Higashinakano, Hachioji-shi, Tokyo 192-0393, Japan*
[2]*Gakushuin University, 1-5-1 Mejiro, Toshima-ku Tokyo 171-0031, Japan*
[3]*Surugadai University, 698 Azu, Hannou-shi Saitama 357-0046, Japan*
[4]*Cybozu, Inc., 2-7-1 Nihonbashi, Chuo-ku Tokyo 103-6028, Japan*

ABSTRACT

An investigation about the relationship between Free/Libre and Open Source Software (FLOSS) developers and their information sources on FLOSS was conducted. In the questionnaire, we asked several questions, such as the year when you got to know FLOSS, the FLOSS you learned for the first time, the way you learned about it. The results disclosed the changes of technological issues as well as the trends of information sources. In this paper, based on the results of the questionnaire, we discussed these changes over the last three decades.

KEYWORDS

Developers' Survey, Chronicles of FLOSS, Magazines as Information Sources

1. INTRODUCTION

In the current IT industry, Open-Source Software (OSS) has been commoditized. It is unimaginable that OSS components are not used in system construction and/or system integration. In addition, information on OSS can be easily obtained from the Internet. OSS, which has its roots in free software, was rapidly developed from the late 1990 's to the 2000' s. However, much of the information at the time was undocumented, especially in Japan. Therefore, clues to know the situation at the time are being rapidly lost.

To keep such information as a form of explicit knowledge instead of implicit knowledge, we launched the FLOSS stories project (Iio, *et al.* 2013) in the late 2013. In our project, we are conducting interviews with the person who knows the state of the time and topics, and are working on collecting it as an oral history. As a part of this project, we conducted a questionnaire survey on OSS developers in Japan asking several questions, e.g. what made OSS developers know about OSS, and what was the source of information about OSS at that time.

2. RELATED WORK

Investigation of OSS developers' actual situation has been one of the main topic of FLOSS research. There were comprehensive surveys such as FLOSS survey (Ghosh, *et al.* 2002), FLOSS-US survey (David, *et al.* 2003), FLOSS-JP/Asia survey (Shimizu, *et al.* 2004), and FLOSS 2013 survey (Robles, *et al.* 2013), which was replicated version of the original FLOSS survey.

Their research questions contained many topics, ranging from not only profile information, such as, gender, age, occupation, academic background, but also their thoughts on licensing, development platform, experience of contribution to FLOSS projects, motivation, expectation, views regarding FLOSS development. Because of that, their questions had become quite complicated. In addition, under current standards, some questions are difficult to ask from the viewpoint of privacy protection.

There have been many studies on FLOSS contributor motivation to participate in OSS development. Von Krogh *et al.* (Von Krogh, *et al.* 2012) summarized the result of their intensive literature review on this topic. In this topic area, researchers have their interests on contributors and developers in the context of software engineering. For instance, Hannebauer and Gruhn focused on the newcomers to FLOSS projects (Hannebauer and Gruhn 2016). However, we have many kind of contributors who provide their talent besides writing source code. Especially in Japan, document translators from English to Japanese are one of the typical contributors. Therefore, we must care about such contributors if we try to disclose the reality of activities regarding FLOSS communities.

3. OVERVIEW OF THE SURVEY

In this section, the items we asked in the questionnaire and how we conducted the survey are described.

3.1 Research Questions

In this survey, we have focused on the relationship between OSS developers in Japan and their information sources.

First question is how and when did they get involved in the OSS development and various activities in OSS communities. Hence, the questionnaire asked the respondents to recall the typical OSS they had met first.

Second question is their information sources at that time. The trend of information sources on information technologies has been changed over these three decades. We wanted to confirm the transformation of that from the respondents' real experiences.

The questions listed in the questionnaire sheet were followings:

1. When did you get to know OSS?
2. What was the OSS which you learned for the first time?
3. How did you learn about it?
4. What were the major information source about OSS at that time?
5. What was the IT related magazine you were reading at that time?

In addition to above questions, we asked gender, age, and occupation as a profile information of respondent.

3.2 Survey Method

The questionnaire was conducted in an event named "Open Source Conference (OSC) 2016 Tokyo/Fall" held at Meisei University, Tokyo, Japan, on 5th and 6th November 2016. The questionnaire was printed in a sheet of A4 paper, and we asked visitors to fill in the form of our questionnaire.

Note that the questionnaire was conducted in Japanese, that is, the questions were written in Japanese and participants wrote their answer in Japanese, as well. All the representations of questions and answers in this paper are translated to Japanese to be acceptable for the foreign people other than Japanese.

4. RESULT OF THE SURVEY

The results of the questionnaire and considerations based on it are shown in this section.

First, demographic data of the responses are explained here. We collected 106 samples (99 males, 6 females, and 1 other). The age of respondents covers wide range from 10 to 62 years. The most frequent age groups were 40–49 years with 34 participants (32 %), 50-59 years with 24 participants (23 %), 30–39 years with 21 participants (20 %), and 20–29 years with 18 participants (17 %).

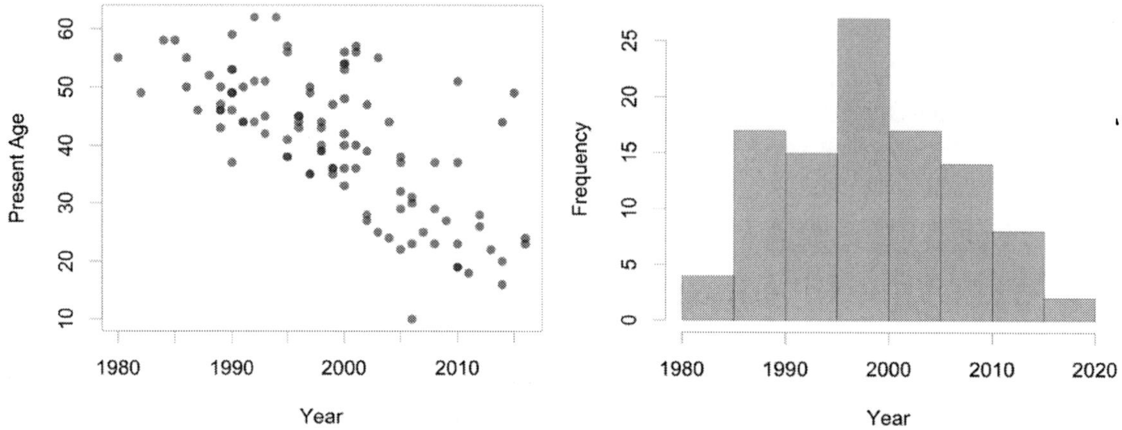

Figure 1. Scatter diagram of years when they got to know OSS for the first time and respondents' present ages (left); histogram of the years (right)

4.1 Q1: Year and Age When They Learned OSS

The responses of question one (Q1), which asked the year of learning OSS, are shown in the Figure 1. The left part of Figure 1 is a scatter graph of answers for Q1 and respondents' present ages. The right part of Figure 1 is a histogram of the years in the responses of Q1.

As you can see in the figure, the years distributed from late 80s' to current, extensively. One peek can be found at late 90s', and it corresponds approximately to the period of the emergence of OSS.

We can discuss their ages when they met OSS, as well. Figure 2 indicates the histogram of ages when they got to know OSS. The ages were calculated from the answer of Q1 and present age in their profile information. Obviously, the histogram has a pointed peak around 20 years old. This implies that many people learn OSS at universities, technical schools, or that when they go out into the world.

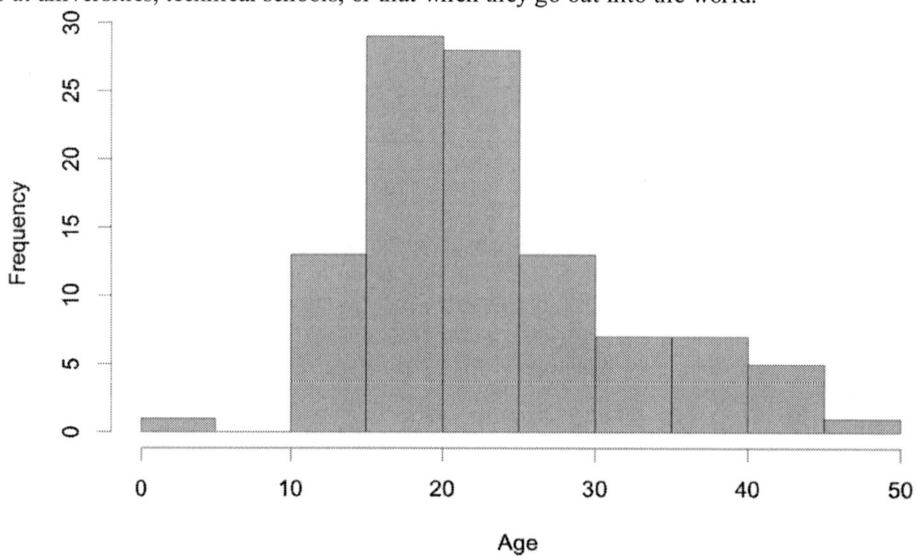

Figure 2. Histogram of Ages When They Got to Know OSS for the First Time

Although the number of participants in their survey is an order of magnitude greater than ours, Robles *et al.* reports similar histogram on age respondents had when they first contributed to FLOSS and that on year which the first contribution to FLOSS took place (Robles, *et al.* 2013).

4.2 Q2: Their First OSS

The question two (Q2) asked what your first OSS was. Table 1 shows the responses of Q2. In the table 1, respondents are classified into five periods in accordance with the answer of Q1 and help to understand the transition of OSS popularity. For instance, in the early periods, Emacs and gcc are the typical OSS of their first OSS. However, after the late 90s', they have gone. In contrast, Linux came to the forefront.

Table 1. Responses of Q2: what was the FLOSS which you Learned for the First Time?

Respondents	FLOSS
2005 — present	Linux(12), LibreOffice(3), WordPress(2), boost, apache, Zabbix, OpenOffice.org, NetCommons, MySQL, MIT-Scheme, Hinemos, Firefox, CyanogenMod, Chromium
2000 — 2004	Linux(11), BSD(3), OSASK(2), apache, Asterisk, XOOPS, Ruby, PostgreSQL, Plone, Plan9, Perl, PHP, OpenOffice.org, MySQL, Mozilla
1995 — 1999	Linux(17), BSD(4), zip, lha, gzip, gcc, apache, Netscape
1990 — 1994	Emacs(5), gcc(4), BSD(3), Linux(2), LATEX(2), xdvi, sqrtf, gnuplot, gawk, ULTRIX/X-10, TEX, FD
— 1989	Emacs(6), gcc(4), tin, gnuplot, f2c, X, TinyBasic, TEX, GNU MANIFEST, Basic, BSD

4.3 Q3: How They Learned about OSS

Figure 3 shows the way the respondent learned about OSS, showing acquisition of information on OSS by communication with other people is dominant.

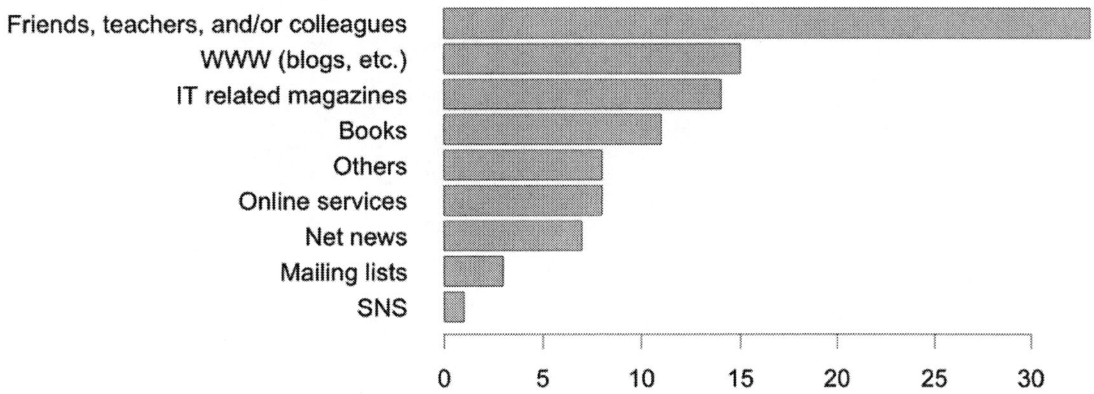

Figure 3. Responses of Q3: how did you Learn about OSS?

4.4 Q4: Major Source of Information on OSS

The question four (Q4) inquires that what were your major source of information on OSS. Figure 4 shows the responses of Q4. Note that Q4 was multiple answers allowed, therefore the summation of the numbers of responses are more than total number of respondents.

Figure 5 indicates the ratio of information sources by age. You can see the trends that the portion of net-news is shrinking and that of WWW is expanding in the figure.

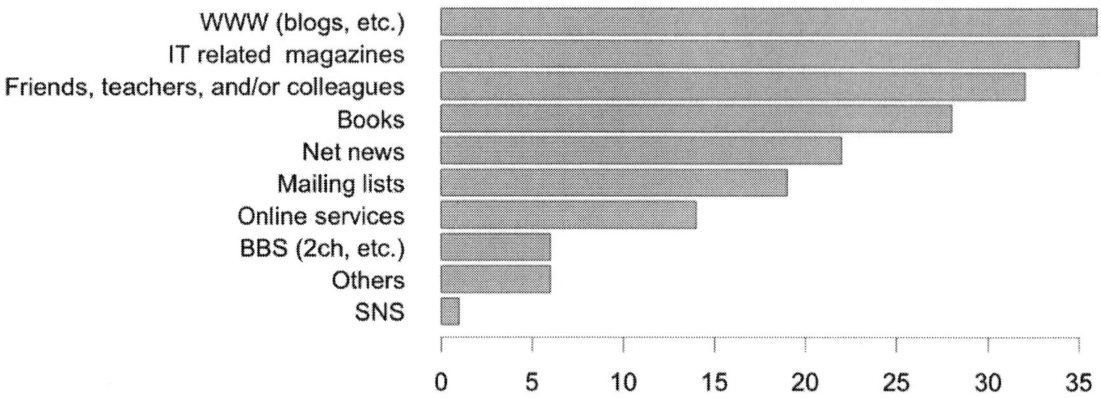

Figure 4. Responses of Q4: what were the Major Information Source About OSS?

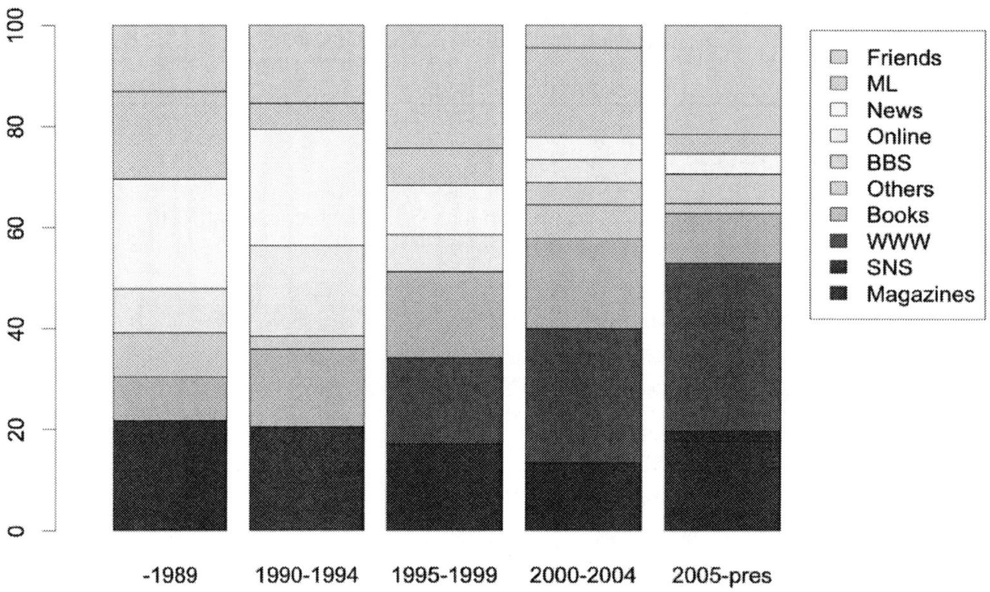

Figure 5. Responses of Q4: what were the Major Information Source About OSS? (in Details)

4.5 Q5: Magazines for Acquiring Information on OSS

The last question (Q5) is about the magazines as their information sources. Table 2 represents the responses of Q5 in the categories classified in the same method of Table 1. There is difference between aggregating data for Q2 shown in Table 1 and that for Q5 shown in Table 2. The difference is treatment of blank answers for each question. The blank answers for Q2 were skipped, so that they are not appearing in Table 1. On the other hand, those of Q5 were counted and they are aggregated in Table 2.

Table 2. Responses of Q5; what was the IT Related Magazines you were Reading at that Time?

Respondents	Magazines
2005 — present	[blank](11), None/Unknown(5), Nikkei Linux(5), Nikkei WinPC (2), Software Design(2), Weekly ASCII(2), Nikkei network, Nikkei computer, Nikkei personal computing, Nikkei PC21, Mac People, Mac Fan, MACPOWER, Interface, I/O, ASCII
2000 — 2004	[blank](7), ASCII(3), Software Design(2), Internet Magazine, Dekiru(possible) series*, Nikkei computer, Nikkei personal computing, Nikkei Linux, Windows 100%, Weekly ASCII, UNIX MAGA- ZINE, TECH Win, Oh!PC, MACPOWER, Linux USER, Interface, DOS/V magazine, BSD magazine, None/Unknown
1995 — 1999	[blank](6), UNIX MAGAZINE(2), Oh! PC(2), Linux Japan(2), DOS/V POWER REPORT(2), ASCII(2), Gamelabo, Nikkei computer, Nikkei Linux, Software Design, PC USER, PC Japan, Oh!FM TOWNS, MdN, Book for using Linux 256 times*, Linux magazine, LOGIN, Hello! PC, None/Unknown
1990 — 1994	UNIX MAGAZINE(5), I/O(4), Transistor Gijutsu(2), UNIX USER (2), UNIX MAGAIZINE(2), Oh! X(2), [blank](2), Micom BASIC Magazine, PROGRAM POCHETTE, Nikkei computer, Nikkei personal computing, Nikkei byte, TECHNOPOLIS, bit, Super ASCII, Software Design, POPCOM, PC Magazine, Oh!FM towns, Inter- face, ASCII DOS/V Issue, ASCII
— 1989	UNIX MAGAZINE(7), ASCII(4), I/O(3), bit(2), Interface(2), Micom BASIC Magazine, Transistor Gijutsu, Paperware BASIC master, Making a Radio*, Nikkei byte, Electronics Review*, UNIX USER, The BASIC, Software Design, RAM, IEEE Computer, Dr.Dobb's Journal, Communications of ACM, C MAGAZINE, [blank]

In the early periods, we can see that they relied on overseas sources like IEEE Computer, Communications of ACM, and Dr. Dobb's Journal. In addition, the numbers of blank entry[1] and that of "None/ Unknown" are increasing along with the progress of the times. It can be considered that the trend implies the transition from paper media to cyber-media such as WWW and SNS.

The proper noun "Nikkei" appearing many times in Table 2 is the name of a typical mass communication media in Japan. It publishes many series of IT related magazines. In Table 2, note that the items marked with asterisk (*) are translated by the authors due to the lack of English titles.

5. CONCLUSIONS

We have conducted the questionnaire on the relationship between FLOSS developers and their information sources. The results of questionnaire disclosed the year when they were joined into OSS community, their first OSS, the way they learned about OSS, major information sources and magazines they read at that time. Especially, it is considered that the trend of their first OSS reflects the trend of technological movement. In addition, the trend of magazines also reflects the changes in acquiring information on technologies.

[1] The case that the answer form of Q5 was blank. It is shown as "[blank]" in Table 2.

REFERENCES

David, P. A., Waterman, A., and Arora. S., 2003. FLOSS-US: The Free/Libre/Open Source Software Survey for 2003. *Technical report, Stanford Institute for Economic and Policy Research,* Stanford, USA.

Ghosh, R. A., Robles, G., and Glott, R., 2002. Software source code survey (free/libre and open source software: Survey and study). *Technical report, Univ. of Maastricht,* The Netherlands.

Hannebauer, C. and Gruhn, V., 2016. Motivation of Newcomers to FLOSS Projects, *The International Symposium on Open Collaboration, OpenSym2016*, Berlin, Germany. doi:10.1145/2957792.2957793

Iio, J., Hatta, M., Kazaana, K., 2015. The FLOSS History in Japan: An Ethnographic Approach, *The International Symposium on Open Collaboration, OpenSym2015,* San Fransisco, CA.

Robles, G., Reina, L. A., Serebrenik, A., Vasilescu, B., and Gonz´alez-Barahona, G. M., 2014. FLOSS 2013: A Survey Dataset about Free Software Contributors: Challenges for Curating, Sharing, and Combining, *The 11th Working Conference on Mining Software Repositories,* Hyderabad, India. doi:10.1145/2597073.2597129

Shimizu, H., Iio, J., and Hiyane, K., 2004. The realities of Free/Libre/Open Source Software developers in Japan and Asia. *First Monday*, 9(11).

Von Krogh, G., Haefliger S, Spaeth, S., and Wallin M. W. Carrotsand Rainbows, 2012. Motivation and Social Practice in Open Source Software Development, *MIS Quarterly,* 36(2).

REMOVING BARRIERS IN EGOVERNMENT: BACK OFFICE ASSESSMENT

Demetrios Sarantis
United Nations University – Operating Unit on Policy-Driven Electronic Governance
Campus de Couros, Rua Vila Flor 166, 4810-445 Guimarães, Portugal

ABSTRACT

Public sector organisations encounter many design options and challenges that must be managed in order to provide more productive and attractive eGovernment interface. There are several eGovernment assessment tools which evaluate countries' eGovernment development according to a variety of perspectives (economic, human, technological etc.), which aim to assist them towards making progress with service innovation and to help them move forward. Those instruments rank countries according to different criteria and at the same time are used by decision makers when devising information and communication policies and allocating resources to implement those policies. Despite their widespread use, current benchmarking and ranking tools have limitations. One of those limitations is that they do not provide adequate support to assess easily and practically national eGovernment back office operation. In this paper, five eGovernment assessment frameworks for computing eGovernment assessment indexes are illustrated and an eGovernment back office capacity assessment framework is proposed which could be applied complementary as a sub-index to existing approaches. Specific measurable dimensions are proposed and analysed.

KEYWORDS

eGovernment, Assessment, Back Office, Integration, Public Administration

1. INTRODUCTION

eGovernment development measurement over the years and across the nations is important in order to analyse the relative and absolute development of eGovernment world-wide. eGovernment development stage varies across countries. Developed economies are relatively advanced in usage of Information and Communication Technologies (ICT) for improving public sector operation and service delivery. However, most developing countries are less advanced and a comparable assessment framework is important for their eGovernment improvements (United Nations, 2017).

eGovernment readiness research has gained significant recognition (Alghamdi, 2011), as multiple initiatives have been undertaken by international organizations, consulting firms, and scholars to measure and operationalize the various aspects of eGovernment status. Much of the research in this area is driven and initiated by specific stakeholders and focuses on divergent sets of indicators. The eGovernment assessment literature has focused predominantly on implementation (Heeks, 2005), security and authentication (Moon, 2002), technology acceptance (Chen, 2003), project planning and design (Gil-García and Pardo, 2005), and procurement and purchasing (Gil-García and Pardo, 2005) issues.

Several frameworks exist for eGovernment readiness assessment. The United Nations eGovernment Development Index (EGDI), the Waseda University-eGovernment Rankings, the World Economic Forum Networked Readiness Index (NRI), the European Commission Digital Economy and Society Index (DESI) and the EU E-government Benchmark Indicators have been used for assessing eGovernment globally and within Europe. These models use a wide range of indicators to assess a community's eGovernment readiness. While the above results are useful for obtaining a representative picture of the supply side (front end), what the public sector offers, they lack coverage in back office indicators.

In this paper, after presenting the basic elements of the above approaches we propose specific eGovernment back office assessment criteria to assess a country's overall eGovernment readiness from a backend perspective. The purpose of this research is to propose a generic back office eGovernment capacity assessment framework that has several distinct aspects that are critical for the countries to assess and subsequently improve their eGovernment back office integration capacity. Discussion and conclusions are illustrated in section four.

2. RELATED WORK - ASSESSING EGOVERNMENT

eGovernment development is assessed across the globe by various methodologies provided by universities, companies, public and private organizations and multi-lateral international institutions. These approaches mainly assess the progress made by each country over a period of time and compare its growth against other countries which have a political and potentially economic impact and which can influence the development of eGovernment services. These assessment efforts serve as a tool for the countries and public institutions to learn from each other, identify areas of opportunities and challenges in eGovernment and accordingly develop appropriate strategies, policies, initiatives. It also helps in assessing the eGovernment readiness of the country and build capacities in the gap areas. Hereinafter we illustrate the basic elements of the most used assessment approaches.

2.1 United Nations eGovernment Development Index (EGDI)

Progress of eGovernment development in United Nations (UN) is assessed by eGovernment Development Index (EGDI) which is a composite index based on weighted average of three indices, the Telecommunications Infrastructure Index (TII), the Human Capital Index (HCI) and the Online Service Index (OSI) (United Nations, 2016). Regarding OSI, which is the primary eGovernment index, data is collected from an independent survey questionnaire that assesses the national online presence of all 193 United Nations Member States. National web presence is assessed in its native language including the national portal, eServices portal and eParticipation portal as well as websites of education, labour, social services, health, finance and environment ministries.

2.2 Waseda University, eGovernment Rankings

The Waseda – IAC International e-Government Ranking uses comprehensive benchmarking indicators to assess the latest developments of eGovernment in the major countries in ICT (Waseda University Institute of E-Government, 2016). In the process of evaluation, researchers found that Information Technology is increasingly widely used in the activities of governments and the applications of ICT have been applied to many fields in various sectors. Many governments around the world are aware of the role of ICT in their administration and management; they have applied ICT to deliver services to citizens, businesses and the government itself, aiming to move traditional government towards an eGovernment model. In order to effectively evaluate the application of new trends in each country, the research team conducts a survey by sending a questionnaire to relevant government officers as well as experts globally. The main assessment indicators are Network Preparedness/Digital Infrastructure, Management Optimization, Online Services/ Applications, National Portal/Homepage, Government Chief Information Officer (GCIO), eGovernment Promotion, eParticipation/ Digital Inclusion, Open Government Data, Cyber Security, The Use of Emerging ICT.

2.3 World Economic Forum Networked Readiness Index (NRI)

The Networked Readiness Index measures the capacity of countries to leverage ICTs for increased competitiveness and well-being (Bilbao-Osorio et al, 2013). It also considers innovation trends of recent years. It is based on four sub-indexes, the Environment sub-index which measures the extent to which a country's market conditions and regulatory framework support ICT development, entrepreneurship and innovation, the Readiness sub-index assesses the country by the extent to which the infrastructure and other factors support the uptake of ICT, the Usage sub-index considers the level of ICT adoption by a society's main stakeholders - government, businesses, and individuals and the Impact sub-index which determines the broad economic and social impacts accruing from ICT.

2.4 European Commission Digital Economy and Society Index (DESI)

The Digital Economy and Society Index (DESI) measures progress of European Union (EU) countries towards a digital economy and society (European Commission, 2017). As such, it brings together a set of relevant indicators on Europe's current digital policy mix. The DESI was developed following the guidelines and recommendations in the OECD's (Organisation for Economic Co-operation and Development) "Handbook on constructing composite indicators: methodology and user guide". The data included in the index are mostly collected by the European Commission services (DG CNECT, Eurostat) and by ad-hoc studies launched by the Commission services. DESI is composed of 5 principal dimensions, each divided into a set of sub-dimensions, which are in turn composed by individual indicators:

- Connectivity dimension which is considered as a necessary condition for the development of a digital society is the ability of its members to connect to the Internet.
- Human Capital Dimension which assures the appropriate skills to take advantage of the Internet and of the myriad of possibilities unravelled by a digital society.
- Use of Internet Dimension which covers the essential engagement in a wide range of online activities.
- Integration of Digital Technology Dimension which is one of the main contributors to enhanced economic growth.
- Digital Public Services Dimension evaluates business and citizen interaction with the Public Sector using digital technologies.

2.5 EU e-Government Benchmark Indicators

European Commission benchmarks a set of seven life events (Codagnone and Undheim, 2008). These life events represent virtually all domains of government. The assessment process consists of four top-level benchmarks, User Centricity - indicates to what extent (information about) a service is provided online, Transparency - indicates to what extent governments are transparent, Cross Border Mobility - indicates to what extent European users can use online services in another country, Key enablers - indicates the extent to which five technical pre-conditions for eGovernment are used.

3. BACK OFFICE INTEGRATION ASSESSMENT FRAMEWORK

The above eGovernment assessment methods are crucial to cross-country comparisons of digital government evolution. Policymakers can use evaluation results to plan digital development policies and implement new innovative services for their citizens. Assessment initiatives also assist governments to monitor the efficiency and effectiveness of public spending (ITU, 2009; United Nations, 2010).

Despite their undeniable usefulness, controversy exists over the coverage of the whole spectrum of eGovernment domain. Most of eGovernment assessment efforts lack a coverage focus on back-office site (Janssen et al., 2004). Furthermore, eGovernment assessment methods become more problematic, when they are based on subjective data collection criteria (studies, interviews, opinions etc.) to calculate assessment indicators. The more sophisticated tools require expensive data collection and complex processing. There is a need in the case of eGovernment back office assessment, for simple, inexpensive, fairly transparent and replicable, and widely accepted and used criteria (Rorissa et al, 2011).

Back office integration has long been an important focus of attention by researchers, policy makers, technologists and public officials. The eGovernment vision is a vision of integrated information and services. This means radical changes are needed in what happens behind the web portal that users see. New public administration processes, different information flows, changed policies and new kinds of citizen and business needs are all part of the integration story.

Silo mentality is a pertinent problem in public administration integration efforts. Lack of appropriate mechanisms for the coordination of the investment in public administration to optimize resources is obvious. There is a reluctance to share data, information and resources and the lack of technical interoperability between systems of different government agencies or even inside the same government remains an issue. The lack of basic common public sector IT architectures has resulted in the development of a diversity of disparate applications (Themistocleous et al, 2005). Lack of open data, data standards and common way of service design are major technical barriers (Lam, 2005).

Based on the study of the existing assessment indicators and the current needs of national eGovernment initiatives we propose specific eGovernment back office capacity indicators, identified in literature, which are relatively easily measurable. Our framework for back office assessment of eGovernment capacity identifies eleven criteria: open standards, ontologies, metadata, document integration, Process Representation, Service Oriented Architecture, Single-Sign-On (SSO) National Portal, Common Platforms, Multiple Devices and Channels, Software Reuse and Public Sector Communication Network. Below we describe the eleven assessment dimensions in detail. We identify the significance of these dimensions and highlight cases and pertinent examples.

3.1 Open Standards

An essential aspect of eGovernment systems architecture is the establishment of the appropriate technical standards. Public Organisations worldwide are gradually adopting open standards to harvest significant benefits, namely interoperability, flexibility, and avoidance of vendor lock-in (Simon, 2005). In general, standards define common elements, such as user interfaces, system interfaces, representations of data, protocols for the exchange of data, and interfaces accessing data or system functions. Public sector system integration is expected to be facilitated by open standards application. Open standards are usually adopted and maintained by a not-for-profit organization, and their ongoing development occurs based on an open decision-making procedure available to all interested parties. Open standards are published and their specification documents are available either freely or at a nominal charge. The intellectual property of an open standard is made irrevocably available on a royalty-free basis and there are no constraints on the re-use of the standard. For example, public administration services and their associated application services can be specified by open standards like Web Ontology Language (OWL), Web Service Modelling Ontology (WSMO), and Business Process Model and Notation (BPMN) (Hofman, 2008).

3.2 Ontologies

Ontologies allow the interoperable information exchange across heterogeneous public sector information systems (PSIS) and they propel the development of eGovernment systems that can be easily integrated to provide seamless services delivery to users. Semantic-based eGovernment systems consist of applications that are implemented on existing conceptual domain model's entities, concepts, processes, laws and regulations. Representation of public sector's concepts through ontologies will facilitate the task of locating specific concepts, and then exploit the relationships to trace other concepts that are linked to them (Sarantis et al, 2011). Thus, the ontologies can be used as a tool that facilitate integration and interoperation to eGovernment systems (Dombeu and Huisman, 2011). Using ontologies, each piece of public sector information is semantically modelled and annotated. Instead of scattering data over numerous functions and procedures in all possible organisations and application, it could be consistently kept in the semantic model.

3.3 Metadata

Metadata, which is defined as 'Data about data' or 'information about information' is a valuable tool in eGovernment applications to make seamless flow of information and services across government and support citizens locating government information and using services more easily (Alasem, 2009). Metadata are used, amongst other for search, exploration, discovery and retrieval of public sector information, as well as to assist in the management of government electronic resources. In other words, metadata is a key to back office integration. Quam (2003) asserted that the importance of metadata and controlled vocabularies in government websites is to give access to a wide range of government information and services through one access point. Ontologies contribute in organizing public sector data on the internet in a way which help users to search and locate information without needing details of public administration structure, and in finding and using government services without knowing which agency delivers them.

3.4 Document Integration

In public administration (PA), documents are the most common input/output for services delivery and they represent the proof that an operation has to been done and must be supported. Document engineering provides the concepts and methods needed to align public administration operation and services. A set of rules for encoding documents in a format that is both human-readable and machine-readable facilitates the reuse of data, standards, or patterns that work, reducing costs and risks while increasing reliability and interoperability. Uniform way of document representation, when the syntax, structure or semantics conform to common pattern or standards, ensures that interaction parties understand and use each other's documents.

In this context, the emergence of eGovernment has resulted in the creation of electronic documents and the information they contain is indeed a valuable asset that must be carefully managed. In this manner, the intra and inter organization structural dependencies should be surpassed, through accurate and reliable electronic document definition and through an effective system to manage them. Public administration documents can be implemented in a modular form, produced by departmental and organisational coordination (Sabucedo et al, 2010).

3.5 Process Representation

Application of a common public administration process representation method advances public organizations' ability to work together to deliver services in a seamless, uniform and efficient manner across whole public sector and information technology systems. Public agencies need to engage in a process of ensuring that their systems, information and processes are illustrated in a uniform way to maximise opportunities for exchange with and reuse by others. Process integration requires a collective mindset, an understanding of how each collaborating agency operates and the development of arrangements which effectively manage business processes that cut across organisational boundaries.

Public administrations are facing specific conditions when they model their business processes and try to improve them. Public sector processes include a lot of interconnected and interdependent services and underlying processes for citizens, companies, and other administrational parties. Simultaneously, public administrations are large organisations with decentralized knowledge about the processes. Usually, there is no organisational unit that has detailed expertise about the entire process landscape.

Application of a common process representation modelling method will allow for a simple representation of the process landscape. The meaning of the constructs will become intuitive and their counterparts in the real world will become easily identifiable. The syntactical rules will be easily comprehensible and process models will become maintainable and comparable (Becker et al, 2007).

3.6 Service Oriented Architecture (SOA)

Public sector organisations can use and benefit from Service Oriented Architecture (SOA) to build open, flexible and collaborative eGovernment services while at the same time lowering ICT costs. SOA is considered one of the promising technologies that provide interoperability and integration between various ranges of services, implemented by different software applications, running on a variety of platforms in government organizations (Yan and Guo, 2010). A Service Oriented Architecture (SOA) approach to eGovernance supports IT with service delivery objectives and allows different government agencies to reprocess developed assets (Behara et al, 2009), shifting from more 'silo' government approaches, towards more back-and front-office integration, via a collaborative approach. It is useful to offer flexible SOA solutions as this can be beneficial for governing, integrating, deploying, securing, and managing services, irrespective of the platforms on which they were created (Behara et al, 2009). SOA diminishes the dependency on back-end applications and reduces the requirement to write code every time there is a change in policy because it can deal with different platforms, and can establish new software that advances the direct collaboration of eGovernment users irrespective of the delivery model (Behara et al, 2009).

3.7 Single-Sign-On (SSO) National Portal

Web portals represent integrated gateways for government service between public administration (PA) and users to provide a single point of contact for services. The goal of eGovernment services is to conduct complete end-to-end solutions for citizens whenever it is possible. As portals integrate services, they certainly improve access to government, reduce service-processing costs, and enable PAs to provide a higher quality of service. The development of web application for eGovernment services has benefits for both government and citizens.

A national eGovernment SSO portal enables login to multi-portals and applications, it establishes a simple and practical interface between citizens, government departments and businesses under a 24/7 model (Corradini et al, 2007). It also enables each participant organisation to continue its own legacy and processing systems.

3.8 Common Platforms

The use of common platforms in public sector can reduce costs through partnership and enhance information sharing. Such platforms allow the combination of disparate information in a variety of data formats, the facilitation of interaction between citizens, businesses, public agencies, collaboration and the sharing of information. Common platforms can be structured by generic and modularised components such as a common framework for citizens' electronic identity management (eID), an electronic payments module, a Public Key Infrastructure (PKI) module (supporting digital signatures and certificates), a public procurement services module, a citizen relationship management (CRM) module etc. The use of those components will enable each public body to improve the quality of service provision, without deep organizational change. For example by using a CRM application as the common front office user interface linked to the existing back office applications, a common view of information held in all public sector back office applications could be achieved.

3.9 Multiple Devices and Channels

Current ICT installations and know-how has been vertically organized around departments with little or not at all common horizontal functionality, hindering thus the development of multi-channel services. eGovernment systems expand their size and structure for distributed, heterogeneous, collaborative interoperability properties within the new service multi-channels eGovernment systems (Ping, 2011). There is a growing need to use multiple service channels within one public service delivery process or to use different channels for different service delivery processes (Pieterson and Dijk, 2006).

Several e-government architectures that have been proposed insofar, namely the European one-stop government, the Federal Enterprise Architecture and the extended Enterprise Application Integration include multi-channel access to e-services as core functionality of the delivery platform. The multi-channel model allows users to gain access to services in a more holistic view through different channels, while ensuring information consistency (Vassilakis et al, 2007). If the channels and back-office processes are integrated, then different channels can complement each other, improving the quality of service and delivery simultaneously. Thus, an environment with full integration of data, systems and processes, not only coexistence, is required.

3.10 Software Reuse

The central idea of this emerging approach is based on reuse of, available in public sector, software building blocks and components to implement new eGovernment systems by assembly, and thus has the advantage of materialising public sector information systems (PSIS) in a shorter time with better quality. Software reuse is expected to improve the productivity and the quality of PSIS to reduce development time and to optimize the use of public money. Over the last years, software reuse has been stressed as a key factor for the developers to improve the productivity and the quality of information systems (Kwon et al, 2015). Software reuse and system integration would be greatly facilitated by having a central repository for standard software components, open to any authorized user with standard access channels, rules and documentation (Bolici et al, 2003).

3.11 Public Sector Communication Network

The Public Sector Communication Network (PSCN) is important in providing a communications hub specifically for electronic government transactions. The aim of these technologies is to support and integrate the operations of business processes and information systems dimension across organizations by providing the necessary standards and protocols all the way through ICT network and communication infrastructure solutions such as the intranet, extranet, internet, and VOIP. Thus, it links PA agencies, hosting their telecommunication services, in a secure and a cost-effective manner. Organization communications should be characterized by a high degree of efficiency and reliability to provide very high transfer speeds and should provide security in the transfer of data using the latest techniques of data transfer protocols to be able to connect to other agencies through the PSCN. The use of such a communication network decreases the transaction costs and enables organizations to focus on their core competencies.

4. DISCUSSION AND CONCLUSION

In the current study, five eGovernment assessment approaches have been explored and the results highlight that a gap exists in the assessment of eGovernment back office operation. There is a need for an eGovernment back office policy to underpin 'transparent' assessment models developed by specific benchmarking organizations (Bakry 2003). Our proposed framework contributes in the research discussion providing an answer on questions such as if the existing eGovernment development indexes are adequate and how can they be improved. Specifically, we delve into eGovernment back office and try to provide an assessment perspective contribution. The proposed Government back office capacity criteria add measurements that assist countries to assess their status and could encourage dialogue among them regarding service collaboration and interoperation.

The proposed framework could become part of the existing eGovernment assessment indexes developing a consensus on a set of eGovernment back office indicators to serve as the basis for collection of ICT measurements that would be comparable at the international level.

A primary audience for this framework is the community of public administration professionals around the world, including national government managers, regional and national public administration institutions and the individuals that lead them, researchers, practitioners etc.

eGovernment experts highlight that a holistic approach is needed to advance sustainable development through the implementation of whole-of-government approaches. They emphasize that a whole-of-government approach should be embedded in the national strategies to encourage collaboration and coordination among ministries and agencies as well as all levels of public administration. To ensure successful implementation of national strategies, governments should provide adequate technical and operational frameworks to support public organisations¨ interoperation. eGovernment programmes should clearly identify expected outcomes and should be assessed based on well and clear defined processes and measurement metrics.

The proposed framework could be used to assess national capacity of back offices of service production advancing their interoperability and improving their integration and service delivery to citizens and enterprises as users. It also provides leeway for eGovernment actors (researchers, politicians, managers, officials etc.) to look for the strategy and options that fit best their specific technical-socio-political environment.

ACKNOWLEDGEMENTS

This paper is a result of the project "SmartEGOV: Harnessing EGOV for Smart Governance (Foundations, methods, Tools) / NORTE-01-0145-FEDER-000037", supported by Norte Portugal Regional Operational Programme (NORTE 2020), under the PORTUGAL 2020 Partnership Agreement, through the European Regional Development Fund (EFDR).

REFERENCES

Alasem, A., 2009. An overview of e-government metadata standards and initiatives based on Dublin Core. Electronic Journal of e-Government, 7(1), pp.1-10.

Alghamdi, I.A., Goodwin, R. and Rampersad, G., 2011. E-government readiness assessment for government organizations in developing countries. Computer and Information Science, 4(3), p.3.

Behara, G.K., Varre, V.V. and Rao, M., 2009. Service oriented architecture for e-governance. BPTrends, October.

Bilbao-Osorio, B., Dutta, S. and Lanvin, B., 2013. The global information technology report 2013. In World Economic Forum (pp. 1-383).

Bolici, F., Cantoni, F., Sorrentino, M. and Virili, F., 2003. Cooperating strategies in e-government. Electronic Government, pp.1069-1070.

Chen, H., 2003. Digital government: technologies and practices. Decision Support Systems, 34(3), pp.223-227.

Codagnone, C. and Undheim, T.A., 2008. Benchmarking eGovernment: tools, theory, and practice. European Journal of ePractice, 1(4), pp.1-15.

Corradini, F., Sabucedo, L.A., Polzonetti, A., Rifón, L.A. and Re, B., 2007, September. A case study of semantic solutions for citizen-centered web portals in eGovernment: the Tecut Portal. In International Conference on Electronic Government (pp. 204-215). Springer, Berlin, Heidelberg.

Dombeu, J.V.F. and Huisman, M., 2011. Combining ontology development methodologies and semantic web platforms for e-government domain ontology development. arXiv preprint arXiv:1104.4966.

European Commission, 2017, Digital Single Market, The Digital Economy and Society Index (DESI)

Gil-García, J.R. and Pardo, T.A., 2005. E-government success factors: Mapping practical tools to theoretical foundations. Government information quarterly, 22(2), pp.187-216.

Heeks, R., 2005. e-Government as a Carrier of Context. Journal of Public Policy, 25(1), pp.51-74.

Hofman, W., 2008, June. eGovernment interoperability with open standards. In Technology Management Conference (ICE), 2008 IEEE International (pp. 1-8). IEEE.

ITU, 2009. Measuring the information society: The ICT development index.

Janssen, D., Rotthier, S. and Snijkers, K., 2004. If you measure it they will score: An assessment of international eGovernment benchmarking. Information Polity, 9(3, 4), pp.121-130.

Kwon, Y., Kim, E. and Lee, N., 2015, July. Key factors on software reuse of e-Government common framework. In Advanced Communication Technology (ICACT), 2015 17th International Conference on (pp. 774-781). IEEE.

Lam, W., 2005. Barriers to e-government integration. Journal of Enterprise Information Management, 18(5), pp.511-530.

Moon, M.J., 2002. The evolution of e- government among municipalities: rhetoric or reality?. Public administration review, 62(4), pp.424-433.

Pieterson, W. and Dijk, J., 2006. Governmental service channel positioning: history and strategies for the future.

Ping, L., 2011, May. Web service-based e-Government public service channels workflow integration and simulation. In Communication Software and Networks (ICCSN), 2011 IEEE 3rd International Conference on (pp. 333-338). IEEE.

Quam, E., 2003. Metadata and taxonomy integration in government portals. Metadata applications and management. International Yearbook of Library and Information Management, 2004, pp.95-108.

Rorissa, A., Demissie, D. and Pardo, T., 2011. Benchmarking e-government: A comparison of frameworks for computing e-government index and ranking. Government Information Quarterly, 28(3), pp.354-362.

Sabucedo, L.M.Á., Rifón, L.E.A., Corradini, F., Polzonetti, A. and Re, B., 2010. Knowledge-based platform for eGovernment agents: A Web-based solution using semantic technologies. Expert Systems with Applications, 37(5), pp.3647-3656.

Sarantis, D., Charalabidis, Y. and Askounis, D., 2011. Towards a public sector interoperability ontology: conceptualization of fundamental entities. In Proceedings of the 5th International Conference on Theory and Practice of Electronic Governance (pp. 259-264). ACM.

Simon, K.D., 2005. The value of open standards and open-source software in government environments. IBM Systems Journal, 44(2), pp.227-238.

Themistocleous, M., Irani, Z. and Love, P.E., 2005, January. Developing e-government integrated infrastructures: a case study. In System Sciences, 2005. HICSS'05. Proceedings of the 38th Annual Hawaii International Conference on (pp. 228-228). IEEE.

United Nations, 2010, United Nations e-Government survey 2010: Leveraging e-Government at a time of financial and economic crisis.

United Nations, 2016. e-Government Survey 2016, e-Government in Support of Sustainable Development

United Nations, 2017, e-Government and its Measurements, UN E-Government EGM Meeting Background Paper.

Vassilakis, C., Lepouras, G. and Halatsis, C., 2007. A knowledge-based approach for developing multi-channel e-government services. Electronic Commerce Research and Applications, 6(1), pp.113-124.

Yan, P. and Guo, J., 2010, May. Researching and Designing the Architecture of E-government Based on SOA. In E-Business and E-Government (ICEE), 2010 International Conference on (pp. 512-515). IEEE.

Waseda University Institute of E-Government, 2016. Waseda University E-Government Ranking.

USABILITY ANALYSIS OF THREE MASSIVE ONLINE OPEN COURSE PLATFORMS

Alex de Souza Paiva, Augusto José Waszczynskyj Antunes das Neves, Beatriz Otto Ramos, Claudia Mara Scudelari de Macedo, Fernanda Domingues and Juliana Bueno
Federal University of Paraná, Brazil

ABSTRACT

Virtual learning environments are an upgrade to the form of acquiring and sharing information. The article aims to conduct a brief analysis on the usability of Massive Online Open Course (MOOC) environments. Three MOOC platforms (Sophia, CK-12 and Curriki) were analyzed and discussed using a systematic bibliographic review according to the fundamentals of Information Design, Universal Design and Usability. A structured form was also applied to collect data regarding the usability of MOOC environments analysed. The comparison among platforms made possible to perform an analysis of the symbolization modes and variable types. Matches and discrepancies under visualization and human-computer interaction characteristics were considered and evaluated.

KEYWORDS

MOOC. Usability. Universal Design

1. INTRODUCTION

The need to reach a growing audience in free course platforms has generated an interest in information technology communities. There are multiple ways of producing a learning object. Among these platforms are those that represent free courses for public access available on the internet, better known as Massive Online Open Course (MOOC).

Regardless of the country of production, these environments are widespread throughout the world. However, the success of MOOC platforms depends on the usability of these electronic learning environments. The international International Organization for Standardisation (ISO) 9241-11.1998 standard defines usability as: "effectiveness, efficiency and satisfaction by which specific users can achieve specific goals in specific environments". It is a broad concept that can be applied in digital media.

A platform to be characterized as a MOOC it necessarily has to be available in an electronic mean and grant free access to all users, it has to contain activities connected to each other and it has to make the user perform actions of multiple choice (Aldahdouh and Osorio, 2016). At the same time, the universal design prescribes that learning objects must be user-friendly, with a user-accessible interface (flexible, consistent, simple and intuitive use), adaptable to any environment and technologically adequate to the available resources (Sonza et al., 2013).

In this context, this research proposes a usability analysis of MOOC platforms, based on the criteria of Engelhart (2002), Van Deer Waarde (1993) and Mijksenaar (1997), applied to the evaluation of symbolic modes and to the differentiating, hierarchical and supportive variables. For this analysis the following platforms were chosen: Sophia, Ck-12 and Curriki.

2. MOOCS AND E-LEARNING TOOLS: DISTANCE LEARNING EDUCATION AND VIRTUAL LEARNING ENVIRONMENTS

Distance Learning Education (DLE) represents a teaching format developed and used for the purpose of democratizing and increasing the ease of access to knowledge (Filatro, 2007). For Moore and Kearsley (2008), when technology is combined with DLE, some benefits emerge: encouraging education in a more inexpensive way in which students have the freedom of choosing the place/time that best suits their personal study and learning needs, allowing the reduction of social discrepancies; the possibility of directing data, information and knowledge to specific audiences; upgrading personal and professional skills/abilities; and to allow access to a learning experience with an international bias.

Among the technologies that make DLE practice viable, the Virtual Learning Environments (VLEs) stand out. For Almeida (2003), VLEs are educational systems/softwares present on the internet that have the aim to support distance learning education activities, which are mediated by information and communication technologies (ICTs). Thus, the VLEs have applicability in face-to-face activities (potentiating extra-classroom interactions) and semi-presential (when face-to-face meetings and DLE activities take place in complementary way), while facilitating dialogue and interaction between the actors of the educational process. Therefore, Student/computer interaction; the possibility of individual attendance to the student; customized control of the learning sequence, pace, and time by students; creativity and attractiveness in the way that study materials are transmitted and exchanged; and evaluating the student individually are advantages that the use of VLEs offer (MORAES, 2002).

One of the main examples of VLE applicability lies in the support for e-learning. For Albino and Bergamaschi (2013), the e-learning tools result from the convergence among teaching, technology and education, which enabled the creation of online educational environments and platforms for web based training. In this context, e-learning provides the use of technologies to spread data, information and knowledge, facilitating the interaction between the system users and the management of study needs.

Among the available e-learning environments are those that emerge as open educational resources (OER). According to Hilen (2006), the OERs represent open and unrestricted digital educational content that is used by the academy for teaching, research and learning purposes. These include learning management systems that assist in the systematization of participants, content, courses and / or learning objects.

The MOOCs are one of the most recent strands of OER. For Pisutova (2012), they represent platforms for the provision of formative content on the internet, which can be accessed by any user who wants to enroll and follow a course. The main characteristics of MOOCs are: openness (work is performed where the users can read and comment on specific contents), costless (the users can participate in courses without paying for it), collaborative (the work is shared with all the users enrolled in the course), values the involvement of users (participants gain from contents published and shared by colleagues) and allows the distribution of content (information produced and/or shared by users may be part of the course but not on the same website). As MOOCs examples: CK12 (www.ck12.org), Curriki (www.curriki.org) and Sophia (www.sophia.org).

CK12 is a foundation that started in 2007 with the objective of bringing quality open educational content for students from all over the world. In 2008 CK12 launched a collection of free Textbooks called Flexbooks. In 2011, after creating the teacher's resources, workbooks, quizzes and assessment tests, all the content was deconstructed into bite-size chunks of information. Soon after the content was broken down and presented in various formats to deliver learning objects in different learning styles that provided a certain level of adaptability (Ck12.org, 2017).

Sophia is an online platform created for any education enthusiast that provides the possibility of including bite size lessons so educators and tutors can use them to teach others in a social network environment. The website covers most educational areas and offers self-paced courses free of charge or at a very low cost (Sophia.org, 2017).

Curriki is an online community where educators, learners and parents can work together to build and share educational material. The platform provides free and open resources with the mission of eliminating the gap of those who have an access to high-quality education and those who do not. With a community of over 10 million global users, Curriki encourages collaboration and the development of educational skills in all kinds of levels (Curriki.org, 2017).

3. UNIVERSAL DESIGN AND USABILITY

The Brazilian Legislation determines that everyone has the right to education and accessibility. To extend this concept, it is necessary to understand how digital media promotes equal access to navigability perspectives. Furthermore, educational technology should achieve full virtual accessibility for all users.

Universal design (UD) is a way to generate environments, services, products and technologies that can be used in a balanced way, offering security and autonomy to the greatest number of people without the need for adaptation or readaptation (Sonza et al., 2013).

Developed at North Carolina State University, UD aims to be egalitarian and reach all audiences, unrestrictedly. There are seven principles that guide digital accessibility practices, regardless of the type of user: compatible use (egalitarian), flexible (adaptable) use, simple and intuitive, noticeable information, tolerance to error (safe), low requirements on physical effort and the size and space for access and use (Sonza et al., 2013, Okimoto et al., 2015). In this context, it can be said that MOOC platforms are examples of learning environments that can democratize the access of all citizens to communication and education: people can register, enroll, access courses and gain new and meaningful knowledge using information technologies (Aldahdouh and Osório, 2016, Ulbricht *et al.*, 2011).

Universal Design is not the only movement to address the issues of digital virtual accessibility. They were also discussed by the World Wide Web (W3C) which is a committee made up of large Internet companies that committed themselves to develop guidelines and rules to make web sites accessible to all types of users (Sonza et al., 2013).

To formulate and maintain these recommendations, the WAI (Web Accessibility Initiative) was created. Some examples of WAI are WCAG 1.0 (1999), that had its content revised in Brazil under Laws 10.098 and 10.048/2000, by Decree 5.296/2004 that regulates such laws. There are also complementary recommendation such as e-MAG (Electronic Accessibility Model) from 2005, and in the updated version of WCAG 2.0 (2008) translated into Brazilian Portuguese in 2014 (Sonza et al, 2013).

These documents relate to the interface design. They contain guidelines that web developers should consider regarding navigation formats. With the suggested structure users from all around the world, just like as in universal design, can get the same technological patterns, visual language even with the use of plugins, programs, or applications (i.e. screen readers for the visually impaired). For these reasons, MOOC platforms have been sought to illustrate the current digital access context.

4. METHODOLOGY

In the current research, the methodology from Conforto, Amaral and Silva (2011) was used as a bibliographic review process, following a script entitled by the author as "RBS Roadmap". The first step of this paper was to define a bibliographic review strategy, to gather information about scientific productions on MOOC platforms and also to find correlated projects.

The research followed the IDEM steps: defining the problem, identifying the primary source, finding ideal keywords for the research, applying inclusion and exclusion criteria, as well as processing results documentation.

The libraries database were chosen according to the location of the object of study (query to the regional collection of the Library System of the Federal University of Paraná, acronym SIBI/UFPR); in publications of the Brazilian Digital Library of Theses and Dissertations, in responsibility of the Brazilian Institute of Information and Technology (Ibict / BDTD); in Scopus library database; and the CAPES journals.

The databases search was held in the first half of April 2017, considering the productions from 2010 onwards. Firstly, the search was to relate the information regarding assistive technology and adaptive teaching both associated to the MOOC platforms.

The data associated with the search were delineated with the access, proximity to the subject of study, and opposing what was predicted, it was necessary to increase the number of keywords to obtain more search results for further discussions.

Based on the theoretical guidelines, a structured form was created to perform an analysis focusing on the usability of MOOC platforms according to the criterion established by Engelhart (2002), Van Deer Waarde (1993) and Mijksenaar (1997). It was established two categories for comparison: symbolization modes and variable types. The platforms were evaluated according to the fulfillment of the presented requirements.

5. RESULTS AND DISCUSSION

The objective of this study was to perform a brief analysis on the usability of Massive Open Online Courses (MOOC) platforms according to a set of pre-established parameters of Universal Web Design.

Taking into consideration only non sensory impairments users, Table 2 shows the scores obtained by each MOOC. A scale of 1 to 3 was created to evaluate each criteria. The score 1 represents a POOR evaluation, representing the features that did not meet the specifications of the analysed criteria; the score 2 represents an AVERAGE evaluation, a result that evidenced the features that are satisfactory but could be improved regarding the analysed criteria; and the score 3 represents an OPTIMAL evaluation, meaning that the feature evaluated on the MOOC meets all requirements of the analysed criteria.

Table 1. Evaluation of Sophia, CK-12 and Curriki platforms based on Engelhart (2002), Van der Waarde (1993) and Mijksenaar (1997) categories

Categories evaluated	Sophia	Ck-12	Curriki
	3-Optimal	**2-Average**	**1-Poor**
1. Symbolization Modes			
Pictorial	3	3	3
Verbal	2	3	3
2. Variable Types			
Differentiating variables			
Colors	2	3	3
Illustrations	3	2	3
Number or Width of columns	3	2	3
Types/Fonts	1	3	3
Hierarchical variables			
Layout Element Position	1	3	3
Sequential Position of the element	2	3	3
Size and Weight of Type	2	2	3
Line Spacing	3	3	3
Alignments	1	2	3
Support Variables			
Box	**3**	**3**	**3**
Shading and Color areas	**2**	**3**	**3**
Lines	**3**	**3**	**3**
Text attributes (italic, bold, etc.)	**1**	**3**	**3**
Responsiveness	**1**	**2**	**3**
Navigation/navigability	**1**	**3**	**3**

Table 1 shows qualitative data about the symbolization modes: Pictorial and Verbal. That is, how images are presented and if there are words associated with them. (Engelhart, 2002; Van der Waarde, 1993; Mijksenaar, 1997).

The use of images (pictorial feature) in Sophia, CK-12 and Curriki platforms was OPTIMAL making it easy for users to identify courses and modules. For this reason, all three platforms evaluated received maximum score (3). In the textual relationship between the reader and the web pages, only the Sophia platform received and AVERAGE score, due to the perceptional quality unsatisfactory when used in different browsers. Furthermore, Sophia depends on constant updates to work properly.

In order to evaluate the Variable Types,, a few groups were organized to facilitate the analysis. The elements in this category were analyzed taking into consideration the result of the interface design influenced by the whole set of the web pages and also by how it is presented to the user.

The Differentiating Variables are the graphic elements that compose the objects accessed on the screen device. They can be splitted into the following categories: colors, illustrations, width and number of columns and types. These elements are the very first visual information that the user sees while accessing a platform. The Hierarchical Variables correspond to the organization of the elements in the visual space, such as the sequence, size and weight of the visual type, the space between lines and the alignments. They create an environment to facilitate users to read and understand information. Support Variables accentuate, emphasize, and organize relationships among the previous types of classes established.

6. CONCLUSION

In the transcription of the items listed in Table 2, there are qualitative data about symbolization modes, which means how the images are presented ("pictorial"), and the "verbal" term means images associated and the direction relations (indicative arrows of the reading path) between screen elements ("schematic") (Engelhart, 2002; Van Deer Waarde, 1993; Mijksenaar, 1997).

The use of images (pictorial) of the Sophia, CK-12 and Curriki platforms was enough to identify available courses and modules satisfactory. For this reason, all three platforms evaluated got maximum score. that reason all received a maximum score, three points. In the textual relationship between the reader and the web pages, only the Sophia platform received partial evaluation, because its provision quality it is not enough when used in more browsers. Furthermore, Sophia depends on constant updates to work properly.

On the schematic symbolization mode, there was no record because of the lack such element in all the platforms evaluated.

In order to evaluate the Types of Variables, groups were organized to give scores related to the expected quality, with the same structure as the initial stage. The result of the interface design is influenced by the whole set of the web page and also how it is presented to the user.

The differentiating variables are the graphic elements that compose the objects on the access device screen: colors, illustrations, width and number of columns, types. At last, they are the very first visual information that the user has contact, except in the case of a visually impaired person.. The hierarchical variables correspond to the organization of the elements in the visual space, such as the sequence, size and weight of the visual type, the space between lines, the alignments, so that the user can read the information and understand it. Support variables accentuate, emphasize, and organize relationships between the previous types of classes established.

During the analysis and scoring items for Sophia Platform, items, it was verified that the settings for pictorial mode did not fully meet all the user needs because there was no uniformity of types, and in verbal mode the colors used were not visualized with enough contrast.

Regarding the types of variables, the colors of the differentiating variables do not follow an identity for the message to the operator, and the types have smaller size than the ideal. The reading process becomes difficult because they present 4 dashboards which make difficult to organize the reading process in sectors, and also the colors do not have a proper contrast with the background colors. The element position in the layout make difficult to browse the page for not having regularity in scrolling the screen and the continuity in the reading hierarchy. This issue occurs again with the sequence of these elements and the incoherence of the courses groups proposed by the platform. Also the alignment of the access buttons to the courses was impaired by this structure. The platform is not responsive, which means that when used on more than one display size or a different device, the web page distorces.

The box and row support variables are appropriate. Shading and color spots do not follow a pattern for all homepage pages. The variation of the text attributes (italic, bold, types) represent an excess of visual information to the user. In conclusion, the platform analysis shows that it meets the browsing expectations, however it is advisable to adapt it to facilitate the access of the elderly or people with visual disabilities related to digital accessibility.

The CK-12 platform presented positive results in the modes of symbolization, pictorial and verbal. In the types of illustrative variables, it showed lack of uniformity for the visualization by the operator. On the other hand, the size was ideal to identify the subject of each course.

It has been programmed semi-responsive and loses quality during zoom in and zoom out, necessary to the user needs related to his reading standard. It has also been programmed using tables which impairs the use of screen reader for visually impaired people.

The hierarchical variables related to size and "weight" of the alignment types are large compared with the text. This does not impede the reading, but it makes it difficult to identify the courses by people with low vision. The Curriki platform had a positive evaluation of the symbolization modes and types of variables. The dashboard is organized according to a logical sequence to courses access, with accessible visualization, good distribution of the colors differentiating variables, and illustrations. The hierarchical and support variables corresponded to the parameters for the ideal visualization of the elements for people without special needs. The responsiveness present on the platform aids in the action of magnifying the images for people with disabilities or low vision.

REFERENCES

Albino, J. and Bergamaschi, S. (2013). Gestão do Conhecimento e EAD: uma reflexão. In: W. Yonezawa and D. Barros, ed., *Ead, tecnologias e TIC*. São Paulo: Cultura Acadêmica, pp. 99-123.

Aldahdouh, A. and Osório, A., 2016. Planning to Design MOOC? Think First. *In The Online Journal of DIstance Education and e-Learning – TOJDEL*, Vol. 4, No. 2, pp 47-57.

Almeida, M, 2003. Educação a distância na internet: abordagens e contribuições dos ambientes digitais de aprendizagem. *In Educação e Pesquisa*, Vol. 29, No. 2, pp 327-340.

Busarelo, R., Quevedo, S. and Vanzin, T. (2011). A comunicação com o aluno surdo. In: V. Ulbricht, T. Vanzin and V. Villarouco, ed., *Ambiente Virtual de aprendizagem inclusivo*. Florianópolis: Pandion, pp. 101-154.

Ck12.org, (2017). *About CK12*. [online] Available at: https://www.ck12info.org/about/mission/?_ga=1.184757097.1963957510.1493233595 [Accessed 17 Apr, 2017].

Conforto, E., Amaral, D. and Silva, S., 2011. Roteiro para revisão bibliográfica sistemática: aplicação no desenvolvimento de produtos e gerenciamento de projetos. *8º Congresso Brasileiro de Gestão de Desenvolvimento de Produto*. Porto Alegre, Brazil, pp. 1-12.

Curriki.org, (2017). *About Curriki*. [online] Available at: http://www.curriki.org/about-curriki/

[Accessed 17 Apr, 2017].

Engelhardt, J., 2002. *The language of graphics: a framework for the analysis of syntax and meaning in maps, charts and diagrams*. Universiteit van Amsterdam, Amsterdam, The Netherlands.

Filatro, A., 2007. *Design instrucional contextualizado: educação e tecnologia*. Editora Senac, São Paulo, Brazil.

Mijksenaar, P., 1997. *Visual function: an introduction to information design*. 010 Publishers, Rotterdam, The Netherlands.

Moore, M. and Kearsley, G., 2008. *Educação a distância: uma visão integrada*. Cengage Learning, São Paulo, Brazil.

Moraes, M., 2002. *Educação a distância: fundamentos e práticas*. Unicamp, Campinas, Brazil.

Morandi, M. and Camargo, L., 2015. Revisão sistemática de Literatura. In: A. Dresch, D. Lacerda and J. Antunes, ed., *Design Science Research: método de pesquisa para avanço da ciência e tecnologia*. Porto Alegre: Bookman, pp. 141-172.

Okimoto, M., Teixeira, S. and Heemann A., 2015. *Design Univesal para Inclusão de Pessoas com Deficiência em Linhas de Produção Industriais: análise estruturada de publicações. In Estudos em Design*, Vol. 23, No. 2, pp. 133-149.

Pisutova, K., 2012. Open education. *Proceedings IEEE International Conference on Emerging e-Learning Technologies and Applications*. Stará Lesná, Slovakia, pp. 297-300.

Sonza, A., Kade, A., Façanha, A., Rezende, A., Nascimento, G., Rosito, M., Bortolini, S. Fernandes, W., 2013. *Acessibilidade e tecnologia assistiva: pensando a inclusão sociodigital de PNEs*. Instituto Federal do Rio Grande do Sul, Bento Gonçalves, Brazil.

Sophia.org, (2017). *About Sophia.* [online] Available at: https://www.sophia.org/about [Accessed 17 Apr,2017].

Ulbricht, V., Vanzin, T. and Villarouco, V., 2011. *Ambiente virtual de aprendizagem inclusivo.* Pandion, Florianópolis, Brazil.

Van der Waarde, K., 1993. A*n investigation intothe suitability of the graphic presentation of patient package inserts.* University of Reading, Reading, United Kingdom.

FACTORS FAVORING THE DEVELOPMENT OF EDUCATIONAL APPS. USABILITY STUDY OF MOBILE APPLICATIONS TO TEACH PROGRAMMING

Miguel García-Iruela and Raquel Hijón-Neira
Department of Computing Science, Universidad Rey Juan Carlos
Móstoles, Madrid, Spain

ABSTRACT

The use of smart-phones and tablets has had a big impact on our habits of handling interactive applications. These devices provide us with plenty of information to consult whenever we want. Developing an application is not difficult even lacking a high level of programming. However, creating high-quality application with good usability and the capacity of engaging the users is doubtless a more demanding task. This article shows the usability study of two educational apps created to teach programming and the experiences carried out with students from university and vocational training. The experiences took place in two countries, within an interval of three years. Through the experiences, we identified several very suitable factors in the development of educational apps, especially in teaching programming.

KEYWORDS

Teaching programming, Usability, Higher Education, Mobile Applications

1. INTRODUCTION

The arrival of mobile phones promoted a dramatic change in our concept of communications. New generations cannot imagine a world without smart-phones and the functionalities that they provide. Although the early smart-phones had many limitations, their hardware nowadays closely approaches that in personal computers. Referring to the increase in power of these devices, Microsoft announced in the Windows Hardware Engineering Conference (WinHEC) a Windows 10 version for devices with ARM processors, very common in smart-phones and tablets. Related to this fact, we made a study about educational applications specific for smart-phones and tablets, and their limitations.

Students often run into difficulties in their training. Many times, these obstacles found generate such anxiety that they become frustrated (Ibáñez, et al., 2014). The use of a technology that is closer and friendlier to them can boost attraction and interest (Ganapathy et al., 2016). There are plenty of mobile applications for this purpose with a wide range of topics. Apps can be created to train the employees of a company or to use a motivational effect to promote exercises such as "Zombies, Run!" (Gillman & Bryan, 2016).

This article presents the usability study of two applications for teaching Java programming, used in two experiences, of two different educational environments, with people from two countries. We implemented these applications in the School of Computer Science at the University of Lisbon and the higher degree of Information Technology for vocational training in Madrid at the Educational Superior Institute (I.E.S.) Clara del Rey. After the experiences, we analyzed the data provided by the students and the experts to investigate the motivations and features of Apps that should be taken into consideration by anyone intending to develop educational applications. Section 2 shows the state of the use of Apps in education. Section 3 presents the applications used in this study and their comparative analysis, section 4 describes the research methodology, and then section 5 analyzes the experimental part. Finally, section 6 summarizes the conclusions.

2. STATE OF THE ART

2.1 Apps in Education

Nowadays, the Information and Communication Technologies (ICT) are playing an important role in our society. ICT refers to technologies that involve the computer and the Internet; these technologies allow processing, storage, transmission and consultation of massive amounts of information. This group of technologies includes local programs, databases, multimedia and online technologies such as forums, blogs, e-learning platforms, social networks, and the like (Jaramillo et al., 2009). In the ICT environment, there is no shortage of information, rather an overabundance (Piscitelli, 2012). Its use in education provides a wide range of possibilities, which has generated a great advance as mediators of the teaching-learning process, allowing the incorporation of very diverse digital contents (Rugeles et al., 2015). These technologies can be used for many activities, from the creation of an educational radio using the podcast platform (Ausín et al., 2016) to teaching people with special needs (Pascuas-Rengifo et al., 2015). This paper focuses on applications for teaching Java programming in higher education.

According to Lan & Sie (2010), learning through mobile devices is a profitable way of accessing educational material at any place and time. In medicine, for instance, several published studies show the benefits of accessing information through mobile applications (Nason et al., 2015; Briz-Ponce et al., 2016). The explosive advance in mobile technologies has dramatically increased the contribution of these devices to the educational field (Lan & Sie, 2010; Hung & Zhang, 2012; Hwang & Tsai, 2010; Liu et al., 2010). The use of mobile applications for learning produce positive impacts (Leinonen et al., 2016), especially for combined learning, social learning, student-centered learning, collaborative learning and project-based learning. Mobile game applications with attractive interfaces encourage the students to spend more time playing, and improve their learning process (Sanchez & Olivares, 2011). For this reason, it is highly recommended that developers of mobile applications for teaching take into account the opinion of students concerning the complexity or the difficulty of using the Apps (Navarro et al., 2016).

A great example of a mobile application developed for teaching is "Accounting Challenge", aimed to teach accounting in a fun way, away from classrooms. By the end of September of 2016 the 23,230 downloads of the App in 90 countries had earned for it three international awards (Seow & Wong, 2016).

An application created to help students of ESL College to learn English contains 852 words, each with seven characteristics: spelling, pronunciation, meaning in the Chinese language, synonyms, antonyms, speech and examples in some sentences. The conclusions of the study show that the experimental group that used the application achieved significantly better results than the control group (Wu, 2014; Wu, 2015).

There are several successful experiences of the use of applications for language learning from English to Japanese. Published results highlight the efficacy of smart-phones and tablets for learning Japanese in an Australian university, where user satisfaction on the use of applications was measured (Ota, 2015). In other educational levels, the game "1910" is an application in which the student plays the role of a journalist reporting the main moments of the Republic's implementation in Portugal (Cruz et al., 2015).

The applications used in the experiences described in this article are oriented to computer science teaching as in Yoo et al. (2016), who conceive applications as learning aids through multimedia elements and previously loaded texts. At this point, the use of applications on mobile devices is justified as a good tool that helps providing access to resources and information in a user-friendly way which today's students are accustomed to (Casillas et al., 2016). Young people are interested in using mobile applications and e-Books (Fojtik, 2015).

2.2 Apps Usability

Currently, no special programming skills are required to develop applications for mobile devices; some tools, such as "App Inventor", greatly simplify the process (A-Ghamdi et al., 2016; Cardoso & Freixo-Nunes, 2015). A more advanced objective is that educational applications should aim to "hook" users and keep their attention to improve the process of teaching (Sanchez & Olivares, 2011).

Two main issues eventually decide whether users will accept the App: usability and the user´s experience. Usability is "the extent to which a product can be used by specified users to achieve specified goals with effectiveness, efficiency and satisfaction in a specified context of use" (ISO, 1998). It very much depends on efficiency and learning experience (Ganapathy et al., 2016). The user´s experience expresses "a person's perceptions and responses that result from the use, or anticipated use, of a product, system or service" (ISO, 1998). For instance, users usually reject e-books where reading is unpleasant and interfaces are not very intuitive. It is not surprising, that the main JISC studies (JISC national e-books observatory project) stress the importance of improving the end-user experience (Muir & Hawes, 2013).

Jou et al., (2016) conclude that developing e-books and Apps that are practical in the education field require converting abstract concepts into real examples, to provide learning activities that hold the user (challengers), to offer multisensory experiences, to establish logical connections between different points of knowledge and to give students solutions to problems. However, a main point is that the result of teaching depends directly on the learning style of each student (Jou et al., 2016).

Another aspect to consider is the requirements of the applications from the point of view of teachers. In this respect, Cherner et al. (2016) offer some guidelines to evaluate them. In our study (this paper), we focused on the assessment of usability and experience as proposed by Hassenzahl (2000, 2004).

3. ANALYSIS OF APPLICATIONS OF THE STUDY

We designed an experiment to evaluate the usability of two applications developed for teaching Java programming by our research group LITE (LITE, 2017) using Android. The aim was to obtain qualitative conclusions about the usability and motivation of educational applications at the Spanish Vocational Training center IES Clara del Rey and at the University of Lisbon (Portugal).

"GoJavaGo" (GoJavaGo, 2017) and "SmartJava" (SmartJava, 2017) are applications created for smart-phones and tablets with Android operating system. Both applications divided the subject in 6 topics: 1. Basics elements, 2. Structured instructions, 3. Subprograms, 4. Recursion, 5. Arrays, and 6. Files. However, their interfaces are completely different.

3.1 Description of the Applications

"GoJavaGo" (Figure 1) has an initial screen similar to an electronic book with a drop-down menu on the right side that allows navigating through the various topics. It has several sections explaining theoretical concepts and examples of Java programming. Additionally, it presents the users with a self-evaluation test at the end of each topic.

When users consult the theory, the menu remains hidden, enabling them to observe the content on full screen, as if the device were a book. The test part is accessed using the right menu in section 7 (entitled How much do you know?). Once inside the section, the App displays a menu with several theme options. The user can choose one option and answer a test with questions type 'test' or 'true/false' format. At the end of each test, users can review the result. Questions answered correctly are displayed while incorrect responses will be displayed in red together with the adequate choice in green. The default language is English, but there is also a Spanish option.

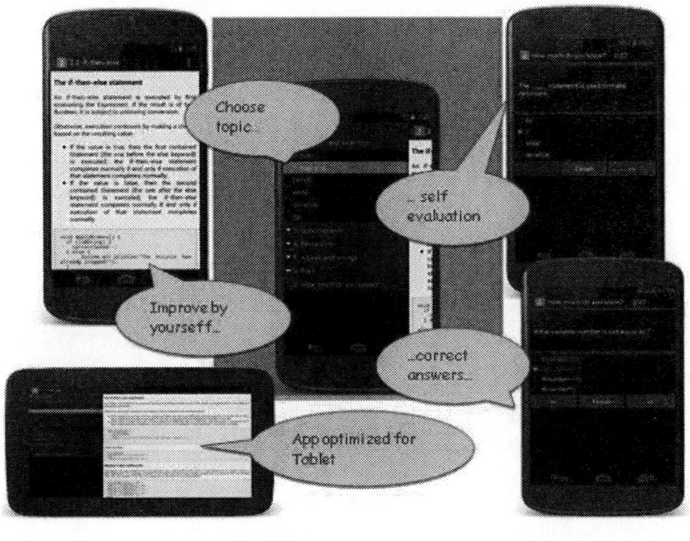

Figure 1. Application "GoJavaGo"

"SmartJava" (Figure 2) has an initial screen with a menu where users can consult the statistics of completed tests (right answers vs attempted by topic), check options (vibration, language, 'true/false' alert) or continue with a new test, select topics, and, in some topics, type of questions.

The topics available are: 1. Pre-form, 2. Introduction, 3. Structured instructions, 4. Subprograms, 5. Recursion, 6 Arrays, 7. Introduction in POO, 8. Time trial test, 9. Resistance test, 10. Failed questions, 11. Later form. Option 1 is a previous form. Options 2 to 7 present questions about the topic. Option 8 is a test to try to answer the maximum number of questions in two minutes. Option 9 is a test that ends when the user fails a question. Option 10 is a test that presents all the questions failed in the previous tests and gives a new chance to answer them. Option 11 offers a form to be filled after finishing all the topics.

The tests offer several types of questions, such as: 1. True or false, 2. Multiple choices or 3. Short answer. True or false questions are answered using the tactile functionality of the device by drawing a "V" for true or an "F" for false (not true). In the questions, there is the possibility of pressing "share", to share it on Facebook or Twitter. The bulb on the top left side of the screen is a link to an embedded web page with additional information related to the question (Figure 2). To unlock the contents, users must necessarily carry out the previous tests.

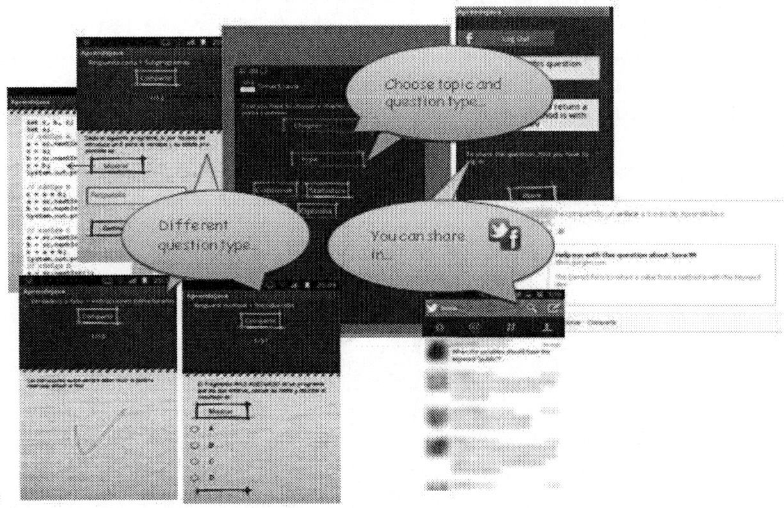

Figure 2. Application "SmartJava"

3.2 Comparison of Applications

For easier comparison of the applications, we present a table with various relevant features (Table 1).

Table 1. Comparison of Applications

Characteristics	Applications	
	Smart Java	GoJavaGo
Theoretical concepts		X
Code examples		X
Embedded web	X	
True or False questions	X	X
Short answer questions	X	
Individual game	Time trial and resistance test	
Incentives	Show statistic	
Multilingual	English/Spanish	English/Spanish
Share questions in social networks	Facebook and twitter	
Recovery failed questions	X	
Review questions		X
Blocked content	X	
Questions with pictures	X	
Web test	Init.& fin.exam linked-Moodle	
Add content	Using xml files or by code	

First, the table compares whether the applications have a part to present theoretical concepts and whether they offer practical examples with code. Only "GoJavaGo" has this section, although "SmartJava" allows, in certain questions, to access an embedded web page with related/additional information. Both applications include 'test' and 'true or false' questions about Java programming. "SmartJava" also has short-answer questions. "SmartJava" has more options. To motivate users, it has individual games like the time trial test and the resistance test. If we mix those games with the option that shows statistics, we obtain a motivational effect to improve and overcome previous marks. "SmartJava" establishes a minimum mark to access the following tests and allows sharing questions on Facebook and Twitter. "SmartJava" uses gamification. Both applications allow question reviewing: "GoJavaGo" checks the whole test showing the solutions while "SmartJava" stores the list of failed questions and presents them in the 'failed questions' test section. Additionally, "SmartJava" offers the option of language change, whereas "GoJavaGo" lacks this option and automatically adapts to the language of the device.

Concerning the interfaces, "GoJavaGo" looks like an electronic book with a formal design, using black and several shades of blue colors, and combining theoretical sections with test sections. In contrast, the "SmartJava" interface simulates a blackboard for menus and a notepad for tests, in reference to these elements usual in classrooms.

4. RESEARCH METHODOLOGY

The experiment consisted of two parts: the experience on the Computer Science Department (C.S.D.) in the Universidade de Lisboa (Portugal) in 2013 and the experience in the IES Clara del Rey (Spain) in 2017.

The Lisbon experience was held on the Superior Computer Science School (C.S.D.) of the Universidade de Lisboa. Twelve experts, 11 men and a woman, with an age range between 23 and 51 years, take part in the experience. All of them used both applications. For each application, firstly it was made a demonstration to each participant; then, they were asked to use the apps performing the tests they included and consulting their contents; finally, they answered the questions in the online test about their experience using the app. The two questionnaires were answered at the end of the all the experiment.

The Madrid experience was held on the Superior Degree of Developing Multiplatform Applications within three weeks of class, 6 hours a week, to learn about Java Programming. Fourteen students, 11 men and 3 women with an age range varying from 19 to 38 years. In this case the teacher offered both applications to his students; students had used the apps both in class and on their free time; finally, they answered the questions on the same online test that on the previous experience.

5. EXPERIMENTATION

5.1 Analysis Presentation

The analysis of the Apps follows the indications given by Hassenzahl (2000, 2004) for the evaluation of interactive products. Therefore, to adequately evaluate the applications, it is advisable to consider aspects such as ergonomics, quality (simplicity, controllability...), hedonic quality (novelty, originality...), beauty and goodness. The data collected are quantitative values, complemented with qualitative inputs provided by the comments of the participants, as recommended by Hassenzahl (2004).

To collect data about the two apps under scrutiny, we asked all students participating in our experiences to complete a final survey. The survey consisted of ten questions, and a final open section for comments (Table 2). Questions 1 to 4 referred to pragmatic qualities, questions 5 to 8, to hedonic qualities, question 9 to appearance and question 10 to satisfaction. All questions rated from 1 to 7, the scheme is similar to previous published surveys and evaluations of usability in interactive products (Cardoso & Freixo-Nunes, 2015; Muir & Hawes, 2013).

Table 2. Items Analyzed in the Hassenzahl´s Evaluation of Interactive Products

Type	Values	
	1	7
Pragmatic Quality	Confusing Impractical Unpredictable Complicated	Structured Practical Predictable Simple
Hedonic Quality	Dull Tacky Cheap Unimaginative	Captivating Stylish Premium Creative
Beauty	Ugly	Beautiful
Goodness	Bad	Good

5.2 Analysis of Results

The evaluation by the students of Lisbon indicates a better pragmatism in "GoJavaGo", but a better hedonic quality in "SmartJava". Both applications reached similar scores in beauty; "SmartJava" rated better in goodness (Figure 3). In the Madrid experience, both Apps reached similar scores in the pragmatic quality, but "SmartJava" surpassed "GoJavaGo" in hedonic, beauty and goodness issues (Figure 4). The overall results resembled those from Lisbon but scores, as a whole, were somewhat lower (note differences in the scale of scores).

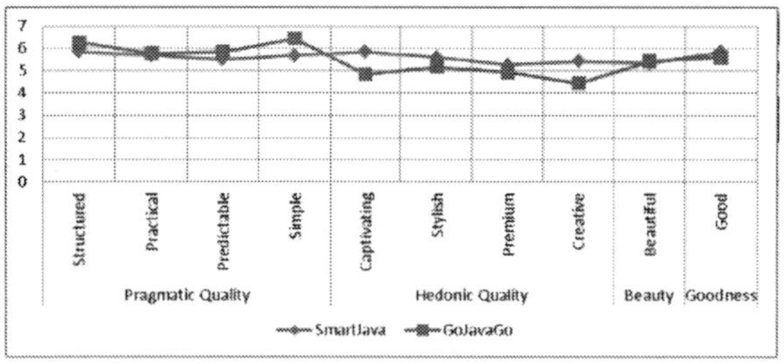

Figure 3. Results of the experience in Lisbon

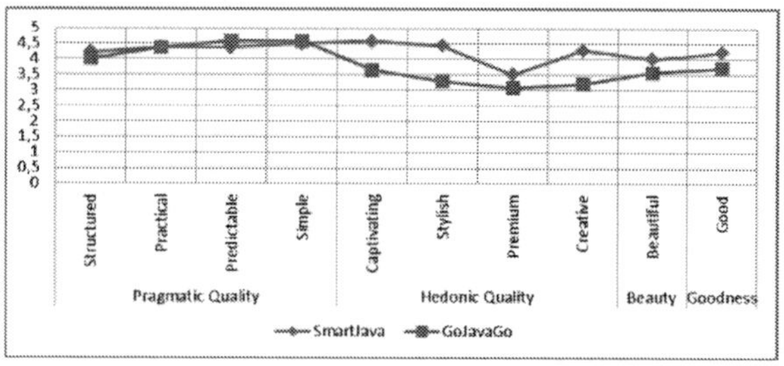

Figure 4. Results of the experience in Madrid

Looking at the overall results of both groups, "GoJavaGo" is more pragmatically valued due to the use of an electronic-book style, easier to use than the "SmartJava" interface. However, "SmartJava" reached better scores in the hedonic section. In beauty and goodness, the participants prefer "SmartJava" because it uses well-known elements of classrooms such as a notebook in tests, a blackboard as background, and chalk strokes to show text and buttons. All these provide a friendlier appearance and, subsequently, a greater user's satisfaction. Looking at figures 3 and 4, the graphs are quite similar, but the second (Madrid) is placed lower in the vertical axis than the first (Lisbon). It is as if the first graph was displaced downwards, obtaining poorer scores in all sections of the Apps. As the first experience dates from 2013 and the second from 2017, we interpret this shift as the result of aging of the Apps; over time, the valuation of the applications decreased paralleling the continuous worldwide improvement in Apps.

Considering possible gender differences, i.e., the scores given by men & women, they are similar (Figure 5).

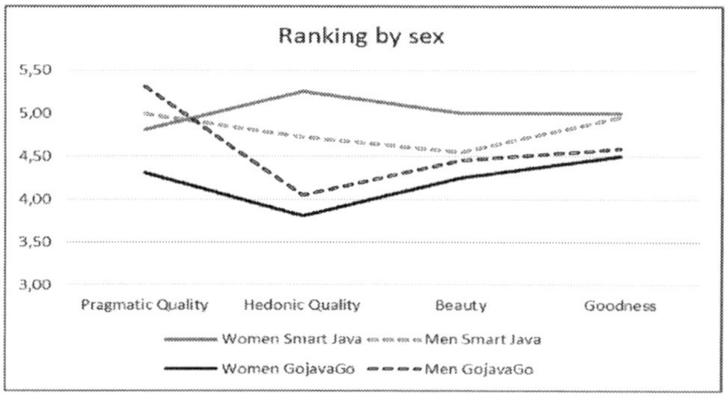

Figure 5. Results by Sex

In detail, men rated higher the pragmatic quality of "GoJavaGo", and women rated higher the hedonic, beauty and goodness sections of "SmartJava". In sum, "SmartJava" is clearly better valued in terms of hedonic appearance and slightly better in goodness and beauty. In contrast, "GoJavaGo" has an advantage in the pragmatic aspect, particularly its simplicity.

6. CONCLUSIONS

Developing applications for Android devices is relatively easy, even for people without extensive programming expertise. The difficult part is creating an application that is not only useful, but also user-friendly. A critical point is that the app should "hook" users (in our case students) and increase the time of use to improve education and training in the computing field. The difficulty is that we must reduce as much as possible the anxiety caused by the obstacles faced along the learning process. Anxiety leads to frustration and, in severe cases, dropping out of school (Ibáñez, et al., 2014). To avoid this problem, developers should implement user-friendly interfaces, to favor usability, coupled with rewarding interactive experiences. It is essential to attract users with beauty, goodness, simplicity, organization of contents, and creativity. We studied these aspects in this research.

This study focused on two applications for Android smart phones and tablets, both aimed at teaching Java programming. We carried out two experiences in higher education. The first in 2013 at the University of Lisbon and later at the high school IES Clara del Rey in Madrid. Despite the small size of the sample, this experiment shows interesting data. After the experiences, we concluded that nationality, sex and differences of training did not significantly influence the results of the surveys for the evaluation of the apps. The graphs plotted in figures 3 and 4 are very similar but we must point out that, in the time lapse separating the experiences, the score of both applications decreased in all topics. We interpret this fact as the logical result of obsolescence, because users are more demanding, in line with the evolution of technology and the App market. Consequently, maintaining the quality and beauty of applications requires continuous updates of interfaces and usability to keep up with the ever growing standards of usability and user satisfaction. The users consider both applications practical, but the simplicity and the ease of use of "GoJavaGo" make it a good choice in terms of usability. In contrast, students (especially women) valued well the beauty, creativity and style of "SmartJava". The use of a notebook appearance for the test, a blackboard for the menu background and print text and buttons as if chalk strokes, all familiar elements in a classroom, gave "SmartJava" a better appearance that was well appreciated in the surveys. Both applications have good quality. For future developments, we strongly recommend a hybridization between them, incorporating the simple interface of "GoJavaGo" and the elements of "SmartJava" that are familiar to users (such as a blackboard, a notepad, etc.) because they create a comfortable environment. Another very important fact revealed in this study is the need of continuously improving the Apps to compensate aging and decrease of appeal by incessant innovation.

ACKNOWLEDGEMENT

This research was supported by Ministerio de Economía y Competitividad (TIN2015-66731-C2-1-R) and Comunidad Autónoma de Madrid (S2013/ICE-2715). We are thankful to IES Clara del Rey and Universidade de Lisboa for giving us the opportunity to realize the experiences.

REFERENCES

A-Ghamdi, S. A. et al., 2016. Using App Inventor 2 in A Summer Programming Workshop: Improvements Over Previous Years. *IEEE Global Engineering Education Conference (EDUCON)*, Abu Dhabi, UAE pp. 383-388.

Ausín, V. et al. 2016. Aprendizaje Basado en Proyectos a través de las TIC. Una Experiencia de Innovación Docente desde las Aulas Universitarias. *Formación universitaria*, Vol. 9, No 3, pp 31-38.

Briz-Ponce, L. et al., 2016. Effects of Mobile Learning in Medical Education: A Counterfactual Evaluation. *Journal of Medical Systems*, Vol. 40, No. 6, pp.1-6.

Briz-Ponce, L. et al., 2016. Learning with mobile technologies – Students' behavior. *Computers in Human Behavior*, Vol. 72, pp. 612-620.

Cardoso, T. and Freixo Nunes, J.M. 2015. DIY M-Learning Apps com o APP Inventor do MIT: A aplicação LHPt (Letra e Hino de Portugal). *XVII Simposio Internacional de Informática Educativa*, Sétubal, Portugal pp. 277-280

Casillas Alvarado, M. A. et al., 2016. Afinidad tecnológica de los estudiantes universitarios. *Innovación Educativa,* Vol 16, pp. 151-175.

Cherner, T. et al., 2016. A detailed rubric for assessing the quality of teacher resource Apps. *Journal of Information Technology Education: Innovations in Practice*, Vol. 15, pp. 117-143.

Cruz, S. et al., 2015. 1910: Um jogo mobile para reviver a Implantação da República em Portugal. *XVII Simposio Internacional de Informática Educativa*. Setúbal, Portugal, pp. 219-226.

Fojtik, R., 2015. Ebooks and mobile devices in education. *4th World Conference on Educational Technology Researches (WCETR) Procedia Social and Behavioral Sciences,* Vol. 182, pp. 742-745

Ganapathy, M. et al., 2016. Malaysian ESL Students' Perceptions on the Usability of a Mobile Application for Grammar Test: A Case Study of ESL Undergraduates in University Sains Malaysia. *3L: The Southeast Asian Journal of English Language Studies,* Vol 22, No 1, pp. 127 -140.

Gillman, A. S. and Bryan, A. D, 2016. Effects of Performance Versus Game-Based Mobile Applications on Response to Exercise. *Annals of Beheavioral Medicine*, Vol 50, No 1, pp. 157-162.

GoJavaGo, (2017). *GoJavaGo Official Website* [online] Available at: http://www.lite.etsii.urjc.es/tools/gojavago/ [Accessed 23 Sept. 2017].

Hassenzahl, M. 2000. Hedonic and ergonomic quality aspects determine a software's appeal. *Proceedings of the CHI 2000 Conference on Human Factors in Computing*. New York: ACM.

Hassenzahl, M. 2004. The Interplay of Beauty, Goodness, and Usability in Interactive Products. *Human-Computer Interaction*, Vol. 19, No 4, pp. 319-349.

Hung, J. and Zhang, K. 2012. Examining mobile learning trends 2003-2008: A categorical meta-trend analysis using text-mining techniques. *Journal of Computing in Higher Education*, Vol. 24, No 1, pp. 1-17.

Hwang, G. and Tsai, C. 2011. Research trends in mobile and ubiquitous learning: A review of publications in selected journals from 2001 to 2010. *British Journal of Educational Technology*, Vol. 42, No 4, pp. 65-70.

Ibáñez, M. B. et al., 2014. Gamification for Engaging Computer Science Students in Learning Activities: A Case Study. *IEEE Transactions on Learning Technologies*, Vol. 7, No. 3, pp. 291-301.

International Organisation for Standardisation (IOS), 1998. ISO9241 Ergonomic, Part 11: Guidance on usability. Geneva, Switzerland.

Jaramillo, P. et al., 2009. Qué hacer con la tecnología en el aula: inventario de usos de las TIC para aprender y enseñar. *Educación y Educadores*, Vol. 12, No. 2, pp. 159-179.

Jou, M. et al., 2016. A study on the usability of E-books and APP in engineering courses: A case study on mechanical drawing. *Computers & Education*, Vol. 92-93, pp. 181-193.

Lan, Y. and Sie, Y. 2010. Using RSS to support mobile learning based on media richness theory. *Computers and Education*, Vol. 55, No 2, pp. 723-732.

Leinonen, T. et al., 2016. Mobile Apps for reflection in learning: A design research in K-12 education. *British Journal of Educational Technology*, Vol. 47, No. 1, pp. 184-202.

LITE, (2017). *LITE Official Website* [online] Available at: www.lite.etsii.urjc.es [Accessed 23 Sept. 2017].

Liu, Y. et al., 2010. Understanding the factors driving m-learning adoption: A literature review. *Campus-Wide Information Systems*, Vol. 27, No 4, pp. 210-226.

Muir, L. and Hawes, G., 2013. The case for e-book literacy: undergraduate students' experience with e-books for course work. *Journal of Academic Librarianship*, Vol. 39, No 3, pp. 260-274.

Nason, G. J. et al., 2015. The use of smartphone applications by urology trainees. *Surgeon-Journal of the Royal Colleges of Surgeons of Edinburgh and Ireland*, Vol. 13, No 5, pp. 263-266.

Navarro-Cota, C. X. et al., 2016. Factores que favorecen la adopción del m-learning. Una Revisión de la Literatura y Propuesta de una Taxonomía. *XVIII Simposio Internacional de Informática Educativa*, Salamanca, Spain. pp. 305-311.

Ota, F., 2015. Effectiveness of Smartphone and Tablet PC Apps for Japanese. *JALLT Journal of Language Learning Technologies*, Vol 44, No 2, pp. 64-82.

Pascuas-Rengifo, Y S. et al., 2015. Tecnologías de la información y las comunicaciones para personas con necesidades educativas especiales. *Entramado*, Vol.11, No 2, pp.240-248.

Piscitelli, A. 2012. *Las TIC No son una caja de herramientas, son una nueva cultura. Red Latinoamericana Portales Educativos (Relpe)*. [online] http://www.relpe.org/las-tic-no-son-una-caja-de-herramientas-son-una-nueva-cultura/ [Accessed 23 Sept. 2017].

Rugeles Contreras, P. A. et al., 2015. El rol del estudiante en los ambientes educativos mediados por las TIC. *Revista Lasallista de Investigación*, Vol. 12, No. 2, pp. 132-138

Sanchez, J., and Olivares, R. 2011. Problem solving and collaboration using mobile serious games. *Computers and Education*, Vol. 57, No. 3, pp. 1943-1952.

Seow, P. S. and Wong, S. P., 2016. Using a Mobile-Gaming App to Enhance Accounting Education. *Journal of Education for Business,* Vol. 91, No 8, pp. 434-439

SmartJava, (2017). *SmartJava Official Website* [online] Available at: http://www.lite.etsii.urjc.es/tools/smartjava/ [Accessed 23 Sept. 2017].

Wu, Q., 2015. Designing a smartphone App to teach English (L2) vocabulary. *Computers & Education*, Vol 85, pp. 170-179.

Wu, Q., 2014. Learning ESL Vocabulary with Smartphones. *3rd Cyprus International Conference on Educational Research (CY-ICER), Procedia Social and Behavioral Sciences*, Vol 143, pp. 302-307.

Yoo, W. S. et al., 2016. Curriculum Development for Computing Education Academy to Enhance High School Students' Interest in Computing. *6th IEEE Integrated STEM Education Conference (ISEC)* Princeton, EEUU pp. 282-284.

ZERO COPY SERIALIZATION USING RMA IN THE HPX DISTRIBUTED TASK-BASED RUNTIME

John Biddiscombe[1], Anton Bikineev[2], Thomas Heller[3] and Hartmut Kaiser[4]
[1]*CSCS, Swiss National Supercomputing Centre, Lugano, Switzerland*
[2]*Kaspersky Lab. Moscow, Russian Federation*
[3]*Friedrich-Alexander-Universität, Erlangen-Nürnberg, Germany*
[4]*Louisiana State University, USA*

ABSTRACT

Increasing layers of abstraction between user code and the hardware on which it runs can lead to reduced performance unless careful attention is paid to how data is transferred between the layers of the software stack. For distributed HPC applications, those layers include the network interface where data must be passed from the user's code and explicitly copied from one node to another. Message passing incurs relatively high latencies (compared to local copies) from the transmission of data across the network, as well as from the injection and retrieval of messages into and out of the network drivers that may be exacerbated by unwanted copies of data being made at different levels of the stack. As memory bandwidth is becoming one of the limiting factors in scalability of codes within a node, and latencies of messaging between nodes, it is important to reduce both memory transfers and latencies wherever possible. In this paper we show how the distributed asynchronous task-based runtime, HPX, has been developed to allow zero-copy transfers of data between arguments in user defined remote function invocations and demonstrate the performance of our network layer in a state-of-the-art astrophysics code.

KEYWORDS

Distributed, Task-based, Asynchronous, Runtime, Network, Serialization

1. INTRODUCTION

The HPX runtime system for parallelism and concurrency (Kaiser et al. 2014) is a C++ library that implements asynchronous execution of task (graphs) using futures as synchronization primitives and extends the C++ API with distributed operations using an Active Global Address Space (Kaiser et al. 2015). Asynchronous task launching is performed using an `async` function that is templated over the function type and over a variadic arguments list; this powerful construct allows the user to define any function - with *any number of arguments* - and invoke it asynchronously, returning a future. The C++ standard introduced this function in C++11 as a means of introducing concurrency into the language; when this feature is extended to allow arbitrary function invocations on remote compute nodes as well as the local node, it introduces the need to serialize the arguments into a buffer (marshalling) for transmission and then deserialize them on reception and pass the function arguments onwards to the call being made. When the arguments are small (in terms of bytes of memory required to represent them), then the arguments can be copied into a memory buffer and transmitted as one using an eager protocol, but when the arguments are larger, performance improves when using remote memory access (RMA) operations (using a rendezvous protocol) between nodes to avoid copies and reduce latency – this technique is employed by nearly all HPC message passing systems such as MPI/MVAPICH (W. Huang), PGAS models like UPC (El-Ghazawi et al.), Legion (Bauer et al. 2012).

In addition to implementing the serialization of arguments and RMA transfer between nodes, HPX is a multithreaded task based runtime that makes use of lightweight threads for fast context switching when suspending (or ending) one task and resuming (or starting) another, this means that our implementation must be thread safe (any thread may invoke a remote function at any time) and in order to be used in HPC applications our solution must give high performance.

2. RELATED WORK

There exist a large number of serialization libraries that are used for RPC purposes (as well as for persisting the state of objects to the filesystem or a database); they can be separated broadly into categories as follows

- Auto generated data requiring an intermediate description and/or pre-processor
- Auto generated but not requiring additional description/compiler
- Manually generated and possibly not strongly typed

Where auto generated means that code necessary to transfer parameters (either streamed/copied/placed) for functions can be generated by using either the native compiler for the system – or the compiler accompanied by an additional preprocessing/compilation step using a tool to transform a user supplied description of structures/data to be transmitted. The principal advantage of using an intermediate description of structures is that serialization between different languages (Java/Python/C++/&etc.) can be handled by the preprocessing step since it can generate different import/export code for each language. A secondary advantage is that it can produce very fast serialization code as the user has supplied type and size information to the preprocessor that makes it easier for the final compilation step to do the right thing. Serializers that fall into this category include Google's protobuf (Google & Varda 2017) and Flatbuffers, Apache thrift (Agarwal et al.) and the charm++ Pack/Unpack (PUP) framework (Kale & Krishnan 1993) and Cap'n Proto (Varda 2015). The principal disadvantage of these libraries is that they require the user to instrument any datatypes that they need to send/receive and/or run a preprocessing step over them before use. In projects that have a limited number of fixed messages/structures/records/types (or vocabulary) this is not a significant workload, but in a runtime system where the user may invoke arbitrary functions with arbitrary parameters, this places an unacceptable burden on the developer, particularly so for projects in their development phase where messages and types can be changing rapidly.

Notable libraries that do not require an intermediate description include the boost serialization library (Boost 1998-2017), the boost MPI library, Cereal. These libraries have the advantage of not requiring additional preprocessing steps and instead require the user to provide a (frequently trivial) serialization function for custom types that usually follows the pattern of Listing 1. (Note that built in types usually have serialization functions provided either as part of the language distribution or the serialization library provides them).

```
template <typename Char>
void serialize(output_archive & ar, const std::string<Char> & s, unsigned) {
    std::uint64_t size = s.size();
    ar << size;
    save_binary(ar, s.data(), s.size() * sizeof(Char));
}
```

Listing 1. Structure of a typical serialization function, an archive object is given a size and binary data, the templated type of the item being serialized allows the compiler to instantiate the correct specialization

The third category that requires manually generating serialization functions includes the MPI library itself and the HPC RPC framework Mercury (Soumagne et al.). With MPI, one can build custom datatypes to represent aggregates of other types and then pass these to the network for transmission, with Mercury one can do the same, but in addition each element may be designated either as a bulk data type or a normal argument. The user must register the function signature and provide a registered memory handle to each bulk data item so that the serialization of arguments can be done using an eager protocol to transfer bulk data handles, followed by a rendezvous phase where each of the bulk arguments is retrieved using an RMA get from the remote node. In this respect, Mercury performs essentially the same operation as the zero copy infrastructure in HPX, however, HPX being based on a C++ solution (rather than C) automates a large part of the function and argument registration to greatly simplify the process and place the burden of work on the compiler instead of the user.

When transferring data via RMA, a memory registration process known as pinning is required on both source and destination buffers. The reason for this is to ensure that when the RMA hardware driver initiates a copy from/into user memory and onto/off the wire, the memory must not have been paged out by the operating system. Registration can be an expensive operation (requiring a kernel level call) and so it is commonplace for networking libraries such as MPI, GASNet (Bonachea 2002), libfabric (Choi et al. 2015) to provide a pool of registered memory or a registration cache so that repeated requests for registration of memory blocks that are in pages of pre-pinned memory do not incur large costs. Memory registration caching can be a cause of problems as it depends on parameters that are system dependent, generally hidden from the user and can cause system instability or poor performance when incorrectly set. In the HPX messaging layer we expose an `allocator` (using a memory `pool`) that provides registered memory and a custom `vector` that makes use of it, and may in turn be used for variables that are frequently transmitted between nodes – this places the memory registration in the user's hands rather than leaving it to the system to make decisions - we will further discuss the serialization process in the following sections. PGAS programming models partition distributed memory such the address space spans all nodes and R/W operations to/from nodes are mapped from those addresses to the relevant node, this allows blocks of memory to be 'assigned' to communication on a per node basis – HPX uses an Id type for objects and localities to map addresses in the same way, but there is no block memory reservation made on any given node to represent objects or data on another node, the AGAS system acts as a distributed memory key value store holding the location of objects in the system.

3. SERIALIZATION

A large number of serialization libraries exist already and the need to re-implement one in HPX was driven by the desire to reduce unwanted memory copies and enable zero copy transfers – to illustrate what can happen in an extreme case Figure 1 shows that 5 copies of data can be created when a transfer is made. We wish to replace this with a single RMA (copy) operation between user variables at each end of a connection (when appropriate), to make this possible, HPX adopts a technique referred to as chunking.

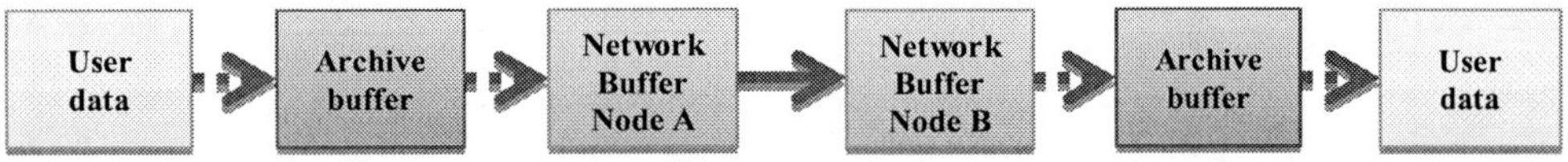

Figure 1. Memory copies that can occur when transferring data from user variables on one node to another

3.1 Serialization with Chunking

To solve the problem of serialization and zero-copy of arguments, HPX uses a chunk-based archive format that differs from 'flat' archives used elsewhere. If we consider the following function invocation where `action` represents a remote method, `locality` the Id of a remote node, `thing` an arbitrary return type (of the action function), and the parameters are typical function arguments, then we would like the small objects to be serialized as usual into a buffer, but the large data vector to be left untouched and instead pass a pointer into the network layer so that it can transfer the object directly without copying. Since the `async` implementation is a variadic template, the compiler can generate the serialization code for us if the type of each parameter is known. User defined types must provide a function of the kind shown in Listing 1, built in types and those provided by the STL are supplied by the HPX library, so `std::vector<float>` is automatically handled. The serialization layer creates an archive object that holds a special `chunker` object responsible for tracking blocks of data inserted into the archive - scalar parameters are inserted directly into the archive, however the vector is specialized to call `save_binary` on its data, which terminates the current chunk and writes a pointer chunk containing the vector's data pointer. The next argument may be another large object or a smaller one and depending on the serialization threshold may generate another pointer chunk or start a new index chunk (where the index tracks the size of data being incrementally written into the archive buffer). The process continues until all arguments are written. The archive therefore contains two objects, a raw buffer and a chunk list, both of which are transmitted across the network together.

```
char x = '5'; double y = 3.1415;
std::vector<float> data(1000000, 2.718);
hpx::future<thing> = hpx::async(action, locality, x, y, data, "string", ...);
```

Listing 2. Example of remote action invocation that benefits from a zero copy parameter

Figure 2. Structure of the chunk based archive generated for a function call similar to that shown in Listing 2, dotted lines delimit how individual sub-elements might be aligned within the index chunks. Pointer chunks always contain a single {pointer, size} entry

3.2 Serialize_Buffer

There is unfortunately a problem with Listing 2 that prevents us using the code exactly as shown - when a function is executed asynchronously, one must be careful when parameters are passed by reference, in case they go out of scope and are destroyed before the function is actually executed (which might happen at some arbitrary time later), so parameters should be *moved* or *copied* into an `async` function. We do not wish to copy the vector as this defeats the purpose of the exercise and we may not wish to move the vector as its data might still be required later on the local node. HPX therefore provides a `serialize_buffer` object that wraps data supplied into a shared pointer and passes it through the `async` API to the parcelport layer in HPX where it is then converted into a pointer chunk for transmission. Listing 3 shows the equivalent form of the function call. Since `serialize_buffer` uses reference count semantics, the network layer will release its reference once it is no longer needed and the sending code may either keep or release its own, with reclamation taking place when no copies are held. If a `serialize_buffer` is used to wrap a vector, it remains the responsibility of the user to ensure that the vector is not destroyed until transmission is complete (when the returned future becomes ready, it is guaranteed that the message has been delivered).

```
hpx::serialize_buffer buff(data_ptr, size);
hpx::future<thing> = hpx::async(action, locality, x, y, buff, "string", ...);
```

Listing 3. A serialize buffer is used to wrap binary data into a form that can be passed by reference using zero-copy

Note that if the remote function does a significant amount of work, the future returned may not become ready until long after the message has been delivered; if the user wishes to reuse buffers immediately after they have been sent, HPX provides an alternative function invocation `async_cb` that allows the user to attach a callback that will be triggered as soon as the parcelport layer has transmitted the data (but before the remote function has completed) – the callback signals that the buffers may be reused.

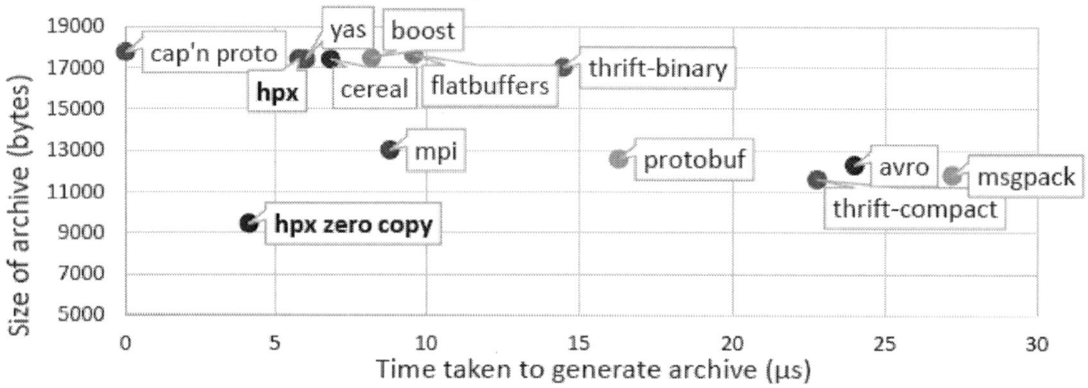

Figure 3. Comparison of serialization libraries. In general, the larger the size, the faster the time, HPX (with zero copy) produces small archives (because pointer chunks are skipped) and achieves good speed for the same reason

Note also that any type that has the traits `hpx::is_bitwise_serializable` may be wrapped in a `serialize_buffer` but if the data is smaller than the zero-copy serialization threshold (default 4KB), the serialization layer can copy data into the index chunk instead of creating a pointer chunk.

In Figure 3 we show the performance of the HPX serialization layer (with and without zero copy enabled) compared to a number of other libraries using an extended version of the '*C++ serialization comparison tool*' (Sorokin 2017). In the example used in the test, the parameters are not large (<20KB) so the advantage of using pointer chunks is not very significant, but it is clear that HPX performs extremely well; with the exception of Cap'nProto, HPX is the fastest library available even with zero copy disabled (when no pointer chunks are created and all data is copied into the archive), with zero copy enabled HPX is both faster and smaller (large data is not copied into the archive). The size of archives falls into 3 bands, with those that copy all data being just under 20KB, those that compress data being 11-13KB and HPX zero copy being the smallest. The Cap'nProto library achieves the best performance because it does not actually do any serialization – the archive is simply a pointer to the raw record structure of the message data. Unfortunately this approach cannot be used in HPX since it would require all functions to be invoked with a single parameter (a struct) and no zero copy of individual elements would be possible. (Note that, if and when static reflection capabilities are added to C++ (Chochlik et al.), serialization should become both faster and simpler for the user as the compiler will be able to do almost everything).

3.3 Parcelport

The serialized archive (data+chunk list) is passed to the parcelport (network layer) in HPX for transmission. The term 'parcel' is used to refer to the abstraction that represents the serialized form of the archive data, plus chunk list, and also a serialized descriptor of the remote function that must be invoked which is inserted at the start of the archive data (first index chunk); the function type is necessary because HPX uses active messages rather than simple data sends to waiting receivers.

The parcelport is responsible for converting the index and pointer chunks into actual messages that are sent. Multiple parcelport implementations exist in HPX, the default one uses MPI to send the parcel and chunks using non-blocking send + receive calls; the header block is transmitted using the eager protocol and if all data fits inside, then nothing more needs to be done. When pointer chunks are present (or the message exceeds the default (but configurable) 4096 byte limit, then an eager message is sent containing as much of the data as possible, and the remaining chunks must be received in a second round of rendezvous receives. MPI might zero copy pointer chunks using RMA or not depending upon how it internally decides to perform the send/receive.

Our new parcelport implementation is based on libfabric (an implementation also exists using infiniband ibverbs) and follows the same basic procedure except that pointer chunks may be registered on the fly and the memory keys passed in the eager header block so that during the second rendezvous round, data is RMA copied from the source into memory registered on the destination side (RMA get operation). The implementation is thread-safe and lock-free and integrates fully into the asynchronous HPX tasking runtime.

3.4 Extension to RMA Chunks

The ability to copy pointer chunks directly from user's variables is a significant advancement over the serialization process used in other libraries and gives a significant performance boost to HPX, but there is still a penalty incurred at both ends – registration of user variable memory on send and of memory to receive them into – we can avoid the registration of a blocks on the receive end, by using pre-registered memory, but this means that we must then copy the data from the registered block into the user's variable – otherwise when the memory is freed, it will not be reclaimed correctly unless we intercept the system malloc and maintain a registration cache for example (this is used by some MPI implementations to improve performance and libfabric also supports this behaviour). The drawbacks to transparently intercepting memory requests in this way are that when data is being frequently allocated and freed by the user and used in messages, the random fragmentation of blocks allocated to the user can lead to excessive pinned memory being reserved by the system since it can only pin whole pages at a time – only by forcing the user to allocate from a particular pool can this be kept under control. We seek a solution that explicitly places control of memory in user's hands and therefore provide an `rma_vector<T>` class that takes its memory from an `rma_allocator` that in turn uses a configurable memory pool provided by the parcelport being used (we aim to support many possible network layers and all have different memory registration handles and APIs so the pool abstraction must be specialized by each parcelport implementation).

Any datatype that is `is_bitwise_serializable` may be stored in an `rma_vector` and will be serialized by the HPX runtime automatically to produce an RMA chunk that stores the memory registration information needed by the network layer. We also provide a templated `rma_object<T>` for individual objects of significant size that can benefit from zero copy.

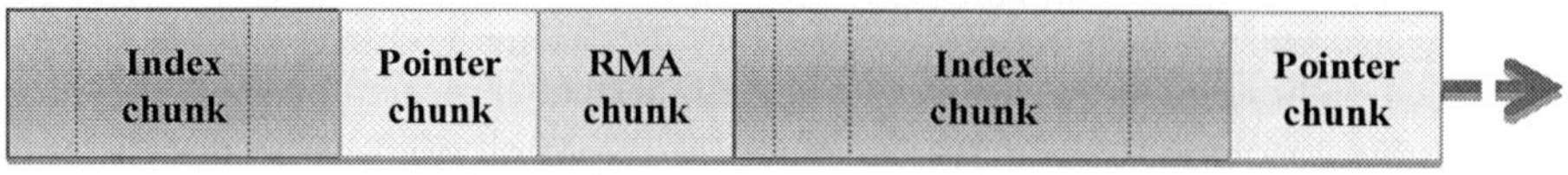

Figure 4. An archive may contain RMA chunks: pointer chunks with additional registered memory handles

The advantages of using an `rma_vector<T>` (or `rma_object<T>`) are that

- Memory is taken from an allocator that is aware of the memory registration API of the network and pinned when the user creates the data structure (or resizes it). It is therefore not pinned/unpinned on the fly during transfer, the RMA chunk constructed during serialization contains the memory handle already.
- The vector is a drop in replacement for `std::vector<T>` with the difference that the copy/assignment constructor makes a shared pointer copy of the internal data so it may be passed as a function parameter without the need to wrap it in a `serialize_buffer`.
- On the receive end of the message, the types of arguments are matched and during deserialization the HPX runtime will construct an `rma_vector<T>` to receive the data into; the received buffer can then be *moved* into the user variable and when freed will be given to the correct allocator for destruction. The user may declare as many or as few RMA capable objects as needed and does not rely on hidden functions intercepting memory requests to manage resources.

Figure 5 shows the performance of our libfabric parcelport compared to the existing MPI parcelport, and also the native OSU benchmark using Cray MPI running on Piz Daint, a Cray XC50 with 12 core Intel Xeon nodes and Aries dragonfly interconnect. The performance improvement over the previous HPX implementation is dramatic and we are able to achieve results close to the native MPI benchmark. It is important to note that the MPI OSU benchmark (Ohio-State-University & Panda 2017) implements a ping-pong of messages between two nodes; the native MPI implementation uses a blocking send and matching receive at each end in alternation and therefore does nothing more than poll the network, receive and return the message. As HPX is a task-based runtime using active messages, a ping-pong operation requires a message from one node to another with the action being to invoke a function that creates a message to send the arguments back. The HPX version of the OSU test therefore includes, parcel creation, serialization, deserialization and task creation/management which is why it does not achieve as high a performance as the native MPI implementation.

Figure 5 shows two important features, the speed improvement of the libfabric parcelport over the MPI parcelport is evident, however the effects of the RMA chunking can be seen when comparing the `serialize_buffer` and `rma_vector` versions of the test. When many threads are used, the cost of pinning and unpinning the memory on send and receive is hidden by the fact that many threads may take part in messaging – with 12 threads active, the two versions produce almost identical results. When only 2 threads are used the pre-pinned version with RMA chunks is on average 40% faster than the pointer chunk version for the larger messages sizes (below 4096 bytes, both use the eager protocol with data copied into the network). The difference between the two versions (lower latency, higher bandwidth) translates into a reduction in the idle or busy wait times of the thread pools in HPX which when running an application, means more time to perform productive work.

4. APPLICATION RESULTS

The performance of the RMA enabled parcelport is evident in the micro-benchmark test, but we wish to also demonstrate that the reduction in idle time translates into improved application performance. We have therefore tested OctoTiger, a 3D octree based, finite-volume AMR hydrodynamics code with Newtonian gravity; it is a successor to previous hydrodynamics codes described in (Kadam et al.) written using the HPX runtime as the parallelism framework for both on node and distributed operation.

Figure 6 shows the number of AMR grids processed per second using different levels of refinement (LoR) with the libfabric and MPI parcelports in HPX – (higher levels of refinement cannot be computed on smaller node counts, and lower levels of refinement show reduced performance on higher node counts); a pattern is clear from the results when the speedup is shown. With the exception of the level 7 LoR on high node counts, we see a performance improvement of between 25% and 50% across the board - at 24,576 cores on 2048 nodes, an improvement of 25% is highly significant, and it should be noted that this improvement is not just the messaging parts of the application, but the entire solve step which includes communication via re-gridding as the mesh is adapted/refined.

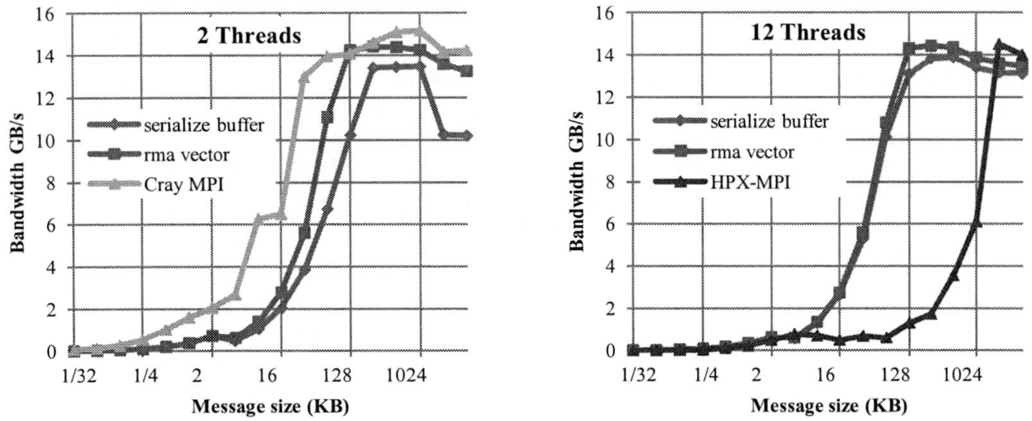

Figure 5. Performance of an HPX version of the equivalent OSU bi-directional bandwidth test between two nodes using the libfabric parcelport in HPX on different thread counts and with/without RMA chunking. Also included on (left) is the OSU micro-benchmark using Cray MPI and on (right), the HPX OSU test with the HPX parcelport implemented using MPI asynchronous calls

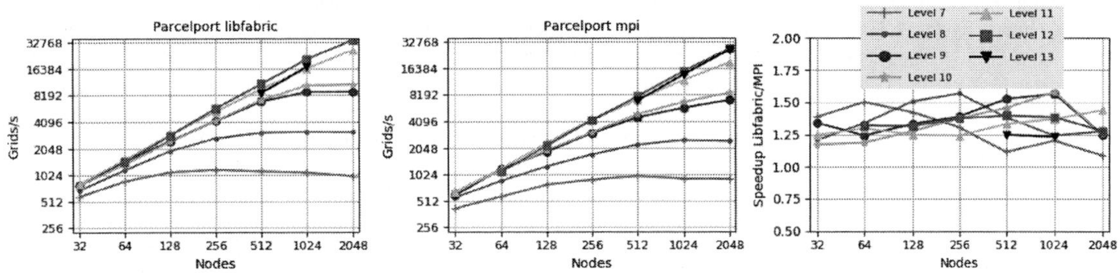

Figure 6. Comparison of the number of AMR grids processed per second for different levels of refinement when using the libfabric (left) and MPI (middle) parcelports with OctoTiger. The speedup (right) achieved when using libfabric compared to MPI. All tests were run using 12 cores per node on the Piz Daint supercomputer at CSCS

5. CONCLUSION

We have demonstrated that the serialization layer in HPX competes well against other libraries available and have extended it to support RMA features that make it possible to perform zero-copy RPC calls in distributed HPX task-based applications. In micro-benchmarks it performs well and this performance extends to improved application performance in large scale runs on state of the art supercomputers. Our implementation relies heavily on the strongly typed features of the C++ language and removes most of the burden of message optimization from the user, placing it instead on the compiler and runtime. This improvement to the HPX parcelport layer opens new opportunities for applications built on the HPX runtime and opens the door to exascale development for them.

ACKNOWLEDGEMENT

This project has received funding from the European Union's Horizon 2020 research and innovation programme under grant agreement No 720270 (HBP SGA1). The authors would like to thank the libfabric developers for their patience and assistance with development.

REFERENCES

Agarwal, A., Slee, M. & Kwiatkowski, M. (2007), Thrift: Scalable cross-language services implementation, Technical report, Facebook. http://thrift.apache.org/static/files/thrift-20070401.pdf

Bauer, M., Treichler, S., Slaughter, E. & Aiken, A. (2012), Legion: Expressing locality and independence with logical regions, *in* 'Proceedings of the International Conference on High Performance Computing, Networking, Storage and Analysis', SC '12, IEEE Computer Society Press, Los Alamitos, CA, USA, pp. 66:1–66:11. http://dl.acm.org/citation.cfm?id=2388996.2389086

Bonachea, D. (2002), Gasnet specification, v1.1, Technical report, Berkeley, CA, USA.

Boost (1998-2017), 'Boost: a collection of free peer-reviewed portable C++ source libraries'. http://www.boost.org/. http://www.boost.org/

Chochlik, M., Naumann, A. & Sankel, D. (2017), 'P0350R0: Static reflection', ISO/IEC C++ Standards Committee Paper. http://www.open-std.org/jtc1/sc22/wg21/docs/papers/2016/p0350r0.pdf

Choi, S.-E., Pritchard, H., Shimek, J., Swaro, J., Tiffany, Z. & Turrubiates, B. (2015), An implementation of ofi libfabric in support of multithreaded pgas solutions, *in* 'Proceedings of the 2015 9th International Conference on Partitioned Global Address Space Programming Models', PGAS '15, IEEE Computer Society, Washington, DC, USA, pp. 59–69. http://dx.doi.org/10.1109/PGAS.2015.14

El-Ghazawi, T., Carlson, W., Sterling, T. & Yelick, K. (2003), *UPC: Distributed Shared-Memory Programming*, Wiley-Interscience.

Google & Varda, K. (2017), 'Protocol buffers', http://code.google.com/apis/protocolbuffers/.

Kadam, K., Clayton, G. C., Motl, P. M., Marcello, D. & Frank, J. (2017), Numerical Simulations of Close and Contact Binary Systems Having Bipolytropic Equation of State, *in* 'American Astronomical Society Meeting Abstracts', Vol. 229 of *American Astronomical Society Meeting Abstracts*, p. 433.14.

Kaiser, H., Heller, T., Adelstein-Lelbach, B., Serio, A. & Fey, D. (2014), HPX: A Task Based Programming Model in a Global Address Space, *in* 'Proceedings of the 8th International Conference on Partitioned Global Address Space Programming Models', PGAS '14, ACM, New York, NY, USA, pp. 6:1–6:11. http://doi.acm.org/10.1145/2676870.2676883

Kaiser, H., Heller, T., Bourgeois, D. & Fey, D. (2015), Higher-level parallelization for local and distributed asynchronous task-based programming, *in* 'Proceedings of the First International Workshop on Extreme Scale Programming Models and Middleware', ESPM '15, ACM, New York, NY, USA, pp. 29–37. http://doi.acm.org/10.1145/2832241.2832244

Kale, L. V. & Krishnan, S. (1993), Charm++: A portable concurrent object oriented system based on c++, *in* 'Proceedings of the Eighth Annual Conference on Object-oriented Programming Systems, Languages, and Applications', OOPSLA '93, ACM, New York, NY, USA, pp. 91–108. http://doi.acm.org/10.1145/165854.165874

Ohio-State-University & Panda, D. K. (2017), 'MVAPICH: MPI over InfiniBand, 10GigE/iWARP and RoCE'. http://mvapich.cse.ohio-state.edu/benchmarks

Sorokin, K. (2017), 'Compare various data serialization libraries for c++'. https://github.com/thekvs/cpp-serializers

Soumagne, J., Kimpe, D., Zounmevo, J. A., Chaarawi, M., Koziol, Q., Afsahi, A. & Ross, R. B. (2013), Mercury: Enabling remote procedure call for high-performance computing., *in* 'CLUSTER', IEEE Computer Society, pp. 1–8. http://dblp.uni-trier.de/db/conf/cluster/cluster2013.html#SoumagneKZCKAR13

Varda, K. (2015), 'Cap'n proto'. https://capnproto.org/

W. Huang, G. Santhanaraman, H. J. Q. G. D. P. (2007), Design and implementation of high performance mvapich2: Mpi2 over infiniband.

INTERNET VOTING USING ZCASH

Pavel Tarasov and Hitesh Tewari
School of Computer Science and Statistics, Trinity College Dublin, University of Dublin, Ireland

ABSTRACT

Voting systems have been around for hundreds of years and despite different views on their integrity, have always been deemed secure with some fundamental security and anonymity principles. Numerous electronic systems have been proposed and implemented but some suspicion has been raised regarding the integrity of elections due to detected security vulnerabilities within these systems. Electronic voting, to be successful, requires a more transparent and secure approach, than is offered by current protocols. The approach presented in this paper involves a protocol developed on blockchain technology. The underlying technology used in the voting system is a payment scheme, which offers anonymity of transactions, a trait not seen in blockchain protocols to date. The proposed protocol offers anonymity of voter transactions, while keeping the transactions private, and the election transparent and secure. The underlying payment protocol has not been modified in any way, the voting protocol merely offers an alternative use case.

KEYWORDS

Blockchain, EVoting, Zcash, zk-SNARK

1. INTRODUCTION

With blockchain steadily striving towards becoming the new system for decentralized payment schemes, amongst other implementations, it is easy to imagine why this technology can be considered an ethical liberator in some senses. Blockchain, although a relatively new concept, has gained enough popularity for applications to emerge such as simplified methods for identification and authentication, the widely known decentralized payment scheme, Bitcoin, and domain systems which reside outside the control of the government or non-governmental organisations (NGOs) (Swan, 2015). The number of blockchain systems is steadily increasing, however the electronic voting domain is slow to adapt with a relatively low number of systems devised so far, based on our observation of the state of the art.

Electronic voting has been a topic of active debate, with significant number of people believing that electronic voting cannot be trusted enough to be used for significant elections due to uncertainty in the authenticity and integrity of the machines and the votes that have been cast using them. On the other hand, people acknowledge that paper solutions are significantly outdated and can be subject to serious manipulation from a coercer. The emergence of blockchains has introduced a new way to construct secure systems which have less inherent security issues present. It is a belief that a successful voting system can be implemented using blockchains, or with a blockchain being one of the main elements present in a hybrid electronic voting scheme (Bradbury, 2014).

In our work, we investigate a new decentralized, anonymous payment scheme called Zcash (Hopwood *et al,* 2016) and create a voting system without altering the inner working of Zcash protocol.

2. STATE OF THE ART

Electronic voting is a topic of much research and several viable schemes have been created to attempt and solve the problem. Here, we present some influential voting protocols and other viable voting schemes as well as the techniques they implement at the core of vote processing, their security issues and analysis that have been done on some of the protocols in this domain. Blockchain voting technologies that have emerged recently are also discussed here, with attention to *Ethereum* (Wood, 2014).

2.1 Influential Electronic Voting Protocols

Electronic voting protocols have been implemented in different elections, ranging from university to government based elections. Many viable protocols have been created since Chaum (Chaum, 2004) first proposed *Votegrity*, one of the first *end-to-end* (E2E) verifiable voting schemes. E2E verifiability means that the voter can verify that their own vote has been cast as intended. The voter would be the assured that their vote has been counted correctly and included in the final tally and that the public members can verify an election externally without being involved in an election. These voting protocols, also provide a way to audit the voter's votes and the ballots prior to picking the candidate and casting the ballot.

Some of the most prominent examples that have stemmed from Chaum's *Votegrity*, which also provide E2E verifiability, are Neff's *Markpledge* (Neff, 2004), *Prêt à Voter* (Ryan *et al*, 2009), *Helios* (Adida, 2008), *Scantegrity* (Carback *et al*, 2010) and *STAR-Vote* (Bell *et al*, 2013). Markpledge was one of the first E2E voting protocols which has been proposed alongside Votegrity, influencing the development of the other schemes mentioned above and more. Helios, a university voting scheme, has undergone security analysis, which uncovered security vulnerabilities with a potential to affect the outcome of the elections. This led to the development of Helios 2.0 (Adida *et al*, 2009) and Helios 3.0 versions, attempting to fix the vulnerabilities posted by Estehghari and Desmedt (Estehghari and Desdedt, 2010). This is a good example of a security vulnerabilities in a voting protocol. A possible attack on Helios 2.0 included cross-site scripting (XSS) through the usage of a browser rootkit, a script capable of monitoring user traffic, capturing passwords entered by the user and get access to the DOM tree of the web page.

Some E2E protocols use public *web bulletin board* (WBB) for posting all the cast ballots for the public to see. Web bulletin boards are used as an authenticated public broadcast channels which, display the cast ballots to the public in an encrypted form, and serve as an important stage for any E2E protocol. Typically, after the voter has cast their vote and received a receipt encrypting their choice in a way that is dependent of what voting protocol used, the encrypted vote is propagated to the WBB (Parsovs, 2015; Heather, 2007, Culcane *et al*, 2015).

The receipt is an important part of the voting protocol, as it allows the user to prove their vote to an authority in case the voter wishes to dispute their vote or prove that they have voted contrary to what the system has recorded. The receipt also allows the user to find their vote and view how the system recorded their vote. These receipts vary from system to system, but typically these receipts are the summary of how the voter voted, which can be presented to the voter in an encrypted or obfuscated manner. As an example, Votegrity summarizes the vote in a print out which prompts the voter to pick the top or the bottom layer of the receipt. The receipt is a laminated piece of paper, which is separated into two layers, which are only readable when these layers are combined and never on their own. The mutual relationship of the pixels on the translucent layers is how the vote becomes readable (Chaum, 2004).

Some electronic voting protocols implement a challenge system, which helps a voter to establish trust in the system. Apollo (Gaweł *et al*, 2016) is an extension of the Helios protocol, however, it avoids some security issues that are inherent in Helios by having voter assistants to verify, lock and audit the vote. The assistants are external to the voting protocol devices that can interact with the election and can be laptops, tablets, or any other external devices. These interact with the session by fetching the personalized string, input by the voter during the start of the session, to fetch the session. The voter that wishes to audit their vote sends the audit code through the voting booth, which in turn opens the encryption of the ballot by posting the randomness encrypted with the session key. Each voting assistant checks the bulletin board and displays the plaintext value of the vote. This procedure may be repeated as many times as the voter wants (Gaweł *et al*, 2016).

Mixing is one of the two predominant techniques that are used in electronic voting protocols and utilizes mix networks (*mixnet*), a protocol that takes in multiple input messages from the users and shuffles these messages in random order before passing them to the next destination (Chau, 1981). Mixnets, in the context of voting, are used to provide a degree of anonymity to the user by obfuscating where the message came from. For example, Zeus (Tsoukalas *et al*, 2013) implements mixing after the election has been closed to break the linkability between the encrypted ballots and the voters who cast them. This is a multi-round procedure which depends solely on the number of mixing proxies available to the system. Each stage of the mixing provides a proof of correct mixing, which can be used to verify that the mixing server is not corrupt.

The second widely used technique is *homomorphic tally*. Cohen and Fischer (Cohen and Fischer, 1985) describe how this can be applied to a voting protocol. Homomorphic tally involves modifications, usually additions and multiplications, to the ciphertext which are preserved upon decryption to reveal the operations that have been done on the ciphertext while recovering the modified decrypted value. Protocols such as Helios 2.0 (Adida *et al*, 2009), STAR-Vote (Bell *et al*, 2013) and several others implement this technique for tallying the votes due to its simplicity both in application and for verification by the public, though the efficiency of these protocols, over mixnets, have been different through the papers where these methods are used.

Protocols such as Zeus (Tsoukalas *et al*, 2013) and Apollo (Gawel *et al*, 2016) use the basis of Helios to build their own voting protocol on, while attempting to tackle some of the security issues that are inherent to Helios. For instance, Apollo tackles the issues of XSS, cross-site forgery, clickjacking and clash attacks with the help of the voting assistants. For example, XSS was possible due to the unchecked URL parameters that meant to obtain the election URL, but if compromised could have pointed to a proxy with malicious script forced to execute on the target machine by the attacker. Ultimately, the attacker could encrypt each choice of the voter correctly, but submit their own ballot instead of the voters when the voter continued to submit their vote. This attack is impossible to detect server-side, but can be detected by the voter if the voter checks the WBB later to find their vote. XSS is in the third place of the top vulnerabilities of web applications as found by OWASP in 2013 (Wichers, 2013) and remains in the same position in OWASPs "Top 10 Application Security Risks" draft of 2017.

2.2 Blockchain for Voting

The conclusion can be made that an electronic voting system must be secure, while allowing for as much transparency as possible to be a working E2E verifiable. Blockchains (Nakamoto, 2008) help to achieve this level of security and transparency, while maintaining privacy and non-malleability of the transactions (Deloitte Nederland Website, 2016; Glass, 2016).

Although different, some elements from the above-mentioned protocols may apply to the concept of blockchain voting. The notion of WBB, where the encrypted votes can be seen by the public members, can persist in blockchain in the form like (Blockchain Website, 2017). Here the blocks of transactions can be observed as well as the height of the blockchain with any other relevant information. Although blockchain is a promising technology, we have not found any relevant papers to date that present a protocol for online voting with blockchains. Examples such as Follow My Vote (Follow My Vote Website, 2017) or TIVI (TIVI Website, 2017) present a seemingly sound voting protocol, however they are presented without any in-depth specification to verify the security of the protocol.

One other noteworthy blockchain technology that could revolutionize electronic voting is Ethereum (Wood, 2014). Ethereum differs from Bitcoin (Nakamoto, 2008) as it serves as a generic platform for creation of custom functionality in the form of contracts. The currency used by Ethereum is *ether* and *gas*. However, the main difference is the fact that the contracts allow for different functionality using the Ethereum Virtual Machine (EVM), while being enforced by the peer-to-peer, decentralized way, inherent to the core structure of blockchain. Ethereum possesses two types of accounts, which is another way of specifying types of users. Human entities use accounts, whereas contracts are accounts which are operated by code on the EVM. Contracts are the agents that bring about the generic functionality of Ethereum and allow one to create custom behavior for one's blockchain application. These applications include, and are not limited to, automatic payments or creation of custom currency, which is worthless outside of the context of the contract application (Wood, 2014; Devcon2 Video, 2016).

3. ZCASH OVERVIEW

Zcash is a decentralized blockchain payment scheme, which aims to provide anonymity of transactions. One of the biggest differences between Zcash and Bitcoin is the proof-of-work system, where Zcash relies on zero-knowledge proofs (Hopwood *et al*, 2016). We present a brief overview of the important concepts of Zcash prior to describing details of the proposed voting protocol.

3.1 Addresses and Transactions

Zcash supports both anonymous and transparent transactions as it has two types of addresses, which differs from the Bitcoins single address. These addresses are, namely, z- address and t-address, where z-address is the address which preserves anonymity in transactions, and t-address resembles the Bitcoins addresses in structure and allows for transparent transactions. The transactions between different addresses ensure the conversion of transparent value into a shielded value and vice versa. The details of shielded values cannot be observed by the public. The transaction between addresses is illustrated by Figure 1.

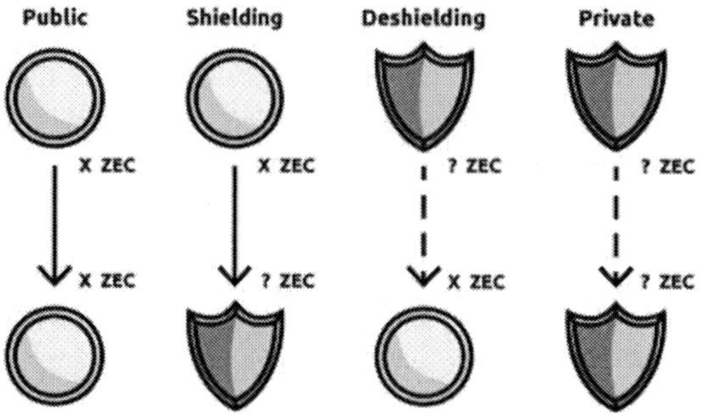

Figure 1. Types of Transactions in Zcash (Peterson, 2016)

Private transactions occur when both, the sender and receiver use z-addresses, which ensures that no entity, outside the entities involved, can view the details and the value of Zcash (ZEC) that are exchanged in the transaction.

The private, z-addresses are generated with the combination of the keys, of which there are a total of 4 keys, which allow for spending, viewing, paying and transmission of secret values between the parties. These keys are namely:

- *Paying key* (a_{pk}): Used as a part to generate payment address.
- *Transmission key* (pk_{enc}): Used to encrypt and decrypt secret values to be passed between the parties involved in a transaction.
- *Spending key* (a_{sk}): Allows spending of ZEC.
- *Viewing key* (sk_{enc}): Establishing keys for viewing the private transaction between involved parties.

The combination of paying key (a_{pk}) and transmission key (pk_{enc}) is what makes up a *z*-address.

Part of spending a ZEC involves revealing a *nullifier* for a ZEC which has a *commitment* in a Merkle tree (Nakamoto, 2008). The commitment is placed on such tree in Zcash, whenever a new ZEC is generated. A nullifier is a serial value for each ZEC which prevents double-spending of the same ZEC. The spending procedure involves locating a commitment on the Merkle tree and ensuring that the nullifier has not yet been revealed, as once the nullifier is revealed, the ZEC is considered spent. The nullifier set is maintained at every full node and newly revealed nullifiers are inserted into the set with each transaction.

A secret pair of keys is established and known as the *ephemeral keys*. The ephemeral keys are established for the transmission of the secret values in private transactions to ensure that only the sender and the recipient can view the transaction. The possession of the private ephemeral key (esk) and the recipient's address is what allows the sender to view the transaction. At the same time, the receiver uses their viewing key (sk_{enc}) and the ephemeral public key (epk) to view the transaction from their end. The ephemeral public key is sent with the transaction, which is the way that the receiver obtains it. Even if a third party obtained this key, they do not have the other keys to view the transaction or derive a key to decrypt the secret values in the transaction.

Part of the transaction, named *JoinSplit* Transfer in Zcash (Hopwood *et al*, 2016), is for the sender to spend their ZEC, which reveals the nullifier for the input ZEC, and generation of the commitments for the new ZEC which will be passed to the receiver as part of the transaction. The values used to generate the ZEC are passed to the receiver after being encrypted with a key established via transmission key (pk_{enc}). These values in a transaction are accompanied, by a zero-knowledge proof to ensure that the transaction is legitimate and follows the rules for a transaction. Finally, the JoinSplit Transfer supports both shielded and transparent values in the same transaction as the transparent value pool in each transaction is dedicated for transparent transactions as well as to hold the miners reward for processing the transaction.

3.2 Zero-Knowledge Proving System

The key to the private transactions is the zero-knowledge proving system. This is because there is a need to transfer the secret values between the involved parties without disclosing these values to each other. To facilitate this transfer, Zcash implements zk-SNARKs (Zero-Knowledge Succinct Non-Interactive Arguments of Knowledge) devised into libsnark library from the designs of Ben-Sasson (Ben-Sasson, *et al*, 2014; Ben-Sasson *et al*, 2013). This construct allows for generation of zero-knowledge proofs given an arbitrary program. The proofs are generated using several steps which are shown in Figure 2.

For this paper, we will not be discussing these steps in details, rather we provide an overview of the zk-SNARK functionality for better understanding of its application in Zcash. The purpose of supplying a proof is to verify the legitimacy of secret values, which are used to generate a ZEC, exchanged during a transaction. Libsnark allows the conversion of programs into proofs of knowledge. The program utilizes a port for a GCC compiler to create a circuit based on monitoring the execution of a program.

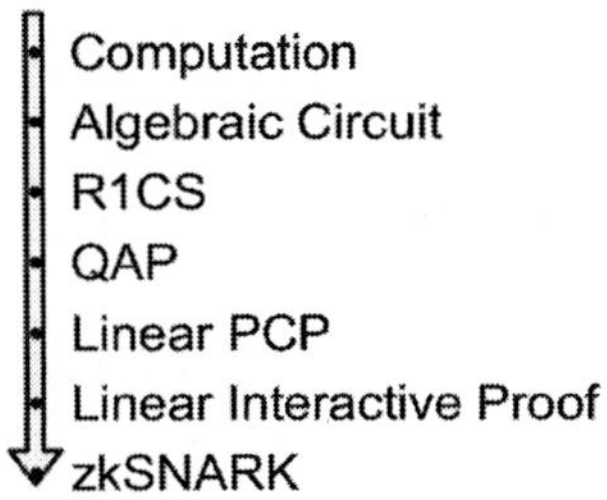

Figure 2. Overview of zk-SNARK Proof Creation (Buterin, 2016)

The core idea is that some universal program circuit is used as input to a generator function, with secret values acting as toxic waste to generate a pair of public keys, which can be distributed to both the proving and the verifying parties. The prover is to use the proving key, public value to be proven and a secret value (witness) as input to a function which generates a proof from the above information.

The verifier obtains the verifier key as well as the proof generated by the prover and using a verification function, whose inputs are verification key, the same public value to be proven and the proof provided by the prover to verify the legitimacy of the proof. The verification function is a simple function which returns either true or false depending on whether the proof has been successfully proven (Lundkyist, 2017).

The generator function is part of a setup procedure and uses toxic waste values as part of the setup stage. The setup phase for ZCash is done once to establish the proving and verification keys. If the toxic waste is not deleted and a party was able to obtain these keys, then the said party would be able to generate fake proofs.

The JoinSplit transfer also provides some proofs as part of the transfer is to generate new ZECs. Some of the things that the proof is used to prove are:

- The total values of input ZECs and output ZECs matches.
- The commitments exist and are valid for the input ZECs.
- The nullifier and the commitment have been calculated correctly.

The proofs are not limited to these three items and the total size of the resulting proof is 296-bytes (Hopwood *et al*, 2016).

4. SYSTEM OVERVIEW

Prior to describing our voting protocol, it is worth mentioning that the underlying Zcash protocol (Hopwood *et al*, 2016) has not been changed in any way. The protocol utilizes basic functions offered by Zcash and creates a platform with the ability to cast votes. The work assumes the following things: assumption of confirmed identity, where the protocol assumes that the identity of a potential voter can be verified, such as employing X.509 certificates (Hazlewood, 2011) and Certificate Authorities (CA) to verify those identities. This is to facilitate legal authorisation of the vote transaction on behalf of the voter. The voting protocol can be separated into four distinct steps: registration, notification, voting, and count/audit.

4.1 Registration

Registration is the first step of the protocol and is required as part of the identity verification step and for audit purposes, to keep track of which voters have cast a ballot, and is a control mechanism to disallow unregistered people to participate in the vote. A potential voter who wishes to participate in an election or a poll visits the registration page, where communication with the server is established transparently. The system needs to authenticate a potential voter and can do so by following the Challange-Handshake Authentication Protocol (CHAP) (Simpsom, 1994) and exchange challenge information and solution.

After successful registration, the voter's email address or an X.509 certificate containing their email address is stored in the database used by the voting system. The overall registration step can be seen in Figure 3.

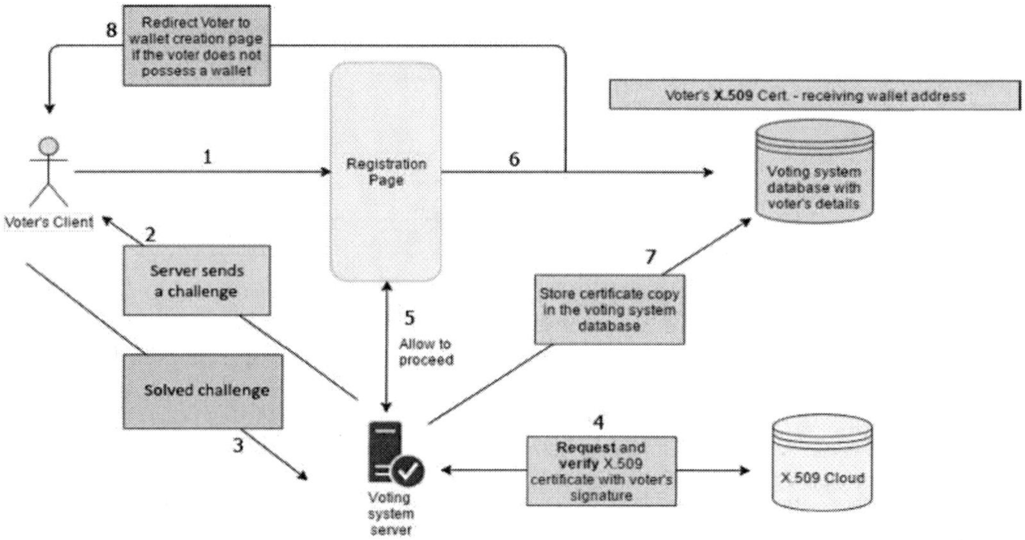

Figure 3. Voter Registration

4.2 Invitation

Invitation step is a small step which sends a one-time unique link to the voter's email to redirect the voter to a unique ballot assigned to them. The voting server issues the invitations only when the administrator of the election issues the details for the election. This is similar to the Zeus protocol (Tsoukalas *et al*, 2013) where the administrator too, inputs the details of the poll as well as the list of the registered users.

The system server obtains the voter details from copies of stored user verification data, such as X.509 certificates, in the server's database and issues the vote links to all the registered voters. The links are active for as long as the election and expire as soon as the election timer has expired. The invitation step can be seen in Figure 4.

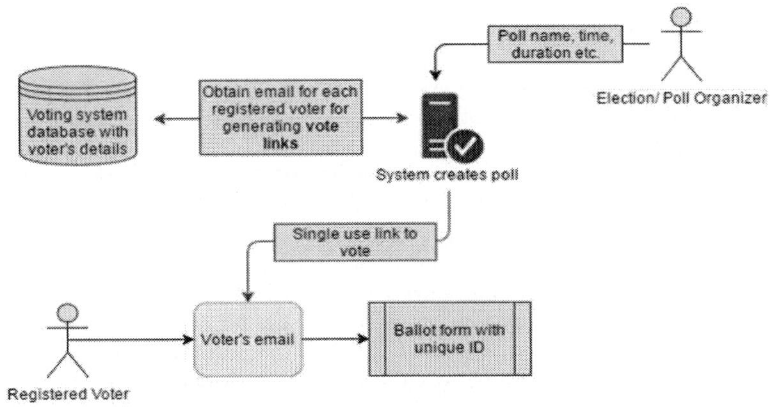

Figure 4. Invitation to Participate in Ballot

4.3 Voting

Once the voter has followed the ballot link, they are redirected to the ballot page. The ballot is a simple interface which contains candidates' names and a checkbox next to the names. The top of the ballot contains a field which requires the voter to input their receiving t-address. The voter generates these addresses to send and receive the tokens. To maintain anonymity, but at the same time adhere to the transparency of the vote, the voter is required to provide a receiving t-address and is required to send the vote with a z-address.

The receiving t-address is provided by the voter on the top of the ballot and can be changed as many times as required by the voter. This is the address which will ensure that the voter receives the vote token which is redirected to the candidate wallet. The voter uses the z-address to ensure that their vote is anonymous.

Once the authorisation takes place, the vote tokens can be generated by the system faucet to send to a ZEC pool, or if there are enough ZECs available, issue them straight from the ZEC pool. The ZEC pool is a system wallet which issues ZECs to the voters once the voter has authorised the vote. Once the voter has authorised the vote, the system changes the voter's status in the database, as well as incrementing the system count of the total votes for the current election. At the same time, a token is sent to the receiving address specified by the voter. The number of issued tokens is tracked by the system and is compared to the total number of votes to ensure that no extra votes have been added into the tally. Fig. 5 outlines the steps taken when the voter casts their vote.

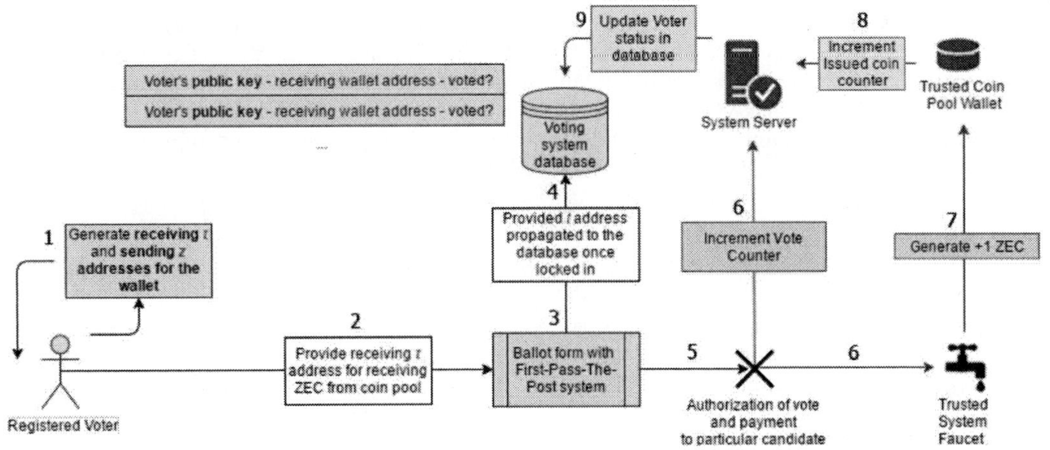

Figure 5. Overview of the Voting Process

4.4 System Variants

The transaction between the candidate and the voter becomes private if the candidate uses z-address. Inherent to the Zcash protocol, z-addresses break the linkability between the ZECs and previous transaction. This means that when the candidate empties their wallet into the ZEC pool, the voter may no longer trace their vote to the ZEC pool. This scheme requires more trust in the system, however it guarantees the privacy of the system i.e. no one can see the details and amounts of the transaction sent to the candidate.

Since private transactions require more complicated setup, there are more internal steps involved in making these transactions. One of the most important pieces of information is the establishment and sharing of ephemeral keys. These keys allow the voter and the candidate both to view the transaction, which is exclusive to the two parties. These keys are established as per key agreement function of Zcash. Internally, the transaction remains the same.

The second variant of the system involves the candidate's receiving with their t-addresses. This is an example of a deshielding transaction and would mean that the candidate's token balance can be observed by the public in real-time. The linkability of the tokens would also be preserved. Linkability in this case means that a token can be traced back to the sender to the ZEC pool, where the tally occurs after an election timer has expired. This can help users determine if their vote has been counted in the tally.

Regardless of the variant used, the JoinSplit transfers of vote tokens from voters to candidates are stored on the blockchain with the appropriate data for each JoinSplit transfer.

4.5 The Tally/Audit

The final stage of the voting protocol is the vote count and the audit which takes place after the count to review the election process and ensure that the integrity of the election has not been compromised. The candidate wallets send all the ZEC vote tokens to the ZEC pool which has ZEC balance of 0 ZEC vote tokens. This requires some trust in the system, however the assumption is that the candidate wallets and a ZEC pool have 0 ZEC vote tokens in the beginning and that candidate wallets send all the collected ZEC vote tokens into the coin pool. The transactions may be more difficult to verify as these are private and the details are only available to the voters and the candidates only. However, if the same party who starts an election holds the ownership of the candidate wallets and may implement verification systems to check each transaction destined for each candidate.

The candidate wallets send all their acquired ZEC vote tokens to the ZEC pool using sending t-address on the candidate's side and a receiving t-address on the side of the ZEC pool. The system declares the end of the election or a poll as soon as the expiry time has been met. After that, no votes are accepted into the count and the system, the unique vote links expire and the ballot forms do not allow to proceed with the submission of the votes.

At this point the number of total votes cast becomes public as well as the number of tokens issued for the voters. The total number of transactions may also be displayed with the total number of voters who participated in the election. It is not in the interest of the candidates to not empty their wallets upon conclusion of the election, or to send an incorrect number of ZEC vote tokens as the system equations will not balance and the election will be considered forfeit. Figure 6 provides an example election with 100 total votes being cast between candidate X and candidate Y.

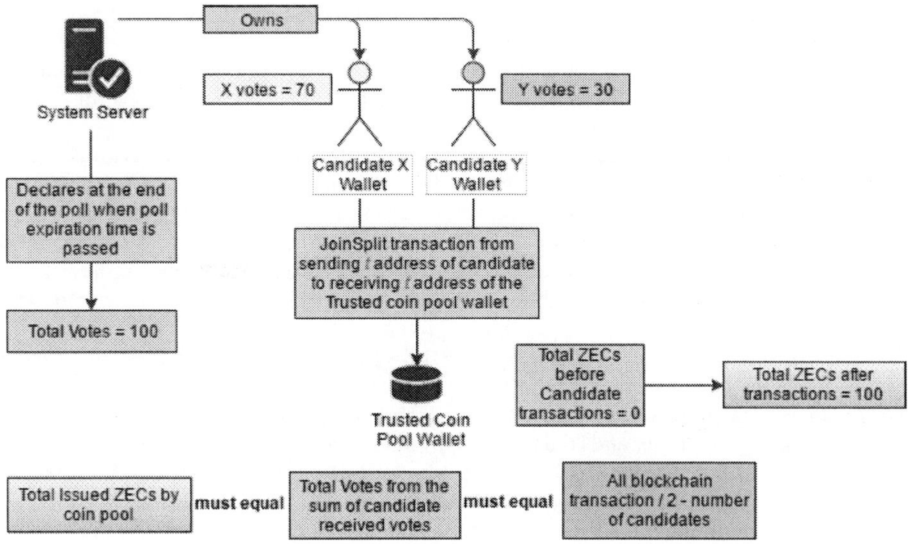

Figure 6. Example of the count and audit of an election

5. SECURITY CONSIDERATIONS

A significant issue with internet voting protocols is compromised voting machines. Since the target platform of the protocol would be user's end devices, such as computers and mobile devices, it is possible for a coercer to influence the outcome of the vote by compromising the voter's device as it would be much easier to achieve than compromising the entire electronic voting scheme. The coercer could infect the voter's machine and influence the voting software installed. The voting software will then be influenced by the coercer's candidate choice. One of the possible ways that a concerned voter can defend against such an attack is to obtain a checksum of the voting application. A checksum can simply be a hashing of the voting software of a specific version which the voter has installed on their device. If the voter's device is compromised then the hash versions will not be the same and the voter can obtain a new copy of the software.

Since our proposed voting protocol does not make any changes to the underlying Zcash protocol, some problems, like double voting i.e. using the same granted vote token to vote for multiple candidates, is inherently absent in the voting protocol. However, since the unique ballot link is sent to a voter's email address, the issue of compromised machine can persist once again. A potential coercer could get access to the voter's email first and attempt to cast a vote on their behalf. Notification systems can be in place to send email confirmation when a vote has been issued by the voter and visually notify the voter of the number of times they have attempted to vote so far.

A major consideration in dealing with Zcash and the automated script assumption is that all the operations deal with ZECs, which have a non-negligible value on the market (CoinGecko Website, 2017). This gives a potential incentive for corrupt voters to attempt to hijack the vote token upon brief arrival to their wallet. The assumption is that the script can detect the specific transaction arriving into the wallet and redirecting it to a candidate immediately. There are several mitigations to avoid ZEC hijacking. First is to deal with the smallest denominations of ZEC (1 zatoshi) to reduce the incentive to steal a whole ZEC as 1 ZEC is 10^8 zatoshis (Hopwood *et al*, 2016). Though the audit calculations for the end of the election may not fail, a rogue transaction to a wallet, not belonging to a candidate may be noticed by the public.

Having mentioned the required balance of values at the end of an election to verify its integrity, a possible attack could be carried out on the system, where a losing candidate does not submit all the received votes. This would cause the election to be forfeit as the total number of ZEC vote tokens does not balance with the total number of votes and ZEC vote tokens issued. This attack could be detected if the candidates were using t-addresses as all the receiving transactions would be visible, however it would pose a problem if the candidate used *z*-address as no public party, except the administrators of the voting system would know if a candidate is misbehaving. A possible mitigation for this attack can disregard the total number of ZEC vote tokens returned to the counting pool, only if this number is less than or exactly equal to the number of total votes. In case of this occurrence, the voters and the administrators can be notified by the system that the votes returned did not match the total number of votes issued.

An alternative solution can implement internal system trackers, which count the number of votes cast for each candidate, and serve the purpose of controlling the amount of ZEC vote tokens returned by the candidates. A tracker for each candidate increments each time a vote has been cast for a candidate and the system expects to withdraw this amount of ZEC vote tokens from the candidate wallet, which would not let a malicious candidate trick the system. These trackers would function even if the candidates used z-addresses. It is also possible to make this tracker public, during the tally period, to notify the public what the expected vote count is.

A question may arise, of what would happen if the system counters have been modified by an attacker. According to the rules of the system, the integrity of the election will be considered compromised and the result will be forfeit. The reality of a decentralized system is that there may be more than one instance of the tracker initialized at a given time, and it may be required that they all need to agree at the end of an election.

One significant attack on the entire blockchain is called 51% attack (Learn Cryptography Website, 2013). This is one of the biggest flaws in blockchain technology. This attack allows an entity with the biggest contribution to block mining to be able to change the contents of the past blocks on the blockchain due to the sheer computer power available to the entity. Other activities would include prevention of some transactions from obtaining a required number of confirmations and preventing people from sending ZEC vote tokens to the candidate addresses. This attack would be difficult to prevent. On one hand, it is possible to pick out several trusted verifiers out of the public volunteers and allow them to confirm the transactions to be included in the blocks. On the other hand, there may be trust issues raised by the participating voters. One other option is to allow any willing public member to participate in a verification pool. This would mean that the voter adds their computing power to the pool of other voter's machines to verify the transactions, however this pool would need to be organized by a trusted party whose actions can be verified in case the party is considered rogue.

6. FUTURE WORK

Having outlined the voting protocol and the basis for its operations, it is important to outline the direction this protocol can take. The Ethereum protocol (Wood, 2014), has been established early in the work as a potential candidate to become the platform for our voting protocol. One of the reasons for this is that Ethereum supports creation of contracts, which are accounts which are operated by the EVM. These contracts can be used to implement a voting scheme. However, voters' anonymity and privacy is an important piece of any voting protocol and is not yet handled by EVM transactions.

Steady advancements in development of the Ethereum platform bring the possibility of creation of this protocol closer. The future Ethereum aims to make use of zk-SNARKs to add privacy and anonymity of transactions. The zk-SNARKs are complex to implement efficiently due to the time taken to generate proofs, which is one of the issues in implementing these today. However, steps towards adoption of zk-SNARKs have already been taken by Ethereum (Hudson, 2017).

Finally, steps have been made to integrate Zcash and Ethereum together in projects such as Zcash over Ethereum (ZoE), however these are still at very early stages (Bowe, 2016; Reitwiessner, 2017).

7. CONCLUSION

A standardized electronic voting solution which would be widely adopted has not yet emerged, and although there are some good candidates, there are inherent security issues which make these protocols unsuitable for elections. The literature identifies a distinct gap in the domain which could be filled by a protocol, using a different technology then the previous protocols. Blockchain offers an inherently more secure platform, and with development of the recent anonymous transaction scheme, namely Zcash, it is finally possible to tackle the anonymity issues of blockchain transactions, which would open a possibility for blockchain voting. Ethereum has offered the smart contract functionality since it first came to pass, however the much-needed anonymity factor has not been present in the protocol so far. The rapid growth of the Ethereum protocol, and its integration with Zcash will most likely come up with the protocol, suitable for wide-spread, cheap voting system. As indicated by the future work on these protocols, voting on blockchain has received the much-needed push in the right direction.

The applications for the proposed protocol are not limited to government elections only. These can be stretched to opinion polls or corporate elections providing a unified platform for voting regardless of the cost or circumstance. The drive behind a cheaper, unified, electronic voting system was the basis for the above protocol, which has potential to grow into a real wide-spread implementation, dealing with assumptions and concerns which limit the current system.

The standardization or adoption of such protocol would be a step towards public approval of electronic voting schemes, provided that the said protocol is secure and has been tested and tried. The release of new protocols, with security issues does not take steps to progress in public approval and, ultimately, replacement of the paper elections.

A major effort has gone into development of a sound voting system and with the rapid developments of blockchain technology and its implementations in various fields, one final push is required to bring a sound electronic solution to one of the humanities basic rights - to vote.

REFERENCES

Adida, B., 2008, July. Helios: Web-based Open-Audit Voting. In *USENIX security symposium*, 17, pp. 335-348).

Adida, B., De Marneffe, O., Pereira, O. and Quisquater, J.J., 2009. Electing a university president using open-audit voting: Analysis of real-world use of Helios. *EVT/WOTE*, *9*(10).

Bell, S., Benaloh, J., Byrne, M.D., DeBeauvoir, D., Eakin, B., Fisher, G., Kortum, P., McBurnett, N., Montoya, J., Parker, M. and Pereira, O., 2013. STAR-Vote: A secure, transparent, auditable, and reliable voting system. *USENIX Journal of Election Technology and Systems (JETS)*, 1(1), p.18-37.

Ben-Saason, E., Chiesa, A., Genkin, D., Kfir, S., Tromer, E., Virza, M., 2014, *libsnark: C++ library for zkSNARK proofs*. Available at: https://github.com/zcash/libsnark

Ben-Sasson, E., Chiesa, A., Genkin, D., Tromer, E. and Virza, M., 2013. SNARKs for C: Verifying program executions succinctly and in zero knowledge. In *Advances in Cryptology–CRYPTO 2013* (pp. 90-108). Springer, Berlin, Heidelberg.

Ben-Sasson, E., Chiesa, A., Tromer, E. and Virza, M., 2013. Succinct Non-Interactive Arguments for a von Neumann Architecture. *IACR Cryptology ePrint Archive*, *2013*, p.879.

Blockchain Website, 2017, *Bitcoin Block Explorer Blockchain*, Available at: https://blockchain.info/

Bowe, S., 2016, *Zcash - zkSNARKs in Ethereum*, Zcash Blog, Available at: https://z.cash/blog/zksnarks-in-ethereum.html

Bradbury D., 2014 *How Block Chain Technology Could Usher in Digital Democracy*. Available at: http://www.coindesk.com/block-chain-technology-digital-democracy/ [Accessed 23 November 2016]

Buterin, V., 2016, *Quadratic Arithmetic Programs: from Zero to Hero*, Medium, Available at: https://medium.com/@VitalikButerin/quadratic-arithmetic-programs-from-zero-to-hero-f6d558cea649#c1fkogp41

Carback, R., Chaum, D., Clark, J., Conway, J., Essex, A., Herrnson, P.S., Mayberry, T., Popoveniuc, S., Rivest, R.L., Shen, E. and Sherman, A.T., 2010. Scantegrity II municipal election at Takoma Park: the first E2E binding governmental election with ballot privacy. 19th USENIX Conf. Secur., pp. 19-35

Chaum, D., 2004. Secret-ballot receipts: True voter-verifiable elections. *IEEE security & privacy*, *2*(1), pp.38-47.

Chaum, D.L., 1981. Untraceable electronic mail, return addresses, and digital pseudonyms. *Communications of the ACM*, *24*(2), pp.84-90.

Cohen, J.D. and Fischer, M.J., 1985. *A robust and verifiable cryptographically secure election scheme* (pp. 372-382). Yale University. Department of Computer Science.

CoinGecko Website, 2017, *Zcash/Bitcoin (ZEC/EUR) Price Chart*", Available at: https://www.coingecko.com/en/price_charts/zcash/btc

Culnane, C., Ryan, P.Y., Schneider, S. and Teague, V., 2015. vVote: a verifiable voting system. *ACM Transactions on Information and System Security (TISSEC)*, *18*(1), p.3.

Deloitte Nederland. 2016, *Blockchain technology: 9 benefits & 7 challenges*", Available at: https://www2.deloitte.com/nl/nl/pages/innovatie/artikelen/blockchain-technology-9-benefits-and-7-challenges.html

Devcon2: Ethereum in 25 Minutes. 2016 Buterin, V., [Online video], YouTube, Ethereum Foundation. Available at: https://www.youtube.com/watch?v=66SaEDzlmP4

Estehghari, S. and Desmedt, Y., 2010. Exploiting the Client Vulnerabilities in Internet E-voting Systems: Hacking Helios 2.0 as an Example. *EVT/WOTE, 10*, pp.1-9.

Follow My Vote Website. 2017, *The Online Voting Platform of The Future - Follow My Vote.* Available at: https://followmyvote.com/

Gaweł, D., Kosarzecki, M., Vora, P.L., Wu, H. and Zagorski, F., 2016, October. Apollo–End-to-End Verifiable Internet Voting with Recovery from Vote Manipulation. In *International Joint Conference on Electronic Voting* (pp. 125-143). Springer, Cham.

Glass, P., 2016 *How secure is blockchain?*, Available at: https://www.taylorwessing.com/download/article-how-secure-is-block-chain.html

Hazlewood, L., 2011, *What is an X.509 Certificate?* Stormpath User Identity API, 2011. Available at: https://stormpath.com/blog/what-x509-certificate

Heather, J., 2007, July. Implementing STV securely in Prêt à Voter. In *Computer Security Foundations Symposium, 2007. CSF'07. 20th IEEE* (pp. 157-169). IEEE.

Hopwood, D., Bowe, S., Hornby, T. and Wilcox, N., 2016. *Zcash Protocol Specification.* Tech. rep. Zerocoin Electric Coin Company.

Hudson, J., 2017, *EIPs*, GitHub Website, Available at: https://github.com/ethereum/EIPs

Learn Cryptography Website, 2013, *51% Attack*, Available at: https://learncryptography.com/cryptocurrency/51-attack

Lundkvist, C., 2017, *Introduction to zkSNARKs with Examples*, ConsenSys Media, Available at: https://media.consensys.net/introduction-to-zksnarks-with-examples-3283b554fc3b

Nakamoto, S., 2008. Bitcoin: A peer-to-peer electronic cash system.

Neff, C.A., 2004. *Practical high certainty intent verification for encrypted votes.*

P. Peterson, 2016, *Anatomy of a Zcash Transaction*", Zcash Blog. Available at: https://z.cash/blog/anatomy-of-zcash.html

Parsovs, A., 2016. Homomorphic Tallying for the Estonian Internet Voting System. *IACR Cryptology ePrint Archive, 2016*, p.776.

Reitwiessner, C., 2017, *An Update on Integrating Zcash on Ethereum (ZoE)*, Ethereum Blog, Available at: https://blog.ethereum.org/2017/01/19/update-integrating-zcash-ethereum/

Ryan, P.Y., Bismark, D., Heather, J., Schneider, S. and Xia, Z., 2009. Prêt à voter: a voter-verifiable voting system. *IEEE transactions on information forensics and security, 4*(4), pp.662-673.

Simpson, W., RFC 1994: PPP Challenge Handshake Authentication Protocol (CHAP), *Obsoletes RFC1334 [LS9 2]. Status: DRAFT STANDARD.*

Swan M., 2015, *Blockchain: Blueprint for a New Economy*, O'Reilly Media, Sebastopol. California.

TIVI Website, 2017, *TIVI Online Voting*, Available at: https://tivi.io/tivi/

Tsoukalas, G., Papadimitriou, K., Louridas, P. and Tsanakas, P., 2013, August. From Helios to Zeus. In *EVT/WOTE*. Washington D.C

Wichers, D., 2013. Owasp top-10 2013. *OWASP Foundation.*

Wichers, D., 2017. Owasp top-10 2017. *OWASP Foundation.*

Wood, G., 2014. Ethereum: A secure decentralised generalised transaction ledger. *Ethereum Project Yellow Paper, 151.*

TRAJECTORIES COMPARING BASED ON MATCHING AND DISTANCE EVALUATION WITHIN STIEFEL AND GRASSMANN MANIFOLDS

Amani Elaoud[1], Walid Barhoumi[1,2], Hassen Drira[3] and Ezzeddine Zagrouba[1]

[1]Université de Tunis El Manar, Institut Supérieur d'Informatique, Research Team on Intelligent Systems in Imaging and Artificial Vision (SIIVA), LR16ES06, Laboratoire de recherche en Informatique, Modélisation et Traitement de l'Information et de la Connaissance (LIMTIC),2 Rue Bayrouni, 2080 Ariana, Tunisia

[2]Université de Carthage, Ecole Nationale d'Ingénieurs de Carthage, 45 Rue des Entrepreneurs, 2035 Tunis-Carthage, Tunisia

[3]IMT Lille Douai, CRISTAL (UMR CNRS 9189), Villeneuve-d'Ascq, France

ABSTRACT

In this paper, we are interested in comparing human trajectories using skeleton information provided by a consumer RGB-D sensor. In fact, 3D human joints given by skeletons offer an important information for human motion analysis. In this context, the use of manifolds has grown considerably in the computer vision community in recent years. The main contribution of this study resides in working jointly with two manifolds. The matching of the trajectories is performed in Stiefel manifold and dissimilarity measure is carried out in Grassmann manifold. Indeed, trajectories of motions are provided by the projection in the Stiefel manifold. Then, the Stiefel distance is used within the dynamic time warping in order to define the appropriate matching between a reference trajectory and a test one. This allows avoiding that the rotation within the motion will be ignored, as it is the case with the Grassmann manifold. Then, the dissimilarity is evaluated using the Grassmann distance to compare motions while being invariant against rotation. Realized experiments on standard challenging datasets prove that the proposed method, for the comparison of human trajectories with different sizes, performs accurately compared to existing manifold-based methods.

KEYWORDS

Trajectories, Human Motion, Manifolds, Grassmann, Stiefel, Matching, Kinect, Skeleton

1. INTRODUCTION

Recognizing and analyzing human actions in videos is a challenging task with very complex actions in the real world (Barhoumi, 2014). Recently, skeleton-based human representations have been intensively studied and kept attracting an increasing attention. Some recent surveys, such as (Presti et Cascia, 2016), (Alashkar et al., 2016) and (Han et al., 2017), together overview this research area. The recent focus on skeleton representation has resulted in a variety of approaches, to conduct research on action recognition (Song et al., 2017) and modeling (Ding et Liu, 2017), tracking (Anjum et al., 2017) and re-identification (Wu et al., 2017). Indeed, the importance of the interpretation of human behavior from skeleton information was firstly reclaimed by (Shotton et al., 2011). We find success of skeleton information in action recognition such as (Vemulapalli et al., 2014) that use skeletal representation to prove the 3D geometric relationships of body parts in Lie group using rotations and translations in 3D space. Besides, (Du et al., 2015) propose a hierarchical recurrent neural network based on skeleton. The input skeleton is divided into five parts according to human physical structure, and a recurrent neural network is applied to classify the actions. Furthermore, a 3D action recognition method (Ke et al., 2017) with skeleton sequences is performed to jointly represent the sequence while incorporating spatial structural information. On the other hand, to deal with tracking issues, (Schubert et al., 2016) present automatic bone parameter estimation for skeleton tracking. The objective is to construct a rough hierarchical skeleton structure to optimize probabilistic skeleton tracking performance. Then, a method based on tracking the position of selected joints in human skeleton with depth videos recorded using Kinect camera is proposed in (Anjum et al., 2017). More recently,

(Wang et al., 2014) extract the skeleton of the human body using the 3D joint positions that are generated via skeleton tracking from the depth map sequence. (Meng et al., 2016) study the human gait from skeleton data using inter-joints distances as spatio-temporal features. Various skeleton-based representations are also used for human re-identification. For instance, (Munaro et al., 2014a) use skeleton information to build a descriptor which can then be classified with an SVM (Support Vector Machine) classifier for one-shot person re-identification through a consumer depth sensor. Recently, deep learning approaches have been customized for re-identification. For instance, (Barbosa et al., 2017) propose a framework through a classification based on CNN architecture.

In recent years, there is a growing attention for the techniques reformulating computer vision problems over non-Euclidean spaces, such as Riemannian manifolds. The study of these manifolds has important consequences for applications such as dynamic textures (Miao et al., 2017), human activity modeling and recognition (Feng et al., 2017), face recognition (Cai et al., 2016) and shape analysis (Amor et al., 2016). For instance, (Turaga et al., 2008) use Stiefel and Grassmann manifolds for analysis applications in computer vision, such as activity recognition, face recognition and shape classification. (Lui et Beveridge, 2011) represent videos as a tangent bundle on a Grassmann manifold for action classification. Videos are expressed as third order tensors and factorized to a set of tangent spaces. Then, tangent vectors are computed between elements on a Grassmann manifold. More recently, (Slama et al., 2014) use Grassmann manifold and model motion for activity recognition from depth sequences. In another work, (Michalczuk et al., 2017) present an application of Grassmann manifold to the evaluation of the human stability based on movements in hip, knee and ankle joints. In general, the use of manifold transforms informations on trajectories, that is why temporal modeling and time-warping solutions have attracted an important interest to compare sequences, trajectories or motions. An emerging solution is to compare two sequences with different sizes. The same person can do the same action with different rates. Indeed, the same activity can greatly decrease recognition performance, if some frames are ignored. The invariance to the temporal rate of execution of action helps to provide an accurate recognition. (Turaga et Chellappa, 2009) propose as a model a Time-Varying Linear Dynamic System (TV-LDS) and Dynamic Time Warping (DTW) for the problem of modeling and recognizing complex activities in time-varying dynamic. (Abdelkader et al., 2011) use the DTW algorithm in order to solve the temporal alignment and to match a given time series with the optimal non-linear warping function. (Amor et al., 2016) propose to use human shape evolution of skeletons as trajectories on Kendall shape manifold via smoothed transported square-root vector fields (TSRVFs). More recently, (Devanne et al., 2016) analyze the trajectory of motion and consider shape variations within a Riemannian manifold to learn step models. They propose to analyze their shape by using the SRVF, where each shape trajectory is viewed as an element of the shape space.

As best we know, all the existing manifold-based methods chose one manifold that is then used for matching as well as for distance evaluation. In this paper, we are interested in using the DTW algorithm, the popular sequence alignment and matching method, especially for two unregulated sequences. Indeed, it can resolve the problem of temporal alignment and it measures the similarity between sequences varied in time in order to be capable of providing superior performance with size variance. The main idea of this work is the projection of a set of videos. Each frame will be a point on a manifold, and construct a trajectory of motion to lay these points. Then, Stiefel distance d_S is applied for the matching in the DTW and then the Grassmann distance d_G is applied for the couples resulting from the matching. We chose to apply in this paper this idea in the framework of human motion analysis, and more precisely for people re-identification which is an important and challenging task. It is helpful for many applications in various domains, like entertainment, medicine and surveillance. As many-to-one matching, between a reference trajectory and a test one, is often used, we opted for the Stiefel manifold in order to avoid invariance against rotation. Indeed, if a rotation-invariant manifold is used during the matching, which is totally spatial, one frame in the reference video can be wrongly matched with many frames in the test video, notably when the filmed persons rotate on themselves. However, as the temporal information is also considered during the assessment of the similarity between two motions, we opted for the Grasssmann manifold which is invariant to rotation.

The remainder of this paper is structured as follows. Proposed method is discussed in Section 2. Section 3 presents experimental results and numerical evaluations. Concluding remarks and ideas for future works are given in Section 4.

2. PROPOSED METHOD

We study the problem of evaluating similarity of human motions using 3D videos generated by an RGBD sensor, especially the Kinect. By representing human body as dynamical trajectories, we study the evolution of their sequences of skeletons as trajectories on the non-linear manifolds. A manifold is a topological space locally similar to the Euclidean space. In this work, we are interested in two relevant manifolds: Stiefel and Grassmann. On the one hand, Stiefel manifold is the set of k-dimensional orthonormal bases in R^n, where $k<n$, represented by V(R^n). We obtain an $n \times k$ matrix Y, such that $Y^t Y = I_K$. To define a Stiefel metric between two elements of this manifold, the Frobenius norm is widely used. In fact, given two elements *P* and *P'* of Stiefel manifold, the Stiefel distance is defined by:

$$d\_S(P, P') = ||P - P'||_F \quad (1)$$

where $||.||_F$ is the standard Frobenius norm. It is equal to the square root of the matrix trace of $M.M^t$, defined by:

$$||M||_F = \sqrt{tr(MM^t)} \quad (2)$$

On the other hand, Grassmann manifold G(R^n) is a quotient space of V(R^n), represented by $V(R^n)/SO(K)$, where *SO(K)* is the orthogonal group of dimension *k*. Two points on a Grassmann manifold are equivalent if one can be mapped into the other one by a rotation matrix: a $k \times k$ orthogonal matrix (Edelman et al., 1998) Then, to define a Grassmann distance, the length of the shortest curve θ connecting the subspaces S and S' generated by point P and the best matched point P* and it is computed according to:

$$d\_G(S, S') = \sum_{i=1}^{n} \theta_i^2 \quad (3)$$

The proposed method ignores the RGB channel and uses only the skeleton data. In fact, given a skeleton sequence, composed of a set of ordered frames that shows a person in motion, we try to measure similarity between trajectories. We start by analyzing shapes of human skeletons, and their temporal evolutions. Since human skeletons are characterized by sets of registered points (or landmarks), each skeleton is characterized by *N* joint points obtained by the Kinect sensor. Note that *N* is equal to 20 (*resp.* 25) in the case of Kinect-Version1 (*resp.* Kinect-Version2) as was described by (Elaoud et al., 2017). Then, each skeleton is projected in the Stiefel manifold. The idea behind using the Stiefel manifold representation is that each skeleton of 3D information can be as a point representation which results the appearance of the trajectories containing these points. Thus, for two videos *V* and *V'* with different sizes, we obtain two trajectories *T* and *T'*. Then, we try to find the most similar point in *T* with each point in *T'* while using the distance *d_S*, what results in defining the best matched couples. For example, as we can see in Figure 1, P_1 in *T* is matched with P_2' in *T'*, P_2 in *T* is matched with P_4' in *T'* ... and P_n in *T* is matched $P_m'$with in *T'*. The matching is continued until the end of the trajectory and we keep the best matched point P_j^* defined by:

$$P_j^* = Minarg_{1 \leq j \leq n} d\_S(P_i, P_j') \quad (4)$$

The next step consists to calculate the distance *d_G* between the matched couples. To do this, the distance *d_G* is computed between (P_1 ,P_2^*), (P_2,P_4^*),... and (P_n,P_m^*). Thus, the dissimilarity *D* is the sum of Grassmann distances d_G(P_1, P), d_G(P_2,P_4^*), ... and d_G(P_n,P_m^*).

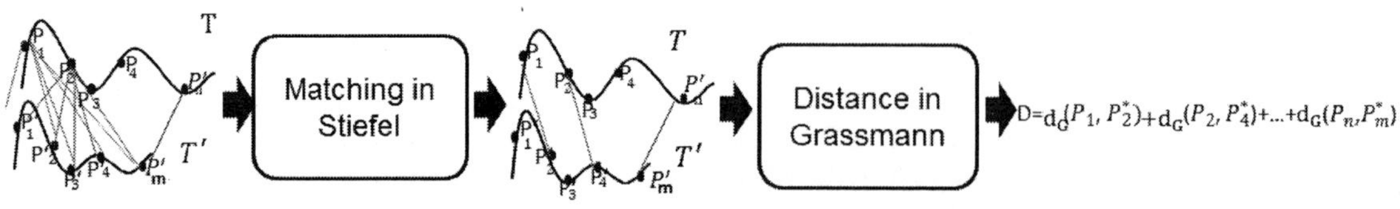

Figure 1. The outline of the proposed method

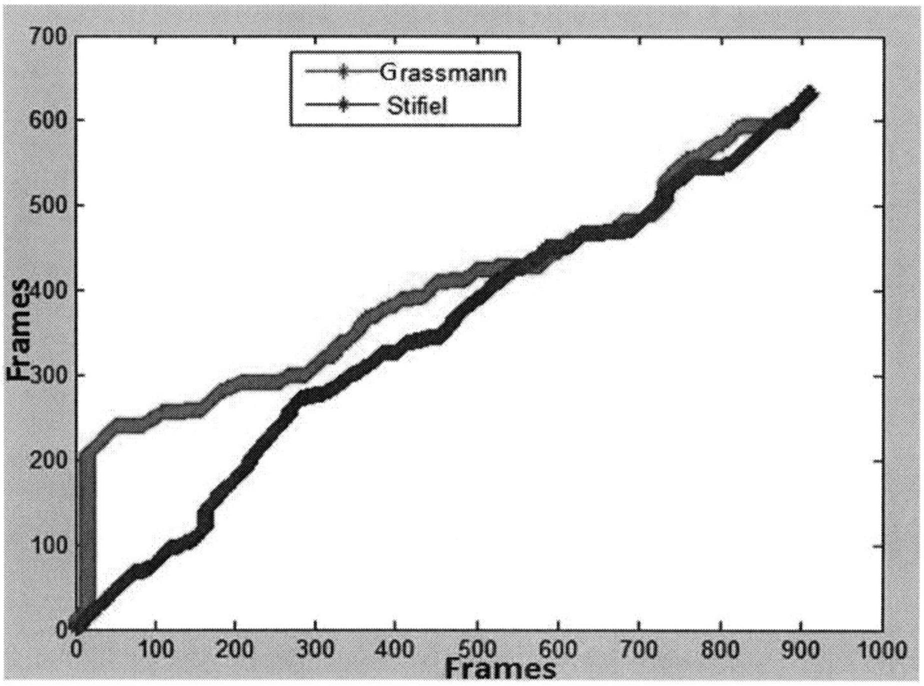

Figure 2. The matching in Stiefel and Grassmann manifolds

As described previously, we explore two different manifolds (Stiefel and Grassmann) using two different metrics in order to calculate dissimilarity between motions. This can be helpful to analyze actions, classifications and re-identification issues. Using the mathematical framework described in the previous sections and the nearest neighbor as a classifier, we can evaluate the dynamic of skeletal data. Thus, in our case, a point on a Stiefel manifold is an orthonormal matrix of size 20×3 that can be viewed as 3-dimensional subspace of R^{20}. By applying the DTW with the Stiefel distance, we obtain the nearest point. The matching in Stiefel is used to guarantee the best matching since Grassmann is known by the ignorance of rotation. As we can see in Figure 2, by ignoring the rotation with Grassmann, we can match many frames (200 frames) with the same frame, if the difference in motion is just a rotation. Then, Grassmann distance d_G (2) is applied for all couples of landmarks already matched (Figure 2). Finally, the dissimilarity D is the sum of matched couples all along trajectories as described in what follows:

```
Input: Two trajectories T and T' using skeleton information

Output: Dissimilarity D between T and T'

Method: Matching of the trajectories in Stiefel manifold and
dissimilarity measurement in Grassmann manifold

BEGIN
D ← 0
/* Browse the trajectory T of size n */
for i=1 to n
/* Identify the point P_j* in T' that matches best the point P_i in T */
Tab ← Null     /* Fill array with matched values with P_i */
min ← 0
index ← 0     /* The index of the min value */
/* Browse the trajectory T' of size m */
      for j=1 to m
            Tab[j] ← d_S(P_i, P_j')
            if  Tab[j]<min
            min ←  Tab[j]
            index ← j
            end
      end
D ← D + d_G(P_i, P*_index)
End
END
```

3. EXPERIMENTS

This work addresses the problem of identifying a person (e.g. in a company, in an airport…) and can reduce the problem of scanning device, waiting in line or remembering user passwords. This method can be used to identify a person by the way of walking (comparison trajectories of motion (Elaoud et al., 2017)). In this section, we present some experimental illustrations, in order to evaluate the proposed method on challenging datasets, such as the BIWI-Lab RGBD-ID dataset (Munaro et al., 2014b). It is a specified RGB-D dataset for re-identification tasks that aims to re-identify different persons in different locations with different appearances. It is divided on 50 training sequences and 56 testing sequences of 50 different people. In the training sets, people repeat the same action in front of a Kinect sensor, like a rotation around the vertical axis, several head movements and two walks towards the camera. 28 people, different of the 50 ones that are present in the training video, have been recorded also in two testing sequences each. These testing sets have been recorded in a different day and in a different location with respect to the training dataset, therefore most subjects have different clothes. Every person has a Still sequence and a Walking sequence in the testing set. For the first set, the Still videos, every person is slightly performing motion in place and for the second set, Walking sequences, every person moves with two walks frontally and two other walks diagonally with respect to the Kinect.

For evaluation purposes, we compute Cumulative Matching Curves (CMC) (Gray et Tao, 2008), which are commonly used for analyzing the re-identification performances. In Figure 3.a and Figure 3.b, we report the CMC curves on Still BIWI-Lab RGBD-ID and Walk BIWI-Lab RGBD-ID datasets, respectively. The reported curves are based on Stiefel distance *d_S*, Grassmann distance *d_G* and matching Stiefel with Grassmann (noted d_M)-based classifications. As shown in Figure 3.a (for the set Still BIWI-Lab RGBD-ID), the distance *d_G* and the distance *d_M* -based classifications performs better results than the one based on *d_S* in most of the cases. The results reported using the distance *d_G* and the distance *d_M* are similar in general.

In fact, the recognition rate starts in rank 2 for both distances with a value of 3.57%. Then, for rank 4, the distance *d_M*-based classification outperforms the distance *d_G*-based classification with a value of 14.28% against 10.71%. For the others ranks, the curves are alternated, such as in rank 20 to 33 the distance *d_G*-based classification outperforms distance d_M-based classifications but in rank 35 to 50 the distance *d_M*-based classification outperforms the one based on the distance *d_G*. Especially, the first distance that reaches 100% for the recognition rate is the *d_M* distance in rank 48 against 92.85% for *d_G*. As shown in Figure 3.b (for the set Walk BIWI-Lab RGBD-ID datasets), the distance *d_G*-based and the distance *d_M*-based classifications perform better results than the one based on *d_S*. The recognition rate at rank 3 is equal to 7.14% for both *d_G* and *d_M*-based classifications. Then, one can see along the CMC curves that the *d_M*-based classification is better than the ones based on the distance *d_G* with a value of 10.71% at rank 4 against 7.14% for the classification based on *d_G*. The results for both distances are close in general, such as the *d_M*-based classification outperforms the *d_G*-based classification in rank 12 to rank 23 but the *d_G*-based classification is the best in ranks 23 to 30. A finer comparison detailed these results and the maximum values are presented in Table 1 and Table 2. This leads us to conclude that it cannot be the best measure in all cases but it has performance for more than half of results. Then, the matching can exist as a measure and can give good results. Thus, as best as we know, it is the first time that this unsupervised method is proposed and can have an important role. As re-identification with Kinect is still recent, there are not many previous approaches in this area to make a complete comparison. To the best of our knowledge, limited efforts have been spent on Kinect-based person re-identification (Munaro et al., 2014a, 2014b). The proposed method in (Munaro et al., 2014a) and (Munaro et al., 2014b) is based on anthropometric measurements that are calculated from the skeleton data and not on the gait. The gait extracted from skeleton for re-identification is more challenging task and has not been sufficiently investigated. We argue that the proposed method is among first efforts to re-identify person based on their gaits using skeleton data.

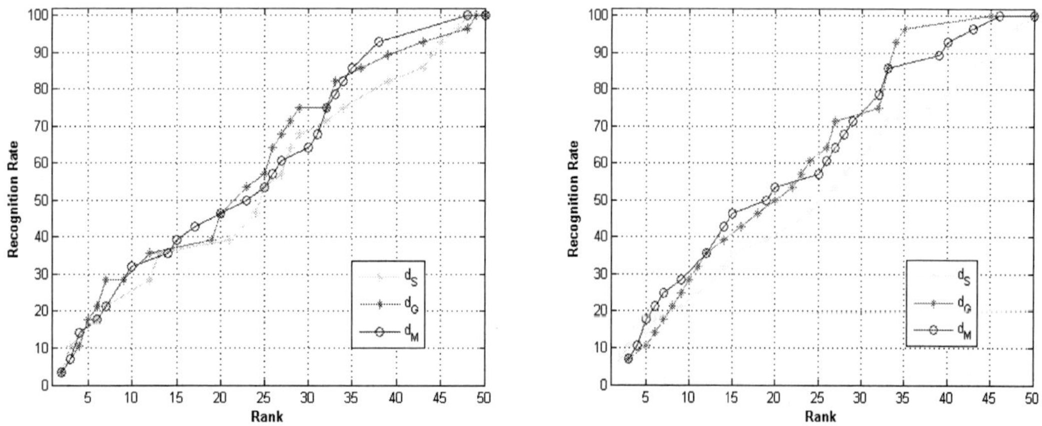

(a) (b)

Figure 3. Re-identification accuracy using Still BIWI-Lab RGBD-ID dataset and Walk BIWI-Lab RGBD-ID dataset

Table 1. Comparison of re-identification results using Still BIWI-Lab RGBD-ID dataset

Rank	D_G	D_M
2-4	10.71%	14.27%
4-9	28.57%	27%
9-11	31%	32.14%
11-14	35.14%	34%
14-20	39.28%	42.85%
20-32	75%	68%
32-34	82%	82.14%
34-48	96.42%	100%
50	100%	100%

Table 2. Comparison of re-identification results using Walk BIWI-Lab RGBD-ID dataset

Rank	D_G	D_M
1-12	32.14%	35.71%
12-23	64.28%	67.85%
24-30	75%	71.42%
30-33	77%	78.57%
33-44	98%	97%
46	100%	100%

4. CONCLUSION

We have presented in this paper an accurate method for comparing human motions using evolutions of skeletons. The proposed method is based on metrics that are independent of the color information and change appearance. Indeed, we used the Riemannian geometry to process skeletal data and their temporal evolutions with a classification performed by closest neighbor. The main contribution of the proposed method resides in working conjointly with two manifolds: Stiefel and Grassmann. The matching of the trajectories is realized in Stiefel manifold and the dissimilarity assessment is performed in Grassmann manifold. This permits to benefit of to two manifolds. This work is tested in the field of re-identification, but it can be applied for others applications such as human action recognition or tracking. Although that the produced matching by our work is not the best in all cases, notably when compared with supervised methods, but this work introduces for the first time the possibility of using two different manifolds for the challenging stages of matching and distance computing. Future work will be focused on more manifolds and different types of distances to be able to provide a good measure of dissimilarity.

REFERENCES

Abdelkader, M.F. et al., 2011. Silhouette-based gesture and action recognition via modeling trajectories on Riemannian shape manifolds. Computer Vision and Image Understanding, 115(3), pp. 439–455.

Alashkar, T. et al., 2016. A Grassmann framework for 4D facial shape analysis. Pattern Recognition, 57, pp. 21–30.

Amor, B.B., Su, J. & Srivastava, A., 2016. Action Recognition Using Rate-Invariant Analysis of Skeletal Shape Trajectories. IEEE Transactions on Pattern Analysis and Machine Intelligence, 38(1), pp. 1–13.

Anjum, M.L., Rosa, S. & Bona, B., 2017. Tracking a Subset of Skeleton Joints: An Effective Approach towards Complex Human Activity Recognition. Journal of Robotics, 2017, pp. 1–8.

Barbosa, I. B. et al., 2017. Looking beyond appearances: Synthetic training data for deep CNNs in re-identification. arXiv preprint arXiv:1701.03153.

Barhoumi, W., 2014. Detection of highly articulated moving objects by using co-segmentation with application to athletic video sequences. Signal, Image and Video Processing, 9(7), pp. 1705–1715.

Cai, Z. et al., 2016. RGB-D datasets using microsoft kinect or similar sensors: a survey. Multimedia Tools and Applications, 76(3), pp. 4313–4355.

Devanne, M. et al., 2016. Learning shape variations of motion trajectories for gait analysis. 2016 23rd International Conference on Pattern Recognition (ICPR).

Ding, W. and Liu, K., 2017. Learning linear dynamical systems with high-order Tensor data for skeleton based action recognition. arXiv preprint arXiv:1701.03869.

Du, Y., Wang, W. & Wang, L., 2015. Hierarchical recurrent neural network for skeleton based action recognition. 2015 IEEE Conference on Computer Vision and Pattern Recognition (CVPR).

Edelman, A., Arias, T.A. & Smith, S.T., 1998. The Geometry of Algorithms with Orthogonality Constraints. SIAM Journal on Matrix Analysis and Applications, 20(2), pp.303–353.

Elaoud, A. et al., 2017. Analysis of Skeletal Shape Trajectories for Person Re-Identification. International Conference Advanced Concepts for Intelligent Vision Systems.

Feng, Y., Lu, B. & Zhang, D., 2017. Multiscale singular value manifold for rotating machinery fault diagnosis. Journal of Mechanical Science and Technology, 31(1), pp. 99–109.

Gray, D. & Tao, H., Viewpoint Invariant Pedestrian Recognition with an Ensemble of Localized Features. Lecture Notes in Computer Science Computer Vision – ECCV 2008, pp. 262–275.

Han, F. et al., 2017. Space-time representation of people based on 3D skeletal data: A review. Computer Vision and Image Understanding, 158, pp. 85–105.

Ke, Q. et al. 2017. A New Representation of Skeleton Sequences for 3D Action Recognition. arXiv preprint arXiv:1703.03492.

Lui, Y.M. & Beveridge, J.R., 2011. Tangent bundle for human action recognition. Face and Gesture 2011.

Meng, M. et al., 2016. Detection of Abnormal Gait from Skeleton Data. Proceedings of the 11th Joint Conference on Computer Vision, Imaging and Computer Graphics Theory and Applications.

Michalczuk, A. et al., 2017. Evaluation of human dynamic balance in Grassmann manifold.

Miao, J. et al., 2017. Manifold Regularized Slow Feature Analysis for Dynamic Texture Recognition. arXiv preprint arXiv:1706.03015.

Munaro, M. et al., 2014. One-Shot Person Re-identification with a Consumer Depth Camera. Person Re-Identification, pp. 161–181.

1. Munaro, M. et al., 2014. 3D reconstruction of freely moving persons for re-identification with a depth sensor. 2014 IEEE International Conference on Robotics and Automation (ICRA).

Presti, L.L. & Cascia, M.L., 2016. 3D skeleton-based human action classification: A survey. Pattern Recognition, 53, pp. 130–147.

Schubert, T. et al., 2016. Automatic bone parameter estimation for skeleton tracking in optical motion capture. 2016 IEEE International Conference on Robotics and Automation (ICRA).

Shotton, J. et al., 2011. Real-time human pose recognition in parts from single depth images. Cvpr 2011.

Slama, R., Wannous, H. & Daoudi, M., 2014. Grassmannian Representation of Motion Depth for 3D Human Gesture and Action Recognition. 2014 22nd International Conference on Pattern Recognition.

Song, S. et al., 2017. An End-to-End Spatio-Temporal Attention Model for Human Action Recognition from Skeleton Data. In. AAAI, pp. 4263–4270.

Turaga, P. & Chellappa, R., 2009. Locally time-invariant models of human activities using trajectories on the grassmannian. 2009 IEEE Conference on Computer Vision and Pattern Recognition.

Turaga, P., Veeraraghavan, A. & Chellappa, R., 2008. Statistical analysis on Stiefel and Grassmann manifolds with applications in computer vision. 2008 IEEE Conference on Computer Vision and Pattern Recognition.

Vemulapalli, R., Arrate, F. & Chellappa, R., 2014. Human Action Recognition by Representing 3D Skeletons as Points in a Lie Group. 2014 IEEE Conference on Computer Vision and Pattern Recognition.

Wang, J., Liu, Z. & Wu, Y., 2014. Learning Actionlet Ensemble for 3D Human Action Recognition. SpringerBriefs in Computer Science Human Action Recognition with Depth Cameras, pp. 11–40.

Wu, A., Zheng, W.-S. & Lai, J.-H, 2017. Robust Depth-based Person Re-identification. . IEEE Transactions on Image Processing, pp. 2588–2603.

GRAPH GENERATION WITH IMPOSED AND FORBIDDEN PATTERNS

Mohamed Amine Omrani[1] and Wady Naanaa[2]
[1]*Faculty of Sciences*
[2]*National Engineering School*
University of Tunis El Manar, LIMTIC laboratory, Tunisia

ABSTRACT

Graphs are considered as a powerful tool to model pairwise relations between objects providing a convenient way to represent various real-world problems. However, the task of building graphs is not obvious, especially when it is surrounded by a set of various structural constraints. In this paper, we cope with constrained graph generation, which we encode as a constraint satisfaction problem, in order to reduce the computational cost required by considering structural constraints while generating graphs.

KEYWORDS

Graph construction; graph generation; constraint satisfaction problem; constraint programming; graph cycle; forbidden pattern

1. INTRODUCTION

A graph is a set of vertices and edges that link vertices together. One of the most attractive features of graphs is their adequacy to model pairwise relationship between objects. Such structural information would be helpful to solve relevant combinatorial problems. From the practical point of view, graphs are considered as a powerful tool frequently used to represent and solve various real-world problems. Indeed, modeling problems using graphs provides a fairly accurate description of the problem at hand. For example, in analytical chemistry, generating all possible molecular graphs formed from a fixed set of atoms involves generating connected graphs, where atoms are represented by vertices and bonds are represented by edges (Omrani and Naanaa, 2016). In telecommunications network planning, base stations and hubs stand for the vertices, while communication links correspond to edges and the network must be constructed in such a way that guarantees a good connectivity between the communicating devices. In transport network, solving the traveling salesman problem (TSP) (Junger and al., 1994) involves constructing a minimal length path which visits every pair of cities. This problem can also be interpreted as a graph construction task, where the cities are the vertices, the paths are edges and weights on the edges represent the distances between cities. The World Wide Web (WWW) can be modeled as a directed graph in which a vertex represents a web page and an edge represents a hyperlink and the study of this graph can provide insight into web algorithms for crawling, searching, and ranking web resources (Lehmberg and al., 2014).

However, graph construction is a ubiquitous problem in itself, a problem which appears embedded within many practical applications and surrounded by a set of non-trivial related tasks distinguishing characteristics of these graphs. Some of these tasks are graph connectivity (Brown and al., 2005), subgraph isomorphism (Deville and al., 2010), forbidden and enforced subgraphs (Genova and al., 2012), all-pairs shortest path problem (APSP) (Williams, 2014) and others. More details on the theoretical challenges of generating random graphs with given constraints can be found in (Hofstad, 2017).

We focus specifically on the issue of forbidding certain patterns to appear as induced subgraphs in the graphs to be constructed. This problem, besides being interesting in its own right, is useful in a variety of situations and is of great interest for biologists, computer scientists, economists, electrical engineers, mathematicians and sociologists. From the theoretical point of view, it has been shown that this problem is NP-complete on general graphs (Garey and Johnson, 1979).

In this work, we describe a new approach to solve a particular variant of constrained graph generation. We propose a framework to generate graphs with a given degree sequence and a given set of imposed subgraphs, while forbidding other small and specific subgraphs, namely small cycles. More concretely, our contribution handles two main structural constraints: the target graphs will be constrained to contain some predefined subgraphs, while some cycles of prescribed lengths are excluded during the generation process. Our interest for forbidding small cycles has been motivated by their importance as basic data structures for a number of information visualization applications and many real-life applications. For example, in analytical chemistry, the molecular graph generation (MGG) problem consists in finding all molecular graphs that are consistent with a dataset derived from different kinds of spectra. In most situations, this dataset requires forbidding small cycles (Meringer, 2013). In information theory, a low-density parity-check (LDPC) code is a linear error correcting code which allows transmitting a message over a noisy transmission channel (MacKay, 2005). Designing high performance LDPC codes is constructed using graphs without short cycle (Bayati, 2009).

The problem of efficiently generating graphs with forbidden cycles constraints has been poorly studied. To the best of our knowledge, in 2009, was published the first polynomial-time algorithm (Bayati, 2009) for randomly generating one graph with n vertices, m edges and no cycle of length larger than ℓ using $O(n^2m)$ operations, where $m = O(n^{1+\alpha})$ and $\alpha \leq 1/2\ell(\ell + 3)$. The work presented in (Melancon, 2001) proposed an algorithm based on a Markov Chain for randomly generating cycle-free digraphs with a given number of vertices.

The present work is intended to further develop the constraint satisfaction approach to graph generation in the direction of forbidding predefined subgraphs during the generation process. The contribution of the paper is two folds. First, we propose a pure constraint-based encoding of the graph generation problem which enables an efficient use of various pieces of information. Second, we show how this encoding is appropriate for imposing predefined subgraphs, and forbidding small cycles from the target graphs during the generation process.

The rest of the paper is organized as follows: In Section 2, we present a theoretical description for the graph generation problem from a structural point of view. Precisely, we recall some notions from graph theory and we briefly describe the constraint satisfaction paradigm. In Section 3, we explain, our pure constrained-patterns-based encoding of the graph generation problem. In particular, we use a combinatorial optimization technique to impose and forbid a particular class of predefined patterns during the generation process. In Section 4, we resort to one of the well-known and powerful constraint solvers, namely, the Mistral solver (Lecoutre, 2008), which is available within the python constraint programming platform Numberjack, developed by Hebrard and al., (2008) to solve the encoded instances. The experimental results obtained from the generation of several real-world constrained graphs instances showed that our approach does indeed work.

2. BASIC NOTIONS

2.1 Graph Theory Notions

To begin with, we give the necessary graph theory background and terminologies employed in this paper.

An undirected graph is a pair $G = (V, E)$ comprising a nonempty finite set V of vertices together with a collection, E, of edges, with $E \subseteq \binom{V}{2}$. A simple graph contains no loops, i.e. an edge that relates a vertex to itself. In a computer network, a pair of computers is in E, if and only if, they are connected by some medium. If E contains multiple copies of an edge, that is E is a multi-set, then G is a multi-graph. The degree of a vertex $v \in V$, denoted by $d(v)$, is the number of edges of E that have v as end-point. A chain in G is a sequence of vertices $(v_1, \ldots, v_\ell)$ such that, for each $1 \leq i < \ell, \{v_i, v_{i+1}\}$, is in E, and we say that ℓ is the length of the chain. A path in G is a chain $(v_1, \ldots, v_l)$ such that $v_i \neq v_j$, for all $i \neq j$. A cycle in G is a path $(v_1, \ldots, v_\ell)$ such that $\ell \geq 3$ and $v_1 = v_\ell$. A cycle in G of length ℓ is called an ℓ-cycle of G. Note that the number of vertices in an ℓ-cycle equals the number of edges. G is connected if, for every $v_i, v_j \in V$, with $i \neq j$, there is a path in G from v_i to v_j.

Now on, we will assume that G is a connected undirected graph with no self-loops. A graph $H = (V', E')$ is called a subgraph of a graph $G = (V, E)$ if $V' \subseteq V$ and $E' = E \cap (V' \times V')$. H is called the subgraph of G induced by V' and will be denoted by $G[V']$. A graph is cycle-free if it does not contain any cycle. An ℓ-cycle-free graph is a graph with no induced cycle of length ℓ. Recall that an ℓ-cycle is a set of ℓ vertices connected in a closed chain.

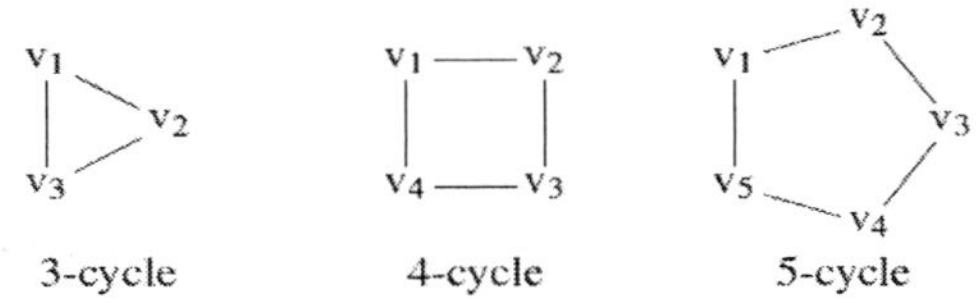

Figure 1. Typical cyclic patterns

2.2 The CSP Approach

2.2.1 Definitions and Notations

First, we recall the definition of a Constraint Satisfaction Problem (CSP) on finite domains as it has been described by Tsang (2014).

A CSP is defined by a triple (X, D, C) where:

- $X = \{x_1, \ldots, x_n\}$ is a finite set of variables.
- $D = \{D_1, \ldots, D_n\}$ is a finite set of value domains so that D_k is the domain of x_k.
- $C = \{C_1, \ldots, C_m\}$ is a set of constraints. Every constraint is a pair (X_k, R_k), where $X_k = \{x_{k_1}, \ldots, x_{k_r}\} \subseteq X$ is the constraint *scope* and $R_k \subseteq D_{k_1} \times \ldots \times D_{k_r}$ is a r-ary *relation* specifying the r-tuples allowed by the constraint.

The *arity* of a constraint is the size of its *scope*. The arity of a problem is the maximum arity over all its constraints. An assignment S is defined by a pair (X_S, V_S), where $X_S = \{x_{S_1}, \ldots, x_{S_k}\} \subseteq X$ is a subset of variables and $V_S = (v_{S_1}, \ldots, v_{S_k}) \in D_{S_1} \times \cdots \times D_{S_k}$ is the sequence of values simultaneously taken by the variables in X_S. Let $S = (X_S, V_S)$ be an *assignment* and let $C_k = (X_k, R_k)$ be a constraint such that $X_k \subseteq X_S$. We say that S satisfies C_K if and only if $(V_S \downarrow X_k) \in R_k$, where $\downarrow$ denotes the projection operator which allows to get the sub-tuple of V_S that assigns values to the variables of X_k. An assignment is consistent if it satisfies all the constraints of the CSP. If it violates one or more constraints, it is said to be inconsistent. If an assignment affects a value to every variable of the CSP then it is said to be complete, otherwise it is a partial assignment. A solution to a CSP is a complete and consistent assignment. A CSP instance may globally be characterized by four parameters, which are the problem arity, the number of variables, the number of constraints, and the size of the largest value domain. These parameters are very influential on the complexity of the solution process and the goal of a good CSP formulation is to keep these parameters as small as possible.

2.2.2 CSP Solving

CSPs are solved by means of dedicated programs called constraint solvers. Constraint solvers are mainly based on filtering techniques, whose role is to remove values, (resp., combinations of values), from the domains of variables, (resp. from the relations defining the constraints), that cannot be part of any solution. Filtering algorithms are based on the notion of local consistency and tends to simplify the problem by reducing the search space based on the notion of local consistency. For this reason, they are crucial for solving large CSPs. CSP solutions can be determined by searching systematically through the possible complete assignments. Systematic search methods are based on backtracking, a form of depth-first search which abandons a branch whenever it determines that no solutions lie further down the branch. This is done by testing the values chosen for variables against a set of constraints. So, many works have been carried out to make the solving of CSPs more efficient by using several variants of Backtracking algorithms (Kumar and Vipin, 1992), such as (Backjumping, Backmarking, Forward Checking and Maintaining Arc Consistency); Filtering techniques based on constraint propagation; Heuristics, and others.

3. GRAPH GENERATION AS A CSP

There are several ways to represent graphs, each has its advantages and drawbacks. Some situations, or algorithms that we want to run with graphs as input/output, call for a particular representation, and others call for a different representation. Here, we use the adjacency matrix to represent graphs within the constraint satisfaction framework.

3.1 The Basic Model

As it has been stated above, a CSP is defined by a triple (X, D, C). For the encoding of graph generation, the variable set, X is composed of two subsets: the adjacency variables set A and the fragment variables set F which will allow to impose subgraphs. The first variable subset, will handle the adjacency of vertices in the graph. Hence, for a graph with n vertices, we create $n \times n$ variables, a variable for each pair of vertices (i, j), which will be referred to by adjacency variables. When $a_{i,j} \neq 0$, this means that there is an edge between i and j, and when $a_{i,j}$ is set to 0, there is no edge from i to j.

Since target graphs are undirected, we post the constraint $a_{i,j} = a_{j,i}$ for each pair $i < j$. To forbid self-loops, we add the constraint $a_{i,i} = 0$, for each $1 \leq i \leq n$. Given the degree $d(i)$ of vertex i, then we can post the constraint $\sum_{j=1}^{n} a_{i,j} = d(i)$, for each row i of matrix A to ensure that the vertices have the correct degree. If a pair of vertices can be related by more than one edge, this will result in a multi-graph and we should have $a_{i,j} \geq 2$, for some pairs (i, j).

3.2 Imposing Subgraphs

As we have seen in the introduction, several structural constraints surround the graph construction process. In what follows, we show that a CSP encoding allows a simultaneous processing of these various constraints. In particular, the challenging task of imposing and forbidding certain predefined subgraphs to appear in the target graph can be encoded in the terms of a CSP.

One of the various ways of constraining the graph generation process consists in imposing some specified subgraphs to appear in the generated graphs. For instance, imposing subgraphs can be helpful for generating molecules in the design of organic synthesis. In this Section, we aim to provide a CSP solution that allows expressing and satisfying this structural constraint during graph generation.

Assume that the target graphs must all contain a predefined graph H as an induced subgraph. Recall that an induced subgraph of graph G (denoted $H \subset G$) is a graph which is isomorphic to some subgraph of G. To enforce such a constraint, we proceed as follows: Every subgraph H is imposed through a specific variable subset denoted by F_H. The domain of each $f \in F_H$, is set to the list of vertices that may correspond to the vertices of H. Thus, the domain of every subgraph variable should be a subset of $\{1, \ldots, n\}$. To achieve enforcing the desired subgraph, we must establish connections between the subgraph variables and the adjacency variables, i.e. the variables of F and those of A. Hence, if a subgraph variable f, which is connected by an edge to another subgraph variable f' in the subgraph H, are respectively assigned to vertices i and j then we must have $a_{i,j} \neq 0$, where $a_{i,j}$ is the adjacency variable encoding the connection between i and j. This constraint is defined, for every fixed $i, j \in D_f \times D_{f'}$, where D_f and $D_{f'}$ denotes the value domains of f and f' respectively, by the following ternary relation:

$$(f \neq i) \vee (f' \neq j) \vee (a_{i,j} \neq 0) \qquad (1)$$

The example depicted in Figure 2 illustrates how the proposed CSP-based approach processes an instance with degree sequence (4,4,4,3,3,2,2) requiring the presence of two cyclic subgraphs, H and H'. A possible assignment of the CSP variables $f_1, \ldots, f_6$ is indicated by the circled values, together with the resulting assembly. Observe that the two imposed fragments are present in the constructed graph and that the degree sequence is met.

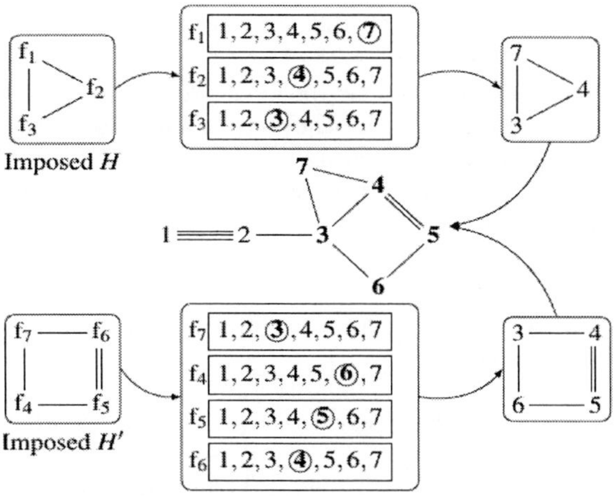

Figure 2. An illustrative example of imposing two predefined subgraphs (***H*** and ***H'***)

3.3 Forbidding Subgraphs

In this Section, we add structural constraints in order to generate ℓ-cycle-free graphs. To simplify the description of these constraints, let us first recall some supplementary graph theoretic notions.

An ℓ-cycle of a graph G is an induced subgraph of G which is isomorphic to a set of vertices connected in a closed chain. A graph G is ℓ-cycle-free if it contains no ℓ-cycle as an induced subgraph.

To forbid cycles with certain lengths in the target graph, we use the notion of cyclic sequence which is simply a tuple of distinct vertices, except for the first and last component of the tuple which are the same (see Figure 3). For instance, $(v_1, v_2, \dots, v_\ell, v_1)$ is a cyclic sequence. To disallow ℓ-cycles in a graph on n vertices, we first generate the list of all possible ℓ-cyclic sequences that can be formed from n vertices, (observe that the size of the ℓ-cycle list is equal to the number of arrangements A_n^ℓ), and then, we create, for each cyclic sequence σ, a constraint that either enforces a pair of successive vertices in σ to be disconnected or enforces the cycle to admit a cord, that is, an edge connecting two non-consecutive vertices of the cycle. This condition can be expressed by the following logical constraint:

$$(\bigvee_{k=1}^{\ell-1} a_{v_k,v_{k+1}} = 0) \vee (a_{v_1,v_\ell}=0) \vee (\bigvee_{1\leq k+1<k'\leq \ell} a_{i_k,i_{k'}} \neq 0) \quad (2)$$

A drawback of the method described above for forbidding cycles is that we are compelled to limit the length of the forbidden cycles, because there are $O(n^\ell)$ cyclic ℓ-sequences that can be formed from a set of n vertices. In what follows, we focus on the generation of a narrowed list of cyclic sequences. We show that an effective elimination of redundant cyclic sequences allows a significant time saving.

Two cyclic sequences are redundant if they correspond to the same cycle. For instance, $(v_1, v_2, \dots, v_\ell, v_1)$ and $(v_2, \dots, v_\ell, v_1, v_2)$ are redundant. Generating all possible cyclic sequences first, and then filtering out those corresponding to identical cycles entails a waste of computation time, and this can be all the more time consuming that the filtering process is executed during the generation process. A more efficient method consists, once again, in the use of a CSP which allows only cyclic sequences that forbid distinct cycles.

The proposed filtering method requires, however, the following notions:

- The *reversed cyclic sequence* σ^R of a cyclic sequence $\sigma = (v_1, v_2, \dots, v_\ell, v_1)$ is the rearranged cyclic sequence $(v_1, v_\ell, v_{\ell-1}, \dots, v_2, v_1)$.
- By *canonical cyclic sequence*, we mean a cyclic sequence $\overline{\sigma} = (\overline{v}_1, \overline{v}_2, \dots, \overline{v}_\ell, \overline{v}_1)$ that verifies $\overline{v}_1 < \overline{v}_k$, for all $1 < k \leqslant \ell$ and $\overline{v}_2 < \overline{v}_\ell$.
- The subset of edges corresponding to the ℓ-cyclic sequence $\sigma = (v_1, v_2, \dots, v_\ell, v_1)$ is $E(\sigma) = \{\{v_k, v_{k+1}\}_{1\leq k\leq \ell-1}\} \cup \{\{v_1, v_\ell\}\}$.
- A pair of cyclic sequence σ and σ' are equivalent if and only if $E(\sigma) = E(\sigma')$.

For instance, $\sigma_1 = (1,2,3,4,5,1)$, $\sigma_2 = (5,1,2,3,4,5)$ and $\sigma_3 = (3,4,5,1,2,3)$ are three equivalent cyclic sequences with $E(\sigma_1) = E(\sigma_2) = E(\sigma_3) = \{\{1,2\},\{2,3\},\{3,4\},\{4,5\},\{5,1\}\}$.

The equivalence relation defined in the last point of the above list induces the partition of the cyclic sequences into equivalence classes. The cyclic sequences that belong to the same equivalence class have the same length, involve the same vertices and induce the same edges. For every length ℓ, $1 \leq \ell \leq n$, and for every ℓ-subset of vertices only one representative cyclic sequence per equivalence class suffices to forbid ℓ-cycles. To show this, we prove that, for all ℓ-cyclic sequence 6, there exists a canonical ℓ-cyclic sequence $\bar{\sigma}$ which is equivalent to σ.

Proposition 1. Any cyclic sequence is equivalent to its reverse.

Proof. Let $\sigma = (v_1, v_2 \ldots, v_\ell, v_1)$ be a cyclic sequence. Recall that the reverse of σ is $\sigma^R = (v_1, v_\ell, v_{\ell-1}, \ldots, v_2, v_1)$. We have therefore

$$E(\sigma) = \{\{v_k, v_{k+1}\}\}_{1 \leq k \leq \ell-1} \cup \{\{v_\ell, v_1\}\}$$

which is the same set as

$$E(\sigma^R) = \{\{v_1, v_\ell\}\} \cup \{\{v_k, v_{k-1}\}\}_{\ell \geq k \geq 2}$$

Proposition 2. Any cyclic sequence has an equivalent canonical cyclic sequence.

Proof. Let $\sigma = (v_1, v_2 \ldots, v_\ell, v_1)$ be any cyclic sequence and let $k^* = \arg\min_{1 \leq k \leq \ell} v_k$ we prove that either $\sigma^- = (v_{k^*}, v_{k^*-1}, \ldots, v_1, v_\ell, \ldots, v_{k^*+1}, v_{k^*})$ or $\sigma^+ = (v_{k^*}, v_{k^*+1}, \ldots, v_\ell, v_1, \ldots, v_{k^*-1}, v_{k^*})$ is a canonical cyclic sequence which is equivalent to σ.

First, let us show that $E(\sigma^-) = E(\sigma^+) = E(\sigma)$. Observe that σ^- is the reversed sequence of σ^+. Then, by Proposition 1, it suffices to verify that $E(\sigma^+) = E(\sigma)$. We have

$$E(\sigma^+) = \{\{v_k, v_{k+1}\}\}_{k^* \leq k \leq \ell-1} \cup \{\{v_\ell, v_1\}\} \cup \{\{v_k, v_{k+1}\}\}_{1 \leq k \leq k^*-1}$$

which can be written as

$$E(\sigma^+) = \{\{v_k, v_{k+1}\}\}_{1 \leq k \leq \ell-1} \cup \{\{v_1, v_\ell\}\}$$

Thus, $E(\sigma^+) = E(\sigma)$.

Now, suppose that neither σ^- nor σ^+ is a canonical cyclic sequence. Since both σ^- and σ^+ meet the condition of starting by the minimal component of σ that is v_k^*, we must have $v_{k^*-1} \geq v_{k^*+1}$ and $v_{k^*+1} \geq v_{k^*-1}$. This results in $v_{k^*-1} = v_{k^*+1}$. But the components of σ are all distinct, hence the contradiction.

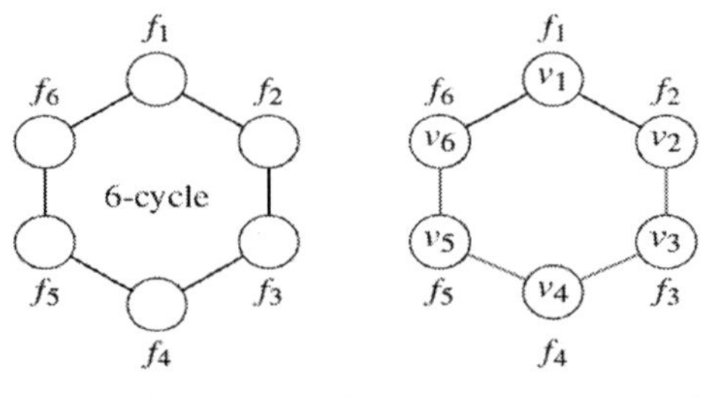

Figure 3. An illustrative example of cyclic sequence σ associated to 6-cycle f

To generate the list of non-redundant cyclic sequences, for each forbidden cycle length ℓ, we resort, once again, to a CSP-based approach. We introduce a new CSP on ℓ variables $f_1, \ldots, f_\ell$, where all the f_i's take their values in $\{1, \ldots, n\}$. Three constraints are used in this CSP. The first constraint imposes that all the variables, that is the f_i's, are different. This can be done using the predefined *Alldifferent()* constraint, which is well handled by the constraint solver. The second constraint imposes a restriction on the first variable f_1, so that it takes the minimum values among all the f_i's to have a canonical sequence. Finally, we add a single constraint which enforces the value assigned to the second variable, f_2 to be smaller than the value assigned to the variable f_ℓ. These constraints ensure the generation of canonical cyclic sequences only.

Table 1 shows the results and the effect of our technique for filtering forbidden cycles of all lengths not exceeding 6. We can see that the number of non-redundant cyclic sequences, denoted by $\bar{A}_n^\ell$, was greatly reduced, reaching a percent as low as 8.33% for cycles of length 6.

Table 1. Filtering cyclic sequences results

	$\ell = 3$		$\ell = 4$		$\ell = 5$		$\ell = 6$	
n	A_n^ℓ	$\bar{A}_n^\ell$	A_n^ℓ	$\bar{A}_n^\ell$	A_n^ℓ	$\bar{A}_n^\ell$	A_n^ℓ	$\bar{A}_n^\ell$
3	6	1	-	-	-	-	-	-
4	24	4	24	3	-	-	-	-
5	60	10	120	15	120	12	720	60
10	720	120	5040	630	30240	3024	151200	12600
20	6840	1140	116280	14535	1860480	1860480	27907200	2325600
30	24360	4060	657720	82215	17100720	1710072	427518000	35626500
40	59280	9880	2193360	274170	78960960	7896096	2763633600	230302800
50	117600	19600	5527200	690900	254251200	25425120	11441304000	953442000

4. EXPERIMENTAL RESULTS

We discuss here the efficiency of the constraint based solution for generating graphs without small cycles. All tests have been done on a PC at 2.0 Ghz and 4 GB of RAM running Ubuntu 12.04 LTS. During graphs generation, we used the *Mistral* solver (Lecoutre , 2008), which is available within the python constraint programming platform *Numberjack*, developed by Hebrard and al., (2008).

Table 2 summarizes the experimental results obtained on some constrained graph generation instances by forbidding cycles of various lengths. The Table reports the number of vertices (n), the degree sequences of the target graphs, the number of generated graph and the computational time in seconds required for each degree sequences. The two last columns of the table report the result obtained by taking into account the forbidden cycles, which are 5-cycles, 4-cycles, 3-cycles or none (none means there is no excluded cycles). These results show that the execution time increases when the length ℓ of the predefined cycle increases.

Table 2. A constrained graphs generation results based on forbidden cycles of small length

n	Degree sequence	Solutions Found		CPU Time	
				A_n^ℓ	$\bar{A}_n^\ell$
6	<2,2,2,2,1,1>	none	31	0.05	0.05
		5-cycle	31	0.04	0.02
		4-cycle	28	0.02	0.01
		3-cycle	27	1.77	0.05
7	<2,2,2,2,2,1,1>	none	167	0.05	0.05
		5-cycle	155	0.18	0.08
		4-cycle	152	0.05	0.02
		3-cycle	147	0.02	0.01
8	<3,3,2,2,2,2,1,1>	none	1074	0.03	0.04
		5-cycle	798	2.48	0.8
		4-cycle	722	0.32	0.1
		3-cycle	652	0.04	0.03
9	<3,3,2,2,2,2,2,1,1>	none	9760	0.06	0.06
		5-cycle	7480	52	17.4
		4-cycle	6820	4.26	1.9
		3-cycle	6380	0.47	0.2
10	<4,4,4,2,2,2,2,2,1,1>	none	70530	0.06	0.06
		5-cycle	15960	407	144.7
		4-cycle	7020	18.5	7
		3-cycle	8520	1.4	0.7
11	<4,3,3,2,2,2,2,1,1,1,1>	none	229916	2.05	2.05
		5-cycle	163658	3216	1284
		4-cycle	132452	204	80.6
		3-cycle	111570	14	7.8

5. CONCLUSION

In this paper, we presented a constrained-based approach to cope with the graph generation problem. In particular, we have presented an effective encoding of graph generation in terms of constraint satisfaction problem allowing the generation of graphs with imposed and forbidden patterns. This study has shown the advantage of imposing and forbidding a set of subgraph patterns through constraint reasoning. A substantial efficiency gains came from a filter rejecting cyclic sequences checks.

As a future work, we plan to equip our constraint by a routine which enables forbidding more complex subgraphs in the target graph. Another track consists in taking into account uncertain data. Such data are frequently encountered in real-world graph generation instances and may be very helpful in narrowing the set of candidate solutions. To this end, we plan to move to a wider constraint reasoning framework, namely, the Valued Constraint Satisfaction Problems (VCSP).

REFERENCES

Bayati, M., Montanari, A., and Saberi, A., 2009. Generating random graphs with large girth. *In Symposium on Discrete Algorithms*. pp. 566–575.

Brown, K. N., Prosser, P., Beck, J. C., and Wu, C. W., 2005. Exploring the use of constraint programming for enforcing connectivity during graph generation. *The 5th workshop on modelling and solving problems with constraints.*

Deville, Y., and Solnon, C., 2010. Solving Subgraph Isomorphism Problems with CP. *Constraints*. pp. 31–25.

Garey, M. R. and Johnson, D. S., 1979. A Guide to the Theory of NP-Completeness (Series of Books in the Mathematical Sciences). *Computers and Intractability*. pp. 340.

Genova, D., and Jonoska, N., 2012. Forbidding and enforcing on graphs. *Theoretical Computer Science*. pp. 108–117.

Hebrard, E., Mahony, E. O., and Sullivan, B. O., 2008. CP and Combinatorial Optimisation in Numberjack. *Integration of AI and OR Techniques in Constraint Programming for Combinatorial Optimization Problems*. pp. 181-185.

Hofstad, R van der., 2017. Random Graphs and Complex Networks, *Cambridge University Press*. pp 306-316.

Junger, M., Reinelt, G. and Rinaldi, G., 1994. *The Traveling Salesman Problem*. Handbook on Operations Research and the Management Sciences North Holland Press, pp. 225-330.

Kumar., and Vipin., 1992. Algorithms for Constraint Satisfaction Problems. *AI Magazine*. pp. 32-44.

Lecoutre, C., 2008. Mistral: A Constraint Satisfaction Library. *In Proceedings of 3th International csp solver competition.*

Lehmberg, O., Meusel, R., and Bizer, C., 2014. Graph Structure in the Web. *Proceedings of the 2014 ACM conference on Web science - WebSci '14*. Indiana, Bloomington, pp.119–128.

MacKay, D. J. C., 2005. Information Theory, Inference, and Learning Algorithms. *Learning*. pp. 1-640.

Melançon, G. ,Dutour, I. and Bousquet, M., 2001. Random Generation of Directed Acyclic Graphs. *Electronic Notes in Discrete Math*. pp. 202-207.

Meringer, M., and Schymanski, EL.,2013. Small Molecule Identification with MOLGEN and Mass Spectrometry. *Metabolites*. pp. 440-462.

Omrani, M. A. and Naanaa, W. A., 2016. Constrained molecular graph generation with imposed and forbidden fragments. *Proceedings of the 9th Hellenic Conference on Artificial Intelligence - SETN '16*. Greece, pp. 1-5.

Tsang, E.P.K., 2014. *Foundations of Constraint Satisfaction*, Edited by Thom Fruehwirth, Books on Demand.

Williams, R., 2014. Faster All-Pairs Shortest Paths Via Circuit Complexity. *Arxiv preprint arXiv:1.1261*. pp. 664–673.

A NOVEL ALGORITHM FOR SCALING DOWN LARGE SOCIAL NETWORKS

Delel Rhouma and Lotfi Ben Romdhane
MARS Research Lab LR17ES05
Higher Institute of Computer Science and Telecom (ISITCom), University of Sousse, Tunisia

ABSTRACT

The outburst of social networks has engendered big data that can't be easily consumed by analyzers. In fact, helping to understand the information content of these huge graphs becomes a fundamental challenge. For that, several techniques have been developed in order to extract a small meaningful representation. Graph coarsening is one of them and its main benefit is to save key characteristics of networks. This paper sets out a multilevel graph coarsening scheme for the management of a community discovering problem. The principal procedure of our algorithm named MMCA (Multi-level Merging Compact Areas) is to merge well connected zones in every level until a stopping criterion is met. Our experimentations on real social networks show the efficiency of our model.

KEYWORDS

Graph; Social Networks; Coarsening; Multi-level

1. INTRODUCTION

The production of data has been multiplied due to Internet applications (web, social networks) as well as technical applications (communication or electricity networks) and scientific ones (statistical physics, biology) [Fortunato and Hric, 2016], [Kaur and Singh, 2016]. So, their analysis becomes more and more necessary. One of the important techniques of social network analysis is community detection [Fortunato, 2010], which has diverse real applications. We mention that this technique serves to partition the graphs in strongly linked clusters. Unfortunately, the ordinary community discovering methods become inapplicable due to social network grows [Yiye et al., 2015]. In fact, these graphs evolve quickly into an inextricable entanglement of nodes and edges called "Big Data". Thus, we need a very scalable algorithm able to deal with the huge amount of networks. One of the solutions is to reduce the graph's size by extracting a small version [Hu and Lau, 2013]. Then, this compressed version is considered as a preliminary step in the community detection process [Yiye et al., 2015]. In this paper, we propose a novel graph coarsening method that aims to produce an approximation representation of the network, while retaining its original structure. Our primordial objective is to cope with the huge amount of data by finding a succinct version of the network. Thus, community detection can be done by examining the tiny representation. Innately, well connected zones in a real network can be considered as a super node because they will not be cut during the graph partition. Thus, we suggest the merge of compact areas. This algorithm is done in a greedy way. Indeed, in each level, the number of nodes and edges is reduced. The rest of the paper is arranged as follows. In Section 2 we provide a literature review of graph's reduction process. The algorithm MMCA, along with preliminary materials, is outlined in Section 3. We report experimental results in Section 4 and we finally conclude the paper by discussing our model and planning future improvements.

2. RELATED WORKS

In the literature, we discover a large range of graphs' reduction methods following various strategies. These algorithms are reviewed and categorized into two main families. In what follows, we denote by n the number of nodes of a graph G and by m the number of edges. First, Graph Sampling which is based on the idea of retrieving a pattern of the initial network [Manos et al., 2013] while maintaining the main properties of the original network. Otherwise, it selects a subset of nodes and/or edges of the original graph [Hu and Lau, 2013]. Usually used techniques are: Vertex sampling, Edge sampling and Traversal based sampling [Hu and Lau, 2013]. This approach is simple, but there is no theoretical proof that the real source network structure is preserved [Manos et al., 2013]. Also, some graph clustering methods have used graph sampling techniques [Jiyoung et al., 2012], [Sercan et al., 2010], [Venu et al., 2011] as a preliminary phase to reduce the huge size of the graph, but results are not encouraging. Thus, this branch of study isn't suitable to our problem since it risks losing the graph structure. Another powerful category is graph coarsening scheme. This paradigm consists in collapsing nodes and edges of the original graph to obtain a hierarchy of decreasing size of the graphs. The selection of the vertices to be contracted can be determinate according to several heuristics. The first implementation of the multi-level scheme is Random Matching (RM) method [Bruce and Robert, 1995]. Its main idea is to match an un-contracted random node u with one of its un-contracted neighbors chosen at random. RM merges these two nodes to have a super node and updates the weights of edges and nodes of the coarsened graph. Although this method is simple and minimizes the number of levels, it has a random strategy which damages the partition result. The time complexity of this method is O(m) [George and Vipin, 1998a]. The second family of coarsening method is Edge Matching (EM). Its fundamental idea is to match nodes according to the weight of edge linking them. One of its popular algorithms is Heavy Edge Matching (HEM). It tries to select matching corresponding to the maximum weight of links to maximize the reduction in weight of the contracted graph. HEM works as follows: an un-contracted vertex u selected randomly is paired with one of its un-contracted neighbours v having the maximum weight of edge (u, v) [George and Vipin, 1998a]. Author proved that this algorithm has a high quality of partition and preserves the graph's topology. There are two other revised methods (HEM* [George and Vipin, 1998b] and LEM [George and Vipin, 1998a]) of HEM adapting the same principal. The time complexity of the methods cited above is O(m) [George and Vipin, 1998a]. The third class is Heavy Clique Matching (HCM) [George and Vipin, 1998a] which consists in collapsing nodes having a high edge density of the super-node. Indeed, this clique will not be cut during the partition phase. So, it procures a good bisection. Concerning its complexity, it is the same as cited upon. A new approach based on modularity is proposed by Karypis [LaSalle and Karypis, 2015]. In fact, the authors proposed an algorithm having a multi-level aspect and suggested three coarsening methods adapted to every law degree distribution of the social network. The first one is MAT (Standard Matching) [LaSalle and Karypis, 2015]. It consists of visiting nodes in a random order and merging them with a neighborhood not yet marked. The condition of merging is the maximization of the variation of modularity. This algorithm works well on graphs having a uniform distribution of degree. To solve this, they developed a new algorithm called M2M (Matching with secondary two-hop Matching) [LaSalle and Karypis, 2015]. M2M has the same principle of MAT except that if all the neighbors of u are marked, it will be merged with one of the neighbors of the neighbors of u. M2M surpasses MAT to generate a reduced graph of small-size (approximately half of the initial size). The third coarsening method is FCG [LaSalle and Karypis, 2015] (First Choice Grouping). Its main idea is; if u belongs to a group of nodes g, then the priority of the addition of v to this group is determined in a similar way (calculate the modularity of the cluster g). This method is adapted to graphs of the power law degree distribution and it allows the fusion of a set of nodes. The three coarsening phases presented above takes O(m + n) time [LaSalle and Karypis, 2015]. In opposite to the previous cited methods which produces disjoint coarsened graph, the algebraic multigrid method (AMG) [Safro et al., 2012] guaranties an overlapped version of the reduced network [Cdric and Ilya, 2009]. It is a coarsening scheme which adapts the measure of connectivity between vertices named "algebraic distance connectivity" (Algebraic distance distinguishes local and non-local edges). It produces an overlapped coarsened graph [Cdric and Ilya, 2009]. This paradigm succeeds in keeping multiple networks' features and produces partitions that are provably good [George and Vipin, 1995]. On the other side, multi-level framework suffers from some limits. The first one is that in most existing methods the contraction is done by merging a pair of nodes. So, the reduction rate in every level of coarsening is smaller than two. The second limit is that in many cases, there are a large portion of well connected components. Reasonably, it is not useful to split them by collapsing only two nodes. Thus, leads to poor quality of graph partition. Motivated by the fact that the graph coarsening paradigm tries to preserve the general structure of the graph and its properties, which is our main objective; we opt for contracting our network in a greedy way.

3. METHODOLOGY

3.1 Problem Statement

We modeled the input social network by an undirected graph $G = (V, E)$ (without loops). In general, each node $v \in V$ represents an individual of the network, links $e \in E$ represent relationships between these individuals. We consider n the number of nodes in G ($n = |V|$) and m the number of edges ($m = |E|$). The main purpose of multi-level graph coarsening is to transform the original graph G_0 in a sequence of smaller graphs $G_1, G_2, \ldots, G_p$ such that: $|V_0| > |V_1| > |V_2| > \ldots > |V_p|$. This process is repeated until: $\frac{|V_{i+1}|}{|V_i|} < \delta$ and $0 < \delta < 1$

3.2 Basic Definitions

Definition 1: (Direct neighbor)
In the graph $G = (V, E)$, the vertex v is a direct neighbor of the node u if v and u are connected by an edge. This relationship is represented by the edge $(v, u) \in E$.

Definition 2: (Vertex border)
It is all the direct neighbors of node v in the graph. This set is noted by $\Gamma(v)$. More formally this set is noted as follows:

$$\Gamma(v) = \{u \in V; \quad (u, v) \in E\}$$

Definition 3: (Vertex degree)
It is the number of nodes located at the boundary of v. Otherwise; it is the border's cardinality of v. More formally it is noted as follows:

$$d(v) = |\Gamma(v)|$$

Definition 4: (The local coefficient of clustering)
The local coefficient of clustering was introduced by Watts and Strogatz [J. and H., 1998] in the context of social network analysis. It is a property of a node v in a graph G. It quantifies how well this node and its neighbors can form a clique (full graph). It is given by the proportion of links between vertices within its neighborhood, divided by the number of links that could possibly exist between them. So, for a node v of degree greater than or equal to 2 we have:

$$cfc(v) = \frac{2|\{e_{jk}\}|}{d(v)*(d(v)-1)}; v_j, v_k \in V, e_{jk} \in E$$

This quantity is between 0 and 1 (1 if the neighborhood is well connected, 0 means that there is almost no connections between neighbors).
Definition 4: (Reduction Rate)
In each level i of coarsening, the reduction factor defines the size of the contraction, i.e. the number of joined nodes. This factor is noted F^* and defined as:

$$F^*(G_i, G_{i+1}) = \frac{|V_i|}{|V_{i+1}|}$$

3.3 The Node Importance Concept

First, we should argue that the choice of nodes to contract where the community detection is done may affect the obtained partition. Second, the number of vertices to merge in every step has a great influence on the reduction's rate. This means, in principle, that we cannot rely on random or simply two nodes to be matched (like other methods quoted in the literature). We have found that, in a social network, a node whose neighbors are also connected (i.e.,"know" one another"), is the most relevant choice which tends to be the most compact core to form a small- group. That's why we have adapted a factor that measures the importance of an individual in a network. It represents the starting point in the formation of a community called "Node Importance" [Rhouma and Ben Romdhane, 2014]. Indeed, the node importance of node u is its tendency to form a compact area. This term combines two concepts: the degree of u and the local coefficient of clustering of this node. This index is noted NI and defined as: $NI(v) = cfc(v) * d(v)$

3.4 Our Algorithm MMCA

Using the fundamental concepts cited above, we introduce a novel algorithm called "**MMCA**" (**M**ulti level **M**erging **C**ompact **A**reas) to find a succinct representation of the graph while saving key characteristics of community detection process. This method is founded on the principle of "multi-level coarsening" paradigm; since the reduced graph is built in a greedy manner until reaching a fixed threshold. **MMCA** is outlined in Algorithm 1 and is described in details in the following paragraph. In order to contract the initial network, we apply the **MCA** Algorithm 2 to every level of coarsening. As a starting point, we mark all the nodes of *G* as un-contracted (*UC*). Next, we assign a score called (Node Importance) "*NI*" to all the nodes of the graph computed by equation 4. Then, we sort them according to their importance in descending order. In the next step, we choose the most important vertex u, which represents the origin of the construction of the areas to merge. In principal, this node is the "most influential" in the remaining non-contracted part of the graph. After, we build the multi-node X formed by the center u and its direct (UC) neighbors. Thereafter, we mark the components of X as contracted. If u has no un-contracted neighbors, it is matched with itself (aggregated by itself). Concerning the resulted graph, we proceed as follows: if two nodes of X have the same neighbor k then we conserve an only one link between them. Similarly, we reproduce the same previous steps until there are no un-contracted nodes. Eventually we end up with a condensed version of the original network. MCA is finished by producing the contracted graph G_i of the first level. We stop the coarsening graph that occurs in a greedy way when our objective function reaches an upper bound (Namely the rate of contraction $F^*(G_i, G_{i+1})$ is less than a given threshold).

Theorem 1: (Time Complexity)

The worst case time complexity of our algorithm is $O(m + n\log^2(n))$ where *n* and *m* denote respectively the number of nodes and the number of edges of *G*.

Theorem 2: (Space Complexity)

The space complexity of our algorithm **MMCA** is $O(m + n)$ where *m* is the number of edges and *n* is the number of nodes in the social network.

Algorithm 1: Multi-level Merging Compact Areas (*MMCA*)

Data: A graph $G = (V, E)$, A threshold δ
Result: A coarsened weighted graph $G_C = (V_C, E_C)$.
Begin
$l \leftarrow 0$
$G_0 \leftarrow G$
repeat
$l \leftarrow l+1$
$G_l \leftarrow MCA(G_{l-1})$
$r \leftarrow F^*(G_l, G_{l-1})$
Until $(r \leq \delta)$;
$G_C \leftarrow G_l$
Return (G_c).
End

```
Algorithm 2: Merging Compact Areas (MCA)
Data: A graph G l = (V l, El)
Result: A graph Gl+1 = (V l+1, El+1)
Begin
   UC ← {v ∈ Vl/v is un-contracted}
   ∀v ∈ UC calculate NIw (v).
   Sort UC in descending order.
   while UC ≠ ∅ do
   v ← First (UC)
    X ← {v}
     for all u ∈ Γv do
     if u ∈ UC then
          X ← X ∪ {u}
     End
     End
   Remove the components of X from UC
  End
   Return G l+1
End
```

4. EXPERIMENTAL RESULTS

The major objective of this section is to analyze experimentally the behavior of *MMCA*. For this, we performed experiments, firstly, to demonstrate its performance as a tool of graph coarsening. Secondly, we use the Index of Jaccard [Broder et al., 1998] in order to assure that the community structure of the original graph is not destroyed during the contraction step. We compare *MMCA* against what is currently well-known: (1) Random Matching (*RM*) which is the basic of coarsening done in random way [Bruce and Robert, 1995]; (2) Heavy Edge Matching (*HEM*) well used model in coarsening and tends to reduce edge cut [George and Vipin, 1998a]; (3) First Choice Grouping (*FCG*) which merges a group of nodes in order to maximize modularity [LaSalle and Karypis, 2015]. Various real-world networks are employed to test our new coarsening scheme.

4.1 Datasets

For our evaluation, we use five different datasets obtained from diverse domains. The characteristics of these graphs are shown in Table 1 and they are taken from the graph mining library SNAP [Leskovec and Krevl, 2014]. As our method deals with undirected graphs, we converted directed social network to un-directed versions (we kept one link between two nodes and we delete self loops). The Facebook [Leskovec and Mcauley, 2012] is a social network composed of "friends lists" gathered from some participants using Facebook applications. Vertices, here, correspond to users and edges exist when there is a relationship between them. In the Route views computer (AS) data [Leskovec et al., 2007], vertices correspond to autonomous systems (AS), and links denote communication between them. It is an undirected internet network. Peer to Peer (P2P) graph [Ripeanu et al., 2002] is created from Gnutella peer to peer network on August 2002. Nodes in the graph refer to hosts and links exist if a pair of computer communicates. Finally, the PGP dataset [Boguna et al., 2004] formed by a giant connected component list of Pretty-Good Privacy users. Nodes, here, denote users and links correspond to a relationship between them.

Table 1. The Characteristics of Datasets

Networks	Nodes	Edges
Facebook	4 039	88 234
AS network	6 474	12 572
P2P 06	8 717	31 525
PGP	10 680	24 316
P2P 04	10 876	39 994

4.2 Effectiveness of MMCA

To prove the efficiency of our model we try to quantify the number of levels generated to coarsen a graph in totality. That's meant to have in the final stage only one node. Figure 1 illustrates that among all experiments, the coarsen level generated by our approach is almost incomparable with that of RM, HEM. In fact, the numbers of edges/nodes for these coarsening schemes have a tendency to diminish very slowly and by a small factor. As intended from theoretical study, methods based on merging only two nodes require an increasing amount of coarsen levels. Especially in the context of power-law degree distribution graphs (many low degree nodes tend to be linked to high degree nodes), we have networks with small reduction rate. So, the total memory consumption increases rapidly. In conclusion, these models need a huge number of levels and an extra memory to store the series of successive coarser graph. MMCA and FCG overcome these two limitations of the multi level framework by contracting a group of nodes. Then, they deal with power law degree distribution networks. As our model and "First Choice Grouping" adopt the same principle, they perform similarly with a slightly exceed of mine in some cases. In almost experiments, the number of generated level for MMCA doesn't exceed 5. To sum up, our model was able to overmaster the weakness of multi level paradigm by a rapid convergence despite the nature of used networks.

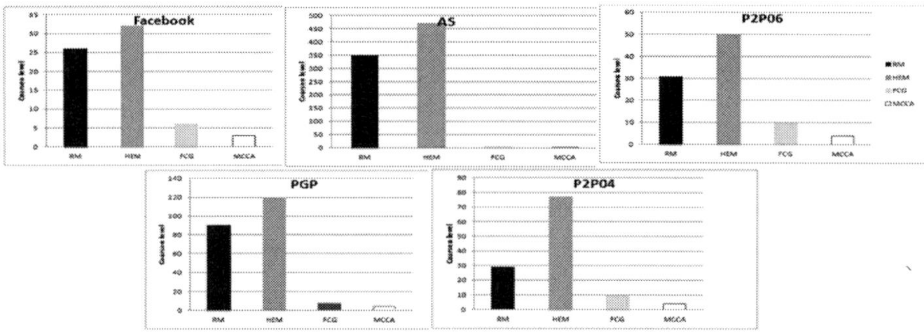

Figure 1. Effectiveness of MMCA for Graph Coarsening Problem

4.3 Application: Community Detection Problem

In this section, we test a concrete application of graph coarsening as well as *MMCA* model to community discovering problem. For this, we use the powerful community detection method named *DOCNet* [Rhouma and Ben Romdhane, 2014]. It is a greedy algorithm discovering overlapped clusters. We notice that we have chosen 0.95 as a minimum coarsening rate (similar to the threshold used in recent work of coarsening scheme [LaSalle and Karypis, 2015]). In the first step, we quantified the scalability of our scheme. Then, we measured the similarity between the partitions generated by DOCNet on both original network and coarsest one in order to present the effect of the multi-level coarsening process (*MMCA*). The most appropriate metric to do this is the index of Jaccard [Broder et al., 1998].

4.3.1 Scalability

In order to show the scalability of *MMCA*, we measured the running time of the community detection algorithm DOCNet directly and after using coarsening schemes and DOCNet. Table 2 demonstrates that, for all datasets, the elapsed time decreased considerably after reducing the size of the original network. MMCA surpasses the others. In fact, our model of contraction shows its effectiveness in facilitating the community discovering task of especially such expensive algorithm. In other words, our algorithm achieves one of its main objectives which are: to make the networks of large size manageable and usable by the ordinary social network analysis methods.

Table 1. Elapsed Time (in Minute) for Community Detection Process

Networks	DOCNet	RM+DOCNet	HEM+DOCNet	FCG+DOCNet	MMCA+DOCNet
Facebook	20	13	12	4	**3**
AS	23	15	15	8	**5**
P2P 06	29	16	14	6	**6**
PGP	34	19	17	10	**7**
P2P 04	41	21	19	11	**8**

4.3.2 Community's Structure Analysis

The Jaccard index (or Jaccard's coefficient) J [Broder et al., 1998] is one of the well known matching criteria in the literature. It describes the ratio between the cardinality (the size) of the intersection of the considered sets and the cardinality of their union. It allows evaluating the similarity between the sets. Given two sets S_1 and S_2, the index is: $J(S_1, S_2) = \frac{|S_1 \cap S_2|}{|S_1 \cup S_2|}$

This score varies between 0 and 1, where one specifies the ideal recovery of the original communities. From the results mentioned in the table 3, we note that the similarity between the two partitions is average. In fact, by applying the index of Jaccard on all our data sets, we see that the partition produced by DOCNnet directly is different from that produced after the contraction of the original network. In almost experiments, we remark that coarsening schemes (RM, HEM, and FCG) exceed somewhat our model. This is explained by the fact that our algorithm misses some improvement during its development. Indeed, merging a group of compact nodes at each step without taking into consideration their number or the weight of links damages, clearly, the quality of reduced networks.

In conclusion, although our *MMCA* algorithm produces contracted networks in a limited number of iterations and guarantees a gain of runtime, its partition quality requires more improvement.

Table 2. Index of Jaccard of the Coarsening Techniques

Networks	RM	HEM	FCG	MMCA
Facebook	0.40	0.39	0.44	0.42
AS	0.32	0.33	0.41	0.33
P2P 06	0.55	0.57	0.61	0.53
PGP	0.44	0.47	0.74	0.45
P2P 04	0.60	0.61	0.71	0.62

5. CONCLUSION

This paper focuses on the problem of graph's size reduction, which is an indispensable tool to resolve the community discovering problem especially in Large Scale Social Network. In order to situate our work, we have summarized the state of the art of graph compression methods. Our main contribution is the suggestion of partition-based coarsening model called *MMCA* (multi-level Merging Compact Areas) which greedily contracts an original network. The basic idea of our proposal is to merge a compact group of nodes until reaching a stopping criterion. Experimental results showed that our algorithm is able to reduce the size of the graph quickly and to speed up the community detection process. On the other hand, although our model provides a similarity measure comparable to existent methods, but it requires some improvements in order to overmatch them.

This work opens many perspectives in this fast-growing field of supporting Mega Scale Social networks. Among these, we can cite two future developments: First, we plan to add an appropriated weight to both links and nodes of the contracted graph which are updated at every step. This procures a concise version of the graph that keeps its almost structural properties. Second, a suggestion of a multi-level community detection framework (Coarsening, partition, un-coarsening) based on our developed coarsening scheme.

REFERENCES

Rhouma and Ben Romdhane (2014). An efficient algorithm for community mining with overlap in social networks. *Expert Syst.Appl.* Vol 41, No 9, pp 4309--4321

Bogunna et al. (2004). Models of social networks based on social distance attachment. *Phys. Rev. E*, Vol (70), pp 561-572.

Broder et al. (1998). Min-wise independent permutations (extended abstract). *STOC '98: Proceedings of the thirtieth annual ACM symposium on Theory of computing*, pp. 327-336, New York, NY, USA: ACM Press.

Bruce, H. and Robert, L. (1995). A multilevel algorithm for partitioning graphs. *In Proceedings of the 1995 ACM/IEEE Conference on Supercomputing. ACM.*

Cdric, C. and Ilya, S. (2009). Comparison of coarsening schemes for multilevel graph partitioning. In T. Stützle (ed.), LION. pages 191–205. *Springer.*

Fortunato, S. (2010). Community detection in graphs. *Physics Reports*, 486:75 –174.

Fortunato, S. and Hric, D. (2016). Community detection in networks: A user guide. *Physics Reports*, 659:1– 44.

George, K. and Vipin, K. (1995). Analysis of multilevel graph partitioning. . In S. Karin (ed.), SC (p./pp. 29), page 29. *ACM.*

George, K. and Vipin, K. (1998a). A fast and high quality multilevel scheme for partitioning irregular graphs. *SIAM Journal on scientific Computing*, (1):359–392.

George, K. and Vipin, K. (1998b). Multilevel k-way partitioning scheme for irregular graphs. *J. Parallel Distrib. Comput.*, 48(1):96–129.

Hu, P. and Lau, W. C. (2013). A survey and taxonomy of graph sampling. *CoRR.*

J., W. D. and H., S. S. (1998). Collective dynamics of 'small-world' networks. *Nature*, (6684):409–10.

Jiyoung et al. (2012). Scalable and memory-efficient clustering of large-scale social networks. pages 705–714. *IEEE Computer Society.*

Kaur, R. and Singh, S. (2016). A survey of data mining and social network analysis based anomaly detection techniques. *Egyptian Informatics Journal*, 17(2):199 – 216.

LaSalle, D. and Karypis, G. (2015). Multi-threaded modularity based graph clustering using the multilevel paradigm. *Journal of Parallel and Distributed Computing*, 76:66 – 80.

Leskovec et al (2007). Graph evolution: Densification and shrinking diameters. *ACM Trans. Knowledge Discovery from Data,* 1(1):1–40.

Leskovec, J. and Krevl, A. (2014). SNAP Datasets: Stanford large network dataset collection. http://snap.stanford.edu/data.

Leskovec, J. and Mcauley, J. J. (2012). Learning to discover social circles in ego networks. *In Advances in Neural Information Processing Systems* 25, pages 539 –547.

Manos et al (2013). Sampling online social networks. *IEEE Trans. Knowl. Data Eng.*, 25(3):662–676.

Ripeanu et al. (2002). Mapping the gnutella network: Properties of large-scale peer-to-peer systems and implications for system design. *IEEE Internet Computing Journal*, 6:2002.

Safro, et al. (2012). Advanced coarsening schemes for graph partitioning. *CoRR.*

Sercan et al. (2010). an efficient community detection method using parallel clique-finding ants. Pages 1–7. *IEEE.*

Venu et al. (2011). Local graph sparsification for scalable clustering. Pages 721–732. *ACM.*

Yiye et al. (2015). Community Discovery: Simple and Scalable Approaches, pages 23–54. *Springer International Publishing.*

EXPERIENCES ON OBJECT TRACKING USING A MANY-CORE EMBEDDED SYSTEM

Laercio Minozzo[1], José Rufino[2,3] and José Lima[2,4]
[1]*Federal University of Technology – Paraná, Medianeira - PR, 85884-000, Brasil*
[2]*Polytechnic Institute of Bragança, 5300-253 Bragança, Portugal*
[3]*Laboratory of Instrumentation and Experimental Particle Physics, University of Minho, 4710-057 Braga, Portugal*
[4]*Centre for Robotics in Industry and Intelligent Systems (CRIIS), INESC-TEC, 4200-465 Porto, Portugal*

ABSTRACT

Object localization and tracking is core to many practical applications, like human-computer interaction, security and surveillance, robot competitions and Industry 4.0. Such task may be computationally demanding, especially for traditional embedded systems, that usually have tight processing and storage constraints. This calls for the investigation of alternatives, including emergent heterogeneous embedded systems, like the Parallella line of single-board-computers (SBCs).
The work presented in this paper explores the use of a Parallella board with a 16-core Epiphany co-processor, to perform real-time tracking of objects in frames captured by a Kinect sensor, based on color segmentation. We addressed several processing strategies, trying to assess which one performed better. We also ran the same code (where applicable) in several models of the Raspberry Pi platform, for comparison. We conclude that effectively exploring the Epiphany co-processor is not trivial, requiring considerable programming effort and suitable applications (CPU-demanding and highly parallelizable), to the extent that simpler development approaches, on more recent SBCs may be more effective.

KEYWORDS

Visual Tracking, Computer Vision, Embedded Systems, Heterogeneous Systems, Parallel / Hybrid Programming

1. INTRODUCTION

Object localization and tracking is a crucial task in several real-world domains, as augmented reality, human-computer interaction, security and surveillance, robot competitions and aerial vehicles, and Industry 4.0 (i-SCOOP, 2017), to name a few. The later, for instance, demands the collaboration between robots and humans; in this context, perception is one of the most important capabilities, that should be applied as fast as possible to guarantee expected/bounded reaction times.

The growth of the processing capacity of embedded systems, and the parallel processing abilities of many moderns Systems-on-Chip, are playing an important role in real-time object localization and tracking, making room for more sophisticated image processing techniques, that are able to exploit the extra processing power available. In this regard, a recent trend is the emergence of energy efficient embedded heterogeneous systems, with powerful co-processors that may be used to accelerate tasks in co-operation with the host processor.

In this work we document preliminary experiences with the Parallella heterogeneous embedded system, connected to a Kinect sensor, towards its use on object tracking. We explored a simple technique (color segmentation), through several programming models, and processing strategies, in order to take advantage of the parallel computing capabilities of the Parallella and its Epiphany co-processor. For those development approaches that would permit it, we extended its evaluation to the full family of Raspberry Pi SBCs, in order to assess the merits of the Parallella in comparison to a popular embedded platform.

The rest of the paper is structured as follows: section 2 provides Background information on object tracking, (heterogeneous) embedded systems, and the Parallella board; section 3 offers a high-level description of the tracking application; section 4 discusses several implementation strategies; section 5 provides the results of the evaluation in the target platforms. Section 6 concludes the paper and points some directions for future work.

2. BACKGROUND

2.1 Object Tracking

There are several algorithms, applications and systems that solve the object tracking problem. In a general way, tracking can be defined as "the problem of estimating the trajectory of an object in the image" (Yilmaz, 2006). Different approaches can be found, depending on the object characteristics and features such as appearance, shape, context/environment or scenario, and the end use.

A well-known object tracking application is surveillance (human body tracking). In some works addressing this topic (Aggarwal, 1999; Gavrila, 1999; Moeslund, 2001), human kinematics provides the implementation basis, namely using articulated object models. Another application is learning the different views of an object, by training a set of classifiers, like support vector machines (Avidan, 2001) or Bayesian networks (Park, 2004).

Object tracking can also be found in such different areas as industrial applications or robotics soccer. Specific examples include manipulators finding objects to perform pick and place operations (helping users in a collaborative task), or mobile soccer robots finding the ball and estimating its position.

Feature selection is the most critical role in tracking. The most desirable property of a visual feature is its uniqueness so objects can be easily distinguished in the environment. Feature selection provides a way to perform image segmentation. This can be achieved using Mean-shift (Comaniciu, 1999), Graph-cut (Shi, 2000) and Active Contours (Caselles, 1995). Another approach is to use the color (RGB or HSV) as a feature for histogram-based appearance representations, while for contour-based representation object edges are usually used as features. In general, many tracking algorithms use a combination of these features (Paschos, 2001).

Ready to use algorithms can be found in well-known applications. Mathworks' Matlab includes the Computer Vision System Toolbox, providing video tracking routines that can be used for tracking a single or multiple objects. Matlab, however, currently runs only on x86-64 bit platforms, preventing its use on most embedded systems. OpenCV (OpenCV, 2017) also offers an API for object tracking. However, this work did not use such API, due to the need of fine-grain control on the code, for parallelization purposes (OpenCV was still used, though for different tasks, like Calibration, Visualization and to support some data types).

2.2 Heterogeneous Embedded Systems

In recent years, advancements in embedded systems and, in particular, the rise of Systems on Chip (SoC) (mostly propelled by the widespread adoption of mobile devices and the emergence of the Internet-of-Things), brought with it a growing processing capacity, coupled with low/modest power requirements. Nowadays, there's a plethora of small single-board computers (SBCs) (board-db, 2017), build around these SoCs. They are usually open-platforms, running an open-source operating system (typically Linux) with standard development tools, offering tremendous flexibility at a relatively low cost. In this regard, the Raspberry Pi (Raspberry Pi Foundation, 2017) line of SBCs is perhaps the most well-established on the market and academia (Brown, 2017), with an enormous ecosystem, covering industry, education and I&D. Moreover, many case studies cover, precisely, object tracking assisted by a Raspberry Pi SBC (Menezes, 2015; Soetedjo, 2016).

Virtually all modern embedded systems include a multi-core CPU, and the same happens with the Raspberry Pi, since the launch of the 4-core Raspberry Pi 2, in early 2015. Therefore, there has been an increasing interest in exploring the parallel computing capabilities of modern SoCs, to accelerate processing on demanding applications, including object tracking (Iszaidy, 2016; Truong, 2017). This trend also extends to heterogeneous embedded systems (Kaeli, 2011), where the main/host processor co-exists with additional devices, from a different architecture, that may be used to execute/accelerate tasks on its behalf. A common example of this is the presence of increasingly powerful Graphical Processing Units (GPUs) in SBCs, usable as numerical co-processors, beyond their native graphical capabilities (NVIDIA, 2011). Another example is provided by the Parallella board (Gwennap, 2011; Olofsson, 2014), that couples a 2-core ARM CPU with a grid co-processor of 16 (or more) Epiphany cores (Adapteva1, 2013).

Due to its specificities, like its memory architecture, the Parallella board often requires a low-level approach to application development. There are, however, many examples that were able to explore its potential. For instance, (Gener, 2015) compared the Parallella with a GPU for spatial domain video filtering, showing that in such scenario the Parallella offers an efficient low-cost and low-power alternative. Taking advantage of the Epiphany co-processor, by using a combination of task and data parallelization, and fine-grained data pipelining, (Brauer, 2016) was able to decrease the processing latency of a typical signal processing chain in more than 50%. (Vaas, 2016) investigated if smart control units used for frequency conversion could benefit from highly parallel hardware accelerators, namely the Epiphany co-processor, and achieved a speedup of 1.78 with a limited increase (9%) on power consumption.

2.3 The Parallella Board

2.3.1 Hardware Details and Architecture

Parallella is a credit card sized, single-board computer developed by Adapteva, targeting high performance with low power consumption (Gwennap, 2011; Olofsson, 2014;). It was made available to general public in late 2013, after successful Kickstarter funding in 2012. There are several models currently available, all offering an Epiphany III MIMD co-processor. This work explores the "Parallella-16 Desktop Computer", with USB 2.0 data ports (as required, to connect a Kinect sensor), and a micro-HDMI port (for visualization).

The Parallella board is a heterogeneous system, with processing elements based on two different architectures. The host component consumes up to 5W, and includes a 32 bit dual-core 667 MHz ARMv7 A9 microprocessor, serviced by 1GB of SDRAM. The co-processor consumes an additional 2W, and consists of a 16-core 2D-grid of 32 bit RISC CPUs, based on the Epiphany III architecture (Adapteva1, 2013). All Epiphany RISC CPUs (eCores or eNodes) interconnect through a Network-on-Chip (eMesh), that provides efficient message passing. eCores run at 600 MHz, with 19.2 GFLOPS aggregated single-precision peak performance (or 2.74 GFLOPS/W, considering that host and co-processor consume up to 7W).

The memory architecture of the Epiphany co-processor does not have an explicit hierarchy and has no caches; it is a distributed shared memory, with a partitioned global address space of 512 KBytes; each eCore is assigned 32 KBytes of local memory (4 banks of 8 KBytes), for code, stack and data; fast inter-eCore local memory access is supported. Buffers shared between the host and the eCores may be created in a 32 MBytes region (8 MBytes usable) of the host main memory; host and eCores may exchange data and synchronize through this shared/external memory, but access to this memory is slow (even for the host). Another data exchange (and the slowest) possibility is for the host to access directly the eCores local memory. Each eCore contains two DMA general purpose channels to ease data transfers to/from other eCores or host memory. The DMA engine works at the same frequency as the eCore RISC CPU and can transfer 64-bits per clock cycle.

2.3.2 Software Environment and Development Frameworks

The Parallella board runs a version of Linux (Ubuntu-based). Applications that take advantage of the Epiphany co-processor may be developed using either the low-level Epiphany Software Development Kit (eSDK) (Adapteva2, 2013), or higher-level frameworks (Parallella, 2017). With the eSDK, eCores are programmable in ANSI C and C++ (partial support), using the GNU-GCC tool chain, the newlib C library for embedded systems and the Epiphany Hardware Utility Library (eLib). Higher-level approaches and frameworks to explore the Epiphany accelerator include, among others, i) ePython (Brown, 2016) (for Python-based parallel programming), ii) OpenSHMEM (Ross, 2016) (particularly suitable to Epiphany's partitioned global address space), iii) OpenMP (OpenMP, 2013) via the OMPi compiler (Spiros, 2015) (for automatic thread-based parallelization via code pragmas), and iv) MPI (MPI, 2015) using the Threaded MPI implementation (Richie, 2015) (for distributed parallel computing on the Epiphany grid based on message passing). This flexibility results from the MIMD nature of Epiphany's architecture, that supports many parallel programming models.

Different approaches may also be mixed, in line with a Hybrid Programming approach, often used in Heterogeneous Systems. At the host-side, the application developed for this work explores conventional POSIX Threads (Pthreads) (Butenhof, 1997), either isolated, or combined with OpenMP threads. For co-processor offloading, both the low-level eSDK eLib and the OMPi compiler were explored.

3. APPLICATION STRUCTURE

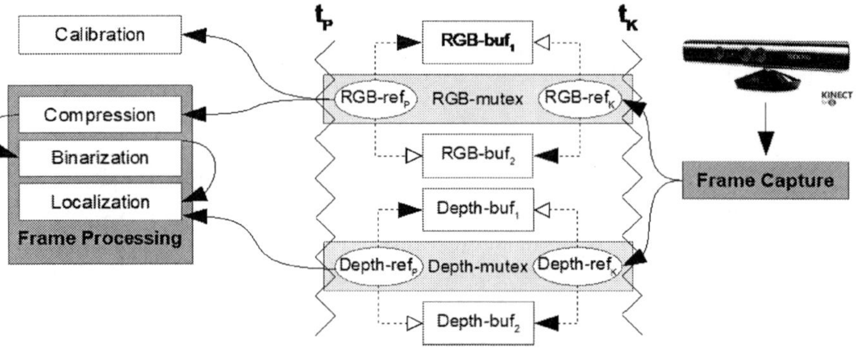

Figure 1. General Structure of the Tracking Application

Figure 1 shows the general structure of the tracking application discussed in this paper. It is based in two threads: t_K, that captures frames from the Kinect sensor; t_P, that performs an initial calibration procedure and then loops through the processing of each frame (it also allows for the visualization of the frames in all stages of processing, using OpenCV). The next sections provide a detailed description of each application component.

3.1 Frame Capture

The t_K thread captures frames from the Kinect sensor via libfreenect (libfreenect, 2017) facilities. This is achieved using two callback functions, one for RGB frames, another for Depth frames. Each callback uses a pair of buffers (<RGB-buf_1, RGB-buf_2>, and <Depth-buf_1, Depth-buf_2>). Each pair of buffers is referenced by a pair of global pointers (<RGB-ref_P, RGB-ref_K>, and <Depth-ref_P, Depth-ref_K>), visible in both t_K and t_P. Pointers RGB-ref_K and Depth-ref_K reference the buffers that t_K will use to receive the next RGB and Depth frames. Pointers RGB-ref_P and Depth-ref_P reference the buffers that hold the previous RGB and Depth frames, to be processed by t_P. The pointers switch the buffers they point to, for every new frame captured. This way there's no need for memory copies that would delay processing the current frame and capturing the next.

A locking mechanism, based on semaphores (RGB-mutex and Depth-mutex) coupled with conditions variables, shared by the two threads, prevents the misuse of the buffers. To switch buffers, t_K performs a non-blocking lock on the semaphore that protects the pointers to the buffers; if the locking succeeds, buffers are switched and the t_P thread is notified; otherwise, if locking fails, it means the t_P thread has previously acquired the lock and is still processing the frame in the other buffer; in this situation, if t_K is fast enough, it will be able to capture a new frame that will overlap the one captured in the previous round.

The t_P thread performs a blocking lock on the same semaphores; when succeeds, it will check, through the condition variables, if buffers were switched (meaning a new frame arrived); if true, it will fully process the frame, and only at the end will release the lock; if buffers were not switched, it will release the lock immediately and will block, awaiting for the condition variable to change.

3.2 Calibration

Generically, the purpose of calibration is twofold: i) to capture the RGB colors of the object to be tracked in the RGB frames; ii) to measure the parallax error between the RGB and Depth frames (due to the separation of their cameras in the Kinect sensor). The work presented in this paper is prototype-level, and therefore only RGB calibration was fully implemented, with Depth calibration planned for future work. RGB calibration is done once, by the t_P thread. It uses an OpenCV-managed window, as shown in Figure 2, where the purple rectangle (drawn by the user) delimits the area containing the relevant colors.

The presence of specific RGB colors in the object is initially represented as True (1) boolean values in a 3D data structure: a RGB cube with $2^8 \times 2^8 \times 2^8$ elements of one boolean byte each, with each element referenced by a specific 3D <R,G,B> coordinate. This RGB cube needs 16 MBytes of storage, which is way beyond the 32 KBytes of local memory available at each Epiphany eCore. Considerable compression is thus needed to make possible storing a full copy of the RGB cube at each eCore local memory, during processing (it is undesirable, for performance reasons, that eCores access the RGB cube outside their local memory).

Figure 2. Initial RGB Calibration

First, the <R,G,B> coordinates are downsized: the Red, Green and Blue channel bytes loose the least significant 3, 2 and 3 bits, respectively: $<R_8,G_8,B_8> \rightarrow <R_5,G_6,B_5>$ (this finds ground on the fact that captured RGB frames usually show some color noise, to the extent that close colors may be considered equal). This bit removal reduces the overall number of <R,G,B> coordinates to $2^5 \times 2^6 \times 2^5 = 2^{16}$. Furthermore, by coding the presence/absence of a specific color with one bit (instead of one byte), the calibration data structure will consume only 64 Kbits (or 8 KBytes), thus perfectly fitting in one local memory bank of an Epiphany eCore. The initial 3D RGB cube thus became a 1D RGB bitmap, indexed by a $R_5G_6B_5$ 2-byte coordinate or color.

3.3 Frame Processing

As Figure 1 shows, t_P processes frames through three different stages: i) (RGB) Compression, ii) (RGB) Binarization, and iii) (RGB+Depth) Localization. The next sections elaborate on these processing stages.

3.3.1 (RGB) Compression

This stage reduces the size of RGB frames. It aims to increase the processing speed of further stages and to allow an RGB frame to be stored into the local memory of each Epiphany eCore (1/16th of the frame, per eCore). Besides reducing the frame size, compression also reduces the color noise.

RGB frame compression is achieved in two phases: 1) the original 640 × 480 frame is downscaled to 320 × 240 (each dimension is halved), by averaging tiles of 2 × 2 adjacent pixels, producing a frame with 1/4th of the size of the original (900 → 225 KBytes); 2) each RGB pixel is downsized from 24 bits to 16 bits, using the same technique applied to the RGB coordinates of the calibration data structure; this reduces the frame in 2/3, going down to 150 KBytes (9,375 KBytes per Epiphany eCore); furthermore, the $R_5G_6B_5$ pixels in the reduced frame may be used as coordinates for direct access to the RGB calibration bitmap. In all implementations (see section 4), these two phases are performed together for each pixel, for performance reasons.

3.3.2 (RGB) Binarization

This stage produces a binary version of the compressed RGB frame, that is, a version with only two colors: white for the pixels belonging to the object being tracked, and black for the remaining pixels – see Figure 3.

This is achieved as follows: for each pixel in the compressed RGB frame, its $R_5G_6B_5$ 16 bit color is used as a coordinate in the RGB calibration bitmap, to check if that pixel color is one of the tracked object colors, detected during the calibration stage. The resulting binary frame will have half the size (75 KBytes) of the compressed frame, once each pixel will now be represented by a single byte (with value 255 or 0).

3.3.3 (RGB+Depth) Localization

This stage takes the <X,Y> coordinates of all object pixels (white pixels) in the binary frame, and computes their average. The outcome is a single <avgX, avgY> pair of coordinates, that should be further corrected by applying the Depth adjustment produced (to do in future work) during the Calibration phase. The resulting <X',Y'> coordinates are then used to retrieve the corresponding Z' Depth coordinate from the Depth frame as follows: to minimize the noise influence, Z' is calculated as the average of all Depth values of a tile of 3 × 3 centered on position <2X', 2Y'> in the Depth frame (note that <X',Y'> refers to a 320 × 240 binary frame, but the Depth frame was not compressed and thus preserves its original 640 × 480 resolution).

Figure 3. Compressed RGB frame and Binary frame

4. PROCESSING STRATEGIES

4.1 Concurrent Processing with Pthreads

Accordingly with the general structure described in section 3, the application developed is multi-threaded, with two main threads: the frame capture thread (t_K), and the frame processing thread (t_P). The reason for this is as follows: by relieving the frame capture thread from frame processing tasks, the capture of frames may be performed at the maximum rate of ≈30 frames per second, as supported by the Kinect sensor. This was confirmed by preliminary tests with the Parallella board: the frame rate of a single thread, running in the ARM host, with frame processing fully performed in the libfreenect callback functions, was always bellow 30 fps.

The t_K and t_P threads are based on the POSIX Threads (Pthreads) standard (Butenhof, D.R., 1997). In addition to using this model as the basic foundation for our application, other processing strategies were inter-mixed, trying to improve the performance of frame processing. These hybrid approaches are addressed next.

4.2 Parallel Processing with OpenMP

OpenMP was explored as a straightforward way for automatic parallelization of all frame processing stages (suitable to parallelization due to independent accesses and processing on data structures involved).

The parallel processing elements available to OpenMP in the Parallella board, and in the Raspberry Pi boards, have some differences. In the Parallella board, OpenMP may be used to take advantage either of the dual-core ARM CPU or of the Epiphany manycore co-processor. In the Raspberry Pi SBCs, OpenMP has only the single/quad-core ARM CPU at its disposal. Differences also extend to the OpenMP implementations used: ARM CPUs were targeted by the native OpenMP facilities of the C/C++ compilers used; the Epiphany 16-core co-processor required the use of OMPi, a separate OpenMP implementation.

In ARM CPUs, OpenMP was used for automatic parallelization of for loops in the Compression, Binarization and Localization (RGB only) stages, by prepending each loop with proper "pragma" directives. For the Compression and Binarization stages, the directive used was `#pragma omp parallel for`, in a single loop in each stage. To compute the average coordinates < avgX, avgY > in the RGB Localization, a more specific directive (reduction) was used: `#pragma omp parallel for reduction (+:sumX,sumY,numElems)`.

When using Epiphany with OMPi, only the Binarization and RGB Localization stages were parallelized, using "pragma" directives for loop parallelization, similar to those used with ARM CPUs. However, these directives were preceded by three additional OMPi specific directives: i) `pragma omp target data map(to:RGBframe,RGBbitmap) map(from:sumX,sumY,numPixels)`, ii) `pragma omp parallel private(RGBbitmap)`, iii) `pragma omp target`. The first two directives ensure the transfer of a copy of the RGB calibration bitmap and 1/16th of the compressed RGB frame to the local (private) memory of the Epiphany cores, and the recovery of the outcome of the RGB Localization. The third directive ensures that subsequent parallel loops execute on the Epiphany device. Unfortunately, OMPi has bugs (yet unresolved) in the Epiphany, that prevent the parallelization of further loops after the first one: subsequent loops execute only in a single of the Epiphany cores, thus much slower than in a single of the host ARM cores. Therefore, this strategy was excluded from evaluation.

4.3 Parallel Processing with the Epiphany SDK

Another processing strategy explored in this work (and its main motivation) was to make use of the low-level Epiphany Software Development Kit (eSDK) for the parallelization of Binarization and Localization (RGB only) on the Epiphany co-processor. This approach allows fine control of the processing resources and data distribution in the, promising good performance, although at the cost of high programming complexity.

In this approach (and, more generally, in any that makes use of the Epiphany device), it becomes crucial to minimize data transfers between the ARM host and the co-processor, and to take the most advantage of data in the small local memory of the eCores (this kind of constraints is typically found when developing applications for heterogeneous systems). These were the primary reasons for having aggressive compression applied to the RGB calibration structure and to the captured RGB frames. Without compression, frame processing could still be offloaded to the Epiphany co-processor, by splitting each original frame (and the calibration structure) into fragments, and processing each one in as much offloading rounds. But that would hardly pay off.

Thus, in this approach, the very first task to perform right after Calibration finishes in the host, is to copy the RGB calibration bitmap to the local memory, at each eCore. This is done once, before starting the main loop, that captures Kinect frames. Then, for each frame acquired and compressed, a 1/16th slice of this frame (taking 9,375 KBytes) is copied to each eCore's local memory. eCores perform further processing in parallel.

Communication between the host and the Epiphany eCores is conducted through a buffer in the 32MB shared memory zone (mapped in the host main memory). The size of this buffer is multiple of 8 (padding was required), once the eCores local memory is 8 byte-aligned and host-device DMA transfers also require this alignment. The application divides the buffer in two regions: i) a control region, for host-device synchronization, and ii) a data region, for host-device data exchanges. In the control region, one byte is used by the host to encode a specific task to be executed by the device; eCores inspect this byte and will act accordingly; when the task is completed, each eCore will change a specific byte flag in the control region; the host actively monitors these flags to know when a task submitted to the Epiphany device has completed. The data region is wide enough to accommodate the different structures that host and device exchange: RGB calibration bitmap, compressed RGB frames, and (partial) RGB localization results. Accordingly, the tasks are device-side functions, that i) grab from the host a copy of the RGB calibration bitmap, ii) grab from the host a specific slice (1/16th) of a RGB compressed frame, and perform binarization on it, and iii) inspect a binary RGB fragment on local memory, and return partial RGB localization data (the number of object points detected, and the sum of its X and Y coordinates), to the host, so it may compute the effective coordinates of the object being tracked, by reduction of the data received from all eCores.

Host-device data transfers are DMA-based, from the perspective of the device. When copying the RGB calibration bitmap, a simple blocking DMA operation is used; this means that each eCore is blocked, waiting for its own DMA controller to finish the transfer. However, when loading a compressed RGB frame slice, it is more efficient to use a non-blocking DMA operation: this allows the DMA controller to grab one line, while the eCore is busy with the binarization of the line previously transferred, effectively overlapping communication and computation (several tests were made, with different number of lines transferred, per DMA operation, and the best performance was achieved with a single line per transfer). Finally, when each eCore returns localization data to the host, it does so using, again, blocking DMA.

Due to restrictions on how the four 8 KBytes banks of local memory may be used, and also to ensure maximum performance on local memory accesses, carefully planning was needed to choose the better storage approach. In an eCore local memory, the first bank (bank 0) stores the interrupt vector, followed by the program code; the stack is assigned to the last bank (bank 3). Thus, banks 1 and 2 are free, and bank 3 fills top-bottom. With this in mind, it was decided to assign the RGB calibration bitmap to bank 1, and the compressed RGB frame slice to banks 2 and 3, alternated (odd lines to bank 2, and even lines to bank 3, taking near 50% of each banks capacity: 9,375 KBytes / 2 = 4,6875 KBytes). This alternation allows the eCore and its DMA controller to access local memory at the same time, without conflicts: the eCore processes (read access) a frame line in a bank, while the DMA controller writes a new line in another bank.

5. EVALUATION

We now present and discuss the evaluation results of the tracking prototype developed, with different combinations of execution platforms and processing strategies. The testing platforms include: a Parallella-16 Desktop Computer, a Raspberry Pi 1 (700 MHz single-core, 512 MBytes RAM), Raspberry Pi Zero (1 GHz single-core, 512 MBytes RAM), a Raspberry Pi 2 (900 MHz quad-core, 1 GByte RAM), and a Raspberry Pi 3 (1.2 GHz quad-core, 1 GByte RAM). The processing strategies are the ones discussed previously (section 4), that may or may not be applicable, depending on the platform. We recall, however, that two POSIX threads are always involved, as per the basic structure of the application. That processing strategy is implicit, and thus omitted in the notation next introduced for the test scenarios. These scenarios are fully described in Table 1

Table 1. Characterization of the evaluated scenarios

Test Scenario	Execution Platform	Processing Strategy (Processing Stages)	Maximum Processing Threads or Cores
Rasp1	Raspberry Pi 1	Pthreads (all)	1
Rasp0	Raspberry Pi Zero	Pthreads (all)	1
Rasp2	Raspberry Pi 2	Pthreads (all)	1
Rasp2(OMP)	Raspberry Pi 2	OpenMP (all)	4
Rasp3	Raspberry Pi 3	Pthreads (all)	1
Rasp3(OMP)	Raspberry Pi 3	OpenMP (all)	4
Parallella	Parallella (host)	Pthreads (all)	1
Parallella(OMP)	Parallella (host)	OpenMP (all)	2
Parallella(eSDK)	Parallella (host) + Epiphany	Pthreads (Compression) + eSDK (Binariz. + Localiz.)	1 + 16
Parallella(OMP+eSDK)	Parallella (host) + Epiphany)	OpenMP (Compression) + eSDK (Binariz. + Localiz.)	2 + 16

Figure 4 shows the evaluation results. They are average times (ms) from the capture and processing of 2000 frame pairs (RGB + Depth). The executables were all generated with the `gcc/gcc+` optimization level `-O2`.

Capture times per frame are shown on the top of the chart, in square brackets. The results reveal that only the Parallella and the Raspberry Pi 3 platforms are able to keep up with the frame generation rate of the Kinect sensor (30 fps), that demands a capture time of no more than 33ms. The other platforms would lose frames.

Processing times are represented in columns (overall value on top, in parentheses), split in Compression time (T_Comp), Binarization time (T_Bin), and Localization time (T_Loc). An extra time component is shown for the Parallella(eSDK) and Parallella(OMP+eSDK) scenarios: T_SharedCopy, as the time spent in transfers from host memory to shared memory (right after Compression and before Binarization). Also, for the same two Parallella scenarios, T_Bin includes the time spent in transfers from shared memory to the local memory of all eCores (that time overlaps with the time spent in the binarization itself, performed in the eCores).

In the Parallella scenarios, it is clear that using the Epiphany co-processor, ensures the smallest Binarization and Localization times (0.7 ms to 0.8 ms, and 0.1 ms). However, overall processing times are penalized by the time spent copying data from the host main memory to the shared memory (2,2 ms and 1,9 ms), to the extent that processing with only one POSIX thread takes less overall time (7,5 ms) than when offloading Binarization and Localization to the co-processor (7,9 ms in Parallella(eSDK)). Only when Compression is also parallelized with OpenMP on the host, does the overall time decreases (to 5,5 ms). However, compared to fully using OpenMP in the host (which takes 5,7 ms), the performance gain is negligible (0,2 ms). Moreover, the decrease of the Compression time to 2.7 ms in the Parallella(OMP+eSDK) scenario is an oddity, once its OpenMP code is exactly the same as in Parallella(OMP), where it takes 4.9 ms; this is most probably a side effect, from the compiler rearranging code or doing other optimizations when OpenMP and eSDK code co-exist.

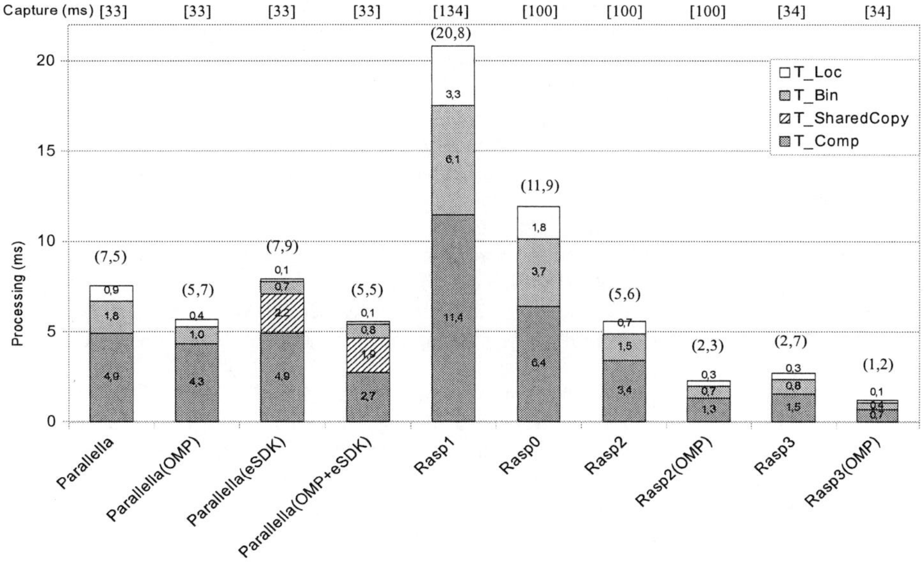

Figure 4. Eval. Results (ms): [frame capture times], (frame processing times), and decomposed frame processing times

Results with the different Raspberry Pi models are more diverse than with the Parallella. With a single CPU-core available, the Raspberry Pi 1 and Zero models are clearly outperformed by the quad-core Raspberry Pi 2 and 3, and by the Parallella platform. However, the Raspberry Pi 2 with a single processing thread (Rasp2 scenario) is already on-par with the best Parallella scenarios and, with four threads (Rasp2(OMP)), it more than halves the processing time (to 2,3 ms). The performance of the Raspberry Pi 3 with a single thread (Rasp3 scenario) is close (2,7 ms) to the best Raspberry Pi 2 scenario (2,3 ms), and with four threads (Rasp3(OMP) scenario), it more than halves the processing time (to 1,2 ms), in line with the Raspberry Pi 2 behavior.

When directly comparing the best Raspberry Pi 3 scenario (Rasp3(OMP)) with the best Parallella scenario (Parallella(OMP+eSDK)), the first attains a speedup of 5,5 / 1,2 = 4,58(3). This performance gap makes sense, once the Parallella(OMP+eSDK) and Parallella(OMP) have similar performance (i.e., using the Epiphany is almost irrelevant), and the Raspberry Pi 3 has twice the number of ARM cores, at double the clock frequency.

Finally, in terms of energy consumption at peak load, running our application, we measured 6,5W in the Parallella(OMP+eSDK) test and 3,6W in the Rasp3(OMP) test (noting that the Kinect sensor has its own external power supply). Thus, the Raspberry Pi 3 draws about half the power of Parallella.

6. CONCLUSIONS AND FUTURE WORK

This paper presented and evaluated an object localization application (based on color segmentation) developed to explore a heterogeneous many-core embedded system. This involved mixing different programming models and processing strategies, including a low-level approach for the Epiphany co-processor. The portability of some of the approaches pursued made possible to evaluate them on a conventional embedded system. This allowed a cross-platform comparison that revealed a lower than expected performance of the many-core system. Clearly, the need for costly data exchanges between the host and co-processor, and the scarce eCores local memory (making time-consuming Compression necessary), acted in Parallella disfavor. Thus, our case study, did not take full advantage of the Parallella co-processor, which requires workloads with higher computation/communication ratios in order to hide the offloading costs. We will pursue our work in object tracking and localization, investigating better ways to unleash the full potential of the Parallella board.

REFERENCES

Adapteva1, 2013. Epiphany Architecture Reference. Available at: http://www.adapteva.com/docs/epiphany_arch_ref.pdf

Adapteva2, 2013. Epiphany SDK Reference Available at: http://adapteva.com/docs/epiphany_sdk_ref.pdf

Aggarwal, J. K. and Cai, Q., 1999. Human motion analysis: A review. Comp. Vision Image Understand., 73, 3, 428–440

Avidan, S., 2001. Support vector tracking. In IEEE Conf. on Computer Vision and Pattern Recognition (CVPR). 184–191

board-db, 2017. The Single Board Computer Database. Available at: https://www.board-db.org/

Brauer, P. et al, 2016. Improving Latency in a Signal Processing System on the Epiphany Architecture. In Procs. of the 24th Euromicro Int. Conf. on Par., Dist.and Net.-Based Processing (PDP 2016), pp. 796-800. Heraklion, Crete, Greece

Brown, E., 2017. hacker board survey. Available at: http://linuxgizmos.com/2017-hacker-board-survey-raspberry-pi-still-rules-but-x86-sbcs-make-gains/

Brown, N., 2016. ePython: An Implementation of Python for the Many-core Epiphany Coprocessor. In Procs. of the 6th Workshop on Python for High-Performance and Scientific Computing (PyHPC'16), pp. 59--66. Piscataway, USA

Butenhof, D.R., 1997. Programming with POSIX Threads. Addison-Wesley

Caselles, V. et al., 1995. Geodesic active contours. In IEEE Int. Conference on Computer Vision (ICCV). 694–699

Comaniciu, D. and Meer, P., 1999. Mean shift analysis and applications. In IEEE International Conference on Computer Vision (ICCV), 2, 1197–1203

Gavrila, D. M., 1999. The visual analysis of human movement: A survey. Comp. Vision Image Understand., 73, 1, 82–98

Gener, Y. S. et al, 2015. Low-cost and low-power video filtering with parallel many cores. In Proceedings of the 9th International Conference on Electrical and Electronics Engineering (ELECO), pp. 921-925. Bursa, Turkey

Gwennap, L. Adapteva, 2011. More Flops, Less Wats. Microprocessor Report

i-SCOOP, 2017. Industry 4.0: the fourth industrial revolution. Available at: https://www.i-scoop.eu/industry-4-0/

Iszaidy, I. et al., 2016. Threading implementation on different hardware for travel time estimation purpose. In Proceedings of the International Conference on Robotics, Automation and Sciences. Ayer Keroh, Malaysia

Kaeli, D., and Akodes, D., 2011. The convergence of HPC and embedded systems in our heterogeneous computing future. In Proceedings of the IEEE 29th Int. Conference on Computer Design (ICCD 2011), pp. 9-11. Amherst, MA, USA

libfreenect, 2017. OpenKinect/libfreenect. Available at: https://github.com/OpenKinect/libfreenect

Menezes, V. et al., 2015. Surveillance and monitoring system using Raspberry Pi and SimpleCV. Conference on Green Computing and Internet of Things (ICGCIoT), pp. 1276-1278. Noida, India, 2015

Moeslund, T. and Granum, E., 2001. A survey of computer vision-based human motion capture. Computer Vision and Image Understanding, 81, 3, 231–268

MPI, 2015. MPI: A Message-Passing Interface Standard, Version 3.1. Message Passing Interface Forum

NVIDIA, 2011. Bringing High-End Graphics to Handheld Devices (Whitepaper)

Olofsson, A. et al, 2014. Kickstarting high-performance energy-efficient manycore architectures with Epiphany. In Proceedings of the 48th Asilomar Conference on Signals, Systems and Computers, pp. 1719-1726. Pacific Grove, CA.

OpenCV, 2017. OpenCV library. Available at: http://opencv.org/

OpenMP, 2013. OpenMP Application Program Interface, Version 4.0. Architecture Review Board

Parallella, 2017. Programming Parallella. Available at: https://www.parallella.org/programming/

Park, S. and Aggarwal, J. K., 2004. A hierarchical bayesian network for event recognition of human actions and interactions. Multimedia Systems, 10, 2, 164–179.

Paschos, G., 2001. Perceptually uniform color spaces for color texture analysis: an empirical evaluation. IEEE Transactions on Image Processing, 10, 932–937.

Raspberry Pi Foundation, 2017. Teach, Learn, and Make with Raspberry Pi. Available at: https://www.raspberrypi.org/

Richie, D., et al., 2015. Threaded MPI Programming Model for the Epiphany. Journal of Comput. Science 9, 94–100

Ross, J., and Richie, D., 2016. An OpenSHMEM Implementation for the Adapteva Epiphany Coprocessor. In Procs. of the 3d Workshop on OpenSHMEM and Related Technologies (OpenSHMEM 2016), pp. 146-159. Baltimore, MD, USA

Shi, J. and Malik, J., 2000. Normalized cuts and image segmentation. IEEE Transactions on Pattern Analysis and Machine Intelligence, 22, 8, 888–905.

Soetedjo, A. and Somawirata, I K., 2016. Implementation of face detection and tracking on a low cost embedded system using fusion technique. In Procs. of the 11th Int. Conf. on Comp. Science & Education, pp. 209-213. Nagoya, Japan

Spiros, N.A. et al., 2015. Targeting the Parallella with OpenMP. In Proceedings of the 21st International Conference. on Parallel and Distributed Computing (Euro-Par 2015), pp. 662-674. Springer, Vienna, Austria.

Truong, M.T.N., and Kim, S., 2017. Parallel implementation of color-based particle filter for object tracking in embedded systems. Journal of Human-centric Computing and Information Sciences, 7(2).

Vaas, S. et al, 2016. Embedded Parallel Computing Accelerators for Smart Control Units of Frequency Converters. In Proceedings of the 29th Int. Conf. on Architecture of Computing Systems (ARCS 2016). Nuremberg, Germany

Yilmaz, A., Omar, J. and Shah, M., 2006. Object Tracking: A Survey. ACM Computing Surveys, 38, 4, Article 13.

BENCHMARKING OF BARE METAL VIRTUALIZATION PLATFORMS ON COMMODITY HARDWARE

Duarte Pousa[*] and José Rufino[*†]
[*]*Polytechnic Institute of Bragança, 5300-253 Bragança, Portugal*
[†]*Laboratory of Instrumentation and Experimental Particle Physics, University of Minho, 4710-057 Braga, Portugal*

ABSTRACT

In recent years, System Virtualization became a fundamental IT tool, whether it is type-2/hosted virtualization, mostly exploited by end-users in their personal computers, or type-1/bare metal, well established in IT departments and thoroughly used in modern datacenters as the very foundation of cloud computing. Though bare metal virtualization is meant to be deployed on server-grade hardware (for performance, stability and reliability reasons), properly configured desktop-class systems are often used as virtualization "servers", due to their attractive performance/cost ratio. This paper presents the results of a study conducted on such systems, about the performance of Windows 10 and Ubuntu Server 16.04 guests, when deployed in what we believe are the type-1 platforms most in use today: VMware ESXi, Citrix XenServer, Microsoft Hyper-V, and KVM-based (represented by oVirt and Proxmox). Performance is measured using three synthetic benchmark: PassMark for Windows, UnixBench for Ubuntu Server, and the cross-platform Flexible I/O Tester. The benchmarks results may be used to choose the most adequate type-1 platform (performance-wise), depending on guest OS, its performance requisites (CPU-bound, IO-bound, or balanced) and its storage type (local/remote) used.

KEYWORDS

Bare Metal Virtualization, Synthetic Benchmarking, Performance Assessment, Commodity Hardware

1. INTRODUCTION

System Virtualization allows a physical host to run (simultaneously) many guest operating systems in self-contained software-defined virtual machines, sharing the host hardware, under control of a hypervisor. It comes in two basic forms: a) in hosted (or type-2) virtualization, an operating system (typically desktop-oriented) hosts virtual machines, along with other applications; this is achieved by type-2 platforms, like VMware Workstation (Vmware-a, 2016) or Oracle VM VirtualBox (VirtualBox, 2016); b) in bare metal (or type-1) virtualization, the platform hypervisor has direct hardware access, ensuring a more efficient use of the underlying resources; an approach is to install a thin hypervisor in the host, along with a management console; this console may be minimal, as in VMware ESXi (Vmware-b, 2016), or a management virtual machine, as in XenServer (XenServer, 2016) or Hyper-V (Hyper-V, 2016); another option is to have a server-class operating system with kernel modules that convert the operating system into a type-1 platform, like in KVM-based (KVM, 2017) approaches, as oVirt (oVirt, 2017) and Proxmox (Proxmox, 2017).

Bare metal virtualization is commonly deployed on server-grade hardware, often vendor-certified for specific type-1 virtualization platforms. This ensures adequate performance, stability and reliability, along with advanced management features, that are essential for mission-critical applications. However, it is usually possible to run most modern type-1 platforms on commodity hardware, and the compromises entailed by such option are acceptable in many scenarios, often related to tight budgets (home labs, public schools, SMEs, etc.).

This paper presents the results of several benchmarks conducted on Windows 10 LTSB and Linux Ubuntu Server 16.04 virtual machines, hosted in well-known bare metal platforms (VMware ESXi, Citrix XenServer, oVirt, Proxmox and Microsoft Hyper-V), running in commodity hardware with reasonable (tough not high-end) configurations. The benchmarks selected for this study include synthetic OS-specific benchmarks (Passmark for Windows, and UnixBench for Linux), and also a cross-platform I/O-centric benchmark (Flexible IO Tester). The later was run with virtual machines deployed both on local and remote storage, and several remote storage options were evaluated (NFS and iSCSI). The same benchmarks were conducted in native instances of the operating systems selected for this study, installed on the same host hardware.

All these test scenarios allowed to gather information that may help answering performance-centric questions, like: what is (are) the most suitable type-1 platforms(s) to host modern Windows and Linux guests in commodity "servers" ? what is the impact on secondary storage IO performance of different guest storage platforms ? what is the impact introduced by each type-1 hypervisor, compared to a native scenario ?

The rest of the paper is organized as follows. Section 2 describes our testbed, including type-1 platforms, guest operating systems and benchmarks selected, as well as hosts, guests and remote storage configuration. Section 3 presents the benchmarking methodology and its results. Section 4 revises related work on benchmarking of virtualization platforms. Section 5 concludes and points directions for future work.

2. TESTBED

2.1 Type-1 Virtualization Platforms

The bare metal virtualization platforms selected for this study range from proprietary and closed source, represented by VMware ESXi 6.0 (Free License) and Hyper-V (Windows Server 2016 Datacenter Edition), to open source implementations: Citrix XenServer 7.0, oVirt 4.1 and Proxmox 4.4. The specific versions of each type-1 platform were the latest ones available when this study began (fall 2016). Bearing in mind the distinction between a virtualization platform and a hypervisor, each of these platforms build on the following hypervisors, respectively: ESXi, Hyper-V, Xen and QEMU/KVM (for both oVirt and Proxmox). These hypervisors rely on different virtualization techniques, some used in combination (Hwang, J. et al, 2013): i) Para-Virtualization (Hyper-V, Xen, KVM); ii) Hardware-Assisted Virtualization, based on ISA extensions like Intel's VT-x and AMD-V (all hypervisors); iii) Full Virtualization (ESXi, Xen, KVM). In our study, the type-1 hypervisors choose automatically the virtualization technique to run each guest. Also, from this point onwards, the concepts of type-1 platform and type-1 hypervisor will be used interchangeably.

2.2 Guest Operating Systems

We conducted benchmarks on a small, yet representative set of guest operating systems (OSs): Microsoft Windows 10 (in its LTSB variant) and Ubuntu Server 16.04 LTS. Both choices play a dual role in this study.

The first OS stands as a modern representative of the Microsoft Windows line of operating systems and is poised to take the leading position in desktop machines. Windows 10 LTSB (Long Term Servicing Branch) is a long-term support version of Windows 10 Enterprise. It is designed for stability, meaning it will seldom (or ever) be updated with new features, but will have security updates and bug fixes for 10 years after its release.

The second OS selected for our study functions as a "proxy" for the many variants of Linux-based OSs, mostly used in infrastructure servers. Canonical's Ubuntu Linux distributions, specifically, have been consistently present at the top of usage rankings. Also, Ubuntu's relevance in the cloud space has been steadily growing, becoming a major player, both at infrastructure layers (IaaS) and as an instance (virtual machine). As with the LTSB Windows variant, a Long Term Support (LTS) Ubuntu version was also selected.

2.3 Benchmarks

Our original goal was to use only multi-platform, free (if possible open-source), and broad scope (i.e., not focused on a single system component) synthetic benchmarks. However, considering the choice of Operating Systems (see above), we were unable to find such a benchmark. Instead, we resorted to PassMark Performance Test v9 (PassMark-a, 2016) for Windows, and UnixBench v5.1.3 (UnixBench, 2016) for Linux. These are not multi-platform (and PassMark is not open-source), but all other requisites are fulfilled.

PassMark generates CPU, 2D graphics, 3D graphics, Disk and Memory ratings, that are combined in a global PassMark score (PassMark-b, 2017). UnixBench is a system (OS-level) benchmark for Unix-like systems, that mostly depends on the OS, libraries and compilers used. It includes tests on General CPU+Memory performance (Dhrystone2), CPU Arithmetic performance (Whetstone), File Copying, Process

Creation & Substitution, Context Switching, System Call Overhead, Shell Scripting and 2D/3D Graphics (unfit to Ubuntu Server and so excluded in our study). An overall system index combines the scores of all tests.

We still considered important to conduct a multi-platform benchmark, even if one component-specific, as a way to establish a comparable baseline between different operating systems executed on the same type-1 virtual hardware. This is accomplished by the Flexible I/O Tester (FIO, 2016) benchmark that was used to assess the impact of different storage options (local disk-based, remote NFS-based, and remote iSCSI-based).

2.4 Host, Guests and Storage Server Specifications

All benchmarks were executed on the same host, with the following configuration: CPU = Intel Skylake i7-6700 (4cores/8threads, 3.4/3.8 GHz); RAM = 32 GB 2133MHz DDR4; OS / Hypervisor Disk = 500 GB SSD; FIO Benchmark Disk = 500 GB SSD (capped to 32GB); Discrete GPU = NVIDIA Quadro 4000M.

Virtual guests were all configured with the same generic virtual hardware, as follows: vCPU = 1 socket, 4 cores/4threads; vRAM = 8 GB; OS vDisk = 32 GB thin provisioned (on top of the Hypervisor SSD); FIO Benchmark local vDisk = 32 GB thick provisioned (on top of the FIO Benchmark Disk); FIO Benchmark remote vDisk = 32 GB ZFS volume (on top of a remote SSD); Passthrough GPU = NVIDIA Quadro 4000M.

To support FIO benchmarking on the virtual guests with remote storage (via NFS and iSCSI), an auxiliary storage server was setup, with the following specifications: CPU = Intel Lynnfield i7-870 (4cores/8threads, 2.9/3.6 GHz); RAM = 16 GB 1333MHz DDR3; OS and Filesystem = FreeNAS v9.10 with ZFS; OS Disk = 16 GB USB3 PenDrive; Auxiliary Disk = 1TB 7200rpm SATA HD; NFS/iSCSI Disk = 256 GB SSD.

To make native and virtual conditions as close as possible, native tests ran with hyperthreading disabled (thus effectively ensuring that only 4 single-threaded cores were available), with RAM limited to 8GB, and using only 32GB of raw space from a separate SSD volume for FIO benchmarks. During guests execution, hyperthreading was enabled in the host system (as is usually done in virtual machine servers), although each guest used only 4 vCores. Also, there was no vCPU binding to real CPU cores. The default types provided by each hypervisor for vCPUs, vDisks and vNICs were used, without hypervisor optimizations or tuning.

All physical machines were connected in an isolated network, through a dedicated 1Gbps Ethernet switch.

3. EVALUATION

3.1 Methodology

Preliminary tests showed some variability on the scores achieved by very specific sub-benchmarks: DiskMark in the case of Passmark, and (Pipe-based) Context Switching in the case of UnixBench, with a Relative Standard Deviation (RSD) up to 7% and 25%, respectively (all other had RSD values below 3%). At the same time, a full run of Passmark and UnixBench complete relatively quickly in our testbed (around 30 minutes and 60 minutes, respectively). Thus, to ensure reliable results, it was decided to execute PassMark and UnixBench six times, on each testing scenario, with the outcome being averages of the six full runs. On the other hand, the time required for a full run of the FIO benchmark was much higher (from 6 to 12 hours, depending on the kind of secondary storage used), but each run produced very similar results (RSD values below 3.25%). Therefore, the outcomes of this benchmark are averages of only three runs.

Other testing conditions, common to all benchmarks, were as follows: i) each full benchmark run was preceded by a OS clean boot, followed by a five minute standby time to reduce any potential noise introduced by the booting phase; ii) before the first and last run, benchmarks conducted on virtual guests also implied a clean boot of the hypervisor (also followed by a five minute stabilization phase); iii) automatic update services were turned off in both operating systems tested, to prevent interference during testing; iv) finally, it should be stated that all benchmarks were run with their own default configurations.

Also, it's worth mentioning that, for each hypervisor, there are usually special drivers that are meant to be installed in guests in order to improve guest's performance at many levels (secondary-storage, 2D graphics, network, etc.). These correspond to VMtools in ESXi, XenTools in XenServer, Virtio drives for KVM-based hypervisors (like oVirt and Proxmox), and Integration Services for Hyper-V. Moreover, for Windows guests, VMware provides an optimization tool (VMware-c, 2016) that allows to disable unnecessary services and features to improve performance, and may be applied to Windows guests regardless of the underlying hypervisor. We have conducted benchmarks with/without the accelerations drivers (both in Windows and Linux guests), and with/without the optimizations offered by the optimization tool (Windows guests only). This paper focus on the results with the accelerations drivers installed, once we believe this is the most common scenario. Also, the effects of VMware's optimization tool are not reported here.

3.2 Results

Figures 1 to 3 provide charts with the consolidated results of the benchmarks conducted in our testbed. Columns represent percentages, relative to absolute scores measured in a native instance. Absolute scores are shown (in parentheses) on the top of the charts (in Figures 1 and 2), or below their vertical axis 100% mark (in Figure 3).

As expected, in general all hypervisors introduce performance penalties, to different extents, depending on the specific benchmark. However, we have observed some situations where virtual instances managed to be faster than the baseline native instance (this was especially true and most visible in UnixBench). Although rarely observed, this behavior is not entirely uncommon. In the right circumstances, type-1 hypervisors may provide faster than native performance, because they may be able to manage hardware resources more efficiently than the guest's kernel (Che, 2008; Henderson, 2009; Vaughan-Nichols, 2013).

3.2.1 PassMark Results

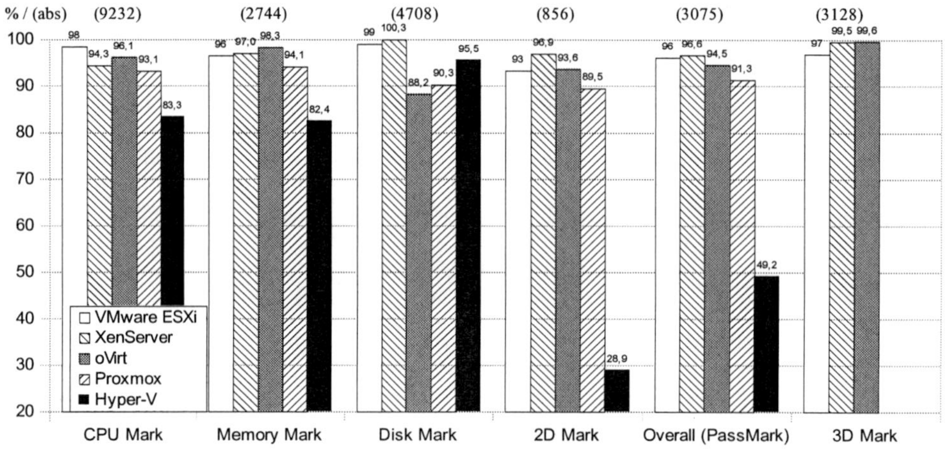

Figure 1. PassMark results (relative to native) for the Windows 10 LTSB guest (all hypervisors)

Figure 1 shows the results of PassMark in Windows 10 LTSB. In the Overall score, VMware ESXi, XenServer and oVirt are on the same league, with relative scores of 96.6%, 96.1% and 94.5% of the absolute native score (3075), whereas Proxmox is right below, with 91.3%, and Hyper-V achieves only 49.2%. This overall ranking is similar to the rankings in some PassMarks's sub-benchmarks, but visibly changes in others. We note that Overall (PassMark) results exclude 3D Mark results because GPU passthrough was not always entirely successful: in Proxmox, the guest gets stuck at 100% CPU utilization during boot, and in Hyper-V the guest halts during GPU compute tests. Thus, 3D Mark results are presented separately, and only for the hypervisors where GPU passthrough to the Windows 10 guest worked flawlessly and 3DMark completed.

In CPUMark, VMware ESXi and oVirt are the top performers, with 98.5% and 96.1% of the absolute native score (9232), thus becoming recommend choices for CPU-bound applications in a Windows 10 guest. XenServer and Proxmox closely follow, with 94.3% and 93.1%, respectively. Hyper-V achieves just 83.3%.

MemoryMark results are relatively homogeneous: except for Hyper-V, all scores are within a margin of 4.2% of each other, between 94.1% and 98.3% of the native score (2744). Hyper-V, lags behind, to 82.4%.

However, Hyper-V exhibits a good performance in DiskMark, attaining 95.5% of the native score (4708), yet still surpassed by ESXi and XenServer, with 99% and 100.3%, respectively, thus with virtually no performance loss. In turn, oVirt and Proxmox, fall to 88.2% and 90.3%, respectively; this may be due to the default Virtio configuration used: it assumes a "native" instead of a "threads" IO mode, meaning no additional IO threads are created by QEMU to handle extra IO load. As such, for Disk-bound applications with IO load similar to DiskMark, running in a Windows 10 guest, instantiated on local hypervisor storage, ESXi and XenServer ensure the very best (if not optimal) performance, with Hyper-V right behind.

Regarding graphical performance, XenServer leads in 2DMark, with 96.9% of the native score (856), slightly above ESXi (with 93.2%), oVirt (with 93.6%) and Proxmox (with 89.5%). Hyper-V, however, shows very poor performance, with a relative score of only 28.9%, that brings down its Overall (PassMark) score.

3DMark, that ran separately, achieved close-to-metal performance in XenServer and oVirt, with a relative score of 99.5% and 99.6% of the native score (3128), respectively. ESXi, with 96.8%, is near. Were 3DMark included on the Overall score, it would confirm VMware ESXi, XenServer and oVirt as the top hypervisors.

3.2.2 UnixBench Results

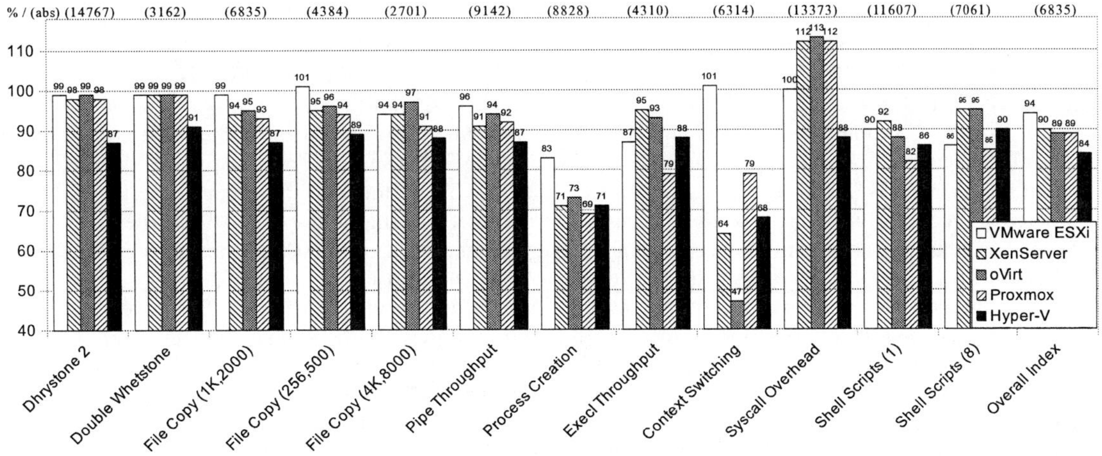

Figure 2. UnixBench results (relative to native) for the Ubuntu Server 16.04 LTS guest (all hypervisors)

Figure 2 presents the results of UnixBench in Ubuntu Server 16.04 LTS. As stated before, UnixBench is an OS-level benchmark, not meant to evaluate (at least directly) hardware components. It generates single and multi-threaded results, and we only provide the later, meaning each test ran in parallel, in 4 separate instances, one per each real/virtual CPU-core. Also, results are presented truncated (integer part only) due to space limits.

In the Overall Index, VMware ESXi leads with 94% of the native index (6835), closely followed by XenServer (90%), and both oVirt and Proxmox (89%), all very near to each other. Hyper-V attains only 84%. Thus, running Linux guests seems a task for which Hyper-V is not as suitable as the other type-1 hypervisors.

In the CPU-related/bound tests (Dhrystone and Whetstone), VMware ESXi, XenServer, oVirt and Proxmox achieve near native performance: between 98% and 99% of the native indexes (14767 and 3162). The dominance of these hypervisors in such tests is in line with was observed in the CPU Mark test. The last rank of Hyper-V in CPU Mark is also transposed to Dhrystone and Whetstone, with only 87% and 91%.

File Copy tests measures "the rate at which data can be transferred from one file to another" (UnixBench, 2016), using various buffer sizes (256, 1024, 4096 bytes) and file sizes (2000, 500, 8000 blocks). They provide clues on file system performance and, indirectly, on secondary storage performance. Taking the average of the relative indexes in these tests, the following hypervisor ranking emerges: VMware Esxi – 97%; oVirt – 95.6%; XenServer – 93.3%; Proxmox – 92.3%; Hyper-V – 88%. For what it's worth, this ranking is only consistent with DiskMark's in VMware ESXi and Proxmox; the other hypervisors exchange rankings.

Pipe Throughput measures the rate at which the same process can write data to a pipe and read it back. This "has no real counterpart in real-world programming" (UnixBench, 2016), and we only provide results for completeness. Much in line with other tests, VMware ESXi is first, and Hyper-V is again the last.

Process Creation, that measures the rate at which a process can fork and reap a child that exits right away, exhibits relatively low scores: VMware ESXi achieves 83% and the other hypervisors fall between 69% and 83%. This test is said to be related to memory bandwidth, due to memory allocations for new processes (UnixBench, 2016). Yet, there's no obvious relation with MemoryMark results, perhaps because of the light nature of the Process Creation benchmark: children die immediately, without changing any variables, and with the parent waiting for their ending; thus, the parent's data segment never gets duplicated, and so, basically, a child needs only a stack and kernel memory for its process control block (the code segment is always shared).

Execl Throughput measures the rate at which a process image (code and data) in RAM may be replaced. This involves reading the new code and data from an executable at the file system (FS), into a memory region. However, in this benchmark, the same (small) executable replaces itself, and so FS caching comes into play. We dare to say that this benchmark ends up evaluating memory bandwidth, and some hypervisors, namely oVirt, Proxmox and Hyper-V, even keep their relative positions from the Process Creation test: oVirt first, then Hyper-V, then Proxmox (VMware ESXi and XenServer, however, exchange places). If we take the average of the Process Creation and Execl Throughput benchmarks, the following ranking emerges: VMware ESXi – 85%; XenServer – 83%; oVirt – 83%; Hyper-V – 79,5%; Proxmox – 74%. These values are more balanced, thus more in line with the Memory Mark scores, although lower by more than 10%.

The Context Switching test measures the rate at which two processes exchange an increasing integer through a pipe. Because both processes strictly alternate execution, this test assesses how fast is context switching (an OS capability important to many real-world applications). It turns out that the results of this test are the most divergent in all UnixBench tests, with a RSD of 22,7%. VMware ESXi is able to sustain faster than native performance, up to 101% of the native index (6314), and Proxmox follows at distance, with 79% score. However, XenServer, Proxmox and Hyper-V only achieve 64%, 47% and 68%, respectively. The oVirt score is intriguing, and deserves further investigation, mostly because, like Proxmox, is KVM-based.

In the Syscall Overhead test, a basic primitive (the `getpid` system call, that returns the ID of the calling process) is repeatedly invoked, so as to measure the cost of entering and exiting the kernel. This time, all hypervisors but Hyper-V exhibit exceptionally good performance, from 100% of the native index (13373) in VMware ESXi, up to 112% / 113% in XenServer and KVM-based hypervisors. Thus, a syscall acceleration mechanism seems to come into play, in the three Linux-based hypervisors. Hyper-V falls behind, at 88%.

Finally, the Shell Scripts (*n*) tests measure the rate at which a process can start and reap a set of $c*n$ concurrent copies of a script that applies a series of transformation to a data file, where c is the number of CPU cores seen by the OS. Once c=4 in our testbed, Shell Scripts (1) and Shell Scripts (8) reach up to 4 and 32 concurrent instances of the child script. Comparing the results from both scenarios, XenServer, oVirt and even Hyper-V, react more favorably to a load increase, hinting at a better scalability under higher load (this is subject to confirmation in future work, when performing benchmarks with more than one virtual machine running).

3.2.3 FIO Results

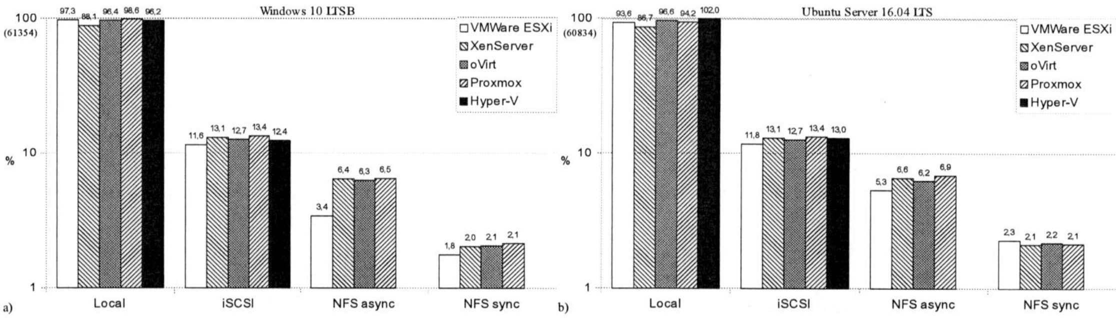

Figure 3. FIO results (relative to native) for a) Windows 10 LTSB, and b) Ubuntu Server 16.04 LTS (all hypervisors)

The charts of Figures 3.a) and 3.b) exhibit the results of FIO in Windows 10 LTSB and Ubuntu Server 16.04 LTS, respectively. FIO's native absolute scores are presented below the chart's vertical axis 100% mark.

Native scores on both OSs are very similar (with a relative difference of ≈ 0,0085%); as such, relative scores in both charts are directly comparable, allowing to confront both OSs for any kind of storage used.

An immediate conclusion is that FIO performance in both OSs is very similar (excluding VMware ESXi over NFS). This supports the following cross-platform conclusions: local SATA SSD storage is ≈10 times faster than the fastest remote storage, provided by the iSCSI protocol; using an NFS share with asynchronous writes (enforced at the ZFS level, on the storage server), ensures approximately half of the performance of an iSCSI volume; finally, NFS with synchronous writes (the default NFS behavior) is roughly one third as fast as asynchronous NFS. We note that results are not provided for Hyper-V and NFS because Hyper-V does not currently support (and likely won't) virtual disks instantiated on NFS shares (Kolomyeytsev, 2015).

Trying to discover which hypervisor(s) offer the best FIO performance, for each kind of storage, we observe that: i) on local storage, all hypervisors provide very good performance (96,2% to 98,6% in Windows, and 93,6% to 102% in Ubuntu), except XenServer (with only 88,1% in Windows, and 86,7%, in Ubuntu); notably, this contradicts XenServer's DiskMark score of 100,3%, above all others; however, XenServer's FIO scores are more in line with UnixBench's File Copy scores, where XenServer was undercut almost just by Hyper-V; ii) with iSCSI, results are very balanced across all hypervisors, and strikingly similar between both OSs; iii) with NFS, results are also balanced, excluding the score produced by the Windows guest on VMware ESXi over NFS asynchronous, that is about half of the other hypervisors.

4. RELATED WORK

We only reference here academic work, that conducted performance studies focused on type-1 hypervisors.

Che et al. (Che, 2008) studied the performance of the Xen 3.1 and KVM-60 hypervisors (supported by a Fedora 8 host), when running the Linpack, LMbench and IOzone benchmarks, to measure floating-point CPU power, OS latencies and memory bandwidth, and file system I/O performance, respectively, on Linux Fedora 8 and Windows XP guests (Linpack only). The physical host was a desktop-class machine, with a dual-core CPU and 2 GB of RAM (1.5 GB for guests). Xen ensured close-to-native Linpack and LMbench performance, and sometimes better than native IOzone performance.

Fayyad-Kazan et al. (Fayyad-Kazan, 2013) conducted a study with Linux instances modified with RT-Preempt realtime preemption patches, on VMware ESXi 5.1, Xen 4.2.1, Hyper-V 2012 and bare metal. The host was workstation/server-class (Xeon CPU), but without hyperthreading capabilities. Guests had only 1 vCPU and 1GB of RAM, a rather limited configuration, but some tests were made with more than one VM running, contrarily to our study, that runs a singles VM at a time. The benchmarks were tailored to evaluate the real-time performance and behavior of real-time OSs (which is a corner case). Xen performance came up very close to native, followed by Hyper-V and ESXi.

Hwang et al. (Hwang, 2013) evaluated the performance of Hyper-V 2008, KVM, VMware ESXi 5.0 and Xen 4.1.2 under hardware-assisted virtualization settings, using microbenchmarks for CPU (Bytemark), memory (Ramspeed), disk (Bonnie++ and FileBench), and network (Netperf), and also application level benchmarks (Linux kernel compilation and freebench). They also ran several VMs and studied their mutual interference. The host used was server-class, with a four core Xeon CPU, 8 GB of RAM, SAS hard disks and 1 Gbps Ethernet NICs. Guests were based on Ubuntu 10.04 LTS, with 1 or 4 vCPUs, 2 GB of RAM for isolated VMs, and 1GB of RAM for simultaneous VMs. Results showed that, overall, VMware ESXi performed the best, followed by a respectable performance of the other three hypervisors.

Graniszewski et al. (Graniszewski, 2016) analyzed the performance of Hyper-V 2008+2012, VMware ESXi 5.1, Oracle VM Server, XenServer 6.1, and Oracle VM Virtualbox, using component-specific benchmarks (nbench for CPU, netperf for network, FileBench for storage, and ramspeed for memory), that ran on an Ubuntu 12.04 guest. A real-word test (Linux kernel compilation) was also performed. Tests were done with one and two vCPUs, and 2GB RAM. The host was desktop-class, with a low-end configuration (dual-core CPU, 4GB RAM, 5400rpm HD). Results put VMware ESXi on the lead, followed by Xen.

5. CONCLUSIONS AND FUTURE WORK

As discussed throughout this paper, the performance characteristics of all the mainstream type-1 virtualization platforms were analyzed, through synthetic benchmarks conducted in guests, with care to avoid resource over-commitment (thus limited to a single guest in operation). The scope of the benchmarks used enabled investigation under multiple workloads aiming at stressing CPU, Memory, local and remote storage, GPU (under passthrough) or even OS (Linux) sub-systems. Ultimately, all the tested type-1 platforms proved that, in the right conditions, there is very little overhead introduced by the hypervisors, with the exception of Hyper-V, the most frequent outlier in our tests. The choice of a type-1 platform, though, is not purely dictated by raw performance, especially when margins between different options are narrow. Other factors, like the technical background of the IT staff, the organization culture, and the IT budget, play perhaps a more decisive role. But if we were to recommend a type-1 virtualization platform, based only on the performance results observed (and their consistency), VMWare ESXi and Citrix XenServer would be our current choices.

While the provided analysis is thorough, there are still many untested scenarios that we intend to cover in future work, such as: i) evaluate the performance of (para)virtualized/SR-IOV network adapters; ii) introduce 10Gigabit Ethernet into the testbed (following the market trend that points to its commoditization) and study its effect on network and remote storage (FIO) benchmarks; iii) go beyond the default configurations for each hypervisor, trying to assess the best combination(s) of critical setting(s) (CPU types, Main Memory paging, IO options); iv) conduct a representative set of real world benchmarks (including Linux kernel compilation, video transcoding, etc.); v) assess the performance in multi-server, multi-VM and over-commitment scenarios, taking advantage of industry standard benchmarks, namely SPEC VIRT_SC 2013 (SPECvirt, 2013); vii) study and compare the impact of features like failover / high-availability support, load balancing, live migration, etc.

REFERENCES

Che, J. et al, 2008. Performance Measuring and Comparing of Virtual Machine Monitors. Proceedings of 2008 IEEE International Conference on Embedded and Ubiquitous Computing. Shanghai, China, pp 381-386.

Fayyad-Kazan, H. et al, 2013. Benchmarking the Performance of Microsoft Hyper-V server, VMware ESXi and Xen Hypervisors. In Journal of Emerging Trends in Computing and Information Sciences, Vol. 4, No. 12, pp 922-933.

FIO, 2016. Flexible I/O Tester. Available at: https://github.com/axboe/fio (Linux source code), http://bluestop.org/fio/ (Windows binaries), (Accessed: October 2016)

Graniszewski, W. and Arciszewski, A., 2016. Performance analysis of selected hypervisors. In International Journal of Electronics and Telecommunications, Vol. 62, No. 3, pp 231-236.

Henderson, T. et al, 2009. Xen-based hypervisors push performance limits. Available at: http://www.networkworld.com/article/2271464/data-center/xen-based-hypervisors-push-performance-limits.html (Accessed: June 2017)

Hwang, J. et al, 2013. A component-based performance comparison of four hypervisors. Proceedings of 2013 IFIP/IEEE International Symposium on Integrated Network Management (IM 2013). Ghent, Belgium, pp 269-276.

Hyper-V, 2016. Try Active Microsoft Hyper-V Server 2016 | TechNet Evaluation Software. Available at: https://www.microsoft.com/en-us/evalcenter/evaluate-hyper-v-server-2016 (Accessed: October 2016)

Kolomyeytsev, A., 2015. Hyper-V: NFS. Available at: https://www.starwindsoftware.com/blog/hyper-v-vms-on-nfs-share-why-hasnt-anyone-thought-of-that-earlier-they-did-in-fact-2 (Accessed: October 2016)

KVM, 2017. Kernel Virtual Machine. Available at: https://www.linux-kvm.org/page/Main_Page (Accessed: January 2017)

oVirt, 2017. oVirt. Available at: https://www.ovirt.org/ (Accessed: January 2017)

PassMark-a, 2016. PassMark PerformanceTest. Available at: http://www.passmark.com/products/pt.htm (Accessed: October 2016)

PassMark-b, 2017. PassMark Formulas. Available at: http://www.passmark.com/forum/performancetest/4599-formula-cpu-mark-memory-mark-and-disk-mark (Accessed: June 2017)

Proxmox, 2017. Server virtualization management with Proxmox VE. Available at: https://www.proxmox.com/en/proxmox-ve (Accessed: January 2017)

SPECvirt, 2013. SPEC virt_sc 2013. Available at: https://www.spec.org/virt_sc2013/ (Accessed: September 2017)

UnixBench, 2016. BYTE Unixbenchmak suite. Available at: https://github.com/kdlucas/byte-unixbench (Accessed: October 2016)

Vaughan-Nichols, J.S., 2013. Yes, virtualization is faster (sometimes) than native hardware. Available at: http://www.zdnet.com/article/yes-virtualization-is-faster-sometimes-than-native-hardware/ (Accessed: June 2017)

VirtualBox, 2016. Oracle VM VirtualBox. Available at: https://www.virtualbox.org (Accessed: October 2016)

VMware-a, 2016. Workstation for Windows – VMware Products. Available at: https://www.vmware.com/products/workstation.html (Accessed: October 2016)

VMware-b, 2016. Free VMware vSphere Hypervisor. Free Virtualization (ESXi). Available at: https://www.vmware.com/products/vsphere-hypervisor.html (Accessed: October 2016)

VMware-c, 2016. VMware OS Optimization Tool. Available at: https://labs.vmware.com/flings/vmware-os-optimization-tool (Accessed: October 2016)

XenServer, 2016. XenServer | Open Source Server Virtualization. Available at: https://xenserver.org (Accessed: October 2016)

BLIND QUALITY ALGORITHM TO ANALYZE STREAMING VIDEO CONTENTS IN 5G NETWORKS

Juan Pedro López[1], Anton Authier[2], David Jiménez[3], José Manuel Menéndez [4] and Nuria Sánchez[5]
[134]Universidad Politécnica de Madrid, Madrid, Spain
[2]École nationale supérieure de l'électronique et de ses applications, Cergy, France
[5]Visiona Ingeniería de Proyectos, Madrid, Spain

ABSTRACT

Internet traffic is growing by an average of 40% a year and video streaming stands for 50% of the traffic. The expansion of new applications and services for video distribution makes users demand video quality and faster loads for contents with higher resolutions. For that reason, it is necessary to improve detection systems with check the received contents and insure comfortable use. The wide variety of technologies for streaming and encoding systems make necessary the implementation of blind quality models that detect errors independently of the transmission source, focused on analyzing the decoded image as consumed by the final user. Additionally, the absence of a video reference in streaming systems oblige the creation of No-Reference quality metrics, because the content is not available to compare the video received with the original source. For that reason, this paper proposes a novel algorithm based on the detection transmission artefacts using visual VQA techniques in order to improve users' Quality of Experience (QoE). The algorithm is based on the detection of main streaming visual errors and artefacts, such as color degradation, frozen frames, complete absence of video or packet losses. The algorithm is included in a quality probe application that is part of a 5G transmission network system for streaming high quality video. The algorithm analyzes the video quality for detecting streaming errors and the application warns the broadcaster for the retransmission of content if necessary. For the evaluation of the algorithm, a database of videos containing different types of errors was used in order to simulate streaming conditions and approach reality. The development of this application is necessary for the introduction of next generation 5G telecommunications networks and the consequent new paradigm of video broadcasting.

KEYWORDS

Streaming, 5G networks, Video Quality, Artefacts, Metrics, QoE

1. INTRODUCTION

Video transmission is one of the dominant applications in the internet nowadays. According to future prediction reports (Cisco Visual Networking Index, 2017), by 2021 it is expected that a million minutes of video content cross the network per second. The new wave in using internet networks is mainly concentrated in viewing contents from different resources, such as Video on Demand (VoD) platforms, which implies that thousands of videos must be accessible at any time. For that reason, users require contents with reasonable quality for sound and image, especially when demanding contents with next generation technical advances, such as increasingly Ultra-High Definition (UHD) resolutions, High Frame Rate (HFR) or High Dynamic Range (HDR) imaging. Finally, users demand mobility, which means that every smartphone is connected to the internet. This connection generates data traffic and the consumption of these data with mobile phone is growing again and again, according to Cisco report (Cisco Visual Networking Index, 2017) global mobile data traffic grew 63 percent in 2016.

In this context, Software-Defined Networking (SDN) (Open Networking Foundation, 2014) and Network Function Virtualization (NFV) (Network Functions Virtualisation, 2012) used in 5G networks appear to be interesting tools for the transformation of the infrastructures used to broadcast contents (Ellerton et al., 2015). The applications and services based on NFV are expected to schedule, coordinate, and control media flows across broadcast and contribution in 5G-network infrastructures. In fact, this way of proceeding consist in virtualizing many of network functions and permit to control media flows. The challenges for 5G mobile networks (Chen & Zhao, 2014) include offering higher capacity, higher data rate, lower latency, lower infrastructure cost, massive using and constantly maintenance of QoE.

The saturation of bandwidth leads to dysfunctions during transmission of data as fluctuation of bitrate, as a consequence of the high amount of information transmitted through the network. This may also be compounded by losses during compression or decompression of content, a light defect in the original content can be amplified during this process. Impacting directly the viewing experience for the user. In order to minimize both the cost and the bandwidth consumption, thus optimizing transmission, the system needs to be able to reconfigure the virtual infrastructure, attending to QoE evaluations.

For that reason, it is primary to evaluate the Quality of Experience (QoE) for the users by using VQA (Video Quality Assessment) and image algorithms. In other words, the module of the system named "quality probe" is able to determine if the content received is a reasonably accurate version of the original one and succeed the users' basic requirements. In the second phase, this quality algorithm is used to inform the broadcast infrastructure that an error has occurred and gives feedback to the adjacent node of the network in order to preserve the quality of the video content. The work collected for this paper focuses on this module that implements metrics for assess quality.

The implementation of a reliable quality model for a video system is a challenge and as a consequence is necessary the identification of most influencing factors (Baraković & Skorin-Kapov, 2013). For that reason, to succeed in that challenge, the following Key Performance Indicators (KPIs) were selected (Reichl, Egger, Schatz, & D'Alconzo, 2010) for developing the model: absence of video, frozen frames detection, throughput, colour errors and packet loss rate.

Much work is developed in the context of Video Quality Assessment (VQA) and QoE definition models. Different some surveys analyze this tasks collecting the proposed metrics for assessing quality focused on visual quality and streaming video technologies, such as the following references (Chikkerur, Sundaram, Reisslein, & Karam, 2011; Garcia & Raake, 2010; Lin & Kuo, 2011; Seufert et al., 2015). The work of Saad (Saad, Bovik, & Charrier, 2014) proposes a blind video quality evaluation model for ubiquitous environments that is non-distortion specific, and works independently of the codec and settings of the video transmitted. This model, used as an example for the work developed in this paper, quantifies motion coherency in video scenes adapting the result to human visual systems.

2. OBJECTIVES

The main objective of this work aims at developing an adaptive and cost-efficient solution available for 5G transport networks based on an algorithm, which is able to analyze image quality independently of the codec and settings of the video transmitted. This solution is part of a broadcast platform that allows a ubiquitous infrastructure integrating network, compute and storage resources, and composes a module for Quality of Experience (QoE) assessment. The purpose of this QoE assessment is to reconfigure dynamically the virtual infrastructure of the content distribution network, in order to minimize both the cost and the bandwidth consumption though transmission optimization.

As the quality assessment reports are generated dynamically, the video reference is not available in the system for comparing to the degraded sequence. For that reason, it is necessary to implement No-Reference (NR) metrics that efficiently detect the four most common transmission errors found in this kind of networks, such as frozen frames, packet loss, absence of video or color errors, at any given point in the network. On the other hand, the disparity of conditions on the video transmitted, such as different resolutions, codecs or bitrate oblige the system to create a blind algorithm that is independent of the conditions of the broadcasted signal. For that reason, the metrics are applied over the decoded video sequence and the streamed flow.

The relevance of the implemented algorithm lies in the consideration of every artefact which might be able to appear when playing a video using streaming technology. Each artefact has its specific features, such as color change, image distortion or specific shapes, and the algorithm should detect this features minimizing the false positives that would reduce the cost and bandwidth. At the end, the application provides the assessment report to the broadcast infrastructure using JSON messages, after evaluation the transmitted signal. These messages are communication to the adjacent network nodes in order to enable bandwidth, routing and quality adaptation control, all over the 5G broadcast network, for service provision.

For evaluating the effectiveness of the quality algorithms, the metrics were tested with sequences included in the ReTRiEVED Video Quality Database (Paudyal, Battisti, & Carli, 2014). These sequences include the most common artefacts that appear when playing video using streaming technology.

3. DESIGN AND IMPLEMENTATION OF THE ALGORITHM

The module known as "Quality Probe", that contains the quality algorithm, operates as a Virtual Network Function (VNF). After testing the quality of the content, it communicates with the monitoring application which take the decision or not to optimize the content delivery allowing the user to enjoy the best quality with the lowest delay, sending a Quality Assessment report through a JSON message, as seen in Figure *1*. Video Quality Assessment (VQA) and monitoring in 5G-Networks.

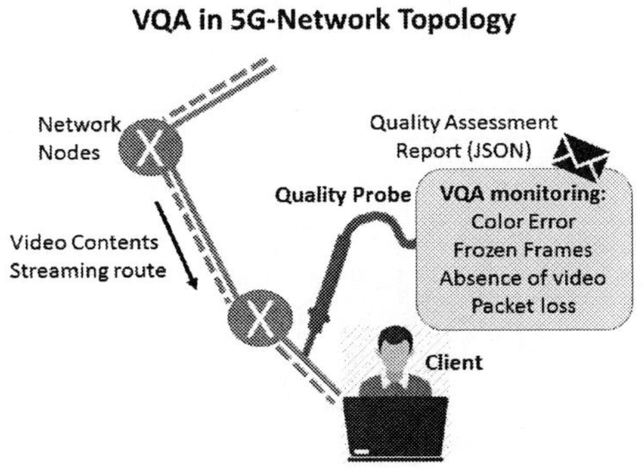

Figure 1. Video Quality Assessment (VQA) and monitoring in 5G-Networks

Network Function Virtualization (NFV) can improve the functioning of traditional networks through service abstraction and by virtualizing functions like computing, storage and resources. In fact, providers implement Virtual Network Functions in software components of the infrastructure like servers or clouds computing systems instead of dedicating hardware especially for this. NFV can pool the signal processing resources in cloud system instead of using dedicated baseband processing units for example. This pooling reduces resource and energy requirements, optimize costs and ensure better performances because of the flexibility of the service. This means that when a network node receives a negative quality report, the system is able to reconfigure, activating only specific terminals in the network instead of activating all the processes as traditional infrastructures would do.

3.1 Algorithms for Artefact Detection

The algorithm which is the basis of the QoE model must detect the basic errors of a typical 5G-network to fulfill the requirements of end users. The design of the algorithm follows the workflow included in Figure *2*. Workflow of VQA Algorithm Implemented, which shows the different paths and transformations applied to the video signal before being processed by the individual quality metrics. In order to be able to detect every issue in a streamed content it is necessary to define which cases mainly occur. This cases include the measurements derived by the metrics implemented for packet loss, color errors or frozen frames detection. First of all, the absence of video is the first step in the process. The metrics use the decoded video composed of captured RGB frames, to obtain the information as the end user receives, simulating the experience by perceived quality.

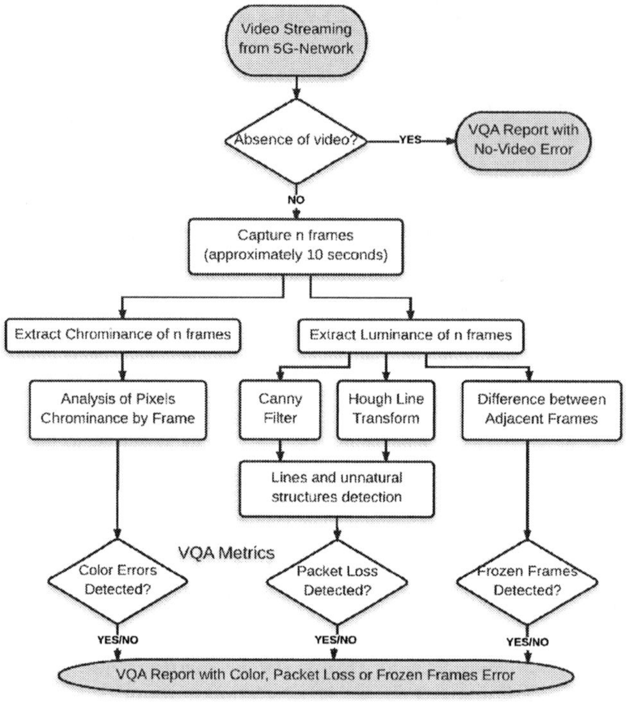

Figure 2. Workflow of VQA Algorithm Implemented

3.1.1 Stalling and Frozen Frames Detection

One of the most common problem occurred when playing a video is the stalling or frozen frames detection. This freezing artefact means that a frame is repeated two or more times instead of changing with temporal evolution according to the frame rate. The code implemented for this detection is based on the comparison between adjacent frames in the video sequence. If a certain percentage of the image remains unchanged then it is considered that the video is frozen, at least one second (25 frames at 25fps or 30 frames at 30fps, for example). The percentage should be carefully chosen to avoid false positives as detecting something frozen whereas it's simply two frame not very different, like in cartoon contents. Furthermore, it is also necessary to consider that in movies we can sometimes see transition screens like black screens or deliberately frozen screens. For that, the code is made in a way that repetition of the detection of frozen frame takes priority over single detection. The formula for detecting individual frozen frames is collected next.

$$frozen.frames(i) \rightarrow if \ \frac{1}{MN}\sum_{y=0}^{N-1}\sum_{x=0}^{M-1}|Y_i(x,y) - Y_{i+1}(x,y)| > \varepsilon$$

where "MxN" are the dimensions of the frame, x and y the spatial coordinates of the pixel, "i" is the number of the frame and "i+1" is the number of the following frame, Y is the luminance function and ε is a threshold approximately 0, in this case 0.1.

3.1.2 Throughput and Color Errors Detection

It is necessary to assure video quality in terms of the average network throughput to fulfill the requirements of end users. Demanded network throughput is important to support the required video quality, avoiding the occurrence of artefacts in form of structures and pixels of unnatural saturated colors that propagate through the frames of the transmitted video sequence. The loss of information is accused both in luminance and chrominance, but the effect in the color component is more visible for human eye, as demonstrated with subjective assessment. For that reason, the algorithm for color error detection is focused on the chrominance component of the decoded image, as seen in the next formula that detects the probability of pixel with values out of the range of natural image colors.

$$f(chrominance(x,y)) = \begin{cases} 1, if\ |chrominance(x,y)| > AChV + \delta \\ 0, otherwise \end{cases}$$

where AChV is the Average Chrominance Value, which is dependent of the number of bits to represent the pixels, for 8 bits this value is 128, chrominance(x,y) is the value of one of the chrominance component of the pixel Cb or Cr, in this case Cb is used because it obtains more accuracy. Finally, δ is a threshold that defines the range of values of chrominance in which the color obtained correspond to a natural image.

$$color.error(i) \rightarrow \frac{1}{MN}\sum_{y=0}^{N-1}\sum_{x=0}^{M-1} f(chrominance(x,y)) > \gamma$$

where "MxN" are the dimensions of the frame, x and y the spatial coordinates of the pixel, "i" is the number of the frame and "i+1" is the number of the following frame, Y is the luminance function and γ is a threshold that indicates the visibility of this factor by the human eye, in this case 0.60 i.e. when 60% of the pixels of the frame are distorted.

The following figure (Figure 3) shows an image corresponding to the sequence with very high throughput "1.r.512.ts", generated with "CrowdRun" original sequence. For this video sequence of 24bppp (8 bits per channel) the value of AChV is 128. Defining δ as 30 for the threshold of natural chrominance values and a γ of 0.6, with a result of 95% of distorted pixels, with is over of the value of γ, then the algorithm detected a color error for this frame. After analyzing all the frames of the array, the probe generates an error inform to give feedback to the streaming system.

Figure 3. Example of Sequence "CrowdRun" (1.r.512.ts) with High Throughput Detected (Right) and the Original (Left)

3.1.3 Packet Loss

During the transmission of the content, some oscillation of the bitrate can appear, typically caused by network congestion, leading to the loss of data. Moreover, almost all contents delivered by streaming are compressed by using compression algorithms (H.264/AVC or H.265/HEVC, for example) which reduce the weight of content to broadcast. This process of compression on the video may amplify the packet loss effect by the propagation of errors through consecutive frames of the sequence. Artefacts included in the image are transmitted through the network and remain visible until the user plays the video. The visualization of Packet loss errors may be present as repeated lines of the frame and undefined structures of color pixels displayed in the areas where information is lost.

This algorithm is able to detect those structures and repeated lines by searching unnatural colored shapes in images, which reflect the areas where packet loss has occurred. In some cases, the information is largely lost and the image is completely changed compared to the original content. For that reason, it is necessary to assure that these structures appear by a degradation process. In this case, some repetitive content like strips or lines appears.

For shape detection, a previous Gaussian filter is used in order to smooth the edges and reduce the possible noise. After that, a canny filter detect the edges included in the image. This filter uses gradient to determine if there are edges (large variation) or not. With a polygonal approximation, we can draw polygons and determine the type of shapes.

The use of the Canny filter allows the edge detection based on techniques of gradient calculation (Islam, Begum, Alam, Amin, & others, 2010). The image is susceptible to the noise present on the raw image, for that reason it is necessary the use of the first derivative of the Gaussian function through the convolution with a Gaussian filter. The result of applying this technique is a smoothly blurred version of the original, whose structures are not affected by the different types of noise that could be present on the image.

Figure 4. Example Of Pixel Unnatural Structures Displayed when Packets Loss Appears (Right) and the Original (Left)

Furthermore, it is possible to check the color inside the detected shape by observing the gradient in the considered area of image. By this way, we can find out artificial colors in the video sequence.

Repeated lines are also common when there are packets lost and most of them are vertical one. By using a Hough Line Transform, it is possible to detect straight lines in an image. And by adding a condition on the angle of the line towards the vertical, the detection is more accurate because the transform only detects straight vertical and horizontal lines, parallel to the framework of the image. The combination of the edge detection technique and the Hough Line transform allow the algorithm to highlight the areas where the image most probably contains this type of error derived by packet loss concurrence. This structures are recognized because they are not common in natural scenes.

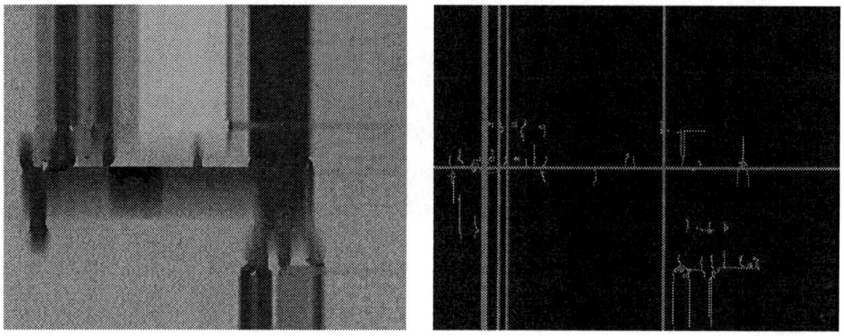

Figure 5. Line Detection with Hough Line Transform in a Frame with Very High Throughput (Right) and the Original Image of Luminance (Left)

4. RESULTS

As mentioned in the objectives section, the sequences included in the ReTRiEVED Video Quality Database were used for testing the algorithm, simulating the most common artefacts as consequence of streaming video in the network. Moreover, sequences with frozen frames were added to these sequences generating the errors with a video editor. The settings of the video sequences used are collected in Table *1*. For more information consult additional descriptions in ReTRiEVED paper (Paudyal et al., 2014).

Table 1. Original Video Sequences detailed on Size in Pixels, FR (Frame Rate), BR (Bit Rate) and length in Seconds

Sequence	Size (pixels)	FR (frames/sec)	BR (Kbps)	Length (s)
Crowdrun (1)	704x576	25	13622	9
Duckstakeoff (2)	704x576	25	7705	9
Parkjoy (5)	704x576	25	11885	8

The videos are characterized with different content and considering key QoS parameters for defining degradation levels: Packet Loss Rate (PLR), Frozen Frames (F) and Throughput (R). For this work, a selection of these sequences were used. The level of impairment or degradation of the sequences selected are collected in Table *2*.

Table 2. Type of Parameter and level of Degradation for the Sequence X (1: Crowdrun, 2: Duckstakeoff, 5: Parkjoy)

Sequence	Degradation	Level of Impairment
X.plr.8.ts	PLR	8% of Packet Loss
X.plr.10.ts	PLR	10% of Packet Loss
X.r.5.ts	R	5Mbps of Throughput
X.r.512.ts	R	512Mbps of Throughput
X.f.50.ts	F	50 frozen frames

The sequences used were streamed in the system and captured by the quality probe to be processed by the QoE algorithm. The significant results obtained from these sequences are collected in Table *3* after being processed by the three main metrics (M2, M3 and M4). Depending on the type of impairment the metric obtains a positive or negative detection of the degradation and quantify the error.

Table 3. Results obtained for Metrics: M1 (Absence of Video), M2 (Frozen frames), M3 (Color errors), M4 (Packet Loss)

Sequence	**M2**	**M3**	**M4**	**Content**
1.plr.8.ts	No error detected	No error detected	Packet Loss error detected in 32 frames	High level of packet loss
1.plr.10.ts	No error detected	No error detected	Packet Loss error detected in 45 frames	Very high level of packet loss
2.plr.8.ts	No error detected	No error detected	Packet Loss error detected in 54 frames	High level of packet loss
2.plr.10.ts	No error detected	No error detected	Packet Loss error detected in 76 frames	Very high level of packet loss
5.plr.8.ts	No error detected	No error detected	Packet Loss error detected in 35 frames	High level of packet loss
5.plr.10.ts	No error detected	No error detected	Packet Loss error detected in 52 frames	Very high level of packet loss
1.r.5.ts	No error detected	Color error detected in 32 frames.	Packet Loss error detected in 12 frames	High level of throughput
1.r.512.ts	No error detected	Color error detected in 65 frames.	Packet Loss error detected in 21 frames	Very high level of throughput
2.r.5.ts	No error detected	Color error detected in 25 frames	No error detected	High level of throughput
2.r.512.ts	No error detected	Color error detected in 62 frames	Packet Loss error detected in 24 frames	Very high level of throughput
5.r.5.ts	No error detected	Color error detected in 35 frames.	Packet Loss error detected in 5 frames.	High level of throughput
5.r.512.ts	No error detected	Color error detected in 72 frames.	Packet Loss error detected in 16 frames	Very high level of throughput
1.f.50.ts	Detected 50 frames	No error detected	No error detected	50 frozen frames
2.f.50.ts	Detected 50 frames	No error detected	No error detected	50 frozen frames
5.f.50.ts	Detected 50 frames	No error detected	No error detected	50 frozen frames

5. CONCLUSIONS

The results obtained with the quality algorithm composed by a collection of metrics demonstrated the validity of the system. The named "Quality Probe" is a necessary module for streaming video contents in 5G networks to fulfill the requirements of end users. The transmission of data by the user device allows the streaming system to improve its performance and ensure to the user a good quality of experience.

Video Quality Assessment enables the analysis of the network state, determining the necessity of providing better quality to the system and the resubmission of low quality video, meaning the convergence between content delivery and 5G networks. The metrics developed for detecting the absence of video, color distortions or frozen frames compose a first approximation to the model that trends expect to be the future 5G multimedia distribution content.

The individual metrics tested with a database of common errors obtain good results for measuring frozen frames, throughput generated errors and packet loss through visual quality techniques, which simulates the perceived experience of the end user, better than QoS traditional metrics, which are not adapted to human eye visualization. First tests highlight the necessity of developing intelligent nodes that are ready to detect common transmission errors to improve the efficiency of 5G networks and increase the users' satisfaction.

The quality algorithm demonstrates the necessity of standardization and deployment of intelligent network nodes that automatically adapt to the 5G network conditions with the objective of improving video transmission, with the enhancement of users' viewing quality.

ACKNOWLEDGEMENT

This work has been partially supported by the EU project "5G Crosshaul: The 5G Integrated fronthaul/backhaul" (grant no. 671598) within the H2020 program (5G Crosshaul Consortium, 2015).

REFERENCES

5G Crosshaul Consortium. (2015). 5G Crosshaul: The 5G Integrated fronthaul/backhaul. http://5g-crosshaul.eu/

Baraković, S., & Skorin-Kapov, L. (2013). Survey and challenges of QoE management issues in wireless networks. *Journal of Computer Networks and Communications, 2013.*

Chen, S., & Zhao, J. (2014). The requirements, challenges, and technologies for 5G of terrestrial mobile telecommunication. *IEEE Communications Magazine*, *52*(5), 36–43.

Chikkerur, S., Sundaram, V., Reisslein, M., & Karam, L. J. (2011). Objective video quality assessment methods: A classification, review, and performance comparison. *IEEE Transactions on Broadcasting*, *57*(2), 165–182.

Cisco Visual Networking Index. (2017). Forecast and methodology, 2016-2021, white paper. *Cisco White Papers, San Jose, CA, USA.*

Ellerton, J., Lord, A., Gunning, P., Farrow, K., Wright, P., King, D., & Hutchison, D. (2015). Prospects for software defined networking and network function virtualization in media and broadcast. In *Annual Technical Conference and Exhibition, SMPTE 2015* (pp. 1–21).

Garcia, M.-N., & Raake, A. (2010). Parametric packet-layer video quality model for IPTV. In *Information Sciences Signal Processing and their Applications (ISSPA), 2010 10th International Conference on* (pp. 349–352).

Islam, M. I., Begum, N., Alam, M., Amin, M. R., & others. (2010). Fingerprint Detection Using Canny Filter and DWT, a New Approach. *JIPS*, *6*(4), 511–520.

Lin, W., & Kuo, C.-C. J. (2011). Perceptual visual quality metrics: A survey. *Journal of Visual Communication and Image Representation*, *22*(4), 297–312.

Network Functions Virtualisation. (2012). Introductory white paper. In *SDN and OpenFlow World Congress, Darmstadt, Germany*. Retrieved from https://portal.etsi.org/nfv/nfv_white_paper.pdf

Open Networking Foundation. (2014). SDN architecture – Issue 1 – ONF TR-502. *SDN Architecture*.

Paudyal, P., Battisti, F., & Carli, M. (2014). A study on the effects of quality of service parameters on perceived video quality. In *Visual Information Processing (EUVIP), 2014 5th European Workshop on* (pp. 1–6).

Reichl, P., Egger, S., Schatz, R., & D'Alconzo, A. (2010). The logarithmic nature of QoE and the role of the Weber-Fechner law in QoE assessment. In *Communications (ICC), 2010 IEEE International Conference on* (pp. 1–5).

Saad, M. A., Bovik, A. C., & Charrier, C. (2014). Blind prediction of natural video quality. *IEEE Transactions on Image Processing*, *23*(3), 1352–1365.

Seufert, M., Egger, S., Slanina, M., Zinner, T., Hobfeld, T., & Tran-Gia, P. (2015). A survey on quality of experience of HTTP adaptive streaming. *IEEE Communications Surveys & Tutorials*, *17*(1), 469–492.

METHODOLOGICAL GUIDE FOR A DATA WAREHOUSING PROCESS

Wilson Castillo-Rojas[1] and Fernando Medina-Quispe[2]

[1]*Informatics Engineering and Computer Science Department, Atacama University, Av. Copayapu 485, Copiapó City, Chile*

[2]*Faculty of Engineering and Architecture, Arturo Prat University, Av. Arturo Prat 2120, Iquique City, Chile*

ABSTRACT

The article describes a methodological guide prepared for the development of a Data Warehousing Process (DWP) in a Chilean University. The goal of this DWP, is to generate indicators of academic productivity. For this, a methodological guide is elaborated, integrating diverse approaches and techniques, such as: specification of information requirements, relational modeling, combined development model of Kimball and Hefesto proposals, ETL process (Extraction, Transformation and Load) with a validation phase of indicators, and integrated and interactive visualizations, for the multidimensional analysis of the indicators with the use of dashboards. In this process, three elements incorporated that, in the opinion of the development team, favored the success and effectiveness of the development of the solution. Firstly, how to specify Key Performance Indicators (KPI) in detail, through the development of a template based on those used to specify information requirements in a software process. Second, to explain the incorporation of a validation phase of the KPI obtained in the ETL process, based on Structured Query Language queries (SQL), and the comparison with the data of the operational systems. Thirdly, integrated visualizations configured with an On-Line Analytical Processing (OLAP) tool, which interactively display the related indicators for the same activity under analysis. Because of this data warehousing process, you get a Business Intelligence (BI) platform based on a DataMart (DM) model with two schemes, one star and another snowflake. The first contains the indicators of teacher productivity, and the second, those of scientific productivity, which satisfy the specifications of the KPI, and defined in agreement with the end users. The methodological guide allowed, on the one hand, the complete development of the process in an appropriate time, and on the other hand, to ensure the quality of the indicators generated through an adequate validation phase.

KEYWORDS

Business intelligence, Data Warehouse, Data Warehousing, DataMart, ETL, OLAP

1. INTRODUCTION

Currently, most organizations use the information to support their strategic decisions. This, in a context of high competitiveness and globalization of markets. In addition, increased data in organizations has created two major problems; The first, to identify the relevant data to follow up the strategy; The second problem, managing a large amount of information by selecting the relevant one for decision making.

The Chilean universities, are not alien to this and are today within a demanding field, with an institutional accreditation system as a process of continuous improvement, and where they must be accountable for all their academic activity. Therefore, universities require not only information systems to provide technological support to their operational processes, but also require computer solutions that provide them with indicators that allow them to measure the performance of their academic and administrative management processes. For this, the use of technologies and tools of massive data analysis is crucial, since they allow the administration and creation of knowledge with the historical information of an organization. Among these technologies are; ETL tools, Data Warehouses (DW), OLAP technology, data mining and others. Technologies and tools that are part of what is now known as BI (Palocsay et al, 2010).

In this context, the article presents and describes an elaborated methodological guide, for the development of a DWP at Arturo Prat University of Chile (UNAP). This DWP, aims at the development of a DM, which allows to obtain indicators of academic productivity of the institution.

The rest of the paper is organized as follows: Section 2 provides a framework for BI concepts and technologies. Section 3 describes in detail the methodological guide carried out for the development of the DWP. Section 4 Presents a use case of the methodological guide described, which corresponds to a DM of academic productivity. In section 5 the conclusions of the work are presented. Finally, section 6 lists the bibliographic references used in the article.

2. BI CONCEPTS AND TECHNOLOGIES

In the modern context, where the consolidation of operational systems and databases that provide technical support in a company, over the years the information accumulated by these systems, becomes large volumes of data. Then comes the need for how to handle it and what to do with it. It's here that the term BI appears, which emerges as a solution to analyze, exploit specific areas of information generating new perspectives and knowledge to support decision making. One of the first definitions of BI appears in Conesa et al (2010) for the year 1958, and then in the 60's give rise to Decision Support Systems (DSS). They then evolve into the Information Systems Executive (ISE), which are more robust systems capable of generating consolidated reports, although these systems fulfill their work in information management, they are still insufficient, since these tools do not have visualization and Exploitation of information, appropriate.

The term BI is formally coined in 1989 by Howard Dresden, a Gartner analyst who defines it as: *"Concepts and methods for improving business decisions using fact-based support systems"* (Venter et al, 2005). Other formal concepts about BI are found in Back (2002) and Golfarelli et al (2004). However, it can be concluded that BI corresponds to the set of strategies and tools focused on the administration and creation of knowledge, through the analysis of existing data in an organization. Although a DW corresponds to the central data repository of an BI system, its design and development are part of what is called DWP.

DW is one of the main technologies of BI, and covers all business areas or processes of the organization. The source of this information comes from different data sources, whether operating systems, calculation templates or plain text files. These data sources are integrated to give it a homogeneous and consistent format. A DW is composed of multidimensional databases called DM, and focus on the analysis of a business area, and provides the necessary indicators (Mazón et al, 2007) (Inmon, 2005).

There are two approaches between the DW and DM concepts; On the one hand, Bill Inmon points out that DM uses a DW to extract information that is stored in a structured form in a relational model, which is known as a top-down approach. On the other hand, Ralph Kimball, poses a dimensional vision for the design of the DW, and states that the union of all the DMs of an organization constitutes the corporate DW, what is known as the bottom-up approach (Kimball et al, 2002).

A classic BI process, it has the following phases and technologies (Vaisman et al, 2014):

1) Specification of strategic requirements; Corresponds to the definition of the BI project, the nature of the business and its purposes, as well as the specification of the KPIs that need to be measured in the organization's processes.
2) ETL process; Has the function of integrating the data coming from the different heterogeneous sources, which may be from transactional systems, text files, spreadsheets, etc. The integration consists of the extraction, transformation, preliminary calculations of the KPI, cleaning and homogenization of data, until the data load in the DW. For this, you can use ETL tools, programming languages and / or SQL relational database.
3) DW; It's the data repository, whose conceptual design is based on a Multidimensional Model (MM). It considers the database as a set of facts or object of analysis, and dimensions that are the points of view from which these facts can be analyzed. The relevant information on the facts is represented by a set of indicators or measures (numerical values). And the descriptive information of each dimension is presented by a set of alphanumeric attributes. The technology used are usually relational databases.
4) Exploitation of the DW; Through data analysis tools such as: OLAP, data mining, report generators and statistical graphs, and in general all types of DSS.

A DWP, corresponds to the process that allows the design, implementation and operation of a DW. Generally, a DWP includes the strategies and technologies described in 1), 2), 3), and 4). In this last point, with respect to the exploitation of the DW, only those that have relation to the online analytical processing (OLAP). Precisely, these are the concepts and technologies used in the work of this article.

3. METHODOLOGICAL GUIDE DESCRIPTION

To develop the DWP, a methodological guide illustrated in Figure 1, with its own variants considered relevant, is elaborated to assure a successful and effective result. As outlined in the introduction, this methodology integrates different approaches and techniques. It consists of four stages: Analysis, MM Design, ETL+V Process, and Analytical Processing.

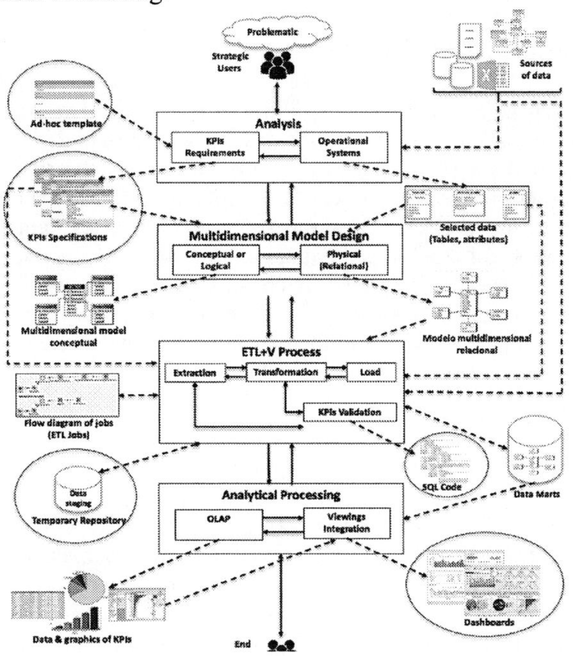

Figure 1. Methodological Guide for the DWP (Own Elaboration)

Each of these stages have defined their inputs and outputs, represented by arrows with segmented line, as can be seen in Figure 1. These stages in turn have a bidirectional sense of operation, which allows to go back to the previous one, or advance to the next, without losing the sense of the DWP. It also establishes the relationship and participation of users, with continuous line arrow and bidirectional, both in the process input and output. The DWP development methodology is based on the classic Kimball DW development model (Kimball et al, 2002), combined with the current Hefesto methodology (Bernabeu, 2010), both of which extract the common phases and merge. It's explained below, each of the stages of the methodological proposal of this work. The bottom-up Kimball approach is used, which means that the DM are built to resolve the specified KPIs.

In this methodology, some elements are considered keys, highlighted in Figure 1 with a circle, these are: ad-hoc template for specifying KPIs, KPI validation with SQL code, and visualizations integrated graphs through the dashboard. This, according to the conclusions of the development team of the DW and the end users, favored the effectiveness and success of the development of the solution.

3.1 Analysis

This initial stage is strongly linked with strategic users. Has two activities; Analysis of KPI requirements, and analysis of operational systems. For the first activity, the entry corresponds to an ad-hoc template designed for the specification of strategic information requirements or KPI. The structure of this template, is considered as one of the key elements in the PDW, and is designed regarding the templates and linguistic patterns of Duran (2000), that are used for the elicitation of information requirements in software projects. This template allows to define and understand clearly, by all strategic users, the indicators obtained, as an interface or tool, in the initial education of the KPI requirements, their analysis, as well as in the validation of each one. The output of this activity is the set of KPIs specified through the designed template.

The second activity of this stage, analysis of the operational systems, its inputs are composed of the data sources of the organization, whether internal or external, plus all information about the data that are available, such as data logical model, metadata, etc. These data sources must be analyzed to check the specified KPIs, and to understand with which data they can perform their calculations, or in case they do not have the ability to obtain them. It has as output this activity, the metadata with the selection of tables, attributes and data, which are necessary to achieve the required KPI.

3.2 Multidimensional Model Design

The outputs of the analysis stage are the inputs in this second stage. There are two activities; The conceptual design and physical (relational) design of the MM or DM, whose outputs correspond to the models under the same name, conceptual and physical respectively. For this, it's necessary to analyze the specified KPIs, together with the metadata of the source sources, to be able to perform the conceptual design.

Also, it's necessary to use a CASE (Computer Aided Software Engineering) tool, where you can use some of the existing graphical notations to diagram the MM, either entity-relationship, UML (Unified Modeling Language), or another. To generate the physical design of the MM, in this case relational since the approach of Kimball is used, it's enough to use the option in the tool CASE to generate it, indicating some parameters like: the database engine, name of the server, and other connection data.

3.3 ETL+V Process

The third stage concerns the classic ETL process, augmented with a fourth activity explicitly incorporated, and called KPI validation. It's the stage that demands the most time, the most complex, and the one that has the most entries and exits. The inputs to this stage are; The KPI specification, the relational MM, the description (metadata) of the selected data, and the original data sources. Their outputs correspond to; Work flow diagram of the ETL process, the temporary repository or staging area, DM loaded with The KPIs, and the validation SQL code.

The ETL+V process, has the function of performing all the extraction and preliminary calculation of the data from the original data sources, which are necessary for the calculation of the KPI, and then be deposited in the relational temporal repository. In this repository, all transformations, calculations, aggregations and validations of data quality are performed. You should also perform the data loading activity to the DM with the already calculated KPIs. However, before loading it's necessary to verify the validity of the KPIs. For this, the validation activity, allows to perform the review of these in an efficient way, using mainly the relational SQL database language to perform the necessary queries, calculations and validations. It's a question of verifying that the obtained KPIs are consistent, with the data integrated in the temporary repository, original data sources, and the DM.

3.4 Analytical Processing

The last stage corresponds to the exploitation and analysis of the information contained in the DM, and for this an OLAP tool is required, with which to generate the multidimensional analysis of the data, and the graphic visualizations of the KPIs. In addition, it's considered as a second activity the integration of visualizations of the different objects of analysis and KPI, using the concept of dashboard (Marcus, 2006), and that allow to provide to end users a comprehensive view of the indicators, through graphical interfaces and interactive reports, of all the information provided by the DM.

4. USE CASE OF METHODOLOGICAL GUIDE IN DWP

4.1 Problematic Description: DataMart of Academic Productivity

In the UNAP, the Institutional Analysis Unit (IAU) is responsible for generating and managing the DM, to be able to provide both qualitative and quantitative reports on the current state of university management of the different areas. On this occasion, the IAU raises the need for the development of a DWP whose objective is to obtain indicators on academic productivity. For this, an analysis of the processes related to academic productivity is carried out. Three fundamental aspects are presented in their activities: teaching, research and linkage with the environment. For this work, agreement is reached to address in the first two labors, since they are the most required in the daily work of the university.

For the teaching activity, the indicators seek to know the distribution of academic staff in the different institutes, venues, faculties and careers of the university, as well as the number of weekly hours devoted to their teaching tasks. It's also important to know the number of full equivalent days that teachers represent in the institution, since it's an indicator that compares with the number of students enrolled, to establish the relationship between them.

As for the research activity, the indicators must allow the scientific production of the university to be established, through measures such as: quantity of publications and research projects carried out by academics from different institutes, venues, faculties and careers. In addition, we seek to determine percentages and rates of increase, between the periods studied. Another important aspect is to know the percentage of teachers with doctor degree who carry out the research work, since with these indicator preventive or incentive measures can be taken.

4.2 Requirements Analysis for KPIs

The taking of requirements is carried out through education techniques, which are used in a software process. A series of executive meetings are held with the two vice chancellors (academic and research), in conjunction with the IAU, to consider the concerns and needs regarding the productivity of academic staff, both in their teaching and research activities. In this way, you can define and specify the required KPIs.

In addition, external requirements, provided by government institutions, are considered, such as: National Accreditation Council (CNA), Information System of Higher Education (SIES), Council of Rectors of Chileans University (CRUCH), and the National Council of Education (CNED). Due to this, an analysis of the reports delivered by these institutions and of their instructions of request of information is made. With both visions, internal and external, the requirements of academic productivity, both teaching and research, are consolidated, using the template ad-hoc requirements, designed for this activity. As a summary, the following is a sample of a teaching KPI, out of a total of fourteen specified (see Figure 2).

Indicator 3	N° Full-time equivalents
Definition or objective	It measures the full-time equivalence, the hours realized by the total of contracted academics.
Periodicity	Annual, semi-annual, monthly
Source	Unit of programming and academic record, Human Resources Unit
Target	External entities: SIES, CNA, CRUCH, CNED, MECESUP projects, Accrediting agencies Internal entities: Rectory, vice-rectories, DFT, Managers, faculties, careers
Dimensions	Branch Year process – semester – month Academic degree Nationality Sex Academic unit Career Education Level Contract type Type of day (full, half-day, etc.)
Formula	$JCE = \frac{\sum TotalJC + TotalJM + TotalJH}{44}$ where: $TotalJC = \left(\sum_{i=1}^{n} AcademicsJC_i\right) * 44$ $TotalJM = \left(\sum_{i=1}^{n} AcademicsJM_i\right) * 22$ $TotalJH = \sum CountHours_i * AcademicsNumberJH_i$ JC = full-time JM = half-day JH = part-time
Observations	For the case of TotalJH, index i represents the number of hours to be multiplied by the number of academics who perform this number of hours.

Figure 2. Indicator: Number of Full-Time Equivalents

It can be observed from this Figure 2, the detailed specification of the indicator that includes not only its description and objective, but also its periodicity, the dimensions involved, to the formulas or metrics, on which the KPIs are calculated. All this information is agreed upon and validated by strategic users, and the template serves as a communication interface throughout the requirements eduction process.

4.3 Operational Systems Analysis

The identification of the sources of data that are necessary for the calculation of the KPIs is continued. For this activity, it's necessary to meet with the Computer and Communications Unit (UNICO) of the institution, together with the IAU, to identify the different models of data involved and select the data sources. After several reviews and analysis of the information systems handled by UNAP, the ones to be used are filtered, resulting in the ones listed in Table 1.

Table 1. Selection of Data Sources to Use

System	Description of the data source
ICON	Accounting and financial system.
SIPER	Personnel System, stores personnel information.
SICDO	Curricular and Teaching System.
GEDO	Online Document Management System.
VRIIP	System that stores research projects, publications and post-graduate programs.

From this activity, the list of the systems containing the data to be used is obtained, and their meta-data, and data logical model. Then, select the tables and attributes that are required for the calculation of KPIs.

4.4 Multidimensional Model Design: Conceptual & Physical

After analyzing the existing requirements and models, two DM are produced. The first one of teaching is of the type Snowflake scheme, where it's done a work of hierarchizing of some dimensions, and reutilization of others. On the other hand, the DM research is a star schema, where the clear majority of its dimensions are created in this work. The list of dimensions used in this DWP, can be seen in Table 2.

Table 2. Dimensions to be used in DM

Dimension	Description
Time	Delivers the temporality to the indicator, has the hierarchies: months, semesters and years.
Academic	It stores the basic information of the academic like: name, date of birth, date of entry, sex and nationality.
Hierarchy	These are: "Associate Professor", "Full Professor", "Assistant Professor", "Instructor", "Without Hierarchy".
Type of contract	It allows knowing the different types of contracts: Full Day, Half Day or Hours.
Academic degree	Degree: Doctorate, Magister, Professional, Licentiate, Technical and Untitled.
Type of activity	Describe the data under which activity you are doing your work: "Teaching" or "Research".
Career	3 different hierarchies: academic unit, location, and level of training.
Type of training	Keep information about the type of subject: General Training or Vocational Training.
Funding Source	Internal (UNAP), or external (public or private).
Knowledge Area	Agricultural and Marine Sciences, Administration and Commerce, Art and Architecture, Natural Sciences and Mathematics, Social Sciences, Law, Humanities, Education, Technology and Health.
Regions	Name of regions
Project Type	The type of project categorizes research or service delivery to a teacher's application for a project.
Project status	Handles the state of the project: adjudicated, in postulation, decreed, or finalized.
Publication format	Manages the status of the project: awarded, in application, Stores the various publication formats: scientific article, chapter of a book, manual or an article review.
Indexing Type	ISI, SCOPUS y SCIELO.
Publication position	Position of the institution in a scientific article.

The indicators of both DM are presented in Figures 3 a) and b), with the respective fact tables made with the indicators specified for the teaching snowflake scheme, and the research star schema.

Figure 3. Facts Tables: a) Teaching, b) Research

4.5 ETL+V Process: Extraction

For this whole process, the Pentaho's Data Integration (PDI or Kettle) tool is used, which allows the ETL process to be modeled with transformation flow diagrams consisting of a set of fixed steps, and encapsulated in integrated flows called job, which allow defining Different execution flows. In the extraction activity, the metadata is used where the selected data sources are registered, in conjunction with the KPI specifications, and the data is extracted and left in an aggregated way, directly in the temporary repository (see Figure 4).

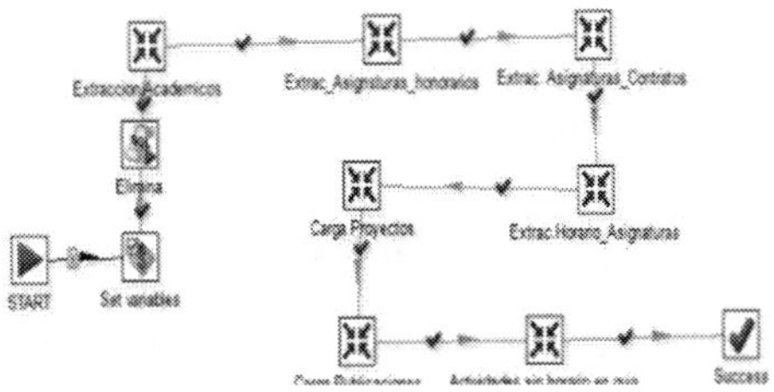

Figure 4. Workflow for the Extraction of Selected Data

4.6 ETL+V Process: Transformation

When designing two DM, it's decided to create a workflow for each one, which allows easier debugging. Figure 5 shows the workflow for the DM that calculates the teaching indicators. In Figure 6, the workflow is presented to calculate the indicators associated with the research activity.

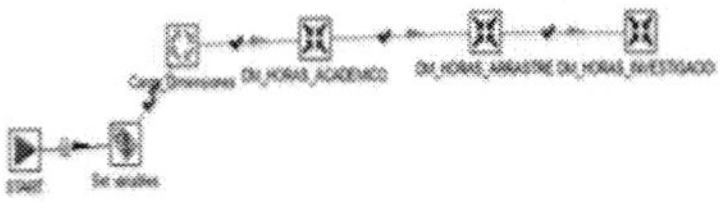

Figure 5. Workflow for Calculating Teaching Indicators

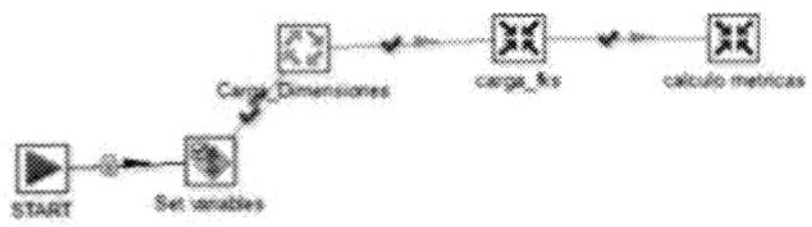

Figure 6. Workflow for Calculating Research Indicators

4.7 ETL+V Process: Load

The load of the fact tables is the most complex part of this stage, where you must carry out the verification of the data loaded in each iteration or change of some node of the transformation. In addition, before loading, must be checked if the estimates obtained are valid in relation to original data.

4.8 ETL+V Process: KPI Validation

It's necessary to verify and validate that the indicators or metrics obtained are the same or like those that can be obtained from the operating systems of origin. For this, it's used like test method, to calculate each indicator by means of SQL instructions to the database of the transactional systems, and then they are compared with results of consultations to the tables of the MM.

4.9 Analytical Processing: OLAP

The results of the DM are presented through the exploitation or visualization of the indicators through the OLAP tool Qlikview. This way, it responds to the requirements defined and raised at the beginning of the project. These results are presented with graphs, which allow visualizing the information and being able to perform the analysis that corresponds. As a sample, a graph of a teaching indicator is shown in Figure 7. In total there are 14 graphs, one for each KPI.

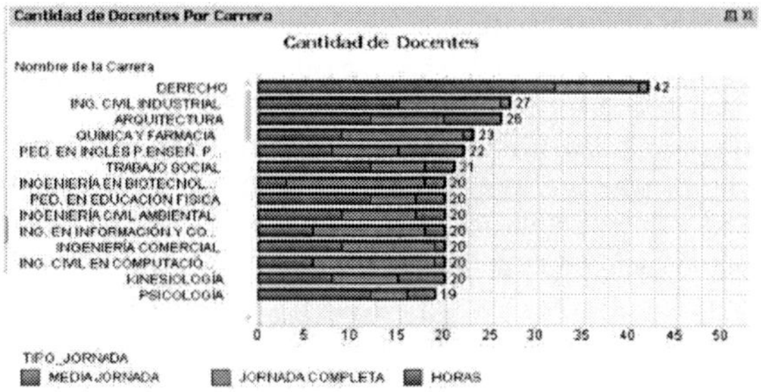

Figure 7. Graph: Number of Teachers per Career

4.10 Analytical Processing: Dashboard

Once the different graphs of the indicators have been generated, they can be integrated into a scorecard format, which allows end users to perform a multidimensional analysis with different controls and interaction mechanisms. The dashboard shown in Figure 8, presents a consolidation of all indicators related to teaching in which, in the extremes, both left and right are the dimensions managed by the model, which can be selected to change the graphs presented inside the panel.

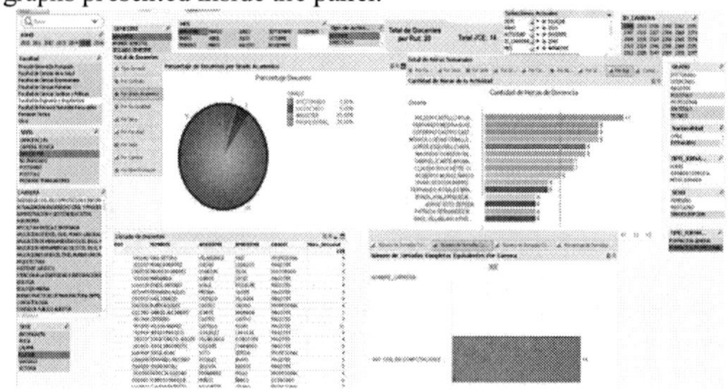

Figure 8. Teaching Indicator Panel

The data highlighted, means the current selections of the model, the ones with a white color are possible selections that are related and the gray color means that those values are not related or linked to the current selection of the information. Figure 9 shows all the indicators of research projects in a dashboard, which can be visualized by different dimensions. The graphics are grouped in a container element in which the tab is displayed on the dimension in which the indicator is shown with some associated graph.

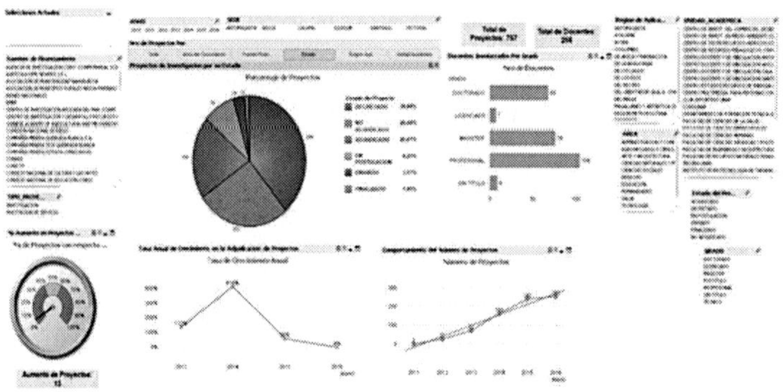

Figure 9. Research Panel Indicators

5. CONCLUSIONS

The final results obtained from this project give an account of the reality in terms of the indicators initially proposed for teaching and research for the academic body of the Institution.

The results generated a great impact on users, since in some cases these indicators were not above the average of the institution, on the contrary, there were cases that the results presented were quite good and acceptable, however, this presentation of the Results, it implies that some attention is given to this, to support decision making from a strategic perspective and thus maintain and improve indicators in general.

Another important aspect, is that the results obtained generate new knowledge to the user about the information and data handles with respect to academics, since with them he can contextualize, compare and orient everything he has already handled previously on this topic.

The proposed methodological guide, allowed to conclude the DWP development, in a successful way and in a timely manner, leaving in evidence the effectiveness of each of the stages established in this one.

REFERENCES

Book

Kimball, R. and Ross, M., 2002. *The Data WarehouseToolkit - The Complete Guide to Dimensional Modeling*. Jhon Wiley and Sons, Inc. Second edition.

Inmon, W. H., 2005. *Building the Data Warehouse*. Jhon Wiley and Sons, Inc. Third edition, ISBN 0-471-08130-2.

Duran, A., 2000. *A Methodological Environment of Requirements Engineering for Information Systems.* PhD thesis University of Seville, Spain.

Journal & Conferences

Back, T., 2002. Adaptive business intelligence based on evolution strategies: some application examples of self-adaptive software. *Information Sciences*. Vol. 148, Issue 1-4, pp. 131-121.

Golfarelli, M., Rizzi, S. and Cella, I., 2004. Beyond Data Warehousing: What's Next in Business Intelligence. *In: Proceedings of the 7th ACM international workshop on data warehousing and OLAP*, pp. 1-6. USA, ISBN 978-0-07-067752-4.

Palocsay, S.W., Markham, I.S. and Markham, S.E., 2010. Utilizing and teaching data tools in Excel for exploratory analysis. *Journal of Business Research*. Vol. 63, Issue 2, pp. 191-206.

Bernabeu, R., 2010. HEFESTO: Metodología para la Construcción de un Data Warehouse. Córdoba, Argentina.

Conesa, J. and Curto, J., 2010. Introduction to Bussiness Intelligence. Barcelona: Ed. UOC, ISBN 978-84-9788-886-8.

Venter, M., 2005. Business Intelligence Initiatives: Failures Versus Success. *Interdisciplinary Journal*. Vol. 4 No 1, ISSN 1684-498X.

Mazón, J. N., Trujillo, J. and Lechtenborger, J., 2007. Reconciling requirement-driven data warehouses with data sources via multidimensional normal forms. *Data & Knowledge Engineering*. Vol. 63, Issue 3, pp. 725-751.

Vaisman, A. and Zimányi, E., 2014. Data Warehouse Systems Design and Implementation. *Springer Series: Data-Centric Systems and Applications XXVI*, 603 p. ISBN 978-3-642-54654-9.

Marcus, A., 2006. Dashboards in Your Future. *The Art of Prototyping*. Vol. 13, Issue 1, pp. 48-60.

MEASURING MESSAGE PROPAGATION AND USER INFLUENCE IN TWITTER DATA

Vishali Narayana, Ashwin Kumar TK and KM George
Department of Computer Science, Oklahoma State University, Stillwater, OK, USA

ABSTRACT

Twitter data has potentially unlimited value and facilitates information diffusion at an exponential rate. Twitter also aids users with a common interest to create a network. Twitter, being a popular micro-blogging network provides an effective way to measure information diffusion in terms of speed, strength and user influence. This paper is based on previous works on models related to topic (information) diffusion and user influence. A topic is defined by a set of keywords. This paper concentrates on the implementation of algorithms for computation of diffusion of a topic in Twitter. The degree of influence of the users who tweet on the topic is also addressed. We have presented two different approaches to compute user influence based on potential of a topic. We compare two diffusion models proposed in the literature, namely potentials and connections. For testing and empirical analyses we gather and analyze tweets related to "*flu*", "*food poisoning*", and "*politics*".

KEYWORDS

Information diffusion; User influence; Topic potential; Degree of Influence; Twitter

1. INTRODUCTION

Online social media generates a prodigious wealth of real-time data and allows millions of people to produce and consume content. It has become a standard platform for information diffusion used by people from all walks of life. The most commonly used social website Twitter facilitates information diffusion at an exponential rate. Twitter is a social network, which allows users to exchange messages of 140 characters or less, known as Tweets. Tweets can be text-based or they can contain multi-media such as images or video and links. In Twitter users who "*follow*" a user can see tweets of that user. The "*follow*" feature allows one to build a network of peers with common interests [Adamic, L. A. and Glance, N. 2005]. Thus, tweets provide a large corpus of text for information mining. There are several information diffusion models present in the literature. Each model attempts to capture specific information from the tweets. One of the models proposed in [TK, A.K. et al, 2015] addresses the propagation of topics and their strengths in Twitter as a function of time. The authors define a concept of potential (which depend on the tweet text) and present formulae to compute the potential. Further they approach user influence from a temporal point of view based on tweets and provide a formula to compute influence of users at a point in time from the potential. This paper presents algorithms to calculate topic potential proposed in [TK, A.K. et al, 2015] and applies them to selected domains and topics. In addition to this we also outline two approaches to assign influence measures to users based on their tweets or retweets and implement them. The objectives of this research are 1) review several diffusion models, 2) develop and test algorithms to build time-series based on the models given in [TK, A.K. et al, 2015] in a Hadoop environment, and 3) to compare the performance of the model against other models. From that viewpoint, this research contributes to big data (Twitter) analytics by developing and validating tools to mine information from tweets. This paper concentrates on implementing algorithms for calculating the strength of information contained in a topic at an instance of time and assign it as the topic potential. A second diffusion model for topics in twitter data outlined in [Yang, J. and Counts, S. 2010] it is used for comparison of results.

2. RELATED WORK

This paper focuses on the general topics of information diffusion and user influence model and hence related research on models has been reviewed. Online networks are more focused on sharing information and have been studied extensively in the context of information diffusion [Asur, S. et al, 2011]. The widely popular use of Twitter have created very large corpus of information for analysis. Several models assume that the information diffuses from one user to another such as spreading of an epidemic [Rogers, E.M. 2010]. There are many investigations done on number of people influenced, the speed and geographic range of propagation [Cha, M. et al, 2010] [Li, C.T. et al, 2013], diffusion flow model [Song, X. et al, 2007] [Yang, J. and Counts, S. 2010], probability of influence [Goyal, A. et al, 2010]. In [Guille, A. et al, 2013], the authors introduced a T-BaSIC model that models the information diffusion through a directed network of users with diffusion function and time-delay parameters. In [Du, N. et al, 2014], a random graph of users is first sampled from the distribution induced by a particular diffusion model and then a function is defined for node reachability in the sampled graph. The expectation of this function is the influence for the random graphs. The authors suggested that a sum over conditional probabilities is used to learn the influence function. The salient features of the models reviewed are summarized in Table I. A more detailed summary can be found in [Zaman, T.R. et al, 2010].

Table 1. Comparison of Various Information Diffusion Models

Model	Graph-based	Regression	Diffusion Measure	Influence Measure	Predictive
Topic Diffusion Model	YES	NO	YES	YES	NO
Predictive Model T-Basic	YES	NO	YES	NO	YES
Diffusion Network Model	YES	YES	YES	NO	NO
Social Graph and Cascade Graph Model	YES	NO	YES	NO	NO
Probabilistic Collaborative Filter model	NO	NO	YES	NO	YES
Indegree, Retweets and Mentions Model	NO	NO	NO	YES	NO
Influence Independent of Diffusion Model	YES	NO	NO	YES	NO
General Threshold Model	YES	NO	YES	YES	YES

3. MODEL DEFINITION AND IMPLEMENTATION

This section provides a formal definition of the topic diffusion model and all the terms used in the model in detail.

3.1 Topic Potential Model

The topic diffusion model proposed in [TK, A.K. et al, 2015] models topic propagation in tweets. The authors introduced a weight associated to every topic called topic potential. A weight associated to the tweet is called tweet potential. The tweets related to a topic form the nodes of a diffusion network. Edges of the network represent retweet relation. User interests, user familiarity, curiosity and several other factors affect the information diffusion [TK, A.K. et al, 2015]. The authors assumed that all the above features affecting the information diffusion are present in the tweets themselves. The authors defined the topic and potential as follows:

Topic: A topic is a set of keywords $L = \{\alpha_1, \alpha_2, \alpha_3, \alpha_4 \ldots\ldots \alpha_k\}$ associated with weights $\gamma_1, \gamma_2, \gamma_3 \ldots\ldots \gamma_k$ with the normalizing condition $-1 <= \sum \gamma_i <= 1$. If $\gamma_i < 0$, then the keyword will influence the topic negatively. (In this paper, when appropriate an n-gram is also used as a keyword).

Level: Each tweet is associated to a level. The levels of the tweets from the diffusion network are computed as follows. The root tweet i.e. original tweet will have a level 0. If a tweet with level 0 is retweeted, then the level of the retweet is $0+1$. In general, if the retweet with level i is retweeted, then the new level becomes $i+1$. In other words, the level captures the depth of a tweet measured by retweets and it is interpreted as velocity of diffusion. The tweet potential is computed based on the levels. The tweet potentials are summed up for detecting the topic potential for particular dates. Information diffusion is calculated by computing the topic's potential. The relevant definitions are listed below:

Potential: A weight called potential *P(tw)* of the tweet *tw* is associated relative to a topic *L*. It is computed as shown in Equation 1. In Equation 1, $I(\alpha_i) = 1$ if keyword α_i is present in the tweet *tw*, 0 otherwise.

$$P_L\,(\mathrm{tw}) = \sum_{1}^{k} \gamma_i\, \mathrm{I}(\alpha_i) \qquad (1)$$

Topic Potential: The potential of a topic *L* at time *t* is calculated as shown in Equation 2. In Equation 2, *L* is the level of tweet *tw* at time *t*. The values at each time contribute to the topic potential time-series.

$$P_L(\mathrm{t}) = \sum p(tw) \qquad (2)$$

3.2 Potential Based User Influence Model

A tweet and its retweets form a tree with the original tweet representing the root and retweets representing the internal nodes. A child node is the retweet of the parent node. Each node also contains the user of the tweet or retweet and the timestamp of the tweet. An example of such representation is shown in Figure 1. The level of the node in the tree corresponds to the level of the tweet or retweets. In this subsection, we define two methods to compute user influence based on the tweet potential.

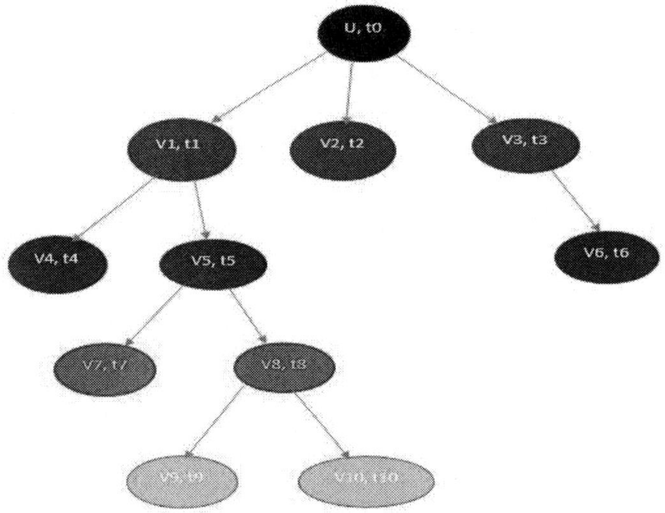

Figure 1. Diffusion network indicating different levels of a tweet at different times

Multi-level Marketing Method: In this method, the potential of a retweet is distributed to all its ancestors. The formula used in this method is shown in Equation 3. In Equation 3, where *A* is the user, *t* is the time, *p(TW)* potential of the tweet, ρ a scale factor and *l* is the level relative to *A*.

$$Influence(A, t) = \sum_{l} p(TW)\rho^{l} \qquad (3)$$

Root-user Method: In this method, only the original user derives credit for all retweets. The formula used is the same as above with the restriction A is the root user.

3.3 Connection Model

The connection model is proposed in [Yang, J. and Counts, S. 2010]. Connected user count is used as diffusion measure. A time-series of connected users is built in the diffusion network model. The date range depends on when the data is collected. When a user 'B' retweets a tweet of user 'A', we say that the users 'B' and 'A' are connected as B → A. The number of such connections is counted for every day to form a time-series. For example, a user 'A' has tweeted or retweeted a tweet on day 1. A user 'B' has retweeted A's tweet or retweet on day 2. We say a connection exists on day 2 from B → A and the count of the connections on day 2 is one. These counts are plotted against the dates to obtain a connection time series graph. This graph is compared with graph of topic potential time-series discussed in the section above, which is one of the objectives of this research.

3.4 Model Implementation

In this section we briefly outline the implementation aspects. We assume that the data is appropriately filtered and grouped. The algorithms developed and implemented use five fields of a tweet, namely text, timestamp, user, owner and owner timestamp. For simplicity, we have assumed that the weight associated to all key words is equal to one.

Potential Computation: A tree called ***User-Tree*** is constructed for the set of tweets or retweets with the same text. The date of tweet or retweet is stored in the node along with the user of the tweet. The root node of the tree is a dummy node. The children at the first level represent the user who created the tweet called root user for that particular tweet and the rest of the users who retweet are connected as descendant nodes to the root user based on their retweets. The levels are calculated for the tweet from the User-Tree on the available dates. For any date multiple levels are possible due to retweets of different users. We construct the levels of a tweet text for the analysis period and store it as a dictionary "*tweet_levels = {date: level}*". Observe that this is equivalent to a time series of tweet levels for a tweet text. To compute the potential time series, the formula defined in the previous section is used.

Connection Computation: Ignore the original tweet. For retweets check if there is a connection on a given date (this_timestamp). If there is no connection on this_timestamp, we add user → owner connection on this_timestamp. If some connections already exist on this_timestamp, we check if this_user (tweeted user) is present in the connections. If the user doesn't exist, we then add the user → owner connection. If the user already exists, we process the next input lines. Finally, we count the number of connections for each day to build the time series.

User Influence Computation: We group all the similar tweets by comparing the tweet_text (text of the tweet) in a tweet_list dictionary. Now, we sort all the tweets based on this_timestamp using an inbuilt sort function in python. For every tweet in the input file, we compare its owner with the user of other tweets. Whenever a match is made, we increase the level by one associated with the parent tweet. Finally, we get the levels of every tweet in the input file. To compute the user influence, we use the formula: $p(TW) = k\rho^l$ where k is the number of key words present in the tweet. This will be the contribution of the tweet to user's influence. This influence will be summed over all tweets based on the scheme (Multi-level marketing or Root-user) used to obtain the user influence.

4. EMPIRICAL RESULTS

In this section we describe the results obtained by analyzing Twitter data collected in three domains, namely flu, food poisoning, and politics. We compute topic potential for different topics in these datasets and compare the results to the connection model of information diffusion.

4.1 Diffusion Measured by Potential

We consider flu as a single topic defined by the keywords given in Table 2. The data used for analysis are in the date range September 9, 2015 to November 26, 2015. All the keywords are given a weight 1. This can be partially justified by the fact that the distribution of the keywords in the tweet corpus can act as weight.

Table 2. Keywords defining Flu topic (Source: CDC[1])

Fever, chills, cough, sore throat, runny nose, stuffy nose, body ache, muscle ache, headache, fatigue, vomiting, diarrhea, aches, water eyes, flushed skin, exhaustion, sneezing, cough, weakness, congestion, oseltamivir, zanamivir, tamiflu, relenza, permavir, rapivab, re: drink fluids, humidifier, gargling salt water, warm blanket, decongestants, cough drops, throat lozenge, acetaminophen, tylenol, ibuprofen, advil, motrin, nuprin, antihistamine, pseudoephedrine, phenylephrine, aspirin, naproxen, aleve, delerium, dizziness

[1] https://www.cdc.gov

We associated three topics with the data related to food poisoning. Topics and defining keywords obtained from the CDC[1] are shown in Table 3.

Table 3. Keywords and topics related to food poisoning data

Topic 1	Topic 2	Topic 3
Headache, nausea, vomiting, body aches, cough, dizziness, tiredness, sweats, hoarseness, fainting, flushing, fainting, sore throat, malaise, anorexia, fatigue, joint pain, back pain, depression, low blood pressure, thirst, muscle cramps, restlessness, rapid heart rate, loss skin elasticity, dry mucous, diarrhea, weakness, anemia, rash, red eyes, jaundice, stiff neck, confusion	Diarrhea, nausea, stomach pain, fever, headache, body aches, dry throat, dizzy, sleepy, fussy, cry, fatigue, abdominal pain, dark urine, jaundice, vomiting, loss of appetite, clay colored stool	Stomach pain, bloody stools, fever, abdominal pain, vomiting, diarrhea, mucus stools, abdominal discomfort, weight loss, dehydration, stomach cramps, bloating, loss appetite, reduced vision, redness, muscle pains, itchy skin, constipation, heart problems, breathing problems, eyes swelling, chills

The third data set we studied is related to politics, which is divided into two topics. The keywords and their topics are obtained from CBS news[2] is shown in Table 4.

Table 4. Keywords and topics related to politics data

Topic 1	Topic 2
Abortion, civil rights, education, families, children, welfare, poverty, principles, values	Budget, economy, corporation, government reform, tax reform, social security, jobs

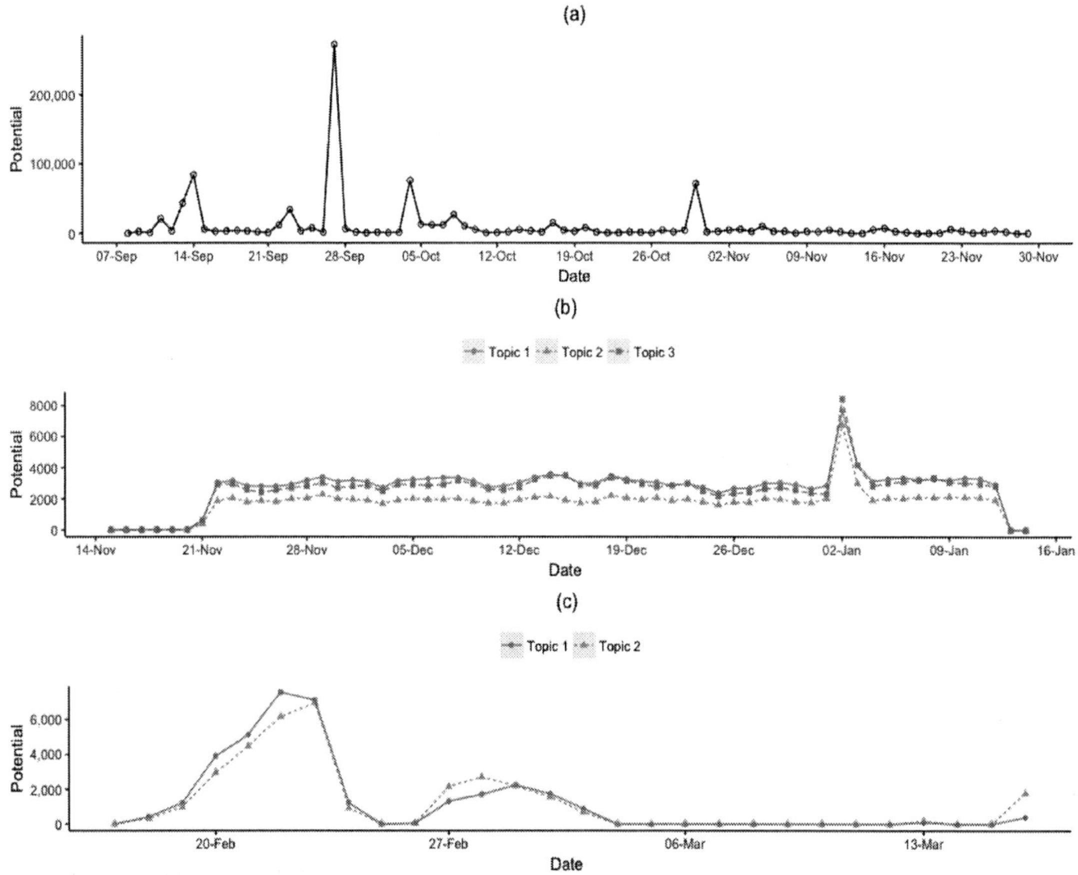

Figure 2. Topic potentials. (a) Flu dataset; (b) Food poisoning dataset; (c) Politics dataset

2 http://www.cbsnews.com

Figure 2 shows the potentials of topics for the flu, food poisoning and politics datasets. Figure 2 (a) shows potential time series for flu dataset with $\rho = 2$. The potential has a peak on September 27, 2015. Figure 2 (b) depicts the topic potential series for the food poisoning data. By examining Figure 2 (b), it is obvious that all topics behave the same including their peaks indicating that same level of keywords are contained in every topic. Figure 2 (c) shows the topic potential for the politics dataset. Potentials of both these topics have similar highs and lows. The peaks could be caused by news stories related to topics in the case of (a) and (c) [Narayana, V. 2017]). In the case of (b), New Year festivities possibly is the reason for the spike.

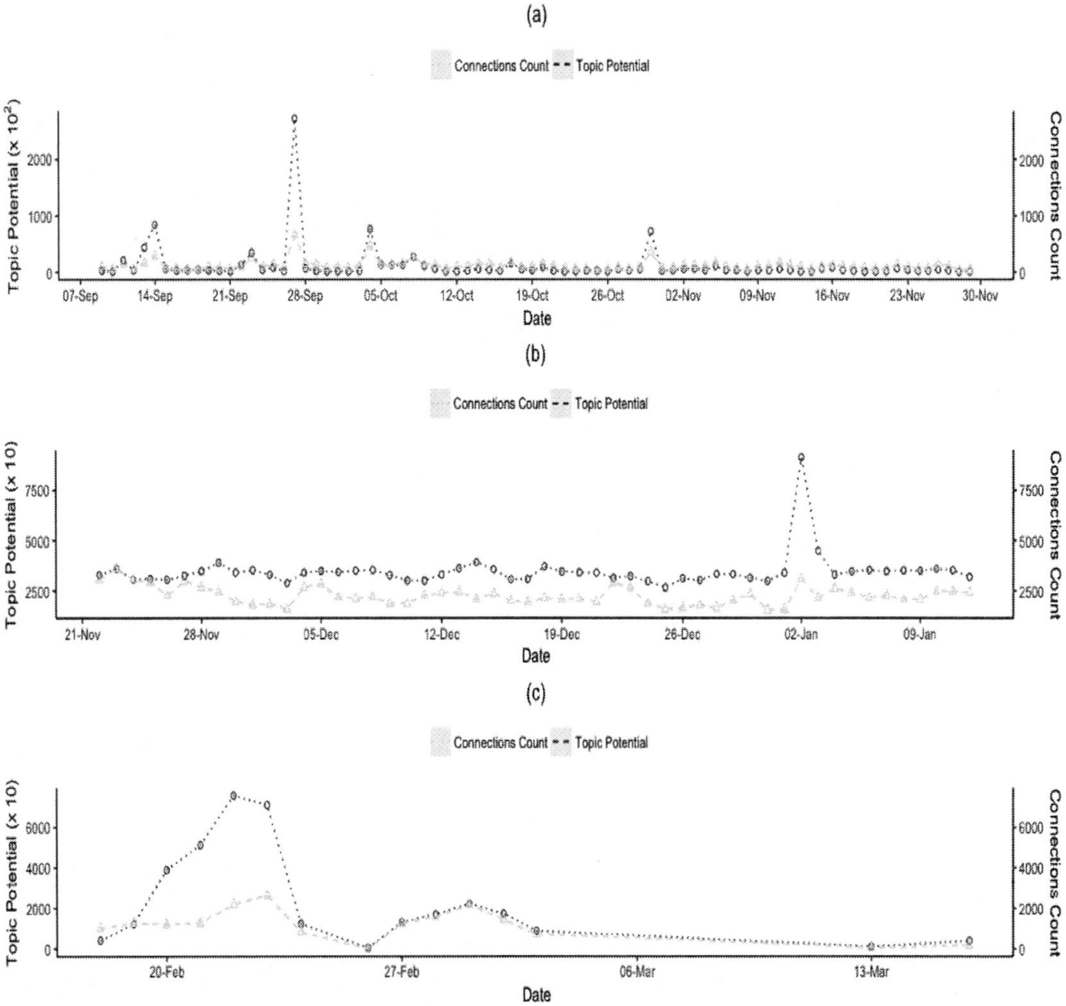

Figure 3. Connections vs. Topic Potential. (a) Flu dataset; (b) Food poisoning dataset; (c) Politics dataset

In Figure 3, the potential model is compared against the connections model. It shows the relation between the connections model and the topic potential model for all topics studied. Each graph in Figure 3 provides quantitative information derived from the tweet text that is useful for time-series based analysis and predictions. The two series represent connections and potential. The peaks in the graph are related to news items or holidays (for details ref to [Narayana, V. 2017]). It can be observed that most of the time, the potential model and connection model move in the same direction. In that sense, they validate each other.

Tweet count is another measure we employed. Figure 4 compares potential against tweet count for one of the data sets (politics). Visual inspection indicates no correlation between topic potential and tweet count. As the potential depends on the keywords, it can measure the sentiment strength of the topics. On the other hand, tweet count measures the user activism in the topic. As such, the two measures serve different aspects of topics.

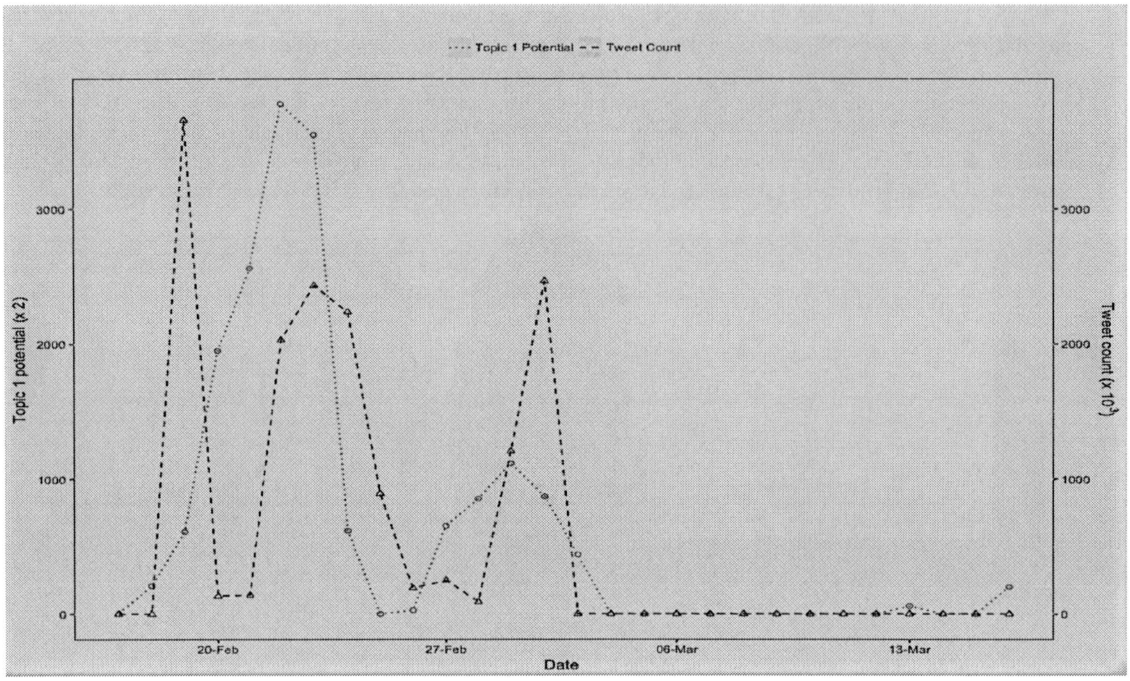

Figure 4. Tweet count vs. Topic 1 potential for politics dataset

4.2 User Influence

User influence measures the influence of a user in Twitter. A twitter user is said to be influential if the user's tweets are retweeted by other users. There are a few researchers who compute the influence of a user based on the number of followers of the user, number of times that user is being mentioned in other users' tweets, and the number of retweets for the tweet posted by the user. In this research, we compute user influence based on different models and provide a comparison. We compute the top five users based on Multi-level Marketing method described in section 3.2 and compare their ranks in other methods. The results are shown in Tables 5, 6, and 7. The results show that the Multi-level Marketing and Root-user method behave the same two out of three cases. They differ substantially from the other three methods, which have substantial difference among them. This occurs because the measurement approaches and data used differ even though same tweet set is used. In practical situations our approach provides an alternative interpretation than just the tweet connections. Also we can observe that the followers and retweets have high correlation.

Table 5. User Influence – Flu data

User	Multi-level marketing rank	Root user rank	Mentions rank	Retweets rank	Followers rank
U1	1	1	1458	8490362	8419574
U2	2	2	1145	61524	1473
U3	3	3	4105	8815444	8769553
U4	4	4	1819	9288452	9278728
U5	5	5	345	2959	949

Table 6. User Influence – Food poisoning data

User	Multi-level marketing rank	Root user rank	Mentions rank	Retweets rank	Followers rank
U1	1	1	13	997	27074
U2	2	7	6	102	4604
U3	3	8	11	4	3353
U4	4	11	1871	218828	28349
U5	5	15	2821	362138	30373

Table 7. User Influence – Politics data

User	Multi-level marketing rank	Root user rank	Mentions rank	Retweets rank	Followers rank
U1	1	1	1191	11023	25743
U2	2	2	1414	553933	27235
U3	3	-	659	5023	3591
U4	4	3	1410	1153	6974
U5	5	-	3021	4055	88203

5. CONCLUSION

The objective of this research is to develop software tools for the analysis of information propagated via microblog medium, which can be termed big data due to their volume and velocity of propagation. In this paper we focus on the Twitter platform. The models use weights and connections and are language independent. Our work makes use of previous work on information diffusion models and user influence models for Twitter data proposed in the literature. We have developed and implemented algorithms to compute topic potential and user influence measure proposed in [TK, A.K. et al, 2015] and the diffusion measure (number of connections) proposed in [Yang, J. and Counts, S. 2010]. Based on the user influence measure defined in [TK, A.K. et al, 2015], we developed and implemented two methods named Multi-Level Marketing and Root User. We have also considered influence measures proposed in [Cha, M. et al, 2010] for comparison. We collected data related to "*flu*", "*food poisoning*", and "*politics*" to test the algorithms. Based on the results obtained by applying our algorithms to the data collected we can make the following claims:

1) Implementation of algorithms works as expected and can be applied to any Twitter data collected in JSON format.
2) Two diffusion models have similar performance in identifying peak points. So the models may be used for corroboration of findings.
3) User influence rankings vary with the models. Keywords could influence ranking.
4) More empirical analysis is required for validation, which is considered future work.

For future work, we propose to implement other models and build an analytic tool set for analyzing Twitter data.

REFERENCES

Adamic, L. A. and Glance, N., 2005. The political blogosphere and the 2004 US election: divided they blog. *Proceedings of the 3rd international workshop on Link discovery*. pp 36-43.

Arias, M. et al, 2013. Forecasting with twitter data. *In ACM Transactions on Intelligent Systems and Technology*, Vol. 5, No. 1, pp 8.

Asur, S. et al, 2011. Trends in social media: Persistence and decay. *Proceedings of 5th International AAAI Conference on Weblogs and Social Media*. pp. 434.

Bakshy, E. et al, 2012. The role of social networks in information diffusion. *Proceedings of the 21st international conference on World Wide Web*. pp. 519-528.

Cataldi, M. et al, 2013. Personalized emerging topic detection based on a term aging model. *In ACM Transactions on Intelligent Systems and Technology*, Vol. 5, No. 1, p.7.

Cha, M. et al, 2010. Measuring user influence in twitter: The million follower fallacy. *Proceedings of the 4th International AAAI Conference on Weblogs and Social Media*. pp. 10-17.

Domingos, P. and Richardson, M., 2001. Mining the network value of customers. *Proceedings of the 7th ACM SIGKDD international conference on Knowledge discovery and data mining*. pp. 57-66.

Du, N. et al, 2014. Influence function learning in information diffusion networks. *Proceedings of International Conference on Machine Learning*. pp. 2016-2024.

Fan, L. et al, 2014. An individual-based model of information diffusion combining friends' influence. *In Journal of Combinatorial Optimization*, Vol. 28, No. 3, pp.529-539.

Fang, X. et al, 2013. Predicting adoption probabilities in social networks. *In Information Systems Research*, Vol. 24, No. 1, pp.128-145.

Gabielkov, M. and Legout, A., 2012. The complete picture of the Twitter social graph. *Proceedings of the ACM conference on CoNEXT student workshop*. pp. 19-20.

Goyal, A. et al, 2010. Learning influence probabilities in social networks. *Proceedings of the 3rd ACM international conference on Web search and data mining*. pp. 241-250.

Guille, A. et al, 2013. Information diffusion in online social networks: A survey. *ACM Sigmod Record*, Vol. 42, No. 2, pp.17-28.

Guille, A. 2013. Information diffusion in online social networks. *Proceedings of the SIGMOD/PODS Ph.D. symposium*. pp. 31-36.

Kwak, H. et al, 2010. What is Twitter, a social network or a news media? *Proceedings of 19th international conference on World Wide Web*. pp. 591-600.

Li, C.T. et al, 2013. Modeling and evaluating information propagation in a microblogging social network. *Social Network Analysis and Mining,* Vol. 3, No. 3, pp.341-357.

Narayana, V. 2017. Message Propagation and Social Influence in Twitter, MS Thesis, Oklahoma State University.

Rogers, E.M. 2010. *Diffusion of innovations*. Simon and Schuster, New York, USA.

Song, X. et al, 2007. Information flow modeling based on diffusion rate for prediction and ranking. *Proceedings of 16th international conference on World Wide Web*. pp. 191-200.

Taxidou, I. and Fischer, P.M. 2014. Online analysis of information diffusion in twitter. *Proceedings of 23rd International Conference on World Wide Web*. pp. 1313-1318.

TK, A.K. et al, 2015. An Empirical Approach to Detection of Topic Bubbles in Tweets. *Proceedings of IEEE/ACM 2nd International Symposium on Big Data Computing*. pp. 31-40.

Tumasjan, A. et al, 2010. Predicting elections with twitter: What 140 characters reveal about political sentiment. *Proceedings of 4th International AAAI Conference on Weblogs and Social Media*. pp. 178-185.

Yang, J. and Leskovec, J. 2010. Modeling information diffusion in implicit networks. *Proceedings of 10th International Conference on Data Mining*. pp. 599-608.

Yang, J. and Counts, S. 2010. Predicting the Speed, Scale, and Range of Information Diffusion in Twitter. *Proceedings of 4th International AAAI Conference on Weblogs and Social Media*. pp. 355-358.

Zaman, T.R. et al, 2010. Predicting information spreading in twitter. *In Workshop on computational social science and the wisdom of crowds*, Vol. 104, No. 45, pp. 17599-601.

Short Papers

USING INFORMATION TECHNOLOGY TO ACCESS MEDICAL EMERGENCY INFORMATION WORLDWIDE

Judith Born[1], Michael Storck[2], Jan Wohlmann[1], Sarah Krudwig[3], Alexander Vogel[4] and Christian Juhra[1]

[1]*University Hospital Muenster, Office for eHealth , Hüfferstraße 73-79, 48149 Münster, Germany*
[2]*Institute of Medical Informatics, University of Muenster, Albert-Schweitzer-Campus 1, 48149 Münster, Germany*
[3]*CompuGroup Medical Deutschland AG , Maria Trost 21, Koblenz, Germany*
[4]*DATATREE AG, Heubesstraße 10, 40597 Duesseldorf, Germany*

ABSTRACT

Due to the increasing mobility of patients, a cross-national information exchange of relevant medical data in case of emergency is becoming more and more important. In Germany, the German Medical Association developed a medical emergency dataset (MED), which provides the possibility to store information on prior diagnoses, medications, allergies and other emergency-relevant information on the German Electronic Health Card. Since the MED can only be decrypted with a German electronic health professional card and cannot be accessed abroad, the objective of this work is to develop a concept for an alternative secure technical solution for a widened access to emergency-relevant patient data via the World Wide Web. This could be achieved with a two-factor authentication via QR-code provided by the patient and an additional authentication provided by an external organization.

KEYWORDS

Health Information Exchange, eHealth, Emergency Treatment, Emergency Dataset

1. INTRODUCTION

A safe, seamless and rapid health information exchange can be critical to the provision of safe and efficient medical care (Finnell and Overhage, 2010; Reis et al, 2017; Shapiro et al, 2007). Particularly in cases of emergency, where the patient may be unconscious and cannot be asked about prior diagnosis, allergies or current medication, this information can be vital.

Accordingly, several studies have shown that providers of emergency medical care have a strong interest in obtaining pre-existing patient information at the point of care (Born et al, 2015; Finnell and Overhage, 2010; Shapiro et al, 2007). However, information is often lacking (Stiell et al, 2003).

In order to facilitate access to vital patient data in case of necessity, there are currently efforts in many countries to improve the availability of electronic patient data in emergencies (Juhra et al, 2017).

In Germany it is defined by law that physicians create emergency datasets on request of their patients from 2018 onwards. As a basis, the German Medical Association developed a medical emergency dataset (MED), which can contain information on prior diagnoses, medications, allergies, implants, contact persons and other relevant emergency information. The MED is intended to be stored on the German Electronic Health Card (EHC) by authorized health professionals.

In addition to the MED, a dataset with information about the locations of important personal patients' statements (called PSP) such as end of life decision can be saved on the EHC. For data protection reasons both datasets – MED and PSP - can only be decrypted with a German electronic health professional card.

Therefore, access to MED and PSP will be limited to the area of Germany exclusively, and the patient data will not be accessible by foreign health professionals when individuals are traveling abroad. In consideration of the rapidly increasing worldwide travel activities – for 2030 1.8 billion international tourist arrivals are forecasted worldwide (World Tourism Organization, 2015) – this is a clear limitation of the utility.

Since a safe exchange of health information across national borders is a particularly relevant as well as complex issue, in 2016 the three-year project Timely Information in Medical Emergencies (T.I.M.E.) started its research in the field of emergency data management. The project is funded by the European Union and the Federal Ministry of Health, Equalities, Care and Aging (MGEPA) of North Rhine-Westphalia. One of its main objectives is to develop a prototype for a secure technical solution for a widened access to emergency-relevant patient data via the World Wide Web and to evaluate its usability.

The technical details of the concept and its intended use within Germany were already described in Storck et al (2017, in press). In this paper, the focus will therefore be on the description of the intended international use.

2. ACCESSING MEDICAL EMERGENCY INFORMATION

2.1 Patient Summery for Emergencies

The Patient Summary for Emergencies (PSE) is based on the MED developed by the German Medical Association (Bundesärztekammer - BÄK) and the gematik for the EHC. An enhanced dataset was developed, which is compatible with the original MED datamodel of the BÄK to ensure interoperability with the emergency dataset on the EHC. Additional information like imaging, discharge letters and laboratory results were added to the dataset under the heading 'Emergency-relevant findings and documents (EFD)', to provide comprehensive information for the practicing emergency physicians.

The prototype is currently developed by CompuGroup Medical (CGM). CGM provides physician information systems for more than 50% of family physicians in Germany. The existing infrastructure and components of CGM will be used for the implementation. Nonetheless, the concept can be generalized and developed in the same manner by other manufacturers.

Figure 1 shows the basic concept of user rights in creating, updating, accessing, and releasing the PSE. All information stored in the PSE is encrypted with state of the art encryption algorithms and can only be accessed by authorized users.

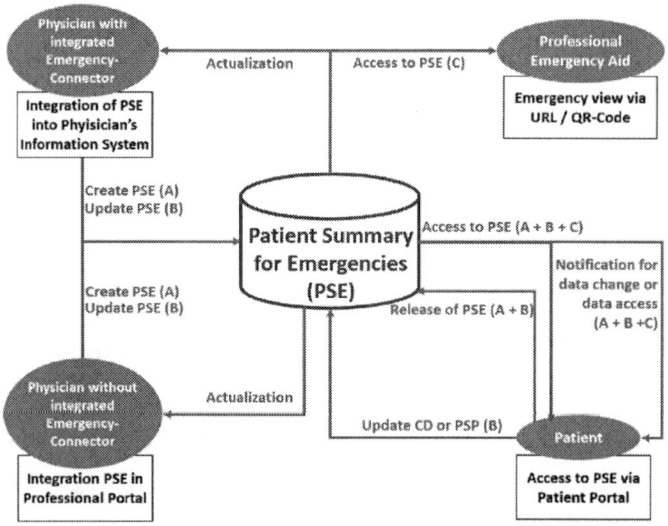

Figure 1. Architecture overview: The physician creates (A) or updates (B) PSE for the patient (left side). The patient has to release the changed PSE (bottom right). The emergency professionals can access the PSE (C upper right)
Source: Storck M. et al, 2017 (in press)

The patients' data is only temporarily stored on the clients' devices. After closing the application but at the latest after three hours the data will be deleted automatically. The access to the personal and medical information is managed by the patient him-/herself. The patient has the possibility to revoke the consent on storing information in the PSE and to delete the data stored in the PSE at any time. The patient receives a notification when his/her information is changed by a physician and has to consent to the new emergency dataset.

2.2 Reading the Emergency Dataset in Case of Emergency Outside of Germany

In order to access the information stored in the PSE considering patient rights to privacy, it must be ensured that only medical professionals can have access to the data. In Germany, this can be accomplished by using a professional registration such as the health professional card or other professional authorizations provided by an organization like the German Medical Association or aid organizations, who can proof the accreditation of the medical professional.

However, since there is no global authorization as a health professional, this concept cannot be used outside of Germany. Two solutions are possible:

- The patient gives full access to his PSE to anybody for a limited period of time. Thus, anybody who scans the QR-Code within the specified period of time can access the whole PSE without any authorization mechanisms in place. This solution provides easy access to the data leaving the level of data security low.
- A second level of authorization can be provided by an external organization, such as a travel insurance company. In this case, the healthcare professional outside of Germany needs to call this organization to get an access code to the patients PSE. Only the combination of the QR-Code and this access code will allow access to the PSE. While the access to the data demands another level of authorization, providing a high level of data security, gaining access to the data is not as easy as in the first solution.

2.3 Evaluation of the Emergency Dataset in Canada

To investigate the usability of the MED in an international context, in 2017 / 2018 a paper-based evaluation study will be conducted together with the University of Victoria (Canada) and the University of British Columbia (Vancouver, Canada). Since the medical emergency datasets were first created in German, for the international evaluation eight randomly selected MEDs were translated into English by a doctoral student of medicine. Every translated MED is to be reviewed by Canadian emergency physicians as well as paramedics on the basis of fictitious emergency scenarios. In addition, a focus group of physicians and paramedics will be conducted to get more information about their perception of the utility of the MED. Moreover, requirements for setting up a globally available emergency dataset will be discussed within the focus group.

3. CONCLUSION

With the increasing mobility of patients, an information exchange of relevant medical data in case of a medical emergency is becoming more and more important. Modern information technology can provide solutions to exchange these data in a secure way cross border. This exchange of personal health data has been promoted by other initiatives like the pilot project Smart Open Services for European Patients (epSOS), a six-year initiative which ended in 2014 (epSOS, n.d.). Even if there are content similarities between the epSOS Patient Summary and the official German MED, the primary application area of patient summaries is in doctors' offices or hospitals. Consequently, the use of this data sharing approach does not appear to be transferable to (pre-hospital) emergency care. Exchanging data cross border implies interoperability standards like IHE XDS. However, such standards addressing the emergency dataset do not exist currently and their development should thus be considered.

Using a two-factor authentication via QR-code provided by the patient and an additional authentication provided by an external organization a secure online access to relevant medical data in case of emergency is possible. If the user wishes easier access to the data in case of emergency, a non-restricted access to the data is also possible. Leaving both options open, the user can decide if he prefers a faster or a more secure access to his relevant medical data in case of emergency.

REFERENCES

Born J. et al, 2015. The Emergency Data Set for the German Electronic Health Card - Which Benefits Can Be Expected? *Studies in health technology and informatics,* Vol. 2015, No. 212, pp. 206-210.

epSOS – Smart open Services for European Patients, n.d.. About epSOS. *URL: http://www.epsos.eu/home/about-epsos.html* [Accessed: 12th July 2017]

Finnell J.T., Overhage J.M., 2010. Emergency Medical Services: The Frontier in Health Information Exchange. *AMIA Annual Symposium Proceedings,* Vol. 2010, pp. 222-226.

Juhra C et al, 2017. NFDM-Sprint. Evaluation der Anlage von Notfalldatensätzen mit Unterstützung der Praxis-EDV in einem Netzwerk von Hausärzten und einem Krankenhaus. *URL: https://nfdm.gematik.de/sites/nfdm_gematik/content/e5/e545/e551/gemAB_NFDM-Sprint_Abschlussbericht_Anlage2_UKM2017.pdf*, pp. 6-8 [Accessed: 6th September 2017]

Reis Z.S.N. et al, 2017. Is There Evidence of Cost Benefits of Electronic Medical Records, Standards, or Interoperability in Hospital Information Systems? Overview of Systematic Reviews. *JMIR Medical Informatics*, Vol. 5, No. 3, pp. e26.

Shapiro J.S. et al, 2007. Emergency Physicians' Perceptions of Health Information Exchange. *Journal of the American Medical Informatics Association,* Vol. 14, No. 6, pp. 700-705.

Stiell A. et al 2003. Prevalence of information gaps in the emergency department and the effect on patientOutcomes. *Canadian Medical Association Journal,* Vol. 169, No. 10, pp. 1023-1028.

Storck M. et al, 2017 (in press). A secure architecture to provide medical emergency dataset for patients in Germany and abroad. *MedInfo 2017.*

World Tourism Organization (UNWTO), 2015. UNWTO Tourism Highlights. URL: http://www.e-unwto.org/doi/pdf/10.18111/9789284416899 *[Accessed: 21st June 2016]*

APPLICATION OF DATA MINING TECHNIQUES ON OLYMPIC DATA

Eric Chagas Farias[1], Marco Aurélio Schünke[1], Paulo Rodrigo Pedroso da Silva[2] and Carlos Mário Dal'Col Zeve[1]
[1]*Universidade Luterana do Brasil (Ulbra) – Curso de Ciência da Computação – Campus Guaíba, Brazil*
[2]*Universidade Luterana do Brasil (Ulbra) – Curso de Educação Física – Campus Guaíba, Brazil*

ABSTRACT

This work seeks to explore the current scenario of news related to the Olympic Games of Rio de Janeiro 2016, using the process of knowledge discovery in databases. With the increase of the news divulged in the scope of the olympic sports, it is tried to relate the most diverse adjacent subjects like Olympic with its games in its totality and with this to identify patterns and relations for the vision of the producers of the content in the disclosure of news on games Olympic. The motivation of this analysis is to be able to understand what the current scenario of news related to the Olympics, how much access to this content in relation to the other inserted in the page, which is the content of these publications about each of the related Issues and who is the producer of this content, which feeling about the content and interest in the interrelation of these issues.

KEYWORDS

Knowledge Discovery, Data Mining, Olympic Games

1. INTRODUCTION

With the 2016 Olympics being held in Brazil, in the city of Rio de Janeiro, an increase in the number of information arising from the dissemination of this event is expected through media vehicles of all genres, such as newspapers, television and mainly on news and social networks.

Based on this information, the present work explores the publications available on the WEB to understand the current scenario of the news that addresses the Olympic games theme in order to discover knowledge related to this domain.

To this end, the official website of the Olympic Games on Facebook, "The Olympic Games", which is one of the fan pages (fan-oriented content pages) with the largest number of followers worldwide and also one of the main To Olympic sports, as well as the official page of the Olympic Games Rio 2016, a Brazilian page created in 2009 especially for the Olympic games based in Brazil, being pertinent to understand the current scenario of publications related to this theme.

1.1 Motivation

The search objective is to understand the current scenario through of publications in official website of the Olympic Games of the Facebook in the Brazil. Official website "Olympic Games" is fan pages with the largest number of followers worldwide and also the social network main to Olympic sports.

The intention is to reveal factors that influence interactions, through the process of knowledge discovery in databases and making use of natural language processing techniques in order to meet the expectation this work.

1.2 Theoretical Grounding

1.2.1 Data Mining

According to Cardoso and Machado (2008), data mining or data mining is one of the techniques used in the discovery of knowledge in databases, and is responsible for revealing knowledge that is implicit in large amounts of information stored in the databases. Being able to predict future events, trends and behaviors based on the analysis found in the information bases, making possible, for example, decision making.

"Data Mining (DM) - is one of the most effective alternatives for extracting knowledge from large volumes of data, discovering hidden relationships, patterns, and generating rules for predicting and correlating data, which can help institutions make faster decisions or , Even to achieve a greater degree of confidence. "(GALVÃO & MARIN, 2009).

Data can be obtained through web crawler, or specific online crawler for social networking site Facebook, which according to Rouse (2016), a crawler is software that scans and stores information, contained in a web page, to attach to a research catalog. Crawlers are scheduled to visit certain sites and update the information previously cataloged or add new discovered pages; complete sites or certain contents can be obtained through this tool.

1.2.2 Processing Data

According to Castro, Mattos and Simões (2009), the process of knowledge discovery begins at the stage in which data are prepared, such as a selection of data to represent the content addressed, or to discard irrelevant content.

Resources are made for information retrieval, showing models of textual collections; Analysis of the data, identifying the terms of the text finding patterns; and a data transformation, which makes the data usable, all techniques used to make data preparation efficient.

For the treatment of data, an Eurekha tool, which second author, Wives (2011), is a software that makes grouping of documents (in English clustering), which groups them based on. These are identified by words or concepts present in the texts.

1.2.3 Natural Language Processing

Natural language processing (PLN) is the ability to process objects of a linguistic nature through computational systems, being a subarea of Artificial Intelligence, which can be defined as the ability to process linguistic data that can be used by humans; Which differs from Corpus linguistics (LC) as the study of the language in large scale use with computerized support and statistical treatment, with the aim of highlighting responses with the different uses of large linguistic data sets, in the identification of Patterns of use and combinatorial of these samples (FINATTO, LOPES & CIRULLA, 2015).

Natural Language Toolkit (NLTK) is a platform built on the Python programming language to work with natural language processing. Composed of a set of text processing libraries, it is able to classify, analyze, catalog and organize semantically the data contained in Corpora.

In order to obtain the statistical data, techniques of analysis of occurrences of words can be used.

2. METHODOLOGY

A Crawler was used to obtain the data, from the obtained data the corpus formation process was applied with the aid of a Web Crawler provided by Facebook, an API that allows making use of Facebook Query Language (FQL) for extraction Content of the social network pages.

In Figure 1, official page of the Olympic Games on Facebook, which has more 10 million Users and which has daily publications. In this stage data were collected from the period 2010 to 2016, in order to outline an overview of the publications considering data from the 2012 Olympics, which occurred in London, and it is possible to relate the publications that occurred before the event, during the event and after the event.

Figure 1. The Olympic Games page

To the work we used Apache web server, the PHP language to implementation of Web Crawler to capture get the messages published. In the messages published were obtained data such as the date and time of the messages, the number of likes and comments of the post.

For the data treatment, the Eurekha tool, developed by Wives (2011), will be used to remove irrelevant or inconsistent terms, so that the information generated can be reliable, for example punctuation, accentuation, articles, prepositions, Some conjunctions and numerals.

In the data mining stage, natural language processing will be used. The Natural Language Toolkit (NLTK) platform will be responsible for the interpretation of the corpus, where techniques for occurrence analysis of words and probabilistic data to the classifications will be used.

Using the N-grams language model, it will be possible to know which word occurs most in the corpus, the two words that occur most together and the three words that occur together, using Unigram, Bigram, and Trigram.

All steps are part of the process of knowledge discovery in database, used as main tool and serving as a guide for the development of the project. Its final step is the evaluation and representation of knowledge, where an area expert will be scaled to analyze the information found in order to discover knowledge by interpreting the patterns and interactions of these themes.

Because of this stage, a corpus was built with two different followings, the first was with the publications of the official page of the Olympic Games on Facebook "The Olympic Games", which has more than 15 million tanned, the main page related to the subject Olympics around the world, counting on posts natively in English. Posts were collected from 2006 to 2016, involving the 2008 Beijing Olympics, London in 2012 and Rio de Janeiro in 2016.

The second follow-up was to create a second corpus with Portuguese posts only for purposes of comparison with the information found in the corpus about the Olympic Games. For the construction of this second corpus a Brazilian page was used, "Rio 2016", which is the official page of the Olympic Games Rio 2016 and has a total of more than 4 million tanned, mostly written in Portuguese, but also Some posts in English; This page was created at the end of 2009, having all your posts accounted for at work.

In the natural language processing stage, NLTK (Natural Language Toolkit) software was used, which is responsible for the accounting of the words in the corpus bringing statistical data and analysis techniques into the word count, the data were processed and as a result we have the 10 Unigram words in order to try to find some pattern, Table 1 shows the frequency of the words that occurred the most, in the "The Olympic Games" fan page found in the corpus:

Table 1. Plot(10) NLTK

Palavras	Frequência
olympic	501
games	250
olympics	177
london	150
winter	129
http	100
rio	98
photo	94
fans	91
youth	89

In Figure 2 shows the 10 Unigran that occurred most in the corpus Rio2016, referring to the posts of the Olympic Games Rio 2016.

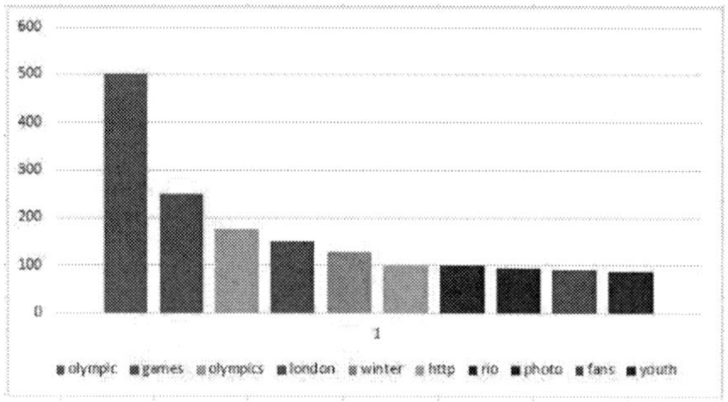

Figure 2. Unigram

In Figure 3 it is evidenced the 10 Bigram that occurred more in the corpus Rio2016, referring to the page posts of Rio 2016 Olympics.

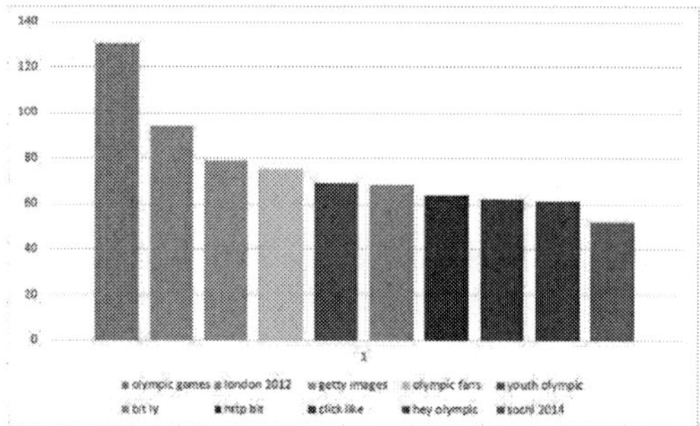

Figure 3. Bigram

In Figure 4 shows the 10 Trigrams that occurred most in the Rio2016 corpus, referring to the Rio 2016 Olympics page posts.

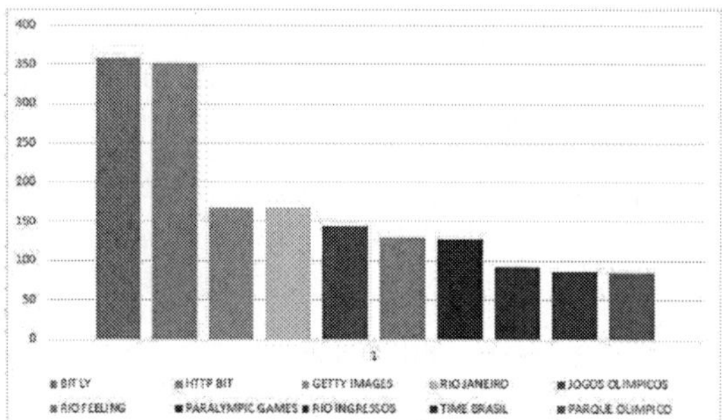

Figure 4. Trigram

In order to identify issues such as feelings and emotions of the people about the Olympics, the Unigram technique was used, using the same data mining tools used to process the postings, in order to account for the words that occurred most in the comments made in the Postings of the page The Olympic Games during the period of the Olympics.

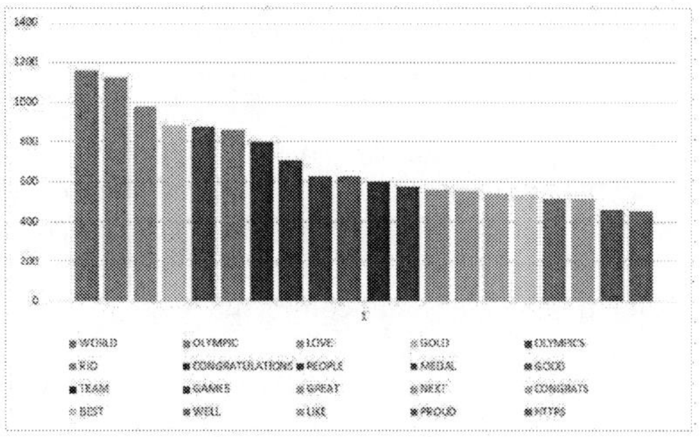

Figure 5. Words that reveal feelings

All the comments made on the page postings during the Olympic Games (05/08/2016 to 08/21/2016) were selected for analysis; Figure 5 shows the 20 words that most occur in comments during the Olympic Games.

3. CONCLUSION

The present work presented the analysis of the current scenario about news related to the Rio 2016 Olympic Games, held in Brazil, since an increase in the information generated on this topic was observed by the various content generators present in the media.

For the task of analysis, the social network Facebook was defined as the object of study, two of its biggest fan pages related to the theme Olympic games identified here, "The Olympic Games" in English and the official page of the Olympic Games "Rio 2016" , The first with 15 million tanned and the second with 4 million, covering a follow-up of interactions relevant to the study.

The use of techniques of data mining, data processing and natural language processing has sought to discover database knowledge, applied to the Olympic games, in order to analyze patterns, and thereby understand what is in evidence in this Scenario, the view of the producers of content on the theme, relation of the main topics covered with the others related to the theme, and also present the feeling present in the comments of the news in relation to the games.

With the application of the technologies raised, it was possible to carry out all the proposed steps, and to answer the questions that make up the objective of the work. It was verified in the analysis of the postings of the page The Olympic Games, the word that occurred more was "Olympic", reinforcing its tendency to deal with the Olympic theme, already the official page of the Olympic Games Rio 2016, the most frequent word was "Rio" ,Reinforcing the reference to the city of Rio de Janeiro as named entity.

Other relevant points were in the analysis of the words that appeared in sequence, where it was possible to perceive that links to other sites are very frequent in the publications, mainly for sites in the purchase of tickets, the site of the Paralympics that was a most frequent subject; Another point still to observe the words together was in the relation of the announcer with the interlocutor, where in the page The Olympic Games this relation showed up with the sequences "Olympic Fans" and "Hey Olympic Fans" indicating that the page was directed Directly to the interlocutor, which did not occur with the official page of the Olympic Games Rio 2016, where the publications were more formatted at the news level.

With the analysis of the statistical data, it was observed that the most frequent words of corpus The Olympic Games together, add up to 14% of all words found in the corpus, while the 100 most frequent ones correspond to 43%, indicating that these words are very frequent In the speech and end up shaping most of the publications being the focal point of the news, same situation for the corpus of the official page of the Olympic Games Rio 2016, with the 10 most frequent words together adding up 13% while the 100 most frequent together represent 30% of the Corpus, this more balanced in the distribution of words, even the word Rio being alone 6% of the whole corpus.

Regarding the comments related to emotions in the page The Olympic Games, the most frequent was "Love", when analyzing the word in its context next to the complete commentary, it was possible to realize that the word occurred related to diverse contexts, first directly to the games And also in actions that the commentators were carrying out, causes, products and purposes. With comments expressing emotions with negative polarity, much is dealt with in relation to the games and to the commentators' sentiment regarding the political and socio-economic conditions of the host country of the 2016 Olympic Games.

With this results presented, the expectation of the work was met, as well as, evidenced the technologies used learned during the course to carry out the study. Presenting the main points related to the Olympic games held in Brazil, with the two main pages of fans of the social network Facebook, being one of the main vehicles of virtual interaction, it was possible to perceive the current scenario of the news related to the Olympic games, the view of the producers Content, their main themes, and adjacent subjects beyond what they think by analyzing the feelings in posts and comments.

REFERENCES

Cardoso, Olinda Nogueira Paes; Machado, Rosa Teresa Moreira. *Gestão do conhecimento usando data mining: estudo de caso na Universidade Federal de Lavras*, Lavras: [Universidade Federal de Lavras], 2008.

Tronchoni, Alex B; Pretto, Carlos O; Rosa, Mauro A; Lemos, Flávio A. Becon. *Descoberta de conhecimento em base de dados de eventos de desligamentos de empresas de distribuição*, Porto Alegre: [Pontifícia Universidade Católica do Rio Grande do Sul], 2010.

Galvão, Noemi Dreyer; MARIN, Heimar de Fatima. *Técnica de mineração de dados: Uma revisão da literatura*, São Paulo: [Universidade Federal de São Paulo], 2009.

CRAWLER Definition. TechTarget, Where Serious Technology Buyers Decide. Disponível em: <http://searchsoa.techtarget.com/definition/crawler> Acesso em: 03 de abril de 2016.

Castro, Flaviana dos santos; MATTOS, Merisandra Côrtes de; SIMÕES, Priscyla Waleska Targino de Azevedo. *Mineração de Textos na Saúde por Meio da Utilização de Ferramenta Eurekha*, Criciúma: [Universidade do Extremo Sul Catarinense], 2007.

EUREKHA. Instituto de Informática da Universidade Federal do Rio Grande do Sul. Disponível em: <http://www.inf.ufrgs.br/~wives/wiki/doku.php?id=eurekha> Acesso em: 03 de abril de 2016.

Finatto, Maria José Bocorny; Lopes, Lucelene; Cirulla, Alena. Processamento de Linguagem Natural, Linguística de Corpus e Estudos Linguísticos: uma parceria bem-sucedida, Uberlândia: [Universidade Federal de Uberlândia], 2015.

NLTK 3.0 documentation. *Natural Language Toolkit*. Disponível em: < http://www.nltk.org/> Acesso em: 03 de abril de 2016.

Hanai, Tuka Al. *Lexical and Language Modeling of Diacritics and Morphemes in Arabic Automatic Speech Recognition*, Cambridge: [Massachusetts Institute of Technology], 2014.

Fonseca, Stella Oggioni da; NAMEN, Anderson Amendoeira. *Mineração em bases de dados do INEP: Uma análise exploratória para nortear melhorias no sistema educacional brasileiro*, rio de Janeiro: [Universidade do Estado do Rio de Janeiro], 2016.

APACHE About. Apache HTTP Server Project. Disponível em: < https://httpd.apache.org/> Acesso em: 15 de maio de 2016.

PHP Documentation. PHP :Hypertext Preprocessor. Disponível em: <http://php.net/> Acesso em: 15 de maio de 2016.

Barbosa, Eduardo Batista de Moraes; SENA, Galeno Jose de. *Data Information System to Promote the Organization Data of Collections – Modeling Considerations by the Unified Modeling Language (UML)* São Paulo: [Universidade Estadual Paulista], 2011.

EXPLORING DATA USE TO IMPLEMENT E-GOVERNMENT IN HIGHER EDUCATION A CASE STUDY

Diego Buenaño-Fernández[1], Sergio Luján-Mora[2] and W. Villegas-Ch[1]
[1]*Facultad de Ingeniería de Ciencias Agropecuarias, Universidad de Las Américas*
Av. de los Granados E12-41y Colimes Quito - Ecuador
[2]*Departament of Software and Computing Systems, University of Alicante*
San Vicente del Raspeig, Alicante, España

ABSTRACT

E-government is a permanent commitment of the central administration to improve the relationship with citizens, through the effective and efficient exchange of services, information and knowledge. All this supported by Information and Communication Technologies (ICT). In the university field, e-government involves the application of ICT in the operational processes (research, teaching and community & service), administrative support and above all in the strategic processes of university management. A fundamental element on which the implementation of e-government platforms is based is the administration of institutional data. From this data it is feasible to obtain crucial information to make strategic decisions that benefit all stakeholders. In this sense, the Data Warehousing (DWH) and the techniques of data mining (DM), are technological tools of support to the management of the data. Universities generate large amounts of data daily, however these data are not being used adequately as a basis for strategic decision making. A common problem that is evident in institutions of higher education is to find computer systems that operate autonomously, this implies that many processes are decoupled and the extraction of information becomes very complicated. This article explores the use of data mining for strategic decision making in private universities in Ecuador. The study is carried out through an analysis of the websites and strategic plans of the institutions, where the use of DM or DWH tools can be identified.

KEYWORDS

E-government; E-governance; Higher Education; Data Mining

1. INTRODUCTION

Institutions of higher education (HEI) are constantly seeking new ways to improve the quality of the services they provide to their stakeholders through the use of information and communication technologies (ICT). This set of initiatives organized as part of strategic planning is entitled electronic government (e-government).

HEI have implemented ICTs in several processes within their own environment such as teaching, learning, research, development, innovation and university management, linkage with society and interaction with students, parents and graduates. The most relevant advances in this area have been in teaching - learning processes online. However, the demand for ICT-based services continues to increase. The adaptation of ICT to e-Government activities in a university can improve the quality of the services it provides, whether external or internal (M.J.V., 2015).

There are several technologies related to information management that are used to support the management of e-government. In the literature reviewed (Kumar et al., 2014) the use of three complementary technologies has been observed: Data Warehousing (DWH), Online Analytical Processing (OLAP) and Data Mining (DM). This article analyzes the implementation of e-government, taking as a case study Ecuadorian universities self-financed and accredited in categories A and B. The methodology is based on a content analysis of the websites of these universities, with the objective of determining the external and internal services offered to their stakeholders.

The content of this work is organized in the following way: Section 2 covers the general concepts of e-Government in higher education; Section 3 describes the case study; Section 4 presents the results of the research, and finally Section 5 presents the conclusions and future work.

2. E-GOVERNMENT IN HIGHER EDUCATION

2.1 E-Government in Higher Education

The concept of governability applied to the university sector is related to an exercise of control in terms of the management of the different centers and departments that make up higher education institutions (Raposo et al., 2006).

The implementation of e-government not only allows the incorporation of value to the primary functions such as: research, community & service and teaching but also becomes a strategy with regard to the innovation, modernization and transformation of university management in terms of both external and internal services (Kumar et al., 2014). These services vary, depending on the vision and mission of each institution and its ability to implement ICT. For this reason we can identify different applications that depend on the characteristics of each educational institution (Dey et al., 2008) and are integrated into their environment through an e-government platform (Raposo et al., 2006).

According to the authors (Sigalés, 2004) (IDC, 2007), it is important to mention that not all experiences of incorporation of ICT in university management have generated the expected results. This is because ICTs have traditionally been implemented as a means of supporting the operations of an organization, rather than with regard to the strategic aspects. In this sense the formulation and management of ICT at the level of a university's strategic direction is key to achieving the e-government objectives (Diligens, 2016).

In Ecuadorian universities, the implementation of e-government platforms has been progressing slowly. The implementation of the organic law on higher education, reformed in 2010 and its Regulation of academic regimes, have prompted significant reforms in terms of the use of ICT in HEI. Such contributions constitute the element of departure for initiated the implementation of e-government in Ecuadorian higher education.

Prior to the adoption of e-government in the university environment, it is important to identify all relevant services relating to HEI, whether internal or external. According to (European Comission, 2008), two groups of stakeholders exist in university environments. On the one hand, external stakeholders consist of individuals or organizations with a particular interest in HEI practices and results. Within this group can be included potential applicants, parents, employers, central government regulatory agencies, national and international accreditation agencies, etc. On the other hand, there are internal users who are part of the operational and academic management of universities. The main stakeholders are students, graduates, administrative staff and academic staff (Dey et al., 2008).

In (Dey et al., 2008), the main applications of e-governance, oriented to both internal and external services in university institutions, are described as follows.

- University to Citizen (U2C) Applications
- University to University (U2U) Applications
- University to Regulators (U2R) Applications
- University to Employee (U2E) Applications

3. CASE STUDY

As a case study, it has been proposed to analyze the Ecuadorian self-financed universities that are in categories A and B. This categorization was carried out by the Council for the Evaluation, Accreditation and Quality Assurance of Higher Education (Consejo de evaluación, acredicatión y aseguramiento de la calidad de la educación superior - CEAACES). This council is in charge of assuring the quality of higher education in the country, through the execution of evaluation, accreditation and categorization processes as they related to HEI.

The web page of CEAACES[1] offers a list of self-financed private universities which are in category A and category B. With this group of ten universities shown in Table 1, the proposed analysis is performed.

The method used for this research consisted of evaluating the websites of each university in order to determine and classify the information and services they offer. This analysis seeks to identify indications that allow the identification of the use of data analysis in the strategic planning of HEI.

This work has taken into account a typology of stakeholders adapted to the situation faced by Ecuadorian universities by emphasizing elements described in related publications (Gaete, 2011), (Karthika, 2013), (European Commission). The typology is based on three criteria:

1. The type of influence that stakeholders have on decision-making.
2. The interests and demands of each group regarding the organization.
3. The level of participation in the processes of the organization.

According to the literature reviewed, two types of relationships between HEIs and their interest groups have been defined: informational relations and transactional relations. Table 1 shows the analysis of these relationships in the ten universities.

Table 1. Information, Communication and Interaction on Websites of Ecuadorian Universities

Information, communication and processes		**Universities**										
		UEES	USFQ	U. CASA GRANDE	U.INTERNACIONAL SEK	UDLA	UNIBE	U. DE LOS HEMISFERIOS	UTEG	UIDE	UTI	**Total universities**
INFORMATION	Scholarships and Financial aid			x	x	x	x		x	x	x	7
	Management reports	x	x	x	x	x	x		x	x	x	9
	Information of academic offer	x	x	x	x	x	x	x	x	x	x	10
	Rates		x	x			x	x			x	5
	Frequent Questions	x							x	x		3
	Institutional Information	x	x	x	x	x	x		x	x	x	9
	Community service		x	x	x	x			x	x	x	7
	Research		x	x	x	x	x	x	x	x	x	9
COMUNICATION	Social networks	x	x		x	x	x	x	x	x	x	9
	University Blogs			x		x				x		3
	Virtual forums											0
	Online suggestions											0
	Information request form		x	x	x	x		x	x		x	7
INTERACTION	Online registration				x		x					2
	Online vocational test			x								1
	Online courses	x	x	x	x	x	x	x		x	x	9
	Online library	x	x	x	x	x	x	X	x	x	x	10
	Online employment opportunities			x		x			x	x		4
	Online administrative procedures											0
	Online practice pre professional registration											0

[1] www.ceaaces.gob.ec

Strategic plans for institutional development (PEDI) were also analyzed to identify the degree of importance that HEIs attach to the implementation and management of e-Government, based on data analysis. Table 2 shows the results obtained. The data were validated at four levels: null (N) when there is no evidence of the use of IT in stakeholder interaction; initial (I) when at least one of the parties makes use of IT tools to store information as an axis of university management; mean (M) when the functionality of an IT tool is not only oriented to automate a process, but also puts it at the service of a group of stakeholders; and finally reached (A), when strategic decisions take into account the interaction of stakeholders with the institution.

Table 2. Inclusion of E-government Strategies in the PEDI of Universities in Study

	Universities								
Axes of university management	UEES	U. CASA GRANDE	U.INTERNACIONAL SEK	UDLA	UNIBE	U. DE LOS HEMISFERIOS	UTEG	UIDE	UTI
Academy and teaching	N	M	I	I	N	N	I	I	I
Research	N	N	N	N	N	N	N	N	N
Community service	N	N	N	I	N	N	N	N	N
Institutional development - governance	I	I	I	I	N	N	I	I	I
Physical and virtual infrastructure	M	M	M	M	I	I	M	M	M
Administrative management	M	M	I	M	I	I	M	M	I

4. DISCUSSION

The information published on the websites of the universities concerned is broad in scope and addressed to both internal and external stakeholders. In terms of academic and admissions offerings, 100% of colleges and universities publish extensive information aimed at student applicants, regulatory agencies, and parents and employers. It is also noted that information on academic offerings is important for internal actors (students and administrative staff), especially in relation to international programs. In this area, the interaction of HEIs with external agents is done through contact forms.

Another source of web publication is related to institutional information (list of authorities, strategic plan, financial reports, salary information, etc.), which responds to a requirement in the Organic Law on Higher Education, which urges universities to publish this information on its electronic portals. This information is essentially useful (100%) for government regulatory agencies and (75%) for parents, researchers, teachers, and administrative staff.

Other information published on university websites refers to services for students. All information related to this topic (student welfare, library, internships and internships, job placement, qualification processes) is of almost exclusive interest to internal stakeholders.

In terms of linkage with the community and research, it is observed that 100% of HEI use their electronic portals exclusively to publish information. In these key operational areas for HEI, it is necessary to implement processes in which stakeholders, both internal and external, interact with institutions. Unfortunately, no user interaction with HEIs has been observed in the analysis of the institutions' websites.

The percentage of universities that make interaction tools available to their stakeholders is low (37%). Few universities have implemented IT tools to automate processes such as online enrollment, internship registration, employment exchange, etc.

Of the sources available for the collection of information, there is evidence that only in two universities (UEES and UDLA), are strategies of data analysis used in the service of strategic planning and decision making. There is no evidence of the implementation and use of DWH and DM techniques that contribute to information management, and thus to e-government strategies.

5. CONCLUSIONS AND FUTURE WORK

For IHEs, web presence is the effective way to communicate with the largest segment of stakeholders, students. Therefore, this article stresses the importance and need to increase web-based services that generate data of the interaction with all stakeholders and thus support the implementation of e-governance strategies in universities. These services should be oriented, on the one hand, to strengthening the internal relations of U2C and U2E and, on the other hand, contributing to the strengthening and creation of external relations in terms of U2U and U2R. In the case of the analyzed study, a significant percentage of university websites publish static information, with little interaction of its stakeholders that is oriented solely to informative reading.

Universities should understand that the implementation of DWH and DM techniques helps them to organize their information at an internal level at, the same time, offers competitive opportunities at the external level. The implementation of a DWH can add strategic intelligence for the taking of decisions, provide a clear vision of historical data, and provide significant support to a university's e-government strategies.

ACKNOWLEDGEMENT

The authors would like to thank to DITC of the Universidad de las Américas for partially funding this research.

REFERENCES

Bhanti, P. et al., 2011. E-Governance in Higher Education: Concept and Role of Data Warehousing Techniques, *In Proceedings of International Journal of Computer Applications*, Vol. 18, No. 1, pp. 15-19.

Dey, S. and Sobhan M., 2008. Conceptual Framework for Introducing e–governance in University Administration, *In Proceedings of the 2nd international conference on Theory and practice of electronic governance ICEGOV*, pp. 433-438.

Diligens, D. Gobierno y gestión estratégica (On line). Available: http://www.duxdiligens.com. (Último acceso: 2017 Agosto 25).

European Commission. 2008, *Higher Education Governance*. Eurydice, Bruselas, Belgium.

Flory, A. et al., 2001. A Design and implementation of a data warehouse for research administration universities. *In Proceedings of the 7th International Conference of European University Information Systems*, pp. 259-267.

Gaete, R., 2011. Relación de las universidades con sus stakeholders en Internet: un modelo de análisis. *Ciencia, docencia y tecnología*, Vol. 22, No. 42, pp. 9-39.

IDC. 2007, *TIC para PYMES*. LID Editorial Empresarial, pp. 50-52.

Karthika, D. and RangaRaj, R., 2013. Survey of E-Governance based Higher Education System in India with Data Mining. *Proceedings of International Journal of Science and Research (IJSR)*, Vol. 2, No. 12, pp. 344-347.

Kumar, M. et al., 2014. Data Warehouse in E-Governance. *International Journal of Engineering Sciences & Research*. Vol. 3, No. 3, pp. 1768-1770.

Morales J., 2015. Modelos de Gobierno TI para Instituciones de Educación Superior. *Revista Politécnica*, Vol. 36, No. 3, pp. 1-6.

Oracle. 2016. Database Data Warehousing Guide. Oracle, (On line). Available: https://docs.oracle.com/. (Last access: 2016 october 10).

Raposo. M. et al,. 2006. E-Governance of Universities: A Proposal of Benchmarking Methodology. *MPRA* Munich Personal RePEc Archive. pp. 1-20.

Sigalés, C., 2004. Formación universitaria y TIC. *Revista de Universidad y Sociedad del Conocimiento*, Vol. 1, No.º 1, pp. 1-12.

UPM. 2016. Current Students. UM, (On linea). Available: http://www.olemiss.edu. (Last access: 2017 August 15).

A COLLABORATIVE LEARNING ENVIRONMENT BASED ON THE SEMANTIC WEB PRINCIPLES

Adriano Ferraz da Costa[1], Cedric Luiz de Carvalho[2] and Deller James Ferreira[2]
[1]*Universidade Estadual de Goiás - UEG Santa Helena de Goiás - GO - Brasil*
[2]*Instituto de Informática - Universidade Federal de Goiás - Goiânia - GO - Brasil*

ABSTRACT

The Semantic Web is a model proposed by Tim Berners-Lee as an extension of the current web. In order to Semantic Web becomes a reality, applications that provide data structures in accordance to its principles are required. On the other hand, in collaborative learning for elementary school, the collaborations should transcend cohort boundaries, making possible content distribution and students interactions among different cohorts at the same school or different cohorts from other schools. Besides, students should access content and collaborative activities adapted to their needs and educational situation. The use of Semantic Web technologies to help educational activities is relatively recent. Here, we highlight that Semantic Web applications can enable students to work in cooperation in an innovative and personalized way. In this work, we implemented an original collaborative environment for teaching and learning that takes advantage of the Semantic Web standards and principles, favoring the process of teaching and learning. This Semantic Web collaborative environment is based on adaptive collaboration scripts and integrated into a semantically structured framework for the creation of augmented virtual communities of learning. A qualitative case study showed the collaborative environment effectiveness in teaching and learning, as well as demonstrated that an adaptable script, designed according to Semantic Web principles, is a valuable educational tool.

KEYWORDS

Collaborative environment; scripts for teaching/learning; semantic web

1. INTRODUCTION

Computer-supported collaborative learning (CSCL) has proven to be effective (Adamson et al., 2014) (Lee et al., 2013). As students collaborate, content becomes easier to be assimilated and learning more enjoyable. In collaborative learning, students not only share their cognitive ability and reduce their mental efforts, but also increase their confidence in the task, leading to a better effective result, especially during the execution of complex tasks (Lee et al., 2013).

Collaboration scripts are used to make collaborative learning more productive (Kobbe, 2007). The development of a collaborative environment that allows the use of multiple collaboration scripts, so that the teacher choose and adapt a collaboration script to be used in a given educational situation is an important issue to be addressed. Wecker and Fischer (Wecker and Fischer, 2011) suggest that ways to adapt collaboration scripts to the current level of students' competence, a specific content, and a given context is a very promising theme to be explored.

The new generation of the Web, the Semantic Web, can be considered a powerful technology for educational settings and implementation of computer-supported collaborative learning (Bittencourt et al., 2009) (Gravier et al, 2012) (Jeremic, 2013) (Li, 2011) (Mangione et al., 2012) (Stojanovic et al., 2001). The Semantic Web is an environment in which human agents and machines communicate by means of a semantic basis (Berners-Lee et al., 2001). The Semantic Web is based on ontologies as a fundamental skeleton.

Some other research works that already incorporate the Semantic Web in teaching and learning processes, using also collaborative methods, can be found in literature. However, we not found any work regarding both adaptive collaboration scripts and Semantic Web principles.

We developed a collaborative environment that allows the teacher to make adaptations on collaboration scripts, aiming better educational outcomes. The teacher is able to create more suitable script configurations, according to distinct educational objectives. Each configuration is linked to a list of relevant activities to a certain educational situation The configuration elaborated by the teacher incorporates the Bloom's taxonomy (Bloom, 1956). In this work, the Bloom's six cognitive domains are used as a basis of educational phases of every collaboration script. The execution order of these phases is defined by the teacher, depending on what activities he wants the students perform during a collaborative episode.

The collaborative environment developed in this work was designed to access the graph-oriented database Neo4j (Neubauer, 2010). From this model, to explore the relationship among data is possible. These relationships among data allow students to perform searches of vital information for the teaching and learning processes. These searches enable the system to return specific information on collaborative activities. Access to this information allows, for example, the teacher use this information to provide better feedback to students. Students can, for example, access relevant information from previous interactions in the same group or from other groups.

Besides this introduction, this work is organized as follows. In Section 2, the developed Collaborative Learning Environments is described. Section 3 shows the case study we conducted. In Section 4, some results are discussed. Finally, in Section 5, we present our conclusions.

2. THE DEVELOPED COLLABORATIVE LEARNING ENVIRONMENT

A virtual learning community was created in the collaborative environment implemented in this work. Members of this community are clustered in groups and can interact with the each other through the Internet. The proposed collaborative learning environment (CLE) is divided into three layers, following the *Model View Controller (MVC)* architectural pattern. Using this architectural pattern, one can map traditional input, processing, and output tasks to web multilayer applications. The use of this pattern contributes to the maintainability of the software.

In the layer called *Model*, we have a list of activities related to the Bloom's taxonomy (Bloom, 1956). The selection of these activities specifies a particular script configuration for system application. In this layer, there are the classes that allow the teacher to establish how the collaborative environment will be used, for example the definition of the script that will be used and the formation of groups.

Each activity has a class, accessed by the *Control* layer, which defines its entities, attributes, rules, and a class of persistence in the database Data Access Object (DAO). In this layer, classes are implemented, enabling interactive visualization of content generated by web components and expressive search that allows a better access to content produced by collaborations

There are screens that provide an interface for user interaction with the software. This interface interacts with the *Control* layer that defines how the received data is interpreted and how they should be presented to the user. This interface is the *View* layer of the MVC architectural pattern.

The CLE was designed to be a script generator based on a list of activities related to the Bloom's taxonomy (Bloom, 1956). The rules for script configuration are also based on the Bloom's taxonomy. An instance of a script is configured based on the six categories of cognitive domain proposed by Bloom. This object determines the steps to be carried out by groups participating in the collaborative process.

The CLE was designed to use a graph-oriented database. This modeling allows creation of nodes and edges and also to assign properties for both nodes and edges. The edges define the type of relationship between nodes. It is possible to search the graph following the relationships between nodes. One can also assign properties to these relationships.

The CLE allows all users to view the collaborations in textual form. The knowledge generated can be displayed in two ways, as Graph Visualization – a graph containing nodes related to a determined theme visualization is shown, the user can view the information saved on a node clicking twice on it; or as Expressive Search – one of the biggest advantages of implementing systems in a graph model is the expressive search, this type of search is more intuitive for humans. The Neo4j (Neubauer, 2010) database allows to make searches from relationships of nodes. This, if implemented in a relational database, would be more difficult to implement and would require more computational processing efforts.

3. THE CLE APPLICATION – A CASE STUDY

The CLE was designed to be an application that can be used in various contexts. Its use is not restricted to a specific subject or content. It makes possible to establish a virtual community. In this case study, a virtual learning community was created, involving two schools. Virtual communities are interesting in educational context because they allow to cluster people with common interests. Thus, they allow interactions and collaborations to be carried out in a context beyond institutional boundaries.

For the application of the collaborative environment, we chose two seventh year classes of an elementary school, involving a total of forty-nine students and one teacher. The teacher assembled groups of four and five students, who worked on notebooks and tablets. The collaborative environment was also applied in a sixth year class of another elementary school, involving seven students and one teacher. Two groups were assembled, one group containing three students and other four students, who used laptops. In both applications, the class duration was fifty minutes.

The students chose to discuss the topic ecology. This is a current topic and it is present in students' daily life. So, it potentially generates many discussions. Besides, this topic involves previous knowledge that most students have. The group discussions on the topic ecology makes emerge many questions and conflicts, that can be better understood by means of collaborative scripts boundaries.

In the adaptive collaboration script we proposed in this research, we used the well-established *Social Script* (Kobbe, 2007). In this case, we expanded it to the six cognitive domains proposed by the Bloom's taxonomy. The *Social Script* is characterized as a strategy to promote argumentative cognitive reasoning. The *Social Script* is based on collaboration by means of making an analysis of a topic, reviewing and performing critical analysis by other groups and finally constructing a new analysis, taking in consideration other groups' criticism. The *Social Script* is a collaborative scheme where students go through these stages sequentially. Besides expanding phases of *Social Script* to the six phases of the Bloom's taxonomy, each phase contains actions associated with it. The teacher, according to different educational situations, chooses the most adequate actions. The proposed script has the following phase sequence:

- Phase 1 – knowledge building: this phase is mapped to the Bloom's cognitive category *knowledge*. The purpose of this phase is to provide students enough material to bring their attention to the content related to the topic ecology. At this stage the students had access to a page in the collaborative environment containing an overview of web links selected by the science teacher.
- Phase 2 – illustrate: this phase is mapped to the Bloom's cognitive category *comprehension*. At this phase, the goal was the students to understand the subject. The students were invited to enter a set of words considered by them to be related to the topic ecology. This brainstorm activity facilitates the following phase *engagement*, because the construction of this list of terms helps users to elaborate the text.
- Phase 3 – analysis: this phase is mapped to the Bloom's cognitive category *application*. In this stage, students were asked to demonstrate their ability to use information received. The students' groups write collaboratively an analysis on the topic discussed.
- Phase 4 – criticizing: this phase is mapped to the Bloom's cognitive category *analysis*. At this stage it is expected that the students are already familiar with content and can identify its main points and perform analysis on them. After this analysis, it was presented to groups an analysis made by another group. The group read this analysis and then wrote a its own critical analysis. This critics was written based on one of the following three aspects: "Here there is a proposal for adjustment of this analysis", "Some aspects are not clear to us yet", and "We have not reached consensus on these aspects".
- Phase 5 – relate: this phase is mapped to the Bloom's cognitive category *synthesis*. During this phase, the set of abstract relations that emerged from students' interactions with content can be mapped in real world situations. The students can describe how the subject content can be related to their daily lives.
- Phase 6 - rewrite analysis: this phase is mapped to the Bloom's cognitive category *evaluation*. This final phase allows a judgment of the acquired knowledge. After writing a review, criticizing, and realized meanings correlations, students were asked to rewrite their initial analysis. It is expected that the group components already have a new perspective on the topics previously pointed out by them.

The interactions of one of the groups in CLE result in a graph. This graph allows exploration of the relationships between nodes. Different searches can be implemented from these relationships. Such searches are known in the context of the Semantic Web as expressive searches. Future implementations from the data generated in collaboration, can allow them to be visible to users' queries relating the cognitive domains with web content. This model also allows assigning scores to the relationships. This favors the recommendation of the best generated learning collaborative material. This model also allows comparisons of collaborations, joint collaborations between different schools, as well as sharing content between different systems.

The collaborative environment presents the search results on collaborations in text form. The teacher took the expressive search tool to view the criticism that the students made based on the aspect "we have reached no consensus on these issues". According to the teacher this information is of great importance because it allowed him to detect the most problematic points, contributing to the preparation of the next class. The teacher read the initial and final analysis text and concluded that there was a remarkable development. He also used the activity as an evaluative activity to constitute students' grades.

4. RESULTS

To evaluate our work, we applied a questionnaire to teachers aiming to get reports on the advantages and drawbacks of the CLE application. The main points of investigation were the advantages of using adaptive collaboration scripts. We also wanted to know if they noticed any advance in cognitive reasoning of the students and if they found beneficial to view the results of the collaboration after performing information search.

The questionnaire answered by the two teachers involved shows that the capacity to adapt scripts is a very positive factor. The teachers easily configured the scripts and the order of execution of the activities chosen by the teachers was efficient, promoting productive interactions among students.

We also applied to the students a questionnaire containing nine questions aiming to examine their motivation to engage in learning activities using the collaborative environment. We also wanted to see if they found easy or difficult to use this computational tool, their opinion concerning its effectiveness on the learning process, as well as the potential of the collaborative environment to foment a learning community.

The students' responses show that the majority of them would like to make their homework collaboratively via the CLE, as well as other activities. This fact reveals a tendency of future intention to use the CLE. This also indicates that the students considered the overall balance of their experience fruitful.

5. CONCLUSIONS

Our approach makes use of Semantic Web technologies to manage collaboration among students. This original CLE contributes to current research in an innovative way, transcending other computer-supported collaborative learning tools. We present a rule-based system for teachers, that help them to develop strategies in the management and facilitation of students' collaborations.

The case study, conducted in this research involving the CLE, aimed to show its effectiveness in teaching and learning process, as well as to demonstrate that adaptable scripts, designed with the use of Semantic Web principles, is a rich and advantageous educational tool. Another important aspect approached in the case study was the integration of technology in teaching and learning process. Students are increasingly acquainted with the technologies and demonstrate ease handling of them. However, the use of technology in schools is not a simple task. The lack of knowledge of educators regarding existing tools and their inability to handle them it is still an obstacle to be overcome.

The results of the case study performed here, evidenced that the developed CLE has the potential to awake educators to the fact that new Semantic Web technologies can be successfully incorporated in teaching and learning processes and pointed out a need to train teachers accordingly.

Analyzing the question posed to the teachers, we could identify that one of them used the tool more profitably than the other, indicating that this second teacher was not so familiar with the pedagogical method and the tool than the first one. This study also shows that the students are highly motivated to use computational tools in their tasks in groups at distance or at computational laboratories.

The CLE application in two elementary schools evidenced its great educational potential. The use of collaborative scripts, based on Semantic Web principles and structured by graph-driven database, proved to be an efficient tool to teachers and students to explore the results of collaborations

We can conclude that the insertion of our collaborative environment in the process of teaching and learning in a primary school class was profitable, relevant and contributed to every day technology to be more present in schools. Its application in two elementary school classes was satisfactory, according to reports from the teachers and students. It is important to highlight that the students in the second school, who attended the study, could view previous collaborations from the first school, expanding the boundaries of traditional collaboration.

The results of the case study unveil that the CLE elaborated here has the potential to foster the creation of virtual learning communities and can be considered a vertical application, highly recommended by the World Wide Web Consortium (W3C) for the Semantic Web to become a reality.

ACKNOWLEDGEMENT

To UEG for the financial support, through its event support program ("Pró-Eventos").

REFERENCES

Adamson, D. et al, 2014. Towards an agile approach to adapting dynamic collaboration support to student needs. *International Journal of Artificial Intelligence in Education*, Vol 24, No. 1, pp. 92–124.

Berners-Lee, T. et al., 2001 . The semantic web. *Scientific American*, Vol. 284, No. 5, pp. 34–43.

Bittencourt, I. et al, 2009. A computational model for developing semantic web-based educational systems. *Knowledge-Based Systems*, Vol. 22, No. 4, pp. 302–315.

Bloom, B. (editor), 1956. *Taxonomy of Educational Objectives. The Classification of Educational Goals, Handbook I: Cognitive Domain*. Longmans, Green, New York.

Gravier, C. et al, 2012. Adaptive system for collaborative online laboratories. *Intelligent Systems*, IEEE, Vol. 17, No. 4, pp. 11–17.

Jeremic, Z. et. al, 2013. Personal learning environments on the Social Semantic Web. *Semantic Web*. Vol. 4, No. 1, pp. 23-51.

Kobbe, L. et al., 2007. Specifying computer-supported collaboration scripts. *International Journal of Computer-Supported Collaborative Learning*, Vol.2, No. 2, pp. 211–224.

Lee, Y. et al. , 2013. Revisit the effect of teaching and learning with technology. *Journal of Educational Technology & Society*. Vol. 16, No. 1, pp.133-146.

Li, Y. et al., 2011. Designing Collaborative E-Learning Environments based upon Semantic Wiki: From Design Models to Application Scenarios. *Journal of Educational Technology & Society*, Vol. 14, No. 4, pp. 49–63.

Mangione, G. et al. , 2012. Conversation-based Learning in the Social Semantic Web. *Journal of e-Learning and Knowledge Society*, Vol 8, No. 2, pp. 45–63.

Neubauer, P., 2010. *InfoQ: Graph Databases, NOSQL and Neo4j*, https://www.infoq.com/articles/graph-nosql-neo4j, last seen on May 2017.

Stojanovic, L. et al., 2001. eLearning based on the semantic web. *In WebNet2001 - World Conference on the WWW and Internet*, pp. 23–27.

Wecker, C. and Fischer, F. , 2011. From guided to self-regulated performance of domain-general skills: The role of peer monitoring during the fading of instructional scripts. *Learning and Instruction*, Vol. 21, No. 6, pp.746–756.

MAILING LISTS ON THE INTERNET - A COLLABORATION TOOL THAT IS STILL ALIVE. THE CASE OF THE REDIRIS LISTS

Antonio Muñoz-Cañavate[1], Alejandro Cordero González[1], Pedro Hípola[2] and Eduardo Alfredo Cardoso Miranda[3]
[1]*Departamento de Información y Comunicación, Facultad de Ciencias de la Documentación y la Comunicación, Universidad de Extremadura, Plazuela Ibn Marwan s/n, 06071 Badajoz, Spain*
[2]*Departamento de Información y Comunicación, Facultad de Comunicación y Documentación, Universidad de Granada, Campus de Cartuja s/n, 18071 Granada, Spain*
[3]*Universidade Lusófona de Humanidades e Tecnologias, Campo Grande, 376, 1749-024 Lisboa, Portugal*

ABSTRACT

The appearance of telematic networks such as Bitnet, Internet, etc., gave rise to the emergence of diverse applications that allowed users to communicate with each other. Email distribution lists were one such application. The possibility of creating open or closed forums, with very specific themes, aimed at people dispersed around the world, who could come into contact at a much lower cost than other communication systems – for example, postal mail or telephone – revolutionized systems of collaboration. However, the arrival of the so-called Web 2.0 with its new category of social media applications which make it easy for users to insert information on Web platforms seems to have called into question the interest of those mailing lists. This paper analyses the validity of such lists through a study of all the email lists managed by the RedIRIS network (Red Española para Interconexión de los Recursos Informáticos – Spanish Network for Interconnection of Informatic Resources) through the information provided by the network's log file that indicates the activity of its lists and the public information on its website. The results include the number of lists created, their permanence, a study by year of their creation, their professional topics, and activity levels. They show that mailing lists are still used effectively as communication tools by the scientific and academic community despite the rise of the aforementioned Web 2.0 social media.

KEYWORDS

Mailing lists, email, Spain, Listserv, RedIRIS

1. INTRODUCTION

Throughout human history, people have used different means to communicate, from mere oral transmission to the new media that have facilitated our access to information and communications technologies.

The development of information and communications technologies and the insertion of information technology into people's daily lives, together with the widespread use of telematic access to networks, led to the creation of such tools as electronic mail, and then mailing and distribution lists. Their development and evolution preceded even the massive expansion of the Internet that took place in the mid-1990s as a consequence of the appearance of the World Wide Web. Many of these lists were managed on non-Internet networks, such as the already extinct Bitnet, dedicated to providing e-mail and file transfer services to the academic community around the world. Castro & Muñoz-Cañavate (1995) analysed the nearly six thousand distribution lists supported by Bitnet, the majority in the field of science and technology, although all disciplines were present. There thus emerged a massive, two-way communications tool in which content – messages – are created by the users themselves, who can interact with people anywhere in the world with whose interests they are related professionally or academically. These systems allow users to communicate with each other at enormous speed and at much lower cost than other forms of communication. Together with the mailing lists, there simultaneously arose other types of electronic forums, one example being the newsgroups, a bulletin board type of system. This alternative to distribution lists would come to be called Usenet, a service that also allowed users to participate in discussions of widely different topics. They differed from mailing lists in their text distribution system. While in a mailing list each message is forwarded to all the list's subscribers, Usenet messages were sent to a series of computers as if they were bulletin boards. Newsgroups were ranked by hierarchies based on levels separated by dots. The system was eventually acquired by Google, and at the moment can be used on the group platforms maintained by, for example, Google (groups.google.com) or Yahoo (groups.yahoo.com). A user must connect to these applications in order to read messages.

Despite their usefulness, research studies of distribution lists in Spain (the country under study in this paper) have been few and far between relative to the enormous volume of studies generated by other social media of the Web 2.0 generation. Two fields which have been studied are Librarianship and Documentation (Hípola, Baiget & Muñoz-Cañavate, 1994; Barrueco, García & Gimeno, 1995; Merlo, 1999; Ontalba, 2009; Cordero & Faba, 2013; Baiget, 2014) and Medicine (Hernández-Borges et al. 1999; Serrano-Castro, Arjona & Guardado, 2004; Rodríguez-Recio & Sendra-Porter, 2007).

Internationally, there have been analyses of a wide variety of aspects. As examples, some studies have analysed their informational potential and current relevance as against other media in certain professional environments (Punjar, Mahesh & Jayakanth, 2014), the content of messages sent to the lists (Waseleski, 2006; Tonta & Karabulut, 2010), and their use as an effective means of conducting studies in different professional sectors since their subscribers are concentrated in specific disciplines (Mushtaq et al., 2014.; Zonfrillo et al., 2014). There has also been debate as to whether mailing lists really are reliable channels for professional communication (Hernández-Borges, Macías & Torres, 1998). Mailing lists have the capacity to maintain accumulated knowledge since the messages sent to them are archived in files that can be consulted at any time, and thus be of service to other sources of information (Kosovsky, 2014).

1.1 RedIRIS

The RedIRIS network (Red Española para Interconexión de los Recursos Informáticos – Spanish Network for Interconnection of Informatic Resources) was configured to act as Spain's academic and research network. It is responsible for providing advanced communications services to the national university and scientific community, consisting of more than 500 institutions. It is funded by the Spanish Government. Its management is carried out by Red.es, a public corporation of Spain's Ministry of Energy.

Its origins date back to 1988 through the IRIS Program (Interconexión de los Recursos Informáticos), and as such was a pioneer in the introduction of the Internet in Spain. The IRIS Program highlighted the need for the tools that would allow data transmission as a cornerstone of the research and training system, and therefore the exchange of information and documentation. The document that was at the origin of the network itself noted that access to academic networks facilitated the work of geographically disperse groups of individuals within a country, and stimulated the flourishing of a true international community with the daily exchange of rivers of information (Ministerio de Educación y Ciencia, 1985).

RedIRIS maintains a large number of distribution lists under the category of collaborative services. These serve to coordinate working groups and/or research projects, to create open forums of general interest to the RedIRIS community, and to foster collaboration with the Latin American academic and research community.

The set of mailing lists managed by RedIRIS is maintained as part of the service called IRISLIST whose mission is to facilitate the exchange of knowledge in Spain's scientific community by means of distribution lists.

The RedIRIS lists are managed using the LISTSERV software, as also of course are the lists of the international network that maintains LISTSERV itself. Its origins go back to the now extinct Bitnet/Earn network. While it is a distributed system, for the end user it appears to be centralized since its various supporting nodes work in coordination. Thus, the use of the Distribute algorithm reduces international data traffic by sending a single message to a national LISTSERV node that is then forwarded to all subscribers to a list in that country.

2. OBJECTIVES, MATERIAL, AND METHODS

The object of study was the set of distribution lists administered by the RedIRIS academic network and managed using the LISTSERV software. The following objectives were set:

a) To determine the total number of distribution lists created and the number of active lists.
b) Description of each list's topics or categories.
c) To study the lists' dates of creation.
d) Knowledge of the lists' activity using one particular indicator: the sent date of the last post.

The data used for the present work were supplied by RedIRIS who gave us the census of all their mailing lists and the log file with the activity of each list. This information made it possible to create a database with details referring to each list, allowing us to study their behaviour and evolution over recent years. The data correspond to the last part of 2015.

We also consulted the Spanish bibliographic database ISOC-CSIC, the international Scopus and Lisa databases, and the RedIRIS website which contains abundant descriptive material on mailing lists in general as a communication resource in the academic world and on the lists it manages in particular.

Data processing was performed using the statistical treatment features of the Excel computer program.

2.1 Results

2.1.1 Total Numbers of Mailing Lists

The file provided by RedIRIS included a total of 546 mailing lists created by the IRIS Network since its inception. Many of the lists have not had continuity in time and have expired because their owners did not renew their subscription, so that such lists are understood as having fallen into disuse. In particular, 152 mailing lists no longer appeared as available on the RedIRIS website, and they had no activity recorded in the log file. There thus remained on the RedIRIS website 394 lists available for the R&D+i community, although 62 of them had no activity registered in the log file but were still available to be used as valid tools. In sum therefore, the number of lists analysed in this paper as available on the RedIRIS website is 394.

In percentage terms, this means that 72.1% of the lists are available to the scientific and academic community, and 60.8% actually have activity registered in the log file. The present study uses the aforementioned 394 lists available on the RedIRIS 2015 website since these are the ones that any interested user can use (whether or not they are active). They also constitute an indicator of the activity levels of this tool.

2.1.2 Thematic Categories of the Lists

Figure 1 shows the weights of the subject areas of the available RedIRIS lists at the time of the study. It should be noted that, while the lists are grouped into thirty categories, many of them are assigned to more than one category. For example, a mailing list within the Documentation category can also be found in the Medicine category if it refers to medical libraries. This figure therefore represents that reality in percentage terms.

The data indicate a preponderance of lists in Medicine and Life Sciences, although, as one can see, there are mailing lists for almost all disciplines.

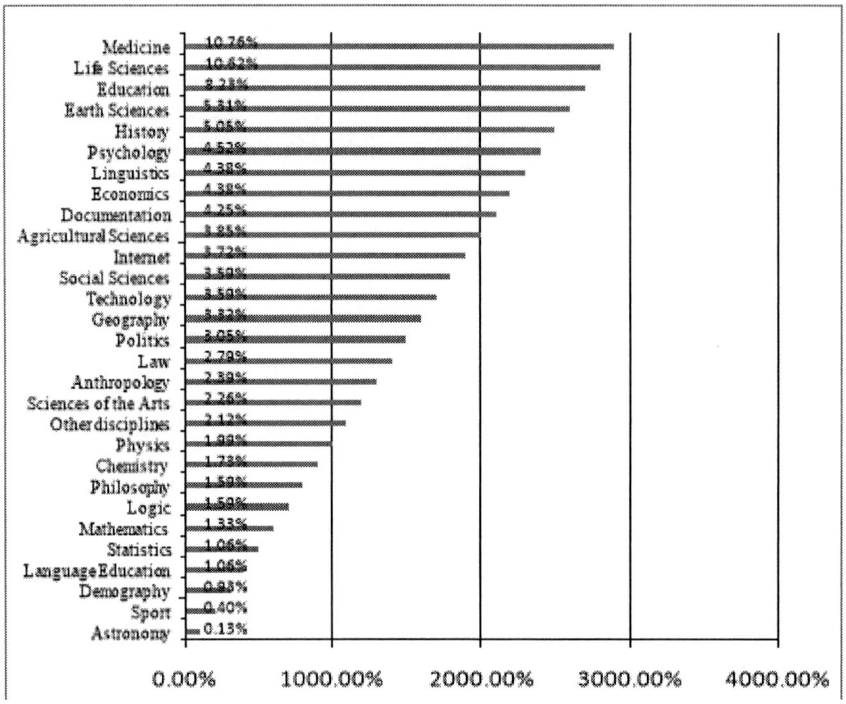

Source: Compiled from RedIRIS data.

Figure 1. Thematic Mailing Lists

2.1.3 Date of Creation of the Lists

With respect to the year of creation of the lists, RedIRIS does not specify the year of creation of 37 of the 394 lists available. The first mailing list was created in 1993. In 1996 there began the spurt in growth of the number of lists – 1997 (12 lists created), 1998 (20 lists), 1999 (30 lists), and 2000 (48 lists). From then on, there was a descent in the creation of new lists, although still with high numbers – 2001 (42 lists) and 2002 (24 lists). The data indicate that, despite the rise of new social media such as Facebook, LinkedIn (with its specialized forums), and Twitter, there continued to be created new mailing lists after 2005 (albeit with smaller numbers) indicative of interest in this tool. Thus, from 2010 to 2012, at the height of the new Web 2.0 context, 32 new mailing lists were created.

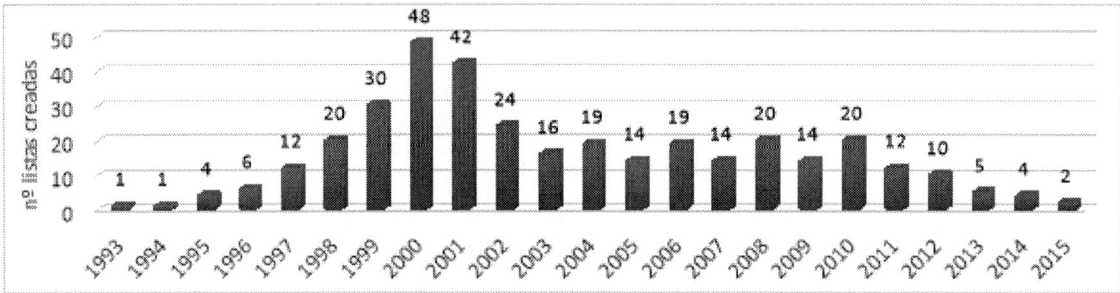

Source: Compiled from RedIRIS data.

Figure 2. Number of Lists Created by RedIRIS Each Year

2.1.4 Latest List Posts

Finally, with regard to the last objective of the present study, the date of the last post to the mailing list is a very relevant datum in that it reflects the real activity of the list. In particular, a mailing list can not be understood as really active if it received no post in the last year. Of the initial 394 lists, only 172 (43.6%) had a post in the last year of the study.

Table 1. Year of the Last Post to the List

Year of the last post	**N° of lists**
Last post was in 2015	172
Last post was in 2014	51
Last post was in 2013	25
Last post was in 2012	15
Last post was in 2011	15
Last post was in 2010	11
Last post was before 2010	15
Not specified by RedIRIS	90
Total	394

Source: Compiled from RedIRIS data.

3. CONCLUSIONS

Mailing lists can be considered to be one of the first social media if one understands this latter term to mean those platforms whose contents are created by the users themselves. Some authors have argued that these tools were disappearing as a means of communication for users interested in specific topics even before the emergence of the better known "Web 2.0" social media such as Facebook, LinkedIn, and Twitter, in which users could use the Web platforms to insert their own content. The emergence of Virtual Communities of Users (VCUs) as antecedents of Facebook, LinkedIn, Twitter, etc. was aimed at bringing together people with common characteristics and making information resources readily available to them. They came to be announced as the tools which were going to eliminate mailing lists (Ontalba, 2002). These VCUs, however, themselves disappeared because of the massive arrival of Web 2.0 based social media, while mailing lists still exist.

This study has shown how mailing lists are still a living and useful mechanism for the Internet user community. Of the 394 lists studied, 62 have become inactive, but 172 (43.6%) have received emails in the past year.

The simplicity of this type of tool and its ease of use, added to its being a system in which the user has to make hardly any effort to stay informed since they receive the posts in their email account, is most likely the main reason for the survival of this system of information and communications.

ACKNOWLEDGEMENT

We are grateful for the help given by Jesús Sanz de las Heras of RedIRIS in carrying out this work.

REFERENCES

Baiget, T. 2014. 20 aniversario de la lista de correo IweTel. *Anuario ThinkEPI*, Vol. 8, pp. 64-69.

Barrueco, J.M. García Testal C. and Gimeno Montoro, M.J. 1996. Las listas de correo como fuente de información en Biblioteconomía y Documentación. *Métodos de Información*, Vol. 3, No. 9.

Castro Castro, C. and Muñoz-Cañavate, A. 1995. Recursos informativos en las redes. Análisis de las listas de discusión gestionadas por un Mail List Manager: el Listserv de la red Bitnet. In *Actas V Jornadas Catalanas de Documentación*, October, 25-27, Barcelona, Spain, pp. 521-528.

Cordero González, A. M. and Faba-Pérez, C. 2013. Comportamiento de las listas de distribución de Documentación de RedIRIS durante la década 2002-2011. *Ibersid*, Vol.7, pp. 157-162.

Hernández-Borges, A., Macías, P. and Torres A. 1998. Are medical mailing lists reliable sources of professional advice? *Medical Informatics*, Vol. 23, No. 3, pp. 231-236.

Hernández-Borges, A.A., Macías-Cervi, P., Gaspar-Guardado, M.A., Torres-Álvarez De Arcaya, M.L., Ruiz-Rabaza, A. and Ormazábal-Ramos, C. 1999. Assessing the relative quality of anesthesiology and critical care medicine Internet mailing lists. *Anesthesia and Analgesia*, Vol.89, No. 2, pp. 520-525.

Hípola, P., Baiget, T. and Muñoz-Cañavate, A. 1994. Iwetel: foro electrónico para profesionales de la información. *IV Jornadas Españolas de Documentacion Automatizada*, octubre, 6-8, Gijón, Spain, pp. 27-33.

Kosovsky, R. 2014. Opera-L and Wikipedia. *Fontes Artis Musicae*, Vol. 61, No. 3, pp. 242-248.

Ministerio de Educación y Ciencia, 1985. *Proyecto IRIS*. Ministerio de Eucación y Ciencia, Madrid.

Merlo Vega, J.A. 1999. Las listas de distribución como herramienta profesional, *Métodos de información*, Vol.6, No. 31, pp.53-6.

Mushtaq, N., Beebe, L.A., Vesely, S.K. and Neas, B.R. 2014. A multiple motive/multi-dimensional approach to measure smokeless tobacco dependence. *Addictive Behaviors*, Vol. 39, No. 3, pp. 622-629.

Ontalba Ruipérez, J.A. 2002. Las comunidades virtuales académicas y científicas españolas: el caso de RedIRIS. *El profesional de la información*, Vol. 11, No. 5, pp. 328-338.

Ontalba Ruipérez, J.A. 2009. Análisis de Contenidos de la Lista de Correo-e Iwe Tel (2001-2007). *El Profesional de la Información*, Vol. 18, No. 1, pp. 50-61.

Pujar, S.M., Mahesh, G. and Jayakanth, F. 2014. An exploratory analysis of messages on a prominent LIS electronic discussion list from India. *DESIDOC Journal of Library and Information Technology*, Vol. 34, No. 1, pp. 23-27.

Rodríguez-Recio, F.J. and Sendra-Portero, F. 2007. Analysis of the Spanish-speaking mailing list RADIOLOGIA. *European Journal of Radiology*, Vol. 63, No. 1, pp. 136-143.

Serrano-Castro, P.J., Arjona Padíllo, A. and Guardado Santervás, P. 2004. Análisis descriptivo de la lista de correo electrónica «Neurología-RedIRIS»: Un instrumento activo, plural y de calidad científica al alcance de la neurología hispanohablante. *Neurologia*, Vol. 19, No. 8, pp. 420-428.

Tonta, Y. and Karabulut, D. 2010. The anatomy of an electronic discussion list for librarians, KUTUP-L: Bibliometric and content analyses of postings. *ELPUB 2010 - Publishing in the Networked World: Transforming the Nature of Communication, 14th International Conference on Electronic Publishing*, pp. 234-244.

Waseleski, C. 2006. Gender and the use of exclamation points in computer-mediated communication: An analysis of exclamations posted to two electronic discussion lists. *Journal of Computer-Mediated Communication*, Vol. 11, No. 4, pp. 1012-1024.

Zonfrillo, M.R., Sauber-Schatz, E.K., Hoffman, B.D. and Durbin, D.R. 2014. Pediatricians' Self-Reported Knowledge, Attitudes, and Practices about Child Passenger Safety. *Journal of Pediatrics*, Vol. 165, No. 5, pp. 1040–1045.

DESIGNING AN EYE TRACKING EXPERIMENT TO DETERMINE COGNITIVE LOAD

Chris Barry, Mairéad Hogan and Ann M. Torres
NUI Galway, Galway, Ireland

ABSTRACT

This paper details an eye tracking study to measure participant cognitive load when interacting with online decision constructs. It elaborates and improves on a pilot study that tested the experiment design. Physiological and subjective measurement of cognitive load is discussed as is a technique to capture participants' thoughts and feelings regarding the interaction. This mixed method approach will generate a more holistic understanding of participants' decision making and rationale.

KEYWORDS

Eye tracking, decision constructs, cognitive load, NASA-TLX

1. INTRODUCTION

This paper describes a research experiment designed to measure, both quantitatively and qualitatively, the cognitive load on participants making decisions on webpages. Several methods will be used to gather data: eye tracking equipment to gather interaction data; a scale to measure subjective cognitive load; and a think-aloud technique to gather thoughts and opinions. This study builds on a pilot conducted to confirm the experiment design and identify improvements to be made in the process. The research evolved from a series of studies into the commercial transactional process that consumers navigate to conclude online purchases.

1.1 Decision Constructs

Users can encounter seven distinct decision constructs throughout the transactional process of an online purchase (Hogan et al., 2014). These constructs form a taxonomy of discrete, mutually exclusive types. In examining this taxonomy, opt-outs were highly problematic for users to navigate as the clarity of the optionality and the level of opacity were challenging. The opt-out encountered in B2C websites was further explored to ascertain the dimensions of option presentation. A desk analysis of 57 websites identified the various dimensions of option presentation, three of which were considered key: default value; question or information framing; and additional persuaders. In an eye tracking pilot study of opt-out decisions the analysis indicates framing to be the most influential dimension in the interaction (Barry et al., 2016). Persuasion particularly appears to be less influential on participants' decision making. Therefore, for the current study, only framing and default value will be considered. Since previous research (Barry et al., 2016) indicates the checkbox to be the most widely used form of decision construct, it is employed in this research.

1.2 Cognitive Load

According to Grimes and Valacich (2015) cognitive load, or mental workload, is viewed as the mental effort and working memory necessary for the completion of a task. It is frequently considered in the development of computer-based learning applications and is acknowledged to impact negatively on learning (Hollender et al., 2010; Martin, 2014). Less research has been conducted on its impact in e-commerce transactions. However, higher cognitive loads negatively affected both the time to complete tasks and user satisfaction in e-commerce applications (Schmutz et al., 2009). Further, higher mental workload corresponds to lower perceived usability for webpages (Longo et al., 2012).

1.3 Eye Tracking

Eye tracking has been used extensively in web usability studies (Djamasbi et al., 2011; Huang and Kuo, 2011; Sivaji et al., 2011) and is frequently used in conjunction with think-aloud techniques. By studying what users look at in an interaction it is possible to determine where they are concentrating their attention (Pernice and Nielsen, 2009). This approach offers powerful insights to the decision making strategies individuals employ. Through the examination of eye movement patterns, conclusions can be made about fundamental aspects of the user's online activity (Day et al., 2006; Glöckner and Herbold, 2011).

2. RESEARCH APPROACH

The pilot study conducted by the authors (Barry et al., 2016) examined how users are impacted by differently designed opt-out decision constructs. It consisted of two parts: tracking eye movement while interacting with several decision constructs; and cued Retrospective Think-Aloud (cued RTA) sessions where the participant retrospectively articulated their thoughts and feelings regarding the interaction. This proposed study builds on the pilot by additionally using a variety of measures to determine the cognitive load on the participant during the interaction. The measurement approach will be three-fold: physiological measures, subjective measures using a subset of the NASA-TLX and attitudinal data identified during the cued RTA sessions.

2.1 Measuring Cognitive Load

2.1.1 Physiological Cognitive Load

Physiological measures can be used to indicate cognitive load based on the assumption that changes occur in the individual's physiological system as the cognitive demands of the task increase (Salmon et al., 2004). For this study, several metrics (blink rate, dwell time and fixation count) from the eye tracking experiments will be used to determine participants' reaction to stimuli (Martin, 2014; Sendurur and Yildirim, 2015). Dwell time denotes the duration of fixations within a particular area of interest (AOI), while fixation count identifies the number of fixations on a specific AOI. As eye tracking metrics can be influenced by factors such as fatigue (Cain, 2007) and age (Martin, 2014) it is recommended that a single measure is not used in isolation (Salmon et al., 2004; Martin, 2014). Hence, it was decided to use primary (dwell time, fixation count) and secondary (blink rate) measures, as well as both qualitative and quantitative subjective measures of cognitive load.

2.1.2 Subjective Cognitive Load

The NASA-Raw Task Load Index (NASA-RTLX) was deemed the most appropriate measurement scale of subjective cognitive load. It derives an estimate of workload that is both reliable and sensitive (Hart and Staveland, 1988). Recent studies (Colligan et al., 2015; Grimes and Valacich, 2015) have used this modified version and found it as effective as the original. Additionally, Hart and Staveland (1988) determined the individual factors (see Table 1) can be used independently to assess various aspects of workload. Studies have also variously adapted the measure using a 5-point scale (Goodman et al., 2005; Smuts et al., 2015), rather than the original 21-point scale.

Table 1. Rating scale definitions for NASA-TLX

Scale	Definition
Mental demand	The level of mental and perceptual activity required for the task
Physical demand	The level of physical activity required for the task
Temporal demand	The level of time pressure felt
Performance	The level of success in reaching the goals of the task
Effort	The level of work, both mental and physical, required
Frustration level	The level of frustration felt during the task

2.1.3 Cued Retrospective Think-Aloud (Cued RTA)

Think-aloud techniques clarify the user's attitudes towards the system and identify problematic elements of the design (Holzinger, 2005). They can be Concurrent Think-Aloud (CTA), where a user articulates their thoughts as they carry out tasks on a system, or Retrospective Think-Aloud (RTA), where the user describes their thought processes after completion of the tasks (Hyrskykari et al., 2008). Cued RTA, rather than relying on memory, requires the user's interaction to be played back to them. It tends to be more effective at eliciting comments than un-cued RTA (Ball et al., 2006). Using eye tracking with cued RTA allows supplementation of eye tracking data (Hyrskykari et al., 2008). Understanding why users focus on particular parts of the screen is important as the reasons can be positive or negative.

3. EXPERIMENT DESIGN

3.1 Lessons Learned from the Pilot

Based on lessons from the pilot study, the final experiment was designed. Three types of data were captured in the pilot: 1) eye tracking data quantified participants' interactions with the decision constructs (e.g., the duration of interaction; the total dwell time; the number of fixations and the mean duration of each fixation); 2) aggregated cued RTA data explained how participants perceived their interactions and afforded a nuanced understanding of participants' internal dialogue; and 3) heat maps (e.g., fixation intensity) provided a visual representation of participants' interaction. This mixed method approach determined which construct variants slow down, or interfere with, decision making and generated a more holistic comprehension of participants' decision making and their rationale. Hence, this process of data collection and analysis will persist in the main study with the addition of assessing cognitive load.

3.2 The Proposed study

This study of 100 participants involves both quantitative (i.e., eye tracking and NASA-TLX) and qualitative (i.e., cued RTA) data. A subset of 20 participants will be selected at random for the cued RTA. The experiment will be explained to the participant and details on the interaction with the equipment and the test material. After calibration, the participants will be presented with a series of 4 opt-out decisions, consisting of both pre-selected and un-selected constructs and using different types of framing. On each screen, they will be told which decision to make (see Figure 1) and to choose and click on the appropriate button (i.e., Change Checkbox or Leave Checkbox). They will then complete the NASA-TLX for the interaction with the decision construct.

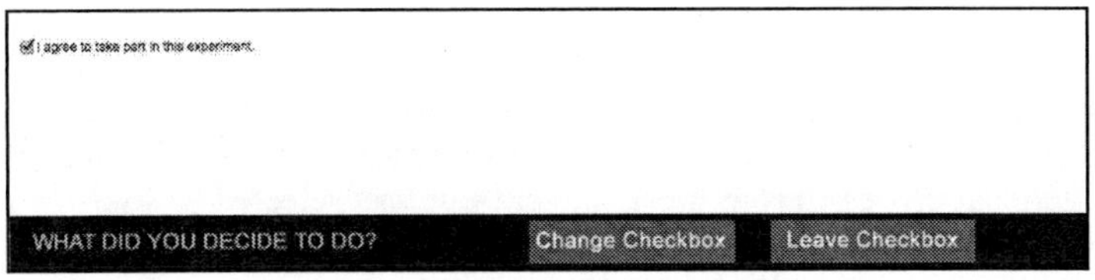

Figure 1. Sample Decision Construct

The participant will be asked to indicate on a rating scale how much each of the relevant factors was impacted by the task. As there is no physical element to the tasks, the subset of factors (see Table 1) chosen for this study are mental demand, performance and frustration level. The more useful 5-point rating scales (Goodman et al., 2005; Smuts et al., 2015) will be used. Given the nature of the tasks, a larger scale would be cumbersome and inappropriate.

For the cued RTA, participants will be shown an animation of their interaction with each decision construct. While they watch the animation, the participant will be asked to articulate the thought processes and feelings they had during the interaction. The interviewer will use prompts to encourage verbalisation (Barry et al., 2016). The prompts ensure all areas of interest are explored rather than directing the conversation in a specific direction. They are most helpful when interacting with participants who are finding it difficult to articulate their thoughts (Monk et al., 1993).

3.3 Analysis of Data

The data analysis will consist of several parts (see Figure 2). The eye tracking data will be used for physiological measures of cognitive load. Blink rate and Eye Point of Gaze (EPOG), which considers fixations, saccades and dwell time, can be used to determine cognitive load. Sensitivity is acceptable if primary parameters, such as fixation count are combined with secondary parameters, such as dwell time (Castor et al., 2003). Therefore, the frequency of fixations and the dwell time for the tasks will be compared. To analyse these factors for the AOI within each webpage, one-way ANOVA will be used to identify the range of participants' physiological cognitive load. The NASA-TLX subscales stand independently (Hart, 2006) and thus can be compared for each task. An overall workload is calculated using the subscales.

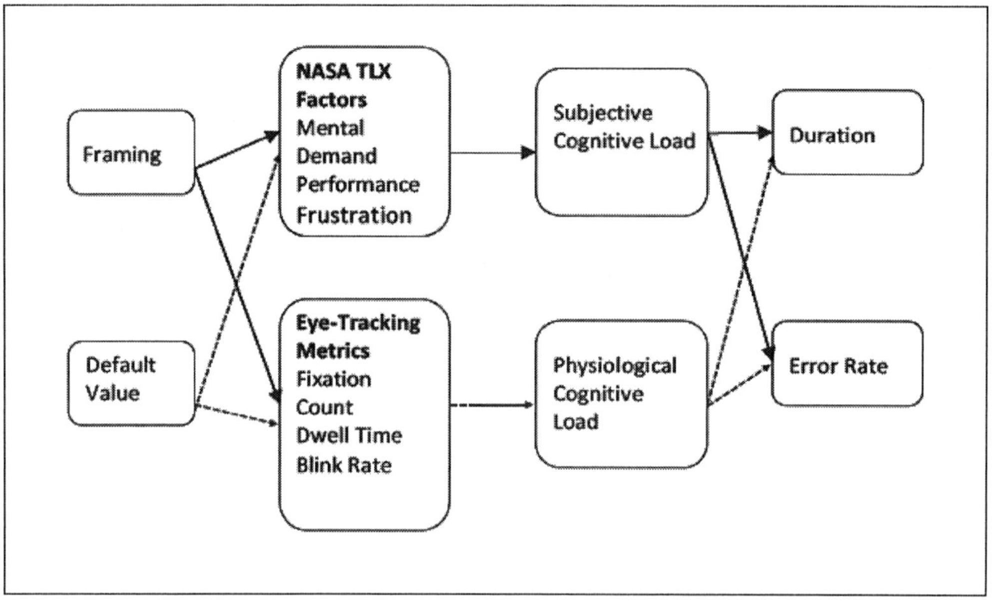

Figure 2. Analysis of Data

4. CONCLUSIONS

This paper has traced the context, development and rationale of a significant study designed to shed light on participants' response to cognitive load during interactions with decision constructs on webpages. The authors have mentioned a taxonomy identifying all decision constructs encountered during the online commercial transactional process. From these, the opt-out was selected to study in more detail, as it caused users particular difficulty and confusion. Cognitive load will be measured both physiologically and subjectively. The exploration of multiple measurements of cognitive load make it possible to gather strong quantitative data on interaction alongside cued RTA which captures, qualitatively, participants' thoughts and feelings during the interaction. This research on decision making during webpage interactions will make an original and novel contribution to the field of information systems development.

REFERENCES

Ball, L. J. et al, 2006. Applying the PEEP method in usability testing. *Interfaces*, Vol. 67, No., pp. 15-19.

Barry, C. et al, 2016. Framing or Gaming? Constructing a Study to Explore the Impact of Option Presentation on Consumers. *Information System Development: Transforming Healthcare Through Information Systems*, Springer International Publishing: 111-124.

Cain, B., 2007. A Review of the Mental Workload Literature. Defence Research and Development Toronto, CANADA.

Castor, M. et al, 2003. GARTEUR Handbook of Mental Workload Measurement. Group for Aeronautical Research and Technology in EURope (GARTEUR) Flight Mechanics Action Group FM AG13.

Colligan, L. et al, 2015. Cognitive workload changes for nurses transitioning from a legacy system with paper documentation to a commercial electronic health record. *International Journal of Medical Informatics*, Vol. 84, No. 7, pp. 469-476.

Day, R. F. et al, 2006. The effect of flash banners on multiattribute decision making: distractor or source of arousal? *Psychology & Marketing*, Vol. 23, No. 5, pp. 369-382.

Djamasbi, S. et al, 2011. Online viewing and aesthetic preferences of generation Y and the baby boom generation: testing user web site experience through eye tracking. *International Journal of Electronic Commerce*, Vol. 15, No. 4, pp. 121-158.

Glöckner, A. and Herbold, A. K., 2011. An eye-tracking study on information processing in risky decisions: Evidence for compensatory strategies based on automatic processes. *Journal of Behavioral Decision Making*, Vol. 24, No. 1, pp. 71-98.

Goodman, J. et al, 2005. How can we best use landmarks to support older people in navigation? *Behaviour & Information Technology*, Vol. 24, No. 1, pp. 3-20.

Grimes, G. M. and Valacich, J. S., 2015. Mind Over Mouse: The Effect of Cognitive Load on Mouse Movement *Thirty Sixth International Conference on Information Systems*, Forth Worth, USA.

Hart, S. G., 2006. Nasa-Task Load Index (NASA-TLX); 20 Years Later. *Proceedings of the Human Factors and Ergonomics Society Annual Meeting*.

Hart, S. G. and Staveland, L. E., 1988. Development of NASA-TLX (Task Load Index): Results of Empirical and Theoretical Research. *Advances in psychology*, Vol. 52, No., pp. 139-183.

Hogan, M. et al, 2014. Theorising and testing a taxonomy of decision constructs. *Journal of Customer Behaviour*, Vol. 13, No. 3, pp. 171-185.

Hollender, N. et al, 2010. Integrating cognitive load theory and concepts of human–computer interaction. *Computers in Human Behavior*, Vol. 26, No. 6, pp. 1278-1288.

Holzinger, A., 2005. Usability engineering methods for software developers. *Communications of the ACM*, Vol. 48, No. 1, pp. 71-74.

Huang, Y.-f. and Kuo, F.-y., 2011. An eye-tracking investigation of internet consumers' decision deliberateness. *Internet Research*, Vol. 21, No. 5, pp. 541-561.

Hyrskykari, A. et al, 2008. Gaze path stimulation in retrospective think-aloud. *Journal of Eye Movement Research*, Vol. 2, No. 4, pp. 1-18.

Longo, L. et al, 2012. The Importance of Human Mental Workload in Web Design. *WEBIST2012 8th International Conference on Web Information Systems and Technologies*.

Martin, S., 2014. Measuring cognitive load and cognition: metrics for technology-enhanced learning. *Educational Research and Evaluation*, Vol. 20, No. 7-8, pp. 592-621.

Monk, A. et al. 1993. *Improving your human-computer interface: A practical technique*. Prentice Hall, New York, USA.

NASA. 1986. "NASA TLX paper and pen manual." http://humansystems.arc.nasa.gov/groups/tlx/paperpencil.html.

Pernice, K. and Nielsen, J., 2009. Eyetracking methodology: How to conduct and evaluate usability studies using eyetracking. *Nielsen Norman Group Technical Report*, Vol., No., pp.

Salmon, P. et al, 2004. Human Factors Design & Evaluation Methods Review

Schmutz, P. et al, 2009. Cognitive Load in eCommerce Applications—Measurement and Effects on User Satisfaction. *Advances in Human-Computer Interaction*, Vol. 2009, No., pp. 1-9.

Sendurur, E. and Yildirim, Z., 2015. Students' Web Search Strategies With Different Task Types: An Eye-Tracking Study. *International Journal of Human-Computer Interaction*, Vol. 31, No. 2, pp. 101-111.

Sivaji, A. et al, 2011. Importance of incorporating fundamental usability with social & trust elements for e-commerce website. *International Conference on Business, Engineering and Industrial Applications (ICBEIA)*.

Smuts, M. et al, 2015. Usability Guidelines for Designing Information Visualisation Tools for Novice Users. *Beyond development. Time for a new ICT4D paradigm? Proceedings of the 9th IDIA conference, IDIA2015*, Nungwi, Zanzibar.

AN APPROACH TO SECURE INFORMATION SHARING IN CRISIS MANAGEMENT

Mohamed Amoud, Siham Younoussi, Ikram Elrhaffari and Ounsa Roudies
SIWeb Team - École Mohammadia d'Ingénieurs (EMI)
Mohammed V University in Rabat. Morocco

ABSTRACT

Crises are dynamic and changing over time, this has far-reaching consequences for design of crisis management information systems. This dynamism causes challenges for security when information sharing, especially in the case of terrorists attacks, because it is impossible to anticipate all the possible changes at design-time. Adaptive security is an applicable solution for this challenge. It is able to automatically select security mechanisms at runtime to preserve the required security level in a changing environment. In this paper we will address the role and importance of information and his secure sharing in crisis management, and propose a self-adaptive security solution for Mobile Devices based on the MAPE-K reference model. The novelty comes from dynamic negotiation of security policies and automatic reconfiguration of security level at runtime in order to be capable of deploying mechanisms adaptive security at different conditions when information sharing during crisis management.

KEYWORDS

Information Sharing, Adaptive Security, Information Security, Security Policies, Crisis Management

1. INTRODUCTION

Events such as *November 2015 Paris attacks, Bardo National Museum attack, Charlie Hebdo* and *Kosher Grocey Store, Algerian Hostage Crisis, Madrid train bombings, and Casablanca bombings* have made abundantly clear the need for greater collaboration and information sharing among government agencies during emergencies. The effectiveness of emergency preparedness and response depends fundamentally on the ability of a wide variety of organizational and professional communities to work together (Timo H. et al. 2011).

One dimension of information security that is increasingly enjoying attention in emergency organizations is that of crisis managers maintaining information security while operating various types of technical devices and complying with organizational security frameworks, such as the information security guidelines (Dan Harnesk et al, 2011). The context of crisis management is a domain which involves rapid and intricate cross-boundary socio-technical communications to manage undefined situations, often under pressure while engaged in the act of rescuing people and saving lives (Harrald, J. R. 2006).

In Information sharing during crisis management, it is not possible to take all the security requirements into account at design time (Benedikt Ley et al, 2014). Hence, this paper addresses the strategic role of the secure information sharing in crisis management, and presents a methodology detailing challenges, key steps and activities to create an adaptive security solution for Information sharing that is able to select security mechanisms and tune their parameters autonomously during crisis management at runtime in order to preserve the required security level in a changing environment.

After the introduction related work is described. Background information is given in Section 3. Section 4 presents our approach for integrating security in Information sharing. Finally, the Conclusion and future work Section close the paper.

2. RELATED WORK

The MAPE-K is commonly utilised as a reference model in different adaptation approaches (Anna Gryszkiewicz, 2012), and thus, elements from the MAPE-K model are emphasised in this section. Elkhodary et al. surveyed three security adaptation approaches in (F. Cuppens, 2014) – namely Extensible Security Infrastructure, The Willow Architecture (R. Adler, et al, 2007) and the Adaptive Trust Negotiation Framework. As the final conclusion, authors notice that any of these approaches support all security objectives but concentrate on specific and pre-selected objectives.

Elrakaiby et al. (Elrakaiby, Y. et al, 2014), present a policy-based approach for automating the integration of security mechanisms into Java-based business applications. They use security@runtime, a Domain-Specific Language (DSL), for the specification of security configurations based on authorization, obligation and reaction policies. Our approach is suitable for using security policies specified in any model since the mapping between the policies and the security functionalities is made at an abstract level of the variability model. We separate the monitoring of changes in the application and the integration of the security functionality following the MAPE-K loop, while they integrate the security functionalities in the same monitoring events.

Many systems, architectures and frameworks currently exist to support such runtime decisions but the challenge we address in this paper lies in moving such a decision from a static design/deployment time decision to a dynamic runtime decision. This concept is at the heart of our methodology which creates an adaptive security solution based on the use of the MAPE- K reference model to dynamic negotiate and deploy of security policies at runtime and monitor the changes in the context in order to be able to react to those changes, what constitutes the novelty of our contributions.

3. BACKGROUND

3.1 Adaptive Security

Building an adaptive security system faces significant challenges (M. Lynne Markus et al, 2012). We expect the adaptive security system to be: -1 self organizing and can deal with different attacks without central control; 2- able to counteract the distributed intelligent attack systems; 3- collaborative and optimized to intelligently safeguard the dynamic systems with low management and maintenance cost. In the IBM's Autonomic Computing vision (Yuan, E. et al, 2012), the autonomic behaviour is achieved by means of the MAPE-K reference model whose phases constitute the adaptation loop (Elkhodary, A. et al, 2007).

Having taken a closer look at characteristics Information Sharing in crisis management, and the adaptive security used to secure dynamic systems, in the next sections we describe the related work and turn to the methodology detailing key steps and activities to create an adaptive security solution for Information sharing.

3.2 MAPE-K Reference Model

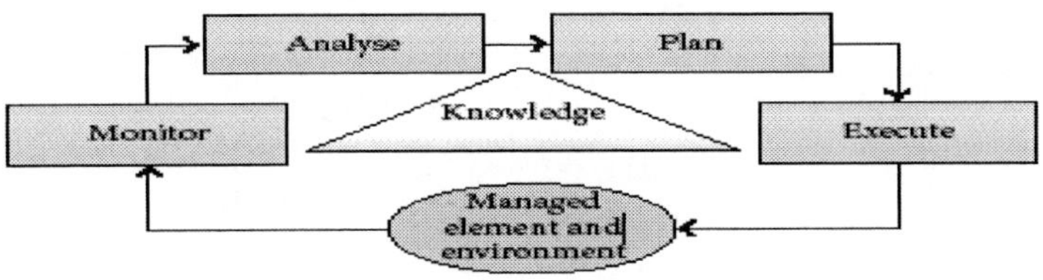

Figure 1. MAPE Adaptation Loop

In the IBM's Autonomic Computing vision (Mazeiar S. et al, 2005), the autonomic behaviour is achieved by means of the MAPE-K reference model (Monitor, Analyse, Plan, Execute, and Knowledge) (Figure 1). The principle of the Monitor phase is to collect information from the managed element. The Analyse phase combines the collected data and possible history data to reveal if requirements are not fulfilled, which causes an adaptation need. Consequently, the Analyse phase calls the Plan phase, which creates the adaptation plan. The adaptation plan contains a decision on how the software will be adapted. Finally, the Execute phase enforces the adaptation plan by means of effectors, which affect the managed element.

4. CHALLENGES AND OUR APPROACH

In this section we describe, in more detail, the main challenges that need to be taken into account in order to dynamically adapt and reconfigure the security level at runtime. We also indicate how our approach copes with these challenges (Yuan, E. et al, 2012), (Mazeiar S. et al, 2005), (Mónica Pinto, 2015), (C. J. Lamprecht, 2012), (R. Adler, et al, 2007), (Knight, J. et al, 2004), (Amoud M. et al, 2016).

4.1 Challenges

Challenge1: Develop secure applications that run on heterogeneous systems.
Challenge2: Dynamic negotiation of security policies for Mobile Devices in crisis management.
Challenge3: Monitor the changes in the context. These changes can be general or can be specific to security. The environment needs to be monitored to react to these changes.
Challenge4: Define a dynamic reconfiguration service to endow applications with self-protection.

4.2 Our Approach

Based on the challenges described before, in this section we describe a methodology to realize an adaptive security solution at runtime that conforms to IBM's Autonomic Computing vision (Mazeiar S. et al, 2005) and which is able to select security mechanisms and tune their parameters autonomously at runtime.

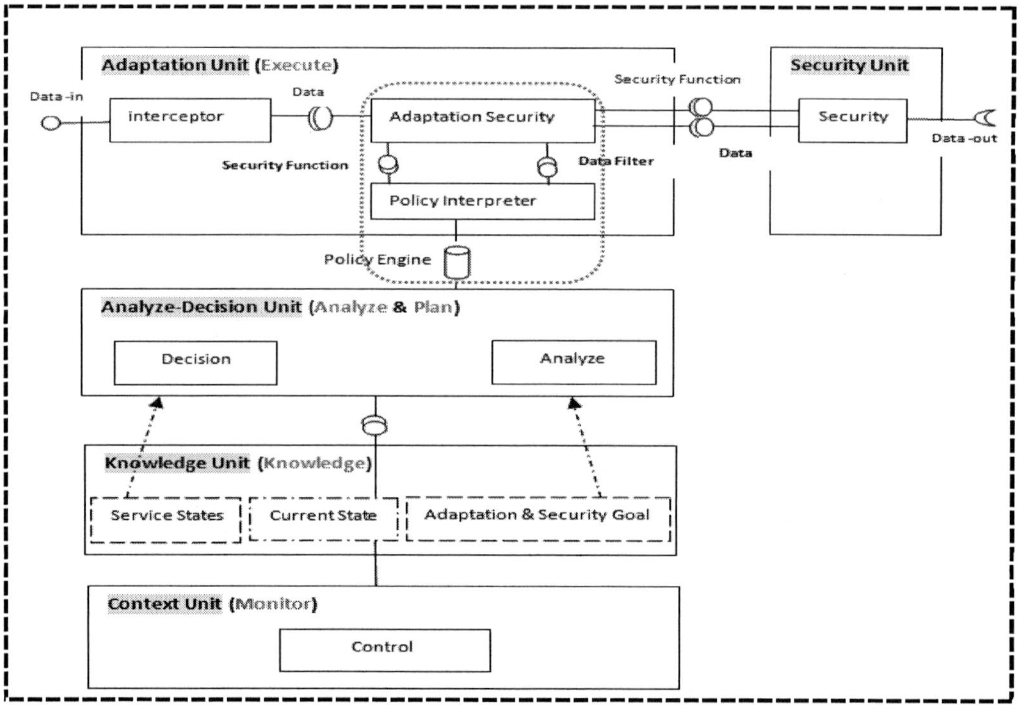

Figure 2. Adaptive Security Architecture

Figures 2 depicts the components of an adaptive security service in dynamic systems which augment a standard security service with adaptive features and new activities supporting the runtime nature of systems assets and products. Furthermore, the design is a realisation of adaptive feedback loop of MAPE-K model.

- **Context Unit:** It is similar to the Monitor component in the MAPE-K Model. It enables the Adaptive Security Service to observe the environment context. Through runtime monitoring of the system context it enables the *Analyze-Decision Unit* to make informed decisions based on the *Current State* of the system.

- **Knowledge Unit**: The shared knowledge includes data such as: -The *Service States* file contains pre-computed data or a system model which represents the interrelationship between security and the environmental concern. - The *Current State* which allows the *Analyze-Decision Unit* to determine the future system state: the change in the relationship, if security is adapted.

- **Analyze-Decision Unit***:* Taking the *Current State* into account the *Analyze-Decision Unit* is thus able to determine the future system state, i.e. the change in the relationship, if security is adapted. The *Analyze* component structures the actions needed to achieve goals and objectives. The *Decision* component determines if and how security should be adapted based on the adaptation *Goal*.

With reference to the *Service States* the *Analyze-Decision Unit* generates a *Policy* which satisfies the adaptation *Goal*.

- **Adaptation Unit**: in some sort, it is the architecture control center. It is a unit whose role is paramount and central. It corresponds to the Executor service in the MAPE-K Model and is responsible for implementing and enforcing the security adaptation at runtime. It is involved in the adaptation process in two key areas : 1) intercepts the source of data in transit to the security unit by forming a checkpoint where security can be adapted; 2) it maps the given Policy rules to the Source Data indicating to the *Security Unit* which Security function to apply to which sets of *Data*.

The block consisting of the *Policy Interpreter* and the P*olicy Engine* modules decide whether or not a new security policy must be negotiated and the changes to be performed in the system security after the negotiation.

The *Policy Interpreter* parses the incoming policy updates, generating appropriately formatted *Security Function* and *Data Filter* pairs as input to the *Adaptation Engine*. Such parsing may include authenticating the sender; policy syntax checking and mapping policy rules to internal security algorithm and *Data filter* representations.

Then the *Adaptation Engine* applies the filter conditions specified in the *Data Filter* to the incoming data from the *Interceptor*. Once filtered, the Data is sent to the *Security Unit* specifying the appropriate *Security Function* to apply to the particular subset of data.

- **Security Unit**: takes source data as input, applies the relevant *security function* to the data and returns the transformed data.

Our methodology applies the whole MAPE adaptation loop for a Dynamic Adaptation of Security in Mobile Devices during crisis management and defines each phase separately to successfully create an Adaptive Security Service.

4.3 Discussion

In terrorist attacks, security influences both how information is presented in a crisis management and how the information systems interact with the crisis management to support information sharing and cooperation. Achieving appropriate security in dynamically changing environments and threat landscapes is not possible by means of static and beforehand selected security mechanisms (Jesus A, 2016). Therefore, information security has to be implemented in a self-adaptive way. In adaptive security, utilised security mechanisms can be changed and modified at runtime, and thus all security related decisions are not bound at design time.

In cases of emergency response, where the time response has to be very short at a certain moment, the reconfiguration must be postponed if and when the instantiating of the adapted security policies would not be strictly necessary for the correct functioning of the system.

Our first objective was to address the role and importance of information and his secure sharing in crisis management, where optimal use can identify and reduce redundant efforts quickly, and improve the effectiveness of the work of the authorities in decision-making, coordination and situational awareness; our second objective was to present an approach for integrating security in Information sharing. The underlying principal focus and driving force in this paper is the desire to move security decisions from a design or deployment time decision to that of a runtime decision, and to identify ways to explore the different ways that adaptive security should be addressed in the design of information systems for crisis management.

5. CONCLUSION AND FUTURE WORK

This paper concentrated on secure sharing of information in crisis management, proposing an Adaptive Security methodology and his architecture at runtime based on the MAPE-K Model. Hence, This approach allows us to: - build secure applications that run in heterogeneous conditions; - dynamically satisfy different security needs at different situations; - monitor the changes in the context in order to be able to react to those changes; - reconfigure the security level of the applications at runtime, and - perform the previous tasks and challenges using an efficient solution that is able to work at runtime.

In light of the diverse scope and novel nature of our research area we highlight an emerging topic: an analysis of how organized criminals have adapted to the digital age by becoming expert at stealing information stored and shared electronically; and integrated solutions for adaptive security in information sharing to combat transnational organized crime.

REFERENCES

Amoud M.; Roudies O., 2016: *MAPE-K-Based Approach for Security @ Runtime*. IEEE International Conference on Software Science, Technology and Engineering (SWSTE), pp. 138-140.

Anna Gryszkiewicz, 2012: *Temporality in the Interaction Design of Information Systems for Crisis Management*. Thesis for the Degree of Licentiate. Sweden.

Benedikt Ley and al. 2014: *Information and Expertise Sharing in Inter-Organizational Crisis Management.* Computer Supported Cooperative Work. Dordrecht, Germany. Springer Science+Business.

C. J. Lamprecht, 2012: '' *Adaptive security* ''. PhD's thesis, Newcastle University.

Dan Harnesk and al. 2011: Multi-Layers of Information Security in Emergency Response. International *Journal of Information Systems for Crisis Response and Management.*

Elkhodary, A.; Whittle, J. 2007: A *Survey of Approaches to Adaptive Application Security*. In Proceedings of the Software Engineering for Adaptive and 65 Self-Managing Systems Workshop, Minneapolis, IEEE, pp. 16–23.

Elrakaiby, Y.; Amrani, M.; Le Traon, Y. 2014: *Security@Runtime: A Flexible MDE Approach to Enforce Fine-grained Security Policies*. Eng. Secur. Softw. Syst., 8364, 19–34.

F. Cuppens: Policy, 2014: *Based Language for Autonomous and Adaptive Security*, The Concordia Institute For I.S. Engineering, Canada.

Harrald, J. R. 2006: *Agility and discipline: Critical success factors for disaster response*. The Annals of the American Academy of Political and Social Science, 256–272.

Jesus Abelarde, 2016, *Security Systems Engineering Approach in Evaluating Commercial and Open Source Software Products*'', SANS Institute InfoSec Reading Room.

Knight, J.; Strunk, E. 2004: *Achieving Critical System Survivability Through Software Architectures*. In Architecting Dependable Systems II, de Lemos R., Gacek C., Romanovsky A., Eds.; Springer Berlin / Heidelberg, pp. 69–91.

M. Lynne Markus and Jane Fedorowicz 2012: *Characterizing and Improving Collaboration and Information-Sharing Across Emergency Preparedness and Response Communities*. 9th Workshop on Positioning Navigationand Communication IEEE. pp 42-46.

Mazeiar Salehie, Ladan Tahvildari. 2005: *Autonomic Computing: Emerging Trends and Open Problems*, Dept.of Elect.Comp.Eng,University of Waterloo.

Mónica Pinto, 2015,'' *Dynamic Reconfiguration of Security Policies in Wireless Sensor Networks*'', Sensors 2015,

R. Adler, D. Schneider, and M. Trapp. 2007, *Development of safe and reliable embedded systems using dynamic adaptation*. Workshop on Model-Driven Software Adaptation, M-ADAPT 2007 at ECOOP, pages 9- 14.

Timo Hellenberg, Pekka Visuri and Lars Nicander. 2011: *Securing Air Traffic*. Published by Aleksanteri Institute, University of Helsinki.

Yuan, E.; Malek, S. 2012, *A taxonomy and survey of self-protecting software systems*. In Proceedings of the IEEE Software Engineering for Adaptive and Self-Managing Systems, Zürich, Switzerland, pp. 109–118,

CONCEPT AND FEASIBILITY TESTS OF SELF-SUSTAINING POWER COMPONENTS FOR AUTONOMOUS SPORT AND HEALTH SENSORS

Hans Weghorn
Baden-Wuerttemberg Cooperative State University Stuttgart, Kronenstrasse 53A, 70174 Stuttgart, Germany

ABSTRACT

Today during sports activities and in health rehabilitation, various electronic monitoring tools are in use quite commonly. Sports persons and patients often are embedded into a personal body sensor network, which traces different parameters of their physiological activity. Heart rate sensors are the most typical devices, but all kinds of meters, e.g., for counting foot steps and pedal turning are often also used in parallel. Concerning power supply, it has commonly established that these sensor devices are autonomously operated as very tiny computer systems from lithium battery cells. Exchanging such sensor batteries from time to time is expensive, the mechanical handling of this step is not very easy due to the small sensor housings, and it has to be regarded that using throwaway batteries represents a waste of resources. In this work an alternative power cell for sport sensors is investigated, which bases on the use of so-called supercapacitors. Advantages of this approach and its possible application range are discussed, while the study is founded on practical experiments from endurance sports. Finally, the study is complemented with concepts for sensor charging including possible smartphone app guidance of its user handling and future self-harvesting of electrical energy by sensors themselves.

KEYWORDS

Sport Monitoring, Patient Monitoring, Body Sensor Network, Wireless Sensor Network, ANT+, Bluetooth LE

1. INTRODUCTION

In general, personal health condition can be improved by controlled physical activities. This plays an important role in our modern and aging societies. Performing personal sports on regular and moderate base from early days on represents a valuable key for preserving an extended period in life with fewer health problems up to higher living ages (Jefferis et al, 2014). All categories of physiological activities are today often monitored with the help of electronic devices and tools for achieving optimal response (Arts and Kuipers, 1994). The simplest variants of such monitoring units are pedometers or smartphones with corresponding software tools (Tudor-Locke and Basset, 2004).

In professional sports better control is achieved by using sports computers, which have either built-in activity sensors or RF-linked sensors (Malkinson, 2009). One of the most well-known samples of this multi-device monitoring are chest straps with an autonomous sensor module for detecting heart beats from skin surface electrodes and producing continuously measures of the heart rate (HR), which are sent to other control units for display, evaluation and recording. Fig. 1 shows three different HR devices, two of them communicate through the so-called Bluetooth LE standard, while the third one (device S) broadcasts its measures through ANT+ radio. The latter can be received by many sports computer and few smartphones, while Bluetooth LE is readable by most modern smartphones. It has been reported earlier that the electrical power consumption of the ANT+ system is lower compared to the Bluetooth LE solution (Weghorn, 2015).

Similar sensors exist for different other physiological measures, which are likely to be traced during sports and health exercises. E.g., tread rate in foot stepping, wheel and pedal turning rate in cycling and other information may be of relevance in such applications. Accordingly, various sensor types are available on the market and a training person can be embedded into a wireless network of short range nodes. In this, a smartphone may act as central control and recording unit and is communicating with several autonomous sensor elements, which are either attached to the body of the sports person or to sports machines.

Since such sensors are constructed as tiny wireless computer modules, they do require also an own electrical power supply. For this, commercial devices use lithium battery cells (B in Fig. 1), which have to be exchanged and disposed as hazardous waste, after they are emptied. This manual exchange is not easy, because the mechanical components are really small and some systems need considerable force and torque for opening and closing the battery mould covers. Fig. 1 shows above each sensor its back case part for the battery cell; for sensor S very small screws have to be handled, which is already inconvenient and complicate for younger people and may render impossible for older people or health patients with reduced sensitivity. Another negative aspect of inconvenience is that these batteries are rather expensive.

The work here discusses first possible alternatives for the use of such lithium batteries. The finding is that supercapacitors as new generation of electronic components allow storing electrical energy in sufficient amount. The specifications of such parts then are validated against the dedicate application in sports and health sensors, next a HR sensor is upgraded in two working stages with the new power cell concept. Extended laboratory and field tests validate in the next step the usability of a supercapacitor-supplied sports sensor in practical operation. The study is complemented with a thorough discussion about the possibilities, how the power cell of the sensor can be recharged with electricity in most convenient way.

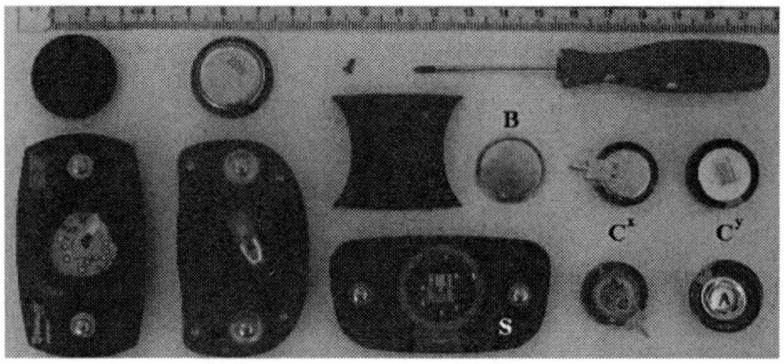

Figure 1. Three different heart rate sensors are visible from backside at bottom left. Above each sensor, its cover for the supply battery is shown; the middle one has to be fixed with four tiny screws. On bottom right, rear and top view of supercapacitors samples are shown, which are possibly feasible for replacing the lithium sensor batteries

2. PROPERTIES OF ELECTRONIC POWER STORAGE COMPONENTS

As evolved through many decades of product generations, body sensors like HR modules are usually equipped with exchangeable batteries as electrical power supply. This simplifies the construction of sensor units at first order, but it stands for a series of disadvantages in handling and in technical sense. Battery exchange is required in any case from time to time. It depends on the power consumption of the sensor electronics, how often this has to take place. The main consumer in body sensors is the RF interfacing; accordingly, a thorough investigation on the communication standards, which have established as the two competing alternative technologies, has unveiled already before the limitations of battery-operated sensors (Weghorn, 2015). This study has shown that one single lithium battery can sustain sufficient electricity for a continuous sensor operation of less than a week, which stands in high contrast to the public advertisements of vendors, who promise operational times of years for such systems. In sports, rare sensor use may require a battery exchange after several months only, but in health monitoring often continuous operation for a longer while is mandatory, which would consequence a battery exchange at least each week.

The handling of battery exchange appears cumbersome for younger people, but it may be even impossible for elder patients with sensitivity impairments. Another critical aspect is the price of such small batteries. Rechargeable batteries would be available, which fit the same size and housing, but their capacity is ten times lower and therefore an exchange would be needed ten times more often as long as no additional internal charging mechanisms are provided. Both types of batteries are very sensitive to deep discharge, and they use to leak in general after longer while, which means that their acid sometimes damages the sensor electronics.

Using batteries has been for a long time the only choice in engineering of unconnected electronics, since switching capacitors didn't provide sufficient storage size. This has changed with the invention and introduction of so-called supercapacitors approximately two decades ago (Conway, 1999). Material sciences and in particular nano technology enabled to increased effective plate surface to an extend, that supercapacitors can reach electrical storage amounts in the order of accumulators or chemical batteries. Their use became popular in high power applications like as boost supply for race cars during, but also recently in smartphone construction such parts were identified as alternative for rechargeable chemical batteries, because these caused increasing problems, in particular some units even exploded in rather sensitive environments.

Fundamentally, there are four basic supercapacitor (SC) types defined, for instance the ones for extreme power delivery during short time intervals. In contrast, body sensors do require low supply voltage and low supply current for a longer while. For this kind of application, electronic parts suppliers have developed so-called memory capacitors, since these are indented for preserving static RAM contents in switched-off computer systems. Since exactly this SC type appears deployable as substitute for coin batteries in body sensors, two specific types have been selected from a electronic parts manufacturer based on certain assumptions: at first, it was estimated from the study in (Weghorn, 2015) together with (USD Labor, 2009), that a capacity of one Farad should provide very roughly the typical operational time in physiological workouts of up to two hours; at second, size dimensions should be similar to the battery cell; another selection criterion was, that the SCs are available from parts suppliers quite regularly, so that mass production would theoretically possible. For each of the two different selected SC parts, which are named here C^x and C^y (Fig 1), a set of 10 samples has been purchased.

With these parts, statistical evaluation of their operational parameters was performed in order to explore their feasibility as power supply in sports body sensors. All the practical tests and calculations were aligned to be used with a HR sensor unit, which most typically represents this device class (unit S in Figure 1) and which works with the ANT+ RF standard, the one that runs at minimal power consumption. From the raw measurement series for the two different types conducted in (Weghorn, 2017), absolute capacities and their variations are derived as listed in Table 1.

Table 1. Calibrated Parameters with Variations for the Selected Memory Capacitor Types

Part	Specified ratings	Calibrated capacity	Standard deviation
C^x	1.50 Farad / 5.5 Volts	1.01 Farad	0.0204 Farad / 2.01%
C^y	1.00 Farad / 5.5 Volts	0.86 Farad	0.0103 Farad / 1.20%

The true absolute capacity of all parts is considerably lower in the experiments here than what is specified in the data sheets. On the other hand, the observed relative capacity range with the concrete samples was found being much lower than the specified range from -20% to 80% out of the data sheets. This may be explained by the fact, that for body sensors only a very limited temperature variation applies.

Energy storage and delivery from SCs suffers from two other disturbing effects with special impact on sports and health applications. The nominal capacity of such parts is specified for a charging time of half an hour. The SC do require this time, because their internal resistance is increasing with electrical load. On the other hand, the base experiments have shown that there is a big variation in self-discharge among the SC samples. Some parts preserve their energy for several days, while others discharge themselves within just one day so far, that they cannot provide the required sensor voltage anymore. Therefore, the SC should always be charged shortly before its use in a workout, but this shouldn't take too long for matter of comfort. Accordingly, a typical minimum time of one minute was assumed and applied in all the experiments here.

3. LABORATORY AND FIELD TESTING OF UPGRADED HR SENSOR

For practical exploration of the improved power cell concept, HR sensor unit S was modified and tested in an extended use series (all major tests in Table 2). The adoption was applied in two elaboration stages, after SC type C^x had been identified as preferable choice, because it was better fitting into the battery mould though minor mechanical modifications were still required. For the first test sequence, the battery was replaced directly by the SC, which means that only the limited voltage band like for the battery from 2.7 up to 3.3 Volts could be harvested. After this, mechanics was improved and the SC was connected through a regulator circuit to the sensor, so that the possible voltage range increased up to 5 Volts or theoretically 10% more.

During the tests in the first phase sometimes severe measurement distortions arose, which were identified as problems with humidity collected inside the sensor; details about this are found in (Weghorn, 2017). The insulation of the sensor was improved together with implementation of the regulation electronics. Specific experiments in both phases have shown, that self-discharge from the inactive sensor are minimal, while the regulation electronics has got small measurable impact. The next biggest sensor test (Fig. 2) was a workout in the run-walk-run mode (Galloway, 2017). This exercise started in the preparation phase with charging the sensor, and then voltage measurements (causing distortion peaks in HR) were performed during the workout in the walking phases with equipment, that was carried during the distance run in a sports rucksack.

Table 2. Documented Major Practical Tests of the HR Sensor with supply by SC Cell

Mode	*Date*	*SC connection*	*Charging*	*Overall duration*	*Voltage decay*
Lab test, no physical strain	April 2017	direct	saturated @3.3V	1hr 9min	0.26V/hr
Slow jogging on nature trail	April 2017	direct	60s @3.3V	1hr 5min	0.26V/hr
Half-marathon competition	May 2017	direct	saturated @3.4V	5hr	test fail
Lab test, no physical strain	June 2017	regulated	60s @3.4V	1hr	0.34V/hr
Jogging on nature trail	June 2017	regulated	60s @5.0V	1hr 5min	0.35V/hr
Run-walk-run trail jogging	June 2017	regulated	60s @5.0V	2hr 16min	Fig. 2
Half-marathon competition	August 2017	regulated	120s @5.0V	3hr 15min	0.36V/hr

This big experiment summarizes all the relevant properties during use of a SC as sensor power cell: the appropriate short charging time is not able to fill the SC completely, which is seen from a sudden voltage drop after charging. The decay rate of approx. 0.3 Volts per use hour, which was measured here throughout the run, confirms all the other measurements. The available voltage band for the sensor operation ranges therefore finally from 4.6 Volts down to 2.8 Volts (2.7 Volts plus 0.1 Volts offset from regulator) and this yields (4.6-2.8)/0.3 equals 6 hours supply time, which is sufficient for most workouts in sports and health.

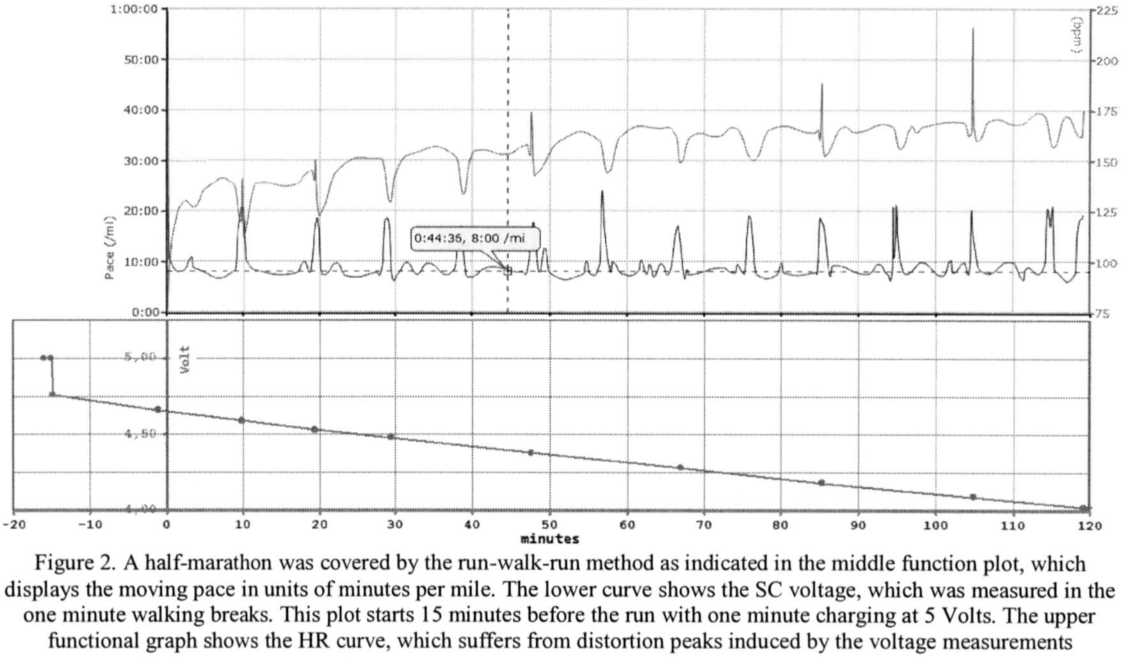

Figure 2. A half-marathon was covered by the run-walk-run method as indicated in the middle function plot, which displays the moving pace in units of minutes per mile. The lower curve shows the SC voltage, which was measured in the one minute walking breaks. This plot starts 15 minutes before the run with one minute charging at 5 Volts. The upper functional graph shows the HR curve, which suffers from distortion peaks induced by the voltage measurements

4. DISCUSSION OF CHARGING MECHANIMS AND PERFORMANCE

So far, all pre-investigations and implementations about using a supercapacitor as power cell in body sensors were based on the assumption that the system is charged via a cable at the typical USB standard voltage. This kind of USB charging was even enforced by European law and manifests a standard since many years for small and intermediate size computerized wireless devices. Of course, this concept requires electrical contacts, which cause efforts in construction and fabrications of the sensors and which needs special handling in daily use. Despite this is quite common for most users now, it doesn't appear as best solution.

In contradiction, in medical applications, which are very sensitive to contact points of any kind, inductive charging was investigated and used already early before (Chen at al. 2008). Inductively loading rechargeable power supplies is actually discussed for electrical urban vehicles, and it is also experiencing its broad market introduction in high ended smartphones. The charging stations for the latter could easily be used for the sport sensors as well. If such supporting devices are unavailable, charging could be also performed by power output from smartphones, which are used during sports or rehabilitation control. A cable solution could work with USB or audio plugs, but modern smartphones are also capable of producing a magnetic RF field through NFC technology. This could supply another system remotely without any cable wire.

Software support of the whole mechanisms presumably improves handling and comfort further. If, e.g., a modern smartphone is used in the workouts together with a special monitoring app anyway, this software can be expanded to guide the user through sensor charging just before the workout for ensuring that all system components work well together. In particular the following sequence is proposed in the preparation phase of a monitored exercise:

1. Sports persons starts smartphone monitoring app for controlling and recording the workout.
2. App performs configuration and communication tests including remotely reading sensor voltages.
3. If required, app asks sports user for manual action (e.g. holding sensor close to the phone cover or plug cable) and activates the charging supply (e.g. NFC field or wired power line outputs).
4. After sufficient charging time (may be derived by AI from workout behavior of the sports person), the process is stopped and the sports user is instructed to start the workout.

Again the sensor charging shouldn't take too long, for better convenience and acceptance this waiting time could be used in parallel for UI interaction between the health or sports app and the exercising person.

The best solution overall would be, if sensor charging can be overcome completely. This kind of advance was addressed already in research in other application fields (Bachmann et al., 2012), in particular body heat can be harvested for supplying wearable devices as reported in (Thielen et al., 2017). Another more obvious solution is using small solar panels as this is practiced since many years in pocket calculators, electronic watches and simple bicycle computers. For sensors mounted on bicycles or other sports machines, solar panels may deliver sufficient energy without special expedient.

In sensors like the HR unit, which are covered during exercising by cloths or shaded due to other effects, intermediate electrical storage is required and again supercapacitors can be used for this. Another opportunity of harvesting energy is mechanical movement: wheel turns are usually detected by flying magnets, these could also induce supply electricity; up/down movements of HR sensors could drive a laterally working generator. There arise manifold possibilities for harvesting energy, the key for the best solution is rooted in the operational mode of each sensor itself as seen in the particular solution samples before.

The indicative parameter combination, which was validated in the experiments here, is that a supercapacitor with one Farad loaded for one minute with a charging voltage of 5 Volts can supply an ANT+ sensor for at least six hours. This is considerably more than what is required in most physical workouts (USD Labor, 2009), but for sensors with the more popular Bluetooth communication standard this time span may be reduced down to securely only two hours. Therefore, it is depending on the dedicate electronics technology inside the sensor, whether higher efforts would be required for the power cell design. Despite this all, using firmly built-in power cells overcomes the series of disadvantages in handling, which were described above, and it reduces efforts in development and fabrication, because the sensor housing can be simplified considerably by having less parts, because requirement for opening and closing became obsolete.

As concluding remark it shall be noted, that this study was aiming to develop draft concepts and critically test their feasibility for the indented purpose. Full implementation of the concepts - especially for improving consumer devices - is left finally to the expert companies from health and sports market.

5. CONCLUSION

The commercially established power supply with tiny lithium batteries in autonomous sports and health sensors has been analyzed, possible alternatives have been considered. Using instead supercapacitors has been identified as better solution and it was implemented into a heart rate monitoring unit as it stands for the most typical sensor of this class. Extended laboratory and field tests - even in street running competitions - have proven that the available parts capacity sustains sufficient energy for the entire duration in typical workouts. It can be expected that the findings are transferable to all other sensor models, like those for tread and turn rate detection, since these are today constructed in very similar scheme like the HR units.

Using supercapacitors as sensor power cell provides a series of advantages. At first, avoiding throw-away components appears much more environment-friendly. Furthermore, operational costs are saved and wrong handling can not destroy sensor electronics due to acid leaking batteries after (deep) discharge. The problem of cumbersome mechanical replacement of batteries is overcome at all. The scheme of recharging the sensor just before the workout may appear inconvenient, but this can be performed with very limited effort and give clearness about the question, whether the sensor will work even in rare use cases. The recharging can be guided and supervised from an interlinked smartphone monitoring software, or it can be a kind of handling automatism, when using sports watches, because these also have to be recharged rather often.

In future investigations in the context here, charging mechanisms for the electrical supply storage in sports and health sensors shall be developed and improved. The final direction of this research will be replacing also the necessity for electrical charging by self-harvesting of electrical energy. Sensors may source their energy from body heat, mechanical movement or solar micro cells, but the explored supercapacitors still will be required for buffering variations in energy input. In the end, the study here yields a good base for designing and dimensioning next generation power supply schemes for health and sports sensor units.

REFERENCES

Arts F.J., and Kuipers H., 1994. The relation between power output, oxygen uptake and heart rate in male athletes. *Int. J. of Sports Medicine*, vol. 15(5), pp 228-231.

Bachmann C., et al., 2012. Low-Power Wireless Sensor Nodes for Ubiquitous Long-Term Biomedical Signal Monitoring. *IEEE Communications Magacine*, vol. 50(1), pp 20-27.

Chen W., et al., 2008. A power supply design of body sensor networks for health monitoring of neonates. *Proceedings of Intelligent Sensors, Sensor Networks and Information Processing, 2008, ISSNIP 2008, 15-18 Dec. 2008, Sydney*, IEEE, pp 255-260.

Conway B.E., 1999. *Electrochemical Supercapacitors, Scientific Fundamentals and Technological Applications.* Springer Science+Business Media, New York, USA.

Galloway J., Run Walk Run: It began in 1974. http://www.jeffgalloway.com/training/run-walk/, last access: July 2017

Jefferis B.J. et al, 2014. Protective Effect of Time Spent Walking on Risk of Stroke in Older Men. *Stroke*, vol. 45, pp 194-199.

Lu M., 2013. *Supercapacitors: Materials, Systems and Applications*. John Wiley and Sons Inc., New Jersey, USA.

Malkinson T., 2009. Current and emerging technologies in endurance athletic training and race monitoring. *Science and Technology for Humanity (TIC-STH).* Toronto, Canada; pp. 581-586.

Thielen M., et al., 2017. Human Body Heat for Powering Wearable Devices: From Thermal Energy to Application. *Energy Conversion and Management,* vol. 131, pp 44-54.

Tudor-Locke C., and Basset D.R., 2004. How many steps/day are enough? Preliminary pedometer indices for public health. *Sports Med.*, vol. 34(1), pp 1-8.

Weghorn H., 2015. Usability and Engineering Aspects of Competing RF Technologies for Communication with Commercial Sports Sensors in Ubiquitous Applications - Experimental Comparison of Power Consumption and Use Cases for ANT+ and Bluetooth Low Energy Sensor Devices. *Proceedings of the 3rd International Congress on Sports Science and Technology Support icSPORTS 2015*, Scitepress, Lisbon, Portugal, pp 263-270.

Weghorn H., 2017. Environment- and User-Friendly Power-Supply Concept for RF-Coupled Health and Sport Sensors. *Proceedings of the IADIS International Conference e-health 2017*, Lisbon, Portugal, pp 11-18.

USD Labor, 2009. Sports and Exercise. *Spotlight on Statistics*, May 2009, https://www.bls.gov/spotlight/2008/sports/, last access: June 2017.

EXAMINATION OF SOCIAL MEDIA GUIDELINES AT UNIVERSITIES IN JAPAN USING AN ARTIFICIAL NEURAL NETWORK

Yukiko Maruyama, Ryozo Kitajima and Ryotaro Kamimura
Tokai University, Hiratsuka Kanagawa, Japan

ABSTRACT

Social media guidelines are complex because they are written in natural language. We adopted the affordance approach and a new type of artificial neural network called potential learning (PL) to classify social media guidelines. As a result, the affordance "editability" was extracted as an important variable. It appears that editability characterizes university guidelines. The conventional method, however, could not be used to classify the guidelines. Therefore, PL is a useful method to analyze data written in natural language such as social media guidelines.

KEYWORDS

Social media guidelines, affordance approach, artificial neural network, potential learning

1. INTRODUCTION

As social media sites increasingly infiltrate our lives, they are used in various situations. For example, they are used as tools for collaborative work in organizations or as tools for gathering and sharing information in emergency situations such as natural disasters. As ways of using social media have diversified, opportunities for users to use social media as a private and social tool have also increased.

As such, users should obtain appropriate skills to use these sites appropriately depending on the situation and their positions. To support users in obtaining skills suitable to the situation, universities are expected to play an important role. Considering the importance of teaching the necessary skills to be responsible social media users in higher education, Takagi et al. suggested incorporating social media guidelines into basic education at universities. Social media guidelines can be effective in shaping students' attitudes towards and use of social media. To consider the possibility of incorporating social media guidelines into university education, it is important to understand the status of existing guidelines. However, university social media guidelines have received scant attention and there are no detailed investigations. While some studies investigated guidelines by focusing on the compositions or words included, in-depth investigations are still needed. Accordingly, this study adopted the affordance approach (Leonardi 2011; Majchrzak & Markus 2013; Treem & Leonardi 2012). Moreover, social media guidelines are written in natural language; thus, a detailed analysis is difficult. To consider this difficulty, we attempted to analyze guidelines using a new type of artificial neural network called potential learning (PL). In this study, we attempt to classify the guidelines as the first step towards a detailed examination of social media guidelines at universities in detail.

2. BACKGROUND

2.1 Studies on Social Media Guidelines

There has been growing research on organizational social media polices. Much of the literature so far has examined social media policies in organizational contexts (e.g., Vaast and Kaganer 2013, O'Connor et al. 2015, Schmidt and O'Connor 2015). However, university social media policies have received scant attention.

Yuki (2014) mentioned that university social media policy differs from organizational policy. The target of organizational social media policy is the workforce. Therefore, a social media policy established by an employer could control employees' social media use. However, the relationship between a university and students is not employment based. A university social media policy should guide students in their social media use. In practice, some universities have established rules regarding students' social media use, referring to them as social media guidelines, which are published on university websites. However, as mentioned, few studies focus on university social media guidelines.

Maruyama (2016) investigated university guidelines published on university websites in Japan. The targets of the survey were 82 national university websites, although only 6 social media guidelines were collected. This suggests that the establishment of social media guidelines is still uncommon for universities. The contexts of the six guidelines collected were examined, with results indicating that existing university social media guidelines focus on preventing trouble, rather than fostering students' skills for appropriate use.

In addition, Haga et al. investigated 98 university guidelines in Japan. They highlighted the following three aspects: 1) the guidelines were categorized into two groups, namely a protocol/platform style and guidebook style. The protocol/platform style has a general format as a guideline, while the guidebook style is written to include ideas to attract students' attention to read it. 2) Both types of guidelines have similar content. 3) The results of text mining show that the guidelines hardly included words related to using social network sites (SNS) in university education and words are important in the relation between university education and SNS.

As mentioned above, a focus on university social media guidelines is lacking in the literature. Even when focused on, detailed examination is absent, as only the compositions or words included in the guidelines are analyzed. To learn more about the status of university social media guidelines, we adopted the affordance approach and a new type of artificial neural network, namely PL.

2.2 Social Media Affordances

Gibson (1977) introduced the concept of affordance to account for how humans perceive their environment. An affordance is perceived as the potential to lead humans to act using certain behavior. The affordance approach highlights users' opportunities for actions in terms of what they can do with ICT systems, rather than the functions provided by these systems. Affordances and the actions provided by them vary according to users' environments and experiences. Therefore, many studies on social media adopt the affordance approach to reveal factors that can affect social media users in various situations. Vaast and Kaganer (2013) adopted the affordance approach in their study on social media policy in organizations. According to them, the "affordance approach suggests that people assimilate and respond to social media based on perceived affordances rather than on a fixed set of features built into the underlying technologies." Therefore, we consider this approach appropriate for our study. This study applies the ten affordances (Table 1) often mentioned in studies on social media.

2.3 Potential Learning

This study adopted a new type of artificial neural network, namely PL (Kamimura 2017, Kitajima 2016), to analyze data on social media guidelines. Artificial neural networks can be used to analyze complex data. As social media guidelines are rulebooks written in natural language, they are too complex to analyze. Therefore, in this study, we decided to adopt the artificial neural network.

We attempted to classify the guidelines by focusing on similarity. Self-organizing maps (SOM) (Kohonen 2001), which can classify data through a neural computational method, are widely used to classify data and as such, are a useful method. However, challenges include difficulty in interpreting a model or the results of the classification. Moreover, SOM treat data uniformly. Based on these characteristics, it is difficult to find variables that strongly influence the results of the classification.

Table 1. Social media affordances

Affordance	Description
persistence	The durability of online expressions and content (Boyd 2014) Social media allow for content previously created and published to remain permanently accessible (Wagner & Majchrzak 2006) Information remains available to users and does not expire or disappear when the poster logs out (Treem & Leonardi 2012)
visibility	The potential audience who can bear witness (Boyd 2014) To make their behaviors, knowledge, preferences, and communication network connections that were once invisible (or at least very hard to see) visible to others (Treem & Leonardi 2012)
association between people	To create and sustain relationships between people (Treem & Leonardi 2012)
association between people and information	To create and sustain relationships between people and information
association between people and organization	To create and sustain relationships between people and organizations (Vaast & Kaganer 2013)
replicability	Content made out of bits can be duplicated (Boyd 2010)
spreadability	The ease with which content can be shared (Boyd 2014)
searchability	The ability to find content (Boyd 2014)
editability	To amend, add to, revise and change content collaboratively (Vaast & Kaganer 2013)
accessibility	The capability of easily reaching content on an SNS (Fox 2016)

To avoid these problems, PL was used. This method is based on SOM, but can classify data by using important variables (There are some kinds of PL and a type, in this study, which classify data by SOM was used. This type is based on a method of Kitajima 2016). PL learns data by paying attention to the variance of variables (Kamimura 2017), and actively uses variables with large variance for the classification. This learning mechanism uses unique variables for the classification, which leads to extracting the key variables. Figure 1 illustrates the concept of PL, which consists of two layers, namely the input layer and output layer. The input layer is configured by input neurons (neurons are shown as circles in Figure 1) and the output layer by output neurons. Input neurons function to import data to the network, namely the input variables. In addition, output neurons show the results of the classification.

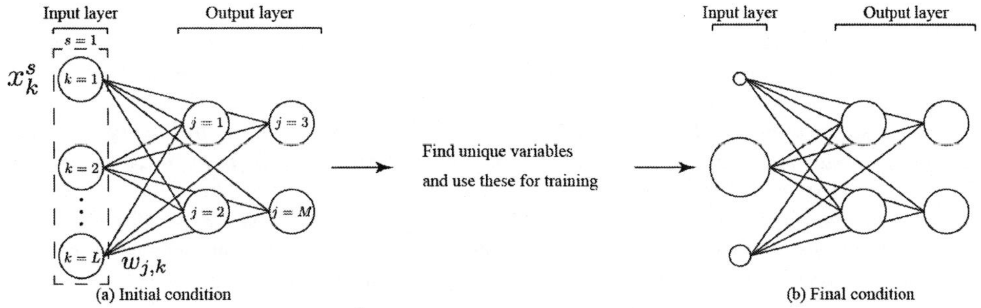

Figure 1. Concept of potential learning

When the original SOM analyzes data, this data is calculated using:

$$\sum_{k=1}^{L}\left(x_k^s - w_{j,k}\right)^2,$$

where x_k^s, L and $w_{j,k}$ denotes data of k th variable in s th pattern, the number of input neurons, and weight connected from the k th input neuron to the j th output neuron. On the other hand, PL then uses a measure of the importance of variables called potentiality ($\emptyset_k^r$) to classify data. Potentiality is computed by the variance of the k th input neuron (v_k). The v_k is defined by:

$$v_k = \frac{1}{M-1}\sum_{j=1}^{M}\left(w_{j,k} - w_k\right)^2,$$

where M denotes the number of output neurons and w_k denotes the average weight of the k th input neuron. The w_k is defined by:

$$w_k = \frac{1}{M}\sum_{j=1}^{M} w_{j,k}.$$

After calculating all v_k, the potentiality of k th input neuron is computed by:

$$\emptyset_k^r = \left(\frac{v_k}{v_{max}}\right)^r,$$

where r is a parameter to emphasize the degree of attention to variables, and PL analyzes data using:

$$\sum_{k=1}^{L} \emptyset_k^r \left(x_k^s - w_{j,k}\right)^2.$$

By using potentiality, data can be classified by paying attention to important variables and a model can be interpreted.

3. METHODOLOGY

3.1 Data Collection

Data were collected through a web page that included links to all Japanese private universities on the Ministry of Internal Affairs and Communications' website (http://www.mext.go.jp/). All university sites linked to the webpages, excepting graduate university sites, discontinued universities, those merged with other universities, and dead links to university sites were the objects of the survey. The total number of objects was 580. From these websites, we investigated content for students in the context of advice or warnings for using social media sites, obtaining 70 social media guidelines. The survey of private university websites was conducted from August to October 2015.

3.2 Data Analysis

The first step of our analysis was interpreting the guidelines in relation to the social media affordances in Table 1 with reference to Vaast and Kaganer's (2013) method. A unit for interpretation was defined as a segment of text no smaller than a sentence and no bigger than a paragraph. Descriptions pertaining to social media in each segment were related to the affordance. For example, from the following description "[a social media site is] media that enables unspecified users to communicate with each other through personal posts using web technology on the Internet (translated by authors)," we can interpret that the action of "communicating with each other" is related to the affordance "association between people." Some segments of text can include several affordances in a single segment. To conduct the analysis using PL, ten data related to each affordance were generated for each guideline. Each data has a value of 0 to 4, which indicates the frequency of each affordance in the guidelines.

The second step of our analysis was text mining using JUMAN, which is software for the morphological analysis of Japanese. A dictionary included in JUMAN has the concepts of "category" and "domain." For example, the word "school" is grouped into the category "place-facility" and domain "education-study." In this study, nouns, verbs, and adjectives in the guidelines were grouped into 11 categories, namely "human," "organization/association," "animal," "artifact-the others," "place-the others," "abstract thing," "name of university," "guideline," "related to penal regulation," "reference," and "SNS-related." The first six categories are original categories in JUMAN's dictionary, while the others were added for the purposes of this study. The Term Frequency-Inverse Document Frequency (TF-IDF) for each category was used as the data for analysis through PL. As such, 70 data sets consisting of 21 data were generated in the first and second steps. These data sets were used as input data in the PL analysis.

The next step of our analysis was classifying the guidelines using PL. In this analysis, the parameter to emphasize the degree of attention to variables, denoted as r in section 2.3, was examined in the range of 10 from 1 from the viewpoint of error. To compare, the same data sets were analyzed using SOM.

4. RESULTS AND DISCUSSION

Figure 2 shows the results of the classification using U-Matrix (Ultsch 1990). In Figure 2, (a) and (b) show the results of the classification through SOM and PL respectively. This figure shows clusters of social media guidelines. The U-Matrix is a popular method for showing results obtained through SOM. It shows clusters by using color. In Figure 2, consecutive hexagons in cold colors represent the clusters. Consecutive hexagons in warm colors breaking into the cold color area represent the boundary.

In Figure 2 (a), there is an unclear area at the lower left. Here, a cluster cannot be extracted. This result suggests that classification through SOM was not adequate.

On the other hand, in Figure 2 (b), two clusters are clearly seen in the U-Matrix using PL. These clusters were named "Group A" and "Group B." This clustering result was obtained when the parameter r was 9.

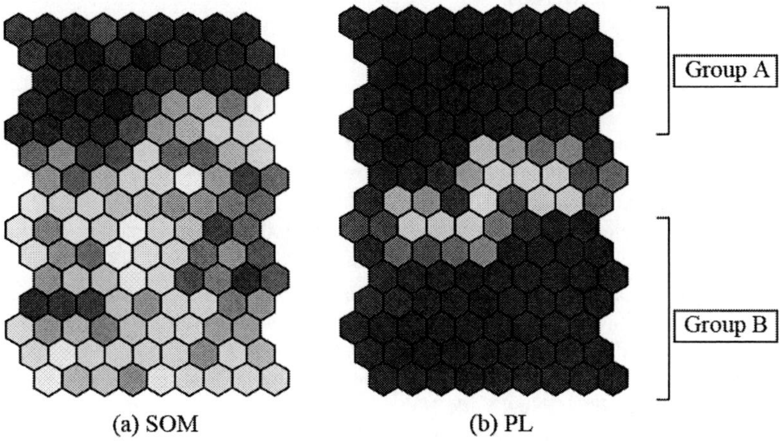

(a) SOM (b) PL

Figure 2. Results of the classification

In addition, the most important variable affecting the results of the classification was extracted. Variable No 15 was obtained. Variable No. 15 indicates the frequencies of the affordance "editability" in each guideline. Group A consisted of social media guidelines that did not contain editability, while Group B consisted of guidelines containing this affordance. Variable No. 15 is regarded as a flag showing whether the affordance editability is contained in the social media guidelines or not. Therefore, the existence of editability affected the classification of guidelines.

Ultimately, 41 guidelines were classified into Group A and 29 into Group B. The guidelines seem to put less emphasis on editability. All guidelines containing editability included statements such as: "If you posted incorrect information, you should immediately correct your post and make it clear you corrected it (translated by authors)."

The university guidelines highlighted a particular facet of editability that related to the ability of "users themselves" to amend social media content. However, Vaast and Kaganer (2013) mentioned that organization policies highlighted a particular facet of editability related to the ability of "others." Therefore, we consider that editability is one affordance that can characterize university guidelines. Thus, by using PL, a useful factor to investigate the guidelines was obtained.

5. CONCLUSION

Social media guidelines are complex, because they are written in natural language. In this study, we adopted the affordance approach and a new type of artificial neural network, namely PL.

As a result, the affordance editability was extracted as an important variable. It seems that editability characterizes university social media guidelines.

Furthermore, the data could not be analyzed using the conventional SOM method. Therefore, PL was confirmed as a useful method to analyze data written in natural language such as social media guidelines.

REFERENCES

Danah, B., 2014, *It's Complicated: The Social Lives of Networked Teens*, Yale University Press, New Haven and London.

Fox, J., 2016, The dark side of social networking sites in romantic relationships. In B. K. Wiederhold, G. Riva, and P. Cipresso (Eds.), *The psychology of social networking: Communication, presence, identity, and relationships in online communities,* DeGruyter Open, Warsaw.

Gibson, J. J., 1977, *The theory of affordances,* In R. Shaw & J. Bransford (Eds.), Perceiving, acting, and knowing: Toward an ecological psychology, 67–82, Lawrence Erlbaum, Hillsdale, N.J.

Haga, T., Otani, T., Sato, T., Takagi, H., and Toyofuku, S., 2015, Pedagogical consideration of guidelines for use of the social networking service (SNS) in university, *Proceedings of IPSJ-SSS 2015,* 149–156.

Kamimura, R., 2017, Collective mutual information maximization to unify passive and positive approaches for improving interpretation and generalization, *Neural Networks*, 90, 56-71.

Kitajima, R., Endou, K., and Kamimura, R., 2016, 入力ニューロンの潜在性に着目した小売店店舗の非継続来店顧客検知モデルの作成 [A Non-Continuous Visitor Detection Model for Supermarkets Focused on the Potentiality of Input Neurons], *オペレーションズ・リサーチ [Operations Research],* 61(2), 88-96. (In Japanese)

Kohonen, T., 2001, *Self-Organizing Maps*, Springer-Verlag Berlin Heidelberg, New York.

Leonardi, P. M., 2011, When flexible routines meet flexible technologies: Affordance, constraint, and the imbrication of human and material agencies, *MIS Quarterly,* 35(1), 147–167.

Majchrzak, A., Wagner, C., and Yates, D., 2006, Corporate wiki users: Results of a survey, *Proceedings of the 2006 International Symposium on Wikis,* New York, NY.

Maruyama, Y., 2016, *An examination of social media guidelines at universities in Japan, Proc. for SITE 2016 Society for Information Technology and Teacher Education International*, 957–961.

O'Connor, K. W., Schmidt, G. B., and Drouin, M., 2015, Helping workers understand and follow social media policies, *Business Horizons,* 59, 205–211.

Schmidt, G. B., and O'Connor, K. W., 2015, Fired for Facebook: Using NLRB guidance to craft appropriate social media policies, *Business Horizons,* 58, 571–579.

Treem, J. W., and Leonardi, P. M., 2012, Social media use in organizations: Exploring the affordances of visibility, editability, persistence, and association, *Communication Yearbook*, 36, 143–189.

Takagi, H., Sato, T., Otani, T., Haga, T., and Toyofuku, S., 2015, A consideration of the potential for development of guidelines for the use of social networking services (SNS) in basic education in university, *IEICE technical report,* 115, 41–46.

Ultsch, A., and Siemon, H. P., 1990, Kohonen's Self-Organizing Feature Maps for Exploratory Data Analysis, *Proceedings of International Neural Networks Conference,* 305–308.

Vaast, E., and Kaganer, E., 2013, Social media affordances and governance in the workplace: An examination of organizational policies, *Journal of Computer-Mediated Communication*, 19, 78–101.

Yuki, D., 2014, Information processing from the perspective of lawyers: 5. Social media legal risk, *Journal of Information Processing Society of Japan*, 55(3), 247–252.

EXTRACTION OF CLASSIFICATION RULES FROM IMBALANCED DATASETS USING GA-ILS

Aouatef Mahani, Sadjia Benkhider and Ahmed Riadh Baba-Ali
University of Sciences and Technology Houari Boumediene, Algeria

ABSTRACT

The classification is a task of Data Mining. It consists of the extraction of a set of rules from large datasets. However, some datasets are imbalanced and they contain majority instances and minority ones. It is worth noting that classical learning algorithms are known to have a bias towards majority class instances. If classification is applied to imbalanced datasets; it is called partial classification. Partial classification approaches are generally based on sampling methods or algorithmic methods. In this paper, we propose a new hybrid approach using a three-phase-rule-based extraction process which takes into account minority and majority instances in imbalanced binary datasets. Our approach has been tested on several imbalanced binary datasets with different values of imbalanced ratio. The obtained results show the efficiency of our approach compared to other results available in the literature.

KEYWORDS

Data Mining, Classification, Imbalanced Datasets, Memetic Algorithm, Iterated Local Search, Genetic Algorithm

1. INTRODUCTION

Classification is a task of Data mining which consists of extracting a model or classifier from large datasets with the aim of attribute the appropriate class to an object according to certain descriptive features [Parpinelli, R.S. et al 2002]. Datasets are divided into two categories: the balanced and the imbalanced datasets. In imbalanced datasets, instances are divided into two sets: majority instances which are the most frequent ones and minority instances which are the less frequent.

Classification algorithms have a bias towards the majority classes [Batista, G. et al 2004]. Consequently, the extracted rules are usually specific to the majority instances, whereas specific rules that predict instances from minority class are usually ignored or treated as noise. Consequently, minority class instances are more often misclassified than those from other classes. In addition, in many applications misclassifying a rare event can result in more serious problems than a common event [Yuchun, T. et al, 2009]. The class imbalance problem is a fundamental problem in machine learning, and it has received much attention recently [Alejo, R. et al, 2007] [Fu, X. et al, 2002]. Consequently, another category of classification appears to deal with this problem known as partial classification [Ali, S. et al, 1998.], nugget discovery [Riddle, P. et al, 1994] or classification problems with imbalanced datasets [Fernández, A. et al, 2007].

This paper is organized in the following manner. Section 2 describes a state of the art about some approaches used for handling the problem of imbalanced datasets. In section 3, we explain the steps of our memetic approach. Results obtained and a comparative study is reported in section 4. Finally, in section 5, we make our concluding remarks and some suggestions of future works are presented.

2. RELATED WORK

A dataset is imbalanced if the number of instances from the different classes is not nearly the same. In imbalanced binary datasets, the imbalanced ratio IR [Wu, G. and Chang, E.Y., 2003] is equal to the fraction between the number of majority instances and the number of minority instances.

The problem of imbalanced datasets appears in many domains such as fraud detection [Walters, S.D. and Wilkinson, W., 1994]. The different approaches used for handling the problem of imbalanced datasets are divided into three groups; data level, algorithm level and hybrid level [Garcìa, S. and Herrera, F., 2009].

Date level approaches consist of resampling the data in order to decrease the effect caused by the imbalance of data [Batista, G. et al 2004.]. The main advantage of these techniques is that they are independent of the used classifier, so they can be considered as preprocessing approaches. These methods are classified into three groups [Batista, G. et al 2004]: undersampling methods [Chyi, Y. M., 2003] [Zhang, J. and Mani, I., 2003] [Liu, X.Y. et al 2006], oversampling methods [Chawla, N.V. et al, 2002] [Batista, G. et al 2004] and hybrid methods combine undersampling and oversampling methods in order to eliminate overfitting [Batista, G. et al 2004] caused by oversampling methods.

Algorithm level approaches are based on modifying the existing complete classification algorithms such as Confidence Proportion Decision Tree approach (CCPDT) [Cieslak, D.N. and Chawla, N., 2008] or proposing specific algorithms such as Rule Learning Algorithm for Skewed Datasets RLSD [Zhang, J. et al, 2004].

Hybrid level approaches are done because some existing methods cannot handle the problem of imbalanced datasets without combination of other techniques, such as ensemble methods classifiers [Polikar, R., 2006] [Rokach, L., 2010] cannot handle the problem of imbalanced datasets [Galar, M. et al, 2012] without any changes or without the integration of sampling techniques such as SMOTEBoost [Chawla, N. V. et al, 2003].

3. THE PROPOSED APPROACH USGA_ILS

The problem of classification is an NP-hard combinatorial problem [Melanie, M., 1996]; we solve it using heuristic or metaheuristic methods. Genetic algorithms have shown their effectiveness and robustness to solve difficult problems. The GA version used is Steady State ssGA [Syswerda, G., 1990]. Different authors [Sun, Y. et al, 2009] recommend the use of ssGA for the design of the Memetic Algorithm MA because they allow the results of Local Search to be kept in the population from one generation to the next. The details GA steps, the representation of the individual are described in [Benkhider, S. and Drias, H., 2013]. The details of our proposed approach are explained in the following:

Phase 1 is called Learning and Sampling phase: the objective of our approach is the extraction of classification rules from imbalanced binary datasets which represent the majority instances and the minority ones. For this reason, we apply this phase in which we develop a learning algorithm based on a genetic algorithm with the aim of extracting the first classifier noted C1, which covers only the majority instances. Consequently, the majority instances which are well classified by the rules of C1 are removed. Therefore, our proposed approach balances the imbalanced dataset and avoids the loss of information contained in the deleted majority instances because they are replaced by the classification rules of C1. Therefore, our approach applies undersampling by classification rules using ssGA. Consequently, our proposed approach is known as USGA (UnderSampling by genetic algorithm). The rules of C1 are extracted using a learning algorithm called sequential covering algorithm. The quality of each rule in this case is evaluated by satisfying specificity (is the percentage of majority instances which are well classified as belonging to the majority class). A rule is the best if it has a high number of well classified majority instances.

Phase 2: In this phase, the same procedure is applied to the obtained balanced dataset using a 5-fold cross validation to construct the classifier C2. In other words, we use five partitions for training and test sets, 80% for training and 20% for testing. C2 is also built by a sequential covering algorithm using memetic algorithm. The algorithm of extraction is the same to the phase 1. Our memetic approach includes the Iterative Local Search method ILS [Lourenco, H. et al, 2003] in the cycle of a genetic algorithm ssGA, we call our approach USGA_ILS. In our contribution the principle modules of ILS are modified as follow:

a. Generation of the initial solution: we apply ILS after crossover or after mutation. Consequently, we don't generate an initial solution. The used solution is the best offspring resulting of crossover or of mutation.

b. Local search: we apply a simple local search in which we modify the value of once attribute selected randomly.

c. Perturbation: The size of a chromosome depends on the number of attributes in a dataset. For this reason, we choose to assign to the strength of perturbation, the values which depend on the number of attributes of the considered dataset. In our tests, we took three possible values to see its impact on the performance of obtained classifiers. The tested values V are: L/4 (25%), L/2 (50%), 3*L/4 (75%).

d. Acceptance criterion: we will test two existing acceptance criteria: random walk and better. We add another which is an alternative of these two acceptance criteria.

e. Termination condition: we will use a fixed number of iterations.

Phase 3: In order to obtain the final classifier noted C3, we merge C1 and C2 at first, and then we process the obtained new classifier by eliminating the contradictory rules and specific rules.

4. EXPERIMENTAL STUDY

The software KEEL (Knowledge Extraction Evolutionary Learning) [Alcalá-Fdez J. et al, 2011] and Weka [Buckland, M. and Gey, F., 1994] are used to obtain the performances of approaches used in comparative study. We use also 38 imbalanced binary datasets from KEEL dataset repository with different IR. Table 1 summarizes the used datasets and shows for each one, the number of instances (#Ex.), number of attributes (#Atts.) and IR. Approaches used in comparative study are Classical ones: C4.5, RIPPER (RIP) [Cohen, W., 1995] and PART and some state of the art ones: SMOTEBOOST (SMB), UnderBagging1 (UB1), AdaC2 (AC2) and Evolutionary under sampling using CHC (CHC). In order to compare different approaches, we use non parametric tests because their usage is strongly recommended in [Demšar J., 2006]. In this paper, we use ***Wilcoxon paired signed rank test*** [Wilcoxon F., 1945] which is used to detect if there is a significant difference between a pair of algorithms and the ***Freidman Aligned-ranks test*** [Hodges, J.L and Lehmann E.L., 1962] which is used as a visualization tool.

Table 1. Characteristics of Used Datasets

Datasets with low imbalance				*Datasets with medium imbalance*				*Datasets with high imbalance*			
Datasets	**#Ex.**	**#Atts.**	IR	**Datasets**	**#Ex.**	**#Atts.**	IR	**Datasets**	**#Ex.**	**#Atts.**	IR
Glass1	214	9	1.82	Glass0123vs456	214	9	3.19	Vowel0	988	3	10.10
Ecoli0vs1	220	7	1.86	Vehicle0	846	18	3.23	Glass016vs2	192	9	10.29
Wisconsin	683	9	1.86	Ecoli1	336	7	3.36	Glass2	214	9	10.39
Pima	768	8	1.90	New-thyroid2	215	5	4.92	Ecoli4	336	7	13.84
Iris0	150	4	2.00	New-thyroid1	215	5	5.14	Yeast1vs7	459	8	13.87
Glass0	214	9	2.06	Ecoli2	336	7	5.46	Shuttle0vs4	1829	9	13.87
Yeast1	1484	8	2.46	Glass6	214	9	6.38	Glass4	214	9	15.47
Vehicle2	846	18	2.52	Yeast3	1484	8	8.11	Abalone9vs18	731	8	16.68
Vehicle3	846	18	2.52	Ecoli3	336	7	8.19	Yeast1458vs7	693	8	22.10
Haberman	306	3	2.68	Page-blocks0	5472	10	8.77	Yeast2vs8	482	8	23.10
Vehicle1	846	18	2.89	Yeast2vs4	514	8	9.08	Yeast4	1484	8	28.41
				Yeast05679vs4	528	8	9.35	Yeast1289vs7	947	8	30.56
								Yeast5	1484	8	32.78
								Yeast6	1484	8	39.15
								Abalone19	4174	8	128.87

In order to set the parameters of genetic algorithm, the number of generations and the value of the population size were tested. As noticed from figure 1, the smallest rank is related to the number of generations equal to 10, and population size equal to 50. Consequently, the used parameters are shown in Table 2.

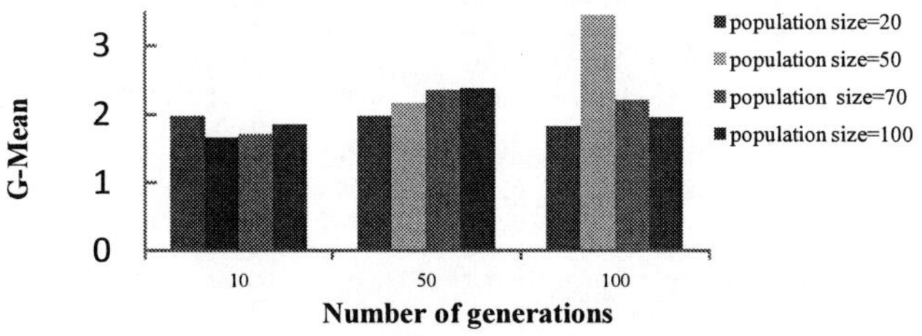

Figure 1. Average Aligned-Ranks for Different Values of Generations Number and Population Size

Table 2. Parameters of Genetic Algorithm

Parameters	
Size of the population	*50*
Number of generations of genetic algorithm	*10*
Crossover probability	*0.9*
Mutation probability	*0.1*

In order to deduce the modules of ILS that give the best parameters, we try these possible cases that are shown in Table 3. For each case, we test three values of strength of perturbation (as we have explained in sub-section 3.3).

After all tests, we find that the best results are obtained by applying CRW/B and for perturbation strength V equal to number of attributes/2 (50%). The Figure 2 show the differences between different cases (we don't give all details of results because the number of pages is limited).

Table 3. Different Cases of Testing ILS

Cases	*Abreviation*
Crossover+Random Walk	CRW
Mutation+Random Walk	MRW
USGA_ILS(Crossover +Better)	CB
USGA_ILS(Mutation+Better)	MB
Crossover +Random Walk/Better	CRW/B
Mutation+ Random Walk/Better	MRW/B

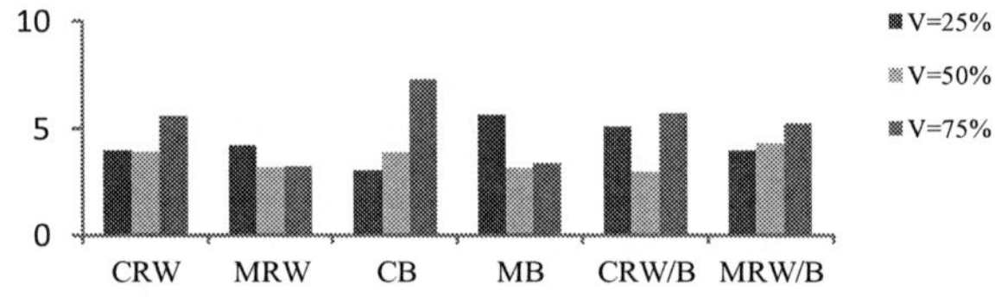

Figure 2. Average Aligned-Ranks for Different Cases

The obtained results of our approaches and other ones are shown in Table 4. We note that the best result in each dataset is stressed in bold-face.

Table 4. Obtained Results

Datasets	**USGA_ILS**	**USGA**	CHC	SMB	AC2	UB1	C4.5	PART	RIP
				Datasets with low imbalance (1.5≤IR≤3)					
Glass1	**0,967**	0,954	0.779	0.799	0.782	0,752	0,731	0,734	0,704
Ecoli0vs1	0,968	0,968	0,979	0,968	0,969	0,979	**0,980**	**0,980**	**0,980**
Wisconsin	**0,989**	0,975	0,966	0,963	0,965	0,961	0,948	0,940	0,952
Pima	**0,987**	**0,987**	0,698	0,743	0,707	0,758	0,706	0,720	0,718
Iris0	0,95	0,950	**1**	0,989	0,989	0,989	0,980	0,980	0,757
Glass0	**0,965**	0,958	0,779	0,814	0,801	0,838	0,791	0,797	0,757
Yeast1	**0,994**	**0,994**	0,655	0,705	0,637	0,722	0,604	0,616	0,647
Vehicle2	**0,957**	0,930	0,778	**0,977**	0,972	0,961	0,938	0,945	0,961
Vehicle3	**0,984**	0,919	0,448	0,741	0,732	0,787	0,679	0,461	0,582
Haberman	**0,984**	0,945	0,385	0,625	0,416	0,661	0,454	0,444	0,500
Vehicle1	**0,964**	0,928	0,448	0,744	0,751	0,760	0,622	0,470	0,674
				Datasets with medium imbalance (3≤IR≤9)					
Glass0123vs456	**0,951**	**0,951**	0,909	0,900	0,901	0,887	0,877	0,473	0,904
Vehicle0	**0,978**	0,941	0,841	0,963	0,943	0,951	0,918	0,935	0,932
Ecoli1	**0,968**	0,968	0,810	0,876	0,876	0,896	0,809	0,828	0,880
New-thyroid2	0,914	0,914	**0,959**	0,968	0,956	0,949	0,868	0,931	0,955
New-thyroid1	0,927	0,901	0,982	**0,983**	0,945	0,963	0,887	0,938	0,900
Ecoli2	**0,952**	**0,952**	0,896	0,904	0,884	0,898	0,855	0,888	0,838
Glass6	**0,912**	0,863	0,890	0,833	0,887	0,897	0,898	0,898	0,900
Yeast3	**0,985**	**0,985**	0,804	0,892	0,910	0,932	0,868	0,802	0,875
Ecoli3	**0,927**	0,912	0,789	0,809	0,847	0,875	0,702	0,731	0,733
Page-blocks0	**0,993**	0,991	0,681	0,934	0,874	0,956	0,919	0,906	0,915
Yeast2vs4	0,941	0,951	0,783	0,874	0,915	**0,953**	0,817	0,811	0,827
Yeast05679vs4	**0,951**	**0,951**	0,630	0,769	0,746	0,786	0,596	0,656	0,838
				Datasets with high imbalance (IR>9)					
Vowel0	**0,97**	0,917	0,896	0,991	0,968	0,947	0,939	0,910	0,945
Glass016vs2	**0,80**	0,84	0,000	0,542	0,408	0,663	0,071	0,241	0,241
Glass2	**0,77**	0,744	0,000	0,754	0,671	0,808	0,476	0,625	0,237
Ecoli4	0,87	0,866	0,918	0,872	**0,927**	0,883	0,701	0,624	0,829
Yeast1vs7	**0,92**	0,915	0,162	0,624	0,698	0,763	0,480	0,311	0,547
Shuttle0vs4	0,98	0,956	0,995	1,00	0,941	0,983	**0,999**	**0,999**	1,000
Glass4	0,73	0,688	0,000	0,898	0,864	0,829	**0,999**	0,866	0,817
Abalone9vs18	0,941	0,941	0,348	0,700	0,025	0,763	**0,999**	0,482	0,574
Yeast1458vs7	**0,92**	0,915	0,000	0,038	0,362	0,615	0,000	0,180	0,000
Yeast2vs8	**0,87**	0,866	0,728	0,718	0,312	0,775	0,000	0,000	0,670
Yeast4	**0,95**	0,951	0,139	0,656	0,008	0,837	0,502	0,556	0,520
Yeast1289vs7	**0,92**	0,9	0,000	0,580	0,565	0,665	0,316	0,364	0,363
Yeast5	0,944	0,944	0,704	0,905	0,875	**0,957**	0,822	0,793	0,875
Yeast6	**0,927**	**0,927**	0,386	0,793	0,595	0,854	0,732	0,712	0,607
Abalone19	**0,921**	0,852	0,000	0,081	0,080	0,658	0,000	0,000	0,000

In the aim to compare approaches, we apply WICOXON'test, where R^+ is the sum of the ranks corresponding to the results for our approach, R- is the sum of the ranks corresponding to the results for other approaches. The measure used in comparison is G-Mean. The results are given in Table 5.

Table 5. Obtained Results

Comparison	R^+	R^-	T	Tested approaches	Comparison	R^+	R^-	T	Tested approaches	Comparison	R^+	R^-	T	Tested approaches
Low imbalanced datasets					***Medium imbalanced datasets***					***High imbalanced datasets***				
USGA					USGA					USGA				
Vs.C45	58	8	8	USGA	vs. C4.5	77	1	1	USGA	vs. C4.5	107	13	13	USGA
Vs.RIP	61	5	5	USGA	vs. RIP	72	6	6	USGA	vs. RIP	114	6	6	USGA
Vs.PART	58	8	8	USGA	vs.PART	69	9	9	USGA	vs. PART	111	8	8	USGA
Vs.AC2	57	9	9	USGA	vs. AC2	69	9	9	USGA	vs. AC2	109	11	11	USGA
Vs.SMB	57	9	9	USGA	vs. SMB	66	16	16	USGA	vs. SMB	105	15	15	USGA
Vs.CHC	61	5	5	USGA	vs. CHC	70	8	8	USGA	vs. CHC	111	6	6	USGA
Vs.UB1	58	8	8	USGA	vs. UB1	59	19	19	Not rejected	vs. UB1	99	21	21	USGA
USGA_ILS					USGA_ILS					USGA_ILS				
Vs.C45	62	4	4	USGA_ILS	Vs.C45	74	4	4	USGA_ILS	vs. C45	113	7	7	USGA_ILS
Vs.RIP	61	5	5	USGA_ILS	Vs.RIP	74	4	4	USGA_ILS	vs. RIP	110	10	10	USGA_ILS
Vs.PART	61	5	5	USGA_ILS	vs.PART	74	4	4	USGA_ILS	vs.PART	114	6	6	USGA_ILS
Vs.AC2	61	5	5	USGA_ILS	vs. AC2	74	4	4	USGA_ILS	vs. AC2	111	9	9	USGA_ILS
Vs.SMB	60	6	6	USGA_ILS	vs. SMB	71	7	7	USGA_ILS	vs. SMB	108	12	12	USGA_ILS
Vs.CHC	62	4	4	USGA_ILS	vs. CHC	72	6	6	USGA_ILS	vs. CHC	111	9	9	USGA_ILS
Vs.UB1	61	5	5	USGA_ILS	vs. UB1	70	8	8	USGA_ILS	vs. UB1	109	11	11	USGA_ILS

For low and high imbalanced datasets, USGA and USGA_ILS are the best in all cases, because the statistical test T is less than the critical value.

For medium imbalanced datasets, USGA is better than all classical approaches, CHC and AC2 because the critical value (13 for 12 datasets and =0.05) is greater than the value of statistical test T. However, there is no significant difference between USGA and approaches UB1 and SMB, because the critical value is bellow than the value of statistical test T. To improve the performance of USGA, we have applied USGA_ILS which is the best of all approaches.

There in fact, these results are due to the principle of our approaches which use an intelligent method of undersampling in the first phase which kept the concept of deleted majority instances in the classifier C1. The rules of C1 are added to the classifier C2 which prevents high misclassification rate of the majority instances. In addition, these results are due to the usage of two different evolutionary phases with respectively two different fitness functions. Each phase favors either majority rules or minority ones and due to ILS method which explores search space. Besides this, the post-processing of the final classifiers removes contradictory rules to avoid the over-fitting and consequently, the performances of our classifier increase.

5. CONCLUSION

Clearly In this paper, we proposed a hybrid algorithm with both a new extraction rule algorithm and undersampling method for imbalanced data classification problems. Based on the original data distribution, our approach removes majority instances in order to balance an imbalanced dataset without losing information. Simulation results on tested datasets with different values of IR show the efficiency of our approach.

Imbalanced learning is a challenging and active research topic in machine learning and data mining. Motivated by the results in this paper, we believe that our approach may provide a significant contribution to this domain. In future work, we are planning to extend our approach to handle multi-classes imbalanced datasets.

REFERENCES

Alcalá-Fdez J. et al, 2011. KEEL data-mining software tool: Data set repository, integration of algorithms and experimental analysis framework. Mult.-Valued Logic Soft Computing, Vol. 17, No. 2–3, pp. 255-287.

Alejo, R. et al, 2007. Improving the performance of the RBF neural networks trained with imbalanced samples. Lecture Notes in Computer Science, Vol. 4507, pp. 162-169.

Ali, S. et al, 1998. Partial classification using association rules. *In Heckerman et al,* pp 115-118.

Batista, G. et al, 2004. A Study of the Behavior of Several Methods for Balancing Machine Learning Training Data. ACM SIGKDD Explorations Newsletter, Vol. 6, No. 1, pp. 20-29.

Beck, K. and Ralph, J., 1994. Patterns Generates Architectures. *Proceedings of European Conference of Object-Oriented Programming.* Bologna, Italy, pp. 139-149.

Buckland, M. and Gey, F., 1994. The Relationship Between Recall and Precision. *Journal of the American Society for Information Science*, Vol. 45, No. 1, pp. 12-19.

Breiman, L. 1996. Bagging predictors. Maching Learning, Vol. 24, pp. 123-140.

Chawla, N.V. et al, 2002. SMOTE: Synthetic Minority Over-Sampling Technique. *Journal of Artificial Intelligence Research*, Vol. 16, pp. 321-357.

Chawla, N. V. et al, 2003. SMOTEBoost: Improving prediction of the minority class in boosting. *In Proceeding of Knowledge Discovery Databases*, pp. 107-119.

Cohen, W., 1995. Fast effective rule induction. *Proceedings of International Conference on Machine Learning.* Morgan Kaufmann, pp. 115-123.

Chyi, Y. M., 2003. Classification analysis techniques for skewed class distribution problem. M. S thesis, Dept. Inform. Manage. Nat. Sun Yat-Sen Univ.

Demšar J., 2006. Statistical comparisons of classifiers over multiple data sets. In *Machine Learning Respiratory*, Vol. 7,pp 1-30.

Fernández, A. et al, 2007. A study of the behaviour of linguistic fuzzy rule based classification systems in the framework of imbalanced data-sets. *Fuzzy Sets and Systems*, Vol. 159, No. 18, pp. 2387–2398.

Fu, X. et al, 2002. Training rbf neural networks on unbalanced data. *In Neural Information Processing*, Vol 2, pp. 1016-1020.

Galar, M. et al, 2012. A review on Ensembles for the class Imbalance Problem: Bagging, Boosting and Hybrid-Based Approaches. *IEEE Transaction System Management, Cy-bern. C: Appl. Rev.*, Vol. 42, No. 4, pp. 463-484.

Garcìa, S. and Herrera, F., 2009. Evolutionary Undersampling for Classification with Imbalance Datasets: Proposals and Taxonomy. *Evolutionary Computation*, Vol. 3, No.17, pp. 275-306.

Hodges, J.L and Lehmann E.L., 1962. *Rank methods for combination of independent Experiments in analysis of variance, Annals of Mathematical Statistics.*

Japkowicz, N. and Stephen, S., 2002. The class imbalance problem: a systematic study. *Intelligent Data Analysis 6*, pp. 429-450.

Liu, X.Y. et al 2006. Exploratory Under Sampling for Class Imbalance Learning. *In Proceeding of International Conference on Data Mining*, Vol. 39, No. 2, pp. 965-969.

Lourenco, H. et al, 2003. Iterated local search. Handbook of metaheuristics, pages 320–353, 2003.

Melanie, M., 1996. An introduction to genetic algorithms, *The MIT Press*.

Parpinelli, R.S. et al 2002. Data mining with an Ant colony optimization algorithm. IEEE trans. On evolutionary Computation, Vol. 6, pp. 321-332.

Polikar, R., 2006. Ensemble based systems in decision making. *IEEE Circuits System Mag*netic, Vol. 6, No. 3, pp. 21-45.

Riddle, P. et al, 1994. Representation design and brute-force induction in a Boeing manufacturing domain. *Applied Artificial Intelligence*, pp. 125-147.

Rokach, L., 2010. Ensemble-based classifiers. *Artificial Intellence Revue,* Vol. 33, pp. 1–39.

Sun, Y. et al, 2009. Classification of imbalanced data: A review. *International Journal of Pattern Recognition and Artificial Intelligence*, Vol. 23, No. 4, pp. 687-719.

Syswerda, G., 1990. A Study of reproduction in Generational and Steady-State Genetic Algorithms. *In Proceeding of Foundation GA*, pp 94-101.

Wang, B.X. and N. Japkowicz, N., 2004. Imbalanced Data Set Learning with Synthetic Samples. *In Proceeding of IRIS Machine Learning Workshop.*

Wilcoxon F., 1945. Individual comparisons by ranking methods. *Biometrics Bull*, Vol. 1, No. 6, pp. 80-83.

Yuchun, T. et al, 2009. SVMs Modeling for Highly Imbalanced Classification. *IEEE Transaction System man, and cybernetics—part b: cybernetics*, Vol. 39, No. 1.

Zhang, J. et al, 2004. Learning Rules from Highly Umbalanced Data Set. *In Proceedings of the fourth IEEE International Conference of Data Mining* (ICDM'04).

Zhang, J. and Mani, I., 2003. KNN Approach to Unbalanced Data Distributions: A Case Study Involving Information Extraction. *In Proceeding of International Conference on Machine Learning (ICML '2003).*

SAMPLING CAR-SHARING DATA TO EVALUATE URBAN TRAFFIC BEHAVIOUR

Andrea Trentini and Federico Losacco
Dipartimento di Informatica
Via Comelico 39, 20135 Milano, Italy

ABSTRACT

Nowadays, in modern countries, urban traffic per se must be addressed as a problem. The “congestion factor” is fought by introducing regulations to reduce private traffic: tolls, dedicated lanes, narrow lanes, low speed limits, reduced parking availability, etc. Some help can come from *car-sharing*, i.e., pools of shared vehicles to be rented for short periods of time. Car-sharing vendors “publish” (not entirely/easily accessible) data about the state of their vehicle pool... Can this data be used to analyse the overall traffic behaviour in town? The authors scraped car-sharing vendors’ websites for a couple of years, made data uniform and then queried and graphed the dataset. Some interesting findings are: the “lung effect” (morning moving-in, evening moving-out); evening peak usage (people using car-sharing instead of taxicabs to go out at night for leisure); vehicle usage (the total number of “busy” vehicles at any time) never goes beyond 70%. Moreover, by combining information about parking locations, movement vectors can be drawn to evaluate frequent paths.

KEYWORDS

Urban Congestion, Traffic Monitoring, Open Data, Public Accountancy, Anti-Pollution Policies

1. INTRODUCTION

Air pollution became a problem with the industrial revolution [Seinfeld and Pandis (2012); Lave and Seskin (2013); Steinle et al. (2013)]. Afterwards, governments begun legislating [US-EPA (2013)] to try and reduce industrial emissions. Air pollution began to decrease as new generations of technologies replaced older ones (see graphs from ARPA, e.g.: http://www.arpalombardia.it/qariafiles/varie/MI_SO2.png). Nowadays urban traffic is perceived to be the main problem of modern countries cities. Governments and local administrations are now addressing the “congestion factor” with regulations [Vanderbilt (2009)] to reduce private traffic, considered the main source of congestion, such as: 1) access tolls for private-car crowded zones; 2) dedicated lanes to public transport/car pools; 3) narrowing lanes (to slow down cars); 4) reducing the number of lanes to deter (by increasing congestion!) private car owners; 5) lowering speed limits (deterrent); 6) reducing parking availability (deterrent). Also, vendors started providing the so called “car-sharing”, i.e., pools of shared (among many users) vehicles to be rented for short periods of time (minutes), usually at higher costs (per day) than standard car rental prices. The car-sharing rationale: 1) parking space is saved since a single parked vehicle serves a lot of users; 2) because of the higher (>private car, <taxicab) costs per use, many users, even if subscribed to the service, would use it wisely, reducing the overall “car mileage load” on the city; 3) it may help in further pollution lowering [Firnkorn and Müller (2011)]. Geolocation and road navigation technologies, combined with widespread mobile connectivity infrastructures have enabled vendors to let users leave (and find) cars anywhere. A smartphone application can track down the position of available cars and lead users to precise parking locations. Location data are stored and secured into vendors’ systems but some data are nonetheless available on the web. **Can this data be used to analyse the overall traffic behaviour in town?** This paper represents an affirmative answer and shows the findings of the authors’ effort in car-sharing data gathering and analysing. A similar work has been described in [Morency et al. (2007)], but in that case the focus was different: identify class of users with access to the internal and complete car-sharing database. Statistical analyses presented here represent mass behaviour and single car behaviour (decoupled from the user). We are not interested in social/economic analyses such as [Fellows and

Pitfield (2000)], our work can be related to [Schmöller et al. (2015)] applied to the Milan context and using only webscraped data. A review on car-sharing studies can be read in [Jorge and Correia (2013)].

1.1 Car-sharing Systems in Milan (Italy)

In Milan there are five (one went bankrupt in 2015) services. They are all similar: 1) a user must subscribe for an annual fee (< 100 €, for some vendor is 0, some include usage minutes as a "welcome package"); 2) the user must install a smartphone application (iOS/Android); 3) the application works using GPS and mobile data; 4) the user can find the car on the application real-time updated map and can even pre-book it (at a cost); 5) some operation can be done via call-centre, often with some added cost; 6) the user approaches the booked car and opens it with a RFID (Radio Frequency IDentification) smart-card or the phone itself (via NFC - Near Field Communication - or RPC – Remote Procedure Call); 7) the car can used at will (usually within time/space limits); 8) when finished the user communicates the "end of service" through the app. Usage fees are by the minute: ~.25 € per minute. Taxicab fees (http://taxiblu.it/cms/tariffe-taxi) are by km (~1 €/km) or hour (~28 €/h) plus an initial fee (between 3.3 € and 6.5 €).

1.2 Open Data vs. "Web-scraping"

Open data is a techno-political movement that pushes governments and public administrations towards transparency: public funded organizational entities should publish information about their internal workings. Info such as expenses, people roles, public activities, law making workflow, public utility structures and commercial info. When available, open-data are usually accessible via websites. Many organizations even dedicate entire websites to open-data only (e.g., data.gov USA, data.gov.uk UK, dati.gov.it Italy). Open data is categorized into classes based on format and licence [Berners-Lee (2009)] and on wider functional aspects [Davies (2010)]. Open-data is usually downloadable in batch or through API (Application Programming Interface). In, luckily rare, cases organizations publish data that can still be called "open", but they also apply some so called "webstacles" (web obstacles) to reduce the usability for the public. In this latter cases a technique called "web scraping" (i.e., programmatically accessing data meant for humans only on standard web pages) can be usefully applied [Trentini (2014)]) to obtain data "obtorto collo" (Latin for "unwillingly").

2. THE QUEST FOR DATA (*WEB-SCRAPING*)

The five car-sharing vendors are: 1) Share'NGo (http://www.sharengo.it); 2) TwistCar (http://twistcar.it, discontinued since 17-Nov-2015); 3) Enjoy (http://enjoy.eni.com); 4) Car2Go (http://www.car2go.com); 5) GuidaMi (http://www.guidami.net). GuidaMi (now GirACI) does not publish data about cars, but it is a small service. The other vendors do publish data about car positions and availability, some of them (Car2go) even offer API (Application Programming Interface) to query data, albeit with some limitations (low query frequency, need for a security key). The authors decided to scrape website data using *wget* [GNU (2009)] in shell scripts or small *python* [Rossum (2016)] programs periodically run on a server. The scripts run every minute and save data into a mongodb [MongoDB Inc. (2016)] database. The 1/min sampling frequency generates 24∗60=1440 samples per day. The heterogeneous data are then intersected into this schema: id=identifier, engine=type of engine (electric, gasoline, etc.), car_plate=plate, service_name=vendor (Enjoy, Twist, etc.), latitude, longitude, date=ISO date (of sample), fuel=fuel level %.

3. DATA ANALYSIS

The following analyses (available cars, average distance from city centre and movements) are based on data gathered between September 2015 and March 2016. They show an evident daily and weekly patterns, i.e.: 1) every day is "cyclical", e.g., night differs from day and office hours represent peaks; 2) there are "seasonal" (weekly) effects: a) days from Monday to Friday are similar to one another; b) Saturday and Sunday are similar; c) Sat-Sun differs from Mon-Fri workdays. To analyse the in-week patterns data were divided into weeks, then Q-Q (Quantile-Quantile) plots were created. These are used to compare if two samples are statistically similar. A Q-Q plot for every day pair (Mon-Tue, Mon-Wed, Mon-Thu, etc.) in every week was generated, originating (7 on 2)=21 Q-Q plots per week. This procedure statistically confirmed the evident (and expected) pattern difference between Mon-Fri and Sat-Sun. Abbreviations: H=Holiday; NH=Non Holiday; stats=computation of (Minimum, 1st Quantile, Median, Mean, 3rd Quantile, Maximum); fivenum=computation of (Minimum, Lower-hinge, Median, Upper-hinge, Maximum).

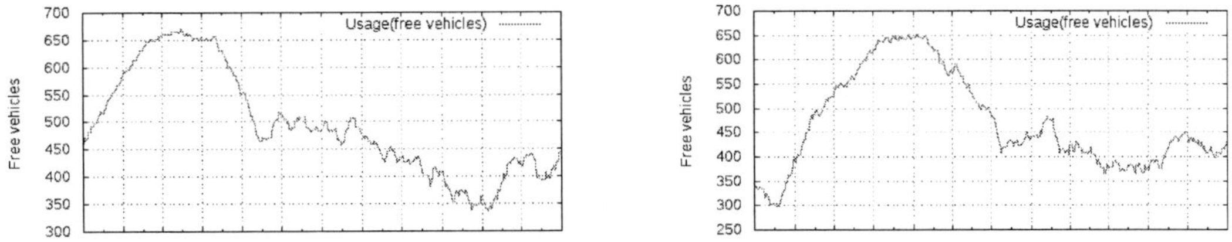

Figure 1. Weekday (left), weekend (right)

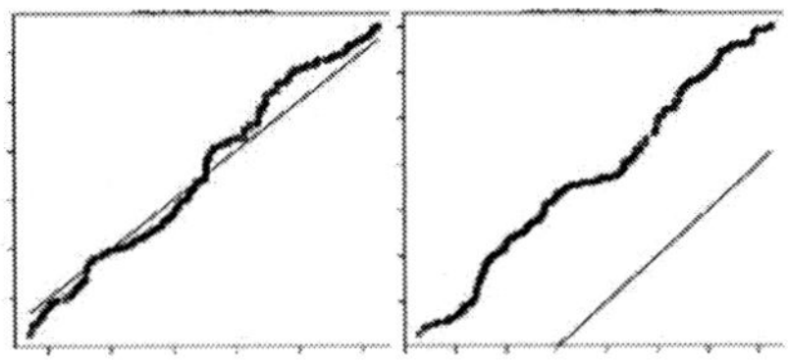

Figure 2. QQ plots: typical NH-NH (top) vs. H-NH (bottom)

3.1 Available Cars

The total number of free cars at a given time *t* is: $CarsAvailable(t) = Sum\ of\ CarAvailable_i(t)\ with\ [i \in Cars]$ (CarAvailable gives 1 if the car is parked, 0 otherwise). When is low it means that many cars are in use. Figure 1 shows the usage for two typical days (00:00-23:59), one weekday and one weekend day. The "late Saturday" (Sunday early morning) usage is clearly visible in the weekend graph. Notable remarks in Figure 1 and on the whole dataset, are: 1) night-time (2AM-7AM) is a peak of free cars; 2) the usage peak (least # of free cars) is 6PM-9PM; 3) morning (8AM-noon) usage is lesser than afternoon (noon-7PM) usage; 4) night-time peak sports a shorter timespan (6AM-8AM) w.r.t. the Mon-to-Fri night-time peaks; 5) there is a usage peak between midnight-2AM, often more substantial than the afternoon peak. Figure 2 depicts the usage Q-Q plots of two day example pairs: 2015-10-05 vs. 2015-09-29 (Tue vs. Mon), near the y=x line → statistically similar; 2015-11-22 vs. 2015-11-17 (Sun vs. Tue), far from the y=x line → statistically different. I.e., (as expected!) users' behaviour on Sunday is different from a weekday.

3.2 Overall Distance from City Centre

At any given time *t*, the distance of a single car is defined by: $CarDistance_i(t) = |CarPosition_i(t) - CityCenterPosition|$, i.e., the module of the vectorial distance between car and centre (lat, long), then the average is computed. Notable remarks in Figure 3 (left is Mon-Fri, right is Sat-Sun, typical days from the dataset, x-axis is 00:00-23:59) are: 1) "lung" effect": average distance decreases during 8AM-6PM and increases during the rest of the day, i.e., people move into the city during daytime and move out of the city otherwise; 2) there is a concentration peak between 11AM-2PM, i.e., during lunchtime users are (on the average) nearer to the city centre; 3) between 8AM-11AM there is an out-movement of people followed by an in-movement, i.e., users move in&out in those hours, not exactly at the same time.

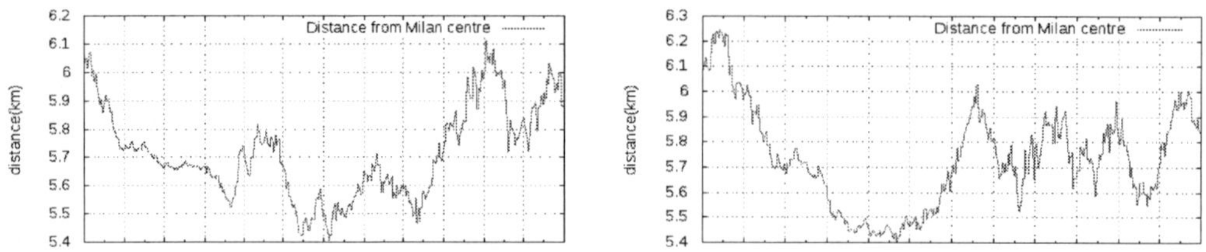

Figure 3. Average Distances: a Typical Weekday (Wed, Left) vs. Weekend Day (Sun, Right)

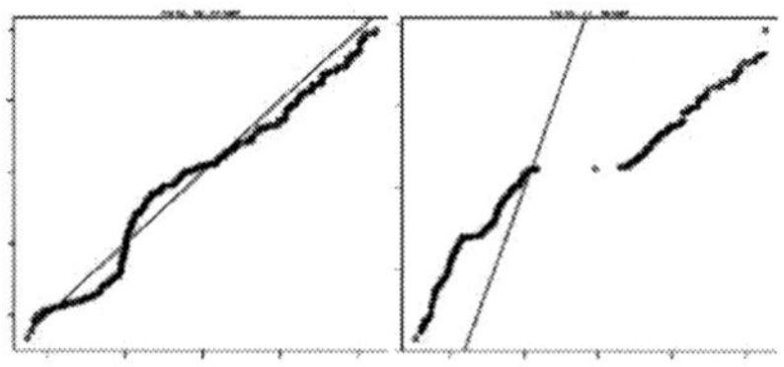

Figure 4. Distances Q-Q Plots: Typical NH-NH vs. H-NH

Figure 4 depicts the distances Q-Q plots of two day pairs taken as example: 2015-10-22 vs. 2015-10-21 (Wed vs. Thu), near the y=x line → statistically similar; 2015-11-15 vs. 2015-11-16 (Mon vs. Sun), far from the y=x line → statistically different, i.e., again, users' behaviour on Sunday is different from a normal weekday. It is also interesting to show the average distance of vehicles "per vendor" (Figure 5), notable remarks are that: 1) Enjoy is always more distant than the others (Car2go and Sharengo); 2) Sharengo (all electrical cars) is always the closest; 3) there has been a "getting near" trend in Car2go cars between 2015 and 2016.

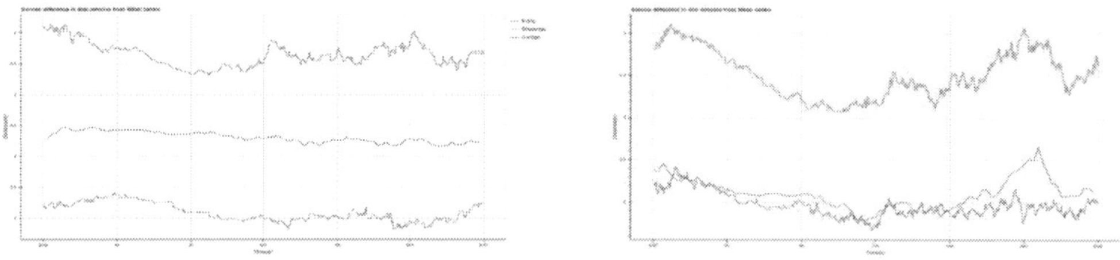

Figure 5. Difference in Average Distances "per Vendor" (Left: 2015/09/06, Right: 2016/02/27)

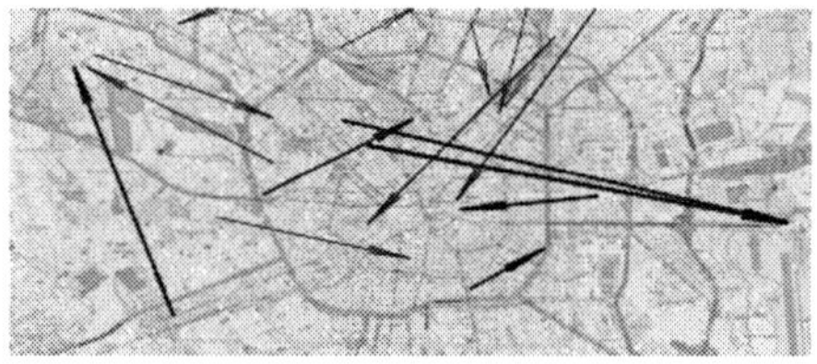

Figure 6. 2015/09/02 08:40, Two Cars Moving from the City Centre Towards the Airport (Rightmost Arrows) in the Morning

3.3 Movements

By pairing subsequent parking points in time a list of "movements" for every car was created, a "movement" is simply a vector between a car "catch" and a "release". The list is composed by records with the following fields: *current_fuel*, *delta_fuel*, *delta_km*, *delta_time*, *end_date*, *end_pos_lat*, *end_pos_lon*, *id_vehicle*, *kmh*, *start_date*, *start_pos_lat*, *start_pos*_lon, *type_vehicle*. Figure 6 shows a very small time-frame (10 min) of car movements, this kind of graph may be used to find patterns and/or visually identify outliers. Of course the same data can be programmatically analysed to identify behaviours, almost in real-time since on average there are less than a hundred records in a ten minutes time-frame.

4. CONCLUSION

This paper describes analyses on web-scraped car-sharing data for Milan, Italy. Since August 2015, scripts run every minute to collect data from car-sharing websites, homogenize them and feed them into a database and graphed. Such a dataset can be enormously useful to stakeholders (citizens, potential car-sharing competitors, public administrations) interested in understanding mobility trends and in designing new sustainable mobility services. The data can also be "almost real-time" analysed to evaluate general behaviour and "situations" (jams, avoided zones, etc.). Data show that: 1) there is an evident usage pattern (# of free cars and average distance from centre) difference between work days and weekends; 2) there are interesting time windows that could be more thoroughly analysed; 3) there is a "lung effect" (people moving-in in the morning and moving-out in the afternoon); 4) there are, of course, places where users go often (e.g. airport, train stations, etc.). The authors are currently analysing "hot spots" and frequency and location of fuel refilling. Additional general analysis work can be thought of, such as: studying congestion zones and times (e.g., to identify badly mobility-wise designed urban zones), correlating car-sharing data with other data (public transport, weather, holidays, strikes, etc.), evaluation of car-sharing vendors' quality of service (in terms of covered zones, vehicle availability, etc.). A final note on the "public availability" of car-sharing data: since car-sharing is often considered a public service (even if provided commercially by private vendors) it could be a good idea to force vendors to supply standard APIs (Application Programming Interface) to access their data, so that third parties (as the authors did) may create value added services.

REFERENCES

Berners-Lee, T. (2009, June). Linked data. http://www.w3.org/DesignIssues/LinkedData.html.

Davies, T. (2010). Open data, democracy and public sector reform: A look at open government data use from data. gov. uk. Practical Participation.

Fellows, N. and D. Pitfield (2000). An economic and operational evaluation of urban car-sharing. Transportation Research Part D: Transport and Environment 5(1), 1–10.

Firnkorn, J. and M. Müller (2011). What will be the environmental effects of new free-floating car-sharing systems? the case of car2go in Ulm. Ecological Economics 70(8), 1519–1528.

GNU (2009). GNU wget. http://www.gnu.org/software/wget.

Jorge, D. and G. Correia (2013). Carsharing systems demand estimation and defined operations: a literature review. €pean Journal of Transport and Infrastructure Research 13(3), 201–220.

Lave, L. B. and E. P. Seskin (2013). Air pollution and human health, Volume 6. Routledge.

MongoDB Inc. (read 2016). http://www.mongodb.com.

Morency, C., M. Trépanier, B. Agard, B. Martin, and J. Quashie (2007). Car sharing system: what transaction datasets reveal on users' behaviors. In Intelligent Transportation Systems Conference, 2007. ITSC 2007. IEEE, pp. 284–289.

Rossum, G. V. (read 2016). http://www.python.org.

Schmöller, S., S. Weikl, J. Müller, and K. Bogenberger (2015). Empirical analysis of free-floating carsharing usage: The munich and berlin case. Transportation Research Part C: Emerging Technologies 56, 34–51.

Seinfeld, J. H. and S. N. Pandis (2012). Atmospheric chemistry and physics: from air pollution to climate change. John Wiley & Sons.

Steinle, S., S. Reis, and C. E. Sabel (2013). Quantifying human exposure to air pollution - moving from static monitoring to spatio-temporally resolved personal exposure assessment. Science of the Total Environment 443, 184–193.

Trentini, A. (2014). Lombardy epa obtorto collo data and anti-pollution policies fallacies. Journal of e-Learning and Knowledge Society 10(2).

US-EPA (2013). History of the clean air act. http://www.epa.gov/air/caa/amendments.html.

Vanderbilt, T. (2009). Traffic: Why We Drive the Way We Do (and What It Says About Us). New York Times.

Reflection Papers

INDICATORS FOR THE EVALUATION OF TECHNOLOGICAL ACTIVITY

Alexandre Lucas[1], Birger Larsen[2], Angel Freddy Godoy Viera[1] and Elías Sanz Casado[3]
[1]Federal University of Santa Catarina – UFSC, Florianópolis, Santa Catarina, Brasil
[2]Aalborg University, Copenhagen, Denmark
[3]Carlos III University of Madrid, Getafe, Madrid, Spain

ABSTRACT

The internet has become a great platform for all kinds of applications and matters relating to the information. This includes information systems, decision-making and of every kind informational indicators. In this context, the use of indicators for the evaluation of scientific and technological activities has been widely adopted to characterize and measure its volume and to identify its main actors and investments. We choose as our focus Institutes of Science, Technology and Innovation (ISTIs). ISTIs are important actors, they work in the "valley of death of innovation", a region with the greatest risks and requirements of investments and needs about the real-time indicators for the evaluation of technological activity. Despite the large volume of information available, there is a perceived lack of applicability of these data for real time decision making. In this paper, we outline our initial work in establishing dynamic Indicators for the Evaluation of Technological Activity (IETAs) and their potential use in real-time decision making, available and accessible via the internet. We will focus on two approaches that involve bibliometric and altmetric data. The first approach is concerned with identifying signs of interest in certain clearly recognized technologies. The second approach is concerned with identifying the terms and phrases that characterize of given technology. Both approaches are going to explore the possibilities offered by the data related to the Web of Science (WoS) and its use as Knowledge Base to apply information retrieval and text mining techniques to unstructured data from technology and other types of relevant reports and only those available and accessible through the internet.

KEYWORDS

Technological Indicators, Real Time Indicators, Evaluation of Technological Activity, Bibliometric, Scientometrics

1. INTRODUCTION

The internet has become a great platform for all kinds of applications and matters relating to the information. This includes information systems, decision-making and of every kind informational indicators. In this context, the use of indicators for the evaluation of scientific and technological activities has been widely adopted to characterize and measure its volume and to identify its main actors and investments. One type of approach is to study scientific production which also may also include patents metrics. Another is statistics of governments and international organization like the OECD that gather information and produce global indicators in their regular reports (González Guitián, Molina Piñeiro, 2008). Despite the large volume of information available, there is a perceived lack of applicability of these data for real time decision making. In this paper, we outline our initial work in establishing dynamic Indicators for the Evaluation of Technological Activity (IETAs) and their potential use in real-time decision making with purpose of presenting the idea to WWW/internet'2017 participants for feedback and exchange of ideas. Clearly explain the nature of the problem, previous work, purpose, and contribution of the paper.

About the importance, relying on patent metrics and government data is not sufficient to make real-time decisions about technology investments. The main challenges are:

- Difficulty in obtaining relevant indicators
- Problems with patent-based indicators
- Velocity of technological innovation and the creation of technological companies and products
- The growth of unstructured data

- How to know if some data or information is about technology?
- Open Science and its influence on the future of scientific indicators of economic activities
- Specific issues for the indicators regarding each country – in our particular case for the countries Brazil, Spain and Denmark

2. INDICATORS FOR THE EVALUATION OF TECHNOLOGICAL ACTIVITY

2.1 Institutes of Science, Technology and Innovation

For our study of IETAs we choose as our case Institutes of Science, Technology and Innovation (ISTIs). ISTIs are important actors within the world of technological development and the innovation ecosystem of each country or even the world. To understand the roles of the involved actors in the phases of development of the technology we use the Technology Readiness Level scale (TRL), initially developed by NASA, but adopted widely by various sectors and organizations including the Horizon 2020 EU program (Mankins, 2009). Figure 1 shows the TRL scale and our analysis of the types of Research, Development and Innovation (R&D&I) activities and relate the relevant actors across phases. Without discussing the limits of each actor's position, with the infographic we want to show that the ISTIs are in the middle of the path of technological development. This interval between the TRL 3 and TRL 7 is also known as the "valley of death of innovation" because it is the region with the greatest risks and requirements of investments (Markham et al., 2010).

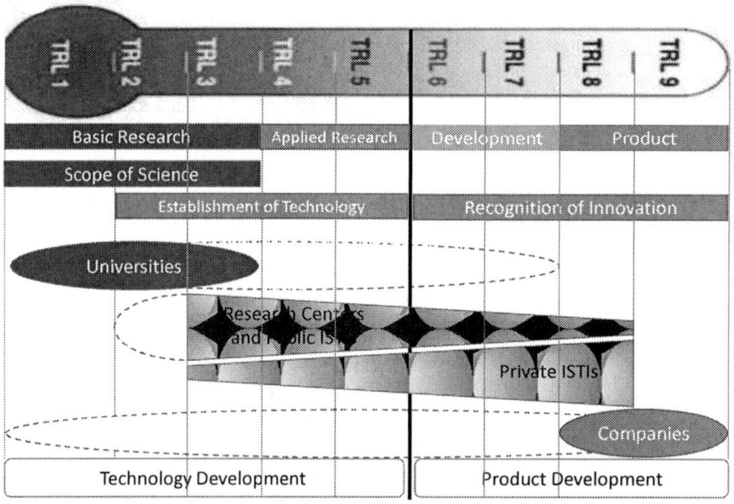

Figure 1. Technology Readiness Level and type of R&D and Innovation and related actors in across phases

2.2 About IETA Research

Our research into IETAs started in June 2017 and is planned to be implemented in 4 main steps:

1. Characterization and conceptualization (defining the concept of 'technology') and state-of-the-art.
2. Study of Information Retrieval and Text Mining approaches that can support the creation of IETAs.
3. Proposal of principal IETA indicators.
4. Application and test of proposed indicators.

In relation to Step 1, we have begun outlining a range of aspects or elements involved in technological activities as shown in Figure 2. In the present paper the research focus is on information related to technological activity and its flow.

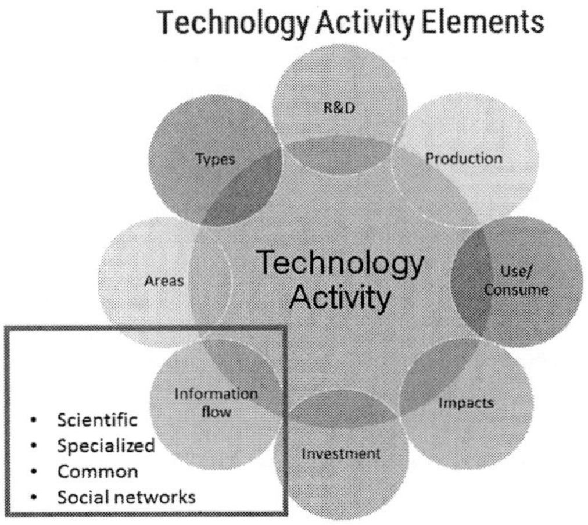

Figure 2. Elements of Technological Activity

2.3 Real-time Indicators

The need for rapid and informed decision-making is increasing fast, and with the current hype around Big Data expectations are building for approaches that can support decision-making in real-time. Figure 3 shows the lifecycle steps of technology development and the perception of development and impact. As can be seen, it may take long while from an incoming grant or investment until production of the first formal results and end reports.

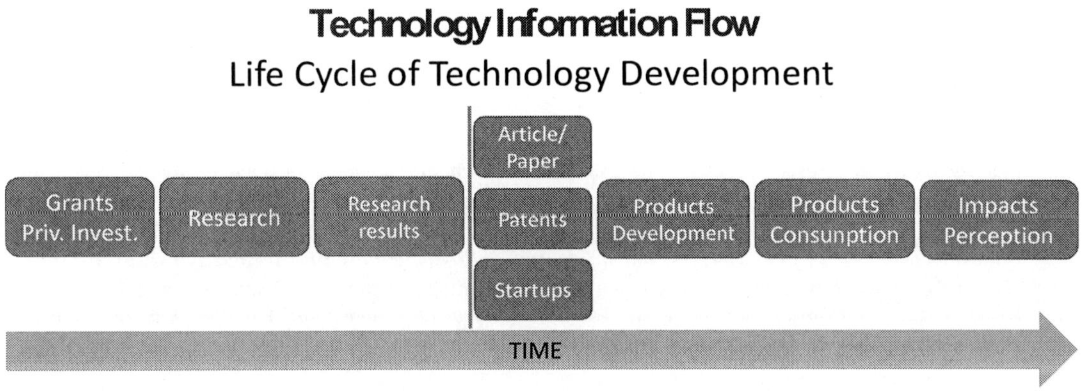

Figure 3. Life cycle of Technology Development

Traditional bibliometric analysis may serve very well for strategic planning or reports of results obtained. However, they may be temporally too late for decisions to be made, e.g for adjustments and perception of the progress of activities. It is with this perspective that our research pursues the ideal of real-time, or near real-time, indicators for the evaluation of technological activity. Maybe its realization is not feasible but the research and ideas in this direction may result in indicators near as short of time and a vision close to "now" of this activity.

2.4 Expected Results

As indicated in Figures. 2 and 3, we consider a wide range of elements and stages of technological activity. In this paper, we will focus on two examples that involve bibliometric and altmetric data.

The first approach is concerned with identifying signs of interest in certain technologies, and we reflect on the possibilities offered in the data related to the Web of Science (WoS). Given a target technology (clearly recognized), expressed as a set of terms as phrases, we may of course search the WoS and analyse publication trends. In addition, the search log of WoS, if made available, can tell us about searcher interest in the target technology (through volume of search terms) as well as which papers are downloaded, e.g a temporal analysis over the last 5 months. These data may be compared to published papers - allowing indicators and monitoring of early interest to be constructed.

The second approach is concerned with identifying the terms and phrases that characterize of given technology. Initial keyword searches can be conducted in WoS, and fields like Title, Abstract, Keywords, Subject Categories, Journal Names, Project/Grant identifications and Authors and Affiliations can be analyzed, e.g. using clustering and visualization, to extract additional prominent terms. The main idea is to give an overview of the technology aspects and the research fields in which they are relevant as well as provide new search terms for further analysis. In addition, the full text links in WoS to local library content may be utilized to download samples of available full text papers and do in-depth analysis of these using e.g. text mining and clustering. From this, we also hope to provide principal insights into procedures for identifying and characterizing technologies - making it easier to so automatically in the future.

3. FUTURE WORK AND CONCLUSION

Our next step is to carry out the two approaches as outlined in the proceeding section. We also plan to apply information retrieval and text mining techniques to unstructured data from technology and other types of relevant reports and only those available and accessible through the internet. This condition is compatible with the movements "open" included the movement called "Open Science"[1].

Our aim with presenting these initial project ideas to WWW/internet'2017 participants is to prompt feedback and to exchange further ideas with the conference participants on how best to proceed.

REFERENCES

González Guitián, M. V., Molina Piñeiro, M. (2008). La evaluación de la ciencia y la tecnología: revisión de sus indicadores. *Acimed: revista cubana de los profesionales de la información y la comunicación en salud*, 6, 2-19.

Mankins, J. C. (2009). Technology readiness assessments: A retrospective. *Acta Astronautica*, 65(9), 1216-1223.

Markham, Stephen K., Stephen J. Ward, Lynda Aiman-Smith, and ANGUS i. Kingon. 2010. "The valley of death the context for scroll theory in product innovation." *Journal of Product Innovation Management* 27(3): 402-17.

OECD (2015), the Frascati Manual 2015: Guidelines for Collecting and Reporting Data on Research and Experimental Development, *The Measurement of Scientific, Technological and Innovation Activities*, OECD Publishing, Paris. DOI: http://dx.doi.org/10.1787/9789264239012-en

[1] http://ec.europa.eu/research/openscience/index.cfm?pg=home&section=monitor

THE DIGITAL MARKETING ENVIRONMENT THROUGH SEARCH ENGINE OPTIMIZATION AND WEB METRICS

José Ramón Saura[1], Pedro R. Palos-Sánchez[2] and Juan José López[3]
[1]Universidad Rey Juan Carlos, Paseo Artilleros, s/n, 28032, Madrid (Spain)
[2] Universidad de Extremadura, Avda. de Elvas, s/n, 06071 Badajoz (Spain)
[3]Universidad a Distancia de Madrid, Vía de Servicio A-6, 15, 28400 Collado Villalba, Madrid (Spain)

ABSTRACT

This study reveals how the fast development of the Internet and the adaptation of traditional marketing to this electronic medium has affected research significantly regarding Digital Marketing (DM) performance over the last decade. As it is well-known, there are different techniques of DM such as Search Engine Optimization (SEO) or Search Engine Marketing (SEM), social media marketing, affiliate marketing or content marketing. However, to establish the main indicators and Web Metrics (WM) for companies, we will focus on the analysis of the techniques of SEO and SEM. Search marketing shares the main indicators with other DM techniques because search engines are the main channel of contact between the user and Internet companies. The difference between visibility with search engines compared to other models in traditional Internet advertising is that the user voluntarily seeks a service, product or information. The accepted thinking in SEO and SEM is that to attract user traffic, it is essential that a website is among the first two or three positions on the first page of the Search Engine Results Page (SERPs), as derived through keyword ranking.
In this study, we focus on the analysis of the main indicators to measure the DM ecosystem by analysing SEO and SEM strategies such as long-tail keywords, click through rates, titles, descriptions or A/B testing. The lack of knowledge of Academics in electronic media, and the skills gap that often exists for marketers in measuring and analyzing DM activities shows that the measurement of DM through technical indicators is a developing art that has not generated consensus between academics about how or what to Measure in academic research.

KEYWORDS

Search Engine Optimization, SEO, Digital Marketing, Web Metrics

1. LITERATURE REVIEW ABOUT SEO AND WEB METRICS

The methodology used in this research is based on the analysis of the current Digital Marketing (DM) performance metrics in use in mid 2016. The study is descriptive and includes commonly practiced DM techniques described in academic studies and industry reports on DM activity. For the development of the research methodology, a selective literature review was performed encompassing SEO and Web Metrics (WM).

A literature review about SEO and WM was conducted. The review served as a basis for derivation of research directions relating to DM measurement. There have been many articles published on these topics in the last few years, suggesting that this is an increasingly popular domain for research. This review is based on relevant articles published between January 2006 and July 2016 related to SEO and WM.

Table 1 below summarizes the literature review. After study the literature review results, it appears at first glance that many of the authors are using similar or identical terminology and covering similar territory. However, this in itself does not confirm that there is consensus in definition or use of the concepts.

Table 1. Literature Review

Search Engine Optimization	Literature Review
Authors	Pauwels, Aksehirli, and Lackman (2016)
	Jarvinen and Karjaluoto (2015)
	Jayaram, Manrai and Manrai (2015)
	Zhuofan, Yong and Bo (2015)
	Leeflang, Verhoef, Dahlström and Freundt (2014)
	Nabout, Bernd, Tanja and Gerstmeier (2012)
	Pierre and Lester (2012)
	Nabout, Skiera, Stepanchuk and Gerstmeier (2012)
Web Metrics	**Literature Review**
Authors	Kent, Carr and Rebeca (2011)
	Chaffey and Patron (2012)
	Germann, Lilien and Rangaswamy (2013)
	Lee (2010)
	Royle and Laing (2014)
	Xu, Frankwick and Ramirez (2016)

2. CONCLUSION

The development of the Internet and electronic commerce involves a change in marketing thinking and practice due to the fact that the traditional marketing has had to develop new techniques for involvement on the Internet. This has resulted in the existence of a gap between the development of new techniques of DM and measurement processes that have to be performed for the correct measurement of results.

Due to the increased use of DM in the last decade and the investment made by companies in the last few years we have conducted an investigation to determine which are the key indicators to which companies should pay attention in order to measure their digital marketing actions.

Nabout, Skiera and Stepanchuk (2012) research presents concerns expressed by companies about the lack of knowledge of what metrics they should use to justify their marketing investments. This remains true despite the many articles published on DM measurement topics in the last few years. Researchers use a great variety of different metrics and indicators to measure the efficiency and effectiveness of DM techniques and calculate profitability (ROI), however, our study shows that little consensus has formed around the use of these indicators or on the definition of the key factors for measuring the DM performance.

In summary, this research presented the main web metrics to measure the performance of DM such as long-tail keywords, click through rates, titles, descriptions, A/B testing or the time per visit. It highlights the most commonly used indicators that might therefore offer potential for growing commonality and comparabilits of results across studies.

The literature shows the importance of using two types of WM as a basis of assessment in DM, (i) quantitative analytical indicators, which allow work on real data, quantifying different goals or conversions and which are the main indicators studied by the authors, (ii) qualitative analytical indicators that are used in DM to show how the user understands a website, helping to define KPIs to understand the on-line buying process and user behaviour.

The lack of knowledge of Academics in electronic media, and the skills gap that often exists for marketers in measuring and analyzing DM activities shows that the measurement of DM through technical indicators is a developing art that has not generated consensus between academics about how or what to measure in academic researches.

REFERENCES

Chaffey, D., & Patron, M. (2012). From WA to DM optimization: Increasing the commercial value of digital analytics. *Journal of Direct, Data and DM Practice*. Vol. 14, No.1, pp30-45. doi: 10.1057/dddmp.2012

Fiorini, P. and Lipsky, L. (2012). Search marketing traffic and performance models. *Journal Computer Standards & Interfaces*, Vol. 34, No. 6, pp517-526. doi:10.1016/j.csi.2011.10.008

Germann, F., Lilien, G., & Rangaswamy, A. (2013). Performance implications of deploying marketing analytics. *International Journal of Research in Marketing*. Vol. 30, No.2, pp114–128. doi: 10.1016/j.ijresmar.2012.10.001

Järvinen, J., Töllinen, A., Karjaluoto, H., & Platzer, E. (2012). Web Analytics and social media monitoring in industrial marketing: Tools for improving marketing communication measurement. *Proceedings of the 41st Academy of Marketing Science Annual Conference*. New Orleans, EEUU, pp. 477-486

Jayaram, J, Manrai, K. y Manrai, S., (2015) Effective use of marketing technology in Eastern Europe: Web analytics, social media, customer analytics, digital campaigns and mobile applications. *Journal of economics. Finance and Administrative science.* Vol. 20, No.39, pp118-132.

Kent, L., Carr, H. and Rebeca A. (2011). Learning web analytics: A tool for strategic communication. Public Relations Review Vol. 37, No.5, pp536–543. doi:10.1016/j.pubrev.2011.09.011

Lee, G. (2010). "Death of "last click wins": Media atribution and the expanding use of media data". *Journal of direct data and digital marketing practice*. Vol.12, No.1, pp16-26. doi: 10.1057/dddmp.2010.14

Leeflang, P, Verhoef, P., Dahsltröm, P. y Freundt, T. (2014). Challengues and solutions for marketing in a digital era. *European Management Journal*. Vol. 32, pp1-12. doi: 10.1016/j.emj.2013.12.001

Nabout, A., Bernd, S., Stepanchuk, T. and Gerstmeier, E. (2012), "An Analysis of the Profitability of Fee-Based Compensation Plans for Search Engine Marketing", *International Journal of Research of Marketing*, Vol. 29, No. 1, pp68-80. doi: 10.1016/j.ijresmar.2011.07.002

Nabout, A., Skiera, B., and Stepanchuk, T. (2012). Return on Quality Improvements in Search Engine Marketing. *Journal of Interactive Marketing*. Vol. 26, No. 3, pp141–154. doi: 10.1016/j.intmar.2011.11.001

Pauwels, Z., Aksehirli, A. and Lackman (2016). Like the ad or the brand? Marketing stimulates different electronic word-of-mouth content to drive online and offline performance. *International Journal of Research in Marketing*. Vol.33 No. 3, pp 639-655. doi: 10.1016/j.ijresmar.2016.01.005

Royle, Jo., Laing, A. (2014). The DM skills gap: Developing a Digital Marketer Model for the communication industries. *International Journal of Information Management*. Vol.34, No.2, pp65–73. doi: 10.1016/j.ijinfomgt.2013.11.008

Xu, Z., Frankwick, J. & Ramirez, E. (2016). Effects of big data analytics and traditional marketing analytics on new product success: A knowledge fusion perspective. *Journal of Business Research*. Vol.69, No.5, pp1562–1566. doi: 10.1016/j.jbusres.2015.10.017

Zhuofan, Y., Shib, Y. and Wang, B. (2015). "Search Engine Marketing, Financing Ability and Firm Performance in E-commerce". *Journal of Marketing Research*. Vol. 55, pp1106-1112. doi: 10.1016/j.procs.2015.07.078

MODELING DATA CLEANING TECHNIQUES FOR BIG DATA

Diana Martinez-Mosquera[1], Sergio Luján-Mora[2] and Fidel Parra[1]
[1]*Departamento de Ciencias de la Ingeniería, Universidad Israel, Quito, Ecuador*
[2]*Department of Software and Computing Systems, University of Alicante, Alicante, Spain*

ABSTRACT

Big Data is currently a popular term, it focuses on high volumes of data processed into relevant information to assist in decision making. A few researches about data cleaning techniques have been adapted to Big Data and we consider that filtering irrelevant data is an important task aimed to reduce hardware and processing time requirements. Moreover, there are separate researches about data cleaning processes in Big Data, thus, our approach proposes to model techniques used for this intent. Since logs can be considered as Big Data we have modeled two different approaches, one to clean a firewall log in a vertical dimension and another to clean a web log in a horizontal dimension. An advantage of our proposal is the use of the Unified Modeling Language, an International Organization for Standardization standard widely accepted since 2005. Consequently, the data cleaning process is composed by logical units that can be replaced or modified by the designer. Thus, the examples demonstrate the integration possibility of several clustering techniques, for example, Levenshtein Distance, Longitudinal Distance, Transposition Invariant Distance, Word Position Invariant Distance, etc.

KEYWORDS

Big, Data, Cleaning, Modeling, UML, Technique

1. INTRODUCTION

Big Data is the used term to describe big volumes of information, which comply with some attributes denoted by V's: Volume, Velocity, Variety, Variability, Viscosity, Virality, Veracity, Viability, Visualization, and Value (Qaiyum, 2016). The constant growing of generated data by companies compelled them to collect terabytes of information; this data has started to be known as Big Data (Cárdenas, 2015).

On the other hand, data cleaning process is related to find and rectify errors and inconsistences (Aye, 2011). We consider the data cleaning process as an important phase, since it reduces the raw data size with the goal of filtering the irrelevant information before analysis. Furthermore, according the common used term Garbage In Garbage Out (GIGO), it is better to fix the wrong data as soon as possible, because it can produce undesired, often nonsensical, results after computation.

Several approaches about Big Data Cleaning have been proposed, for instance: Cleanix system, developed for cleaning relational Big Data, through data cleaning tasks, such as abnormal value detection and correction, incomplete data filling, de-duplication, and conflict resolution (Wang et al., 2015). A big data online cleaning algorithm based on dynamic outlier detection, for real-time data processing (Diao et al., 2015). A cleaning framework for Big Data to identify similar objects and link them using context and usage patterns (Liu, 2015). A generic semantic-based framework that uses parallelized processing model for big data cleansing process, it mainly allows to identify data items and generate correlations between datasets (Wang et al., 2014). All of these separated researches can be modeled to simplify their understanding; however, we did not find a research about modeling the data cleaning process for Big Data. Therefore, our research consists in using the stereotypes and icons proposed by a previous research, for modeling Extract, Transform and Load (ETL) processes using the Unified Modeling Language (UML) (Trujillo, 2013), applied to the data cleaning process for Big Data. Extract task gathers data from external sources; Transform task manipulates collected data, cleaning is addressed on this task to remove unnecessary data and Load task loads the data to permanent storage.

Since logs can be considered as Big Data (Khalifa et al., 2016), we have taken as example a firewall sample dataset from a real environment to present how to model a data cleaning technique in a vertical dimension, discarding columns, and to demonstrate the versatility of the model we have used a web log in a horizontal dimension, discarding rows. After applying UML and the stereotypes for modeling ETL processes, we composed the data cleaning process into separated logical units. Hence, it is also possible to integrate different techniques into any logical unit (Luján-Mora, 2001). This paper is organized with the following structure; section 2 summarizes our modeling data cleaning for Big Data proposal based on a previous research for modeling ETL processes using UML; section 3 presents case study for two data cleaning techniques, one of them for security logs and the another for web logs; conclusions and future work are shown in section 4.

2. METHOD

In this section, we present our approach to model a data cleaning process for Big Data. We will briefly explain some used terms and concepts to be used in our proposal: UML, the Unified Modeling Language is a standard defined by ISO/IEC 19505-2:2012 revision 2, for modeling business and similar processes. Stereotype, is a type of extensibility mechanism in the Unified Modeling Language (UML) that allows designers to create new model elements, derived from existing ones. UML package is the used term to group elements, and to provide a namespace. We propose the use of stereotypes, according the approach for modeling ETL process in data warehouses (Trujillo, 2013), for modeling data cleaning processes in Big Data, thus, every phase will be composed of UML packages to help the designer to separate the process into different logical units that can be replaced or modified according his requirements. Logical units are represented by icons and their meanings states in Table 1.

Table 1. Stereotypes and icons (Trujillo, 2013)

Stereotype	Description	Icon
Aggregation	Aggregates data based on some criteria	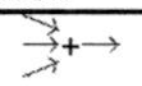
Conversion	Changes data type and format or derives new data from existing data	A→B
Filter	Filters and verifies data	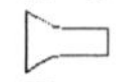
Incorrect	Reroutes incorrect data	
Join	Joins two data sources related to each other via some attributes	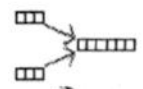
Loader	Loads data into an ETL process target	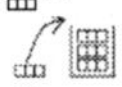
Log	Logs activity of an ETL mechanism	
Merge	Integrates two or more data sources with compatible attributes	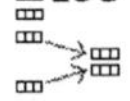
Surrogate	Generates unique surrogate keys	123→
Wrapper	Transforms a native data source into a record based data source	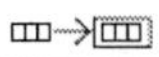

3. CASE STUDY

In order to explain how to use our proposal, in this section we have modeled two data cleaning processes examples. The first of them regards to an automatic data cleaning process for security logs, it enables to discard irrelevant data in a vertical dimension, that is, columns are deleted from the logs; to demonstrate the versatility of our approach, another data cleaning technique for web logs has been modeled, there, not useful data are deleted in a vertical dimension, that is, rows are deleted from the logs. Both examples could be modeled into logical units, facilitating their understanding and offering to the designer the possibility to replace or modified any unit.

3.1 Modeling Data Cleaning Process for Security Logs

In this example, we have modeled an automatic data cleaning process for security logs (Martinez-Mosquera, 2017) with some variations to facilitate the comprehension. The datasets consist in a final user report and a firewall log with two main features: Data format are structured or semi-structured, to identify every separated field and must be in the same language as it enables the use of data clustering techniques.

The first phase is extracting the header fields from several user reports, avoiding header names duplication, for this phase, the used icon is "Filter" as it is shown in Figure 1, since this stereotype filters and verifies data according Table 1. The result of this process is a file that contains the merged report headers regarding to the useful data of the firewall log; hence, this file will be used as a filter rules file. In this case the used icon is "Merge", since it represents the integration of two or more data sources with compatible attributes, as it can be observed in Figure 1.

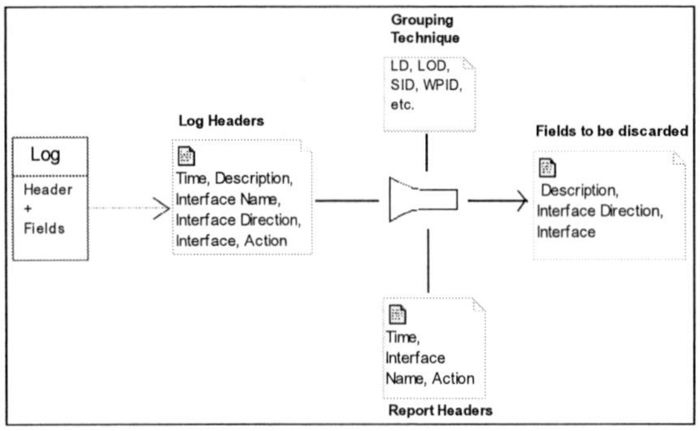

Figure 1. Filtering and Merging User Final Report Headers

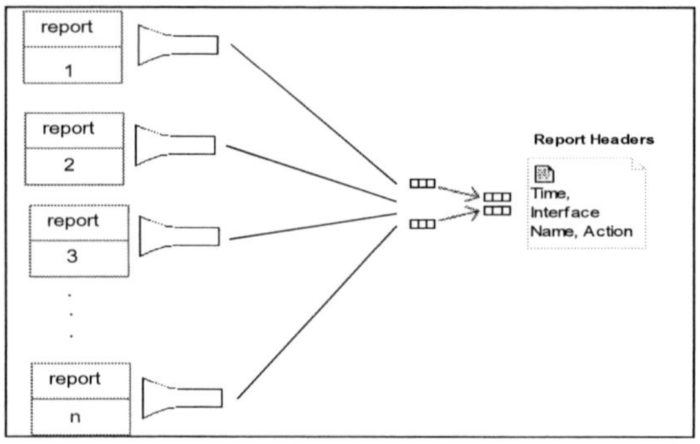

Figure 2. Filtering firewall raw log headers

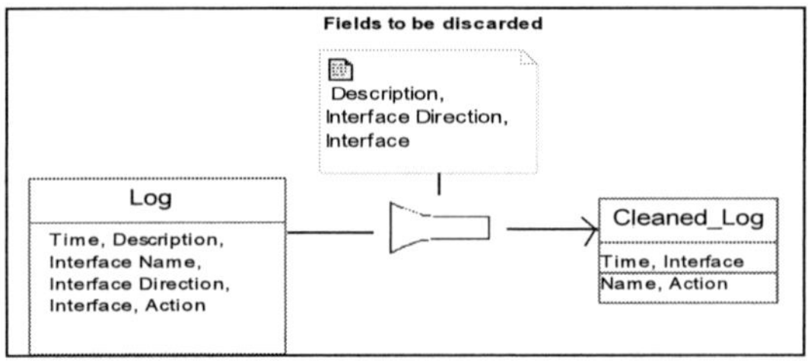

Figure 3. Data cleaning process for security log

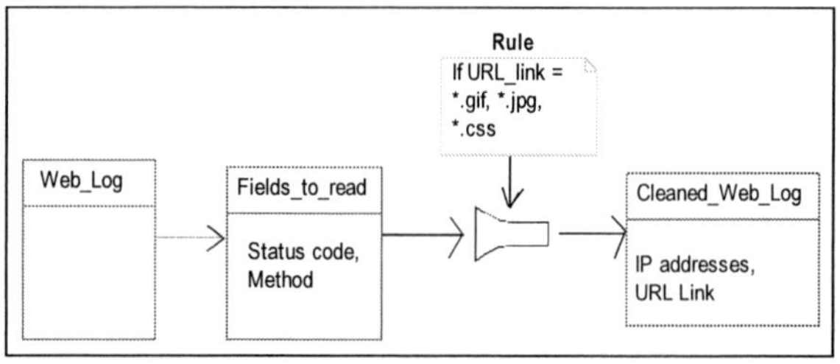

Figure 4. Data cleaning process for web log

In Figure 2, as first step the raw log generated by a firewall will be filtered to separate only log headers. Then, the log headers are filtered according the generated filter rules file, for the comparison of every field name some data clustering technique can be used, for instance: Levenshtein Distance (LD), Longitudinal Distance (LOD), Transposition Invariant Distance (TID), Word Position Invariant Distance (WPID), etc. (Luján-Mora, 2001); the log headers file becomes in a file with header fields to be discarded. In this phase, only the filter icon was used and we can verify the utility of logical units, since Clustering Techniques can be modified and the model will not be affected. In Figure 3, we present the final phase of the data cleaning process, where the file with header fields to be discarded is used to filter the irrelevant fields from the raw logs and to produce the cleaned log. Here, only the filter icon had to be used.

3.2 Modeling Data Cleaning Process for Web Logs

In Figure 4, we have used an algorithm proposed in a research about web log cleaning, the used dataset is the access.log file from an Apache server, the log records are composed basically for user IP number or domain name, time, type of access method, GET, POST, etc., and the page address to be accessed. The main idea is to eliminate references to style files, graphics or sound files considered as unnecessary data for mining web usage patterns (Aye, 2011) (Humm, 2017). As we can observe, the modeling of this process is intuitive and very easy to implement, thus, the data cleaning technique is modeled in a simple way, using only a filter icon, but with a strong support for designers.

4. CONCLUSIONS

In this paper, we have modeled two data cleaning techniques for Big Data using the stereotypes of the approach for ETL process in data warehouses. We could verified, an automatic data cleaning process can be represented into UML packages in a simple way, helping designers to tackle its solutions and improving the understanding of their approaches, since every phase can be composed by logical units, the model offers the facility of replacing or modifying according the designer requirements. As future work, we are working for modeling an entire Big Data ecosystem at the Conceptual, Logical and Physical level; automatizing the model transformation through the use of Query, View, Transformation (QVT) and incorporating the use of Object Management Group (OCL) standard for defining detailed transformation processes.

REFERENCES

Aye, T., 2011. Web log cleaning for mining of web usage patterns. *Proceedings of 3rd International Conference Computer Research and Development (ICCRD*), vol. 2, pp. 490-494. doi: 10.1109/ICCRD.2011.5764181.

Cárdenas A., Manadhata P., Rajan S., 2015. Big Data Analytics for Security. *IEE Security & Privacy*, pp. 74-76. doi: 10.1109/MSP.2013.138.

Diao Y., Liu K. Y., Meng X., Ye X., He K., 2015. A Big Data Online Cleaning Algorithm Based on Dynamic Outlier Detection. *Proceedings of International Conference on Cyber-Enabled Distributed Computing and Knowledge Discovery (CyberC)*, pp. 230-234. doi: 10.1109/CyberC.2015.68.

Humm, B. G., & Ossanloo, H. A, 2017. Semantic search engine for software components. *Proceedings of 13th International Conference on Applied Computing (AC).*

Khalifa S., Elshater Y.,Sundaravarathan K., Bhat A., Martin P., Iman F., Rope D., McRoberts M., Statchuk C., 2016. The Six Pillars for Building Big Data Analytics Ecosystems. *In Canada Journal ACM Computing Surveys, vol. 49.* pp. 33:1-33:35. doi: 10.1145/2963143.

Liu H. and T. K. A. Kumar and J. P. Thomas, 2015. Cleaning Framework for Big Data - Object Identification and Linkage. *Proceedings of IEEE International Congress on Big Data*, pp. 215-221. doi: 10.1109/BigDataCongress.2015.38.

Luján Mora S., Palomar Sanz M., 2001. Reducing Inconsistency in Integrating Data from Different Sources. *Proceedings of 2001 International Database Engineering and Applications Symposium (IDEAS)*, pp. 209-218. doi: 10.1109/IDEAS.2001.938087.

Martinez-Mosquera D., Luján-Mora S., López G., Santos L., 2017. Data Cleaning Technique for Security Logs Based on Fellegi-Sunter Theory. *Proceedings of Xth SIGSAND/PLAIS Eurosymposium'2017 Information systems: research, development, applications, education.* doi: http://dx.doi.org/10.1007/978-3-319-66996-0_1.

Trujillo J., Luján-Mora S., 2003. A UML Based Approach for Modeling ETL Processes in Data Warehouses. *Proceedings of International Conference on Conceptual Modeling (ER)*, pp. 307-320. doi: 10.1007/978-3-540-39648-2_25.

Qaiyum, S., Aziz, I. A., & Jaafar, J. B., 2016. Analysis of Big Data and Quality-of-Experience in High-Density Wireless Network. *Proceedings of 3rd International Conference Computer and Information Sciences (ICCOINS)*, pp. 287-292. doi: 10.1109/ICCOINS.2016.7783229.

Wang, Hongzhi and Li, Mingda and Bu, Yingyi and Li, Jianzhong and Gao, Hong and Zhang, Jiacheng, 2015. Cleanix: A Parallel Big Data Cleaning System. *SIGMOD Rec,* vol. 44, pp. 35-40. doi:10.1145/2935694.2935702.

Wang J., Song Z., Li Q., Yu J., Chen F., 2014. Semantic-based intelligent data clean framework for big data. *Proceedings of IEEE International Conference on Security, Pattern Analysis, and Cybernetics (SPAC)*, pp. 448-453. doi: 10.1109/SPAC.2014.6982731.

USER INTERACTION USING MOTION SENSITIVE DEVICES: A STUDY ABOUT BUTTON´S DIMENSION WITH KINECT AND WIIMOTE

André Constantino da Silva, Luis Otávio Alves Nascimento and Vinícius Simões dos Santos Silva
Grupo de Pesquisa em Mobilidade e Novas Tecnologias de Interação (IFSP)
Instituto Federal de Educação, Ciência e Tecnologia do Estado de São Paulo – Câmpus Hortolândia
Avenida Thereza Ana Cecon Breda s/n, Vila São Pedro, Hortolândia – SP, Brasil

ABSTRACT

New equipment and user interaction software emerged and became popular in the last decade and the interaction with each equipment has peculiarities that must be considered. This paper presents a study based on user testing to investigate the dimensions of buttons when interact with Kinect and WiiMote, two motion-sensitive devices. Our data show that, in the interaction with small dimensions buttons, the time and the number of mistakes are higher than compared with other dimensions, mainly in the interaction using WiiMote; our findings for WiiMote is close to the literature but we did not find the same for Kinect; but volunteers preferred to interact with buttons that have large dimensions instead of the smaller ones.

KEYWORDS

User Interaction, Motion-sensitive Device, Usability

1. INTRODUCTION

New equipment and user interaction software have emerged in the last decade, allowing users to interact in many ways with digital content; we can mention the Kinect, a motion-sensitive device, and the WiiMote, the motion-sensitive control of the Wii console, that allow users interact with an application through gestures. Based on reports from the Gartner group, Kugler (2008) describes that one of the major challenges for Information and Communication Technology in the next 25 years is the natural and non-tactile interfaces and automatic speech recognition. This challenge, coupled with the tendency to gradually switch the mouse over emerging alternative interfaces that work with facial recognition, movement and gestures (Hayes, 2008), brings new challenges to Human-Computer Interaction area. The interaction with each equipment has peculiarities that must be considered in the user interface design, resulting in the need to investigate solutions to allow users interact with the available equipment.

In this context, our work aims to investigate the relationship between the characteristics of user interface components and usability when users interact with motion-sensitive devices. This paper presents a study that investigate the dimensions of buttons, identifying minimum values considering as good for usability that is composed by effectiveness, efficiency and user satisfaction (ISO 9241, 1997). The Section 2 describes presents a literature review; the methodology and discussion are presented on Section 3, and Section 4 presents our final considerations.

2. LITERATURE REVIEW

Modality is the used term to define a mode what the user data input or a system output is expressed. Bernsen's (2008) defines that modality, or, more explicitly, a modality of information representation, is a form of representing the information in some medium. Thus, a modality is defined by its medium and its particular 'form' of representation. One example is gestures: "an expressive, significant movement of the body, that is, physical movement of the fingers, hands, arms, head, face or body that has the intention of passing information or interacting with the environment" (Karpov et al., 2008, p. 156). Karpov et al. (2008) define three categories for gesture recognition technology: (i) *pen-based recognition* (involves recognizing gestures from 2D input devices, such as a pen or touchscreen); (ii) *hardware tracker-based recognition* (using of hardware devices that can process input gesture, such as WiiMote); and (iii) *vision-based recognition* (using cameras that capture images and algorithms that interpret them, such as Kinect).

About mouse, gestures, GUI interface and Natural User Interface, Teiche et al. (2009) emphasize that the mouse and the GUI interface were one of the main reasons for the great penetration of computers in the society; but the interaction technique is indirect and based on recognition. The Natural User Interface with multi-touch screens is intuitive, contextualized and evocative and the changing from GUI to gesture-based interface will continue to make computers an integral but discreet part of our lifestyle. Hamilton et al. (2012) describe that the modes of interaction based on pen, multitouch, and mouse + keyboard are fundamentally different. Thus, direct comparisons of performance are difficult to perform, and few quantitative studies have been done. Considering this, in our previous work (Silva *et al.*, 2015), we investigated the usability attributes when the user interacts with Google Maps and Google Street View using Kinect and WiiMote. Results of this work corroborates the Bernsen´s claim (2008): two interaction modes are not equivalent because modalities differ from each one in relation to the strengths and weaknesses of expressiveness and also in relation to the perceptual systems, cognitive and emotional human being. One of the identified problems was related to the difficult to trigger some buttons in the studied applications; so, we have formulated the following question "What are the dimensions for a button to have a good usability when users will interact with gesture-based devices?". The next Section presents our study trying to answer it.

3. MATERIAL AND METHODS

Our methodology is based on user testing with volunteers interacting with an application to trigger the highlighted button following a predetermined sequence (sequential, random and reverse order) in total of nine buttons for each following size of buttons: 45px height 30px width (considered as small size); 60px height by 90px width (considered as medium sized); and 100px height by 150px width (considered as large size). The application logs the user's mistakes and completed task (to measure effectiveness) and time (to measure the efficiency). To collect user satisfaction, we develop a post-test questionnaire composed by 10 questions.

To map the user's movements captured by Kinect in mouse actions, we use the tool Orchestra version 3.2; while to map the movements captured by the WiiMote in mouse actions, we use the tool TouchMote version 1.0b13. For both devices, the user need to move her/him arm (in case of Orchestra, the hand must be open; and in case of TouchMote, the user must to move the hand that is holding the control) to move the pointer. To trigger the button, in the case of Orchestra, the user must to close and open the hand; and in the case of TouchMote, the user must press one of the WiiMote button. We consider that the gestures to perform a pointer movement or button trigger are simple; so, we do not evaluate it.

Ten volunteers (V01 to V10) participated in the study who performed the task for the three buttons sizes using Kinect and WiiMote; half using the Kinect firstly, and the other half using the WiiMote firstly. Regarding the volunteers, all of them was youngers (aged between 16 and 20 years), 4 males and 6 females, all use computer in everyday activities (mainly for entertainment and to study): the majority (6 volunteers) uses computers for more than five hours per week and four volunteers use computers from one to five hours per week. Eight volunteers answered that did not have Kinect, though six volunteers said they have used previously. About WiiMote, nine volunteers said they never had used the Wii console, though four have played Wii and therefore had used the WiiMote. Therefore, profile data shows that there is a balance between users who have never used the Kinect and the Wii and users with previous experience.

Table 1 presents the interaction time for each volunteer to perform the task considering the three buttons dimensions in each device. The average time to interact with medium sized buttons with Kinect was less than the average time for the small and the large buttons. But with the WiiMote, the average time to interact with large size buttons was less than the average time for the small and the medium ones. But when we analyzed the shortest time for each volunteer considering the three dimensions using Kinect, we identified that 4 volunteers (V02, V03, V08, V09) had the shortest time when interacting with medium sized buttons; 3 volunteers (V05, V06, V07) had the shortest time when interacting with small size buttons; and 3 volunteers (V01, V04, V10) in interact with large size buttons. This finding is not similar for interacting using WiiMote: all volunteers had the shortest time when interacting with large size buttons, as we expected. The longest interaction using Kinect for 4 volunteers (V02, V06, V07, V09) was interacting with large size buttons, for 3 volunteers (V01, V04, V05) was interacting with medium sized buttons, and for 3 volunteers (V03, V08, V10) was interacting with small size buttons. Using WiiMote, the longest interaction for 8 volunteers (V01, V02, V03, V04, V05, V06, V08, V09) was interacting with small size buttons, and for 2 volunteers (V07, V10) was interacting with medium sized buttons. The results for Kinect were not expected; we waited for a similar result from using Kinect and using WiiMote, and less time interacting with large buttons.

Table 1. Time Collected in the User Testing

		Kinect			WiiMote	
	Small	Medium	Large	Small	Medium	Large
V01	187.444,0	257.195,0	129.103,0	120.351,0	112.395,0	99.288,0
V02	199.328,0	177.409,0	349.086,0	308.611,0	152.062,0	123.798,0
V03	231.632,0	156.986,0	188.353,0	423.965,0	63.877,0	46.955,0
V04	110.050,0	112.967,0	102.484,0	120.351,0	112.395,0	99.288,0
V05	107.318,0	126.262,0	123.034,0	87.451,0	74.637,0	41.499,0
V06	170.700,0	210.458,0	317.975,0	101.228,0	50.669,0	40.090,0
V07	200.751,0	239.441,0	293.926,0	214.222,0	221.970,0	113.045,0
V08	201.029,0	136.774,0	156.132,0	254.985,0	114.709,0	64.513,0
V09	262.005,0	253.520,0	463.700,0	385.772,0	178.789,0	94.638,0
V10	119.113,0	114.464,0	100.042,0	115.492,0	157.161,0	46.525,0
Average	199.328,0	156.986,0	172.242,5	167.286,5	113.552,0	79.575,5

The number of mistakes of each volunteer when interact by Kinect and by WiiMote are showed at Table 2. The average of mistakes was lower when the volunteers interact with large buttons on both devices. But, in the Kinect, the average of mistakes in interact with medium sized buttons was greater than interact with small buttons. The smallest number of mistakes using Kinect for 4 volunteers (V01, V06, V07, V09) was interacting with small size buttons; for 3 volunteers (V02, V04, V08) was interacting with medium sized buttons; and for 3 volunteers (V03, V05, V10) was interacting with large size buttons. Using WiiMote, the smallest number of mistakes for 9 volunteers (V01, V02, V03, V04, V05, V07, V08, V09, V10) was interacting with large size buttons. For one volunteer (V06), the smallest number of mistakes was interacting with medium sized buttons.

The largest number of mistakes using Kinect for 5 volunteers (V02, V03, V04, V08, V10) was interacting with small size buttons; for 3 volunteers (V01, V05, V07) was interacting with medium sized buttons; and for 2 volunteers (V06, V09) was interacting with large size buttons. Using WiiMote, the largest number of mistakes for 9 volunteers (V01, V02, V03, V04, V05, V06, V07, V08, V09) was interacting with small size buttons; for 1 volunteer (V10) the same number of mistakes was made in the case of small size buttons and medium sized buttons. The results for WiiMote is expected: interact with large size buttons consumes less time and fewer mistakes. But the same results were not found for Kinect, that had similar results for the different button sizes.

Table 2. Number of Mistakes Collected in the User Testing

		Kinect			Wii	
	Small	Medium	Large	Small	Medium	Large
V01	19	38	20	102	82	41
V02	28	20	25	219	56	40
V03	38	28	24	1.319	140	26
V04	25	18	23	102	82	41
V05	25	30	20	39	20	8
V06	26	31	51	17	3	5
V07	39	52	47	84	46	26
V08	22	11	20	55	36	16
V09	59	64	114	77	31	15
V10	20	13	8	20	20	6
Average	25,5	28,0	23,5	80,5	41,0	21,0

Analyzing Table 3, we noticed that the large size buttons had a better acceptance by the volunteers, both when interacting with the WiiMote and Kinect, although little difference between the results in the case of interaction with Kinect, but of great differences in the case of interaction with the WiiMote.

The last question of the post-test questionnaire was about the volunteer preferred button size. For both equipment, 9 volunteers preferred large size buttons over medium sized and small size. One volunteer prefers medium-sized buttons over large size and small size.

Table 3. Answers for the Post-test Questionnaire

	Kinect					WiiMote				
Questions	SD	D	NAD	A	SA	SD	D	NAD	A	SA
Small size										
I triggered the highlighted button on the first time	0	2	1	5	2	1	2	4	2	1
It was fast to trigger the buttons in the order	1	2	1	5	1	2	2	3	2	1
The size made it easy to press	2	1	1	5	1	3	0	1	4	2
Medium sized										
I triggered the highlighted button on the first time	0	1	1	5	3	0	1	3	6	0
It was fast to trigger the buttons in the order	1	1	3	4	1	1	1	1	4	3
The size made it easy to press	0	1	1	5	3	0	0	0	3	7
Large size										
I triggered the highlighted button on the first time	0	1	1	5	3	0	0	2	5	3
It was fast to trigger the buttons in the order	0	0	1	2	7	0	1	1	1	7
The size made it easy to press	0	0	1	1	8	0	1	0	1	8

SD - Strongly disagree; D – Disagree; NAD - Neither agree nor disagree; A – Agree; SA – Strongly agree.

4. FINAL CONSIDERATIONS

Our data show that, in the interaction with small dimensions buttons (45px height 30px width), the time and the number of mistakes are higher (60px height by 90px width, and 100px height by 150px width), mainly in interacting using WiiMote. The data collected in interacting using WiiMote is close to the literature: users make fewer errors and lower time to trigger larger buttons. But, similar results were not found for Kinect; maybe the not expected results could be related with the settings since this equipment uses vision-based recognition and light, background, and skin color may influence results. Regarding user opinion, volunteers preferred to interact with buttons that have large dimensions instead of the smaller ones. Future work will continue the study with more volunteers, to study other user interface components (e.g. combo box and select box), and how the distance between the components can impact on usability, and finally, to develop some guidelines for designers that build applications that will be interacted by motion-sensitive devices.

REFERENCES

Bernsen, N. O., 2008. Multimodality Theory. *In Multimodal User Interfaces: From signal to interaction*, Springer-Verlag Berlin Heidelberg, Berlin, Germany, pp. 5-28.

Hamilton, W. et al, 2012. High-Performance Pen + Touch Modality Interactions: A real-time strategy game eSports context. *Proceedings of Annual ACM Symposium on User Interface Software and Technology (UIST 2012)*, Cambridge, USA, pp. 309-318.

Hayes, B, 2009. Gartner's Seven IT Grand Challenges. *In Communications of the ACM*, Vol. 51, No. 7, pp. 10.

ISO 9241, 1997. *ISO 9241-11: Ergonomic requirements for office work with visual display terminals (VDTs)*. Part 11 — Guidelines for specifying and measuring usability. International Organization for Standardization, Genève, Italy.

Karpov, A. et al, 2008. Two SIMILAR Different Speech and Gestures Multimodal Interfaces. *In Multimodal User Interfaces: From signal to interaction*, Springer-Verlag Berlin Heidelberg, Berlin, Germany, pp. 155-184.

Kugler, L., 2008. Goodbye, Computer Mouse. *In Communications of the ACM*, Vol. 51, No. 9, pp. 56.

Silva, A. C. da et al, 2015. Identifying Interaction Problems on Web Applications Due to the Change of Input Modality: a study about Kinect, Google Maps and Google Street View. *Proceedings of 14th International Conference WWW/Internet* Maynooth, Ireland, pp. 192-196.

Teiche, A. et al, 2009. *Multitouch Technologies*. NUI Group.

Posters

E-LEARNING AS A STRATEGY FOR IMPLEMENTATION OF PUBLIC POLICIES

Juliana Macedo Reis Mercês and Profa Dra Marcia Maria Pereira Rendeiro
Rio de Janeiro State University - UERJ
524, São Francisco Xavier Street, Block E, room 2013. Maracanã. Rio de Janeiro – RJ. Brazil

ABSTRACT

The Federal Government of Brazil created the Open University of the Unified Health System (UNA-SUS) as a complementary strategy to the Continuing E-health Education Policy (PNEPS),to meet the training and continuing education needs of SUS workers, through the E-Learning modality, as a way of professional updating. UNA-SUS from Rio de Janeiro State University(UNA-SUS / UERJ), developed courses for E-Learning, self-instructional, free and open access to the public interested in the following topics: (a) National Policy on Comprehensive Health LGBT Population; (b) Endocrine-Metabolic Diseases and Nutrition; (c) Judicialization of Health in Home Care and (d) Approach of Violence in home care. The objective of this study was to analyze the applicability of the use of a e-learning course in a country of continental dimensions such as Brazil, to know the profile of the students, the level of satisfaction related to the stimulus to the reflection about the practical situations and the level of knowledge acquired. In addition, the scope of the courses in the national territory was investigated. We used the secondary data extracted from the Arouca Platform and the Self-Assessment Questionnaire from each course and educational offer.The data were organized into Excel spreadsheets and analyzed. Thus, based on the data analyzed, it was possible to conclude that E-learning and the free offer for any professional interested in the themes offered is an excellent strategy to overcome geographical barriers, promote health and support the implementation of public policies, especially in countries with continental dimensions, such as Brazil. Furthermore, the pedagogical choice incorporated in the courses obtained a positive evaluation of the students for providing reflection on practical situations and acquisition of important knowledge for professional practice.

KEYWORDS

e-Learning; e-Health; Public Policy; Continuing Education

1. INTRODUCTION

The E-learning (EAD) has shown an exponential expansion in the last decade, being implemented in a globalized way.Qualified because it allows overcoming the distance, expansion of educational offerings for people who can not study in person, curricular enrichment and decrease of displacement, generating time and production savings, it is seen as a fundamental and strategic tool for knowledge dissipation and information democratization , as well as professional updating, representing great assistance in the task of permanent formation of professionals geographically distant.

According to Niskier (1999, p.16-17), e-learning results in the combination of distance education and communication processes, allowing a large number of people and groups to reach several technological resources.

In Brazil, this modality has been growing intensely and according to data from the Census of Higher Education 2014, conducted by the National Institute of Studies and Educational Research Anísio Teixeira (INEP), the number of students in this modality reached 1.34 million in 2014, which represents a share of 17.1% of total enrollment in higher education (INEP, 2014).

In view of this scenario and in complement to the strategy of the Policy of Continuing Education in Health (PNEPS) - "to promote changes in the educational processes of health professionals, with a view to integrating human resources management with the needs of the population's health services" BRASIL, 2014) - the Ministry of Health (MS), through Decree No. 7,385 of December 8, 2010, created the Open University of the Unified Health System (UNA-SUS) with the purpose of meeting the training and continuing education needs of SUS workers, through the distance education modality as a vehicle for professional updating (BRASIL, 2010).

UNA-SUS is composed of a Network of Public Universities of higher education, affiliated to the Ministry Health and accredited by the Ministry of Education to ensure the best execution of the actions and programs of the Federal Government related to the education of health professionals.

UNA-SUS Rio de Janeiro State University (UNA-SUS / UERJ), is part of the Network of Universities that offer free courses and programs of specialization, improvement and other forms of qualification, in the format of E-learning and semi -presential, tutored and self-instructional.

Within this context, UNA-SUS / UERJ offers four courses at the e-learning modality, in Moodle environment, and self-instructional, in which there is no mediation or help from an online tutor, so the student is responsible for the built of his learning: (a) National Policy on Comprehensive Health LGBT; (b) Endocrine-Metabolic Diseases and Nutrition; (c) Judicialization of Health in Home Care and (d) Approach of Violence in Home Care.

The courses aim to enhance the implementation of Public Policies related to the theme and have as target professionals and health managers linked to the SUS, however they were made available to anyone interested in the subject, having as central focus the dissemination of information and normative content on the Policies and other aspects of the referring legislation in a pleasant way, facilitating the understanding.

They were developed in Moodle environment, with linear navigation and proof of certification at the end of the course.

The teaching and learning strategy was based on Andragogy science, in which teaching learning is adult-oriented, independence and self-management learning. Learning is done through perception or experience, an action that stimulates and transforms content to encourage assimilation, learn by doing. (Somera, Junior Somera and Rondina, 2010).

With this, the course uses the methodology of problematization, problem solving and real tasks of common occurrences in the daily life of the professionals with the objective of developing competences for the professional performance.

In this perspective, the objective of this study was to analyze the applicability of the use of a e-learning course in a country with continental dimensions such as Brazil, considering it to be a strategic action to overcome the geographic barriers and to facilitate the learning, to spread ideas and to present a Policy.

Thus, this study analyzed the profile of the students, the level of knowledge acquired and the evaluation of the students about the stimulus to reflection on the practical situations, as well as the geographical reach of all the offers of the above mentioned courses.

2. METHODS

It is a qualitative quantitative, exploratory, cross-sectional study. We use secondary data, extracted from the Self-Assessment Questionnaire for Courses - applied by UNA-SUS / UERJ by optionally completing online forms to identify:(1) student profile; (2) level of knowledge on the subject and (3) stimulation to reflection about practical situations.

Level of knowledge on the subject and stimulation of reflection about the practical situations were analyzed by closed questions, in which the student indicates his satisfaction through the gradients - insufficient, regular, good and great - and open questions, recording his opinion regarding the course.

In addition, the national database of the Arouca Platform was used, which allows to check conditions on the courses offered by the Network of Institutions that are part of UNA-SUS, to explore the national scope of each course and its offerings.

The data were organized in spreadsheets of the Excel Program and analyzed in percentage.The questionnaires contained open questions for qualitative analysis about students' satisfaction with the applied methodology and the importance of content related to professional activities.

3. RESULTS

60,598 people enrolled in the courses. From this universe, 16,195 volunteers answered voluntarily the questionnaires, optionally filled out, of the following offers: three offers of the National Policy on Comprehensive Health LGBT course, an offer of the Endocrine-Metabolic Diseases courses and Nutrition and Hearing Health Care and two courses offerings Judicialization of Health in Home Care and the Approach of Violence in Home Care (Table 1.)

Table 1. Enrollments in Courses of the UNA-SUS/UERJ

Course	Offer date	Enrolled
Approach of Violence in Home Care	07/30/13 – 09/10/15	2.827
Approach of Violence in Home Care	08/04/16 – 07/10/17	4.422
Judicialization of Health in Home Care	08/02/13 – 11/10/15	4.179
Judicialization of Health in Home Care	08/04/16 – 07/10/17	2.601
National Policy on Comprehensive Health LGBT	05/11/15 - 10/19/15	12.644
National Policy on Comprehensive Health LGBT	07/15/15 – 02/17/16	6.783
National Policy on Comprehensive Health LGBT	04/06/16 – 01/22/17	15.111
Endocrine-Metabolic Diseases and Nutrition	07/12/16 – 04/17/17	11.931

According to the data, it is a mainly young public, predominantly in the age group of 21 to 30 years and is sprayed in several areas of health, with preeminence for Nursing (Table 2).

Table 2. Demographic Profile – Numbers: Extracted from the Self-Assessment and Profile Forms applied in

Course	Age (21-35 years old)	Profession Predominant -Nurse
Approach of Violence in Home Care	49,5%	30,3%
Approach of Violence in Home Care	61%	22,8%
Judicialization of Health in Home Care	58%	21,6%
Judicialization of Health in Home Care	74,91%	21,5%
National Policy on Comprehensive Health LGBT	72,7%	24,8%
National Policy on Comprehensive Health LGBT	76,7%	20,4%
National Policy on Comprehensive Health LGBT	77,9%	19,6%
Endocrine-Metabolic Diseases and Nutrition	53%%	17,4%

The data indicated that 72.21% qualified as Great (higher degree) the self-perception of knowledge about the contents of the course. It is worth mentioning that 69.76% revealed that the methodology adopted stimulates reflection about practical situations.

According to data from the Arouca Platform, students are present throughout the national territory, showing that e-learning is an excellent strategy to facilitate the dissemination of knowledge, especially in countries with continental dimensions such as Brazil (Figure 1).

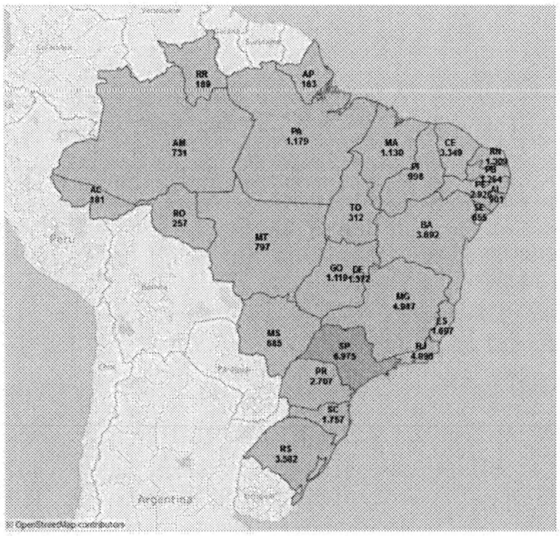

Figure 1. Distribution of Registered Professionals per unit of Federation of Performance

The qualitative analysis of the open answers was rich, with positive opinions of the students regarding the applied pedagogical methodology:

"I had never heard of this policy and I understood my responsibility as a professional with this part of the population" (National Policy on Comprehensive Health LGBT)

"All the time the course questions our position in the matter of prejudice and professionalism". (National Policy on Comprehensive Health LGBT)

"First of all, the training initiative on Policy Attention on Comprehensive Health LGBT and the theoretical and practical involvement, with relevant reflections for the professional activities that sometimes exclude, for acting with the invisibility of populations and carrying social marks that guide and condition our practices" (National Policy on Comprehensive Health LGBT)

My knowledge was certainly improved and my attendance was improved upon new knowledge acquired in the course." (Endocrine-Metabolic Diseases and Nutrition)

"The course was very good and brought very pertinent and up-to-date information on the subject, with practical application". (Endocrine-Metabolic Diseases and Nutrition)

"The course was very helpful in every way and I will apply what I learned in professional practical life." (Approach of Violence in Home Care)

The course was good and practical and offered us a basis on a theme so much alive today and to some extent demystifying what for many managers sounds like a penalty to Judicialization of Health". (Judicialization of Health in Home Care);

Very well directed because it is a subject that has ample discussion. The references were very good and helped in understanding the theme and complementation. (Judicialization of Health in Home Care).

4. CONCLUSION

In view of the results presented and the objective proposed for this study, we can observe that the assignment of a course in the E-learning modality can be considered an additional and strategic tool to overcome geographical barriers because it has reached the target audience, health professionals and managers of SUS, as well as other sectors interested in the themes.

The positive evaluation and results achieved so far demonstrate that E-learning has the potential to be used as a strategy for the implementation of Policies, for allowing a fast diffusion of ideas, reaching actors from different sectors, overcoming distance and facilitating the process , in addition to providing the Continuing Education of SUS health professionals.

REFERENCES

Arnaldo Niskier, 1999. Loyola. E-learning: tecnologia da esperança. São Paulo, Brasil, p.16-17.

BRASIL. Portaria GM/MS nº 1.996, from August 20, 2007. Provides guidelines for the implementation of the National Policy on Continuing Education in Health and provides other measures. Diário Oficial da União, Executive Power Brasília, DF, n. 162, Aug. 22,2007. Seção 1.

______. Portaria GM/MS nº 278, de February 27, 2014. It establishes guidelines for the implementation of the Continuing Education Policy in Health, within the Ministry of Health (MS). Diário Oficial da União, Executive Power , Brasília, DF, Feb 28, 2014. Section 1, p. 59-60.

INEP - National Institute of Educational Studies and Research Anísio Teixeira.Census of Higher Education 2014 - Statistical Notes. [Internet] Brasil; Avaiable in: http://eaesp.fgvsp.br/ensinoeconhecimento/centros/cia/pesquisa

Somera, Elizabeth; Junior Somera, Renato Somera; Rondina, João Marcelo. A proposal of andragogy for continuing education in the health area. Archive Science Health; 17(2):101-107, apr.-june. 2010.

Arouca platform. Distribution of professionals enrolled in Courses of the UNA-SUS System per unit of the Federation of actuation. [internet] Brasil: Open University of the Unified Health System. (UNA-SUS); [Updated in Sept 01, 2015]. Avaiable in: http://www.unasus.gov.br/page/una-sus-em-numeros/una-sus-em-numeros

SELF-TESTING IN PROGRAMMING BASICS LEARNING

Olga Mironova
School of Information Technologies, Department of Software Science, Tallinn University of Technology
Akadeemia tee street, 15A, Tallinn 12618, Estonia

ABSTRACT

The general purpose of this paper is to demonstrate the technique in teaching programming basics to novices. This technique is one of the components of the worked out teaching strategy, which is applied in the introductive programming course for non-IT first year university students. Considered technique is based on testing system in learning e-environment. This approach is quite controversial, but it greatly helps beginners to understand the structure of the program and learn syntax.

KEYWORDS

Programming, Novices, Self-Test

1. INTRODUCTION

Computer Science and its significant part – programming develop rapidly. Contemporary young generation wants to get modern and perspective knowledge and apply it on practice. Teachers' aim is to provide them with such kind of knowledge using experience, knowledge and pedagogical and didactical strategies.

However, it is necessary to note that all learners can be conditionally divided into two groups. The first group includes learners who *want to learn* and the second group is learners who *have to learn* programming. In addition, these two groups can be divided into subgroups: *can* and *cannot*. It is important here that the last division is division *only* according to learners' opinion.

The focus group of the present research is learners, who *have to learn* programming, but, on their opinion, *are not be able to learn*. In general, this group consists of university non-IT students, who have introductive computer science course in their curriculum.

The author's experience in teaching programming to novices is more than 10 years and unfortunately it should be noted, that the focus group size does not decrease. To train such students, additional techniques and strategies are required, not only for the transfer of knowledge, but also for motivation.

2. METHODOLOGY

Programming teaching and learning are complicated processes. As was mentioned in paper (Sohail Iqbal Malik & Jo Coldwell-Neilson, 2016), the key challenge in learning programming is to acquire different sets of skills at the same time. In recent years, the demand for programmers and student interest in programming have grown rapidly, and introductory programming courses have become increasingly popular. Learning to program is hard however (Anthony Robins et al., 2003).

The author of this paper is totally agrees with this statement that it is not possible to teach programming using PowerPoint (Guzdial M, 2015). Practice is one of the most important steps in learning the art of computer programming. (Cheanga B. et al., 2003). It should not be expected from non-IT students and especially from the beginners that they immediately start to write a program code after the first explanations. In addition, it is not possible to put students to write a program if they do not know how to start. The author attempts to suggest the alternative way for novices to practice in programming.

The introductive programming course is aimed to non-IT students from economics, social, chemistry and civil engineering faculties at Tallinn University of Technology, Estonia. The main programming language is Python (Python, 2017). This course is realized in Moodle (Moodle, 2017) environment and tries maximally using its opportunities.

2.1 The Self-Testing System

Different tests with different question types are offered to students during the learning process (Cunningham, G.K. 1998, Ward, A.W., Murray-Ward, M., 1999). It should be noted, that all of them develop students' certain skills. However, the author tries to avoid multiple-choice questions with one correct answer. The explanation here is simply: students can generally respond to these type of questions quite quickly and unfortunately, often do not think.

True/false questions teach students read the sentence carefully. Unfortunately, nowadays, when information can be obtained not only from books, this important kind of skill is lost among the young generation.

Matching questions teach students to compose sentences properly. Students memorize the order of words in the sentence and then correctly use it in practice. This type of tests is useful for memorizing such typical language constructs as conditional statements and iterations.

Short answer or fill-in-the-blank tests greatly help learners to learn programming language syntax, see and understand logical links in the text of the program.

In addition, tests, where students have to make the program text out of sentences and arranging them in the correct order, teach students to see and understand a model of the proposed tasks (Figure 1).

```
for i in range(n+1):

x = a + i*h

y = 2*x + 1

h = (b - a) / n; print(' X', '\t', ' Y')

print (round(x, 2), '\t', round(y, 2))

def Fun(a, b, n):

Fun(-5, 5, 20)
```

Figure 1. Make the program text out of sentences

The combination of these types of questions teaches students on a par with practices. It should be noted that on the first stages of learning programming, when students' knowledge and skills are not enough for coding, these tests are very useful.

2.2 The Experiment

To check the correctness of the chosen approach the author has conducted the experiment with students, their learning materials and practical assignments.

Students, who were aware of the experiment, were randomly divided into two groups G1 and G2 and both groups got two practical assignments: A and B. During the preparation before the task A G1 learners got tests and learning materials. G2 students got only learning materials. During the preparation before the task B instructors did the opposite: G1 learners got learning materials and G2 students got tests and learning materials. The preparation time and conditions were the same.

The experiment result shows that students' group, who had to solve preparation tests, coped with the task better that another one. In the first case, this is the group G1 (Table. 1), in the second case, this is the group G2 (Table. 2).

Table 1. Evaluation of the assignment A

	Assignment A					
	"0"	"1"	"2"	"3"	"4"	"5"
G1	0%	0%	0%	6%	9%	84%
G2	0%	0%	6%	50%	41%	3%

Table 2. Evaluation of the assignment B

	Assignment B					
	"0"	"1"	"2"	"3"	"4"	"5"
G1	0%	3%	16%	44%	38%	0%
G2	0%	0%	0%	3%	9%	88%

Students' feedback also shows that they have benefited from this type of assignment (Table 3).

Table 3

Learning material	Percentage of utility
Conspectus	8%
Example	23%
Homework	27%
Test	**42%**

2.3 Discussion

Described teaching technique is quite controversial, but it is useful at the beginning of coding, when students just learn the basics. Afterwards, when each student has his/her own programming style, it is not so useful. In addition, these tests bring some attractiveness and dynamic into "boring programming" and raise students' motivation.

3. CONCLUSION

Described teaching technique is based on testing system in learning e-environment. Different test types greatly help learners to understand basic programming concepts and learn syntax faster.

Students name different reasons with the aim to justify their "*not be able*" position. However, the authors' practice shows that if the teaching approach is properly selected and applied, good results are achievable.

ACKNOWLEDGEMENT

The author thanks anonymous reviewers for their comments and suggestions and students for participating in the experiment.

REFERENCES

Cheanga, B. et al., 2003. On automated grading of programming assignments in an academic institution. *Computers & Education*, 41, pp. 121–131

Cunningham, G.K. 1998. *Assessment in the Classroom.* Bristol, PA: Falmer Press

Guzdial, M., 2015. What's the Best Way to Teach Computer Science to Beginners? *Communications of the ACM*, Vol. 58, no. 2, pp 12-13

Malik, S., Coldwell-Neilson J., 2016. A model for teaching an introductory programming course using ADRI. *Education and information technologies.* DOI 10.1007/s10639-016-9474-0

Moodle, 2017. Open-source learning platform. Available at: https://moodle.org/

Python programming language, 2017. Available at: https://www.python.org/

Robins, A. et al., 2003. Learning and Teaching Programming: A Review and Discussion. *Computer Science Education*, Vol. 13, No. 2, pp 137–172

Ward, A.W., Murray-Ward, M.,1999. *Assessment in the Classroom.* Belmont, CA: Wadsworth Publishing Co.

AUTHOR INDEX

Agresta, T. 3
Aleksieva-Petrova, A. 95
Amoud, M. 272
Arfeen, I. 103
Arvanitozisis, D. 47
Authier, A. 213
Baba-Ali, A. 289
Baihan, M. 3
Bandeira, D. 23
Barhoumi, W. 171
Barry, C. 267
Belesioti, M. 47
Benkhider, S. 289
Biddiscombe, J. 151
Bikineev, A. 151
Born, J. 241
Buenaño-Fernández, D. 251
Bueno, J. 135
Castillo-Rojas, W. 221
Cheng, G. 3
Chochliouros, I. 47
Cordero González, A. 261
Corseuil, E. 79
Costa, G. 71
da Costa, A. 256
da Costa, C. 15, 23, 39
da Silva, A. 314
da Silva, D. 39
da Silva, G. 79
da Silva, M. 31
da Silva, P. 245
Dardamanis, A. 47
das Neves, A. 135
de Araújo, A. 31
de Assis, G. 71
de Carvalho, C. 256
de Macedo, C. 135
Demurjian, S. 3
Domingues, F. 135
Dorothee, A. 95
Drira, H. 171
Elaoud, A. 171
Elrhaffari, I. 272
Fajardo, J. 47
Farias, E. 245
Ferreira, D. 256
Franzis, A. 3
Garcés, R. 111
Garcia Lloreda, J. 47
García-Iruela, M. 142
George, K. M. 230
Giannoulakis, I. 47
Hatta, M. 120
Heller, T. 151
Hijón-Neira, R. 142
Hípola, P. 261
Hogan, M. 267
Hundertmark, S. 55
Iio, J. 120
Ivson, P. 79
Jaramillo-Alcázar, Á. 111
Jiménez, D. 213
Juhra, C. 241
Kafetzakis, E. 47
Kaiser, H. 151
Kaltenthaler, D. 63
Kamimura, R. 283
Kazaana, K. 120
Ketsmur, M. 87
Khodashenas, P. 47
Kitajima, R. 283
Kostopoulos, A. 47
Kourtis, A. 47
Kröger, P. 63
Krudwig, S. 241
Kumar TK, A. 230
Larsen, B. 303
Lima, J. 195
Llanes, K. 79
Lohrer, J. 63
López, J. 307
López, J. 213
Losacco, F. 295
Lucas, A. 303
Luján-Mora, S. 251, 310
Mahani, A. 289
Martinez-Mosquera, D. 310
Maruyama, Y. 283
Medina-Quispe, F. 221
Menéndez, J. 213

Mercês, J. 321
Minozzo, L. 195
Miranda, E. 261
Mironova, O. 325
Mohti, W. 103
Muñoz-Cañavate, A. 261
Naanaa, W. 179
Narayana, V. 230
Nascimento, D. 79
Nascimento, L. 314
Obermaier, H. 63
Omrani, M. 179
Onofrio, A. 3
Paiva, A. 135
Palos-Sánchez, P. 307
Parra, F. 310
Petrov, M. 95
Pousa, D. 205
Rabello, T. 39
Ramos, B. 135
Rendeiro, M. 321
Rhouma, D. 187
Righi, R. 15, 23, 39
Rivera Sanchez, Y. 3
Rodrigues, M. 87
Roehrs, A. 23
Romdhane, L. 187
Romero, J. 47
Rosero, J. 111
Roudies, O. 272
Rufino, J. 195, 205
Saboor, A. 103
Saettler, A. 79
Sánchez, N. 213
Sanz Casado, E. 303
Sarantis, D. 127
Saura, J. 307
Schmidt, D. 39
Schünke, M. 245
Sfakianakis, E. 47
Silva, V. 314
Souza, M. 71
Spiliopoulou, A. 47
Storck, M. 241
Tarasov, P. 159
Teixeira, A. 87
Tewari, H. 159
Times, V. 31
Toris, A. 3
Torres, A. 267
Trentini, A. 295
Tsukagoshi, K. 120
van der Meijden, C. 63
Viera, A. 303
Villegas-Ch, W. 251
Vogel, A. 241
Weghorn, H. 277
Wichman, M. 23
Wohlmann, J. 241
Wunsch, G. 15
Younoussi, S. 272
Zagrouba, E. 171
Zeve, C. 245
Zumstein, D. 55

International Association for Development of the Information Society (IADIS)
Rua Sao Sebastiao Da Pedreira
No. 100, 30, 1050-209
Lisbon, Portugal

ISBN 978-1-5108-5324-9

CURRAN ASSOCIATES INC.
proceedings.com